MORPHOLOGICAL TYPOLOGY

In this radically new approach to morphological typology, the authors set out new and explicit methods for the typological classification of languages. Drawing on evidence from a diverse range of languages, including Chinantec, Dakota, French, Fur, Icelandic, Ngiti, and Sanskrit, the authors propose innovative ways of measuring inflectional complexity. Designed to engage graduate students and academic researchers, the book presents opportunities for further investigation. The authors' data sets and the computational tool that they constructed for their analysis are available online, allowing readers to employ them in their own research. Readers can access the online computational tool through www.cambridge.org/stump_finkel.

GREGORY STUMP is Professor of Linguistics in the Department of English at the University of Kentucky.

RAPHAEL A. FINKEL is Professor of Computer Science in the Department of Computer Science at the University of Kentucky.

In this series

106 SHARON INKELAS and CHERYL ZOLL: *Reduplication: doubling in morphology*
107 SUSAN EDWARDS: *Fluent aphasia*
108 BARBARA DANCYGIER and EVE SWEETSER: *Mental spaces in grammar: conditional constructions*
109 MATTHEW BAERMAN, DUNSTAN BROWN and GREVILLE G. CORBETT: *The syntax–morphology interface: a study of syncretism*
110 MARCUS TOMALIN: *Linguistics and the formal sciences: the origins of generative grammar*
111 SAMUEL D. EPSTEIN and T. DANIEL SEELY: *Derivations in minimalism*
112 PAUL DE LACY: *Markedness: reduction and preservation in phonology*
113 YEHUDA N. FALK: *Subjects and their properties*
114 P. H. MATTHEWS: *Syntactic relations: a critical survey*
115 MARK C. BAKER: *The syntax of agreement and concord*
116 GILLIAN CATRIONA RAMCHAND: *Verb meaning and the lexicon: a first phase syntax*
117 PIETER MUYSKEN: *Functional categories*
118 JUAN URIAGEREKA: *Syntactic anchors: on semantic structuring*
119 D. ROBERT LADD: *Intonational phonology second edn.*
120 LEONARD H. BABBY: *The syntax of argument structure*
121 B. ELAN DRESHER: *The contrastive hierarchy in phonology*
122 DAVID ADGER, DANIEL HARBOUR and LAUREL J. WATKINS: *Mirrors and microparameters: phrase structure beyond free word order*
123 NIINA NING ZHANG: *Coordination in syntax*
124 NEIL SMITH: *Acquiring phonology*
125 NINA TOPINTZI: *Onsets: suprasegmental and prosodic behaviour*
126 CEDRIC BOECKX, NORBERT HORNSTEIN and JAIRO NUNES: *Control as movement*
127 MICHAEL ISRAEL: *The grammar of polarity: pragmatics, sensitivity, and the logic of scales*
128 M. RITA MANZINI and LEONARDO M. SAVOIA: *Grammatical categories: variation in romance languages*
129 BARBARA CITKO: *Symmetry in syntax: merge, move and labels*
130 RACHEL WALKER: *Vowel patterns in language*
131 MARY DALRYMPLE and IRINA NIKOLAEVA: *Objects and information structure*
132 JERROLD M. SADOCK: *The modular architecture of grammar*
133 DUNSTAN BROWN and ANDREW HIPPISLEY: *Network morphology: a defaults-based theory of word structure*
134 BETTELOU LOS, CORRIEN BLOM, GEERT BOOIJ, MARION ELENBAAS and ANS VAN KEMENADE: *Morphosyntactic change: a comparative study of particles and prefixes*
135 STEPHEN CRAIN: *The emergence of meaning*
136 HUBERT HAIDER: *Symmetry breaking in syntax*
137 JOSÉ A. CAMACHO: *Null subjects*
138 GREGORY STUMP and RAPHAEL A. FINKEL *Morphological typology: from word to paradigm*

Earlier issues not listed are also available.

CAMBRIDGE STUDIES IN LINGUISTICS

General editors: P. AUSTIN, J. BRESNAN, B. COMRIE, S. CRAIN,
W. DRESSLER, C. J. EWEN, R. LASS, D. LIGHTFOOT, K. RICE,
I. ROBERTS, S. ROMAINE, N. V. SMITH

Morphological Typology: From Word to Paradigm

MORPHOLOGICAL TYPOLOGY

FROM WORD TO PARADIGM

GREGORY STUMP
and
RAPHAEL A. FINKEL
University of Kentucky

CAMBRIDGE
UNIVERSITY PRESS

University Printing House, Cambridge CB2 8BS, United Kingdom

Published in the United States of America by Cambridge University Press, New York

Cambridge University Press is part of the University of Cambridge.

It furthers the University's mission by disseminating knowledge in the pursuit of education, learning and research at the highest international levels of excellence.

www.cambridge.org
Information on this title: www.cambridge.org/9781107029248

© Gregory Stump and Raphael A. Finkel 2013

This publication is in copyright. Subject to statutory exception and to the provisions of relevant collective licensing agreements, no reproduction of any part may take place without the written permission of Cambridge University Press.

First published 2013

Printed by CPI Group (UK) Ltd, Croydon CR0 4YY

A catalogue record for this publication is available from the British Library

Library of Congress Cataloguing in Publication data
Stump, Gregory T. (Gregory Thomas), 1954–
Morphological Typology : from word to paradigm / Gregory Stump and Raphael
A. Finkel, University of Kentucky.
   pages   cm
Includes bibliographical references.
ISBN 978-1-107-02924-8
1. Grammar, Comparative and general – Morphology. 2. Grammar, Comparative and general – Morphosyntax. 3. Typology (Linguistics)   I. Finkel, Raphael A., author. II. Title.
P241.S78   2013
415'.9–dc23

                                                                2012047530

ISBN 978-1-107-02924-8 Hardback

Additional resources for this publication at www.cambridge.org/9781107029248

Cambridge University Press has no responsibility for the persistence or accuracy of URLs for external or third-party internet websites referred to in this publication, and does not guarantee that any content on such websites is, or will remain, accurate or appropriate.

Contents

	List of tables	*page* xi
	List of figures	xxii
	List of abbreviations	xxiii
	Introduction	1
1	**Principal parts**	9
1.1	The traditional notion of principal parts	9
1.2	Principal parts in linguistic theory and in language typology	15
1.3	Some preliminary assumptions	25
2	**Plats**	40
2.1	Plats and their parts	40
2.2	The representation issue	51
3	**A typology of principal-part systems**	53
3.1	A typology of principal-part systems	53
3.2	Criterion A: How many principal parts are needed to determine a lexeme's IC membership?	54
3.3	Criterion B: How many dynamic principal parts are needed to determine a given cell in a lexeme's realized paradigm?	58
3.4	Criterion C: To what extent are particular realized cells favored as optimal static principal parts?	62
3.5	Summary	77
4	**Inflection-class transparency**	79
4.1	Introduction	79
4.2	Conjugation classes in Fur	84

4.3	Deviations from maximal transparency in Fur verb paradigms	88
4.4	A first measure of IC transparency: IC predictability	94
4.5	A fourth criterion of IC transparency	99
4.6	A second measure of IC transparency: cell predictability	99
4.7	IC transparency and the No-Blur Principle	103
4.8	IC transparency as a dimension of typological variation	107
4.9	IC predictability, cell predictability, and entropy as measures of an inflection-class system's complexity	109
4.10	Conclusions	114
5	**Grammatically enhanced plats**	**117**
5.1	Sanskrit declension	118
5.2	Measuring the IC complexity of the hearer-oriented declensional plat	119
5.3	Grammatical disambiguation of distinguishers in the Sanskrit declensional plat	132
5.4	The effects of enhancing principal parts with gender specifications and/or stem demarcations	143
5.5	Conclusions	155
6	**Impostors and heteroclites**	**165**
6.1	Impostors and plat construction	165
6.2	Heteroclites and plat construction	175
7	**Stems as principal parts**	**182**
7.1	Principal parts can be indexed stems as well as realized cells	182
7.2	The morphology and phonology of French verbs	184
7.3	Themes, stems, and conjugation classes in French	192
7.4	Static principal-part analysis	202
7.5	Dynamic principal-part analysis	204
7.6	IC predictability and cell predictability	204
7.7	Cross-linguistic comparison	214
7.8	Stem referrals and principal parts	215
7.9	Conclusions	221
8	**The Marginal Detraction Hypothesis**	**225**
8.1	Introduction	225
8.2	Detraction from an IC's predictability	226

8.3	Conjugation classes in Icelandic	228
8.4	Plats and subplats	230
8.5	IC predictability and amassed vs singleton conjugation classes	233
8.6	The isomorphic ideal	237
8.7	Distillations and amassed vs singleton conjugations	243
8.8	Discussion	248
8.9	French evidence for the Marginal Detraction Hypothesis	254
9	**Inflection classes, implicative relations, and morphological theory**	**262**
9.1	Two kinds of lexical representation and two kinds of inflectional rule	262
9.2	Two canonical extremes for a theory of inflection	263
9.3	A hybrid conception of inflectional morphology	271
10	**Entropy, predictability, and predictiveness**	**295**
10.1	Definitions	295
10.2	Entropy applied to plats	297
10.3	The effect of type frequency	301
10.4	Static near-principal parts	305
10.5	Inflection-class entropy measures	311
10.6	Summary	313
11	**The complexity of inflection-class systems**	**314**
11.1	Implicative relations and the complexity of IC systems	314
11.2	Measurable correlates of an IC system's complexity	317
11.3	Complexity as a typological variable of IC systems	325
11.4	Conclusions	339
12	**Sensitivity to plat presentation**	**344**
12.1	Common features of each inflection class	344
12.2	Rules of sandhi	348
12.3	Multiple stem segments	350
12.4	Morphophonemes	351
12.5	More rules of sandhi	352
12.6	Morphophonological rules	353
12.7	Surface-form representation	356
12.8	Multiple stems	359

12.9	Stem forms	361
12.10	Additional syntactic data	362
12.11	Dealing with impostors	363
12.12	Conclusions	366
13	**The Principal-Parts Analyzer**	**368**
13.1	Input format	368
13.2	Output sections	373
13.3	Algorithms	378
	Glossary	380
	References	391
	Index	398

Tables

1.1	Principal parts of five Latin verbs	*page* 12
1.2	The formation of the tenses of verbs, from the present, the perfect, the supine, and the infinitive (Grant 1823: 92)	13
1.3	Four hypothetical IC systems	22
1.4	A hypothetical IC system	24
1.5	Realized paradigms of two Old Norse verbs	27
1.6	Realized paradigm of Old Norse ÞURFA 'need'	28
1.7	A hypothetical IC system F	30
1.8	Static principal parts for system F	30
1.9	Adaptive principal parts for system F	31
1.10	The adaptive principal parts for system F in tabular form	32
1.11	Dynamic principal parts for system F	33
1.12	Representations of static, adaptive, and dynamic principal-part sets for system F in Table 1.7	34
1.13	Plat for the principal-part analysis of Ngiti verbs	36
1.14	Twenty-six optimal static principal-part analyses for Ngiti	38
2.1	Plat representing a hypothetical system of ICs	41
2.2	Plat representing a hypothetical system of ICs in which the property sets τ and υ have identical exponence	42
2.3	The declension of Sanskrit AŚVA 'horse'	43
2.4	Realized present indicative active paradigms of two Sanskrit verbs, in phonemic representation	45
2.5	Realized present indicative active paradigms of two Sanskrit verbs, in morphophonological representation	45
2.6	Partial realized paradigms of two verbs in Ngiti	47
2.7	The declension of AŚVA 'horse' compared to that of MANAS 'mind'	48
2.8	Principal parts of some English verbs	50
3.1	Subject prefixes in Kwerba verb morphology	54

xii *Tables*

3.2	Koasati affirmative agreement morphology	56
3.3	Numbers of optimal principal parts in the verb systems of ten languages	57
3.4	An optimal dynamic principal-part analysis for Fur verbs	59
3.5	Average cell predictor numbers and dynamic principal-part numbers for ten systems of conjugation	61
3.6	The four tense systems in Classical Sanskrit	62
3.7	Conjugation classes in the present and aorist systems	62
3.8	Morphological marks of the conjugation classes of the Sanskrit present and aorist systems	63
3.9	Present-system conjugations in Sanskrit (present indicative active forms)	64
3.10	Aorist-system conjugations in Sanskrit (aorist indicative active forms)	65
3.11	Indicative forms of the *ubhayapadin* verb RUDH 'obstruct'	68
3.12	Indicative forms of the *parasmaipadin* verb BHĪ 'fear'	69
3.13	Indicative forms of the *ātmanepadin* verb ĪKṢ 'see'	70
3.14	Exemplars of the thirty-eight Sanskrit "conjugations" in our sample plat	71
3.15	The nineteen distillations in the Sanskrit plat	72
3.16	The nineteen distillations in our Sanskrit plat	73
3.17	Optimal static principal-part sets in Tuḷu	74
3.18	Degrees of morphosyntactic focus in ten conjugational systems	76
3.19	Two hypothetical IC systems: A and B	76
3.20	Degrees of morphosyntactic focus in the two hypothetical IC systems A and B in Table 3.19	76
3.21	Three dimensions of typological variation in principal-part systems	77
3.22	Typological contrasts among ten systems of conjugation	78
4.1	Plat and irreducible inferences for a hypothetical inflectional system each of whose ICs is maximally transparent	82
4.2	Plat and irreducible inferences for a hypothetical inflectional system whose ICs are maximally opaque	83
4.3	Plat of Fur conjugations	86
4.4	Abbreviations for the twelve MPSs realized by Fur verb forms and the distillations of these property sets	87

4.5	The three alternative optimal dynamic principal-part analyses for Conjugation IIA in Fur	87
4.6	The exponence of distillations 1–9 in Conjugation IIA in Fur	88
4.7	Number of optimal dynamic principal parts for each Fur conjugation class	89
4.8	A representative optimal dynamic principal-part analysis for Conjugation IVB in Fur	89
4.9	The sole optimal dynamic principal-part analysis for Conjugation IIIE in Fur	89
4.10	The two optimal dynamic principal-part analyses for Conjugation IIID in Fur	90
4.11	The sole optimal dynamic principal-part analysis for Conjugation IIIA in Fur	90
4.12	Cell predictor numbers for Fur conjugation classes	91
4.13	Numbers of optimal dynamic principal-part analyses for Fur conjugations	92
4.14	Maximum possible number of optimal dynamic principal-part analyses for Fur verbs	93
4.15	The two alternative optimal dynamic principal-part analyses for Conjugation IIC in Fur	93
4.16	Ratio of actual to possible optimal dynamic principal-part analyses	94
4.17	The eighteen optimal dynamic principal-part analyses for Conjugation IIB in Fur	96
4.18	The sole optimal dynamic principal-part analysis for Conjugation IVA in Fur	97
4.19	IC predictability compared with criteria (6a–c) in the analysis of Fur verbs	98
4.20	Cell predictability in all conjugations in Fur	101
4.21	Average cell predictability in conjugations with high IC predictability in Fur	102
4.22	Affixal exponents of Fur inflection	105
4.23	Number of dynamic principal parts needed to identify each Fur conjugation	106
4.24	IC predictability in three languages	108
4.25	Abbreviations for the twelve distillations realized by Comaltepec Chinantec verb forms	111

xiv Tables

4.26	Abbreviations for the twenty-one distillations realized by Icelandic verb forms	113
4.27	Automatically generated optimal dynamic principal-part analyses for Fur verbs	115
5.1	Hearer-oriented declensional plat for Sanskrit	120
5.2	The six optimal static principal-part sets for the hearer-oriented declensional plat	122
5.3	Optimal dynamic principal parts (circled) for Declensions DC1 and DC5 in the hearer-oriented declensional plat	124
5.4	Optimal dynamic principal-part analyses for the hearer-oriented declensional plat	125
5.5	Cell predictability and IC predictability of the declensions in the hearer-oriented declensional plat	127
5.6	Predictiveness of the nominative singular cell in the hearer-oriented declensional plat	131
5.7	Average predictiveness of distillations in the hearer-oriented declensional plat	132
5.8	Unenhanced and fully enhanced versions of the realized paradigm of Sanskrit AŚVA 'horse'	133
5.9	The declension of MANAS 'mind'	134
5.10	Disambiguation of the principal part ⟨Xas, {nom sg}⟩	135
5.11	The declension of DĀNA 'gift'	136
5.12	The declension of NĀMAN 'name'	136
5.13	Disambiguation of the principal part ⟨Xa, {voc sg}⟩	137
5.14	Disambiguation of the principal part ⟨X$ā$, {nom sg}⟩	138
5.15	Disambiguation of the principal part ⟨Xas, {nom sg}⟩	140
5.16	The declension of NADĪ 'river'	141
5.17	The masculine declension of BALIN 'strong'	141
5.18	Disambiguation of the principal part ⟨X$ī$, {nom sg}⟩	142
5.19	The declension of ALI 'bee'	143
5.20	The declension of MATI 'intellect'	143
5.21	The declension of ŚUKRAŚOCIS 'brilliant'	144
5.22	Disambiguation of the principal part ⟨Xis, {nom sg}⟩	146
5.23	Plat of declensional distinguishers for Sanskrit enhanced with specifications of gender and stem delimitation	148
5.24	Optimal static principal-part analyses for the four types of plats in (3)	150
5.25	Optimal dynamic principal-part analyses of Sanskrit declensions for the four types of plats in (3)	152

5.26	Average cell and IC predictability for the four types of plats in (3)	154
5.27	Average predictiveness of cells realizing the distillations of Sanskrit nominal paradigms for the four types of plats in (3)	158
5.28	Class identifiers (CI) and optimal co-predictors (OCP, shaded) under an analysis lacking specifications for gender or stem delimitation	159
5.29	Class identifiers (CI) and optimal co-predictors (OCP, shaded) under an analysis with specifications for stem delimitation but lacking gender specifications	160
5.30	Class identifiers (CI) and optimal co-predictors (OCP, shaded) under an analysis with gender specifications but lacking specifications for stem delimitation	161
5.31	Class identifiers (CI) and optimal co-predictors (OCP, shaded) under an analysis with specifications for both gender and stem delimitation	163
6.1	Neuter declension DC6 of the *i*-stem KRĪḌI 'playing' and neuter declension DC22 of the *in*-stem BALIN 'powerful'	169
6.2	Cell predictabilities and IC predictability of DC22 (the *in*-stem declension [neuter forms]) in the Sanskrit declensional universe, excluding and including DC6 (the *i*-stem declension [neuter forms])	170
6.3	Declension DC1 of the masculine *a*-stem AŚVA 'horse' and declension DC2 of the neuter *a*-stem DĀNA 'gift'	171
6.4	Declension DC1 of the masculine *a*-stem ŚŪLINA 'Indian fig-tree' and masculine declension DC21 of the *in*-stem BALIN 'powerful'	173
6.5	Sanskrit declension plat modified by the inclusion of the *ina* subtype of DC1	174
6.6	The heteroclite inflection of Czech PRAMEN 'spring, source'	176
6.7	Czech declensional plat	177
6.8	Czech declensions and the themes of their exemplars (in morphophonological representation)	178
6.9	IC predictability of Czech declensions without and with the PRAMEN declension	179
6.10	Cell predictabilities of KOST, KOTEL$_1$, and KOTEL$_2$ without and with PRAMEN	180

6.11	Static principal-part analyses for Czech declensions, without and with the heteroclite declension of PRAMEN	181
7.1	Latin declensional endings	183
7.2	Seventy-two conjugations (each named after an exemplar) and their models in *Bescherelle* (2006)	185
7.3	The forty-nine cells in a French verb's synthetic paradigm	187
7.4	Hearer-oriented plat of French verb terminations (concrete phonological analysis)	188
7.5	Speaker-oriented plat of French verb terminations (abstract phonological analysis)	189
7.6	The indexed stems in a French verb's synthetic paradigm	190
7.7	Indexed stems of eight French verbs in the concrete and abstract analyses	191
7.8	Themes of seventy-two French verbs	193
7.9	Identical French conjugations	195
7.10	Concrete plat of stem formatives for seventy-two French conjugations	196
7.11	Abstract plat of stem formatives for seventy-two French conjugations	199
7.12	Optimal static principal-part analyses for French (concrete analysis)	202
7.13	Optimal static principal-part analyses for French (abstract analysis)	203
7.14	Overview of optimal dynamic principal-part analyses of French conjugations (concrete analysis)	205
7.15	Overview of optimal dynamic principal-part analyses of French conjugations (abstract analysis)	206
7.16	Cell predictabilities and IC predictability of sixty-four French conjugations (concrete analysis)	208
7.17	Cell predictabilities and IC predictability of fifty-seven French conjugations (abstract analysis)	210
7.18	Paradigm transparency in four languages	214
7.19	Stem-referral for seventy-two French conjugations	217
7.20	Optimal static principal-part analyses for French (stem-referral analysis)	220
7.21	Cell predictabilities and IC predictability of fifty-seven French conjugations (stem-referral analysis)	222
8.1	A simple example of detraction from IC predictability	226
8.2	Synthetic paradigm of Icelandic BÍTA 'bite'	229

8.3	Distinctions among the Weak conjugations in Icelandic	229
8.4	Indicative present endings in the Weak conjugations in Icelandic	230
8.5	Distinctions in stem vocalism among the Strong conjugations in Icelandic	231
8.6	Indicative present endings in the Strong conjugations in Icelandic	232
8.7	The 162 conjugations in this study (based on Jörg 1989)	234
8.8	A fragment of the plat for Icelandic verbs	236
8.9	Amassed and singleton conjugations in Icelandic	238
8.10	IC predictability of Weak amassed conjugations calculated in: A. isolation, and in three larger universes: B. all Weak conjugations, C. all amassed conjugations, and D. all conjugations	241
8.11	IC predictability of Strong amassed conjugations calculated in: A. isolation, and in three larger universes: B. all Strong conjugations, C. all amassed conjugations, and D. all conjugations	242
8.12	IC predictability of Weak singleton conjugations calculated in: A. isolation, and in three larger universes: B. all Weak conjugations, C. all singleton conjugations, and D. all conjugations	244
8.13	IC predictability of Strong singleton conjugations calculated in: A. isolation, and in three larger universes: B. all Strong conjugations, C. all singleton conjugations, and D. all conjugations	245
8.14	Average IC predictability of different conjugations (from Tables 8.10–8.13)	246
8.15	How singleton and amassed conjugations detract from each other's IC predictability (Weak and Strong universes contrasted)	247
8.16	How singleton and amassed conjugations detract from each other's IC predictability (Weak/Strong universes contrasted with amassed/singleton universes)	247
8.17	A hypothetical plat (property sets V and Z have isomorphic patterns of exponence)	248
8.18	A hypothetical plat (patterns of exponence of all property sets are isomorphic)	248

xviii *Tables*

8.19	Grouping of morphosyntactic property sets into distillations in the Weak conjugations	249
8.20	Grouping of morphosyntactic property sets into distillations in the Strong conjugations	249
8.21	Grouping of morphosyntactic property sets into distillations in all conjugations	250
8.22	Grouping of morphosyntactic property sets into distillations in all Weak conjugations	250
8.23	Grouping of morphosyntactic property sets into distillations in all Strong conjugations	250
8.24	Grouping of morphosyntactic property sets into distillations in all amassed conjugations	251
8.25	Grouping of morphosyntactic property sets into distillations in all singleton conjugations	251
8.26	The third-person singular and third-person plural past-tense forms of six Old English verbs	253
8.27	Type frequencies of seventy-two French conjugations	254
8.28	The subplat of singleton conjugations in French (concrete plat: distillations shaded)	256
8.29	IC predictability of marginal conjugations in: A. the universe of marginal conjugations, and B. the universe of all conjugations	257
8.30	IC predictability of central conjugations in: A. the universe of central conjugations, and B. the universe of all conjugations	258
8.31	Distillations required by the full French concrete plat and by the marginal and central subplats	259
8.32	Average IC predictabilities for the French subplats when marginal conjugations are those with three or fewer members, and central conjugations those with four or more	260
9.1	A fragment of the English conjugational system	263
9.2	Conjugation-class diacritics and stems for the fragment of English in Table 9.1	264
9.3	Rules of exponence for the fragment of English in Table 9.1	265
9.4	Differences between the PWPM and PEM hypotheses	265
9.5	Realized declensional paradigms of nine Sanskrit nominals	269

9.6	Six declension classes and their superclasses in Sanskrit	274
9.7	Indexed stems for nine Sanskrit nominal lexemes	276
9.8	Rules of stem formation and stem selection for nine Sanskrit nominals	282
9.9	Two principal-part analyses for nine Sanskrit lexemes	287
9.10	Schematic realized paradigms for the nine declension classes exemplified in Table 9.5	290
9.11	Proof of (34a)	293
9.12	Proof of (36b)	293
10.1	Entropy values	296
10.2	Finnish *i*-stem and *e*-stem nouns	297
10.3	Conditional entropy (×100) of MPS (column) given MPS (row), from Table 10.2	298
10.4	Conditional entropy (×100) of MPS (column) given MPS (row), from Table 10.2, omitting the redundant MPS {partPl}	298
10.5	Entropy values (×100) for Sanskrit nominals	299
10.6	MPS entropy measures for Finnish *i*-stem and *e*-stem nouns	300
10.7	Entropy values (×100) for Finnish nouns with artificial type frequency	301
10.8	Entropy values (× 100) for Icelandic verbs	302
10.9	Entropy values (× 100) for Icelandic verbs, using type frequency	304
10.10	Entropy values (× 100) for French verbs	306
10.11	Entropy values (× 100) for French verbs, using type frequency	307
10.12	Simple heuristic for static near-principal parts for Icelandic verbs, using type frequency	308
10.13	Simple heuristic for static near-principal parts for French verbs	309
10.14	Simple heuristic for static near-principal parts for French verbs, using type frequency	309
10.15	Simple heuristic for static near-principal parts for Sanskrit nominals	310
10.16	Lookahead heuristic for static near-principal parts for French verbs	310
10.17	Inflection-class predictable entropy (4-ICBE) (×100), Finnish nouns	311

10.18	Inflection-class predictive entropy (ICVE) (×100), Finnish nouns	312
11.1	Two hypothetical plats and their associated implicative rules	318
11.2	Hypothetical Plat C and implicative rules for IC I	319
11.3	Hypothetical Plat D and implicative rules for IC I	320
11.4	Hypothetical Plat E and implicative rules for IC I	321
11.5	IC predictability of Plats A–E in Tables 11.1–11.4	323
11.6	The 4-system entropy (× 100) of Plats A–E	324
11.7	Two hypothetical plats	324
11.8	The number of MPSs and distillations in the paradigms defined by twelve inflectional systems	326
11.9	The size of optimal static principal-part sets for twelve inflectional systems	328
11.10	Density of optimal static principal-part sets for twelve inflectional systems	328
11.11	Sixty-four French conjugations	330
11.12	Size and number of optimal dynamic principal-part sets for sixty-four French conjugations	331
11.13	Average size of alternative optimal dynamic principal-part sets for twelve inflectional systems and average ratio of actual to possible optimal dynamic analyses	332
11.14	Cell predictor number and cell predictiveness, both averaged across ICs, for twelve inflectional systems	333
11.15	IC predictability of sixty-four French conjugations	335
11.16	Linear transformations from the ten complexity measures to the composite scale of morphological complexity in Figure 11.3	339
11.17	Two hypothetical IC systems and their irreducible inferences and formal descriptions	342
12.1	Finnish i-stem and e-stem nouns	345
12.2	Finnish i-stem and e-stem nouns, themes removed	345
12.3	Cell and inflection-class predictability, Finnish nouns, themes removed	346
12.4	Entropy values (×100) for Finnish nouns, themes removed	346
12.5	Finnish i-stem and e-stem nouns, themes removed, with templates	347
12.6	Finnish i-stem and e-stem nouns, themes removed, sandhi rules	349

12.7	Finnish *i*-stem and *e*-stem nouns, two stems, sandhi rules	350
12.8	Finnish *i*-stem and *e*-stem nouns, two stems, sandhi rules, morphophoneme	352
12.9	Finnish *i*-stem and *e*-stem nouns, two stems, more sandhi rules, morphophoneme	353
12.10	Fragment of a plat of English verbs in phonemic transcription	354
12.11	Fragment of a plat of English verbs in morphophonological representation	355
12.12	Fragment of a plat of French verbs	357
12.13	Fragment of a plat of French verbs in phonemic transcription	358
12.14	Stems for three French verbs	360
12.15	Stems for the French verb fragment	361
12.16	Plat of French verb fragment with multiple stems, in phonemic transcription	362
12.17	Referral patterns for the French verb fragment	363
13.1	PPA input format of Finnish *i*-stem and *e*-stem nouns	369

Figures

1	A Sudoku puzzle	*page* 2
1.1	The adaptive principal parts for system F in tree form	32
2.1	Analysis of Sanskrit *aśvas* 'horse' (nom sg), *aśve* (loc sg) and *aśveṣu* (loc pl)	43
4.1	Cell predictability in all conjugations in Fur	102
4.2	Cell predictability in all conjugations in Comaltepec Chinantec	110
4.3	Cell predictability in all conjugations in Icelandic	112
5.1	IC and cell predictability for the unenhanced plat of Sanskrit declensions	129
5.2	IC and cell predictability for Sanskrit declensions in a plat with specifications for stem delimitation but lacking gender specifications	155
5.3	IC and cell predictability for Sanskrit declensions in a plat with gender specifications but lacking specifications for stem delimitation	156
5.4	IC and cell predictability for Sanskrit declensions in a plat fully enhanced with specifications for both gender and stem delimitation	157
7.1	Predictabilities of French conjugations (concrete analysis)	212
7.2	Predictabilities of French conjugations (abstract analysis)	213
8.1	The nesting of universes in our first set of calculations	240
8.2	Mutual detractiveness between Weak and Strong conjugations in singleton and amassed universes	243
11.1	Average IC predictability of twelve IC systems	336
11.2	Average cell predictability of twelve inflectional systems	336
11.3	Average 4-MPS entropy ($\times$ 100) of twelve IC systems	338
11.4	The relative complexity of twelve IC systems according to ten measures	340

Abbreviations

1, 2, 3	first, second, third person
A	accusative case (in tables)
acc	accusative case (in morphosyntactic property sets)
Ab	ablative case (in tables)
abl	ablative case (in morphosyntactic property sets)
conj	conjugation
D	dative case (in tables)
dat	dative case (in morphosyntactic property sets)
dc	declension
du	dual
fem	feminine gender
fut	future tense
G/gen	genitive case
GEND	gender
H	high tone
I/ins	instrumental case
IC	inflection class
Impf	imperfect tense/aspect (in tables)
impf	imperfect tense/aspect (in morphosyntactic property sets)
impv	imperative mood
ind	indicative mood
inf	infinitive
iness	inessive (in tables)
itr	intransitive
L	low tone
L/loc	locative case
M	mid tone
masc	masculine gender
MPS	morphosyntactic property set
N/nom	nominative case

xxiii

neut	neuter gender
NUM	number
Part	partitive (in tables)
PER	person
pl	plural
PPA	principal-parts analyzer
ptcp	participle
pres	present tense
sg	singular
sbjv	subjunctive mood
TNS	tense
tr	transitive
V/voc	vocative case

Introduction

Sudoku puzzles such as the one in Figure 1 are (as we write this) all the rage. (If you have never worked one of these puzzles – and we expect that you have – the idea is to fill each empty square with a number between 1 and 9, inclusive, in such a way that no number is repeated in any row, any column, or any of the nine 3 × 3 squares of which the puzzle is composed.) In this book, we are, in a sense, concerned with Sudoku puzzles of a different kind. In a Sudoku puzzle of the familiar kind, the numbers provided in the puzzle's initial state give enough information to deduce all of the numbers that appear once the puzzle is successfully completed. A table of a language's inflectional paradigms is in some ways similar to a completed Sudoku puzzle: many of the forms occupying an inflectional paradigm's "squares" (we call them "cells" rather than "squares") are predictable, so that the paradigm can be given a less redundant (or redundancy-free) representation in which only certain particular cells are filled; the word forms occupying these particular cells allow one to predict all the forms that are omitted, just as the numbers in a Sudoku puzzle's initial state allow one to predict the missing numbers. Word forms that satisfy this requirement function as "principal parts" for the paradigm table. (Analogously, we might call the numbers in a Sudoku puzzle's initial state its principal parts.)

Principal parts have a long history in language pedagogy. In particular, they are helpful for learning and using languages with inflection-class systems. In such languages, lexemes belonging to the same syntactic category inflect for the same sets of morphosyntactic properties but do so with different morphology, according to their membership in one or another conjugation or declension. (Inflection-class systems might therefore be likened to books of Sudoku puzzles, with each inflection class requiring a different solution.)

But the interest of principal-part systems does not begin and end with language pedagogy. Principal parts have theoretical interest as well, because they hint at – and to an extent reify – the complex network of implicative relations affiliating the different cells in a lexeme's paradigm. Such relations help language users to learn, recognize, and produce a lexeme's full array of

Figure 1. *A Sudoku puzzle*

forms. Principal parts "work" because they participate in implicative relations that are certainties rather than mere probabilities. There are, to be sure, relations of mere probability in morphology: for instance, if one encountered a new verb with infinitive *dring* and past participle *drung*, one would expect its past-tense form to be either *drang* (compare *sang* and *rang*) or *drung* (compare *stung* and *flung*), but one could not be sure which is right. On the other hand, one could be certain that its present participle is *dringing*: in English, if a verb with infinitive X has a present participle, it is invariably X*ing*.[1]

The networks of implicative certainties upon which principal parts depend exhibit considerable typological variation, and it is in terms of this variation that we define an inflection-class system's relative complexity. Our goal in this book is to develop this conception of complexity as an objective, measurable property of inflection-class systems. To this end, we investigate implicative relations in inflectional morphology from both formal and typological perspectives, addressing questions such as:

(a) How do languages vary with respect to their networks of implicative certainties? How do different inflection classes within a single language vary in this respect?

(b) What makes a word form predictable? What makes a word form predictive? How do predictability and predictiveness vary across inflection classes within a single language? How do they vary across languages?

---

[1] Rare is the verb that has an infinitive but no present participle, though there are examples, e.g. *beware* and (for some speakers) *use to* /jus tu/ (as in *I didn't use to go there*).

(c) How can the predictability and predictiveness of a lexeme's forms be measured?
(d) How are the implicative relations among a paradigm's cells to be represented? What is their theoretical status, and what are their implications for a general theory of inflectional morphology?
(e) How do these factors figure in the conception and quantification of an inflection-class system's complexity?

The hypothesis that linguistic subsystems can be meaningfully said to vary in complexity has drawn considerable interest in recent work in language typology (Baerman *et al.* 2010; Dahl 2004; Hawkins 2004; Miestamo *et al.* 2008; Nichols 1992, 2007; Nichols *et al.* 2006); the dimensions and degrees of such variation are an important focus of current research. In developing the notion of linguistic complexity as it specifically relates to inflection-class systems, we compare the individual inflection classes in a language's inflectional system according to the manner and extent of their deviation from canonical ideals of maximal transparency and maximal opacity; the criteria for these comparisons in turn inform a more general comparison of whole inflection-class systems. We define the complexity of an inflection-class system as the extent to which it inhibits motivated ("certain") inferences about a lexeme's full paradigm from subsets of the forms in this paradigm.

This definition might be taken to imply that an inflection-class system that is more complex (in our sense) has a greater "cost" – that it is more difficult to learn, that it complicates the production and comprehension of utterances, and that it makes lexemes' lexical representations more intricate. Though we would be surprised if this proved not to be the case, our thesis is not that complex inflection-class systems are costly in a psycholinguistic sense. Rather, we regard relative complexity (in our sense) as an objectively observable property of inflection-class systems. The motivated inferences in terms of which we define an inflection-class system's complexity are relations of logical implication, and as such, are directly detectable by computational means. Moreover, we shall see that an inflection-class system may be complex (in our sense) for one or more of a variety of reasons. Accordingly, we will, in this course of this book, propose ten measurable correlates that allow an inflection-class system's complexity to be seen as a multifaceted but quantifiable typological variable.

Our discussion and conclusions are based on evidence from a wide range of languages with complex inflectional systems. In analyzing these systems, we make extensive use of the Principal-Parts Analyzer (PPA), a computational tool that we have devised specifically for generating principal-part analyses and for measuring patterns of predictability, predictiveness, and entropy in an inflection-class system's paradigms.

In Chapter 1, we examine the traditional notion of **principal parts** and consider the factors involved in giving this notion theoretical and typological substance. We distinguish three principal-part schemes: the lexemes in a static scheme have the same members of their paradigms as principal parts; in an adaptive scheme, a lexeme's principal parts are ordered, defining a path through a kind of flowchart determining its inflection-class membership; in a dynamic scheme, lexemes have unordered principal parts which vary in number from one inflection class to another.

In Chapter 2, we develop the notion of a **plat**, a format for modeling a language's system of inflection classes; models in this format constitute our central objects of analysis in identifying and measuring an inflection-class system's degree of complexity. As we show, the construction of plats raises a crucial representational issue: what is actually modeled by a model of a language's inflection classes? In addressing this issue, we draw a critical conceptual distinction between hearer-oriented and speaker-oriented plats.

In Chapter 3, we present a preliminary typology of principal-part systems. Traditionally, morphological typology has focused on the properties of individual word forms, involving such criteria as degree of synthesis and degree of fusion (Greenberg 1960); but in a language's inflectional system, the properties of entire paradigms are of considerable typological interest. We propose three typological criteria for a preliminary classification of inflection-class systems: (i) the number of principal parts needed to determine a lexeme's paradigm, (ii) the number of principal parts needed to determine a given cell in a lexeme's paradigm, and (iii) the extent to which certain cells enjoy a privileged status as determinants of lexemes' inflection-class membership. We apply these criteria to compare the principal-part systems of a range of languages, including Comaltepec Chinantec (Oto-Manguean; Mexico), Dakota (Siouan; USA), Fur (Nilo-Saharan; Sudan), Icelandic, Koasati (Muskogean; USA), Kwerba (Trans-New Guinea; Irian Jaya), Latin, Ngiti (Nilo-Saharan; DR Congo), Sanskrit, and Tuḷu (Dravidian; India). These criteria are observable correlates of an inflection-class system's complexity.

In Chapter 4, we discuss **inflection-class transparency**. An inflection class is transparent to the extent that a member lexeme's full inventory of inflected forms may be inferred from subsets of that inventory. In the paradigm of a lexeme belonging to a maximally transparent inflection class, each cell allows every other cell to be deduced; a paradigm of this sort needs only a single principal part, and any of its cells can serve as this principal part. The relative transparency of inflection classes that deviate from this ideal intuitively depends on three criteria: all else being equal, inflection class A with member lexeme *a* is more transparent than inflection class B with member lexeme *b* (1) if the number of principal parts required to deduce a given cell in *a*'s paradigm is, on average, lower than the number of principal parts required to deduce a given cell in *b*'s paradigm; (2) if there are more alternative principal-part analyses for *a* than for *b*; and (3) if *a*'s paradigm has fewer unpredictable cells than *b*'s paradigm. We give formal substance to these intuitive criteria by proposing precise measures of **inflection-class predictability** and **cell predictability**. We demonstrate these measures with evidence from Fur. We show that the deviation of Fur's conjugation classes from maximal transparency is irreconcilable with the No-Blur Principle (Cameron-Faulkner & Carstairs-McCarthy 2000). The proposed measures of inflection-class predictability and cell predictability afford a precise account of cross-linguistic differences in inflection-class transparency, as we demonstrate in a comparison of the conjugational system of Fur with those of Comaltepec Chinantec and Icelandic. Both of these measures are correlates of an inflection-class system's complexity.

In Chapter 5, we show that a cell's predictability and its **predictiveness** may be enhanced by supplementing its phonological realization with additional grammatical information. In particular, we show that in Sanskrit gender specifications tend to heighten both a cell's predictability and its predictiveness; information about stem delimitation also tends to heighten a cell's predictiveness (though not its predictability). Cell predictiveness is another correlate of an inflection-class system's complexity.

In Chapter 6, we discuss two phenomena that complicate the investigation of paradigms' implicative relations: *impostors* (lexemes one or more of whose realizations exhibit morphology that can be analyzed in two different ways, making them ambiguous with respect to their inflection-class membership) and *heteroclites* (lexemes that follow the patterns of different inflection classes in different parts of their paradigms). We draw a distinction between motivated and unmotivated inferences about a lexeme's paradigm of word forms; this distinction is essential to our characterization of an inflection-class system's complexity.

In the conceptual framework developed in Chapters 1 through 6, we regard a lexeme's principal parts as a subset of the cells within its paradigm. In Chapter 7, we discuss an alternative possibility: that a lexeme's principal parts are a subset of the indexed stems upon which its realizations are based. As we show, some inflectional systems favor this alternative conception of principal parts. We elaborate this idea with extensive evidence from the French verb system, whose conjugation-class distinctions are almost entirely expressed by differences in the formation and alternation of stems (Bonami & Boyé 2002). We show that the framework developed in earlier chapters is straightforwardly generalizable to accommodate stem-based principal-part systems.

In Chapter 8, we discuss the **marginal detraction hypothesis**, according to which marginal inflection classes (those with very few members) tend to detract most strongly from the predictability of other, more central inflection classes. Drawing on the evidence of Icelandic verb conjugation, we present an empirical finding that supports this hypothesis. On their own, central (i.e. nonmarginal) conjugations in Icelandic allow the morphosyntactic property sets in a verb's paradigm to be grouped into a comparatively small number of **distillations** (where a distillation is a set S of morphosyntactic property sets such that members of S are isomorphic in their realization across inflection classes); this phenomenon enhances the predictability of a verb's inflection-class membership from a relatively small number of word forms in its paradigm. Marginal conjugations, however, allow fewer morphosyntactic property sets to be grouped together, detracting from the predictability of other conjugations. This finding implies that as languages evolve historically, they are constantly subject to a kind of tension: on one hand, morphological innovations that minimize the number of distillations in a language enhance the predictability of its paradigms, and the number of distillations can be reduced by eliminating marginal inflection classes; yet, the persistence of marginal inflection classes is favored by the fact that they are inherently more predictable than central inflection classes. An inflection-class system's number of distillations is another observable correlate of its complexity.

The feasibility of deducing all of the cells in a lexeme's paradigm from a small subset of these cells raises an important question about the definition of a language's inflectional morphology: should it be defined by means of rules of exponence (which deduce the realization of a given cell K in the paradigm of a lexeme L from L's stem(s) together with the morphosyntactic property set associated with K), or should it instead be defined by means of implicative rules (which deduce the realization of a given cell in the paradigm of a lexeme L from the realizations of one or more other cells in L's paradigm)? In Chapter 9, we compare these approaches – the **exponence-based approach** (Anderson 1992; Matthews 1972; Stump 2001; Zwicky 1985) and the **implicative approach** (Ackerman *et al.* 2009; Blevins 2006) – arguing that they differ in their strengths and that they are not mutually exclusive. We propose a hybrid approach in which implicative rules are derived as theorems of an inflectional system's exponence-based definition; we illustrate with a fragment of Sanskrit declensional morphology.

Recent research on morphological complexity (Ackerman *et al.* 2009; Milin *et al.* 2009; Moscoso del Prado Martín *et al.* 2004) has employed the information-theoretic measures of **entropy** and **conditional entropy** (Shannon 1951) as a way of quantifying the degree to which cells in a lexeme's paradigm are predictable. Principal parts are those cells in a paradigm that reduce the conditional entropy of every remaining cell to zero. In Chapter 10, we compare entropy measures with our measures of predictability and predictiveness. In our discussion, we focus particular attention on the relevance of type frequency in applying all these measures. We demonstrate that measures of entropy, predictability, and predictiveness reveal different patterns and are therefore complementary as elucidations of an inflection-class system's complexity.

In Chapter 11, we discuss the general program of investigating complexity as a dimension of typological contrast, and we situate our approach to the complexity of inflection-class systems within this general program. We draw together the various correlates of inflection-class system's complexity:

(a) the number of distillations the system has
(b) the size of the system's optimal static principal-part sets
(c) the density of the system's optimal static principal-part sets (given (a) and (b))
(d) the average size of optimal dynamic principal-part sets for the system's inflection classes
(e) the average ratio of actual to possible optimal dynamic principal-part sets for the system's inflection classes
(f) the average number of principal parts required to deduce the realization of a given cell in a lexeme's paradigm
(g) a cell's average predictiveness
(h) the average inflection-class predictability of the system's inflection classes
(i) the average cell predictability of the system's inflection classes
(j) what we call the system's m-system entropy.

As we show, these measures quantify subtly different aspects of a paradigm's implicative structure; all are therefore informative as components of an inflection-class system's complexity.

In Chapter 12, we devote additional discussion to the technical task of constructing plats for investigating principal parts, implicative relations, and the complexity of inflection-class systems. We revisit the choices introduced in Chapter 2 and describe how these choices affect the measures introduced in Chapters 4 and 5.

8 *Introduction*

The research on which this book rests is informed by a range of computational algorithms, all of which are embodied in the Principal-Parts Analyzer (PPA). In Chapter 13, we present the formal details of the PPA: form of input, form of output and algorithms employed. We have made the PPA freely available at the following website, along with the plats employed in our research: www.cambridge.org/stump_finkel.

During the preparation of this book, we have presented our work on the typology of inflection-class systems in a number of places; see Finkel & Stump (2006a,b; 2007; 2008a,b; 2009; 2010; 2011a,b; 2012) and Stump (2010). We wish to thank the organizers of the following conferences for inviting us to present our work in progress:

- 12th International Morphology Meeting, Budapest, 2006.
- Conference on Analogy in Grammar: Form and Acquisition, Max Planck Institute for Evolutionary Anthropology, 2006.
- Southeast Morphology Meeting, University of Surrey, 2008.
- Décembrettes 6: Colloque International de Morphologie – Morphologie et classes flexionnelles, Université de Bordeaux, 2008.
- Workshop on Morphological Complexity: Implications for the Theory of Language, Harvard University, January 22, 2010.
- Workshop on Morphology and Formal Grammar, Université Paris Diderot, 2010.
- Workshop on Quantitative Measures in Morphology and Morphological Development, Center for Human Development, UC San Diego, 2011.
- Workshop on the Challenges of Complex Morphology to Morphological Theory, Linguistic Society of America Summer Institute, Boulder, 2011.
- Conference on Morphological Complexity, British Academy, 2012.

At these conferences and elsewhere, we have benefited from the comments and suggestions of a number of people; we wish to convey our particular thanks to Farrell Ackerman, Adam Albright, Matthew Baerman, Jim Blevins, Olivier Bonami, Gilles Boyé, Dunstan Brown, Greville Corbett, Andrew Hippisley, Rob Malouf, Fermín Moscoso del Prado Martín, and Andrea Sims. Olivier Bonami also kindly supplied a database of French conjugations of which we have made extensive use.

1 *Principal parts*

We regard the complexity of an inflection-class system as the extent to which it inhibits motivated inferences about a lexeme's full paradigm of forms from subsets of those forms. Because principal parts are a crystallization of the implicative relations among different cells in a lexeme's paradigm, they are a good starting point for an examination of inflection-class systems' complexity. In this chapter, we consider principal parts both in their traditional pedagogical function (§1.1) and in the broader context of linguistic theory and typology (§1.2). In §1.3, we expound some preliminary assumptions about the nature of principal parts and implicative relations.[1]

1.1 The traditional notion of principal parts

The notion of principal parts depends on the logically prior notion of an inflectional paradigm. This concept has been defined in different ways by different people. For complete clarity, we define the **paradigm** of a lexeme L as a complete set of cells for L, where each **cell** is the pairing of L with a complete and coherent **morphosyntactic property set** (MPS) for which L is inflectable.[2] Given any such MPS σ, we represent the pairing of L with σ as ⟨L, σ⟩. The cell

---

[1] Portions of this chapter first appeared, in somewhat different form, in Finkel & Stump (2007), © Springer Science+Business Media B.V. 2007. Used with kind permission from Springer Science+Business Media B.V. Other portions of this chapter first appeared, in somewhat different form, in R. Finkel & G. Stump (2009), used with kind permission of Oxford University Press.
    The data sets that we have employed in this chapter are:

principal.A	principal.C	principal.E	principal.ngiti
principal.B	principal.D	principal.F	principal.norse

These are available at the *Morphological Typology* website www.cambridge.org/stump_finkel.

[2] All boldface words are technical terms, some of our own invention. We gather their definitions in the glossary. See pp. xxiii–xxiv for a complete list of the abbreviations that we employ.

⟨L, σ⟩ is expressed morphologically as a word form *w*; *w* is in this context the **realization** of L, of σ, and of ⟨L, σ⟩. For example, the paradigm of the English verb BE[3] is a set containing such cells as these:[4]

⟨BE, {1sg pres ind}⟩
⟨BE, {3sg pres ind}⟩
⟨BE, {3sg past ind}⟩
⟨BE, {3sg irrealis}⟩
⟨BE, {past ptcp}⟩.

These cells have the respective realizations *am*, *is*, *was*, *were*, and *been*. A lexeme's **realized cells** are pairings of its realizations with the MPSs that they realize. The realized cells of the lexeme BE include these pairs:

⟨*am*, {1sg pres ind}⟩
⟨*is*, {3sg pres ind}⟩
⟨*was*, {3sg past ind}⟩
⟨*were*, {3sg irrealis}⟩
⟨*been*, {past ptcp}⟩.

Thus, we also say that ⟨*am*, {1sg pres ind}⟩ realizes ⟨BE, {1sg pres ind}⟩, and so on. The complete set of a lexeme's realized cells constitutes its **realized paradigm**. We find it useful to define the related notion of a syntactic category's **paradigm schema**: the set of complete and coherent MPSs realized by the paradigms of specific lexemes belonging to that syntactic category. For instance, the paradigm schema of a Latin noun is this set:

{{nom sg} {nom pl}
 {voc sg} {voc pl}
 {gen sg} {gen pl}
 {dat sg} {dat pl}
 {acc sg} {acc pl}
 {abl sg} {abl pl}
 {loc sg} {loc pl}}.

---

[3] Here and throughout, we follow the conventional practice of representing lexemes in small capital letters.

[4] A **morphosyntactic property** is the specification of an inflectional category by one of its permissible values. For example, the morphosyntactic property 'NUMBER: singular' is a specification of the inflectional category of number. Where there is no risk of ambiguity, we abbreviate the morphosyntactic property C: *v* (where C is an inflectional category and *v* is one of C's permissible values) as *v*.

Given these notions, we define a lexeme's principal parts as in (1):

(1) The **principal parts** of a lexeme L are a set of cells in L's realized paradigm from which one can reliably deduce the remaining cells in L's realized paradigm.

It is important to regard principal parts as realized cells (as in (1)) rather than as mere word forms. Consider, for example, the Latin noun AGER 'field'. Traditionally, this lexeme is regarded as having the forms *ager* and *agrī* as its principal parts, but these realizations do not work as principal parts if we do not know what property sets they are associated with. For instance, if we did not know that *agrī* is genitive and not dative, we might wrongly assume that AGER inflects like PATER 'father', whose singular paradigm includes the realizations *pater* and *patrī*, which are respectively nominative singular and dative singular. Accordingly, when we say that *ager* and *agrī* are a set of principal parts for AGER, we must understand this statement as shorthand for saying that this lexeme has the realized cells ⟨*ager*, {nom sg}⟩ and ⟨*agrī*, {gen sg}⟩ as a principal-part set.

Principal parts are useful for learning languages whose inflection, like that of Latin, is structured around a system of **inflection classes** (ICs).[5] In such languages, different members of the same part of speech exhibit inflectional differences that do not follow straightforwardly from their meaning, their syntax, or their phonology. In formal grammatical descriptions, these differences are accounted for by assigning members of the same part of speech to different ICs (traditionally called "conjugations" for verbs and "declensions" for nominal lexemes such as nouns and adjectives), and it is precisely a lexeme's membership in a particular IC that its principal parts allow one to infer. In languages in which all members of a given part of speech inflect alike, there is no use for principal parts; in such languages, each lexeme has at most a single principal part, which is informative only to the extent that it identifies the phonology of the lexeme's root or stem. That is, principal parts are no more useful in a language without ICs (such as Turkish) than in a language that lacks inflectional morphology altogether (such as Mandarin Chinese).

The use of principal parts as a means of identifying a lexeme's IC membership (and hence the full content of its realized paradigm) has a long history in

---

[5] An inflection class is a class J of lexemes such that (i) J's members are distinguished by a common pattern of inflection and (ii) membership in J has no syntactic significance; conjugation classes and declension classes are inflection classes. An **IC system** for a syntactic category C is a set S of ICs such that every lexeme belonging to C belongs to some IC in S.

12 *Principal parts*

Table 1.1. *Principal parts of five Latin verbs*

Conjugation	$\sigma_1 = \{\text{1sg pres ind active}\}$	$\sigma_2 = \{\text{1sg perf ind active}\}$	$\sigma_3 = \{\text{first supine}\}$	$\sigma_4 = \{\text{pres active inf}\}$
1st	⟨*laudō*, σ_1⟩	⟨*laudāvī*, σ_2⟩	⟨*laudātum*, σ_3⟩	⟨*laudāre*, σ_4⟩
2nd	⟨*moneō*, σ_1⟩	⟨*monuī*, σ_2⟩	⟨*monitum*, σ_3⟩	⟨*monēre*, σ_4⟩
3rd	⟨*dūcō*, σ_1⟩	⟨*dūxī*, σ_2⟩	⟨*dūctum*, σ_3⟩	⟨*dūcere*, σ_4⟩
3rd (*-iō*)	⟨*capiō*, σ_1⟩	⟨*cēpī*, σ_2⟩	⟨*captum*, σ_3⟩	⟨*capere*, σ_4⟩
4th	⟨*audiō*, σ_1⟩	⟨*audīvī*, σ_2⟩	⟨*audītum*, σ_3⟩	⟨*audīre*, σ_4⟩

language pedagogy. For instance, in his *Institutes of Latin Grammar* (1823: 91), John Grant says:

> There are four principal parts of a [Latin] verb, whence all its other parts are formed, viz. *o* of the present, *i* of the preterite, *um* of the supine, and *re* of the infinitive: as, *Amo, amavi, amatum, amare;* and these are sometimes called its conjugation.

In our terms, Grant's "*o* of the present, *i* of the preterite, *um* of the supine, and *re* of the infinitive" mean cells in a verb's realized paradigm: (i) the first-person singular present indicative active, (ii) the first-person singular perfect indicative active, (iii) the first supine, and (iv) the present active infinitive. Thus, the Latin verbal lexemes LAUDĀRE 'praise', MONĒRE 'warn', DŪCERE 'lead', CAPERE 'take', and AUDĪRE 'hear' have the principal parts in Table 1.1.

Generations of Latin students have learned that by memorizing these four forms for a given Latin verb, one can predict all of the other forms in its paradigm. The principles supporting these predictions are the **implicative relations** that exist among the cells of a lexeme's realized paradigm; these are relations of the type "the realized cell ⟨*w*, σ⟩ determines the realized cell ⟨*x*, τ⟩" (or, more generally, of the type "the realized cells ⟨w_1, σ_1⟩, ..., ⟨w_n, σ_n⟩ determine the realized cell ⟨*x*, τ⟩"). For instance, Grant identifies the implicative relations in which a Latin verb's principal parts participate by means of Table 1.2.

In this table, Grant suggests that each unknown cell in a Latin verb's realized paradigm can be deduced by reference to a single principal part, and this suggestion is mostly true. For instance, the first-person singular perfect indicative active form in *-ī* implies a first-person singular pluperfect indicative active form in *-eram* (e.g. *laudāvī, monuī, dūxī, cēpī, audīvī* imply *laudāveram, monueram, dūxeram, cēperam, audīveram*), a first-person singular perfect

Table 1.2. *The formation of the tenses of verbs, from the present, the perfect, the supine, and the infinitive (Grant 1823: 92)*

		Names of the tenses
I. From -*o* are formed,	-*bam*,	Imperf. Indic.
	-*bo*,	Fut Indic. of the 1st and 2d Conjugation.
	-*am*,	Pres. Subj. of the 2d; Pres. Subj. and Fut Indic. of 3d and 4th.
	-*em*,	Pres. Subj. of the 1st.
	-*ns*,	the Present participle.
	-*dus*,	the Fut. Participle, Passive.
	-*dum, -di, -do*,	the Gerunds.
II. From the -*i* are formed,	-*ram*,	the Plup. Indic.
	-*rim*,	the Perf. Subj.
	-*ro*,	the Fut. Subj. [= future perfect; cf. pp. 83f]
	-*ssem*,	the Plup. Subj.
	-*sse*,	the Perf. Infinit.
III. From -*um* are formed,	-*u*,	the second Supine.
	-*us*,	the Perf. Participle, Passive.
	-*rus*,	the Future Participle.
IV. From the infinitive, whether in -*re*, -*le*, or -*se*, are formed the imperative, by cutting off the final syllable; and the imperfect of the subjunctive, by adding -*m* to it.		

subjunctive active form in -*erim* (e.g. *laudāverim, monuerim, dūxerim, cēperim, audīverim*), and so on. On the other hand, inferences from the "*o* of the present" in Table 1.2 also sometimes refer to a lexeme's present-system conjugation-class membership; given that a verb's present active infinitive reliably reveals its present-system conjugation-class membership, such inferences should be seen as involving simultaneous reference to two principal parts – the "*o* of the present" and the present active infinitive. For instance, a lexeme's first-person singular present indicative active form in -*ō* and its present active infinitive in -*re* together determine its first-person singular imperfect indicative active form in -*bam*, its first-person singular future indicative active form in -*bō* (1st and 2nd conjugations) or -*am* (3rd and 4th conjugations), and so on, as in (2). Table 1.2 does not make explicit reference to finite forms other than those in the first-person singular, but Grant presumably regards these forms as deducible from the corresponding first-person singular forms (together with the present active infinitive in the case of nonperfect tenses). Thus, principal parts are predictors: individually or in combination, they allow all remaining cells in a lexeme's realized paradigm to be deduced.

(2)   Principal parts

σ_1 = {1sg pres ind active}	σ_2 = {pres active inf}		σ_3 = {1sg impf ind active}	σ_4 = {1sg fut ind active}
$\langle laudō, \sigma_1 \rangle$	$\langle laudāre, \sigma_2 \rangle$	→	$\langle laudābam, \sigma_3 \rangle$	$\langle laudābō, \sigma_4 \rangle$
$\langle moneō, \sigma_1 \rangle$	$\langle monēre, \sigma_2 \rangle$	→	$\langle monēbam, \sigma_3 \rangle$	$\langle monēbō, \sigma_4 \rangle$
$\langle dūcō, \sigma_1 \rangle$	$\langle dūcere, \sigma_2 \rangle$	→	$\langle dūcēbam, \sigma_3 \rangle$	$\langle dūcam, \sigma_4 \rangle$
$\langle capiō, \sigma_1 \rangle$	$\langle capere, \sigma_2 \rangle$	→	$\langle capiēbam, \sigma_3 \rangle$	$\langle capiam, \sigma_4 \rangle$
$\langle audiō, \sigma_1 \rangle$	$\langle audīre, \sigma_2 \rangle$	→	$\langle audiēbam, \sigma_3 \rangle$	$\langle audiam, \sigma_4 \rangle$

In pedagogical contexts, language learners memorize principal parts as an easy way to memorize whole paradigms. Because of this specific purpose, principal parts are, in pedagogical contexts, assumed to have three characteristics that are not necessitated by definition (1). First, a lexeme L is assumed to have a **unique** set of principal parts; that is, although there may be various subsets of cells in L's realized paradigm from which L's full realized paradigm is predictable, the label "principal parts" is reserved for only one of these subsets, whose identity is agreed upon as a matter of convention. Thus, it is customarily agreed that Latin AGER 'field' has the nominative singular and genitive singular cells as its unique set of principal parts, although its full realized paradigm is also predictable from other sets of cells (such as its nominative singular and its genitive plural). This assumption of uniqueness makes things easier for the language learner, who is not asked to pick and choose among alternative principal-part sets.

Second, the principal-part sets used in language pedagogy are **uniform**, in the sense that lexemes belonging to the same syntactic category are assumed to have the same cells in their realized paradigms as their principal parts. Thus, in Latin textbooks, all nouns are (like AGER) conventionally assumed to have their nominative singular and genitive singular cells as their principal parts, regardless of the declension to which they belong. If a system of principal parts is uniform in this sense, we call it a "static" system of principal parts (Finkel & Stump 2007: 41; see §1.4.2 below).

Finally, principal-part sets prescribed for use in language pedagogy are chosen so as to be **optimal**; that is, they are as small as possible while still (a) fulfilling the objective of predicting a lexeme's entire realized paradigm and (b) satisfying the requirement of uniformity. In Latin, for example, the nominative singular and genitive singular cells in a noun's realized paradigm generally suffice to predict the full paradigm, but ordinarily, neither the nominative singular cell nor the genitive singular cell alone suffices. As the examples in (3) show, AGER 'field' patterns with PATER 'father' in the nominative singular but with AMĪCUS 'friend' in the genitive singular; both the nominative singular and the genitive singular cells in AGER's realized paradigm are therefore necessary to distinguish its declension-class membership. (In certain instances, a noun's declension-class membership is determined by a single cell in its realized paradigm; for instance, the nominative singular form *cornū* of the noun CORNŪ 'horn' immediately identifies it as a member of the fourth declension. In such cases, the requirement of uniformity outweighs the requirement of optimality, so CORNŪ traditionally has two principal parts – ⟨*cornū*, {nom sg}⟩, ⟨*cornūs*, {gen sg}⟩.)

(3) Nominative singular and genitive singular realizations of three Latin nouns

	Nominative singular	Genitive singular
AMĪCUS 'friend'	*amīcus*	*amīcī*
AGER 'field'	*ager*	*agrī*
PATER 'father'	*pater*	*patris*

Despite the fact that principal-part sets are, in traditional pedagogy, unique, uniform, and optimal, nothing in definition (1) necessitates these characteristics; as we shall see, it is desirable to suspend these assumptions once we begin considering principal parts in a theoretical and typological perspective.

Although the theoretical and typological significance of ICs has been widely discussed (Aronoff 1994; Carstairs 1987; Dressler *et al.* 2006; Stump 2001), that of principal parts has generally received little attention.[6] Yet, because they concisely epitomize the system of implicative relations among the cells in a realized paradigm, principal parts have considerable interest in the domains of linguistic theory and typology; we present a preliminary justification of this perspective in §1.2.

1.2 Principal parts in linguistic theory and in language typology

In the theoretical realm, principal parts are relevant for representing lexemes' IC membership and for deducing their realized paradigms (§1.2.1); in the domain of language typology, they afford a precise means of comparing the kinds of implicative networks exhibited by the inflectional systems of different languages (§1.2.2).

---

[6] An important exception is Brown & Evans 2010, who present an unsupervised machine learning method for distinguishing Russian declension classes from input paradigms. The performance of this method is relatively unaffected if cells exhibiting default inflectional patterns are omitted from the input paradigms, but performance is degraded if principal parts are omitted.

1.2.1   Principal parts and the lexicon

Principal parts are an idealization of an important feature of language acquisition, namely the fact that language learners rely on the implicative relations among the cells in a lexeme's realized paradigm to deduce that paradigm's full inventory of cells. This feature of language acquisition is clearly revealed by the incidence of "faulty" inferences both in the speech of language learners and in the diachronic evolution of languages. Thus, a child who asks *What if he bees silly?* is drawing on the usually reliable implicative relation in (4). Ultimately, the child learns that this relation is not invariably reliable, since it does not hold in the paradigms of BE, HAVE, DO, and SAY. Similarly, the past tense of DIVE has, in many varieties of English, evolved from *dived* to *dove* thanks to the implicative pattern in (5), which is supported by verbs like DRIVE, RIDE, RISE, and WRITE (although not by CLIMB, CHIME, PRIDE or SLIDE).

(4)   ⟨/X/, {inf}⟩ → ⟨/Xz/, {3sg pres ind active}⟩[7]

(5)   ⟨/XaɪY/, {inf}⟩ → ⟨/XoʊY/, {past}⟩

The implicative relations in (4) and (5) are less than fully general; as such, they are subject to overgeneralization in the speech of children and may, over time, engender divergent dialectal developments.[8] But many of the implicative relationships in a language's inflectional system are exceptionless, defining patterns to which generations of speakers adhere with unfailing regularity. For instance, the pattern in (6) (supported by verbs such as CUT, HIT, HURT, PUT, and SHUT) is exceptionless; so are the Latin patterns in (7)

(6)   ⟨X*t*, {inf}⟩ & ⟨X*t*, {past ptcp}⟩ → ⟨X*t*, {past tense}⟩

(7)   (a) ⟨X*ī*, {1sg perf ind active}⟩ → ⟨X*istī*, {2sg perf ind active}⟩
        (b) ⟨X*e*, {pres active inf}⟩ → ⟨X*em*, {1sg impf sbjv active}⟩
        (c) ⟨X*um*, {first supine}⟩ → ⟨X*ūrus*, {fut active ptcp}⟩

Principal parts are a skeletal representation of those aspects of a lexeme's inflection that remain unpredictable once the effects of such exceptionless patterns have been factored out. They distill whole networks of reliable inferences into concise signatures (irreducible signatures, if the pedagogical assumption of optimality is maintained; §1.1). The traditional principal parts of CAPERE

---

[7] /Xz/ is adjusted where necessary to /Xs/ or /Xəz/ by automatic phonology.

[8] Innovations such as *he bees* and *he dove* are sometimes characterized as analogical, but we avoid this terminology because of the logical distinction between rule-based inference and true analogy; see Albright & Hayes 2003; Ernestus & Baayen 2003, 2004; and Chandler 2010 for relevant discussion.

(the realized cells of *capiō*, *cēpī*, *captum*, and *capere*) predict all of its other forms, yet are themselves unpredictable.

The frequency of "faulty" inferences such as *he bees* and *he dove* reveals the psychological reality of implicative relations among the cells of a lexeme's paradigm. It is reasonable to assume that language users make many non-faulty inferences as well (even though inferences that are not faulty are not easily detectable, since the forms that they introduce are difficult to distinguish from forms that are heard and learned individually, without inferences). In view of this conclusion, one might try to develop a theory of morphology that attributes central importance to a lexeme's principal parts and to the implicative relations that affiliate them with the other cells in the lexeme's realized paradigm. For instance, one might entertain the following hypothesis:

The **pure word-and-paradigm morphology (PWPM)** hypothesis

Axiom 1. The realization rules that define a language's inflectional morphology are purely **implicative rules** (expressing implicative relations among realized cells).

Axiom 2. The **stored principal-part (SPP) hypothesis**: a lexeme L's entry in the mental lexicon includes a set of principal parts for L.

Axiom 3. Because a lexeme's IC membership is determined by its principal-part set, neither **IC diacritics** such as '1st conjugation' and '2nd declension' nor inflectional stems such as *laudā-* and *amīc-* are stored in the mental lexicon, nor do they figure in the formulation of realization rules.

According to the PWPM hypothesis' first axiom, a language's inflectional morphology is defined purely by means of implicative rules such as those in (6) and (7); thus, the PWPM hypothesis explicitly excludes rules of exponence such as (8). (See Ackerman *et al.* 2011; Blevins 2006; Robins 1959; and Wurzel 1984 for specific approaches to inflectional morphology that conform to Axiom 1; for approaches making essential use of rules of exponence, see Anderson 1992; Matthews 1972; Stump 2001; and Zwicky 1985.)

(8)   Sample **rule of exponence**. A verbal lexeme's 2sg perfect indicative active form is the result of suffixing the exponent *-istī* to its perfect stem.

According to the PWPM hypothesis' second axiom (the SPP hypothesis), a lexeme's entry in the mental lexicon includes a set of principal parts serving to identify the lexeme's IC membership. This hypothesis is compatible with psycholinguistic evidence that full word forms are lexically stored for irregular lexemes and for regular lexemes of sufficiently high frequency (Alegre & Gordon 1999; Baayen *et al*. 1997, 2002, 2003, 2007; Bybee 1995; Hare *et al*. 2001; Prasada & Pinker 1993). The SPP hypothesis makes, however, a somewhat stronger claim – that the lexical entry of a given lexeme L contains at least enough cells in L's realized paradigm to determine all of the remaining realized cells. As it is formulated above, the SPP hypothesis admits a conception of principal parts that is significantly less restrictive than the pedagogical conception. It entails neither that each lexeme has a unique lexically listed principal-part set, nor that the realized cells belonging to lexically listed principal-part sets are uniform across lexemes belonging to the same syntactic category, nor that lexically listed principal-part sets are optimal. In addition, it does not entail that language users will necessarily agree on which principal parts they store for a given lexeme.

The PWPM hypothesis' third axiom excludes the use of IC diacritics and inflectional stems in lexical entries and in the formulation of realization rules. Thus, it entails that there is no generalization about stems that cannot be reduced to a generalization about whole word forms, and that sensitivities to a lexeme's IC membership are in fact sensitivities to its principal-part set. This entailment is not an unreasonable notion, since principal-part sets may be more informative than diacritic indices about the degrees of similarity among ICs. For example, the Latin verbs CAPERE 'seize' and AUDĪRE 'hear' belong to different conjugations (traditionally labeled the third and fourth conjugations), but the similarity of their principal parts *capiō* and *audiō* (see again Table 1.1) entails numerous parallelisms in their inflection, in accordance with the patterns in Grant's table (Table 1.2); these are the parallelisms in (9). Representing the IC membership of CAPERE and AUDĪRE by means of principal parts rather than by IC labels highlights this kind of inflectional kinship.

(9) | | |
|---|---|
| Imperfect indicative active: | *capiēbam, capiēbās*, etc. *audiēbam, audiēbās*, etc. |
| Present subjunctive active: | *capiam, capiās*, etc. *audiam, audiās*, etc. |
| Future indicative active: | *capiam, capiēs*, etc. *audiam, audiēs*, etc. |
| Present participle: | *capiēns* *audiēns* |
| Future passive participle: | *capiendus* *audiendus* |
| Gerund (accusative form): | *capiendum* *audiendum* |

The PWPM hypothesis entails that language users deduce the unstored cells in a lexeme's realized paradigm from the stored cells (that is, from the lexeme's principal parts), and that they do this by employing implicative rules applying to fully inflected word forms, without reference to stems, affixes or IC diacritics.

This hypothesis is not obviously untenable. In Chapter 9, however, we reject it, arguing instead

(a) that the rules involved in the definition of a language's inflectional morphology include rules of stem selection and rules of exponence whose application to the stem of a lexeme L is conditioned by L's IC diacritic; and
(b) that implicative rules are deducible from this definition and are used by language users to assign newly encountered lexemes to the appropriate IC.

We maintain a neutral stance with respect to the SPP hypothesis. We nevertheless feel that the notion of lexical storage provides a useful way of understanding the concept of principal parts. There is no question that language users store some realized cells of the lexemes they use. On the assumption that they use these stored cells to deduce the other, unstored cells in these lexemes' realized paradigms, the question naturally arises: how many of a lexeme's realized cells are stored? At one extreme, there could be full storage. At the opposite extreme, there could be storage of the minimum of realized cells needed to deduce the remaining, unstored cells. Optimal principal parts embody this notion of a lower extreme.

Although the notion of lexical storage affords a useful way of understanding the notion of principal parts, it is not the only way of conceiving the role of principal parts in a language's inflectional morphology. We return to this issue in Chapter 9.

1.2.2 Principal parts in language typology
As an expression of the implicative relations that exist among the members of a given lexeme's realized paradigm, principal parts constitute an important domain of typological variation in morphology.

Since Friedrich von Schlegel (1808) first articulated his classification of languages according to morphological types (a classification extended by Humboldt [1836] and refined by Sapir [1921]), research on morphological typology has tended to focus on the structure of individual word forms and on their external syntax. For instance:

- Greenberg (1960) employs ten indices for the typological classification of morphological systems: (i) morphemes per word, (ii) degree of agglutination, (iii) ratio of root morphemes to words, (iv) ratio of derivational morphemes to words, (v) ratio of inflectional morphemes to words, (vi) ratio of prefixes to words, (vii) ratio of suffixes to words, and the extent to which (viii) word order, (ix) nonconcordial inflection,

and (x) concordial inflections are used to express significant relations between words in a sentence.
- Nichols (1992: 64f) suggests that the complexity of a language's inflectional morphology is a function of the extent to which it employs head or dependent marking in expressing the subject–verb relation (with a nominal subject and with a pronominal subject), the relation between a verb and its direct or indirect object (with a nominal object and with a pronominal object), the possessor–possessed relation (with a nominal possessor and with a pronominal possessor), and the adjective–noun relation. (See Nichols *et al.* 2006 for related discussion.)
- Juola (1998) equates a language's morphological complexity with the extent to which a word's parts participate in regular relationships with the word's syntactic contexts. On this view, morphological complexity is measurable through the application of compression algorithms to sample corpora.
- In his investigation of the negative correlation hypothesis ("If one component of language is simplified then another must be elaborated"), Shosted (2006: 1) employs inflectional synthesis as his primary metric of morphological complexity; see de Groot (2008) and Nichols (2009) for similar perspectives.
- Kusters (2008) distinguishes three classificatory criteria in the domain of inflectional morphology: (a) degree of economy (the number of categories expressed by a word), (b) degree of transparency (the extent to which morphosyntactic properties and their exponents are biunique), and (c) degree of isomorphy ("The more the order in the morphological domain is computable and motivated by the order in the semantic or syntactic domain, the more isomorphic the morphology is", p. 13).

The criteria that we propose extend the focus of typological classification from the form or syntax of individual words to the structure of whole realized paradigms and the implicative relations that they embody. This new, paradigm-based approach to the typological classification of inflectional systems draws together two themes in contemporary language typology. First, it draws on work asserting the status of linguistic complexity as a measurable variable for the comparison of grammatical systems. Everyone who has learned more than a single language has sensed that one language may be more complex than another in some respect; recent research (Dahl 2004; Hawkins 2004; Miestamo *et al.* 2008; Sinnemäki 2011) suggests that this feeling is not merely a naïve intuition, but actually correlates with objectively measurable properties of human language. Whether one can rank entire languages according to their complexity is (and will, we think, inevitably remain) a matter of debate, but this issue is ultimately irrelevant to the more tractable question of whether two IC systems (or other well-delineated grammatical subsystems) can differ in complexity. Our conviction is that this latter question is susceptible to empirical investigation; but in order to investigate this issue, one needs to be clear about criteria. What does it mean for an IC system to be complex? How would we recognize a complex IC system if we saw one?

Our consideration of these issues brings in a second important theme in contemporary linguistic typology: the notion that differences among grammatical systems can be most clearly calibrated with respect to canonical points of reference (Corbett 2005, 2007, 2009). By articulating the logical distinction between maximally simple and maximally complex IC systems, we can more clearly identify the dimensions along which actual IC systems vary between these two extremes.

Our objective in this monograph is to propose a clear conception of an IC system's complexity, as the extent to which it inhibits motivated inferences about a lexeme's full realized paradigm from subsets of its cells. We shall see that an IC system may be complex (in this sense) for one or more of a variety of reasons. Consider, for example, the hypothetical IC systems in Table 1.3, in which ρ, σ, and τ represent distinct MPSs; I through IV represent distinct ICs; each of **a** through **i** represents the exponence[9] of a particular MPS in a particular IC. (We call a matrix of this sort a **plat**; as we show later, representing IC systems as plats facilitates the analysis of implicative relations among a realized paradigm's cells.) As scrutiny of the four plats in Table 1.3 reveals, the imaginary IC systems that they represent are complex for different reasons. System A is complex because the exponences of its ρ-cells (shaded), though deducible from other cells, are themselves unpredictive: the fact that a lexeme has a ρ-cell with exponence **a** reveals nothing about its other cells (i.e. reveals nothing about the lexeme's IC membership); the ρ-cells in system A therefore would not be much good as principal parts. By contrast, system B is complex because the (shaded) exponences of certain cells (the ρ-cells

---

[9] Here and throughout, we maintain the following terminological distinction. An **exponent** is a minimal morphological realization of some set of one or more morphosyntactic properties; it is minimal in the sense that no proper subpart of it is itself an exponent. The **exponence** of a MPS in some word form is the full set of exponents of that property set in that word form. Thus, the exponence of the property set {1sg present perfective indicative active} in Latin *laudāvī* 'I have praised' is *-vī* (= the exponent *-v* of the perfective active and the exponent *-ī* of the first-person singular present perfective indicative active).

Table 1.3. *Four hypothetical IC systems*

System A				System B		
	ρ	σ	τ		ρ	σ	τ
I	a	b	f	I	a	d	f
II	a	c	g	II	b	d	f
III	a	d	h	III	c	e	g
IV	a	e	i	IV	c	e	h

System C				System D		
	ρ	σ	τ		ρ	σ	τ
I	a	e	g	I	a	c	e
II	b	e	h	II	a	d	f
III	c	f	h	III	b	d	e
IV	d	f	g	IV	b	c	f

In System A, the shaded cells are unpredictive; in System B, the shaded cells are unpredictable; in System C, a row's shaded cell is predictable only by reference to both of the other cells in that row; and in System D, no shaded cell is predictable except by reference to the two other cells in its row.

in ICs I and II and the τ-cells in ICs III and IV), though perfectly predictive, are unpredictable: no matter how much one knows about the exponences of the other cells in their paradigms, one cannot motivatedly deduce the exponence of these particular cells (which must therefore be principal parts). System C is complex for a different reason. Though all of its cells are both predictive and predictable, there is an asymmetry: the exponences in the σ- and τ-cells are all predictable from that of the corresponding ρ-cell, the (shaded) exponences of a realized paradigm's ρ-cell can only be inferred by simultaneous reference to the exponences of both the corresponding σ-cell and the corresponding τ-cell. Thus, it takes more information to infer the exponence of a lexeme's ρ-cell than to infer the exponence of its σ- and τ-cells; put another way, only certain of the cells in system C are optimal principal parts. System D is complex for yet a different reason: here, all cells are predictive, all are predictable, and all may be optimal principal parts; in this system, however, no IC allows a lexeme's optimal principal-part set to have fewer than two members.

These hypothetical examples show that there are different ways in which an IC system may inhibit motivated inferences about a lexeme's full realized paradigm from subsets of that paradigm's cells. It is therefore necessary to see an inflection-class system's complexity as a multifaceted property. We will accordingly present several measurable correlates of this complexity; these correlates will afford precise, objective comparisons of actual IC systems with respect to different facets of their complexity.

Some of the correlates of this complexity involve optimal principal-part sets. All else being equal, IC system X is more complex than IC system Y:

(i) if the optimal principal-part sets for X's lexemes are larger than those for Y's lexemes;
(ii) if deducing a given cell in a lexeme's realized paradigm requires simultaneous reference to more optimal principal parts in X than in Y; and
(iii) to the extent that X's ICs exhibit less regularity than Y's ICs in the ways in which realized cells are inferred from optimal principal parts.

By these measures, the IC system of Icelandic verbs possesses greater complexity than that of verbs in Tuḷu (Southern Dravidian), as the following facts show:

(i) Icelandic verbs require eight principal parts while Tuḷu verbs require two.[10]
(ii) Verbs in some Icelandic conjugations have realized paradigms in which the content of a given cell may only be deduced by simultaneous reference to two, three, or even four of its principal parts; by contrast, deducing a form in a Tuḷu verb's realized paradigm never involves reference to more than one of its principal parts.
(iii) In the realized paradigm of a given Tuḷu verb, there is always one cell that determines all of the remaining cells in the paradigm; across all conjugations, the identity of that determinant cell is (in the optimal analysis) always one of only two possibilities. In Icelandic, by contrast, the patterns of deduction are much less regular across conjugations.

The properties of a language's optimal principal-part sets are not, however, the only correlates of its IC system's complexity; some such correlates pertain directly to the implicative relations embodied by a language's realized paradigms, independently of any principal-part analysis to which such paradigms may be subject. Optimal principal-part sets are, after all, an idealization of language learners' reliance on the implicative relationships among the cells in a lexeme's realized paradigm as a means of deducing that lexeme's full inventory of realized cells. They are an idealization in the sense that they constitute the very minimum

---

[10] Here we refer to static rather than adaptive or dynamic principal parts; see §1.3.6 for discussion of this distinction.

Table 1.4. *A hypothetical IC system*

	System E		
	ρ	σ	τ
I	a	e	g
II	b	e	g
III	c	f	h
IV	d	f	h

The shaded cells are optimal principal parts.

number of cells in a realized paradigm upon which a language learner could draw as a basis for inferring the realized paradigm as a whole. In actual language learning, learners needn't necessarily base their inferences on this bare minimum. Indeed, many if not all of the cells in a realized paradigm participate in the sorts of implicative relations that optimal principal-part sets idealize; the mere fact that cell K_1 can be deduced from cell K_2 does not guarantee K_2's status as a principal part in some optimal principal-part analysis.

Consider the hypothetical IC system E in Table 1.4, whose optimal principal parts are shaded. Although a lexeme L belonging to IC I in Table 1.4 has its realized paradigm's ρ-cell (with exponence **a**) as its optimal principal part, a learner can, upon encountering L's σ-cell (with exponence **e**), immediately infer L's τ-cell (with exponence **g**); that is, both (10a) and (10b) are valid inferences[11] about system E, even though (10b) (unlike (10a)) makes no reference to any optimal principal part. Thus, not all inferences are based on optimal principal-part sets; rather, they are based on a realized paradigm's implicative relations, some of which engage a lexeme's optimal principal-part set and others of which might not.

(10)   Where L_x is L's realization with exponence x,
      (a) $\langle L_a, \rho \rangle \rightarrow \langle L_e, \sigma \rangle$
      (b) $\langle L_e, \sigma \rangle \rightarrow \langle L_g, \tau \rangle$

Because some of the implicative relations embodied by a language's realized paradigms do not directly involve optimal principal-part sets, some of the

---

[11] Naturally, inferences of this sort can only be drawn with full confidence if one has already encountered all of a language's contrasting ICs; for system E, for instance, one can only be completely confident of the inferences in (10) if there are no unencountered conjugations beyond I–IV. For this reason, language learners do sometimes draw unreliable inferences, though unreliable patterns of inference are generally rejected (or restricted in some fashion) when contradictory evidence is encountered.

correlates of an IC system's complexity involve implicative relations among paradigmatic cells, without any necessary reference to optimal principal parts. Thus, all else being equal, IC system X is more complex than IC system Y

(iv) if the realized cells in Y's paradigms are more predictable than those in X's paradigms, and
(v) if the realized cells in Y's paradigms are more predictive than those in X's paradigms.

In order to apply these criteria in a precise way, we need measures of a realized cell's predictability and its predictiveness. We propose explicit set-theoretic measures of these sorts in Chapters 4 and 5; in Chapters 10 and 11, we compare the measures with an alternative, information-theoretic measure. We believe that all of these measures are relevant as objective correlates of the notion of an IC system's complexity. In the coming chapters, we introduce other correlates as well, ultimately combining them in a summary presentation of this notion in Chapter 11.

1.3. Some preliminary assumptions

Our analyses of the complexity of IC systems rest on certain empirical assumptions about the nature of a language's system of implicative relations; we present these assumptions here.

1.3.1 *If two lexemes belong to the same syntactic category but to contrasting ICs, their principal-part sets may be different.*

Traditional principal-part analyses often adhere to the assumption of uniformity (§1.1), according to which lexemes belonging to the same syntactic category have parallel sets of optimal principal parts (as, for instance, in the case of Latin verbs in Table 1.1). In this purely **static** scheme for optimal principal-part sets, lexemes belonging to the same syntactic category are all alike: if one verbal lexeme has its first-person singular present indicative active cell and its infinitive cell as its optimal principal parts, then so do all of the other verbal lexemes. And one can, of course, always simply stipulate that all members of a given category employ the same cells in their paradigms as principal parts, then give all lexemes principal-part sets that are sufficiently large that no matter what morphological peculiarities a given lexeme might possess, its principal-part set allows the remaining forms in its realized paradigm to be deduced. But in many languages with IC systems, certain members of a given syntactic category may have realized paradigms that are optimally deduced from one set of principal parts, while other members of that same category have realized paradigms that are optimally deduced from some distinct set of principal parts. That is, lexemes in a given syntactic category may participate in patterns of deduction that are sufficiently different as to involve optimal principal-part sets that differ in number and/or identity.

Plausible cases of this sort can even be cited from traditional grammatical descriptions. In his grammar of Old Norse, Wimmer (1871) proposes different principal-part analyses for strong verbs and weak verbs. A strong verb has four optimal principal parts (p. 93): the infinitive present, the first-person singular preterite indicative, the first-person plural preterite indicative, and the preterite participle, e.g. the cells of *bjóða*, *bauð*, *buðum*, and *boðinn* in the realized paradigm of BJÓÐA 'offer'. By contrast, it is unnecessary to specify four principal parts for weak verbs, since their morphology is more predictable than that of strong verbs. Accordingly, a weak verb has three optimal principal parts (p. 114): the infinitive present, the first-person singular preterite indicative, and the preterite participle, e.g. the cells of *dœma*, *dœmda*, and *dœmdr* in the realized paradigm of DŒMA 'deem'. That is, the realized paradigms of weak verbs differ from those of strong verbs in that their first plural preterite indicative cells are deducible from their first singular preterite indicative cells, e.g. ⟨*dœmda*, {1sg preterite ind}⟩ → ⟨*dœmdum*, {1pl preterite ind}⟩. (Compare the full strong and weak realized paradigms in Table 1.5, where shaded cells represent the principal-part sets proposed by Wimmer.) As this example suggests, different subclasses of a given syntactic category may possess different degrees of predictability; for this reason, they may differ in the number of principal parts that they require.

In the foregoing example, the cells serving as optimal principal parts in a weak verb's realized paradigm are a proper subset of those serving as optimal principal parts in a strong verb's realized paradigm. But it can also happen that different ICs of a given syntactic category participate in implicative patterns that are substantially different, so that their optimal principal parts must be chosen rather differently.[12] Thus, consider the Old Norse verb ÞURFA 'need' in Table 1.6. For this verb, neither the strong sort of optimal principal-part set nor the weak sort is sufficient to predict its full realized paradigm, because ÞURFA belongs to the small class of "preterite–present" verbs, whose preterite tense forms follow the weak conjugation but whose present-tense forms have the morphology typical of a strong verb's preterite-tense forms. Thus, if

---

[12] This observation is the fundamental motivation for the adaptive and dynamic approaches to principal-part analysis, which we introduce in §1.3.6.

Table 1.5. *Realized paradigms of two Old Norse verbs*

Present

Conjugation	Example		1sg	2sg	3sg	1pl	2pl	3pl		1sg	2sg	3sg	1pl	2pl	3pl
			Indicative							Subjunctive					
Strong	BJÓÐA 'offer'		*býð*	*býðr*	*býðr*	*bjóðum*	*bjóðið*	*bjóða*		*bjóða*	*bjóðir*	*bjóði*	*bjóðim*	*bjóðið*	*bjóði*
Weak	DŒMA 'deem'		*dœmi*	*dœmir*	*dœmi*	*dœmum*	*dœmið*	*dœma*		*dœma*	*dœmir*	*dœmi*	*dœmim*	*dœmið*	*dœmi*

Preterite

Conjugation	Example		1sg	2sg	3sg	1pl	2pl	3pl		1sg	2sg	3sg	1pl	2pl	3pl
			Indicative							Subjunctive					
Strong	BJÓÐA 'offer'		*bauð*	*bautt*	*bauð*	*buðum*	*buðuð*	*buðu*		*byða*	*byðir*	*byði*	*byðim*	*byðið*	*byði*
Weak	DŒMA 'deem'		*dœmda*	*dœmdir*	*dœmdi*	*dœmdum*	*dœmduð*	*dœmdu*		*dœmda*	*dœmdir*	*dœmdi*	*dœmdim*	*dœmdið*	*dœmdi*

Conjugation	Example	Imperative			Inf	Participle (masc)
		2sg	1pl	2pl		
Strong	BJÓÐA 'offer'	*bjóð*	*bjóðum*	*bjóðið*	*bjóða*	*boðinn*
Weak	DŒMA 'deem'	*dœm*	*dœmum*	*dœmið*	*dœma*	*dœmdr*

Source: Zoëga 1910: 541–542.
Shaded cells represent the principal-part sets proposed by Wimmer 1871.

Table 1.6. Realized paradigm of Old Norse ÞURFA 'need'

	Indicative						Subjunctive					
	1sg	2sg	3sg	1pl	2pl	3pl	1sg	2sg	3sg	1pl	2pl	3pl
Present	þarf	þarft	þarf	þurfum	þurfuð	þurfu	þurfa	þurfir	þurfi	þurfim	þurfið	þurfi
Preterite	þurfta	þurftir	þurfti	þurftum	þurftuð	þurftu	þyrfta	þyrftir	þyrfti	þyrftim	þyrftið	þyrfti

Imperative	Infinitive	Participle (neut)
—	þurfa	þurft

Source: Zoëga 1910: 543.

ÞURFA's optimal principal-part set were assumed to be of either the weak or the strong type, it would look like a weak verb's principal-part set and would therefore yield incorrect inferences about ÞURFA's present-tense forms; clearly, preterite-present verbs such as ÞURFA must have finite present-tense cells as well as a preterite-tense cell among their optimal principal parts. Accordingly, the cells serving as optimal principal parts in a preterite–present verb's realized paradigm are neither a subset nor a superset of those serving as optimal principal parts in the realized paradigm of a strong verb: a preterite-present verb requires fewer principal parts realizing the preterite tense than a strong verb does, but unlike a strong verb, it does require principal parts realizing the present tense. As this example shows, different ICs of a given syntactic category may participate in a language's implicative relations in different ways.

1.3.2 An inflectional system's principal parts may be chosen according to one of three schemes

The Old Norse evidence might be seen as motivating optimal principal-part schemes that are different from the static scheme. One alternative is an **adaptive** scheme, in which each lexeme has an ordered sequence of optimal principal parts: in this scheme, lexemes do not necessarily have parallel sets of principal parts, but the form of a lexeme's nth principal part invariably determines the morphosyntactic property set realized by the $(n + 1)$th principal part in its sequence. Another alternative is a **dynamic** scheme, in which the optimal principal parts of lexemes in a given category are neither necessarily parallel nor ordered.

The choice among these three alternative schemes (static, adaptive, and dynamic) has important consequences for any cross-linguistic comparison of paradigms' implicational structure. For instance, lexemes typically need more optimal principal parts in the static scheme than in the dynamic. Here, we present a preliminary discussion of the properties and consequences of these alternative schemes for optimal principal-part sets.

The static scheme for optimal principal-part sets

Traditional principal-part analyses often employ the static scheme, in which the same set of MPSs identifies the optimal principal parts for every IC. Imagine a language having the IC system F in Table 1.7. For this language, we might propose the principal-part analysis schematized in Table 1.8, in which the exponence of each principal part is shaded. This analysis follows the static scheme: the same three realized cells (the ρ-cell, the σ-cell, and the τ-cell) serve as principal parts in each IC. As principal parts, these three cells are

30 *Principal parts*

Table 1.7. *A hypothetical IC system F*

	System F			
	ρ	σ	τ	υ
I	a	e	i	m
II	b	e	i	m
III	c	f	j	n
IV	c	g	j	n
V	d	h	k	o
VI	d	h	l	o

Table 1.8 *Static principal parts for system F*

	ρ	σ	τ	υ
I	a	e	i	m
II	b	e	i	m
III	c	f	j	n
IV	c	g	j	n
V	d	h	k	o
VI	d	h	l	o

Shaded cells are static principal parts.

adequate: in any realized paradigm in any of the six ICs in this language, the ρ-, σ-, and τ-cells uniquely determine all of the other realized cells in the paradigm. As a principal-part set, the ρ-, σ-, and τ-cells are also **minimal** in the sense that there is no proper subset of this set that is adequate. By contrast, the τ- and υ-cells do not constitute an adequate principal part set (because these cells distinguish neither ICs I and II nor ICs III and IV), and the set containing the ρ-, σ-, τ-, and υ-cells, though adequate, is not a minimal principal-part set.

Given the intersecting realizations of the MPSs ρ, σ, and τ and the ICs I–VI in Table 1.8, lexical listings for lexemes in this language must specify a set of three static principal parts, as in (11), where L_x represents that realization of L bearing the exponence x.

(11) Sample static principal-part specifications:

For lexeme L belonging to IC I: {⟨L_a, ρ⟩, ⟨L_e, σ⟩, ⟨L_i, τ⟩}
For lexeme M belonging to IC IV: {⟨M_c, ρ⟩, ⟨M_g, σ⟩, ⟨M_j, τ⟩}
For lexeme N belonging to IC VI: {⟨N_d, ρ⟩, ⟨N_h, σ⟩, ⟨N_l, τ⟩}

Some preliminary assumptions 31

Table 1.9. *Adaptive principal parts for system F*

	ρ	σ	τ	υ
I	a	e	i	m
II	b	e	i	m
III	c	f	j	n
IV	c	g	j	n
V	d	h	k	o
VI	d	h	l	o

Shaded cells are adaptive principal parts.

The adaptive scheme for optimal principal-part sets

Instead of an analysis based on the static principal-part scheme, we could design an analysis based on the adaptive scheme. Now, all lexemes have the same member of their realized paradigm as their first principal part, but the exponence of principal part n determines the MPS realized by principal part $n + 1$. For the system F, we might propose the analysis in Table 1.9. In this analysis, the MPS ρ identifies the first principal part of a given lexeme L; we call ρ the **root property set**. If L's exponence for ρ is **a**, then we need go no further: this exponence unequivocally identifies L as a member of IC I. On the other hand, if L's exponence for ρ is **c**, then the MPS σ identifies L's second principal part; if L's exponence for σ is **f**, then L belongs to IC III. But if L's exponence for ρ is **d**, then property set τ (rather than σ) identifies L's second principal part; if L's exponence for τ is **k**, then L belongs to IC V.

In this adaptive scheme, a lexeme L's optimal sequence of principal parts can be represented as a path through a tree in which (i) each principal part $\langle L_x, \phi \rangle$ of lexeme L corresponds to a subpath from the MPS ϕ to the exponence **x** of ϕ and (ii) the path's endpoint is L's IC. Thus, the principal-part analysis in Table 1.9 may be represented as in Figure 1.1 (or equivalently, as in Table 1.10). In this analysis, no lexical item needs a sequence of three principal parts; indeed, some lexemes have a single principal part (those belonging to ICs I and II), and others have two (those belonging to ICs III–VI), as in (12).

(12) Sample adaptive principal-part specifications:

   For lexeme L belonging to IC I: $\langle\langle L_a, \rho \rangle\rangle$
   For lexeme M belonging to IC IV: $\langle\langle M_c, \rho \rangle, \langle M_g, \sigma \rangle\rangle$
   For lexeme N belonging to IC VI: $\langle\langle N_d, \rho \rangle, \langle N_l, \tau \rangle\rangle$

32 *Principal parts*

Table 1.10. *The adaptive principal parts for system F in tabular form*

Principal parts				IC
First		Second		
Morphosyntactic property set	Exponence	Morphosyntactic property set	Exponence	
ρ	a			I
	b			II
	c	σ	f	III
			g	IV
	d	τ	k	V
			l	VI

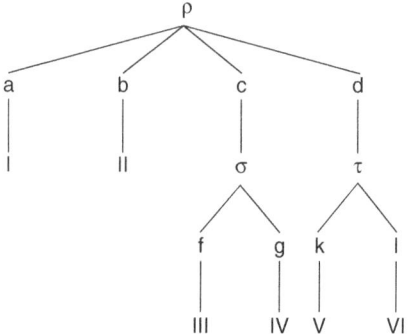

Figure 1.1. *The adaptive principal parts for system F in tree form*

In a principal-part analysis in the static scheme, adequacy and minimality are reckoned with respect to the same set of realized cells for all ICs; in the analysis in Table 1.8, this set contains a lexeme's realized ρ-, σ-, and τ-cells. In a principal-part analysis in the adaptive scheme, each IC J is individually associated with a sequence of realized cells, the first of which realizes the root property set; adequacy and minimality are then reckoned separately for each IC J with respect to its own sequence of cells. In the analysis in Table 1.9, ρ is the root property set. A sequence containing only the realized ρ-cell is an adequate and minimal principal-part sequence for ICs I and II, since the realized ρ-cell in either of these ICs uniquely determines all of the other cells in its paradigm. For ICs III–VI, by contrast, a sequence containing only the realized ρ-cell is inadequate; instead, a larger sequence containing both the realized ρ- and σ-cells is an adequate and minimal principal-part sequence for ICs III and IV, and a sequence containing both the realized ρ- and τ-cells is an adequate and minimal principal-part sequence for ICs V and VI. Thus, while a principal-part analysis in the static scheme has a single set of realized cells that is adequate and minimal across all ICs, a principal-part analysis in the adaptive scheme has an adequate and minimal sequence of realized cells for each IC J such that (i) each sequence begins with the cell $\langle L_x, \phi_1 \rangle$ realizing the root property set ϕ_1 and (ii) the sequence's nth cell $\langle L_y, \phi_n \rangle$ either determines L's membership in J or determines the MPS of the sequence's $(n + 1)$th cell.

The dynamic scheme for optimal principal-part sets

Yet a third way of conceiving of principal parts organizes them in the dynamic scheme. In this scheme, principal parts are neither linearly ordered nor necessarily parallel from one IC to another. System F in Table 1.7 could have the dynamic principal-part analysis in Table 1.11. Here, each IC has only a single principal part. Thus, if a lexeme L has exponence **a** for the MPS ρ, we deduce that L belongs to IC I; if L has exponence **f** for property set σ, we deduce that L belongs to IC III; if L has **k** as its exponence for the property set τ, we deduce that L belongs to IC V; and so on.

Like the adaptive scheme, the dynamic scheme associates each individual IC with its own set of MPSs relative to which adequacy and minimality are reckoned. But while the sets of MPSs associated with a language's ICs must all contain the root property set in the adaptive scheme, there is no such requirement in the dynamic scheme. Thus, in the dynamic analysis of principal parts in Table 1.11, the principal-part set containing only the realized ρ-cell is adequate and minimal for ICs I and II, the set containing only the realized σ-cell is adequate and minimal for ICs III and IV, and the set containing only the

Table 1.11. *Dynamic principal parts for system F*

	ρ	σ	τ	υ
I	a	e	i	m
II	b	e	i	m
III	c	f	j	n
IV	c	g	j	n
V	d	h	k	o
VI	d	h	l	o

Shaded cells are dynamic principal parts.

realized τ-cell is adequate and minimal for ICs v and vi. Thus, the criteria of adequacy and minimality vary according to which of the three principal-part schemes is at issue.

The dynamic scheme is, in a sense, the most parsimonious conception of principal parts, since it allows a smaller inventory of optimal principal parts than is possible under the static or adaptive conceptions. In the static scheme, each lexeme requires three principal parts, as in (11). In the adaptive scheme, each lexeme requires either one or two principal parts, as in (12). In the dynamic scheme, by contrast, each lexeme requires only one principal part, as in (13).

(13)   Sample dynamic principal-part specifications:
       For lexeme L belonging to IC I: $\{\langle L_a, \rho \rangle\}$
       For lexeme M belonging to IC IV: $\{\langle M_g, \sigma \rangle\}$
       For lexeme N belonging to IC VI: $\{\langle N_l, \tau \rangle\}$

That said, it is also clear that the dynamic scheme necessitates a somewhat more complicated kind of representation for a lexeme's principal-part set. In both the static and adaptive schemes, a lexeme's principal-part set can simply be represented as a list of word forms; the MPSs associated with a lexeme's principal parts needn't be specified in individual principal-part lists, but can be given a single, general statement – either as a list of MPSs (in the static scheme) or as a decision tree (in the adaptive scheme). Thus, the static and adaptive principal-part specifications in (11) and (12) may be abbreviated as in Table 1.12. But the dynamic scheme does not afford any analogous abbreviation: there is no choice but to represent a lexeme L's principal-part set as a set of explicitly specified cells in L's realized paradigm, as in Table 1.12.

Table 1.12. *Representations of static, adaptive, and dynamic principal-part sets for system F in Table 1.7*

	Principal-part set (static scheme)			Principal-part sequence (adaptive scheme)		Principal-part set (dynamic scheme)
Lexeme L, IC I:	$\{\langle L_a, \rho \rangle,$	$\langle L_e, \sigma \rangle,$	$\langle L_i, \tau \rangle\}$	$\langle \langle L_a, \rho \rangle \rangle$		$\{\langle L_a, \rho \rangle\}$
abbreviation	$\langle L_a,$	$L_e,$	$L_i \rangle$	$\langle L_a \rangle$		(none)
Lexeme M, IC IV:	$\{\langle M_c, \rho \rangle,$	$\langle M_g, \sigma \rangle,$	$\langle M_j, \tau \rangle\}$	$\langle \langle M_c, \rho \rangle,$	$\langle M_g, \sigma \rangle \rangle$	$\{\langle M_g, \sigma \rangle\}$
abbreviation:	$\langle M_c,$	$M_g,$	$M_j \rangle$	$\langle M_c,$	$M_g \rangle$	(none)
Lexeme N, IC VI:	$\{\langle N_d, \rho \rangle,$	$\langle N_h, \sigma \rangle,$	$\langle N_l, \tau \rangle\}$	$\langle \langle N_d, \rho \rangle,$	$\langle N_l, \tau \rangle \rangle$	$\{\langle N_l, \tau \rangle\}$
abbreviation:	$\langle N_d,$	$N_h,$	$N_l \rangle$	$\langle N_d,$	$N_l \rangle$	(none)

In summary, the specification of a lexeme's optimal principal parts depends upon which of these three conceptions of optimal principal parts one employs. Under the static conception, a lexeme's principal-part specification is a set of realized cells (abbreviated as a sequence of word forms) realizing a set of MPSs that is uniform across ICs. Under the adaptive conception, a lexeme's principal-part specification is a sequence of realized cells (abbreviated as a sequence of word forms) realizing one path through a hierarchy such as that in Figure 1.1 and Table 1.10, where the MPSs realized by a given sequence of principal parts needn't remain uniform from one IC to the next. Finally, under the dynamic conception, a lexeme's principal-part specification is an unordered set of realized cells whose MPSs needn't remain uniform across ICs. Thus, the traditional conception of Latin principal parts in Table 1.1 is a static conception, but one could just as well develop a principal-part analysis for Latin verbs following the adaptive or dynamic scheme.

1.3.3 There may be more than one optimal principal-part analysis for the lexemes in a given inflectional system

Whether one employs the static, the adaptive, or the dynamic scheme, the same plat typically admits alternative optimal principal-part analyses. We have devised a computer program, the Principal-Parts Analyzer (PPA),[13] which, given a plat as input, calculates all possible optimal principal-part analyses that it admits. Thus, consider the plat for verb conjugations in Ngiti (Nilo-Saharan; DR Congo) given in Table 1.13. The exponences in this plat specify the two aspects of a verb form's inflection that distinguish its IC membership: the segmental quality of its stem-initial vowel and the tone of its stem-final vowel.

When we run the PPA on the Ngiti plat, we find twenty-six different optimal static principal-part analyses; each consists of three members, which we tabulate in Table 1.14. Each row represents an alternative static principal-part analysis admitted by Ngiti. Thus, analysis 1 treats the static principal parts across all of the conjugations as consisting of the imperative singular, the perfective narrative past, and the second nominalized stem; analysis 2 takes the three principal parts as consisting of the imperative singular, the imperfective near future, and the second nominalized stem; and so forth. As Table 1.14 shows, some of the word forms in a Ngiti verbal paradigm are not fit to serve as optimal principal parts in the static scheme. In particular, the infinitive, the imperfective past habitual, and the imperfective past conditional are either too easily predicted or not predictive enough to figure as one of the principal parts in

---

[13] We discuss our software tools in Chapter 13.

Table 1.13. *Plat for the principal-part analysis of Ngiti verbs*

Conjugation	Infinitive	Imperative singular	Imperative plural	Perfective present	Perfective recent past	Perfective intermediate past	Perfective remote past	Perfective narrative past	Imperfective near future	Imperfective distant future	Imperfective past continuous	Imperfective past habitual	Imperfective past conditional	Subjunctive	Nominalized stem1	Nominalized stem2	Example (infinitive form)
v1a	αL	αL	αL	αL	αL	αL	αL	αL	αL	αL	αL	αH	αL	αL	αL	αL	*idzi-ta* 'to push'
v1b	βL	βL	βL	βL	βL	βL	βL	βL	βH	βH	βL	βH	βL	αH	βL	βL	*obhi-ta* 'to cultivate'
v2a.tr	αM	αM	αM	αL	αL	αL	αL	αM	αM	αM	αM	αH	αL	αM	αM	αL	*ada-ta* 'to cross'
v2a.itr	αM	αM	αM	αL	αL	αL	αL	αM	αM	αM	αM	αH	αL	αM	αM	αM	*upo-ta* 'to climb'
v2b.tr	βM	βM	βM	βL	βL	βL	βL	βL	βM	βM	βL	βH	βL	βM	βM	βL	*ɔdɔ-ta* 'to guard'
v2b.itr	βM	βM	βM	βL	βL	βL	βL	βL	βM	βM	βL	βH	βL	βM	βM	βM	*ʌdzi-ta* 'to cry'
v3.tr	αM	αLM	αM	αM	αM	αM	αM	αM	αM	αM	αM	αH	αL	αM	αLM	αM	*ʌdhɔ-ta* 'to pour'
v3.itr	αM	αLM	αM	αM	αLM	αLM	αM	αL	αL	αM	αL	αH	αL	αL	αM	αM	*ʌdhɔ-ta* 'to sleep'
v4.tr	αH	αLM	αLM	αLM	αLM	αLM	αLM	αH	αH	αH	αH	αH	αL	αH	αLM	αM	*andi-tá* 'to write'
v4.itr	αH	αLM	αLM	αLM	αLM	αLM	αLM	αH	αH	αH	αH	αH	αL	αH	αLM	αLM	*akpé-tá* 'to whistle'

Source: Kutsch Lojenga 1994: 217ff.

Notes: L = low tone, M = mid tone, H = high tone; α = stem-initial /a/, |I| or |U|; β = stem-initial |O|. According to the principles of Ngiti vowel harmony, the archisegment |I| is realized as /i/ or /ɨ/; |U|, as /u/ or /ʉ/; and |O|, as /o/ or /ɔ/. See Kutsch Lojenga (1994: 62ff) for a discussion of these principles.

any optimal static analysis. Other word forms, on the other hand, seem heavily informative, either because they are unpredictable or because they are heavily predictive (or both); notice in particular that in every one of the optimal principal-part analyses deduced by our program, the second nominalized stem must function as one of the static principal parts in this language.

This Ngiti example is typical in the sense that for any principal-part analysis proposed for a language – whether static, adaptive, or dynamic – there are nearly always alternative analyses of the same kind to choose from. In some cases there is a good basis for favoring one of these analyses over another; in other cases the choice among these competing analyses is arbitrary. On the assumption that lexical representations involve principal parts, it is, of course, perfectly imaginable that different speakers of the same language might apply different principal-part analyses in their lexical representation of the same lexeme.

Extensive scrutiny reveals that inflectional systems vary widely in exactly how many alternative optimal principal-part analyses they admit. In our view, this variation is a significant criterion for the typological comparison of IC systems.

In summary, we have examined traditional principal parts as a concise reification of the implicative relations by which a realized paradigm's cells are affiliated with one another. Principal parts are of both theoretical and typological interest. Their usefulness in investigating the properties of different IC systems can be maximized by abandoning three requirements that have traditionally been placed on principal-part sets in language pedagogy: the requirement of uniqueness (that the label "principal parts" be, by convention, reserved for only one of a lexeme's adequate principal-part analyses), the requirement of uniformity (that the "principal parts" of a lexeme L be the same cells in L's realized paradigm as in the realized paradigms of all other lexemes sharing L's syntactic category), and the requirement of optimality (that a lexeme's set of "principal parts" be as small as it can be, given the requirement of uniformity).

With the assumptions presented in this section, we now turn to a discussion of plats, a format for representing IC contrasts that is central to our investigation of principal parts and implicative relations.

Table 1.14. *Twenty-six optimal static principal-part analyses for Ngiti*

principal-part analysis	Infinitive	Imperative singular	Imperative plural	Perf. present	Perf. recent past	Perf. intermediate past	Perf. remote past	Perf. narrative past	Imperf. near future	Imperf. distant future	Imperf. past continuous	Imperf. past habitual	Imperf. past conditional	Subjunctive	Nominalized stem 1	Nominalized stem 2
1		✓						✓								✓
2		✓							✓							✓
3				✓					✓							✓
4					✓				✓							✓
5						✓			✓							✓
6				✓			✓									✓
7		✓			✓					✓						✓
8										✓						✓
9						✓				✓						✓
10					✓		✓			✓						✓
11										✓	✓					✓
12		✓														✓
13		✓		✓										✓		✓
14					✓									✓		✓
15						✓								✓		✓
16														✓		✓

2 Plats

In this chapter, we develop the notion of a 'plat', a format for the representation of IC systems that is essential for identifying and measuring differences in their complexity. We discuss some of the analytic options that arise when we construct plats to analyze IC systems in real languages, and we explain and justify our choices with respect to these options (§2.1). We conclude with a discussion of the representation issue, the fundamental question of what plats actually represent (§2.2).[1]

2.1 Plats and their parts

In analyzing implicative relations in a language's inflectional system, it is useful to adopt as a fundamental object of analysis a matrix in which (i) distinct MPSs are represented as columns, (ii) distinct ICs are represented as rows, and (iii) the exponence of MPS σ in IC J is specified at the intersection of row J and column σ. We call a matrix of this specific sort a plat (§1.2.2). An example is the hypothetical system of ICs represented in Table 2.1, in which ρ, σ, and τ represent three distinct MPSs, I–VI represent six different ICs, and each of **a–l** represents the inflectional exponence realizing a particular MPS in a particular IC.

A plat reveals implicative relations and provides a concrete basis for principal-part analysis. The plat in Table 2.1, for example, shows that if the ρ-cell in the realized paradigm of a lexeme L has exponence **a**, then L belongs to IC I, L's σ-cell has exponence **f**, and L's τ-cell has exponence **j**. Moreover, it shows that the optimal principal part of a lexeme L belonging to IC I is its realized ρ-cell (with exponence **a**), since this cell is both unpredictable from any other cell in L's realized paradigm and predictive of every other cell in that paradigm; the clearest

---

[1] The data sets that we have employed in this chapter are:
  plats.3MPS   plats.5MPS
These are available at the *Morphological Typology* website www.cambridge.org/stump_finkel.

Table 2.1. *Plat representing a hypothetical system of ICs*

	ρ	σ	τ
I	a	f	j
II	b	f	j
III	c	g	k
IV	d	h	l
V	e	i	k
VI	e	i	l

examples of optimal principal parts exhibit both of these characteristics. But an optimal principal part does not have to be predictive by itself. For instance, the τ-cell (with exponence **l**) of a lexeme L belonging to IC VI is an optimal principal part for L since it belongs to both of L's optimal principal-part sets ({τ-cell, ρ-cell} and {τ-cell, σ-cell}), but by itself, the τ-cell predicts neither L's ρ-cell nor its σ-cell (at most narrowing the choice of ICs to IV and VI). An optimal principal part also does not have to be completely unpredictable; it only has to be as difficult to predict as any alternative cell. Thus, the ρ-cell (with exponence **c**) in the realized paradigm of a lexeme L belonging to IC III is by itself adequate as an optimal principal part for L even though it is predicted by L's σ-cell (with exponence **g**); by the same token, the σ-cell is by itself adequate as an optimal principal part for L even though it is predicted by L's ρ-cell.[2]

2.1.1 Redundant MPSs

A first question that arises concerning the construction of plats is whether every MPS associated with a plat's ICs must be included in the plat. In some cases, the task of analyzing principal parts can be simplified by ignoring certain cells in a lexeme's realized paradigm. Consider the hypothetical plat in Table 2.2, in which the exponence of the MPS υ is, in every IC, identical to that of property set τ. Any inference that can be drawn from or about the υ-cell in a lexeme's realized paradigm can be equally drawn from or about its τ-cell. Thus, we needn't include any υ-cell in a principal-part analysis of the plat in Table 2.2, since we can always regard the corresponding τ-cell as its proxy. We can also

---

[2] The fact that the ρ-cell is an optimal principal part for members of conjugation I doesn't force us to pick the ρ-cell as a principal part for conjugation III. That is, we may choose to abandon the pedagogical assumption that principal-part sets are uniform across all ICs (§1.1); see §1.3.6–7 for further discussion.

Table 2.2. *Plat representing a hypothetical system of ICs in which the property sets τ and υ have identical exponence*

	ρ	σ	τ	υ	ϕ
I	a	c	f	f	h
II	a	c	g	g	i
III	a	d	f	f	h
IV	b	d	g	g	i
V	b	e	f	f	h
VI	b	e	g	g	i

ignore the ϕ-cells: although the exponence of ϕ is not identical to that of τ, it is isomorphic to it. That is, there is an isomorphism *j* such that in any IC in Table 2.2, if the τ-cell has exponence *x*, then the ϕ-cell has exponence *j(x)*; this isomorphism is such that *j*(**f**) = **h** and *j*(**g**) = **i**.

We can articulate this observation in general terms as follows. Where the MPSs $\sigma_1, \ldots, \sigma_n$ are such that the exponence of σ_k is isomorphic to that of σ_1 for all *k* ($1 \leq k \leq n$), we call σ_1 the **distillation** of $\sigma_1, \ldots, \sigma_n$. (Note that by this definition, σ qualifies as a distillation if there is no other property set whose exponence is isomorphic to that of σ.) When σ_1 is the distillation of $\sigma_1, \ldots, \sigma_n$, we treat σ_1 by itself as the representative of each of $\sigma_1, \ldots, \sigma_n$. Thus, in the above example, the property sets τ, υ, and ϕ are isomorphic in their exponence; τ is therefore the distillation of τ, υ, and ϕ, and column τ can therefore be regarded as representative of columns υ and ϕ.

2.1.2 Kinds of exponences

A second, quite complex question concerning the construction of plats is the question of how an IC's exponences are to be represented. In the simplest case, an IC's exponences are simply affixes; for instance, the conjugation of English weak verbs might be represented by a row containing *-s*, *-ed*, and *-ing* in the appropriate columns. But exponences are rarely this simple.

Very often, a lexeme's inflection involves stem modifications, either alone or in combination with affixes, which may themselves exhibit greater or lesser degrees of fusion with the stems with which they join. Thus, consider the declension of the Sanskrit noun AŚVA 'horse'. In Table 2.3, each word in its realized paradigm is broken into two parts: the initial substring *aśv*, which remains phonologically invariant across all of the words in the paradigm; and

Table 2.3. *The declension of Sanskrit* AŚVA *'horse' (stem* aśva-; *theme* aśv; *distinguishers in bold italics)*

	Nom	Voc	Acc	Ins	Dat	Abl	Gen	Loc
Sg	aśv***as***	aśv***a***	aśv***am***	aśv***ena***	aśv***āya***	aśv***āt***	aśv***asya***	aśv***e***
Du	aśv***au***	aśv***au***	aśv***au***	aśv***ābhyām***	aśv***ābhyām***	aśv***ābhyām***	aśv***ayos***	aśv***ayos***
Pl	aśv***ās***	aśv***ās***	aśv***ān***	aśv***ais***	aśv***ebhyas***	aśv***ebhyas***	aśv***ānām***	aśv***eṣu***

Stem	Affix
aśv	a s
theme	distinguisher

Stem	Affix
aśv	a / e — i
theme	distinguisher

Enlarged stem		Affix
Stem	i	
aśv	a / e	su / ṣu
theme		distinguisher

Figure 2.1 *Analysis of Sanskrit* aśvas *'horse' (nom sg),* aśve *(loc sg) and* aśveṣu *(loc pl)*

a final substring in bold italics, which serves to distinguish each word form from other word forms in the paradigm. We refer to the invariant portion *aśv* as the paradigm's **theme** and the variable portions in bold italics as its **distinguishers**.

In the simplest case, a word form's theme coincides with its stem, and its distinguisher is an inflectional affix; for instance, in the paradigm of the English verb WALK, the third-person singular present indicative form *walks* has *walk* as both its theme and its stem and *-s* as both its distinguisher and its inflectional affix. But themes and distinguishers cannot, in general, be respectively identified with stems and affixes. In the Sanskrit example, the theme is *aśv* but the stem is traditionally (and with good motivation) regarded as *aśva-*. Moreover, the distinguisher of the locative singular word form *aśve* is *e*, but the relevant inflectional affix is in this case *-i*, which combines with the final *a* of the stem *aśva-* to yield *e*, in accordance with a rule of automatic sandhi. And the distinguisher of the locative plural word *aśveṣu* is *eṣu*, but its affix is *-su*, whose sibilant undergoes retroflexion when it joins with the modified stem form *aśve-*. Thus, the distinguishers of the words in Table 2.3 are not, in general, inflectional affixes, but are instead the result of combining the stem's final vowel with an inflectional affix, as illustrated in Figure 2.1. For the analysis of principal parts in a fusional language such as Sanskrit, it is useful to employ a plat in which exponences are distinguishers rather than affixes, since distinguishers include stem segments whose patterns of alternation are as significant an expression of IC membership as affixes.

Returning to the plat for English verbs, consider now the conjugation of the verbs SHRINK, DRINK, and SINK. There are at least two possibilities for the representation of the past-tense and past participial exponences of this conjugation. On one hand, these exponences might be equated with the distinguishers *-ank* and *-unk*; alternatively, they might be represented as nonconcatenative processes of vowel modification (orthographically, *i* → *a* and *i* → *u*). These are not equivalent choices: under the distinguisher analysis, SWIM does not belong to the same conjugation as SHRINK, DRINK, and SINK, but instead has its own conjugation; under the process analysis, SWIM belongs to the same conjugation as SHRINK, DRINK, and SINK.

A threefold choice exists for representing the past participial exponences of verbs such as SHUT, SELL, and CLING. Under a distinguisher analysis, these three verbs have distinct past participial exponences: SHUT has empty exponence, SELL has the distinguisher *-old*, and cling has the distinguisher *-ung*. Under a process analysis, they again have distinct past participial exponences: SHUT has empty exponence, SELL has a vowel-modification process combined with a suffix, and CLING has a different vowel-modification process. But neither of these analyses takes account of the fact that the verbs are alike insofar as their past participles are identical to their past-tense forms; thus, one might represent the past participial exponence of each of these verbs in the same way, as a pointer to its past-tense form.

An orthogonal issue concerns the use of orthography in representing an IC's exponences. This representation is appropriate for a language whose orthography unambiguously represents all of its phonological contrasts, but not many languages fall into this category. Consider, for example, the conjugation of the French verbs PLACER 'put', MANGER 'eat', and CHANTER 'sing'. The Larousse *Dictionnaire du français contemporain* (1971) assigns these verbs to distinct conjugation subclasses because of their orthographic difference: before a suffix spelled with initial *a* or *o*, PLACER uses a cedilla (*plaçons* 'we put', *plaçais* 'you put') while MANGER uses the sequence *ge* (*mangeons*, *mangeais*) and CHANTER requires no special spelling (*chantons*, *chantais*). Thus, orthographically, these three verbs have different distinguishers: *-çons/-çais* vs *-eons/-eais* vs *-ons/-ais*. In speech, however, PLACER, MANGER, and CHANTER are identical in their inflection: all three have the distinguishers /ɔ̃/ and /ɛ/, (/plasɔ̃ plasɛ/, /mɑ̃ʒɔ̃ mɑ̃ʒɛ/, /ʃɑ̃tɔ̃ ʃɑ̃tɛ/). Thus, a phonetic or phonemic transcription provides a clearer basis than orthography for representing inflectional exponence in a plat for the analysis of French conjugation classes.

Table 2.4. *Realized present indicative active paradigms of two Sanskrit verbs, in phonemic representation*

	1sg	2sg	3sg	1du	2du	3du	1pl	2pl	3pl
DVIṢ 'hate'	dvéṣ-mi	dvék-ṣi	dvéṣ-ṭi	dviṣ-vás	dviṣ-ṭhás	dviṣ-ṭás	dviṣ-más	dviṣ-ṭhá	dviṣ-ánti
DUH 'milk'	dóh-mi	dhók-ṣi	dóg-dhi	duh-vás	dug-dhás	dug-dhás	duh-más	dug-dhá	duh-ánti

Source: Whitney 1889: §612b,c.

Table 2.5. *Realized present indicative active paradigms of two Sanskrit verbs, in morphophonological representation*

	1sg	2sg	3sg	1du	2du	3du	1pl	2pl	3pl
DVIṢ 'hate'	dvéṣ-mi	dvéṣ-si	dvéṣ-ti	dviṣ-vás	dviṣ-thás	dviṣ-tás	dviṣ-más	dviṣ-thá	dviṣ-ánti
DUH 'milk'	dóh-mi	dóh-si	dóh-ti	duh-vás	duh-thás	duh-tás	duh-más	duh-thá	duh-ánti

But phonological representations of a lexeme's exponences may themselves involve greater or lesser degrees of abstraction. Consider, for example, the realized present indicative active paradigms of the Sanskrit verbs DVIṢ 'hate' and DUH 'milk' in Table 2.4. These two realized paradigms appear to be very different: that of DVIṢ involves three different stem forms (*dvéṣ*, *dvék*, and *dviṣ*) while that of DUH involves five (*dóh*, *dhók*, *dóg*, *duh*, and *dug*); moreover, the verbs seem to involve different distinguishers (e.g. *-ékṣi/-éṣṭi* vs *dhókṣi/dógdhi*) and different suffixes (e.g. *-ṭi/-ṭás* vs *-dhi/-dhás*).

In view of these differences, it is not obvious that DVIṢ and DUH should be regarded as belonging to the same conjugation class. But the word forms in Table 2.4 exhibit the effects of numerous morphophonological operations to which the roots *dviṣ* and *duh* are subject. The operations in question are those in (1):

(1) Some morphophonological operations affecting forms of DVIṢ 'hate' and DUH 'milk'
    (a) *ṣ* becomes *k* before *s*   (Whitney 1889: §226e)
    (b) *s* become *ṣ* after *k* before a vowel   (§180)
    (c) *t(h)* becomes *ṭ(h)* after *ṣ*   (§197)
    (d) *duh* becomes *dhuk* before *s*   (§§155, 159, 222a)
    (e) the sequence *h-t(h)* becomes *g-dh*   (§160)

If the effects of these operations are factored out, the realized paradigms in Table 2.4 have the morphophonological representations in Table 2.5, which reveal the full inflectional parallelism of DVIṢ and DUH; given this more abstract mode of representation, it is clear that the two verbs belong to the same IC

46 *Plats*

(the Sanskrit second conjugation). Such cases show that morphophonological operations may obscure the fundamental morphological patterns embodied by a lexeme's realized paradigm; for this reason, it may be desirable to abstract away the effects of these operations.

Because plats are intended to show the points of contrast among an inflectional system's ICs, it is desirable to omit nondistinctive portions of an IC's exponence. Consider, for example, the system of verb inflection in Ngiti, a Nilo-Saharan language spoken in the Democratic Republic of the Congo (Kutsch Lojenga 1994). Table 2.6 lists partial realized paradigms of two verbs in Ngiti: the verbs 'push' (a member of conjugation v1a) and 'write' (a member of conjugation v4.tr). The representative forms given here include the second-person singular and first-person plural inclusive forms across a range of different tense/aspect/mood combinations as well as several nonfinite forms. As the forms in the table show, the realizations of 'push' and those of 'write' have a fair amount of morphology in common – the 2sg prefix *ny-*, the 1pl inclusive prefix *k-*, the recent-past/past-habitual suffix *-na^L*, and so on. Ultimately, the only inflectional differences between conjugations involve the tone of the stem-final vowel. (There is also, however, a correlation between verbs' conjugation-class membership and the segmental quality of their stem-initial vowel; for instance, the initial vowel segments of verbs in the v1a and v4.tr conjugations are either high or unrounded.) We can therefore abstract away the rest of the morphology of these forms in constructing the Ngiti plat (given above as Table 1.13). In this plat, the exponence for a given MPS σ in a given conjugation J simply specifies (a) the range of stem-initial vowels exhibited by members of J and (b) the tone of a verb's stem-final vowel in the realization of σ in J.

As the foregoing evidence implies, the implicative relations among a paradigm's realized cells sometimes pertain to the entire word forms occupying those cells (as in the case of Sanskrit declensions) but in other cases more narrowly involve the stems upon which those word forms are based (as in the case of Ngiti conjugations). In the following chapters, much of our discussion will concern inflectional systems of the former type, but we will return to stem-based implicative relations in Chapter 7. In Chapter 12, we return to the issue of selecting exponences in plat construction to demonstrate how dramatically a change in the representation of an IC's exponences can affect the resulting analysis of its network of implicative relations.

2.1.3 Grammatical information

As we have seen, exponences are diverse things: they can be (i) concrete or abstract phonological representations (of affixes or of distinguishers or of

Table 2.6. *Partial realized paradigms of two verbs in Ngiti*

		Imperative	present	recent past	Perfective		
					intermediate past	remote past	narrative past
2sg	'push' (v1a)	i^{H}dzi^L	ny-i^{L}dzi^L	ny-i^{L}dzi^L-na^L	ny-i^{H}dzi^L-na^H	ny-i^{H}dzi^L	ny-i^{M}dzi^L
	'write' (v4.tr)	a^{H}ndi^{LM}	ny-a^{L}ndi^{LM}	ny-a^{L}ndi^{LH}-na^L (1)	ny-a^{H}ndi^{LM}-na^H	ny-a^{H}ndi^{LM}	ny-a^{M}ndi^H
1pl incl	'push' (v1a)	k-i^{L}dzi^L	k-i^{L}dzi^L	k-i^{L}dzi^L-na^L	k-i^{H}dzi^L-na^H	k-i^{H}dzi^L	k-i^{M}dzi^L
	'write' (v4.tr)	k-a^{L}ndi^{LM}	k-a^{L}ndi^{LM}	k-a^{L}ndi^{LH}-na^L (1)	k-a^{H}ndi^{LM}-na^H	k-a^{H}ndi^{LM}	k-a^{M}ndi^H

1. LM → LH by tone sandhi.

		near future	distant future	Imperfective		past conditional
				past continuous	past habitual	
2sg	'push' (v1a)	ny-i^{M}dzi^L-na^M	ny-i^{M}dzi^L-ya^M	ny-i^{M}dzi^L-na^M	ny-i^{M}dzi^H-na^L	ny-i^{H}dzi^L-na^M
	'write' (v4.tr)	ny-a^{M}ndi^H-na^M	ny-a^{M}ndi^H-ya^M	ny-a^{M}ndi^H-na^M	ny-a^{M}ndi^H-na^L	ny-a^{H}ndi^L-na^M
1pl incl	'push' (v1a)	k-i^{M}dzi^L-na^M	k-i^{M}dzi^L-ya^M	k-i^{M}dzi^L-na^M	k-i^{M}dzi^H-na^L	k-i^{H}dzi^L-na^M
	'write' (v4.tr)	k-a^{M}ndi^H-na^M	k-a^{M}ndi^H-ya^M	k-a^{M}ndi^H-na^M	k-a^{M}ndi^H-na^L	k-a^{H}ndi^L-na^M

		Infinitive	Subjunctive	Nominalized Stem1	Nominalized Stem2
'push' (v1a)		i^{M}dzi^L-ta^M	r-i^{M}dzi^L	n-i^{H}dzi^L	n-i^{H}dzi^L
'write' (v4.tr)		a^{M}ndi^H-ta^H	r-a^{M}ndi^H	n-a^{H}ndi^{LM}	n-a^{H}ndi^M

Source: Kutsch Lojenga 1994: 455–511.

48   Plats

Table 2.7. *The declension of* aśva *'horse' compared to that of* manas *'mind'*
(stems aśva-, manas-; *themes* aśv, man; *distinguishers in bold italics)*

	Nom	Voc	Acc	Ins	Dat	Abl	Gen	Loc
Sg	aśv*as*	aśv*a*	aśv*am*	aśv*ena*	aśv*āya*	aśv*āt*	aśv*asya*	aśv*e*
Du	aśv*au*	aśv*au*	aśv*au*	aśv*ābhyām*	aśv*ābhyām*	aśv*ābhyām*	aśv*ayos*	aśv*ayos*
Pl	aśv*ās*	aśv*ās*	aśv*ān*	aśv*ais*	aśv*ebhyas*	aśv*ebhyas*	aśv*ānām*	aśv*eṣu*
Sg	man*as*	man*as*	man*as*	man*asā*	man*ase*	man*asas*	man*asas*	man*asi*
Du	man*asī*	man*asī*	man*asī*	man*obhyām*	man*obhyām*	man*obhyām*	man*asos*	man*asos*
Pl	man*āṃsi*	man*āṃsi*	man*āṃsi*	man*obhis*	man*obhyas*	man*obhyas*	man*asām*	man*aḥsu*

suprasegmental properties), (ii) morphophonological operations, (iii) pointers to other exponences, or (iv) combinations of these. Minimally, a plat should associate each exponence (of whatever sort) with a MPS and an IC, as in Tables 2.1 and 2.2. But if associations of this minimal sort are supplemented with additional grammatical information, then their usefulness in deducing other members of their paradigm is sometimes enhanced.

The paradigms of the Sanskrit nouns aśva 'horse' and manas 'mind' in Table 2.7 afford a clear example. With these paradigms in mind, consider the following question: If a Sanskrit nominal lexeme L_1 has a nominative singular form ending in *as*, which other members of L_1's paradigm can we deduce? If we only know that L_1's nominative singular form ends in *as*, there is very little that we can deduce, since L_1's paradigm may follow either the pattern of aśva or the altogether distinct pattern of manas. But suppose that we additionally know that L_1 is neuter. In that case, the paradigm of L_1 cannot follow that of aśva, whose declensional pattern is restricted to masculine nominals; indeed, the only possibility is that L_1 belongs to the declension of manas (a neuter noun).

Suppose now that the nominal lexeme L_2 has a nominative singular form ending in *as* such that the *a* is stem-final and the *s* is suffixal; in that case, we can immediately infer that L_2 belongs to the declension of aśva (and hence is masculine), since the aśva declension presumes a stem ending in *a*, whereas the manas declension presumes a stem ending in *as*.

As this example shows, information about gender and about stem delimitation can enhance a realized cell's value as a principal part; other kinds of supplementary grammatical information afford similar enhancements. Thus, when we construct plats for analyzing an IC system's implicative relations, we must choose whether to supplement the basic associations (of exponences with MPSs and ICs) with additional grammatical information, and if so, what kinds of information to include. We return to this issue in Chapters 5 and 12.

2.1.4 Omitted lexemes

On first consideration, one might expect that the patterns embodied by a language's principal parts only relate to lexemes whose inflection is in some sense regular. This expectation, however, is certainly not justified, since principal-part analysis reveals systematic inflectional properties exhibited even by very irregular lexemes. Consider first the Latin irregular verb FERRE 'bear'. According to John Grant's principal-part analysis for Latin (§1.1), this verb has as its principal parts the realized cells of *ferō, tulī, lātum*, and *ferre*. Notwithstanding the suppletiveness of these forms, the implicative patterns described by Grant (see Table 1.2) correctly predict all the realized cells, including ⟨*tulistī*, {2sg perf ind active}⟩, ⟨*ferrem*, {1sg impf sbjv active}⟩, and ⟨*lātūrus*, {fut active ptcp}⟩. As these examples suggest, the principal parts correctly entail the various domains of suppletion within the paradigm of FERRE; despite the suppletiveness of this paradigm, its conformity to the implicative patterns of Latin verb paradigms is in fact completely regular.

An even more telling example is afforded by the verb COEPISSE 'begin', which lacks present-system (present, imperfect, and future as well as some nonfinite) realizations. Its four traditional principal parts are therefore the realized cells in (2), where ⟨Ø, σ⟩ represents the absence of any realization for σ.

(2) ⟨Ø, {1sg pres ind active}⟩
⟨*coepī*, {1sg perf ind active}⟩
⟨*coeptum*, {first supine}⟩
⟨Ø, {pres active inf}⟩

From (2), Grant's implicative patterns predict the realized cells ⟨*coepistī*, {2sg perf ind active}⟩ and ⟨*coeptūrus*, {fut active ptcp}⟩, but may also be seen as predicting ⟨Ø, {1sg impf sbjv active}⟩. These inferences are entirely correct. Thus, just as a suppletive principal part licenses the inference of other, similarly suppletive cells, so a principal part consisting of an empty realized cell licenses the inference of other empty cells, all in accordance with a single general network of implicative relations.

So principal-part analysis can be relevant even for very irregular lexemes. But should we require every inflecting lexeme in a language to engage with that language's system of implicative relations? Consider the case of English verbs. In English, ordinary verbs never require more than three principal parts. Traditionally, these are the realized cells of the bare infinitive, the indicative past tense, and the past participle, as in Table 2.8. The bare infinitive cell determines all of a verb's present-tense cells (whether indicative, subjunctive, or imperative: *she walks, that she walk, walk!*) as well as that of its present

Table 2.8. *Principal parts of some English verbs*

$\sigma_1 = \{\text{inf}\}$	$\sigma_2 = \{\text{ind past tense}\}$	$\sigma_3 = \{\text{past ptcp}\}$
$\langle walk, \sigma_1 \rangle$	$\langle walked, \sigma_2 \rangle$	$\langle walked, \sigma_3 \rangle$
$\langle prove, \sigma_1 \rangle$	$\langle proved, \sigma_2 \rangle$	$\langle proven, \sigma_3 \rangle$
$\langle make, \sigma_1 \rangle$	$\langle made, \sigma_2 \rangle$	$\langle made, \sigma_3 \rangle$
$\langle break, \sigma_1 \rangle$	$\langle broke, \sigma_2 \rangle$	$\langle broken, \sigma_3 \rangle$
$\langle eat, \sigma_1 \rangle$	$\langle ate, \sigma_2 \rangle$	$\langle eaten, \sigma_3 \rangle$
$\langle see, \sigma_1 \rangle$	$\langle saw, \sigma_2 \rangle$	$\langle seen, \sigma_3 \rangle$
$\langle sing, \sigma_1 \rangle$	$\langle sang, \sigma_2 \rangle$	$\langle sung, \sigma_3 \rangle$
$\langle come, \sigma_1 \rangle$	$\langle came, \sigma_2 \rangle$	$\langle come, \sigma_3 \rangle$
$\langle go, \sigma_1 \rangle$	$\langle went, \sigma_2 \rangle$	$\langle gone, \sigma_3 \rangle$
$\langle put, \sigma_1 \rangle$	$\langle put, \sigma_2 \rangle$	$\langle put, \sigma_3 \rangle$

participle (*walking*), and the indicative past-tense cell determines the irrealis cell (whose realization is identical: *If I walked there tomorrow, I'd be late*).

Although one can regard the three principal parts in Table 2.8 as determining all of the cells in the realized paradigm of an ordinary English verb, there are special verbs for which the implicative pattern fails. For instance, the verb HAVE has a special third-person singular present indicative form that is not predictable from its bare infinitive cell in the usual way: contrast *she has* with *she halves*. The same is true of SAY and DO: contrast *she says* /sɛz/ and *she does* /dʌz/ with *she plays* /pleɪz/ and *she chews* /tʃuz/.[3] The verb BE is even more problematic for the principal-part analysis in Table 2.8. Not only is its third-person singular present indicative form unpredictable from its bare infinitive cell in the usual way (contrast *be*/*she is* with *see*/*she sees*), but it is alone among English verbs in that (i) it has a special first-person singular present indicative form (*am*); (ii) its default present indicative form is distinct from its bare infinitive form (*are* vs *be*); (iii) it has two distinct indicative past-tense forms (*she was, they were*); and (iv) it exhibits an overt difference between the indicative past singular and the irrealis (*she was, if she were*).

Notwithstanding these complications, these special cases do not invalidate the principal-part analysis exemplified by Table 2.8. The verbs HAVE, SAY, and DO do, however, present a choice: Should they be seen as members of a tiny subclass that alone requires a fourth principal part (the realized cell of the third-

---

[3] Similarly, the Latin verbs DŪCERE 'lead', DĪCERE 'say', and FACERE 'do' have the special imperative singular realizations *dūc*, *dīc* and *fac*, which by the usual implicative pattern should have a final *e* (as in *pōne!* 'put!').

person singular present indicative), or should they instead simply be seen as lexical exceptions to the otherwise very general implicative pattern associated with Table 2.8? In our view, the latter option is better motivated. Although the third-person singular present indicative cells in the realized paradigms of HAVE, SAY, and DO are not predictable in the usual way, these cells fail to afford any predictions of their own. If one simply assumes that the third-person singular present indicative cells in the realized paradigms of HAVE, SAY, and DO are stored lexically (an assumption motivated both by their high frequency and their morphophonological exceptionality; Prasada & Pinker 1993, Alegre & Gordon 1999), then the realizations */hævz/, */seɪz/, and */duz/ that would otherwise be inferred from the principal parts of HAVE, SAY, and DO can simply be assumed to be overridden by the lexically listed cells of *has*, *says* /sɛz/, and *does* /dʌz/. Similar remarks hold for the verb BE. In view of both the high frequency of their use and the idiosyncrasy of their morphology, we assume that the realized cells of *is*, *am*, *are*, past indicative *was*/*were*, and irrealis *were* are lexically listed; on that assumption, their incompatibility with the system of implicative relations can be attributed to an override of inferred cells by lexically listed cells.

Modal verbs, such as MUST, CAN, and SHALL, constitute an entire subclass of verbs that seem at odds with the principal-part analysis in Table 2.8. Because modal verbs lack both infinitives and participles, the analysis in Table 2.8 is clearly inapplicable to them. But modal verbs possess at most two forms (one present, one past, e.g. *can*/*could*) and they are both frequent in use and irregular in their morphophonology, so it is plausible to assume that the realized cells of all modal verb forms are lexically listed and therefore needn't engage in any way with the system of implicative relations implied by Table 2.8.

2.2 The representation issue

When assembling a plat in order to investigate a language's ICs, we are immediately confronted with an issue of representation: what do plats actually represent? Logically, the exponences in a plat, and hence the plat itself, may represent one of at least two realities. On one hand, the exponences may represent audible phonological expressions, either in full phonetic detail or with the effects of automatic phonology factored out. In this case, the plat represents the IC contrasts that are directly perceivable by language users and that might be used in determining a newly encountered lexeme's IC membership. In a plat of this sort, the past-tense cells of the English READ and SAY conjugations are alike, containing the distinguisher /ɛd/ of /ɹɛd/ (vs /ɹid/) and /sɛd/ (vs /seɪ/). We call this sort of plat a **hearer-oriented** plat.

On the other hand, the exponences in a plat may represent the patterns of morphological marking that distinguish one IC from another. In this case, the plat instead represents the IC contrasts that the language user recognizes as morphologically significant and that could potentially be used in deducing a known lexeme's realized paradigm from principal parts. In a plat of this sort, the past-tense cells of the READ and SAY conjugations are different: that of READ contains the morphophonological rule /i/ → /ɛ/, while that of SAY contains both a rule of vowel laxing and the *-d* suffix. We call this sort of plat a **speaker-oriented** plat.

In general, a speaker-oriented plat differs from a hearer-oriented plat in that it incorporates morpholexical as well as purely phonological information about the ICs that it includes. This general difference is reflected in various more specific ways. The exponences in a speaker-oriented plat may impose specific requirements on the stems of the lexemes whose inflection the plat portrays; for instance, the morphophonological rule /i/ → /ɛ/ in the past-tense cell of the READ conjugation requires that members of this conjugation (e.g. READ, LEAD, SPEED, FEED) have a stem containing /i/. The exponences in a hearer-oriented plat do not impose requirements of this sort.

A hearer-oriented plat may contain ambiguities that are resolved in a corresponding speaker-oriented plat. In the hearer-oriented plat described above, the distinguisher /ɛd/ is ambiguous, appearing in the past-tense cells of both the READ and SAY conjugations. This ambiguity is absent in the speaker-oriented plat. By the same token, a hearer-oriented plat may make distinctions that are absent from a corresponding speaker-oriented plat. For instance, a hearer-oriented plat may distinguish the /ɛpt/ in *swept*, the /ɛnt/ in *meant* and the /ɛlt/ in *felt*, but the past-tense inflection of all three verbs might be represented as '/i/→/ɛ/, /-t/' in a speaker-oriented plat.

In any study involving the analysis of plats, it is essential to be clear about which sort of plat one employs, since the two sorts of plats may, upon analysis, yield different kinds of results. We address this representation issue again in Chapter 5 (as part of a discussion of the consequences of enriching a plat with extra grammatical information), in Chapter 6 (as part of a discussion of the effects of IC imposture and heteroclisis), in Chapter 7 (in constructing alternative plats for the French conjugational system), and in Chapter 12 (in a general discussion of options for plat construction and their consequences).

3 A typology of principal-part systems

As a preliminary to investigating the relative complexity of IC systems, we employ the notion of principal parts as a basis for typological comparison. We examine three significant dimensions of variation among principal-part systems: (i) the number of (static, adaptive, or dynamic) principal parts needed to determine a lexeme's realized paradigm; (ii) the number of dynamic principal parts needed to determine a given cell in a lexeme's realized paradigm; and (iii) the degree to which certain realized cells are favored in an IC system's optimal static principal-part sets. Logically, dimensions (i) and (ii) are correlates of an IC system's complexity. Variation in dimension (iii) is, as we shall see, logically orthogonal to IC systems' variation in complexity; nevertheless, (iii) exhibits an intriguing correlation with another correlate of complexity.[1]

3.1 A typology of principal-part systems

In elucidating the dimensions of typological variation among languages' principal-part systems, we focus on the principal parts of verbs, since cross-linguistically, verbs tend to exhibit the widest variety in their systems of IC distinctions; nevertheless, the general principles under discussion here apply equally in the analysis of principal parts for other lexical categories. The criteria and distinctions discussed here provide an important foundation for the typological discussion of IC transparency in Chapter 4 and for the broader notion of an IC system's complexity developed in Chapter 11.

---

[1] Portions of this chapter first appeared, in somewhat different form, in Finkel & Stump 2007. Used with kind permission from Springer Science+Business Media B.V.

The data sets that we have employed in this chapter are:

typology.A	typology.fur	typology.latin
typology.B	typology.icelandic	typology.ngiti
typology.comaltepec-chinantec	typology.koasati	typology.sanskrit
typology.dakota	typology.kwerba	typology.tulu

These are available at the *Morphological Typology* website, www.cambridge.org/stump_finkel.

We apply each of our criteria to some or all of ten languages, whose principal parts we analyze computationally. These languages (and our sources for them) are:

Comaltepec Chinantec (Oto-Manguean; Mexico)	Pace 1990
Dakota (Siouan; USA)	LaFontaine & McKay 2005
Fur (Nilo-Saharan; Sudan)	Jakobi 1990
Icelandic (Indo-European)	Jörg 1989
Koasati (Muskogean; USA)	Kimball 1991
Kwerba (Trans-New Guinea; Irian Jaya)	De Vries & De Vries 1997
Latin (Indo-European)	Wheelock 1963
Ngiti (Nilo-Saharan; DR Congo)	Kutsch Lojenga 1994
Sanskrit (Indo-European)	Whitney 1889
Tuḷu (Dravidian; Karnataka, Kerala)	Brigel 1872

3.2 Criterion A: How many principal parts are needed to determine a lexeme's IC membership?

There are languages in which all verbs are alike in their inflection; Turkish verbs are alike in this way (Göksel & Kerslake 2005: 69ff). In such languages, no verbal principal parts are even necessary, since there is no conjugation-class variation from one verb to another. There are also languages that require only a single principal part. In Kwerba, the only piece of verb morphology that distinguishes one conjugation from another is subject agreement: this morphology is abstracted from the rest of the verbal morphology in Table 3.1. Here, a verb can be said to have any one of its cells expressing first- or second-person plural

Table 3.1. *Subject prefixes in Kwerba verb morphology*

Conjugation	Singular		Dual	Plural		
				1	2	3
I	a		ac	ec	ac	naN
II	Diminutive: naN	Augmentative: a	aN	eN	aN	naN
III	naN	a	aN	e	a	a
IV	naN	a	aN	era	ara	ara

N.B.: N is a nasal stop homorganic with the following consonant.
Source: De Vries & De Vries 1997: 18–21.

subject agreement as its only principal part, since this form (in whatever tense/ mood) decisively indicates which of the four conjugations that verb belongs to.

Some languages have a system of ICs requiring a larger number of principal parts. But the exact number and identity of principal parts required for a given category of lexemes in a given language depends on whether one employs the static, the adaptive, or the dynamic principal-part scheme (§1.3.2). For instance, verbs in Koasati require at least two static principal parts, but only a single dynamic principal part, as the schematic representation of Koasati agreement morphology in Table 3.2 shows. In most cases, a Koasati verb's second-person singular cell suffices to reveal its conjugation-class membership. But three conjugations, here represented as 3A.KA, 3A.KI, and 3A.KO, are not distinguished in the second-person singular; they are, however, distinguished in the first-person singular. Thus, in a static scheme of principal parts, a Koasati verb's realized paradigm has two optimal principal parts: the cells expressing first-person singular and second-person singular subject agreement. (There are actually several such cells – there are first-person singular and second-person singular cells in each of the language's combinations of tense, aspect, mood, and evidentiality. In principle, any pairing of a first-person singular cell with a second-person singular cell would work as an optimal static principal-part set.) In a dynamic scheme, by contrast, each verb in Koasati has a single optimal principal part: in most conjugations, a second-person singular cell, but in the particular case of verbs belonging to the 3A.KA, 3A.KI, and 3A.KO classes, a first-person singular cell. (Here again, the existence of such cells in each of the language's combinations of tense, aspect, mood, and evidentiality expands the range of second-person singular and first-person singular cells from which these optimal dynamic principal parts might be chosen.)

In general, principal-part analyses defined according to the static scheme involve the most principal parts, and analyses defined according to the dynamic scheme involve the fewest. For the languages whose systems of conjugation we consider here, the numbers of optimal principal parts are shown in Table 3.3, broken down according to the static, adaptive, and dynamic schemes. Thus, a Kwerba verb has one optimal principal part no matter whether one employs the static, the adaptive, or the dynamic principal-part scheme. By contrast, Fur has five optimal principal parts in the static scheme, but a maximum of only three optimal principal parts in the adaptive and dynamic schemes.

Because we regard the complexity of an IC system as the extent to which the system inhibits motivated inferences about a lexeme's full paradigm of realized cells from subsets of its cells, the size of a lexeme's optimal principal-part set is a correlate of the complexity of the IC system of which it is part: the more principal parts a lexeme requires, the more limited the options for inferring the entirety of that

Table 3.2. *Koasati affirmative agreement morphology*

Conjugation	Form of root	1sg	2sg	3	1pl	2pl	Example
1A	R	R-li	is-R	R	il-R	has-R	Í:MON 'gather'
1B	R	R-li	R<s>	R	R<l>	R<has>	Ó:TIN 'gather'
2AI	R	R-li	R-ci	R	R-hili	R-háci	PÍ:SIN 'suckle'
2AII	Xli	Xli-li	X-ci	Xli	X-hili	X-háci	INCOKFOLÓHLIN 'be dizzy'
2B	Xli:ci	Xli:ci-li	X:ci<ci>	Xli:ci	X:ci<hili>	X:ci<haci>	IMMAMMÍ:CIN 'be good-hearted'
2C	R	R-li	R<ci>	R	R<li>	R<haci>	HOFNÁN 'smell something'
3A.KA	Xka	Xka-li	X-hiska	Xka	X-hilka	X-háska	TANÍHKAN 'gamble'
3A.KI	Xki	Xki-li	X-hiska	Xki	X-hilka	X-háska	FÍ:KIN 'pay'
3A.KO	Xko	Xko-li	X-hiska	Xko	X-hilka	X-háska	ÍSKON 'drink'
3B	R	R-li	R-íska	R	R-ilka	R-áska	PAKAMA:CIN 'tame'
3CI	R	R-li	R-tíska	R	R-tilka	R-táska	MIKKON 'be a king'
3CII	R	R-l-o	R-tísk-o	R-o*	R-tilk-o	R-task-o	SNÁ:H-Q 'be rich'

(The 2sg cells for 3A.KA, 3A.KI, 3A.KO are boxed.)

* paucal R-k-o, plural R-h-o.

N.B.: Y<Z> represents the result of infixing Z in Y.

Exponents of optimal dynamic principal parts are shaded. Unlike other 2sg forms, the boxed forms are not optimal dynamic principal parts.

Source: Kimball 1991: 56–89.

Table 3.3. *Numbers of optimal principal parts in the verb systems of ten languages*

	Number of conjugations in our sample	Number of optimal static principal parts (= static principal-part number)	Depth of optimal adaptive principal parts		Number of optimal dynamic principal parts	
			Maximum	Average over all ICs	Maximum	Average over all ICs (= dynamic principal-part number)
Kwerba	4	1	1	1.00	1	1.00
Koasati	12	2	2	1.25	1	1.00
Tulu	6	2	2	1.67	1	1.00
Dakota	20	2	2	1.26	2	1.25
Sanskrit	38	3	2	1.76	2	1.16
Ngiti	10	3	3	2.40	2	1.60
Latin	19	4	3	2.21	3	1.74
Fur	19	5	3	2.32	3	1.58
Comaltepec Chinantec	67	5	4	2.39	4	1.84
Icelandic	162*	8	4	2.34	4	1.56

* Jörg 1989 lists 162, but there are only 146 distinct ICs.

lexeme's realized paradigm; inferences from a smaller number of realized cells are sometimes unmotivated. Henceforth, we sometimes refer to a lexeme's number of optimal static or dynamic principal parts as its **static** or **dynamic principal-part number**. In a natural extension of this terminology, we regard the static and dynamic principal-part numbers shared by lexemes belonging to an IC J as those of J itself. Similarly, we regard the static principal-part number shared by the ICs in an IC system as that of the system itself, and we average the dynamic principal-part numbers of the ICs constituting an IC system to arrive at the dynamic principal-part number of the system itself. In Chapter 11, we discuss the status of an IC system's principal-part numbers as measurable correlates of its complexity.

3.3 Criterion B: How many dynamic principal parts are needed to determine a given cell in a lexeme's realized paradigm?

Criterion B distinguishes two canonical extremes between which IC systems range. In an IC system at one extreme, each cell in a lexeme's realized paradigm is determined by a single dynamic principal part; in this case, we say that the realized paradigm, its IC, and the system as a whole are **thin**. At the opposite extreme is an IC system in which a lexeme's realized cells can only be determined by simultaneous reference to every one of its principal parts; in this case, the realized paradigm, its IC, and the system as a whole are **thick**. Most principal-part systems do not embody either of these extremes, but are situated somewhere between them; their individual ICs may vary with respect to "thickness," as may an individual paradigm from one cell to another.

Consider, for example, the system of Fur conjugations,[2] whose nine distillations are numbered in (1). One of the 1,492,992 possible optimal dynamic principal-part analyses for this system is represented in Table 3.4. On the table's vertical axis, each of the nineteen conjugations is listed with a schematic representation of an optimal dynamic principal-part set. For example, Conjugation IIB is listed with the schematic principal-part set {1,3}, reflecting the fact that in this conjugation, a lexeme L's principal parts are the cells realizing distillations 1 and 3. The nine distillations are listed on the horizontal axis. In the column headed by distillation d, each row lists the principal part(s) necessary for deducing the cell realizing d in a lexeme's realized paradigm in this analysis; principal parts are again represented by the number of the distillation they realize. Thus, as an IC, Conjugation IIA is thin as can be: in the analysis portrayed in Table 3.4, a verbal lexeme belonging to this IC has one principal part, which suffices to determine

---

[2] We present a detailed discussion of this system in §4.2.

Table 3.4. An optimal dynamic principal-part analysis for Fur verbs

		Third person									
		Nonthird person			Singular			Plural nonhuman			Average number of principal parts required to deduce a realized cell
Conjugations	Optimal dynamic principal-part set	sbjv Dist 1	perf Dist 2	pres Dist 3	sbjv Dist 4	perf Dist 5	pres Dist 6	sbjv Dist 7	perf Dist 8	pres Dist 9	
I1A	{3}	3	3	3	3	3	3	3	3	3	1.00
I1B	{1,3}	1	1	3	1	1	3	1	1	3	1.00
I1C	{3}	3	3	3	3	3	3	3	3	3	1.00
I2A	{6}	6	6	6	6	6	6	6	6	6	1.00
I2B	{6}	6	6	6	6	6	6	6	6	6	1.00
I2C	{3}	3	3	3	3	3	3	3	3	3	1.00
II1A	{3}	3	3	3	3	3	3	3	3	3	1.00
II1B	{1,3}	1	1	3	1	1	3	1	1	3	1.00
II2A	{1,3}	3	3	3	3	3	3	3	3	3	1.00
II2B	{6}	6	6	6	6	6	6	6	6	6	1.00
IIIA	{4}	4	4	4	4	4	4	4	4	4	1.00
IIIB	{4,7}	4	4	4	4	4	4	7	4	4	1.00
IIIC	{1,4}	1	1,4	4	4	1,4	4	1,4	4	4	1.33
IIID	{1,5,7}	1	5	1	1	5	1	7	1	1	1.00
IIIE	{2,5}	2,5	2	2	2,5	5	2	2,5	2	2	1.33
IVA	{1,2}	1	2	1	1	2	1	1,2	1	1	1.11
IVB	{4,7}	4	4	4	4	4	4	7	4	4	1.00
IVC	{1,5,7}	1	5	1	1	5	1	7	1	1	1.00
IVD	{1}	1	1	1	1	1	1	1	1	1	1.00

every cell in the lexeme's realized paradigm. And even though Conjugation IIB has two optimal dynamic principal parts and Conjugation IIID has three, these conjugations are also thin, requiring no more than a single principal part to determine any given cell. Conjugation IIIE is somewhat thicker, requiring both of its principal parts to determine the cells realizing the subjunctive distillations.

(1)   The nine distillations in Fur verb inflection
1 {non3 sbjv}
2 {non3 perf}
3 {non3 pres}
4 {3sg sbjv}
5 {3sg perf}
6 {3sg pres}
7 {3pl nonhuman sbjv}
8 {3pl nonhuman perf}
9 {3pl nonhuman pres}

In the rightmost column of Table 3.4 is the number of principal parts required to determine a given realized cell, averaged across the cells realizing the nine distillations in a given IC. We call this average the IC's **cell predictor number**. Two factors for the calculation of an IC's cell predictor number should be carefully noted. First, any realized cell that is itself a principal part in some analysis is "deducible" from itself in that analysis – that is, if a cell is a principal part in some analysis, it can never require more than a single principal part in order for it to be deduced in that analysis. Second, the same cell may be deducible from a single principal part on one optimal analysis but may only be deducible from two (or more) principal parts in another optimal[3] analysis; for example, an alternative to the principal-part set {1, 5, 7} for Conjugation IVC is the principal-part set {4, 5, 7}, which requires two principal parts (the cells realizing distillations 4 and 5) in order to determine the cell realizing distillation 1. This means that Conjugation IVC has 1.00 as its cell predictor number under the analysis {1, 5, 7}, but 1.11 under the analysis {4, 5, 7}. Where no particular analysis is specified, we regard an IC's cell predictor number as the lowest of the available alternatives.

The ten languages under discussion here vary in exactly how many dynamic principal parts are necessary to deduce a given realized cell. The conjugational systems of Kwerba, Koasati, and Tuḷu are uniformly thin; that of Icelandic is

---

[3] Recall that a principal-part analysis for a lexeme L in a given (static, adaptive or dynamic) scheme is optimal if there is no other analysis in that scheme requiring fewer principal parts to determine L's IC membership. This optimality does not exclude the possibility that two optimal analyses for L in a given scheme might differ with respect to the number of principal parts necessary to deduce a given cell in L's realized paradigm.

Table 3.5. *Average cell predictor numbers and dynamic principal-part numbers for ten systems of conjugation*

	Average cell predictor number	Dynamic principal-part number
Comaltepec Chinantec	1.08	1.84
Dakota	1.00	1.25
Fur	1.04	1.58
Icelandic	1.09	1.56
Koasati	1.00	1.00
Kwerba	0.75	1.00
Latin	1.04	1.74
Ngiti	1.02	1.60
Sanskrit	1.02	1.16
Tuḷu	1.00	1.00

much thicker, with the determination of certain cells requiring reference to three principal parts in some optimal dynamic analyses. But if one averages the cell predictor numbers of all ICs within a given system, the resulting number is in general low. In Table 3.5 are the averages for the ten languages under scrutiny. (The initially surprising Kwerba average is below 1.00 because one of the four distillations for Kwerba verbs has the same exponence in all four ICs and can therefore be deduced without reference to any principal parts.)

A comparison of these average cell predictor numbers with the languages' dynamic principal-part numbers (repeated here from Table 3.3) reveals a difference between the inference of a full realized paradigm and that of an individual realized cell: the dynamic principal-part number tends to be higher than the average cell predictor number, because it often takes more information to determine an entire paradigm than a single cell. These facts recall the Low Entropy Conjecture (Malouf & Ackerman 2010c), according to which paradigms tend universally to exhibit low expected conditional entropy. These facts suggest a finer formulation of this conjecture, according to which the determination of a given realized cell involves lower expected conditional entropy than the determination of the full paradigm to which it belongs.

Because we regard the complexity of an IC system as the extent to which the system inhibits motivated inferences about a lexeme's full paradigm of realized cells from subsets of its cells, an IC's cell predictor number is a correlate of the complexity of the IC system of which it is part: the more cells it takes to deduce a given cell in a realized paradigm, the more limited the options for inferring the paradigm as a whole. We draw together this and other strands of our discussion in the general account of an IC system's complexity in Chapter 11.

3.4 Criterion C: To what extent are particular realized cells favored as optimal static principal parts?

In many IC systems, IC distinctions are particularly clear in the inflectional expression of particular MPSs. In such systems, the cells realizing those property sets are particularly likely to act as optimal principal parts. Sanskrit presents a rather elaborate case of this sort.

According to the traditional analysis, verbs in Classical Sanskrit inflect in four different tense systems, each of which subsumes one or more tense/mood combinations, as in Table 3.6. In this analysis, a Sanskrit verb's inflection is not determined by its membership in a single conjugation class; rather, each of the systems in Table 3.6 has a set of conjugation classes peculiar to it. The present system, for example, has the conjugations in Table 3.7a, and the aorist system has the conjugations in Table 3.7b. Each of these conjugations requires

Table 3.6. *The four tense systems in Classical Sanskrit*

Present system	Aorist system	Perfect system	Future system
present indicative	aorist indicative	perfect indicative	future indicative
imperfect indicative	precative		conditional
optative			
imperative			

Source: Whitney 1889: §§527ff.

Table 3.7. *Conjugation classes in the present and aorist systems*

(a) Present system conjugations		(b) Aorist-system conjugations	
Thematic (stem in -*a*)	Athematic (stem not in -*a*)	Asigmatic (stem lacks *s* suffix)	Sigmatic (stem has *s* suffix)
1st	2nd	root aorist	*s*-aorist
4th	3rd	thematic aorist	*iṣ*-aorist
6th	5th	reduplicated aorist	*siṣ*-aorist
10th	7th		*sa*-aorist
	8th		
	9th		

Source: Whitney 1889: §§527ff.

Table 3.8. *Morphological marks of the conjugation classes of the Sanskrit present and aorist systems*

		Conjugation	Affix	Vocalism of root/stem
Present system	thematic	1	suffix -*a*	root strong if possible
		4	suffix -*ya*	root unchanged
		6	suffix -*a*	root weak
		10	suffix -*aya*	root strong if possible
	athematic	2	none	stem shows gradation if possible
		3	reduplicative prefix	stem shows gradation if possible
		5	suffix -*no*/-*nu*	stem shows gradation if possible
		7	infix -*na*-/-*n*-	stem shows gradation if possible
		8	suffix -*o*/-*u*	stem shows gradation if possible
		9	suffix -*nā*/-*nī*	stem shows gradation if possible
Aorist system	asigmatic	root	none	stem shows gradation if possible
		thematic	suffix -*a*	root weak
		reduplicated	redup. prefix+suffix -*a*	root weak
	sigmatic	s	suffix -*s*	stem shows gradation if possible
		iṣ	suffix -*iṣ*	stem shows gradation if possible
		siṣ	suffix -*siṣ*	root strong if possible
		sa	suffix -*sa*	root unchanged

Source: Whitney 1889: §§527ff.

a particular stem form; we summarize these requirements in Table 3.8 and give examples of conjugation in Tables 3.9 and 3.10. The lexeme BHŪ 'become' belongs to the first conjugation in Table 3.7a, which accounts for the present-system realizations in Table 3.9; BHŪ also belongs to the root-aorist conjugation in Table 3.7b, which accounts for its aorist-system realizations in Table 3.10.

Correlations can in some cases be found between a verb's conjugation-class membership in the present system and its conjugation-class membership in the aorist system; for instance, verbs in the tenth present-system conjugation generally inflect as members of the reduplicated aorist conjugation. In general, however, a verbal lexeme's IC membership in one of these systems is independent

Table 3.9. *Present-system conjugations in Sanskrit (present indicative active forms)*

Conjugation	Exemplar	Singular			Dual			Plural		
		1	2	3	1	2	3	1	2	3
THEMATIC										
1st	BHŪ 'become'; stem *bhava-*	*bhavā-mi*	*bhava-si*	*bhava-ti*	*bhavā-vas*	*bhava-thas*	*bhava-tas*	*bhavā-mas*	*bhava-tha*	*bhava-nti*
4th	DIV 'play'; stem *dīvya-*	*dīvyā-mi*	*dīvya-si*	*dīvya-ti*	*dīvyā-vas*	*dīvya-thas*	*dīvya-tas*	*dīvyā-mas*	*dīvya-tha*	*dīvya-nti*
6th	TUD 'strike'; stem *tuda-*	*tudā-mi*	*tuda-si*	*tuda-ti*	*tudā-vas*	*tuda-thas*	*tuda-tas*	*tudā-mas*	*tuda-tha*	*tuda-nti*
10th	CUR 'steal'; stem *coraya-*	*corayā-mi*	*coraya-si*	*coraya-ti*	*corayā-vas*	*coraya-thas*	*coraya-tas*	*corayā-mas*	*coraya-tha*	*coraya-nti*
ATHEMATIC										
2nd	I 'go'; stems *e-/i-*	*e-mi*	*e-ṣi*	*e-ti*	*i-vas*	*i-thas*	*i-tas*	*i-mas*	*i-tha*	*y-anti*
3rd	HU 'sacrifice'; stems *juho-/juhu-*	*juho-mi*	*juho-si*	*juho-ti*	*juhu-vas*	*juhu-thas*	*juhu-tas*	*juhu-mas*	*juhu-tha*	*juhv-ati*
5th	SU 'press out'; stems *suno-/sunu-*	*suno-mi*	*suno-ṣi*	*suno-ti*	*sun-vas*	*sunu-thas*	*sunu-tas*	*sunu-mas*	*sunu-tha*	*sunv-anti*
7th	RUDH 'obstruct'; stems *ruṇadh-/rundh-*	*ruṇadh-mi*	*ruṇat-si*	*ruṇad-dhi*	*rundh-vas*	*rund-dhas*	*rund-dhas*	*rundh-mas*	*rund-dha*	*rundh-anti*
8th	KṚ 'do, make'; stems *karo-/kuru-*	*karo-mi*	*karo-ṣi*	*karo-ti*	*kur-vas*	*kuru-thas*	*kuru-tas*	*kur-mas*	*kuru-tha*	*kurv-anti*
9th	KRĪ 'buy'; stems *krīṇā-/krīṇī-*	*krīṇā-mi*	*krīṇā-si*	*krīṇā-ti*	*krīṇī-vas*	*krīṇī-thas*	*krīṇī-tas*	*krīṇī-mas*	*krīṇī-tha*	*krīṇ-anti*

Source: Whitney 1889: §§599ff.

Table 3.10. *Aorist-system conjugations in Sanskrit (aorist indicative active forms)*

Conjugation	Exemplar	Singular			Dual			Plural		
		1	2	3	1	2	3	1	2	3
ASIGMATIC										
root aorist	BHŪ 'become'; stem *bhū-*	*a-bhūv-am*	*a-bhū-s*	*a-bhū-t*	*a-bhū-va*	*a-bhū-tam*	*a-bhū-tām*	*a-bhū-ma*	*a-bhū-ta*	*a-bhūv-an*
thematic aorist	TUṢ 'be happy'; stem *tuśc-*	*a-tuṣa-m*	*a-tuṣa-s*	*a-tuṣa-t*	*a-tuṣā-va*	*a-tuṣa-tam*	*a-tuṣa-tām*	*a-tuṣā-ma*	*a-tuṣa-ta*	*a-tuṣa-n*
reduplicated aorist	JAN 'give birth'; stem *jījana-*	*a-jījana-m*	*a-jījana-s*	*a-jījana-t*	*a-jījanā-va*	*a-jījana-tam*	*a-jījana-tām*	*a-jījanā-ma*	*a-jījana-ta*	*a-jījana-n*
SIGMATIC										
s-aorist	NĪ 'lead'; stem *naiṣ-*	*a-naiṣ-am*	*a-naiṣ-īs*	*a-naiṣ-īt*	*a-naiṣ-va*	*a-naiṣ-ṭam*	*a-naiṣ-ṭām*	*a-naiṣ-ma*	*a-naiṣ-ṭa*	*a-naiṣ-ur*
iṣ-aorist	PŪ 'cleanse'; stem *pāviṣ-*	*a-pāviṣ-am*	*a-pāvī-s*	*a-pāvī-t*	*a-pāviṣ-va*	*a-pāviṣ-ṭam*	*a-pāviṣ-ṭām*	*a-pāviṣ-ma*	*a-pāviṣ-ṭa*	*a-pāviṣ-ur*
siṣ-aorist	YĀ 'go'; stem *yāsiṣ-*	*a-yāsiṣ-am*	*a-yāsī-s*	*a-yāsī-t*	*a-yāsiṣ-va*	*a-yāsiṣ-ṭam*	*a-yāsiṣ-ṭām*	*a-yāsiṣ-ma*	*a-yāsiṣ-ṭa*	*a-yāsiṣ-ur*
sa-aorist	DIŚ 'point'; stem *dikṣa-*	*a-dikṣa-m*	*a-dikṣa-s*	*a-dikṣa-t*	*a-dikṣā-va*	*a-dikṣa-tam*	*a-dikṣa-tām*	*a-dikṣā-ma*	*a-dikṣa-ta*	*a-dikṣa-n*

Source: Whitney 1889: §§824ff.

of its IC membership in any other system – that is, neither ordinarily allows the other to be directly deduced. Thus, the pattern of aorist inflection exhibited by BHŪ is shared by verbs whose present-system inflection follows a conjugation other than the first (e.g. HRĪ 'be ashamed' belongs to the third present-system conjugation, SAGH 'be equal to' to the fifth conjugation, GUR 'greet' to the sixth conjugation, and TṚD 'split, bore' to the seventh conjugation); by the same token, several first-conjugation verbs form their aorist differently from BHŪ (e.g. DHVAS 'scatter' follows the thematic aorist conjugation, KḶP 'be adapted' the reduplicated aorist conjugation, RAKṢ 'protect' the *s*-aorist conjugation, ŚAṄK 'doubt' the *iṣ*-aorist conjugation, and KRUŚ 'cry out' the *sa*-aorist conjugation).

Conjugation-class distinctions therefore multiply in Sanskrit. The future- and perfect-tense systems also contribute to this proliferation, though less dramatically than the present- and aorist-tense systems. For purposes of future-system inflection, Sanskrit verbs fall into two classes: in the future-tense forms of verbs in the *seṭ* ('with *i*') group, the future-tense suffix *-sya* (sandhi form *-ṣya*) is preceded by the "linking vowel" *i*, which is absent from the future-tense forms of verbs in the *aniṭ* ('without *i*') group – *bhav-i-ṣya-ti* 's/he will become', *śro-ṣya-ti* 's/he will hear'.[4] The perfect system distinguishes between a synthetic inflection with various subtypes and a periphrastic inflection; to a large extent, phonological criteria suffice to determine which inflectional pattern a verb follows in the perfect.

The cross-classification of the four tense systems' conjugation classes is further complicated by the decay of the system of voice distinctions inherited by Classical Sanskrit. In the prehistory of Sanskrit, middle verb forms were used to describe actions that are in some sense self-directed, while active verb forms were used to describe events or states of affairs not involving self-directed action. For instance, *pacāmahe* 'we cook' (middle) describes the speakers cooking for themselves, while *pacāmas* 'we cook' (active) describes the speakers cooking for someone else. Not all verbs participate in this distinction, since some verbs have an inherently middle meaning (e.g. 'lie down') and others always inherently lack a middle meaning (e.g. 'seem'). During the attested history of Sanskrit, the active/middle distinction is progressively bleached of this semantic significance, yet a three-way distinction persists among verbs: some verbs (labeled *parasmaipadin* 'word for another') only have active forms, while others (*ātmanepadin* 'word for self') only have middle forms, and still

---

[4] The appearance of this linking vowel is grammatically conditioned; it cannot simply be attributed to a rule of phonologically conditioned epenthesis.

others (*ubhayapadin* 'word for both') exhibit full active and middle paradigms. Usage reveals that the active/middle distinction is a largely arbitrary aspect of Classical Sanskrit grammar, often no more expressive of any semantic content than an inanimate noun's status as masculine, feminine, or neuter.[5] Tables 3.11, 3.12, and 3.13 present the indicative subparadigms of the *ubhayapadin* verb RUDH 'obstruct', the *parasmaipadin* verb BHĪ 'fear', and the *ātmanepadin* verb ĪKṢ 'see'.

These facts might lead one to suppose that a Sanskrit verb requires at least four principal parts: one reflecting its present-system conjugation, a second reflecting its perfect-system conjugation, a third for its aorist-system conjugation, and a fourth for its future-system conjugation. Moreover, *parasmaipadin* and *ātmanepadin* verbs seemingly require an additional stipulation that an expected principal part does not exist (e.g. that BHĪ lacks a middle principal part, and that ĪKṢ lacks an active principal part).

In actuality, the situation is not quite that complex. Even though a verb's conjugation in one tense system generally cannot be directly predicted from its conjugation in another tense system, it is often possible to draw inferences from the combination of conjugations that a verb follows in two or three of the tense systems. For this reason, three[6] static principal parts suffice to account for all of the "conjugations" in our sample plat of Sanskrit finite verb inflections. In this plat, each "conjugation" consists of an attested combination of four traditional conjugations, one each from the present-, perfect-, aorist-, and future-tense systems; thus, one of our "conjugations" (to which the *ubayapadin* verb DĀ 'give' belongs) is a conflation of the third present-system conjugation, the perfect conjugation for roots in *ā*, the root-aorist conjugation, and the future conjugation of verbs in the *aniṭ* class. Our sample plat has thirty-eight[7] such "conjugations," whose exemplars are classified according to their present-system and aorist-system inflection in Table 3.14, where the abbreviations (P), (Ā), and (P, Ā) identify *parasmaipadin*, *ātmanepadin*, and *ubhayapadin*

---

[5] Middle inflections are nevertheless important for the expression of passive voice. In the present system, passives are formed by means of a special suffix -*yá* that creates a stem with a thematic conjugation; the desinences of present-system passives are uniformly those of the middle voice. In the other tense systems, ordinary middle-voice forms can be used in a passive sense; the aorist system does, however, present a wholly isolated, third-person singular passive form. (Cf. Whitney 1889: §998.)

[6] One or more additional principal parts might be necessitated by a verb's various nonfinite forms, which we leave aside for present purposes.

[7] We do not claim that this sample is an exhaustive representation of every "conjugation" in Sanskrit; it is not. We are nevertheless confident that, as regards the phenomena at issue here, our sample plat accurately reflects the properties of Sanskrit conjugation.

Table 3.11. *Indicative forms of the* ubhayapadin *verb* RUDH *'obstruct'*

Tense system	Conjugation	Tense	Person	Active			Middle		
				Singular	Dual	Plural	Singular	Dual	Plural
Present	7th	Present	1	*runadhmi*	*rundhvas*	*rundhmas*	*rundhe*	*rundhvahe*	*rundhmahe*
			2	*runatsi*	*runddhas*	*runddha*	*runtse*	*rundhāthe*	*runddhve*
			3	*runaddhi*	*runddhas*	*rundhanti*	*runddhe*	*rundhāte*	*rundhate*
		Imperfect	1	*aruṇadham*	*arundhva*	*arundhma*	*arundhi*	*arundhvahi*	*arundhmahi*
			2	*aruṇas ~aruṇat*	*arunddham*	*arunddha*	*arunddhās*	*arundhāthām*	*arunddhvam*
			3	*aruṇat*	*arunddhām*	*arundhan*	*arunddha*	*arundhātām*	*arundhata*
Aorist	s-Aorist	Aorist	1	*arautsam*	*arautsva*	*arautsma*	*arutsi*	*arutsvahi*	*arutsmahi*
			2	*arautsīs*	*arauddham*	*arauddha*	*arudddhās*	*arutsāthām*	*aruddhvam*
			3	*arautsīt*	*arauddhām*	*arautsus*	*aruddha*	*arutsātām*	*arutsata*
Perfect	Synthetic	Perfect	1	*rurodha*	*rurudhiva*	*rurudhima*	*rurudhe*	*rurudhivahe*	*rurudhimahe*
			2	*rurodhitha*	*rurudhathus*	*rurudha*	*rurudhiṣe*	*rurudhāthe*	*rurudhidhve*
			3	*rurodha*	*rurudhatus*	*rurudhus*	*rurudhe*	*rurudhāte*	*rurudhire*
Future	s-Future	Future	1	*rotsyāmi*	*rotsyāvas*	*rotsyāmas*	*rotsye*	*rotsyāvahe*	*rotsyāmahe*
			2	*rotsyasi*	*rotsyathas*	*rotsyatha*	*rotsyase*	*rotsyethe*	*rotsyadhve*
			3	*rotsyati*	*rotsyatas*	*rotsyanti*	*rotsyate*	*rotsyete*	*rotsyante*

Source: Whitney 1889: §§683ff.

Table 3.12. *Indicative forms of the* parasmaipadin *verb* BHĪ *'fear'*

Tense system	Conjugation	Tense	Person	Active Singular	Dual	Plural
Present	3rd	Present	1	bibhemi	bibhīvas	bibhīmas
			2	bibheṣi	bibhīthas	bibhītha
			3	bibheti	bibhītas	bibhyati
		Imperfect	1	abibhayam	abibhīva	abibhīma
			2	abibhes	abibhītam	abibhīta
			3	abibhet	abibhītām	abibhayus
Aorist	s-Aorist	Aorist	1	abhaiṣam	abhaiṣva	abhaiṣma
			2	abhaiṣīs	abhaiṣṭam	abhaiṣṭa
			3	abhaiṣīt	abhaiṣṭām	abhaiṣus
Perfect	Synthetic	Perfect	1	bibhāya ~ bibhaya	bibhyiva	bibhyima
			2	bibhetha ~ bibhayitha	bibhyathus	bibhya
			3	bibhāya	bibhyatus	bibhyus
Future	s-Future	Future	1	bheṣyāmi	bheṣyāvas	bheṣyāmas
			2	bheṣyasi	bheṣyathas	bheṣyatha
			3	bheṣyati	bheṣyatas	bheṣyanti

Source: Whitney 1889: §§642ff.

verbs, respectively. (In the plat itself, we use "no" as the exponence of middle MPSs in *parasmaipadin* conjugations and of active MPSs in *ātmanepadin* conjugations.) Note that in the aorist, each of the verbs BHID 'split', YUJ 'join', SU 'press out', and HĀ 'abandon' follows one conjugation in its active subparadigm and a different conjugation in its middle subparadigm; for example, BHID has active forms in the thematic aorist and middle forms in the *s*-aorist conjugation.

Our plat of Sanskrit conjugations has forty-five optimal static principal-part analyses, each involving three principal parts. The MPSs expressed by the three principal parts are far from random: in every analysis, one principal part realizes a property set in (2a), another realizes a property set in (2b), and a third realizes a property set in (2c). Considered in the context of the full set of nineteen distillations in our Sanskrit conjugation plat (listed in Table 3.15), these property sets seem to embody an overarching generalization: that a Sanskrit verb's optimal static principal parts necessarily include (a) a cell realizing an active present-system distillation (recall that imperatives belong to the present

70 *A typology of principal-part systems*

Table 3.13. *Indicative forms of the* ātmanepadin *verb* īkṣ *'see'*

Tense system	Conjugation	Tense	Person	Middle Singular	Dual	Plural
Present	1st	Present	1	īkṣe	īkṣāvahe	īkṣāmahe
			2	īkṣase	īkṣethe	īkṣadhve
			3	īkṣate	īkṣete	īkṣante
		Imperfect	1	aikṣe	aikṣāvahi	aikṣāmahi
			2	aikṣathās	aikṣethām	aikṣadhvam
			3	aikṣata	aikṣetām	aikṣanta
Aorist	iṣ-Aorist	Aorist	1	aikṣiṣi	aikṣiṣvahi	aikṣiṣmahi
			2	aikṣiṣṭhās	aikṣiṣāthām	aikṣiḍhvam
			3	aikṣiṣṭa	aikṣiṣātām	aikṣiṣata
Perfect	Periphrastic	Perfect	1	īkṣāṃ cakre	īkṣāṃ cakṛvahe	īkṣāṃ cakṛmahe
			2	īkṣāṃ cakṛṣe	īkṣāṃ cakrāthe	īkṣāṃ cakṛdhve
			3	īkṣāṃ cakre	īkṣāṃ cakrāte	īkṣāṃ cakrire
Future	s-Future	Future	1	īkṣiṣye	īkṣiṣyāvahe	īkṣiṣyāmahe
			2	īkṣiṣyase	īkṣiṣyethe	īkṣiṣyadhve
			3	īkṣiṣyate	īkṣiṣyete	īkṣiṣyante

Source: Whitney 1889: §§734ff.

system), (b) a cell realizing a present or perfect middle distillation, and (c) a cell realizing an aorist indicative active distillation. This generalization is exactly right. In particular, it is not an artifact of our choice of the MPSs in (2) to represent their respective distillations: as Table 3.16 shows, the five numbered distillations containing the MPSs in (2a) only contain active present-system property sets; the three containing the MPSs in (2b) only contain present or perfect middle property sets; and the three containing the MPSs in (2c) only contain aorist indicative active property sets. Cells realizing perfect active, aorist middle or future distillations are never optimal static principal parts.

(2a)   1 {1sg pres ind active}
          2 {1du pres ind active}
          3 {3pl pres ind active}
          6 {1sg impf ind active}
          7 {3pl impv active}

Table 3.14. *Exemplars of the thirty-eight Sanskrit "conjugations" in our sample plat*

				AORIST CONJUGATIONS			
		Root	Thematic	Reduplicated	s	iṣ	siṣ	sa
P R E S E N T	1st	BHŪ (P) 'become'	GAM (P) 'go'	KLP (Ā) 'be ordered'; PAT (P) 'fall'	NĪ (P) 'lead'; SMṚ (P) 'remember'	BĀDH (Ā) 'repel'; BUDH (P) 'wake'; HAS (P) 'laugh'	GAI (P) 'sing'; YĀ (P) 'go'	KRUŚ (P) 'shriek'
	2nd		VAC (P) 'speak'			VAS (Ā) 'clothe'		DVIṢ (P, Ā) 'hate'
C O N J U G A T I O N S	3rd	DĀ (P, Ā) 'give'			BHṚ (P, Ā) 'support'; HĀ (Ā) 'abandon'		HĀ (P) 'abandon'	
	4th		TUṢ (P) 'be pleased'					
	5th		ĀP (P) 'obtain'; ŚAK (P) 'be able'		SU (Ā) 'press out'	AŚ (Ā) 'pervade'; SU (P) 'press out'		
	6th							DIŚ (P) 'point'
	7th		BHID (P) 'split'; PIṢ (P) 'crush'; YUJ (P) 'join'	RIC (P, Ā) 'evacuate'	BHID (Ā) 'split'; BHUJ (Ā) 'eat, enjoy'; RUDH (P, Ā) 'obstruct'; YUJ (Ā) 'join'	HIṂS (P) 'injure'		
	8th				KṚ (P, Ā) 'make'; TAN (P, Ā) 'stretch'			
	9th		PUṢ (P) 'strengthen'		KRĪ (P, Ā) 'buy'	KLIŚ (P) 'torment'; MUṢ (P) 'rob'; PŪ (P, Ā) 'cleanse'		
	10th							

Table 3.15. *The nineteen distillations in the Sanskrit plat*

	Indicative					Imperative
	Present	Imperfect	Perfect	Aorist	Future	
Active	1SG, 1DU, 3PL	1SG	1sg, 2sg, 3sg, 1du	*1sg, 2sg, 1du*	1sg	3PL
Middle	**1sg, 2sg**		**1sg**	*1sg, 2sg*	1sg	

Shaded distillations are optimal principal parts in one or another analysis. The distillations in (2a) are given in small caps; those in (2b) in boldface; and those in (2c) in italics.

(2b) 4 {1sg pres ind middle}
      5 {2sg pres ind middle}
    12 {1sg perf ind middle}

(2c) 13 {1sg aorist ind active}
    14 {2sg aorist ind active}
    15 {1du aorist ind active}

These facts show that, in Sanskrit, certain realized cells are favored loci for the realization of IC distinctions; these cells are the best candidates for inclusion in an optimal static principal-part set.

Not all IC systems exhibit this property so clearly. Tuḷu verb inflection involves the seven distillations[8] labeled **a–g** in Table 3.17; cells serving as optimal static principal parts may realize any of these distillations but **g** (= {1sg fut negative}). The optimal static principal-part sets for Tuḷu verbs consist of two cells; there are ten such sets, as indicated in the table. In this system, the different pairs of optimal static principal parts seem to conform to a very loose morphosyntactic generalization – that at least one of the principal parts must realize an affirmative distillation – but this generalization is not strictly true. Distillation **b** includes mainly negative MPSs ({3sg neut pres affirmative} is its only affirmative member), and {**b, f**} is an optimal dynamic principal-part set.

---

[8] In Tuḷu, the {1sg pres affirmative} distillation contains all (and only) affirmative present property sets except that of the 3sg neuter; the {3sg neut pres affirmative} distillation contains all negative present property sets; the {1sg perfect affirmative} distillation contains all (and only) perfect property sets; the {1sg impf affirmative} distillation contains all (and only) affirmative imperfect property sets; the {1sg impf negative} distillation contains all (and only) negative imperfect property sets; the {1sg future affirmative} distillation contains all (and only) affirmative future property sets; and the {1sg fut negative} distillation contains all (and only) negative future property sets.

Table 3.16. *The nineteen distillations in our Sanskrit plat*

		Present		Imperfect		Optative		Imperative		Perfect		Aorist		Future	
		active	middle	active	middle	active	middle	active	middle	active	middle	active	middle	active	middle
Singular	1	a	e	f	e	a	e	f	e	h	l	m	p	r	s
	2	a	d	a	d	a	e	b	d	i	l	n	q	r	s
	3	a	d	a	d	a	e	a	d	j	l	n	q	r	s
Dual	1	b	d	b	d	a	e	f	e	k	l	o	q	r	s
	2	b	e	b	e	a	e	b	e	k	l	o	p	r	s
	3	b	e	b	e	a	e	b	e	k	l	o	p	r	s
Plural	1	b	d	b	d	a	e	f	e	k	l	o	q	r	s
	2	b	d	b	d	a	e	b	d	k	l	o	q	r	s
	3	c	e	b	e	a	e	g	e	k	l	o	q	r	s

Distillations are labeled **a–s**; the appearance of distillation x in a given cell means that the corresponding MPS belongs to x.

Table 3.17. *Optimal static principal-part sets in Tuḷu*

		Negative		Affirmative			
		g 1sg future	f 1sg imperfect	e 1sg future	d 1sg perfect	c 1sg imperfect	b 3sg neuter present
Affirmative	a 1sg present	✓	✓			✓	
	b 3sg neuter present	✓	✓			✓	
	c 1sg imperfect				✓		
	d 1sg perfect	✓		✓			
	e 1sg future	✓					
Negative	f 1sg imperfect						

Distillations are labeled **a**–**g**; ✓ designates an optimal static principal-part set, e.g. {**a**, **f**}.

We therefore distinguish two canonical extremes between which a given IC system is situated. At one extreme is an IC system possessing a single optimal static principal-part set; this system is **morphosyntactically focused**, in that the distillation realized by each principal part is constrained to uniqueness. At the opposite extreme is an IC system every one of whose distillations may be realized by an optimal static principal part in one or another analysis; this system is **morphosyntactically unfocused**, in that the distillations realized by a lexeme's optimal static principal parts are morphosyntactically unconstrained. The Sanskrit conjugational system is closer to being morphosyntactically focused than that of Tuḷu.

The IC systems that most closely approximate the ideal of total morphosyntactic focus are those in which certain realized cells are principal parts in every optimal static analysis. In our model of Icelandic conjugations, lexemes require eight optimal static principal parts. There are sixty alternative analyses; in every one of these analyses, the cells realizing the MPSs in (3a–d) are principal parts, and the remaining four principal parts realize one MPS from each of (3e–h). Thus, the Icelandic conjugational system exhibits an especially strong morphosyntactic focus on a verb's second-person singular imperative, second participle, first-person plural past subjunctive, and second-person singular past indicative cells; these are "hot spots" where IC distinctions are especially likely to be expressed morphologically.

(3) (a) {2sg impv}
     (b) {2nd ptcp}
     (c) {1pl past sbjv}
     (d) {2sg past ind}
     (e) {2sg pres ind}
          {3sg pres ind}
     (f) {1sg past ind}
          {3sg past ind}
     (g) {2pl impv}
          {2pl pres ind}
          {1sg pres sbjv}
     (h) {inf}
          {1pl impv}
          {1st ptcp}
          {1pl pres ind}
          {3pl pres ind}

Because IC systems exhibit morphosyntactic focus to varying degrees, we propose to measure a system's degree of focus as $1 - [i/(j \cdot k)]$, where i is the number of distinct distillations realized by optimal static principal parts, j is the number of optimal static principal-part sets, and k is the number of members in each set; we call this number an IC system's **morphosyntactic focus number**. For the ten IC systems under consideration, this measure yields the results in Table 3.18; the higher an IC system's morphosyntactic focus number, the more morphosyntactically focused it is.

Table 3.18 reveals an interesting correlation: in these conjugation systems, the morphosyntactic focus number directly reflects the number of optimal static principal-part sets. This is not a logically necessary correlation: in principle, IC systems with the same morphosyntactic focus number should be able to vary in their number of optimal static principal-part sets, as is the case with the hypothetical IC systems in Table 3.19. As Table 3.20 shows, lexemes in system A have three optimal static principal-part sets, each with two members – {ρ-cell, σ-cell}, {σ-cell, υ-cell}, and {τ-cell, υ-cell}; in system B, by contrast, lexemes have two optimal static principal-part sets, each with three members – {ρ-cell, σ-cell, τ-cell} and {ρ-cell, σ-cell, υ-cell}. Systems A and B both have the morphosyntactic focus number 0.33, but they differ in their number of optimal static principal-part sets. It is therefore unexpected that the optimal static principal-part sets of the IC systems in Table 3.18 should covary in number so strictly with these systems' morphosyntactic focus numbers.

76 *A typology of principal-part systems*

Table 3.18. *Degrees of morphosyntactic focus in ten conjugational systems*

	i distillations employed in optimal static principal-part sets	j optimal static principal-part sets	k distillations in each optimal static principal-part set	$1 - [i/(j \cdot k)]$ (morphosyntactic focus number)
Icelandic	16	60	8	0.97
Sanskrit	11	45	3	0.92
Latin	13	24	4	0.86
Tuḷu	6	10	2	0.70
Comaltepec Chinantec	10	6	5	0.67
Ngiti	6	6	3	0.67
Fur	7	4	5	0.65
Dakota	2	1	2	0.00
Koasati	2	1	2	0.00
Kwerba	1	1	1	0.00

Table 3.19. *Two hypothetical IC systems: A and B*

	System A				System B			
	ρ	σ	τ	υ	ρ	σ	τ	υ
I	a	d	g	i	a	c	e	g
II	a	e	h	i	b	c	e	h
III	b	e	g	j	b	c	f	g
IV	b	d	g	k	a	d	e	h
V	c	f	h	k	b	d	e	h

Table 3.20. *Degrees of morphosyntactic focus in the two hypothetical IC systems A and B in Table 3.19*

Hypothetical IC system	i distillations employed in optimal static principal-part sets	j optimal static principal-part sets	k distillations in each optimal static principal-part set	$1 - [i/(j \cdot k)]$ (morphosyntactic focus number)
A	4	3	2	0.33
B	4	2	3	0.33

If two IC systems differ in their degree of morphosyntactic focus, but are otherwise alike (in their number of distillations, in their static and dynamic principal-part numbers, in their average cell predictor number), neither clearly inhibits motivated inferences about a lexeme's full paradigm of realized cells more than the other. Thus, though we regard an IC system's degree of morphosyntactic focus as a significant dimension of cross-linguistic variation, we do not regard it as a necessary correlate of system complexity; the dimension of variation that it defines is orthogonal to that of an IC system's complexity.

3.5 Summary

We have proposed three dimensions of variation among principal-part systems; these define the three oppositions in Table 3.21.

In Table 3.22, we summarize our classification of the ten systems of conjugation according to the three criteria in Table 3.21. Amidst the variation among these systems, there are some significant patterns. First, the systems vary widely with respect to the average number of realized cells required to distinguish a lexeme's IC membership. Second, they vary much less widely with respect to the average number of realized cells required to determine a given cell in a lexeme's realized paradigm; moreover, an IC system's average cell predictor number is less – often much less – than its dynamic principal-part number (except in cases in which both are simply 1.00). The size of a system's dynamic principal-part number does not correlate directly with that of its average cell predictor number; for instance, Ngiti and Sanskrit both have 1.02 as their average cell predictor number, but Ngiti's dynamic principal-part number (1.60) is much higher than that of Sanskrit (1.16). An IC's static and dynamic principal-part numbers and its cell predictor number are logical

Table 3.21. *Three dimensions of typological variation in principal-part systems*

	Dimension	Opposition		
a.	Optimal principal parts per paradigm:	many	↔	few
b.	Cell predictor number, averaged across ICs:	high	↔	low
c.	IC system:	morphosyntactically focused	↔	morphosyntactically unfocused

Table 3.22. *Typological contrasts among ten systems of conjugation*

	Dynamic principal-part number	Average cell predictor number	Morphosyntactic focus number
Comaltepec Chinantec	1.84	1.08	0.67
Latin	1.74	1.04	0.86
Ngiti	1.60	1.02	0.67
Fur	1.58	1.04	0.65
Icelandic	1.56	1.09	0.97
Dakota	1.25	1.00	0.00
Sanskrit	1.16	1.02	0.92
Koasati	1.00	1.00	0.00
Tuḷu	1.00	1.00	0.70
Kwerba	1.00	0.75	0.00

correlates of its complexity, a point to which we return in Chapter 11; as the evidence presented here shows, they measure different facets of an IC system's complexity.

While morphosyntactic focus is not a logically necessary correlate of an IC system's complexity, it exhibits a correlation deserving further empirical scrutiny: the degree of an IC system's morphosyntactic focus seems to covary with its number of optimal static principal-part sets.

4 *Inflection-class transparency*

4.1 Introduction

In Chapter 3, we examined optimal dynamic principal-part systems in several languages and identified three dimensions of typological variation among these systems. Measures of two of these dimensions – (i) number of optimal principal parts per paradigm and (ii) cell predictor number – are objective correlates of an inflection-class system's complexity. In this chapter, we discuss two additional correlates, related to but distinct from (i) and (ii): these are the measures of IC predictability and cell predictability.[1]

Both types of predictability depend on the implicative relations that integrate the cells in a realized paradigm. In Chapter 1, we described a realized paradigm's implicative relations as valid patterns of inference relating the paradigm's cells; (1) represents a relation of this sort in Latin. We call such relations **W-relations** – 'W' being a mnemonic for 'word', because realized cells contain whole word forms, as in (1).

(1) ⟨portāre, {pres active inf}⟩ → ⟨portā, {2sg pres active impv}⟩

We now introduce implicative relations of a more general kind: valid patterns of inference by which the exponence of one MPS is deduced from that of some set of (one or more) other MPSs. Where X is a variable over stems, *y* is some

---

[1] Portions of this chapter first appeared, in somewhat different form, in R. Finkel & G. Stump (2009), used with kind permission of Oxford University Press.

The data sets that we have employed in this chapter are:

transparency.1opt
transparency.2opt
transparency.comaltepec-chinantec
transparency.fur
transparency.fur-affixes
transparency.fur-tones
transparency.maxOpaque
transparency.maxTransparent
transparency.opaque
transparency.partitioned
transparency.unpartitioned

These are available at the *Morphological Typology* website www.cambridge.org/stump_finkel.

exponence, and σ is some MPS, let X:y represent the word form consisting of stem X with exponence y, and let ⟨X:y, σ⟩ represent a realized cell pairing X:y with σ. We then represent implicative relations of this more general kind by means of formulas such as

$$\langle X{:}y, \sigma\rangle \rightarrow \langle X{:}z, \tau\rangle,$$

according to which the presence of a cell instantiating ⟨X:y, σ⟩ in a lexeme's realized paradigm implies the presence of a cell instantiating ⟨X:z, τ⟩; (2) represents a relation of this sort. We call implicative relations of this latter sort **R-relations**: 'R' is a mnemonic for 'rule', because the patterns of exponence over which such relations are defined are intuitively like realization rules; that is, (2) can be read as meaning that if a rule realizing the property set {pres active inf} applies to stem X to yield Xāre, then a rule realizing the property set {2sg pres active impv} applies to X to yield Xā. (In Chapter 9, we give formal substance to this intuitive understanding of R-relations.)

(2)   ⟨Xāre, {pres active inf}⟩ → ⟨Xā, {2sg pres active impv}⟩

Whereas W-relations pertain to the cells of individual realized paradigms, R-relations generalize over whole classes of such cells; for instance, the W-relation in (1) concerns the realized paradigm of Latin PORTĀRE 'carry', but the R-relation in (2) concerns the present active paradigms of all Latin verbs belonging to the first conjugation. Indeed, in those instances in which the same exponence is used to express the same MPS in more than one IC, R-relations may generalize over two or more ICs; for instance, the R-relation in (3) pertains to both the first and second conjugations in Latin. W-relations may in general be seen as instantiations of R-relations; for example, (1) is an instantiation of (2).

(3)   ⟨Xbō, {1sg fut active ind}⟩ → ⟨Xre, {pres active inf}⟩

In general, both W-relations and R-relations may be represented formulaically as in (4). In the representation of a W-relation, the stem variable X is necessarily instantiated by a specific stem; in the representation of an R-relation, X is necessarily uninstantiated. In either sort of representation, singleton sets are interchangeable with their members; thus, the formula '{⟨X:w, σ⟩} → {⟨X:y, τ⟩}' is equivalent to '⟨X:w, σ⟩ → ⟨X:y, τ⟩'.

(4)   (a) $\{\langle X_1, \sigma_1\rangle, \ldots, \langle X_i, \sigma_i\rangle\} \rightarrow \{\langle X_{i+1}, \sigma_{i+1}\rangle, \ldots, \langle X_n, \sigma_n\rangle\}$
       (b) $\{\langle X_1, \sigma_1\rangle, \ldots, \langle X_i, \sigma_i\rangle\} \leftrightarrow \{\langle X_{i+1}, \sigma_{i+1}\rangle, \ldots, \langle X_n, \sigma_n\rangle\}$

In an implicational relation represented as in (4a), if the cells $\langle X_1, \sigma_1\rangle, \ldots, \langle X_i, \sigma_i\rangle$ appear in a lexeme's realized paradigm, then the cells $\langle X_{i+1}, \sigma_{i+1}\rangle, \ldots,$

⟨X_n, σ_n⟩ do as well; in a biconditional relation represented as in (4b), the cells ⟨X_1, σ_1⟩, ..., ⟨X_i, σ_i⟩ appear in a lexeme's realized paradigm if and only if the cells ⟨X_{i+1}, σ_{i+1}⟩, ..., ⟨X_n, σ_n⟩ do as well. Where $S_1 \to S_2$ is a valid W- or R-relation, $S_1 \to S_2$ is **reducible** iff either (i) there is a proper subset S′ of S_1 such that S′ $\to S_2$ is a valid relation or (ii) S_2 is not a singleton set; otherwise, $S_1 \to S_2$ is **irreducible**.

R-relations are helpful for understanding the ways in which a language's ICs differ from one another. Drawing on the method of canonical typology (Corbett 2005, 2007, 2009), we distinguish two canonically opposed extremes between which individual ICs may situated; these are the canonical extremes of maximal transparency and maximal opacity. A **maximally transparent IC** is an IC in whose realized paradigms each cell's exponence determines that of every other cell; given any two cells K_1, K_2 in a realized paradigm belonging to an IC of this sort, there is an R-relation deducing K_1 from K_2.[2] For example, every IC in the hypothetical plat in Table 4.1a is maximally transparent; accordingly, every possible implicative relation among an IC's cells holds true in this plat. By contrast, in a **maximally opaque IC**, no realized paradigm has any cell or combination of cells whose exponence determines the exponence of any other cell; in a realized paradigm belonging to an IC of this sort, there are no R-relations deducing any cell from any other cell or combination of cells.[3] In the hypothetical inflectional system in Table 4.2, every IC is maximally opaque. In a natural extension of this terminology, we will also refer to a lexeme's realized paradigm as being maximally transparent (or maximally opaque) if that lexeme belongs to a maximally transparent (or maximally opaque) IC. In a maximally transparent paradigm belonging to IC J, each pairing of a property set with an exponence is unique across all ICs to the paradigms of members of J; thus, if a lexeme L's realized paradigm is maximally transparent, any cell in this paradigm may serve as L's sole dynamic principal part.

The hypothetical plats in Tables 4.1 and 4.2 highlight an important fact about principal parts: what drives up the number of principal parts required by an IC system is the similarity of its ICs. If the exponences of two ICs are very different, then it is easy to distinguish them with a small number of principal parts, perhaps with only a single one; unusual inflectional patterns therefore tend not to require more principal parts. But an IC system requires more principal parts to the extent that its ICs differ minimally in their exponence,

---

[2] Corbett 2009 discusses the characteristics of a canonical system of ICs; in a canonical system, each IC is maximally transparent.
[3] Trivially, each cell is of course self-determining, even in the paradigms of a maximally opaque IC.

Table 4.1. *Plat and irreducible inferences for a hypothetical inflectional system each of whose ICs is maximally transparent*

(a)	ρ	σ	τ	(b)			
I	a	b	c	⟨X:a, ρ⟩ → ⟨X:b, σ⟩	⟨X:g, ρ⟩ → ⟨X:h, σ⟩	⟨X:m, ρ⟩ → ⟨X:n, σ⟩	⟨X:s, ρ⟩ → ⟨X:t, σ⟩
II	d	e	f	⟨X:a, ρ⟩ → ⟨X:c, τ⟩	⟨X:g, ρ⟩ → ⟨X:i, τ⟩	⟨X:m, ρ⟩ → ⟨X:o, τ⟩	⟨X:s, ρ⟩ → ⟨X:u, τ⟩
III	g	h	i	⟨X:b, σ⟩ → ⟨X:a, ρ⟩	⟨X:h, σ⟩ → ⟨X:g, ρ⟩	⟨X:n, σ⟩ → ⟨X:m, ρ⟩	⟨X:t, σ⟩ → ⟨X:s, ρ⟩
IV	j	k	l	⟨X:b, σ⟩ → ⟨X:c, τ⟩	⟨X:h, σ⟩ → ⟨X:i, τ⟩	⟨X:n, σ⟩ → ⟨X:o, τ⟩	⟨X:t, σ⟩ → ⟨X:u, τ⟩
V	m	n	o	⟨X:c, τ⟩ → ⟨X:a, ρ⟩	⟨X:i, τ⟩ → ⟨X:g, ρ⟩	⟨X:o, τ⟩ → ⟨X:m, ρ⟩	⟨X:u, τ⟩ → ⟨X:s, ρ⟩
VI	p	q	r	⟨X:c, τ⟩ → ⟨X:b, σ⟩	⟨X:i, τ⟩ → ⟨X:h, σ⟩	⟨X:o, τ⟩ → ⟨X:n, σ⟩	⟨X:u, τ⟩ → ⟨X:t, σ⟩
VII	s	t	u	⟨X:d, ρ⟩ → ⟨X:e, σ⟩	⟨X:j, ρ⟩ → ⟨X:k, σ⟩	⟨X:p, ρ⟩ → ⟨X:q, σ⟩	⟨X:v, ρ⟩ → ⟨X:w, σ⟩
VIII	v	w	x	⟨X:d, ρ⟩ → ⟨X:f, τ⟩	⟨X:j, ρ⟩ → ⟨X:l, τ⟩	⟨X:p, ρ⟩ → ⟨X:r, τ⟩	⟨X:v, ρ⟩ → ⟨X:x, τ⟩
				⟨X:e, σ⟩ → ⟨X:d, ρ⟩	⟨X:k, σ⟩ → ⟨X:j, ρ⟩	⟨X:q, σ⟩ → ⟨X:p, ρ⟩	⟨X:w, σ⟩ → ⟨X:v, ρ⟩
				⟨X:e, σ⟩ → ⟨X:f, τ⟩	⟨X:k, σ⟩ → ⟨X:l, τ⟩	⟨X:q, σ⟩ → ⟨X:r, τ⟩	⟨X:w, σ⟩ → ⟨X:x, τ⟩
				⟨X:f, τ⟩ → ⟨X:d, ρ⟩	⟨X:l, τ⟩ → ⟨X:j, ρ⟩	⟨X:r, τ⟩ → ⟨X:p, ρ⟩	⟨X:x, τ⟩ → ⟨X:v, ρ⟩
				⟨X:f, τ⟩ → ⟨X:e, σ⟩	⟨X:l, τ⟩ → ⟨X:k, σ⟩	⟨X:r, τ⟩ → ⟨X:q, σ⟩	⟨X:x, τ⟩ → ⟨X:w, σ⟩

Table 4.2. *Plat and irreducible inferences for a hypothetical inflectional system whose ICs are maximally opaque*

(a)	ρ	σ	τ	(b) (none)
I	a	a	a	
II	b	a	a	
III	a	b	a	
IV	a	a	b	
V	b	b	a	
VI	b	a	b	
VII	a	b	b	
VIII	b	b	b	

with some pairs of ICs contrasting in one cell and others in other cells, as in Table 4.2.

In natural languages, ICs tend not to embody either of the extremes in Tables 4.1 and 4.2, but instead fall somewhere in between; more specifically, languages vary according to where their individual ICs fall on the continuum from maximal transparency to maximal opacity. In this chapter, we examine **IC transparency** – the degree of an IC's approximation to the ideal of maximal IC transparency. This concept is central to understanding the more general notion of an IC system's complexity. We regard the complexity of an IC system as the extent to which it inhibits motivated inferences about a given lexeme's realized paradigm from subsets of that paradigm's cells; an IC system's complexity is therefore inversely proportional to the overall transparency of its individual ICs.

While the criteria discussed in Chapter 3 distinguish broadly different types of principal-part systems, the measures proposed here afford a finer-grained differentiation among ICs within a single system. At least four intuitive criteria might be employed in assessing the relative transparency of ICs that deviate from maximal transparency. All else being equal, IC A is more transparent than IC B:

(a) if the number of dynamic principal parts needed to distinguish lexemes belonging to A from lexemes belonging to other ICs is smaller than the number needed to distinguish lexemes belonging to B from other lexemes;
(b) if the number of principal parts needed to deduce a given cell in the realized paradigms of A's member lexemes is, on average, lower than the number of principal parts needed to deduce a given cell in the realized paradigms of B's members;

(c) if there are more alternative optimal principal-part analyses for the realized paradigms of A's members than for those of B's members; and

(d) if the realized paradigms of A's members have fewer cells whose realization cannot be predicted than the realized paradigms of B's members.

We justify these criteria with evidence from Fur (Nilo-Saharan; Sudan) and give them formal substance by proposing precise measures of IC predictability and cell predictability. After presenting the general features of Fur's system of verb conjugation (§4.2), we demonstrate the ways in which its ICs deviate from maximal transparency (§4.3). As a way of quantifying the varying extents to which Fur's conjugations deviate from maximal transparency, we propose measures of IC predictability (§4.4) and cell predictability (§§4.5, 4.6). We show that Fur's deviation from maximal transparency is irreconcilable with the No-Blur Principle (Cameron-Faulkner & Carstairs-McCarthy 2000), according to which the affixes competing for the realization of a particular paradigmatic cell either uniquely identify a particular IC or serve as the default affixal realization of that cell (§4.7). The proposed measures of IC predictability and cell predictability afford a precise account of cross-linguistic differences in IC transparency, as we demonstrate in a comparison of the conjugational system of Fur with the conjugational systems of Icelandic and Comaltepec Chinantec (§4.8). We summarize our conclusions in §4.9.[4]

4.2 Conjugation classes in Fur

We begin with an overview of the system of conjugation classes in Fur.[5] Minimally, a Fur verb form has three components: (a) a subject prefix expressing person (nonthird or third), number (singular or plural), and (in the third-person plural) the human/nonhuman distinction; (b) the verb root exhibiting inflectional tone marking, and (c) a tense/aspect/mood (TAM) suffix (or the significative absence thereof) expressing the present, the perfect or the subjunctive. Verbs' inflectional exponents exhibit considerable cumulation: the tone inflection of a verb form's root may vary according to both its agreement properties and its TAM properties, and the realization of TAM properties may be sensitive to the agreement properties that they accompany. Verb forms in the third-person plural additionally exhibit (d) a number marker; in some instances,

---

[4] Some of the material in this chapter is presented in Finkel & Stump 2009 with a focus on examples from Comaltepec Chinantec.

[5] For a discussion of a comparably complex system of case inflections in another Nilo-Saharan language, see Baerman (2012).

a single portmanteau suffix serves simultaneously as components (c) and (d). Jakobi (1990: 102ff) analyzes Fur verbs into nineteen conjugation classes according to their realization of components (b), (c), and (d) – in particular, according to (b) the pattern of tone alternation that their roots exhibit, (c) the subjunctive and perfect suffixes that they exhibit, and (d) the particular number markers that they exhibit in the third-person plural.

Table 4.3 lists these nineteen conjugations (along with an exemplar of each conjugation) and their distinctive patterns of exponence. As this table shows, a root's tone alternations involve various combinations of high (H), low (L), and falling (F) tones. Suffixes may exhibit low tone (marked by a grave accent diacritic `) or high tone (marked by the absence of any diacritic); Ø represents the significative absence of a TAM suffix. In third-person plural forms with a single suffix, that suffix is a portmanteau expression of TAM and agreement; in plural forms with two suffixes, the first suffix is an expression of TAM properties and the second an expression of number.

In the inflection of Fur verbs, there are twelve different MPSs. We number these twelve property sets 1 through 12, where the significance of each number is as in Table 4.4. These twelve MPSs fall into nine distillations: MPS 10 falls into distillation 7, MPS 11 into distillation 8, and MPS 12 into distillation 9.

To determine whether there are any maximally transparent paradigms in Fur, we consider all optimal dynamic principal-part analyses for Fur's nineteen conjugations; the full set of analyses is given in Table 4.27 in the appendix to this chapter (§4.11).

The optimal dynamic principal-part analyses reveal that all conjugations in Fur deviate from maximal transparency to some extent. Consider, for example, Conjugation 11A. This conjugation has the three alternative principal-part analyses reproduced in Table 4.5. In this table, the nine distillations in a lexeme's paradigm are given (as 1–9) on the horizontal axis. Each row represents a different optimal principal-part analysis. Principal parts are represented as circled distillation numbers. If a principal part Ⓜ is listed in the column headed by a distillation M in a given analysis, the realization of M is deducible from Ⓜ in that analysis. Thus, Table 4.5 shows that for verbs belonging to Conjugation 11A in Fur, any present-tense cell (whether the nonthird-person present-tense cell 3, the 3sg present-tense cell 6, or the 3pl nonhuman present-tense cell 9) allows all of the other cells in the realized paradigm to be deduced. This implication arises because each of the distillations 3, 6, and 9 has an exponence in Conjugation 11A that is unique to that conjugation. Table 4.6 reproduces the exponences of distillations 1–9 in Conjugation 11A; a comparison of these exponences with those given in the full plat of Table 4.3 reveals that each of

Table 4.3. *Plat of Fur conjugations*

Conjugation	Exemplar	Nonthird person			Third person								
					Singular			Plural					
								Nonhuman			Human		
		Sbjv	Perf	Pres	Sbjv	Perf	Pres	Sbjv	Perf	Pres	Sbjv	Perf	Pres
I1A	BUUŋ 'descend'	LH-ò	LH-ò	LH-èl	HH-ò	HH-ò	HH-èl	HH-òl	HH-ùl	HH-èl-à/ì	LH-òl	LH-ùl	LH-èl-à/ì
I1B	JAAN 'wait'	LH-ò	LH-ò	LF-∅	HH-ò	HH-ò	HF-∅	HH-òl	HH-ùl	HH-è	LH-òl	LH-ùl	LH-è
I1C	IRT 'shake'	LH-ò	LH-ò	LH-ì	HH-ò	HH-ò	HH-ì	HH-òl	HH-ùl	HH-è	LH-òl	LH-ùl	LH-è
I2A	TALL 'chew'	HH-ò	HH-ò	HH-èl	LL-ò	LL-ò	LL-èl	LL-òl	LL-ùl	LL-èl-à/ì	HH-òl	HH-ùl	HH-èl-à/ì
I2B	FUUL 'spin'	HH-ò	HH-ò	HF-∅	LL-ò	LL-ò	LL-∅	LL-òl	LL-ùl	LL-è	HH-òl	HH-ùl	HH-è
I2C	KIR 'cook'	HH-ò	HH-ò	HH-ì	LL-ò	LL-ò	LL-ì	LL-òl	LL-ùl	LL-è	HH-òl	HH-ùl	HH-è
II1A	RII 'snatch'	LH-ì	LH-ì	LH-iti	HH-ì	HH-ì	HH-iti	HH-i-A(l)	HH-i-è	HH-iti-A(l)	LH-i-A(l)	LH-i-è	LH-iti-A(l)
II1B	TIIR 'meet'	LH-ì	LH-ì	LF-∅	HH-ì	HH-ì	HF-∅	HH-i-A(l)	HH-i-è	HH-è	LH-i-A(l)	LH-i-è	LH-è
II2A	*FAUL 'open'	HH-ì	HH-ì	HH-iti	LL-ì	LL-ì	LL-iti	LL-i-A(l)	LL-i-è	LL-iti-A(l)	HH-i-A(l)	HH-i-è	HH-iti-A(l)
II2B	*KAUN 'grind'	HH-ì	HH-ì	HF-∅	LL-ì	LL-ì	LF-∅	LL-i-A(l)	LL-i-è	LL-è	HH-i-A(l)	HH-i-è	HH-è
IIIA	ARR 'measure'	HH-ì	HH-à	HH-èl	LH-ì	LH-à	LH-èl	LH-è	LH-e	LH-èl-à	HH-è	HH-e	HH-èl-à
IIIB	AWI 'pound'	HH-ò	HH-ò	HH-èl	HH-ò	LH-ò	LH-èl	LH-è	LH-e	LH-èl-à	HH-è	HH-e	HH-èl-à
IIIC	DUS 'tear' (tr)	HH-ò	HH-ò	HH-èl	LF-∅	LH-ò	LH-èl	LH-è	LH-e	LH-èl-à	HH-è	HH-e	HH-èl-à
IIID	*KAIR 'stop' (itr)	HF-∅	HH-à	HH-èl	LF-∅	LH-à	LH-èl	LH-è	LH-e	LH-èl-à	HH-è	HH-e	HH-èl-à
IIIE	*TAI 'hold, seize'	HF-∅	HH-à	HH-èl	LF-∅	LH-ò	LH-èl	LH-è	LH-e	LH-èl-à	HH-è	HH-e	HH-èl-à
IVA	JUM 'cover'	HF-∅	HH-ò	HH-èl	LH-ò	LH-ò	LH-èl	LH-Al	LH-e	LH-èl-à	HH-Al	HH-e	HH-èl-à
IVB	BUL 'find'	HH-ò	HH-ò	HH-èl	LH-ò	LH-ò	LH-èl	LH-Al	LH-e	LH-èl-à	HH-Al	HH-e	HH-èl-à
IVC	JUUŋ 'terrify'	HF-∅	HH-à	HH-èl	LH-à	LH-à	LH-èl	LH-Al	LH-e	LH-èl-à	HH-Al	HH-e	HH-èl-à
IVD	KUR 'touch'	HH-à	HH-à	HH-èl	LH-à	LH-à	LH-èl	LH-Al	LH-e	LH-èl-à	HH-Al	HH-e	HH-èl-à

Shaded cells represent dynamic principal parts in one optimal principal-part analysis. The morphophoneme A is realized as /o/ if the preceding root vowel is high (/i,u/) and otherwise as /a/.
The root forms in the 'Exemplar' column exclude tone markings; starred forms in this column are underlying phonological representations proposed by Jakobi.
Source: Jakobi 1990:103–113.

Table 4.4. *Abbreviations for the twelve MPSs realized by Fur verb forms and the distillations of these property sets*

Abbreviation	Property set	
$\underline{1}$	non3 sbjv	
$\underline{2}$	non3 perfect	
$\underline{3}$	non3 pres	
$\underline{4}$	3sg sbjv	
$\underline{5}$	3sg perfect	Distillations
$\underline{6}$	3sg pres	
$\underline{7}$	3pl nonhuman sbjv	
$\underline{8}$	3pl nonhuman perfect	
$\underline{9}$	3pl nonhuman pres	
$\underline{10}$	3pl human sbjv	(included in distillation $\underline{7}$)
$\underline{11}$	3pl human perfect	(included in distillation $\underline{8}$)
$\underline{12}$	3pl human pres	(included in distillation $\underline{9}$)

Table 4.5. *The three alternative optimal dynamic principal-part analyses for Conjugation* 11A *in Fur*

Alternative principal-part analyses	Distillations								
	$\underline{1}$	$\underline{2}$	$\underline{3}$	$\underline{4}$	$\underline{5}$	$\underline{6}$	$\underline{7}$	$\underline{8}$	$\underline{9}$
③	③	③	③	③	③	③	③	③	③
⑥	⑥	⑥	⑥	⑥	⑥	⑥	⑥	⑥	⑥
⑨	⑨	⑨	⑨	⑨	⑨	⑨	⑨	⑨	⑨

the present-tense cells in the paradigm of a lexeme belonging to this conjugation bears an exponence that is absolutely distinctive of this conjugation. By contrast, none of the non-present-tense cells in Conjugation 11A is distinctive in this way, making them comparatively unsuitable as principal parts. Thus, paradigms belonging to Conjugation 11A have some transparency, but they would have more if they had more cells as predictive as the three present-tense cells in Table 4.6.

All Fur conjugations deviate from maximal transparency. The exact nature and extent of this deviation vary rather widely; for instance, not all conjugations exhibit the particular pattern of deviation exhibited by Conjugation 11A. In the following section, we consider the consequences of these various deviations in detail.

Table 4.6. *The exponence of distillations 1–9 in Conjugation* IIA *in Fur (present-tense cells shaded)*

				Morphosyntactic property sets				
1	2	3	4	5	6	7	8	9
LH-o	LH-ò	LH-èl	HH-o	HH-ò	HH-èl	HH-òl	HH-ùl	HH-èl-à/ì

4.3 Deviations from maximal transparency in Fur verb paradigms

It is rare for every cell in a realized paradigm to possess the sort of unique exponence that unambiguously identifies that paradigm's IC.[6] In the paradigms of Fur verbs, many cells are to some extent uninformative; that is, they have either a limited capacity or no capacity at all to serve as optimal principal parts. Such limitations are reflected in the fact that nearly half of the conjugations in Fur require more than one dynamic principal part, as Table 4.7 shows.

One such conjugation is Conjugation IVB. In the paradigm of a verb belonging to this conjugation, the realization of distillation 4 (i.e. the 3rd-person singular subjunctive cell, whose exponence is LH-ò) uniquely determines the realization of distillations 1, 2, 3, 5, 6, 8, and 9, since no matter what the conjugation, the implicative relations in (5) hold true in Fur. Even so, the realization of distillation 4 does not uniquely determine the realization of distillation 7 in the paradigm of a verb belonging to this conjugation – nor does the realization of any other distillation. For this reason, the realization of distillation 7 must itself simply be stipulated as a principal part for Conjugation IVB, as in Table 4.8.

(5) ⟨X:LH-ò, 4⟩ → ⟨X:HH-ò, 1⟩
     ⟨X:LH-ò, 4⟩ → ⟨X:HH-ò, 2⟩
     ⟨X:LH-ò, 4⟩ → ⟨X:HH-èl, 3⟩
     ⟨X:LH-ò, 4⟩ → ⟨X:LH-ò, 5⟩
     ⟨X:LH-ò, 4⟩ → ⟨X:LH-èl, 6⟩
     ⟨X:LH-ò, 4⟩ → ⟨X:LH-e, 8⟩
     ⟨X:LH-ò, 4⟩ → ⟨X:LH-èl-à, 9⟩

As Tables 4.5 and 4.8 show, Conjugations IIA and IVB differ in that the former requires only one principal part, while the latter requires two. Still, the two conjugations are alike in that neither has any cell whose exponence can only be deduced by simultaneous reference to more than one principal part; that is, none

---

[6] Still, this situation does arise. For example, Comaltepec Chinantec (Oto-Manguean; Mexico) possesses four maximally predictable conjugations; see Finkel & Stump (2009) for details.

Table 4.7. *Number of optimal dynamic principal parts for each Fur conjugation class*

Fur conjugation classes	Number of dynamic principal parts needed to identify a conjugation
I1A, I1C, I2A, I2B, I2C, II1A, II2A, II2B, IIIA, IVD	1
I1B, II1B, IIIB, IIIC, IIIE, IVA, IVB	2
IIID, IVC	3

Table 4.8. *A representative optimal dynamic principal-part analysis for Conjugation IVB in Fur*

Principal parts	Distillations								
	1	2	3	4	5	6	7	8	9
④,⑦	④	④	④	④	④	④	⑦	④	④

Table 4.9. *The sole optimal dynamic principal-part analysis for Conjugation IIIE in Fur*

Principal parts	Distillations								
	1	2	3	4	5	6	7	8	9
②,⑤	②,⑤	②	②	②,⑤	⑤	②	②,⑤	②	②

of the cells in the paradigm of a lexeme belonging to Conjugation IVB requires reference to both principal parts ④ and ⑦ in order for its exponence to be inferred.

Other conjugations, however, show less transparency in this regard. Consider, for example, Conjugation IIIE, whose sole optimal principal-part analysis is given in Table 4.9. In this table (and others below), if a given row R lists the pair ⓜ, ⓝ of principal parts in the column headed by distillation $\underline{M}$, then the realization of $\underline{M}$ can only be deduced by simultaneous reference to ⓜ and ⓝ in the optimal principal-part analysis represented in row R. Thus, the realization of distillation $\underline{2}$ in the paradigm of a verb belonging to Conjugation IIIE can be used by itself to deduce the realization of four other distillations; there are three cells, however, whose realization can only be deduced by simultaneous reference to the realization of distillations $\underline{2}$ and $\underline{5}$.

Table 4.10. *The two optimal dynamic principal-part analyses for Conjugation* IIID *in Fur*

	Distillations								
Principal parts	1	2	3	4	5	6	7	8	9
①, ⑤, ⑦	①	⑤	①	①	⑤	①	⑦	①	①
④, ⑤, ⑦	④, ⑤	⑤	④	④	⑤	④	⑦	④	④

Table 4.11. *The sole optimal dynamic principal-part analysis for Conjugation* IIIA *in Fur*

	Distillations								
Principal parts	1	2	3	4	5	6	7	8	9
④	④	④	④	④	④	④	④	④	④

So Conjugations IVB and IIIE differ in that the latter (unlike the former) involves cells whose realization is deducible only by simultaneous reference to more than one principal part. They are alike in that they both have optimal principal-part analyses involving only two principal parts. Two conjugations, however, require three principal parts. One of these is Conjugation IIID, whose two optimal principal-part analyses are given in Table 4.10.

When a paradigm deviates from maximal transparency, the uninformativeness of certain of its realizations may necessitate two or more dynamic principal parts; some but not all such analyses may involve deducing certain nonprincipal parts by simultaneous reference to more than one principal part. But uninformativeness needn't always lead to the postulation of more than one principal part. In some instances, it simply imposes limits on the range of alternative analyses. For instance, a single principal part can be postulated for a verb belonging to Conjugation IIIA, but this must be distillation 4, as in Table 4.11. The number of optimal principal-part analyses for Conjugation IIA in Table 4.5 is likewise limited by the uninformativeness of its nonpresent-tense cells.

The examples presented here show that the uninformativeness of one or more cells in a lexeme's realized paradigm may have at least three kinds of effects on the principal-part analysis of that lexeme:

(a) If the cells in a lexeme L's realized paradigm are sufficiently uninformative, it may be necessary to appeal to two or more principal parts in order to distinguish L's IC membership.

(b) In the realized paradigm of a lexeme with more than one principal part, the uninformativeness of one or more cells may necessitate simultaneous reference to more than one principal part in order to deduce a given cell.

(c) The uninformativeness of one or more cells in a lexeme's realized paradigm may limit the number of alternative optimal principal-part analyses to which that paradigm is subject.

These effects therefore imply the three criteria of IC transparency in (6):

(6) Three criteria of IC transparency
All else being equal, the IC of realized paradigm A is more transparent than that of realized paradigm B:
(a) if the number of dynamic principal parts required to distinguish A's IC membership is smaller than the number required to distinguish B's IC membership (§3.2);
(b) if the number of principal parts needed to deduce a given cell in A is, on average, lower than the number of principal parts needed to deduce a given cell in B (cf. §3.4); and
(c) if there are more alternative optimal principal-part analyses for A than for B.

The transparency of Fur conjugations clearly varies according to the criteria in (6). A single principal part suffices to distinguish most ICs, but some require two principal parts and a couple require three. By criterion (6a), the conjugations in row A of Table 4.12 are most transparent and those in row C, least transparent.

Conjugations whose optimal analysis requires two or three principal parts may vary in the extent to which they require simultaneous reference to more than one principal part in deducing a cell's realization. The rightmost column of Table 4.12 shows the average number of principal parts needed to deduce

Table 4.12. *Cell predictor numbers for Fur conjugation classes*

Fur conjugation classes	Dynamic principal-part number	Cell predictor number
A. I1A, I1C, I2A, I2B, I2C, II1A, II2A, II2B, IIIA, IVD	1	1.00
B. I1B, II1B, IIIB, IVB	2	1.00
C. IIID, IVC	3	1.00
D. IVA	2	1.11
E. IIIC, IIIE	2	1.33

Table 4.13. *Numbers of optimal dynamic principal-part analyses for Fur conjugations*

Conjugation	Number of principal parts	Number of optimal dynamic principal-part analyses
II1B	2	18
I1B	2	12
IVC	3	4
I1A, III1A, II2A	1	3
I1C, I2A, I2C, IVD	1	2
IVB	2	2
IIID	3	2
I2B, II2B, IIIA	1	1
IIIB, IVA, IIIC, IIIE	2	1

a cell's realization in each conjugation in Fur. The conjugation classes in rows A–C house verbs each of whose realizations can always be deduced by reference to a single principal part; those in the remaining two rows house verbs whose realizations must be deduced by simultaneous reference to more than one principal part. According to criterion (6b), the conjugations in row D and especially row E are less transparent than those in rows A–C.

Table 4.13 relates to criterion (6c). Here the different conjugations are arranged in decreasing order according to the number of optimal principal-part analyses that they afford. The conjugation allowing the largest number of optimal principal-part analyses is II1B, which allows eighteen optimal analyses. Succeeding rows show conjugations allowing fewer analyses, with the bottom rows showing conjugations allowing only a single optimal principal-part analysis.

The application of criterion (6c) is complicated, however, by the fact that a paradigm is open to more alternative principal-part analyses the more principal parts it has. Where lexeme L has k principal parts and n is the number of distillations for which L inflects, the largest possible number of optimal principal-part analyses for L is the binomial coefficient of n and k, that is,

$$\binom{n}{k} = \frac{n!}{k!(n-k)!}$$

By this measure, the maximum possible number of optimal principal-part analyses for a Fur verb varies according to the number of principal parts it has, as in Table 4.14. Although the paradigm of a lexeme belonging to Conjugation I1C and that of a lexeme belonging to Conjugation IIID both have

Table 4.14. *Maximum possible number of optimal dynamic principal-part analyses for Fur verbs*

Number (k) of principal parts	Maximum possible number $9!/(k!(9-k)!)$ of optimal dynamic principal-part analyses
1	9
2	36
3	84

Table 4.15. *The two alternative optimal dynamic principal-part analyses for Conjugation I1c in Fur*

Principal parts	Distillations								
	1	2	3	4	5	6	7	8	9
③	③	③	③	③	③	③	③	③	③
⑥	⑥	⑥	⑥	⑥	⑥	⑥	⑥	⑥	⑥

two alternative optimal principal-part analyses (reproduced in Tables 4.15 and 4.10), the latter paradigm is substantially less transparent: because it has three principal parts, its two optimal analyses constitute a mere 2.4 percent of the eighty-four possible analyses that three principal parts would maximally allow; by contrast, Conjugation I1c has only a single optimal dynamic principal part, so that its two optimal analyses constitute a more impressive 22 percent of the nine possible analyses that a single principal part would allow. Thus, (6c) should be interpreted as meaning that the IC of paradigm A is more transparent than that of paradigm B if the ratio of actual principal-part analyses to logically possible analyses (given a paradigm's number of principal parts) is higher for paradigm A than for paradigm B. Table 4.16 gives the full set of such ratios for Fur in decreasing order; as this table reveals, Fur verbs show considerable variation in the ratio of actual to possible principal-part analyses.

By the criteria listed in (6), Fur verb conjugations exhibit widely varying degrees of IC transparency. Nearer to the high extreme, that of maximal transparency, is Conjugation II1b: in this conjugation, lexemes have paradigms each of whose realizations can be inferred by reference to a single principal part, and half of their logically possible principal-part analyses are actual. Nearer to the opposite extreme are Conjugations IIIc and IIIe: lexemes in these conjugations require two principal parts; on average, they require reference to 1.33 principal

94 Inflection-class transparency

Table 4.16. *Ratio of actual to possible optimal dynamic principal-part analyses*

Conjugation	Number of principal parts	Number of optimal analyses	Ratio of actual analyses to possible analyses (%)
II1B	2	18	50
I1A	1	3	33
I1B	2	12	33
II1A	1	3	33
II2A	1	3	33
I1C	1	2	22
I2A	1	2	22
I2C	1	2	22
IVD	1	2	22
I2B	1	1	11
II2B	1	1	11
IIIA	1	1	11
IVB	2	2	5.6
IVC	3	4	4.8
IIIB	2	1	2.8
IIIC	2	1	2.8
IIIE	2	1	2.8
IVA	2	1	2.8
IIID	3	2	2.4
Average	1.58	3.26	17

parts to deduce each cell in their realized paradigm; and only 2.8 percent of their possible principal-part analyses are actually valid. Between these extremes, other conjugations exhibit a range of intermediate degrees of IC transparency.

4.4 A first measure of IC transparency: IC predictability

Although the criteria in (6) are useful for distinguishing degrees of IC transparency, we would like to give more explicit content to the notion of IC transparency than these criteria allow. We therefore propose a precise measure of **IC predictability**. Intuitively, the predictability of a lexeme L's IC is the ratio of adequate (though not necessarily optimal) dynamic principal-part sets among all nonempty subsets of cells in L's realized paradigm. Thus, (i) let M_L be the set of cells in the realized paradigm P_L of some lexeme L and (ii) let M_L' be the set $\{N : N \subseteq M_L$ and N is an adequate dynamic principal-part set for $P_L\}$; the IC predictability ICP_L of L's IC is then calculated as in (7). This measure calculates the fraction of the nonempty members of M_L's power set $\wp(M_L)$ that are adequate (though not necessarily optimal) sets of dynamic principal parts for L.

(7)
$$\text{ICP}_L = \frac{|M_L'|}{|\wp(M_L)\setminus\emptyset|}$$

We refine this measure of IC predictability in two ways. The first refinement is motivated by the fact that in any case in which two or more members of the set M_L realize MPSs belonging to the same distillation, the measure defined in (7) is skewed in favor of higher IC predictability. We therefore prefer to define IC predictability in terms of cells realizing distinct distillations rather than in terms of the full set of realized cells in P_L. Thus, let D_L be any maximal subset of M_L whose members realize distinct distillations, so that D_L' is the set $\{N : N \subseteq D_L$ and N is an adequate dynamic principal-part set for $P_L\}$. We then calculate the predictability ICP_L of lexeme L's IC as in (8) rather than as in (7).

(8)
$$\text{ICP}_L = \frac{|D_L'|}{|\wp(D_L)\setminus\emptyset|}$$

The second refinement in the calculation of IC predictability stems from the fact that where N is a large subset of D_L, N is generally very likely to be an adequate principal-part set for P_L. That is, the subsets of D_L that are best for distinguishing varying degrees of predictability among a language's ICs tend to be the smaller subsets of D_L. We therefore relativize the definition of IC predictability to our calculation on subsets of D_L having no more than m members. Thus, for any collection C of sets, we use $_m[C]$ to represent $\{s \in C : |s| \leq m\}$. We accordingly calculate the predictability ICP_L of L's IC as in (9) rather than as in (8). As a matter of practice, we generally set $m = 4$; when we deviate from this practice, we say so explicitly.

(9)
$$\text{ICP}_L = \frac{|_m[D_L']|}{|_m[\wp(D_L)\setminus\emptyset]|}$$

This measure of IC predictability accounts for all three of the criteria in (6). Consider first criterion (6a). By this criterion, Conjugation 11A (whose member

96 *Inflection-class transparency*

lexemes only require one dynamic principal part) is more transparent than Conjugation IIID (whose lexemes require three dynamic principal parts). This difference reflects a measurable contrast in IC predictability: Conjugation IIA has IC predictability 0.780, whereas Conjugation IIID has IC predictability 0.051.

By criterion (6b), Conjugation IVB (Table 4.8) exhibits greater IC transparency than Conjugation IIIE (Table 4.9): although lexemes in both conjugations require two dynamic principal parts, each cell in the realized paradigm of a lexeme belonging to Conjugation IVB can be deduced from a single principal part, whereas three of the cells in the realized paradigm of a lexeme belonging to Conjugation IIIE can only be deduced by simultaneous reference to two principal parts. This difference reflects a measurable contrast in the IC predictability of the two conjugations: the IC predictability of Conjugation IVB is 0.200, while that of IIIE is 0.137.

Consider finally criterion (6c), which associates greater IC predictability with a greater number of alternative IC analyses. By this criterion, Conjugation II1B exhibits greater IC predictability than Conjugation IVA, since the former allows the eighteen optimal principal-part analyses reproduced in Table 4.17,

Table 4.17. *The eighteen optimal dynamic principal-part analyses for Conjugation* II1B *in Fur*

Principal parts	Distillations								
	1	2	3	4	5	6	7	8	9
1,3	1	1	3	1	1	3	1	1	3
1,6	1	1	6	1	1	6	1	1	6
1,9	1	1	1,9	1	1	1,9	1	1	9
2,3	2	2	3	2	2	3	2	2	3
2,6	2	2	6	2	2	6	2	2	6
2,9	2	2	2,9	2	2	2,9	2	2	9
3,4	4	4	3	4	4	3	4	4	3
3,5	5	5	3	5	5	3	5	5	3
3,7	7	7	3	7	7	3	7	7	3
3,8	8	8	3	8	8	3	8	8	3
4,6	4	4	6	4	4	6	4	4	6
4,9	4	4	4,9	4	4	4,9	4	4	9
5,6	5	5	6	5	5	6	5	5	6
5,9	5	5	5,9	5	5	5,9	5	5	9
6,7	7	7	6	7	7	6	7	7	6
6,8	8	8	6	8	8	6	8	8	6
7,9	7	7	7,9	7	7	7,9	7	7	9
8,9	8	8	8,9	8	8	8,9	8	8	9

Table 4.18. *The sole optimal dynamic principal-part analysis for Conjugation* IVA *in Fur*

Principal parts	Distillations								
	1	2	3	4	5	6	7	8	9
①,②	①	②	①	①	②	①	①,②	①	①

while the latter only allows the single optimal principal-part analysis reproduced in Table 4.18. This difference reflects a measurable contrast in the IC predictability of these two conjugations: the predictability of a member of Conjugation II1B is 0.753, while the predictability of a member of IVA is merely 0.180.

Applying the measure of IC predictability to all of the conjugations in Fur yields the results in Table 4.19. For each conjugation J, Table 4.19 juxtaposes J's IC predictability with J's optimal dynamic principal-part number, J's cell predictor number, and the ratio of actual to possible optimal dynamic principal-part analyses for J, given its number of principal parts. As the table shows, the ICs of paradigms requiring more than one principal part generally have low IC predictability; the ICs of paradigms whose individual cells can (on average) only be deduced by reference to more than one principal part have low IC predictability; and the ICs of paradigms exhibiting a low proportion of actual to possible principal-part sets have low IC predictability.

Inspection of Table 4.19 reveals one point at which the gradient of IC predictability breaks sharply, abruptly falling from nearly 0.592 to 0.200; this break is indicated by the dotted line. The optimal principal-part number of the conjugations above this break is mostly 1, while that of the conjugations below the break is always more than 1. The cell predictor number of the conjugations above the break is always 1, whereas three of the conjugations below the break have cell predictor numbers higher than 1. And for each of the conjugations above the dotted line, more (often many more) than 11 percent of the logically possible principal-part analyses are valid; by contrast, for each of the conjugations below the break, the ratio of actual to possible principal-part analyses never attains six percent. Why are conjugations divided into these two predictability classes? We believe that this break is best understood with respect to a final criterion of IC transparency and, correspondingly, a second predictability measure.

Table 4.19. *IC predictability compared with criteria (6a–c) in the analysis of Fur verbs*

IC	IC predictability	Dynamic principal-part number n	Cell predictor number	Number p of optimal dynamic analyses	Ratio of p to the number of possible principal-part sets of cardinality n
ɪɪA	0.780 (199 out of 255)	1	1.00	3	33.3% of 9 possible analyses
ɪɪ1A	0.780 (199 out of 255)	1	1.00	3	33.3% of 9
ɪɪ2A	0.780 (199 out of 255)	1	1.00	3	33.3% of 9
ɪ2A	0.773 (197 out of 255)	1	1.00	2	22.2% of 9
ɪɪ2B	0.769 (196 out of 255)	1	1.00	1	11.1% of 9
ɪɪ1B	0.753 (192 out of 255)	2	1.00	18	50.0% of 36
ɪ1C	0.616 (157 out of 255)	1	1.00	2	22.2% of 9
ɪ2C	0.616 (157 out of 255)	1	1.00	2	22.2% of 9
ɪVD	0.616 (157 out of 255)	1	1.00	2	22.2% of 9
ɪɪɪA	0.612 (156 out of 255)	1	1.00	1	11.1% of 9
ɪ2B	0.608 (155 out of 255)	1	1.00	1	11.1% of 9
ɪ1B	0.592 (151 out of 255)	2	1.00	12	33.3% of 36
ɪVB	0.200 (51 out of 255)	2	1.00	2	5.6% of 36
ɪVA	0.180 (46 out of 255)	2	1.11	1	2.8% of 36
ɪɪɪC	0.137 (35 out of 255)	2	1.33	1	2.8% of 36
ɪɪɪE	0.137 (35 out of 255)	2	1.33	1	2.8% of 36
ɪɪɪB	0.114 (29 out of 255)	2	1.00	1	2.8% of 36
ɪVC	0.094 (24 out of 255)	3	1.00	4	4.8% of 84
ɪɪɪD	0.051 (13 out of 255)	3	1.00	2	2.4% of 84
Avg	0.485				

4.5 A fourth criterion of IC transparency

We now consider a fourth criterion of IC transparency, supplementing the three given earlier in (6). All else being equal, the IC of paradigm A is more transparent than that of paradigm B if A has fewer unpredictable cells than B. We say that a cell K is **unpredictable** in the paradigm of some lexeme L if and only if no other cell or combination of cells in L's realized paradigm is informative about K's realization. This criterion has considerable intuitive appeal; as yet, however, we have no direct way of demonstrating a cell's unpredictability. While dynamic principal-part analyses (such as those in Tables 4.5, 4.8–4.11, etc.) show which cells have predictable realizations in paradigms belonging to the conjugations at issue, they do not show which cells have unpredictable realizations. One might suppose that if cell K is stipulated as a principal part in every optimal principal-part set for some IC J, then K's realization is unpredictable in J. For example, the cells associated with distillations 2 and 5 would, on this supposition, have unpredictable realizations in Conjugation IIIE (Table 4.9). This reasoning is not valid, however. Even if cell K is stipulated as a principal part in every optimal principal-part analysis for some IC J, its realization may nevertheless be inferable from one or more nonoptimal principal-part sets for J. We therefore propose a second measure of IC transparency, that of cell predictability.

4.6 A second measure of IC transparency: cell predictability

Cell predictability measures the predictability of a realized cell's exponence from that of the other cells in its paradigm (whether or not these are optimal principal parts). Intuitively, the predictability of a cell $\langle w, \sigma \rangle$ in a lexeme L's realized paradigm P_L is the ratio of (a) to (b), where (a) is the number of nonempty subsets of P_L's cells whose realization uniquely determines $\langle w, \sigma \rangle$ and (b) is the number of all nonempty subsets of P_L's cells. Thus, (i) let M_L be the set of cells in the realized paradigm P_L of some lexeme L, (ii) let D_L be any maximal subset of M_L whose members realize distinct distillations, and (iii) where $\langle w, \sigma \rangle$ is a cell in P_L, let $D_{\langle w, \sigma \rangle}$ be the set $\{N : N \subseteq D_L \text{ and } N \text{ uniquely determines the realized cell } \langle w, \sigma \rangle \text{ in } P_L\}$. The cell predictability $\text{CELLP}_{\langle w, \sigma \rangle}$ of P_L's cell $\langle w, \sigma \rangle$ is then calculated as in (10).

(10)
$$\text{CELLP}_{\langle w,\sigma \rangle} = \frac{|_m[D_{\langle w,\sigma \rangle}]|}{|_m[\wp(D_L)\backslash \varnothing]|}$$

Here, too, a refinement must be made. Because a realized cell always uniquely determines itself, the inclusion of $\langle w, \sigma \rangle$ in any member of $D_{\langle w, \sigma \rangle}$ invariably enhances cell predictability, thereby diminishing distinctions in the cell predictability measures of different cells. We therefore exclude $\langle w, \sigma \rangle$ from all members of $D_{\langle w, \sigma \rangle}$ in calculating cell predictability. For any collection C of sets, we use $[C]_{-\langle w, \sigma \rangle}$ to represent the largest subset of C such that no member of $[C]_{-\langle w, \sigma \rangle}$ contains $\langle w, \sigma \rangle$. Cell predictability is then calculated as in (11).

(11)
$$\text{CELLP}_{\langle w,\sigma \rangle} = \frac{|[_m[D_{\langle w,\sigma \rangle}]]_{-\langle w,\sigma \rangle}|}{|[_m[\wp(D_\text{L})\setminus\emptyset]]_{-\langle w,\sigma \rangle}|}$$

By this measure, the cells in the paradigms of Fur verbs have the cell predictability in Table 4.20, where we present the conjugations in order of decreasing average cell predictability. Average cell predictability and IC predictability are listed in the table's rightmost two columns. The measures in Table 4.20 are represented graphically in Figure 4.1. In this figure, distillations are listed on the horizontal axis in order of decreasing average cell predictability; conjugations are listed on the vertical axis in order of decreasing IC predictability; and the lightness of a cell's shading represents its degree of cell predictability. The interpretation of each shade of gray is given at the bottom edge of the picture, and the shades on the left edge indicate the average cell predictability for each conjugation.

The graphic representation in Figure 4.1 reveals two things about cell predictability especially clearly. First, the cell realizing distillation 8 (3pl nonhuman perfect) is highly predictable in all conjugations. Second, Fur ICs fall into two groups: those in which the cells realizing present-tense distillations (3, 6, and 9) are less predictable than the remaining cells, which are highly predictable; and those in which the cells realizing the nonpresent-tense distillations (other than 8) are much less predictable than the present-tense cells, which are highly predictable. The former group contains the conjugations in Jakobi's classes I and II; the latter contains the conjugations in her classes III and IV.

The measure of cell predictability sheds new light on the major break in the gradient of IC predictability in Table 4.19; this break emerges particularly clearly in Figure 4.1. This break corresponds well with the appearance of unpredictable cells (i.e. cells whose cell predictability is zero). The conjugations above the dotted line in Table 4.20 have no unpredictable cells; six of the seven conjugations beneath the dotted line have either one or two unpredictable cells. (The cell predictability measures of unpredictable cells are shaded in Table 4.20; these are the black cells in Figure 4.1.)

Table 4.20. Cell predictability in all conjugations in Fur

IC	1	2	3	4	5	6	7	8	9	Avg	IC predictability
I1A	0.994	0.994	0.650	0.994	0.994	0.650	0.994	0.994	0.650	0.879	0.780 (199 out of 255)
i11A	0.994	0.994	0.650	0.994	0.994	0.650	0.994	0.994	0.650	0.879	0.780 (199 out of 255)
I12A	0.994	0.988	0.650	0.988	0.988	0.650	0.988	0.988	0.650	0.876	0.780 (199 out of 255)
I2A	0.988	0.975	0.650	0.975	0.975	0.638	0.975	0.975	0.638	0.866	0.773 (197 out of 255)
i12B	0.975	0.969	0.644	0.969	0.969	0.632	0.969	0.969	0.650	0.861	0.769 (196 out of 255)
i11B	0.951	0.951	0.644	0.951	0.951	0.644	0.951	0.951	0.650	0.849	0.753 (192 out of 255)
I1C	0.988	0.988	0.393	0.988	0.988	0.393	0.988	0.988	0.650	0.818	0.616 (157 out of 255)
I2C	0.988	0.982	0.393	0.982	0.982	0.393	0.982	0.982	0.650	0.815	0.616 (157 out of 255)
IVD	0.393	0.810	0.994	0.393	0.718	0.988	0.650	0.988	0.988	0.769	0.616 (157 out of 255)
IIIA	0.393	0.804	0.988	0.387	0.644	0.982	0.644	0.982	0.982	0.756	0.612 (156 out of 255)
I2B	0.975	0.969	0.393	0.969	0.969	0.380	0.969	0.969	0.650	0.805	0.608 (155 out of 255)
i1B	0.951	0.951	0.393	0.951	0.951	0.393	0.951	0.951	0.650	0.793	0.592 (151 out of 255)
IVB	0.393	0.706	0.988	0.135	0.798	0.975	0.000	0.975	0.975	0.661	0.200 (51 out of 255)
IVA	0.135	0.135	0.994	0.393	0.393	0.988	0.135	0.988	0.988	0.572	0.180 (46 out of 255)
IIIC	0.135	0.380	0.988	0.000	0.638	0.975	0.135	0.975	0.975	0.578	0.137 (35 out of 255)
IIIE	0.233	0.135	0.994	0.491	0.000	0.988	0.135	0.988	0.988	0.550	0.137 (35 out of 255)
IIIB	0.491	0.638	0.988	0.000	0.798	0.975	0.000	0.975	0.975	0.649	0.114 (29 out of 255)
IVC	0.301	0.393	0.994	0.393	0.135	0.988	0.000	0.988	0.988	0.575	0.094 (24 out of 255)
IIID	0.233	0.491	0.994	0.393	0.000	0.988	0.000	0.988	0.988	0.564	0.051 (13 out of 255)
Avg	0.658	0.750	0.757	0.650	0.731	0.751	0.603	0.979	0.807	0.743	0.485

Shading indicates cells whose realization is unpredictable.

102 *Inflection-class transparency*

Table 4.21. *Average cell predictability in conjugations with high IC predictability in Fur*

1	2	3	4	5	6	7	8	9	Avg cell predictability	IC predictability
0.882	0.948	0.620	0.878	0.927	0.616	0.921	0.978	0.705	0.831	0.691

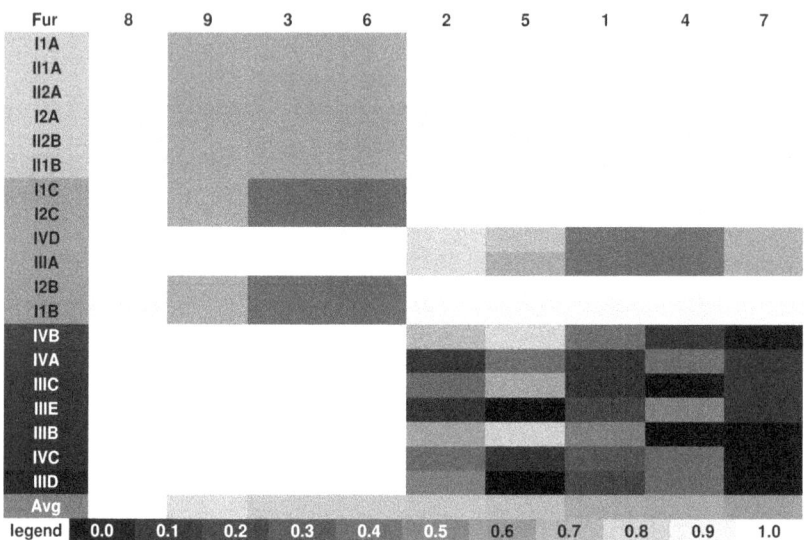

Figure 4.1. *Cell predictability in all conjugations in Fur (numbered distillations on the horizontal axis, ICs on the vertical axis; lighter shade represents higher cell predictability)*

But what of Conjugation IVA, which is below the dotted line but has no unpredictable cells? Despite the absence of any unpredictable cell in its paradigm, Conjugation IVA is still remarkable for the low predictability of certain of its cells. In conjugations with high IC predictability (those listed above the dotted line in Table 4.20), the cells associated with distillations 1, 2, and 7 (the nonthird-person subjunctive, the nonthird-person perfect, and the third-person plural nonhuman subjunctive) tend to have high cell predictability; as Table 4.21 shows, these cells have 0.882, 0.948, and 0.921 as their average cell predictabilities in the conjugations with high IC predictability. In Conjugation IVA, by contrast, the cells associated with these three distillations each have a cell predictability of 0.135.

Thus, the cell predictability measure reveals an important fact about IC predictability: low cell predictability (including cell unpredictability) degrades IC predictability. Because this is so, the correlation between IC predictability and average cell predictability is strong. Inevitably, an unpredictable cell must be a dynamic principal part. In addition, cells with low predictability are likely to be principal parts; in the case of Conjugation IVA, the cells associated with distillations $\underline{1}$ and $\underline{2}$ (both low in predictability) must both be principal parts in the sole optimal dynamic principal-part analysis for this conjugation (see Table 4.18). (Distillation $\underline{7}$ is also low in predictability in Conjugation IVA, but as Table 4.18 shows, the realization of distillation $\underline{7}$ is deducible by simultaneous reference to the realization of distillations $\underline{1}$ and $\underline{2}$ in this conjugation.)

We conclude that the extent of an IC's deviation from maximal transparency is susceptible to two types of objective measure: IC predictability and cell predictability. Together, these measures account for the four intuitive criteria of IC transparency.

4.7 IC transparency and the No-Blur Principle

There can be no doubt that IC transparency helps the language user, both in the domain of language learning and in that of lexical storage. Nevertheless, the facts presented above raise doubts about the extent to which IC transparency is necessary in human language. In particular, they cast doubt on the No-Blur Principle, a hypothesis that portrays the avoidance of IC opacity as a structural principle of natural language.

Cameron-Faulkner & Carstairs-McCarthy (2000: 816) formulate the No-Blur Principle as in (12).

(12) The No-Blur Principle
Among the rival affixes for any inflectional cell [affixal exponents of the same MPS in different ICs – S&F], at most one affix may fail to be a class-identifier, in which case that one affix is the class-default for that cell.

This principle entails that all of the affixal exponents for the inflection of lexemes belonging to a particular category fall into two classes: class identifiers and class-defaults.

(13) (a) A CLASS-IDENTIFYING affix is one that is peculiar to one IC, so that it can be taken as diagnostic of membership in that class.
(b) A CLASS-DEFAULT affix is one that is shared by more than one IC, and all of whose rivals (if any) are class identifiers.
(Cameron-Faulkner & Carstairs-McCarthy 2000:815; cf. also
Carstairs-McCarthy 1994)

If all affixes must be either class identifiers or class-defaults (as the No-Blur Principle asserts), then any lexeme that inflects by means of a class-identifier needs only one dynamic principal part: the word containing that class-identifier suffices to indicate which IC the lexeme belongs to. The only other situation is one in which none of the words in a lexeme's paradigm contains a class-identifier; in that case, the lexeme's words must inflect entirely by means of class-default affixes. But if at most one affix in a set of rival affixes may fail to be a class-identifier, then there can be at most one IC whose inflection is based entirely on class-default affixes. This, therefore, is the only IC whose members could have more than one principal part. That is, the No-Blur Principle entails (14):

(14) Of all the ICs for lexemes of a given syntactic category, at most one requires more than one principal part.

As Cameron-Faulkner & Carstairs-McCarthy formulate it, the No-Blur Principle only constrains affixal exponence, and in Fur, conjugation classes are distinguished by both affixal and non-affixal morphology. Clearly, though, if one ignores the tone alternations represented in Table 4.3, the affixal part of Fur inflection (given in Table 4.22) decisively disconfirms the No-Blur Principle.

The number of dynamic principal parts necessitated by a Fur conjugation class depends on whether one takes account of tonality. The two possibilities are given in Table 4.23. In this table, the left-hand column indicates the number of dynamic principal parts needed to identify each conjugation if only affixes are taken into account; the right-hand column indicates the number required if root tonality as well as affixes are taken into account.

As the first column of Table 4.23 shows, only two of the nineteen conjugations have a class-identifier among their affixal exponents. By the assumptions of the No-Blur Principle, all of the other affixes in each column of Table 4.22 should be the class-default for the MPS represented by that column; but this means that every one of the MPSs in Table 4.22 has more than one class-default – contrary to the assumptions of the No-Blur Principle.

Cameron-Faulkner & Carstairs-McCarthy (2000) discuss an apparently similar instance from Polish in which a particular MPS (locative singular) seemingly has more than one class-default, namely the suffixes *-e* and *-u*. They argue, however, that these two suffixes actually constitute a single default, since they are in complementary distribution: *-e* only appears in combination with a lexeme's special "minority" stem alternant, and *-u* appears elsewhere. In this way, they claim, the Polish evidence can be reconciled with the No-Blur Principle.

Table 4.22. *Affixal exponents of Fur inflection*

Conj	Examples	Nonthird person			Third person									
					Singular			Plural						
								Nonhuman			Human			
		Sbjv	Perf	Pres	Sbjv	Perf	Pres	Sbjv	Perf	Pres	Sbjv	Perf	Pres
I1A	BUUŋ 'descend'	-o	-ô	-èl	-o	-ô	-èl	-òl	-ùl	-èl-à/-ì	-òl	-ùl	-èl-à/-ì
I1B	JAAN 'wait'	-o	-ô	-∅	-o	-ô	-∅	-òl	-ùl	-ê	-òl	-ùl	-ê
I1C	IRT 'shake'	-o	-ô	-ì	-o	-ô	-ì	-òl	-ùl	-ê	-òl	-ùl	-ê
I2A	TALL 'chew'	-o	-ô	-èl	-o	-ô	-èl	-òl	-ùl	-èl-à/-ì	-òl	-ùl	-èl-à/-ì
I2B	FUUL 'spin'	-o	-ô	-∅	-o	-ô	-∅	-òl	-ùl	-ê	-òl	-ùl	-ê
I2C	KIR 'cook'	-o	-ô	-ì	-o	-ô	-ì	-òl	-ùl	-ê	-òl	-ùl	-ê
II1A	RII 'snatch'	-i	-î	-iti	-i	-î	-iti	-i-A(l)	-i-ê	-iti-A(l)	-i-A(l)	-i-ê	-iti-A(l)
II1B	TIIR 'meet'	-i	-î	-∅	-i	-î	-∅	-i-A(l)	-i-ê	-ê	-i-A(l)	-i-ê	-ê
II2A	*FAUL 'open'	-i	-î	-iti	-i	-î	-iti	-i-A(l)	-i-ê	-iti-A(l)	-i-A(l)	-i-ê	-iti-A(l)
II2B	*KAUN 'grind'	-i	-î	-∅	-i	-î	-∅	-i-A(l)	-i-ê	-ê	-i-A(l)	-i-ê	-ê
III A	ARR 'measure'	-i	-à	-èl	**-i**	-â	-èl	-ê	-e	-èl-à	-ê	-e	-èl-à
III B	AWI 'pound'	-o	-ô	-èl	-o	-ô	-èl	-ê	-e	-èl-à	-ê	-e	-èl-à
III C	DUS 'tear' (tr)	-o	-ô	-èl	-∅	-ô	-èl	-ê	-e	-èl-à	-ê	-e	-èl-à
III D	*KAIR 'stop' (itr)	-∅	-à	-èl	-∅	-à	-èl	-ê	-e	-èl-à	-ê	-e	-èl-à
III E	*TAI 'hold, seize'	-∅	-à	-èl	-∅	-à	-èl	-ê	-e	-èl-à	-ê	-e	-èl-à
IV A	JUM 'cover'	-∅	-ô	-èl	-∅	-ô	-èl	-Al	-e	-èl-à	-Al	-e	-èl-à
IV B	BUL 'find'	-o	-à	-èl	-o	-à	-èl	-Al	-e	-èl-à	-Al	-e	-èl-à
IV C	JUUŋ 'terrify'	-∅	-à	-èl	-o	-à	-èl	-Al	-e	-èl-à	-Al	-e	-èl-à
IV D	KUR 'touch'	**-à**	-à	-èl	-à	-à	-èl	-Al	-e	-èl-à	-Al	-e	-èl-à

Only the two affixal exponents in shaded boxes are class identifiers.
Shaded cells represent dynamic principal parts in one optimal principal-part analysis.
The root forms in the 'Examples' column exclude tone markings; starred forms in this column are underlying phonological representations proposed by Jakobi.
Source: Jakobi 1990:103–113.

Table 4.23. *Number of dynamic principal parts needed to identify each Fur conjugation*

Conjugation	Number of dynamic principal parts	
	With only affixes taken into account	With tonality and affixes both taken into account
IIIA, IVD	1 (class-identifier)	1
I1A, I1C, I2A, I2B, I2C, II1A, II2A, II2B	2	1
I1B, II1B, IIIB, IIIC, IIIE, IVA, IVB	2	2
IIID, IVC	3	3

This same strategy will not work for Fur, however. Notice, for example, that in the nonthird-person perfect, some conjugations exhibit a low-toned -à suffix and others exhibit a low-toned -ò suffix. Yet, the paradigms of conjugations exhibiting the -à suffix may exhibit exactly the same pattern of stem tonality as those of conjugations exhibiting the -ò suffix. For instance, Conjugations IIIE and IVA differ in that the first shows the -à suffix and the second shows the -ò suffix; yet, these two conjugations exhibit precisely the same pattern of stem tonality, and the two suffixes are therefore in contrastive rather than complementary distribution. More generally, for each of the five sets of conjugations listed in (15), the only differences in exponence between the conjugations are affixal, and none of the distinguishing affixes is a class-identifier. These facts lead inevitably to the conclusion that the No-Blur Principle cannot be maintained.

(15) (a) I1A, I1C and II1A
 (b) I1B and II1B
 (c) I2A, I2C and II2A
 (d) IIIB and IVB
 (e) IIID, IIIE, IVA, and IVC

The theoretical antecedent of the No-Blur Principle is the Paradigm Economy Principle (Carstairs 1987), which Carstairs-McCarthy (1991: 222) formulates as in (16):

(16) Paradigm Economy Principle
 There can be no more inflectional paradigms for any word-class in any language than there are distinct "rival" inflectional realizations available for that morphosyntactic property-combination where the largest number of rivals compete.

As with the No-Blur Principle, it is intended that this principle relate specifically to affixal inflection; thus, it entails that the maximum number of conjugations in Fur should be no larger than the maximum number of affixes that compete to realize the same property set in Fur verbal inflection. Just as the Fur evidence fails to confirm the predictions of the No-Blur Principle, it likewise fails to confirm the predictions of the Paradigm Economy Principle. In Fur, the largest number of rival suffixes for the inflection of a particular MPS is six (in both the nonthird-person subjunctive and the third-person singular subjunctive; cf. Table 4.22) – far fewer than the total number of conjugations (of which there are nineteen). While the benefits of paradigm economy for language learning cannot be doubted, these facts show that paradigm economy is not clearly enforced by any linguistic constraint.

Accordingly, evidence from languages such as Fur raises similar doubts about Albright's (2002, 2008) single surface base hypothesis:

> [T]he single base hypothesis means that for one form in the paradigm (the base), there are no rules that can be used to synthesize it, and memorization is the only option. Other forms in the paradigm may be memorized or may be synthesized, but synthesis must be done via operations on the base form. Since we are assuming here a word-based model of morphology, the base is a fully formed surface member of the paradigm, and for this reason, I will call this the *single surface base* hypothesis.   (Albright 2002: 11)

Albright acknowledges that in order to synthesize forms in a complex inflectional paradigm, it is sometimes necessary to refer to multiple, local bases; this might be taken to suggest that the paradigms of a richly inflected language can be subdivided into sectors such that each sector S has a base by which the single surface base hypothesis is satisfied within S. But it is not clear that the single surface base hypothesis can be maintained even in this weakened form, since as we have seen, some of the cells in a realized paradigm are only deducible by simultaneous reference to two or more principal parts within that paradigm. (See Finkel & Stump 2007 for additional relevant discussion.)

4.8 IC transparency as a dimension of typological variation

The Fur facts demonstrate that languages tolerate considerable variation in the amount of IC transparency that they exhibit. In addition, there is considerable variation across languages in the relative transparency of their paradigms. Thus, consider the facts in Table 4.24, in which the IC transparency of Fur's verb paradigms is juxtaposed with that of verbs in Icelandic (Germanic; Iceland) and Comaltepec Chinantec (Oto-Manguean; Mexico).

Table 4.24. *IC predictability in three languages*

	Fur	Icelandic	Comaltepec Chinantec
Conjugations	19	162*	67
Distillations	9	21	12
Optimal principal-part number, averaged across conjugations	1.58	1.56	1.84
Cell predictor number, averaged across conjugations	1.04	1.09	1.08
Number of alternative dynamic principal-part analyses for a conjugation, averaged across conjugations	3.26	28.18	5.96
Ratio of actual to possible optimal dynamic principal-part analyses, averaged across conjugations (%)	17.3	23.9	20.3
IC predictability, averaged across conjugations	0.485	0.570	0.391
Average cell predictability, averaged across conjugations	0.743	0.845	0.815

*Jörg 1989 lists 162, but there are only 146 distinct ICs.

The three languages vary considerably in their number of distillations and conjugations. On average, Fur and Icelandic require approximately the same number of dynamic principal parts (between 1.5 and 1.6) in order to deduce a verb's conjugation-class membership; Comaltepec Chinantec requires a substantially higher number (over 1.8). On average, the three languages require approximately the same number of principal parts in order to deduce a given word form in a given verb paradigm (between 1.0 and 1.1). They differ considerably, however, in their ratios of actual to possible principal-part analyses, ranging from 17 percent (Fur) to 24 percent (Icelandic). Their average IC predictability ranges from 0.391 (Chinantec) to 0.570 (Icelandic); by contrast, it is Fur that shows the lowest average cell predictability (0.743), and Icelandic, the highest (0.845).

The conjugational system of Fur is what we call a **condensed** system, in which the least predictable cells tend to be confined to the same regions in the paradigms of lexemes belonging to different ICs. In particular, the least predictable cells in all of the conjugations that Jakobi assigns to groups I and II are in the present tense (distillations 3, 6, and 9); by contrast, the least predictable cells in the conjugations that Jakobi assigns to groups III and IV are (a) the subjunctive and perfect of both the nonthird person and the third-person singular (distillations 1, 2, 4, and 5) and (b) the subjunctive of the nonhuman third-person plural (distillation 7). Figure 4.1 shows these facts particularly clearly.

Comaltepec Chinantec presents a similarly condensed system, as Figure 4.2 shows. In this figure (as in Figure 4.1), distillations are listed on the horizontal axis in order of decreasing average cell predictability and conjugations are listed on the vertical axis in order of decreasing IC predictability; the numbering of distillations is given in Table 4.25. As condensed systems, the Fur conjugations and those in Comaltepec Chinantec contrast with conjugational systems such as that of Icelandic, which is **diffuse** rather than condensed. In Figure 4.3 (whose distillation numbers are given in Table 4.26) the least predictable cells are not confined to the same regions in the paradigms of different lexemes, but are widely dispersed among the cells of paradigms.

4.9 IC predictability, cell predictability, and entropy as measures of an inflection-class system's complexity

Several researchers have drawn attention to the utility of the information-theoretic notion of conditional entropy as a way of elucidating the implicative relations among a paradigm's parts; see in particular Moscoso del Prado Martín *et al.* (2004), Milin *et al.* (2009), Ackerman *et al.* (2009), and Malouf & Ackerman (2010a, b, c, 2011a,b). This conception of a paradigm's implicative structure affords another way of quantifying the complexity of ICs; we discuss it in detail in Chapter 10. In anticipation of that discussion, we here point out some important differences between conditional entropy and the notions of IC and cell predictability presented in this chapter.

Consider a simple example. Suppose that there is a syntactic position in which an English word form is to be used; in the absence of any other information, this syntactic position might be represented as in (17a). The entropy of this position can be intuitively equated with the difficulty of guessing what word is to occupy this position; the entropy is in this case very high – any word is possible. But if one knows something about the position's syntactic context, then its entropy, conditioned by this additional information, is lower. Thus, suppose that the position is preceded by the degree adverb *very*, as in (17b); in that case, we can be reasonably sure that the word occupying the position is not (for example) a finite verb form. If we know even more about the position's syntactic context, as in (17c), then the position's conditional entropy is still lower; in (17c), the empty position must seemingly be occupied by a determiner, adjective or adverb possessing gradable semantics (as in *with very few* ..., *with very good* ... or *with very nearly* ...). Moreover, the candidates for the position in (17c) are not all equally likely. In the *Corpus of Contemporary American English* (Davies 2008–present), *little* is more than twice as likely as any other word in the position

Figure 4.2. *Cell predictability in all conjugations in Comaltepec Chinantec (Numbered distillations on the horizontal axis, ICs on the vertical axis; lighter shade represents higher cell predictability)*

Table 4.25. *Abbreviations for the twelve distillations realized by Comaltepec Chinantec verb forms*

Abbreviation	Property set
1	1sg progressive
2	1pl progressive
3	2nd-person progressive
4	3rd-person progressive
5	1sg intentive
6	1pl intentive
7	2nd-person intentive
8	3rd-person intentive
9	1sg completive
10	1pl completive
11	2nd-person completive
12	3rd-person completive

in (17c); the odds that the missing word is *little* are therefore fairly good, and this probability reduces the entropy of the position in (17c) still further.

(17)   (a) ___   (b) *very* ___   (c) *with very* ___

Suppose, now, that a past-tense word form must be inferred for the realized paradigm of an unfamiliar English verbal lexeme L. Without any additional information about L's paradigm, it is difficult to guess what word form should be situated in cell (18a). But if we know one of the paradigm's other cells, as in (18b), the conditional entropy of ⟨ ___, {past}⟩ is reduced; given the inflection of BITE, WRITE, INVITE, or FIGHT, the past-tense counterpart of infinitive /daɪt/ is most likely /dɪt/, /doʊt/, /daɪtəd/, or /dɔt/. The additional paradigmatic context in (18c) reduces the conditional entropy of ⟨ ___, {past}⟩ effectively to zero.

(18)   (a) ⟨ ___, {past}⟩
         (b) ⟨ /daɪt/, {inf}⟩, ⟨ ___, {past}⟩
         (c) ⟨ /daɪt/, {inf}⟩, ⟨ ___, {past}⟩, ⟨/daɪtəd/, {past ptcp}⟩

Despite the superficial parallelism of (17) and (18), there is a fundamental difference. In the case of (17), no amount of extra context will ever reduce the target word's conditional entropy to zero; in this respect, (17) is typical of word positions in syntax. By contrast, it is normal for a realized cell to be uniquely determined by one or more of the other cells in its paradigm (either alone or in

Figure 4.3. *Cell predictability in all conjugations in Icelandic (Numbered distillations on the horizontal axis, ICs on the vertical axis; lighter shade represents higher cell predictability)*

Table 4.26. *Abbreviations for the twenty-one distillations realized by Icelandic verb forms*

Abbr.	Property set	Abbr.	Property set	Abbr.	Property set
1	Infinitive	8	2sg present indicative	15	3sg past indicative
2	2sg imperative	9	3sg present indicative	16	1pl past indicative
3	1pl imperative	10	1pl present indicative	17	2pl past indicative
4	2pl imperative	11	2pl present indicative	18	1sg present subjunctive
5	1st participle	12	3pl present indicative	19	1sg past subjunctive
6	2nd participle	13	1sg past indicative	20	3sg past subjunctive
7	1sg present indicative	14	2sg past indicative	21	1pl past subjunctive

combination). If a realized cell is not predictable, then it must have the status of a principal part and is likely stored in the lexicon; but the large majority of realized cells are predictable. Inflectional paradigms are small, closed systems whose internal structure is highly integrated, and it is for this reason that their implicative structure is open to the kind of set-theoretic measures that we have presented in this chapter. Syntactic structures simply are not open to any comparable kind of measure; it would be absurd to search through a word's syntactic context for a set of "principal parts" that would uniquely determine its syntagmatic distribution.

Thus, two approaches to elucidating the notion of an IC system's complexity can be distinguished. One approach employs the information-theoretic measure of conditional entropy, which is well suited for quantifying the degree to which a given form is expected or unexpected in a particular linguistic context (whether this be a syntagmatic or a paradigmatic context). The other approach employs the set-theoretic measures of IC and cell predictability. Unlike conditional entropy, these measures are not applicable across a variety of domains, precisely because they measure a singularly distinctive property of inflectional paradigms, namely the strong implicative affiliation of their realized cells. Where conditional entropy measures the degree of likelihood that certain forms will cooccur, the set-theoretic measures of IC and cell predictability measure the proportion of cases in which cooccurrence is certain. Unlike the measure of conditional entropy, the latter measures are predicated on the assumption that each realized paradigm has sets of cells that fully determine the paradigm as a whole. On this assumption, it is not surprising that when conditional entropy measures are applied to paradigms, the results tend to be low (Malouf & Ackerman 2010c); indeed, the expectation is that the conditional entropy of paradigms and their cells is always reducible to zero if conditioned by the right cells, that is, a set of principal parts. Entropy measures are compatible with the possibility that there are no motivated inferences in inflectional morphology, only unmotivated inferences that have a greater or lesser probability of being confirmed; the IC and cell predictability measures, by contrast, depend on the more restrictive premise that there are motivated inferences in inflectional morphology – that the architecture of IC systems inevitably makes some inferences certain.

4.10 Conclusions

In this chapter, we have introduced the concept of IC transparency – the extent to which the realized paradigms of an IC's member lexemes deviate from the canonical ideal of maximal transparency. We have shown that within a given language, paradigms belonging to different ICs may vary widely in their IC transparency. Examining evidence from Fur, we have proposed four criteria for assessing the degree of a language's deviation from maximal transparency. The criteria correlate well with the measures of IC predictability and cell predictability: an IC that is more transparent by the four criteria generally exhibits higher IC predictability and higher cell predictability. We have shown that the No-Blur Principle, a proposal whose effect is to constrain the incidence of IC opacity, is too strong; it is irreconcilable with the patterns of IC opacity observable in languages such as Fur. Finally, we have cited evidence from Comaltepec Chinantec and Icelandic which, when juxtaposed with the Fur evidence, highlights the status of IC transparency as a dimension of typological variation.

It is initially somewhat unexpected that languages should vary in the extent of their deviation from maximal transparency, given the apparent benefits of IC transparency for language learning and lexical storage. But IC transparency is by no means the only property of inflectional systems that may confer benefits on the language user, and it is sometimes at cross purposes with other such properties. For instance, when contrasting ICs employ the same exponence in certain realized cells (e.g. the suffix -*s* in the third-person singular present indicative cells of *sings*, *brings*, *stings*, and *dings*, whose past-tense counterparts are all different), that identity of exponence makes the learning of those cells easier, but it lowers the transparency of the ICs involved. To fully understand the cross-linguistic variability of IC transparency, it will be necessary to understand the ways in which IC transparency conflicts with, counterbalances, or compensates for other properties of inflectional systems.

4.11 Appendix

Table 4.27. *Automatically generated optimal dynamic principal-part analyses for Fur verbs*

Conjugation	Principal-part analysis	Distillations									Cell predictor number
		1	2	3	4	5	6	7	8	9	
I1A	③	③	③	③	③	③	③	③	③	③	1.00
	⑥	⑥	⑥	⑥	⑥	⑥	⑥	⑥	⑥	⑥	1.00
	⑨	⑨	⑨	⑨	⑨	⑨	⑨	⑨	⑨	⑨	1.00
I1B	①,③	①	①	③	①	①	③	①	①	③	1.00
	①,⑥	①	①	⑥	①	①	⑥	①	①	⑥	1.00
	②,③	②	②	③	②	②	③	②	②	③	1.00
	②,⑥	②	②	⑥	②	②	⑥	②	②	⑥	1.00
	③,④	④	④	③	④	④	③	④	④	③	1.00
	③,⑤	⑤	⑤	③	⑤	⑤	③	⑤	⑤	③	1.00
	③,⑦	⑦	⑦	③	⑦	⑦	③	⑦	⑦	③	1.00
	③,⑧	⑧	⑧	③	⑧	⑧	③	⑧	⑧	③	1.00
	④,⑥	④	④	⑥	④	④	⑥	④	④	⑥	1.00
	⑤,⑥	⑤	⑤	⑥	⑤	⑤	⑥	⑤	⑤	⑥	1.00
	⑥,⑦	⑦	⑦	⑥	⑦	⑦	⑥	⑦	⑦	⑥	1.00
	⑥,⑧	⑧	⑧	⑥	⑧	⑧	⑥	⑧	⑧	⑥	1.00
I1C	③	③	③	③	③	③	③	③	③	③	1.00
	⑥	⑥	⑥	⑥	⑥	⑥	⑥	⑥	⑥	⑥	1.00
I2A	⑥	⑥	⑥	⑥	⑥	⑥	⑥	⑥	⑥	⑥	1.00
	⑨	⑨	⑨	⑨	⑨	⑨	⑨	⑨	⑨	⑨	1.00
I2B	⑥	⑥	⑥	⑥	⑥	⑥	⑥	⑥	⑥	⑥	1.00
I2C	③	③	③	③	③	③	③	③	③	③	1.00
	⑥	⑥	⑥	⑥	⑥	⑥	⑥	⑥	⑥	⑥	1.00
II1A	③	③	③	③	③	③	③	③	③	③	1.00
	⑥	⑥	⑥	⑥	⑥	⑥	⑥	⑥	⑥	⑥	1.00
	⑨	⑨	⑨	⑨	⑨	⑨	⑨	⑨	⑨	⑨	1.00
II1B	①,③	①	①	③	①	①	③	①	①	③	1.00
	①,⑥	①	①	⑥	①	①	⑥	①	①	⑥	1.00
	①,⑨	①	①	①,⑨	①	①	①,⑨	①	①	⑨	1.22
	②,③	②	②	③	②	②	③	②	②	③	1.00
	②,⑥	②	②	⑥	②	②	⑥	②	②	⑥	1.00
	②,⑨	②	②	②,⑨	②	②	②,⑨	②	②	⑨	1.22

116　*Inflection-class transparency*

Table 4.27. (*cont.*)

Conjugation	Principal-part analysis	Distillations									Cell predictor number
		1	2	3	4	5	6	7	8	9	
	③,④	④	④	③	④	④	③	④	④	③	1.00
	③,⑤	⑤	⑤	③	⑤	⑤	③	⑤	⑤	③	1.00
	③,⑦	⑦	⑦	③	⑦	⑦	③	⑦	⑦	③	1.00
	③,⑧	⑧	⑧	③	⑧	⑧	③	⑧	⑧	③	1.00
	④,⑥	④	④	⑥	④	④	⑥	④	④	⑥	1.00
	④,⑨	④	④	④,⑨	④	④	④,⑨	④	④	⑨	1.22
	⑤,⑥	⑤	⑤	⑥	⑤	⑤	⑥	⑤	⑤	⑥	1.00
	⑤,⑨	⑤	⑤	⑤,⑨	⑤	⑤	⑤,⑨	⑤	⑤	⑨	1.22
	⑥,⑦	⑦	⑦	⑥	⑦	⑦	⑥	⑦	⑦	⑥	1.00
	⑥,⑧	⑧	⑧	⑥	⑧	⑧	⑥	⑧	⑧	⑥	1.00
	⑦,⑨	⑦	⑦	⑦,⑨	⑦	⑦	⑦,⑨	⑦	⑦	⑨	1.22
	⑧,⑨	⑧	⑧	⑧,⑨	⑧	⑧	⑧,⑨	⑧	⑧	⑨	1.22
II2A	③	③	③	③	③	③	③	③	③	③	1.00
	⑥	⑥	⑥	⑥	⑥	⑥	⑥	⑥	⑥	⑥	1.00
	⑨	⑨	⑨	⑨	⑨	⑨	⑨	⑨	⑨	⑨	1.00
II2B	⑥	⑥	⑥	⑥	⑥	⑥	⑥	⑥	⑥	⑥	1.00
IIIA	④	④	④	④	④	④	④	④	④	④	1.00
IIIB	④,⑦	④	④	④	④	④	④	⑦	④	④	1.00
IIIC	①,④	①	①,④	④	④	①,④	④	①,④	④	④	1.33
IIID	①,⑤,⑦	①	⑤	①	①	⑤	①	⑦	①	①	1.00
	④,⑤,⑦	④,⑤	⑤	④	④	⑤	④	⑦	④	④	1.11
IIIE	②,⑤	②,⑤	②	②	②,⑤	⑤	②	②,⑤	②	②	1.33
IVA	①,②	①	②	①	①	②	①	①,②	①	①	1.11
IVB	①,⑦	①	①,⑦	⑦	①,⑦	①,⑦	⑦	⑦	⑦	⑦	1.33
	④,⑦	④	④	④	④	④	④	⑦	④	④	1.00
IVC	①,②,⑦	①	②	①	①	②,⑦	①	⑦	①	①	1.11
	①,⑤,⑦	①	⑤	①	①	⑤	①	⑦	①	①	1.00
	②,④,⑦	②,④	②	②	④	②,⑦	②	⑦	②	②	1.22
	④,⑤,⑦	④,⑤	⑤	④	④	⑤	④	⑦	④	④	1.11
IVD	①	①	①	①	①	①	①	①	①	①	1.00
	④	④	④	④	④	④	④	④	④	④	1.00

5   *Grammatically enhanced plats*

Plats play a central role in our analyses of the implicative relations that connect the cells in a realized paradigm. In Chapter 2 we raised the representation issue: what, exactly, do plats represent? We drew a distinction between hearer-oriented and speaker-oriented plats: hearer-oriented plats represent the phonetic or phonological distinctions among ICs that language users directly perceive and that they use in determining a newly encountered lexeme's IC membership; speaker-oriented plats represent the IC distinctions that language users regard as morphologically significant and that they could potentially use in deducing a known lexeme's realized paradigm from principal parts. In this chapter, we explicitly contrast a hearer-oriented plat with a speaker-oriented plat representing the same IC system; specifically, we present an analysis of the implicative relations exhibited by Sanskrit declension classes in a hearer-oriented plat, then in a speaker-oriented plat incorporating "extra" grammatical information. We introduce the characteristics of Sanskrit declension in §5.1. Our initial analysis of the hearer-oriented declensional plat involves various measures of IC complexity, including the measures of IC and cell predictability introduced in Chapter 4 as well as a new measure, that of cell predictiveness (§5.2). We propose two grammatical enhancements of the declensional plat: the enhanced, speaker-oriented plat includes information about a nominal lexeme's gender and identifies stem boundaries within an IC's distinguishers (§5.3). We show that including this extra information diminishes the IC complexity of the Sanskrit declensional system. In particular, the inclusion of gender specifications heightens both predictability and predictiveness; information about stem delimitation heightens predictiveness but not predictability (§5.4). We summarize our conclusions in §5.5.[1]

---

[1] The data sets that we have employed in this chapter are:

    enhanced.sanskrit-both   enhanced.sanskrit-plain
    enhanced.sanskrit-gender enhanced.sanskrit-stem

These are available at the *Morphological Typology* website www.cambridge.org/stump_finkel.

118 *Grammatically enhanced plats*

5.1   Sanskrit declension

Sanskrit nominal expressions (including nouns, adjectives, and pronouns) inflect for eight cases (nominative, vocative, accusative, instrumental, dative, ablative, genitive, and locative) and three numbers (singular, dual, and plural). Certain case/number combinations are, however, systematically syncretized: the nominative, vocative, and accusative of the dual; the instrumental, dative, and ablative of the dual; the genitive and locative of the dual; the nominative and vocative of the plural; and the dative and ablative of the plural.

A nominal's gender (masculine, feminine or neuter) is sometimes reflected in its inflection. Most declensions are restricted to particular genders; for example, the *a*-stem declensions exclude feminines, whether these be inherently feminine nominals (feminine nouns and pronouns) or adjectives inflecting for feminine gender agreement. The difference between a declension associated with one gender and a declension associated with another gender is sometimes very slight; for instance, the declensions of MĀTṚ 'mother' (feminine) and PITṚ 'father' (masculine) differ only in the accusative plural. In some of the consonant-stem declensions, masculine and feminine forms are alike in their inflection.

By analyzing the realized paradigms of Sanskrit nominals into themes and distinguishers, we arrive at the inventory of the thirty-eight major declension classes listed and exemplified in (1). The unique series of distinguishers corresponding to these classes are given in full in the hearer-oriented plat in Table 5.1.

We emphasize that this plat represents the major declension classes; each of the patterns in Table 5.1 is regularly embodied by the paradigms of several (in many cases, hundreds or even thousands) of lexemes. There are irregular nouns with idiosyncratic or hybrid (heteroclite) paradigms that we simply leave aside, since the patterns that they embody do not clearly figure in the language's productive declensional morphology. (We will, however, return to the problems posed by such lexemes in Chapter 6.)

(1)   The thirty-eight major declension classes in Sanskrit, with exemplars

DC1	AŚVA 'horse' (masc)	DC23	TUDAT$_m$ 'striking' (masc)
DC2	DĀNA 'gift' (neut)	DC24	TUDAT$_n$ 'striking' (neut)
DC3	SENĀ 'army' (fem)		DHĪMAT$_n$ 'intelligent' (neut)
DC4	ALI 'bee' (masc)	DC25	DHĪMAT$_m$ 'intelligent' (masc)
DC5	MATI 'intellect' (fem)	DC26	ŚREYAS$_m$ 'better' (masc)
DC6	VĀRI 'water' (neut)	DC27	ŚREYAS$_n$ 'better' (neut)
DC7	PAŚU 'tethered animal' (masc)		MANAS 'mind' (neut)
DC8	DHENU 'cow' (fem)	DC28	VIDVAT$_m$ 'knowing' (masc)
DC9	MADHU 'honey' (neut)	DC29	VIDVAT$_n$ 'knowing' (neut)

DC10 NADĪ 'river' (fem)
DC11 VADHŪ 'bride' (fem)
DC12 DHĪ 'thought' (fem)
DC13 BHŪ 'ground' (fem)
DC14 PITṚ 'father' (masc)
DC15 MĀTṚ 'mother' (fem)
DC16 DĀTṚ$_m$ 'giver' (masc)
DC17 SVASṚ 'sister' (fem)
DC18 DĀTṚ$_n$ 'giver' (neut)
DC19 RĀJAN 'king' (masc)
DC20 NĀMAN 'name' (neut)
DC21 BALIN$_m$ 'strong' (masc)
DC22 BALIN$_n$ 'strong' (neut)

DC30 SUMANAS$_m$ 'benevolent' (masc)
    SUMANAS$_f$ 'benevolent' (fem)
DC31 ŚUKRAŚOCIS$_m$ 'having brilliance' (masc)
    ŚUKRAŚOCIS$_f$ 'having brilliance' (fem)
DC32 ŚUKRAŚOCIS$_n$ 'having brilliance' (neut)
DC33 DĪRGHĀYUS$_m$ 'long lived' (masc)
    DĪRGHĀYUS$_f$ 'long lived' (fem)
DC34 DĪRGHĀYUS$_n$ 'long lived' (neut)
DC35 MARUT 'wind' (masc)
    SARIT 'stream' (fem)
DC36 JAGAT 'world' (neut)
DC37 PRATYAK$_m$ 'west' (masc)
DC38 PRATYAK$_n$ 'west' (neut)

5.2 Measuring the IC complexity of the hearer-oriented declensional plat

We find several measures useful in assessing the complexity of an IC J in the hearer-oriented declensional plat. We have already employed some of these measures in other contexts:

(a) the number of principal parts needed to deduce the realized paradigm of a lexeme belonging to J (cf. §3.2) – J's optimal principal-part number;

(b) the average number of optimal dynamic principal parts needed to deduce a given cell in the realized paradigm of a lexeme belonging to J (cf. §§3.4, 4.3) – J's cell predictor number;

(c) the number of alternative optimal dynamic principal-part analyses allowed by the realized paradigm of a lexeme belonging to J (§4.3);

(d) J's IC predictability (§4.4); and

(e) the average cell predictability of a lexeme belonging to J (§4.6).

Each of these measures helps elucidate the notion of IC complexity. In particular, we propose that each contributes to a canonical conception of IC complexity according to which a canonically complex IC

- has a high optimal principal-part number;
- has a high cell predictor number;
- has a small number of alternative analyses;
- has low IC predictability; and
- contains lexemes with low average cell predictability.

Consider now the application of these measures to the hearer-oriented declensional plat.

Table 5.1. Hearer-oriented declensional plat for Sanskrit

Declension class	Singular									Dual			Plural					
	N	V	A	I	D	Ab	G	L	NVA	IDAb	GL	NV	A	I	DAb	G	L
DC1	as	a	am	ena	āya	āt	asya	e	au	ābhyām	ayos	ās	ān	ais	ebhyas	ānām	eṣu
DC2	am	a	am	ena	āya	āt	asya	e	e	ābhyām	ayos	āni	āni	ais	ebhyas	ānām	eṣu
DC3	ā	e	ām	ayā	āyai	āyās	āyās	āyām	e	ābhyām	ayos	ās	ās	ābhis	ābhyas	ānām	āsu
DC4	is	e	im	inā	aye	es	es	au	ī	ibhyām	yos	ayas	īn	ibhis	ibhyas	īnām	iṣu
DC5	is	e	im	yā	aye	es	es	au	ī	ibhyām	yos	ayas	īs	ibhis	ibhyas	īnām	iṣu
DC6	i	i	i	inā	ine	inas	inas	ini	inī	ibhyām	inos	īni	īni	ibhis	ibhyas	īnām	iṣu
DC7	us	o	um	unā	ave	os	os	au	ū	ubhyām	vos	avas	ūn	ubhis	ubhyas	ūnām	uṣu
DC8	us	o	um	vā	ave	os	os	au	ū	ubhyām	vos	avas	ūs	ubhis	ubhyas	ūnām	uṣu
DC9	u	u	u	unā	une	unas	unas	uni	unī	ubhyām	unos	ūni	ūni	ubhis	ubhyas	ūnām	uṣu
DC10	ī	i	īm	yā	yai	yās	yās	yām	yau	ībhyām	yos	yas	īs	ībhis	ībhyas	īnām	īṣu
DC11	ūs	u	ūm	vā	vai	vās	vās	vām	vau	ūbhyām	vos	vas	ūs	ūbhis	ūbhyas	ūnām	ūṣu
DC12	īs	īs	iyam	iyā	iye	iyas	iyas	iyi	iyau	ībhyām	iyos	iyas	iyas	ībhis	ībhyas	iyām	īṣu
DC13	ūs	ūs	uvam	uvā	uve	uvas	uvas	uvi	uvau	ūbhyām	uvos	uvas	uvas	ūbhis	ūbhyas	uvām	ūṣu
DC14	ā	ar	aram	rā	re	ur	ur	ari	arau	ṛbhyām	ros	aras	ṝn	ṛbhis	ṛbhyas	ṝṇām	ṛṣu
DC15	ā	ar	aram	rā	re	ur	ur	ari	arau	ṛbhyām	ros	aras	ṝs	ṛbhis	ṛbhyas	ṝṇām	ṛṣu
DC16	ā	ar	āram	rā	re	ur	ur	ari	ārau	ṛbhyām	ros	āras	ṝn	ṛbhis	ṛbhyas	ṝṇām	ṛṣu
DC17	ā	ar	āram	rā	re	ur	ur	ari	ārau	ṛbhyām	ros	āras	ṝs	ṛbhis	ṛbhyas	ṝṇām	ṛṣu
DC18	ṝ	ṛ	ṝ	ṛṇā	ṛṇe	ṛṇas	ṛṇas	ṛṇi	ṝṇī	ṛbhyām	ṛṇos	ṝṇi	ṝṇi	ṛbhis	ṛbhyas	ṝṇām	ṛṣu
DC19	ā	an	ānam	nā	ne	nas	nas	ni	ānau	abhyām	nos	ānas	nas	abhis	abhyas	nām	asu
DC20	a	a	a	nā	ne	nas	nas	ni	nī	abhyām	nos	āni	āni	abhis	abhyas	nām	asu
DC21	ī	in	inam	inā	ine	inas	inas	ini	inau	ibhyām	inos	inas	inas	ibhis	ibhyas	inām	iṣu
DC22	i	i(n)	i	inā	ine	inas	inas	ini	inī	ibhyām	inos	īni	īni	ibhis	ibhyas	inām	iṣu
DC23	an	an	antam	atā	ate	atas	atas	ati	antau	adbhyām	atos	antas	atas	adbhis	adbhyas	atām	atsu

DC24	at	at	at	atā	ate	atas	atas	ati	ati	antau	adbhyām	atos	anti	anti	adbhis	adbhyas	atām	atsu
DC25	ān	an	antam	atā	ate	atas	atas	ati	ati	antau	adbhyām	atos	antas	atas	adbhis	adbhyas	atām	atsu
DC26	ān	an	āṃsam	asā	ase	asas	asas	asi	asi	āṃsau	obhyām	asos	āṃsas	asas	obhis	obhyas	asām	aḥsu
DC27	as	as	as	asā	ase	asas	asas	asi	asi	asī	obhyām	asos	āṃsi	āṃsi	obhis	obhyas	asām	aḥsu
DC28	vān	van	vāṃsam	uṣā	uṣe	uṣas	uṣas	uṣi	uṣi	vāṃsau	vadbhyām	uṣos	vāṃsas	uṣas	vadbhis	vadbhyas	uṣām	vatsu
DC29	vat	vat	vat	uṣā	uṣe	uṣas	uṣas	uṣi	uṣi	uṣī	vadbhyām	uṣos	vāṃsi	vāṃsi	vadbhis	vadbhyas	uṣām	vatsu
DC30	ās	as	asam	asā	ase	asas	asas	asi	asi	asau	obhyām	asos	asas	asas	obhis	obhyas	asām	aḥsu
DC31	is	is	iṣam	iṣā	iṣe	iṣas	iṣas	iṣi	iṣi	iṣau	irbhyām	iṣos	iṣas	iṣas	irbhis	irbhyas	iṣām	iḥsu
DC32	is	is	is	iṣā	iṣe	iṣas	iṣas	iṣi	iṣi	iṣī	irbhyām	iṣos	īṃṣi	īṃṣi	irbhis	irbhyas	iṣām	iḥsu
DC33	us	us	uṣam	uṣā	uṣe	uṣas	uṣas	uṣi	uṣi	uṣau	urbhyām	uṣos	uṣas	uṣas	urbhis	urbhyas	uṣām	uḥsu
DC34	us	us	us	uṣā	uṣe	uṣas	uṣas	uṣi	uṣi	uṣī	urbhyām	uṣos	ūṃṣi	ūṃṣi	urbhis	urbhyas	uṣām	uḥsu
DC35	t	t	tam	tā	te	tas	tas	ti	ti	tau	dbhyām	tos	tas	tas	dbhis	dbhyas	tām	tsu
DC36	t	t	t	tā	te	tas	tas	ti	ti	tī	dbhyām	tos	nti	nti	dbhis	dbhyas	tām	tsu
DC37	yaṅ	yaṅ	yañcam	īcā	īce	īcas	īcas	īci	īci	yañcau	yagbhyām	īcos	yañcas	īcas	yagbhis	yagbhyas	īcām	yakṣu
DC38	yak	yak	yak	īcā	īce	īcas	īcas	īci	īci	īcī	yagbhyām	īcos	yañci	yañci	yagbhis	yagbhyas	īcām	yakṣu

Table 5.2. *The six optimal static principal-part sets for the hearer-oriented declensional plat (principal parts are checked (✓))*

	\multicolumn{11}{c}{Distillations}										
	Singular						Dual			Plural		
	N	V	A	I	D	L	NVA	IDAb	GL	NV	A	I	G
a.	✓	✓	✓								✓		
b.	✓	✓					✓				✓		
c.	✓	✓								✓	✓		
d.	✓		✓								✓		✓
e.	✓						✓				✓		✓
f.	✓									✓	✓		✓

5.2.1 The Sanskrit plat's optimal principal-part numbers

The optimal principal-part numbers of the plat's ICs can be calculated on the basis of optimal static or optimal dynamic principal-part sets.[2]

There are six optimal static principal-part sets for the plat in Table 5.1; these are shown in Table 5.2. Every set has four principal parts, always including the nominative singular and accusative plural cells; the other two cells in the set consist of either the vocative singular cell or the genitive plural cell plus one of the cells in (2). These results entail that the nominative singular and accusative plural cells in a Sanskrit nominal lexeme's realized paradigm generally carry the most information about that lexeme's declension-class membership, that the vocative singular and genitive plural cells carry somewhat less information, and the three cells in (2) are also informative.

(2)   accusative singular cell
      nominative/vocative/accusative dual cell
      nominative/vocative plural cell

Under an optimal dynamic principal-part analysis of the plat, most declensions have only a single principal part, and none has more than two. Consider,

---

[2] Both the static and the dynamic principal-part analyses presented here abstract away from a problem arising from specific lexemes that we term 'impostors'. An example is the DC25 adjective BHAGAVAT 'prosperous', whose nominative singular form *bhagavān* bears an accidental similarity to the nominative singular form of the DC28 adjective VIDVAT 'knowing' (nom. sg. *vidvān*). The theme for BHAGAVAT is *bhagav*, whereas the theme for VIDVAT is *vid*. The final *v* on *bhagav* causes its nominative singular form to mimic a DC28 nominative singular form, whose distinguisher begins with a *v*. Impostor lexemes complicate the principal-part analysis of both their own IC and the mimicked class. We discuss these complications in Chapter 6.

Measuring IC complexity 123

for example, the analyses of declensions DC1 and DC5 in Table 5.3; these are the declensions of AŚVA 'horse' (masc) and MATI 'intellect' (fem). In Table 5.3, each row represents a principal-part analysis for DC1 or DC5; the principal parts in these analyses are checked. Each subsequent column is headed by a MPS; in each analysis, the word form realizing a given property set is deducible from the principal part listed below that property set. In declension DC1, only a single principal part is necessary, either the nominative/vocative/accusative dual form (e.g. *aśvau*, numbered ⑦ in Table 5.3) or the accusative plural form (*aśvān*, numbered ⑩). In declension DC5, two principal parts are necessary, and there are eighteen pairs that work as these two principal parts.

The full complement of optimal dynamic analyses is summarized in Table 5.4. In the analyses in Table 5.4, declensions vary in the number of principal parts they require. The large majority require only one, but some require two; none requires more than two. One especially revealing feature of Table 5.4 is the difference between declensions DC23 and DC25. Although these two masculine declensions differ only in the nominative singular (TUDAT 'striking': *tudan* vs DHĪMAT 'intelligent': *dhīmān*), their dynamic principal-part profiles are extremely different: TUDAT has a single optimal dynamic principal-part set with a single member (its nominative singular cell), but DHĪMAT has eleven optimal dynamic principal-part sets, each with two members (one member must be its nominative singular cell, the other may be the realization of any other distillation besides the vocative singular); moreover, most of DHĪMAT's analyses have a cell predictor number of 1.31. These are superficially surprising facts, but they reveal something essential about inflection classes: the more similar they are, the more complex the task of distinguishing them. It is not an IC's inflectional idiosyncrasy that diminishes its transparency; it is the IC's inflectional similarity to other ICs.

5.2.2 The Sanskrit plat's cell predictor numbers

Consider again declension DC5 in Table 5.3. In some of the optimal dynamic principal-part analyses for DC5, it is possible to deduce each nonprincipal part from one of the two principal parts. For instance, if the principal parts are ⟨*matim*, {acc sg}⟩ (numbered ③) and ⟨*matyā*, {ins sg}⟩ (numbered ④), then the nominative singular cell is deducible from the former and the accusative plural cell is deducible from the latter. In other analyses, some nonprincipal parts can only be deduced by simultaneous reference to both principal parts; for instance, if the principal parts are ⟨*matis*, {nom sg}⟩ (numbered ①) and ⟨*matyā*, {ins sg}⟩ (numbered ④), then the accusative singular cell can only be deduced by simultaneous reference to both principal parts. Three other declensions in

Table 5.3. *Optimal dynamic principal parts (circled) for Declensions* DC1 *and* DC5 *in the hearer-oriented declensional plat (In each analysis, the word form realizing a given property set is deducible from the principal part listed below that property set.)*

Declension class	Optimal principal-part number	Cell inference number	Alternative analyses	Optimal dynamic principal parts	Singular						Dual			Plural				
					N	V	A	I	D	L	NVA	IDAb	GL	NV	A	I	G	
DC1	1	1.00	2	⑦	⑦	⑦	⑦	⑦	⑦	⑦	⑦	⑦	⑦	⑦	⑦	⑦	⑦	
				①	①	①	①	①	①	①	①	①	①	①	①	①	①	
DC5	2	varies from 1.00 to 1.62 according to the analysis	18	①,④	①	①,④	①,④	④	①,④	①,④	①,④	①,④	④	①,④	④	①,④	④	
				①,⑪	①	①,⑪	①,⑪	⑪	①,⑪	①,⑪	①,⑪	①,⑪	⑪	①,⑪	⑪	①,⑪	⑪	
				②,④	②,④	②	②,④	④	②,④	②,④	②,④	②	④	②,④	④	②,④	④	
				②,⑪	②,⑪	②	②,⑪	⑪	②,⑪	②,⑪	②,⑪	②	⑪	②,⑪	⑪	②,⑪	⑪	
				③,④	③	③	③	④	③	③	③	③	④	③	④	③	④	
				③,⑪	③	③	③	⑪	③	③	③	③	⑪	③	⑪	③	⑪	
				④,⑤	⑤	⑤	⑤	④	⑤	⑤	⑤	⑤	④	⑤	④	⑤	④	
				④,⑥	④,⑥	④,⑥	④,⑥	④	④,⑥	⑥	④,⑥	④,⑥	④	④,⑥	④	④,⑥	④	
				④,⑦	⑦	⑦	⑦	④	⑦	⑦	⑦	⑦	④	⑦	④	⑦	④	
				④,⑧	④,⑧	④,⑧	④,⑧	④	④,⑧	④,⑧	④,⑧	⑧	④	④,⑧	④	⑧	④	
				④,⑩	⑩	⑩	⑩	④	④,⑩	⑩	⑩	⑩	④	⑩	④	⑩	④	
				④,⑪	④,⑪	④,⑪	④,⑪	⑪	④,⑪	④,⑪	④,⑪	④,⑪	⑪	④,⑪	④	④,⑪	④	
				⑤,⑪	⑤	⑤	⑤	⑪	⑤	⑤	⑤	⑤	⑪	⑤	⑪	⑤	⑤	
				⑥,⑪	⑥,⑪	⑥,⑪	⑥,⑪	⑪	⑥,⑪	⑥	⑥,⑪	⑥,⑪	⑪	⑥,⑪	⑪	⑥,⑪	⑪	
				⑦,⑪	⑦	⑦	⑦	⑪	⑦	⑦	⑦	⑦	⑪	⑦	⑪	⑦	⑦	
				⑧,⑪	⑧,⑪	⑧,⑪	⑧,⑪	⑪	⑧,⑪	⑧,⑪	⑧,⑪	⑧	⑪	⑧,⑪	⑪	⑧	⑪	
				⑩,⑪	⑩,⑪	⑩,⑪	⑩,⑪	⑪	⑩,⑪	⑩,⑪	⑩,⑪	⑩	⑪	⑩,⑪	⑪	⑩	⑪	

Table 5.4. *Optimal dynamic principal-part analyses for the hearer-oriented declensional plat*

Declension	Optimal principal-part number n	Cell predictor number	Number p of optimal dynamic analyses	Ratio of p to the number of possible principal-part sets of cardinality n
DC1	1	1.00	2	15.4% of thirteen possible analyses
DC2	1	1.00	1	7.7% of thirteen possible analyses
DC3	1	1.00	6	46.2% of thirteen possible analyses
DC4	1	1.00	1	7.7% of thirteen possible analyses
DC5	2	1.00	18	23.1% of seventy-eight possible analyses
DC6	2	1.00	19	24.4% of seventy-eight possible analyses
DC7	1	1.00	1	7.7% of thirteen possible analyses
DC8	2	1.00	18	23.1% of seventy-eight possible analyses
DC9	1	1.00	8	61.5% of thirteen possible analyses
DC10	1	1.00	5	38.5% of thirteen possible analyses
DC11	1	1.00	5	38.5% of thirteen possible analyses
DC12	1	1.00	11	84.6% of thirteen possible analyses
DC13	1	1.00	10	76.9% of thirteen possible analyses
DC14	2	1.00	3	3.8% of seventy-eight possible analyses
DC15	2	1.00	3	3.8% of seventy-eight possible analyses
DC16	2	1.00	3	3.8% of seventy-eight possible analyses
DC17	2	1.00	3	3.8% of seventy-eight possible analyses
DC18	1	1.00	10	76.9% of thirteen possible analyses
DC19	1	1.00	4	30.8% of thirteen possible analyses
DC20	1	1.00	3	23.1% of thirteen possible analyses
DC21	1	1.00	5	38.5% of thirteen possible analyses
DC22	1	1.00	1	7.7% of thirteen possible analyses
DC23	1	1.00	1	7.7% of thirteen possible analyses
DC24	1	1.00	6	46.2% of thirteen possible analyses
DC25	2	1.00	11	14.1% of seventy-eight possible analyses
DC26	1	1.00	3	23.1% of thirteen possible analyses
DC27	1	1.00	4	30.8% of thirteen possible analyses
DC28	1	1.00	5	38.5% of thirteen possible analyses
DC29	1	1.00	5	38.5% of thirteen possible analyses

Table 5.4. (*cont.*)

Declension	Optimal principal-part number *n*	Cell predictor number	Number *p* of optimal dynamic analyses	Ratio of *p* to the number of possible principal-part sets of cardinality *n*
DC30M	1	1.00	4	30.8% of thirteen possible analyses
DC31M	1	1.00	4	30.8% of thirteen possible analyses
DC32	1	1.00	4	30.8% of thirteen possible analyses
DC33M	1	1.00	3	23.1% of thirteen possible analyses
DC34	1	1.00	3	23.1% of thirteen possible analyses
DC35	1	1.00	4	30.8% of thirteen possible analyses
DC36	1	1.00	4	30.8% of thirteen possible analyses
DC37	1	1.00	6	46.2% of thirteen possible analyses
DC38	1	1.00	6	46.2% of thirteen possible analyses

Table 5.1 have alternative analyses that yield different cell predictor numbers; for the remaining declensions, the large majority, every analysis has a cell predictor number of 1.

5.2.3 Alternative analyses for ICs in the Sanskrit plat

As Table 5.4 shows, the declension classes in the Sanskrit plat vary in the number of optimal dynamic principal-part analyses they afford: some only have one; most have multiple analyses, nineteen being the maximum (for DC6).

5.2.4 IC predictability and cell predictability in the Sanskrit plat

Applying these two measures to the hearer-oriented plat in Table 5.1, we obtain the results in Table 5.5. As these figures show, Sanskrit declensional paradigms and their individual cells vary widely in their predictability. For instance, DC1 has a much higher IC predictability than DC5; this disparity recalls the observation in Table 5.3 that DC1 requires only a single dynamic principal part but that DC5 requires two. The average cell predictability in the Sanskrit declensional plat is 0.903. The average cell predictability of six distillations is shaded in Table 5.5: the cells realizing these six distillations have an average cell predictability that is below the overall average of 0.903, and these cells all emerge as principal parts in some or all of the optimal static analyses in Table 5.2 – the nominative singular, vocative singular, accusative singular, nominative/vocative/accusative dual, nominative/vocative plural, and accusative plural cells. These are therefore canonical as principal parts insofar as they are in general the least

Table 5.5. Cell predictability and IC predictability of the declensions in the hearer-oriented declensional plat

Declension class	Cell predictability																	Average	IC predictability
	Singular						Dual				Plural								
	N	V	A	I	D	L	NVA	IDAb	GL	NV	A	I	G						
DC1	0.668	0.979	0.977	0.977	0.977	0.977	0.666	0.996	0.996	0.676	0.666	0.977	0.996					0.887	0.758
DC2	0.660	0.980	0.971	0.971	0.971	0.971	0.670	0.990	0.990	0.668	0.668	0.971	0.990					0.882	0.753
DC3	0.969	0.969	0.967	0.967	0.967	0.967	0.977	0.996	0.996	0.977	0.967	0.967	0.996					0.976	0.976
DC4	0.975	0.975	0.974	0.292	0.974	0.975	0.974	0.991	0.976	0.974	0.282	0.991	0.986					0.872	0.478
DC5	0.970	0.970	0.969	0.292	0.969	0.970	0.969	0.976	0.986	0.969	0.292	0.976	0.991					0.869	0.475
DC6	0.916	0.282	0.916	0.987	0.977	0.977	0.916	0.995	0.977	0.916	0.916	0.995	0.292					0.851	0.477
DC7	0.976	0.975	0.975	0.292	0.975	0.976	0.975	0.992	0.977	0.975	0.282	0.992	0.996					0.874	0.478
DC8	0.971	0.970	0.970	0.292	0.970	0.971	0.970	0.977	0.987	0.970	0.292	0.977	0.996					0.870	0.475
DC9	0.977	0.980	0.977	0.987	0.977	0.977	0.977	0.995	0.977	0.977	0.977	0.995	0.999					0.983	0.984
DC10	0.974	0.975	0.972	0.987	0.972	0.972	0.972	0.976	0.990	0.972	0.987	0.976	0.994					0.978	0.980
DC11	0.977	0.971	0.969	0.984	0.969	0.969	0.969	0.977	0.986	0.969	0.984	0.977	0.990					0.976	0.977
DC12	0.995	0.995	0.995	0.995	0.995	0.995	0.995	0.999	0.995	0.995	0.995	0.999	0.995					0.996	0.996
DC13	0.999	0.990	0.990	0.990	0.990	0.990	0.990	0.999	0.990	0.990	0.990	0.999	0.990					0.992	0.993
DC14	0.990	0.989	0.514	0.989	0.989	0.989	0.514	0.997	0.989	0.514	0.000	0.997	0.997					0.805	0.155
DC15	0.990	0.989	0.514	0.989	0.989	0.989	0.514	0.997	0.989	0.514	0.000	0.997	0.997					0.805	0.155
DC16	0.990	0.989	0.514	0.989	0.989	0.989	0.514	0.997	0.989	0.514	0.000	0.997	0.997					0.805	0.155
DC17	0.990	0.989	0.514	0.989	0.989	0.989	0.514	0.997	0.989	0.514	0.000	0.997	0.997					0.805	0.155
DC18	0.990	0.990	0.990	0.990	0.990	0.990	0.990	0.999	0.990	0.990	0.990	0.999	0.999					0.992	0.993
DC19	0.874	0.874	0.873	0.996	0.996	0.996	0.873	0.996	0.996	0.873	0.873	0.996	0.996					0.939	0.908
DC20	0.866	0.875	0.866	0.990	0.990	0.990	0.866	0.990	0.990	0.874	0.874	0.990	0.990					0.935	0.903
DC21	0.875	0.874	0.874	0.994	0.989	0.989	0.874	0.997	0.989	0.874	0.874	0.997	0.927					0.933	0.909

Table 5.5. (cont.)

Declension class	Cell predictability															IC predictability
	Singular						Dual				Plural				Average	
	N	V	A	I	D	L	NVA	IDAb	GL	NV	A	I	G			
DC22	0.875	0.239	0.875	0.995	0.990	0.990	0.875	0.999	0.990	0.875	0.875	0.999	0.292	0.836		0.447
DC23	0.000	0.875	0.874	0.997	0.997	0.997	0.874	0.997	0.997	0.874	0.874	0.997	0.997	0.873		0.274
DC24	0.875	0.875	0.875	0.999	0.999	0.999	0.875	0.999	0.999	0.875	0.875	0.999	0.999	0.942		0.909
DC25	0.000	0.875	0.872	0.995	0.995	0.995	0.872	0.995	0.995	0.872	0.872	0.995	0.995	0.871		0.272
DC26	0.793	0.795	0.791	0.995	0.995	0.995	0.791	0.995	0.995	0.791	0.872	0.995	0.995	0.907		0.848
DC27	0.795	0.874	0.793	0.997	0.997	0.997	0.793	0.997	0.997	0.793	0.793	0.997	0.997	0.910		0.850
DC28	0.843	0.843	0.843	0.999	0.999	0.999	0.843	0.928	0.999	0.843	0.875	0.928	0.999	0.918		0.886
DC29	0.843	0.843	0.843	0.999	0.999	0.999	0.875	0.928	0.999	0.843	0.843	0.928	0.999	0.918		0.886
DC30	0.714	0.795	0.714	0.999	0.999	0.999	0.714	0.999	0.999	0.714	0.795	0.999	0.999	0.880		0.792
DC31	0.999	0.997	0.678	0.997	0.997	0.997	0.678	0.997	0.997	0.678	0.678	0.997	0.997	0.899		0.766
DC32	0.999	0.997	0.678	0.997	0.997	0.997	0.678	0.997	0.997	0.678	0.678	0.997	0.997	0.899		0.766
DC33	0.928	0.927	0.645	0.997	0.997	0.997	0.645	0.927	0.997	0.645	0.678	0.927	0.997	0.870		0.742
DC34	0.928	0.927	0.645	0.997	0.997	0.997	0.678	0.927	0.997	0.645	0.645	0.927	0.997	0.870		0.742
DC35	0.999	0.999	0.678	0.999	0.999	0.999	0.678	0.999	0.999	0.678	0.678	0.999	0.999	0.900		0.766
DC36	0.999	0.999	0.678	0.999	0.999	0.999	0.678	0.999	0.999	0.678	0.678	0.999	0.999	0.900		0.766
DC37	0.875	0.875	0.875	0.999	0.999	0.999	0.875	0.999	0.999	0.875	0.875	0.999	0.999	0.942		0.909
DC38	0.875	0.875	0.875	0.999	0.999	0.999	0.875	0.999	0.999	0.875	0.875	0.999	0.999	0.942		0.909
Average	0.867	0.900	0.829	0.918	0.988	0.988	0.815	0.987	0.992	0.814	0.694	0.985	0.957	0.903		0.702

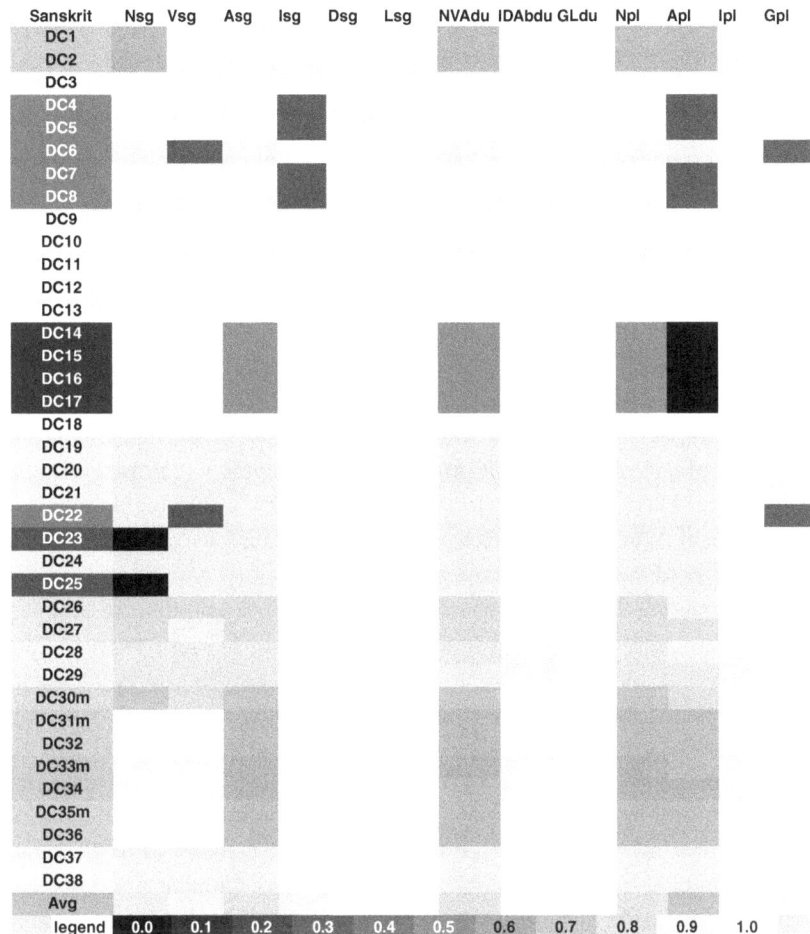

Figure 5.1. *IC and cell predictability for the unenhanced plat of Sanskrit declensions (distillations are on the horizontal axis, ICs on the vertical axis; lighter shade represents higher predictability)*

predictable cells in a Sanskrit nominal paradigm. As the dark-outlined boxes in Table 5.5 show, the nominative singular and accusative plural cells are unpredictable in certain declensions, for which they must be principal parts.

The results in Table 5.5 can be seen more transparently in Figure 5.1, where declensions are listed on the vertical axis and distillations are listed on the horizontal axis. The shading of the declension numbers on the left side of the figure indicates IC predictability, and the shading under a given property set indicates its cell predictability in each declension; in each case, the darker the shading, the lower the predictability.

5.2.5 Cell predictiveness

We now propose an additional measure of IC complexity, that of cell predictiveness. Within a realized paradigm, the **predictiveness** of a given cell s is the fraction of non-s cells that are fully determined by s. For example, the PPA represents the predictiveness of the nominative singular cell in each declension as in Table 5.6, where the appearance of 1 in a column headed by a distillation σ means that a realized paradigm's nominative singular cell suffices to determine its σ-cell, and 0 means that it does not suffice: in some declensions (e.g. DC1), the nominative singular cell is not a **predictor** of any other cell; in other declensions (e.g. DC36), the nominative singular cell is a predictor of some cells but not others; and in still others (e.g. DC2), it is a predictor of every other cell. (In this last case, we say that the nominative singular cell is an **IC identifier**, that is, it unambiguously reveals the IC membership of the lexeme it expresses.)[3]

By computing the predictiveness of each cell in a paradigm from each IC, we arrive at the predictiveness averages in Table 5.7. On average, the most predictive cells (shaded in Table 5.7) are the accusative singular, the nominative/vocative/accusative dual, the nominative/vocative plural and the accusative plural, each of which emerges as a principal part in some or all of the static analyses given earlier in Table 5.2; these are therefore fully canonical as principal parts, since they are both low in predictability (indeed, they are on average the least predictable cells in Table 5.5) and high in predictiveness. By contrast, the nominative singular and vocative singular are not fully canonical as principal parts: though low in predictability, they are not especially predictive. The genitive plural, which emerges as a principal part in half of the static analyses in Table 5.2, is the least canonical principal part in those analyses: it is quite predictable and not very predictive.

Up to now, our focus has been on the hearer-oriented declensional plat. We now turn to speaker-oriented plats, supplementing the purely phonological distinguishers in Table 5.1 with grammatical information whose effect is to reduce the IC complexity of the Sanskrit declensions.

---

[3] IC identifiers are what Carstairs-McCarthy (1994) terms 'class identifiers'.

Table 5.6. *Predictiveness of the nominative singular cell in the hearer-oriented declensional plat*

Declension class	Distillations													Predictiveness of Nsg cell
	Singular					Dual			Plural				
	N	V	A	I	D	L	NVA	IDAb	GL	NV	A	I	G	
DC1	X	0	0	0	0	0	0	0	0	0	0	0	0	0.000
DC2	X	1	1	1	1	1	1	1	1	1	1	1	1	1.000
DC3	X	0	0	0	0	0	0	0	0	0	0	0	0	0.000
DC4	X	0	0	0	0	0	0	0	0	0	0	0	0	0.000
DC5	X	0	0	0	0	0	0	0	0	0	0	0	0	0.000
DC6	X	0	1	1	1	1	1	1	1	1	1	1	0	0.833
DC7	X	0	0	0	0	0	0	0	0	0	0	0	0	0.000
DC8	X	0	0	0	0	0	0	0	0	0	0	0	0	0.000
DC9	X	1	1	1	1	1	1	1	1	1	1	1	1	1.000
DC10	X	0	0	0	0	0	0	0	0	0	0	0	0	0.000
DC11	X	0	0	0	0	0	0	1	0	0	0	1	0	0.167
DC12	X	1	1	1	1	1	1	1	1	1	1	1	1	1.000
DC13	X	0	0	0	0	0	0	1	0	0	0	1	0	0.167
DC14	X	0	0	0	0	0	0	0	0	0	0	0	0	0.000
DC15	X	0	0	0	0	0	0	0	0	0	0	0	0	0.000
DC16	X	0	0	0	0	0	0	0	0	0	0	0	0	0.000
DC17	X	0	0	0	0	0	0	0	0	0	0	0	0	0.000
DC18	X	1	1	1	1	1	1	1	1	1	1	1	1	1.000
DC19	X	0	0	0	0	0	0	0	0	0	0	0	0	0.000
DC20	X	1	1	1	1	1	1	1	1	1	1	1	1	1.000
DC21	X	0	0	0	0	0	0	0	0	0	0	0	0	0.000
DC22	X	0	1	1	1	1	1	1	1	1	1	1	0	0.833
DC23	X	1	1	1	1	1	1	1	1	1	1	1	1	1.000
DC24	X	1	1	1	1	1	1	1	1	1	1	1	1	1.000
DC25	X	1	0	0	0	0	0	0	0	0	0	0	0	0.083
DC26	X	1	0	0	0	0	0	0	0	0	0	0	0	0.083
DC27	X	0	0	0	0	0	0	0	0	0	0	0	0	0.000
DC28	X	1	1	1	1	1	1	1	1	1	1	1	1	1.000
DC29	X	1	1	1	1	1	1	1	1	1	1	1	1	1.000
DC30	X	1	1	1	1	1	1	1	1	1	1	1	1	1.000
DC31	X	0	0	0	0	0	0	0	0	0	0	0	0	0.000
DC32	X	0	0	0	0	0	0	0	0	0	0	0	0	0.000
DC33	X	0	0	0	0	0	0	0	0	0	0	0	0	0.000
DC34	X	0	0	0	0	0	0	0	0	0	0	0	0	0.000
DC35	X	1	0	1	1	1	0	1	1	0	0	1	1	0.667
DC36	X	1	0	1	1	1	0	1	1	0	0	1	1	0.667
DC37	X	1	1	1	1	1	1	1	1	1	1	1	1	1.000
DC38	X	1	1	1	1	1	1	1	1	1	1	1	1	1.000
Average														0.408

132 *Grammatically enhanced plats*

Table 5.7. *Average predictiveness of distillations in the hearer-oriented declensional plat*

Singular						Dual			Plural			
N	V	A	I	D	L	NVA	IDAb	GL	NV	A	I	G
0.408	0.522	0.943	0.504	0.647	0.559	0.890	0.336	0.471	0.877	0.785	0.384	0.351

5.3 Grammatical disambiguation of distinguishers in the Sanskrit declensional plat

We can now enhance the distinguishers in Table 5.1 by introducing two sorts of information: (i) specifications of gender and (ii) demarcations of the boundary between a word form's stem and its affix. The inclusion of this information effectively converts the hearer-oriented plat in Table 5.1 into a speaker-oriented plat.

To understand the way in which we enhance the plat, consider first the realized paradigm of the Sanskrit noun AŚVA 'horse'. In its unenhanced form, this paradigm is as in Table 5.8a; in its most fully enhanced form, it is as in part (b) of the table. In both parts of the table, the paradigm's distinguishers are given in bold italics; these are the exponences of masculine *a*-stem nouns in Sanskrit. Unlike its unenhanced counterpart, the enhanced paradigm in Table 5.8b specifies the masculine gender of AŚVA by including *M* as part of each distinguisher; in addition, it uses '+' to demarcate the boundary of stem and affix within each distinguisher. Two sorts of complication arise in demarcating the boundary between a word form's stem and its affix: (i) a word may lack any inflectional affix, and (ii) morphological fusion may obscure this boundary. In Table 5.8b, we address these complications by (i) allowing a word to be equated with its stem, as in the case of vocative singular *aśva+M*; and (ii) identifying instances of stem-affix fusion by the omission of '+', as in locative singular *aśveM*, in which *e* represents the combination of stem-final *a* with suffix -*i* by a well-motivated rule of sandhi. Similar instances of fusion arise in the instrumental singular (also involving *e*), the dative and ablative singular (where *ā* represents the fusion of a stem-final *a* with a suffix-initial *ā*) and the instrumental plural (where *ai* represents the fusion of a stem-final *a* with a suffix-initial *ai*). Our analysis does assume stem alternations before affixes that are observed in several declensions, e.g. the alternants *aśv-* and *aśvā-* before the affixes -*au* and -*bhyām*.

It is reasonable to suppose that the addition of this information about gender and stem boundaries to the Sanskrit plat will diminish its IC complexity. Moreover, it is likely that information of these two different sorts will diminish its complexity in different ways. To test that possibility, we constructed three new plats: a fully

Table 5.8. *Unenhanced and fully enhanced versions of the realized paradigm of Sanskrit* AŚVA *'horse'* (*declension* **DC1**; *stem* aśva-; *theme* aśv-; *distinguishers in bold italics*)

		N	V	A	I	D	Ab	G	L
(a) Unenhanced	Sg	aśvas	aśva	aśvam	aśvena	aśvāya	aśvāt	aśvasya	aśve
	Du	aśvau	aśvau	aśvau	aśvābhyām	aśvābhyām	aśvābhyām	aśvayos	aśvayos
	Pl	aśvās	aśvās	aśvān	aśvais	aśvebhyas	aśvebhyas	aśvānām	aśveṣu
(b) Fully enhanced	Sg	aśva+s**M**	aśva+**M**	aśva+m**M**	aśvena**M**	aśvāya**M**	aśvāt**M**	aśva+sya**M**	aśve**M**
	Du	aśv+au**M**	aśv+au**M**	aśv+au**M**	aśvā+bhyām**M**	aśvā+bhyām**M**	aśvā+bhyām**M**	aśvay+os**M**	aśvay+os**M**
	Pl	aśvā+s**M**	aśvā+s**M**	aśvā+n**M**	aśvais**M**	aśve+bhyas**M**	aśve+bhyas**M**	aśvān+ām**M**	aśve+ṣu**M**

134 *Grammatically enhanced plats*

Table 5.9. *The declension of* MANAS *'mind' (declension* DC27; *stem* manas-; *theme* man; *distinguishers in bold italics*)

	N	V	A	I	D	Ab	G	L
Sg	man*as*	man*as*	man*as*	man*asā*	man*ase*	man*asas*	man*asas*	man*asi*
Du	man*asī*	man*asī*	man*asī*	man*obhyām*	man*obhyām*	man*obhyām*	man*asos*	man*asos*
Pl	man*āṃsi*	man*āṃsi*	man*āṃsi*	man*obhis*	man*obhyas*	man*obhyas*	man*asām*	mana*ḥsu*

enhanced, speaker-oriented plat, a plat enhanced only by the inclusion of gender information, and a plat enhanced only by the demarcation of stems.

5.3.1 Disambiguation by means of gender information

In Sanskrit, enhancing a principal part with a gender specification can elevate it from a nonpredictor to a predictor of one or more cells or indeed from a nonidentifier to an IC identifier. Consider, first, a nominative singular nominal having a theme X and the distinguisher *as*. This word form could belong to the same declension as AŚVA 'horse' (Nsg *aśvas*; full paradigm Table 5.8a) or to the same declension as MANAS 'mind' (Nsg *manas*; full paradigm Table 5.9). Thus, as a principal part, ⟨X*as*, {nom sg}⟩ is not an identifier because it fails to distinguish members of the AŚVA declension from members of the MANAS declension. But it becomes an IC identifier if its gender is specified. On the one hand, members of the AŚVA declension are, without exception, masculine; by contrast, members of the MANAS declension are, without exception, neuter. Thus, if ⟨X*asM*, {nom sg}⟩ (where M = masculine) is a principal part, then it is an IC identifier of the AŚVA declension. In this case, the gender specification disambiguates the unadorned principal part ⟨X*as*, {nom sg}⟩, allowing each of the other cells in its realized paradigm to be deduced, as in Table 5.10.

In many cases, however, a gender specification fails to produce an identifier. Consider a vocative singular nominal having a theme X and the distinguisher *a*. This word form could belong to the declension of AŚVA 'horse' (DC1, Vsg *aśva*; full paradigm Table 5.8a), that of DĀNA 'gift' (DC2, Vsg *dāna*; full paradigm Table 5.11), or that of NĀMAN 'name' (DC20, Vsg *nāma*; full paradigm Table 5.12). With the principal part ⟨X*aN*, {voc sg}⟩ specified as neuter, this ambiguity is only partly resolved. This gender specification excludes the possibility that X*a* belongs to the AŚVA declension, but it fails to determine whether X*a* belongs to the DĀNA declension or the NĀMAN declension, which both consist of neuter nominals. Even so, the addition of the neuter gender specification does convert ⟨X*aN*, {voc sg}⟩ into a predictor of its paradigm's nominative, vocative, and accusative plural

Table 5.10. *Disambiguation of the principal part ⟨Xas, {nom sg}⟩*

Grammatical information	Declension class	Morphosyntactic property sets and their distinguishers																	
		Singular								Dual				Plural				
		N	V	A	I	D	Ab	G	L	NVA	IDAb	GL	NV	A	I	DAb	G	L
(i) none	DC1	as	a	am	ena	āya	āt	asya	e	au	ābhyām	ayos	ās	ān	ais	ebhyas	ānām	eṣu
	DC27	as	as	as	asā	ase	asas	asas	asi	asī	obhyām	asos	āṃsi	āṃsi	obhis	obhyas	asām	ahsu
(ii) gender	DC1	asM	aM	amM	enaM	āyaM	ātM	asyaM	eM	auM	ābhyāmM	ayosM	āsM	ānM	aisM	ebhyasM	ānāmM	eṣuM
	DC27	asN	asN	asN	asāN	aseN	asasN	asasN	asiN	asiN	obhyāmN	asosN	āṃsiN	āṃsiN	obhisN	obhyasN	asāmN	ahsuN

In (i), the principal part ⟨Xas, {nom sg}⟩ belongs to either **DC1** or **DC27**, but is not an identifier for either of these, nor is it a predictor of any of the shaded exponences.

In (ii), the principal part ⟨XasM, {nom sg}⟩ is an identifier of **DC1**.

136 *Grammatically enhanced plats*

Table 5.11. *The declension of* DĀNA *'gift' (declension* **DC2**; *stem* dāna-; *theme* dān; *distinguishers in bold italics)*

	N	V	A	I	D	Ab	G	L
Sg	dān*am*	dān*a*	dān*am*	dān*ena*	dān*āya*	dān*āt*	dān*asya*	dān*e*
Du	dān*e*	dān*e*	dān*e*	dān*ābhyām*	dān*ābhyām*	dān*ābhyām*	dān*ayos*	dān*ayos*
Pl	dān*āni*	dān*āni*	dān*āni*	dān*ais*	dān*ebhyas*	dān*ebhyas*	dān*ānām*	dān*eṣu*

Table 5.12. *The declension of* NĀMAN *'name' (declension* **DC20**; *stem* nāman-; *theme* nām; *distinguishers in bold italics)*

	N	V	A	I	D	Ab	G	L
Sg	nām*a*	nām*a*[1]	nām*a*	nām*nā*	nām*nas*	nām*ne*	nām*nas*	nām*ni*[2]
Du	nām*nī*[3]	nām*nī*[3]	nām*nī*[3]	nām*abhyām*	nām*abhyām*	nām*abhyām*	nām*nos*	nām*nos*
Pl	nām*āni*	nām*āni*	nām*āni*	nām*abhis*	nām*abhyas*	nām*abhyas*	nām*nām*	nām*asu*

[1] Also nām*an*.
[2] Also nām*ani*.
[3] Also nām*anī*.

cells, since these are alike in the DĀNA and NĀMAN declensions. These facts are schematized in Table 5.13.

As these examples show, a gender specification may disambiguate a principal part either by making it an IC identifier or by making it a cell predictor. But gender specifications do not always have this strong an effect. Consider now a nominative singular word form having a theme X and the distinguisher ā. This word form may belong to any of the six declension classes listed in Table 5.14. With the principal part ⟨XāM, {nom sg}⟩ specified as masculine, the choice of possible declension classes is limited to three, but this principal part is neither an identifier nor a predictor, as Table 5.14 shows.

The idea of including gender in the specification of a principal part may strike some as questionable, given that in many languages, a noun's gender may be determined by its declension-class membership; see Corbett (1991). But a language user might in any event employ the gender of a known nominal lexeme as a factor in deducing that lexeme's realized paradigm from its principal parts.

Table 5.13. *Disambiguation of the principal part* ⟨Xa, {voc sg}⟩

Morphosyntactic property sets and their distinguishers

Grammatical information	Declension class	Singular							Dual			Plural					
		N	V	A	I	D	Ab	G	L	NVA	IDAb	GL	NV	A	I	DAb	G	L
(i) none	DC1	as	a	am	ena	āya	āt	asya	e	au	ābhyām	ayos	ās	ān	ais	ebhyas	ānām	eṣu
	DC2	am	a	am	ena	āya	āt	asya	e	e	ābhyām	ayos	āni	āni	ais	ebhyas	ānām	eṣu
	DC20	a	a	a	nā	ne	nas	nas	ni	nī	abhyām	nos	āni	āni	abhis	abhyas	nām	asu
(ii) gender	DC1	asM	aM	amM	enaM	āyaM	ātM	asyaM	eM	auM	ābhyāmM	ayosM	āsM	ānM	aisM	ebhyasM	ānāmM	eṣuM
	DC2	amN	aN	amN	enaN	āyaN	ātN	asyaN	eN	eN	ābhyāmN	ayosN	āniN	āniN	aisN	ebhyasN	ānāmN	eṣuN
	DC20	aN	aN	aN	nāN	neN	nasN	nasN	niN	niN	abhyāmN	nosN	āniN	āniN	abhisN	abhyasN	nāmN	asuN

In (i), the principal part ⟨Xa, {voc sg}⟩ belongs to either DC1, DC2 or DC20, but is not an identifier for any of these, nor is it a predictor of any of the shaded exponences.

In (ii), the principal part ⟨XaN, {voc sg}⟩ belongs to either DC2 or DC20, but it is not an identifier for either of these; it is a predictor of the NVpl and Apl exponences but not of any of the shaded exponences.

Table 5.14. *Disambiguation of the principal part $\langle X\bar{a}, \{\text{nom sg}\}\rangle$*

Grammatical information	Declension class	Morphosyntactic property sets and their distinguishers																
		Singular								Dual						Plural					
		N	V	A	I	D	Ab	G	L	NVA	IDAb	GL	NV	A	I	DAb	G	L
(i) none	DC3	ā	e	ām	ayā	āyai	āyās	āyās	āyām	e	ābhyām	ayos	ās	ās	ābhis	ābhyas	ānām	āsu
	DC14	ā	ar	aram	rā	re	ur	ur	ari	arau	ṛbhyām	ros	aras	ṝn	ṛbhis	ṛbhyas	ṝṇām	ṛṣu
	DC15	ā	ar	aram	rā	re	ur	ur	ari	arau	ṛbhyām	ros	aras	ṝs	ṛbhis	ṛbhyas	ṝṇām	ṛṣu
	DC16	ā	ar	āram	rā	re	ur	ur	ari	ārau	ṛbhyām	ros	āras	ṝn	ṛbhis	ṛbhyas	ṝṇām	ṛṣu
	DC17	ā	ar	āram	rā	re	ur	ur	ari	ārau	ṛbhyām	ros	āras	ṝs	ṛbhis	ṛbhyas	ṝṇām	ṛṣu
	DC19	ā	an	ānam	nā	ne	nas	nas	ni	ānau	abhyām	nos	ānas	nas	abhis	abhyas	nām	asu
(ii) gender	DC3	āF	eF	āmF	ayāF	āyaiF	āyāsF	āyāsF	āyāmF	eF	ābhyāmF	ayosF	āsF	āsF	ābhisF	ābhyasF	ānāmF	āsuF
	DC14	āM	arM	aramM	rāM	reM	urM	urM	ariM	arauM	ṛbhyāmM	rosM	arasM	ṝnM	ṛbhisM	ṛbhyasM	ṝṇāmM	ṛṣuM
	DC15	āF	arF	aramF	rāF	reF	urF	urF	ariF	arauF	ṛbhyāmF	rosF	arasF	ṝsF	ṛbhisF	ṛbhyasF	ṝṇāmF	ṛṣuF
	DC16	āM	arM	āramM	rāM	reM	urM	urM	ariM	ārauM	ṛbhyāmM	rosM	ārasM	ṝnM	ṛbhisM	ṛbhyasM	ṝṇāmM	ṛṣuM
	DC17	āF	arF	āramF	rāF	reF	urF	urF	ariF	ārauF	ṛbhyāmF	rosF	ārasF	ṝsF	ṛbhisF	ṛbhyasF	ṝṇāmF	ṛṣuF
	DC19	āM	anM	ānamM	nāM	neM	nasM	nasM	niM	ānauM	abhyāmM	nosM	ānasM	nasM	abhisM	abhyasM	nāmM	asuM

In (i), the principal part $\langle X\bar{a}, \{\text{nom sg}\}\rangle$ belongs to either **DC3**, **DC14**, **DC15**, **DC16**, **DC17** or **DC19**, but it is not an identifier for any of these, nor is it a predictor for any of the shaded exponences.

In (ii), the principal part $\langle X\bar{a}M, \{\text{nom sg}\}\rangle$ belongs to either **DC14**, **DC16** or **DC19**, but it is not an identifier for any of these, nor is it a predictor for any of the shaded exponences.

5.3.2   Disambiguation by means of stem demarcation

Specifying gender is one way to disambiguate an ambiguous principal part. Another way is to specify the stem on which the principal part is based. Morphologically, the nominative singular form *aśvas* consists of the stem *aśva-* followed by the suffix *-s*; thus, the distinguisher *as* of the nominative singular form *aśvas* might be represented morphologically as *a+s*, since it consists of a stem-final vowel plus a consonantal suffix. By contrast, the nominative singular form *manas* consists of the stem *manas-* and no suffix at all; thus, the distinguisher *as* of the nominative singular form *manas* might be represented morphologically as *as+*, since it consists of a stem-final vowel-consonant sequence. Accordingly, if the cell ⟨X*as*, {nom sg}⟩ is instead represented as ⟨X*a+s*, {nom sg}⟩, then it becomes an identifier of the AŚVA declension. Thus, stem demarcation and gender specification do an equally good job of disambiguating the principal part ⟨X*as*, {nom sg}⟩, as Table 5.15 shows. In other cases, however, gender specification does a better job; and in still others, stem demarcation does a better job. Consider an example of each of these latter two sorts.

A nominative singular form consisting of a theme X and the distinguisher *ī* is ambiguous. On the one hand, this word form could belong to the same declension as NADĪ 'river' (**DC10**, Nsg *nadī*; full paradigm Table 5.16) or to the same declension as the masculine forms of the adjective BALIN 'strong' (**DC21**, masculine Nsg *balī*; full masculine paradigm Table 5.17). Thus, the principal part ⟨X*ī*, {nom sg}⟩ fails to distinguish members of the NADĪ declension from members of the masculine declension of BALIN. Specifying the stem of X*ī* does not eliminate this ambiguity, since the *ī* is stem-final in both of the nominative singular forms *nadī* and *balī*. But the paradigm in Table 5.17 is restricted to masculine nominals; thus, if the gender of the nominative singular form X*ī* is specified as feminine, then it becomes an identifier of the NADĪ declension **DC10**. In this case, a gender specification disambiguates an ambiguous principal part, but a stem demarcation does not; this difference is schematized in Table 5.18.

But now consider a nominative singular nominal having a theme X and the distinguisher *is*. This word could belong to the same declension as ALI 'bee' (**DC4**, Nsg *alis*; full paradigm Table 5.19), to that of MATI 'intellect' (**DC5**, Nsg *matis*; full paradigm Table 5.20) or to those of ŚUKRAŚOCIS 'brilliant' (**DC31**, **DC32**, Nsg *śukraśocis* in all three genders; full paradigm Table 5.21). Thus, the principal part ⟨X*is*, {nom sg}⟩ fails to distinguish members of the ALI declension from members of either the MATI declension or the ŚUKRAŚOCIS declensions. If the gender of the principal part X*is* is specified as masculine, a

Table 5.15. *Disambiguation of the principal part* ⟨*Xas*, {nom sg}⟩

Grammatical information		Declension class	Morphosyntactic property sets and their distinguishers																			
			Singular								Dual					Plural						
			N	V	A	I	D	Ab	G	L	NVA	IDAb	GL	NV	A	I	DAb	G	L			
(i)		DC1	as	a	am	ena	āya	āt	asya	e	au	ābhyām	ayos	ās	ān	ais	ebhyas	ānām	eṣu			
none		DC27	as	as	as	asā	ase	asas	asas	asi	asī	obhyām	asos	āṃsi	āṃsi	obhis	obhyas	asām	ahsu			
(ii)		DC1	asM	aM	amM	enaM	āyaM	ātM	asyaM	eM	auM	ābhyāmM	ayosM	āsM	ānM	aisM	ebhyasM	ānāmM	eṣuM			
gender		DC27	asN	asN	asN	asāN	aseN	asasN	asasN	asiN	asiN	obhyāmN	asosN	āṃsiN	āṃsiN	obhisN	obhyasN	asāmN	ahsuN			
(iii)		DC1	a+s	a+	a+m	ena	āya	āt	a+sya	e	+au	ā+bhyām	ay+os	ā+s	ā+n	ais	e+bhyas	ān+ām	e+ṣu			
stem		DC27	as+	as+	as+	as+ā	as+e	as+as	as+as	as+i	as+ī	o+bhyām	as+os	āṃs+i	āṃs+i	o+bhis	o+bhyas	as+ām	ah+su			
(iv)		DC1	a+sM	a+M	a+mM	enaM	āyaM	ātM	a+syaM	eM	+auM	ā+bhyāmM	ay+osM	ā+sM	ā+nM	aisM	e+bhyasM	ān+āmM	e+ṣuM			
both		DC27	as+N	as+N	as+N	as+āN	as+eN	as+asN	as+asN	as+iN	as+iN	o+bhyāmN	as+osN	āṃs+iN	āṃs+iN	o+bhisN	o+bhyasN	as+āmN	ah+suN			

In (i), the principal part ⟨*Xas*, {nom sg}⟩ belongs to either DC1 or DC27 but is not an identifier of either, nor is it a predictor of any of the shaded exponences.
In (ii), the principal part ⟨*XasM*, {nom sg}⟩ is an identifier for DC1.
In (iii), the principal part ⟨*Xa+s*, {nom sg}⟩ is an identifier for DC1.
In (iv), the principal part ⟨*Xa+sM*, {nom sg}⟩ is an identifier for DC1.

Grammatical disambiguation of distinguishers in Sanskrit   141

Table 5.16. *The declension of* NADĪ *'river' (declension* **DC10**; *stem* nadī-; *theme* nad; *distinguishers in bold italics)*

	N	V	A	I	D	Ab	G	L
Sg	nad*ī*	nad*i*	nad*īm*	nad*yā*	nad*yai*	nad*yās*	nad*yās*	nad*yām*
Du	nad*yau*	nad*yau*	nad*yau*	nad*ībhyām*	nad*ībhyām*	nad*ībhyām*	nad*yos*	nad*yos*
Pl	nad*yas*	nad*yas*	nad*īs*	nad*ībhis*	nad*ībhyas*	nad*ībhyas*	nad*īnām*	nad*īṣu*

Table 5.17. *The masculine declension of* BALIN *'strong' (declension* **DC21**; *stem* balin-; *theme* bal; *distinguishers in bold italics)*

	N	V	A	I	D	Ab	G	L
Sg	bal*ī*	bal*in*	bal*inam*	bal*inā*	bal*ine*	bal*inas*	bal*inas*	bal*ini*
Du	bal*inau*	bal*inau*	bal*inau*	bal*ibhyām*	bal*ibhyām*	bal*ibhyām*	bal*inos*	bal*inos*
Pl	bal*inas*	bal*inas*	bal*inas*	bal*ibhis*	bal*ibhyas*	bal*ibhyas*	bal*inām*	bal*iṣu*

large measure of ambiguity remains: as a masculine principal part, ⟨X*is*M, {nom sg}⟩ could still belong either to the ALI declension or to the masculine declension of ŚUKRAŚOCIS; because these declensions differ inflectionally except in the nominative singular, ⟨X*is*M, {nom sg}⟩ would, by itself, be neither an identifier nor a predictor. Suppose now, on the other hand, that the gender of the nominative singular principal part is unspecified but that its stem is specified as ending in *i*: ⟨X*i*+*s*, {nom sg}⟩. This principal part cannot belong to the ŚUKRAŚOCIS declensions (which involve a stem in *is*) but may belong to either the ALI declension or the MATI declension; yet, because the latter declensions are very often alike in their inflection, this principal part, though not an identifier, is nevertheless a predictor of most of the cells in its paradigm. Thus, in this case, a stem demarcation is more informative than a gender specification, as Table 5.22 shows.

To facilitate our investigation of the effects of enhancing an IC's principal parts, we modify the declensional distinguishers in Table 5.1 as in Table 5.23. Because certain ICs contain both masculines and feminines (specifically **CD30**, **CD31**, **CD33**, and **CD35**), we must now subdivide each of them into a masculine subclass and a feminine subclass, the former expressed by masculine distinguishers, the latter by feminine distinguishers.

Table 5.18. *Disambiguation of the principal part ⟨Xī, {nom sg}⟩*

					Morphosyntactic property sets and their distinguishers													
			Singular							Dual			Plural					
Grammatical information	Declension class	N	V	A	I	D	Ab	G	L	NVA	IDAb	GL	NV	A	I	DAb	G	L
(i) none	DC10	ī	i	īm	yā	yai	yās	yās	yām	yau	ībhyām	yos	yas	īs	ībhis	ībhyas	īnām	īṣu
	DC21	ī	in	inam	inā	ine	inas	inas	ini	inau	ibhyām	inos	inas	inas	ibhis	ibhyas	inām	iṣu
(ii) gender	DC10	īF	iF	īmF	yāF	yaiF	yāsF	yāsF	yāmF	yauF	ībhyāmF	yosF	yasF	īsF	ībhisF	ībhyasF	īnāmF	īṣuF
	DC21	īM	inM	inamM	ināM	ineM	inasM	inasM	iniM	inauM	ibhyāmM	inosM	inasM	inasM	ibhisM	ibhyasM	ināmM	iṣuM
(iii) stem	DC10	ī+	i+	ī+m	y+ā	y+ai	y+ās	y+ās	y+ām	y+au	ī+bhyām	y+os	y+as	ī+s	ī+bhis	ī+bhyas	ī+ām	ī+ṣu
	DC21	ī+	in+	in+am	in+ā	in+e	in+as	in+as	in+i	in+au	i+bhyām	in+os	in+as	in+as	i+bhis	i+bhyas	in+ām	i+ṣu
(iv) both	DC10	ī+F	i+F	ī+mF	y+āF	y+aiF	y+āsF	y+āsF	y+āmF	y+auF	ī+bhyāmF	y+osF	y+asF	ī+sF	ī+bhisF	ī+bhyasF	ī+āmF	ī+ṣuF
	DC21	ī+M	in+M	in+amM	in+āM	in+eM	in+asM	in+asM	in+iM	in+auM	i+bhyāmM	in+osM	in+asM	in+asM	i+bhisM	i+bhyasM	in+āmM	i+ṣuM

In (i), the principal part ⟨Xī, {nom sg}⟩ belongs to either DC10 or DC21 but is not an identifier of either, nor is it a predictor of any of the shaded exponences.
In (ii), the principal part ⟨XīF, {nom sg}⟩ is an identifier for DC10.
In (iii), the principal part ⟨Xī+, {nom sg}⟩ belongs to either DC10 or DC21 but is not an identifier of either, nor is it a predictor of any of the shaded exponences.
In (iv), the principal part ⟨Xī+F, {nom sg}⟩ is an identifier for DC10.

Table 5.19. *The declension of* ALI *'bee' (declension* **DC4***; stem* ali-*; theme* al*; distinguishers in bold italics)*

	N	V	A	I	D	Ab	G	L
Sg	al*is*	al*e*	al*im*	al*inā*	al*aye*	al*es*	al*es*	al*au*
Du	al*ī*	al*ī*	al*ī*	al*ibhyām*	al*ibhyām*	al*ibhyām*	al*yos*	al*yos*
Pl	al*ayas*	al*ayas*	al*īn*	al*ibhis*	al*ibhyas*	al*ibhyas*	al*īnām*	al*işu*

Table 5.20. *The declension of* MATI *'intellect' (declension* **DC5***; stem* mati-*; theme* mat*; distinguishers in bold italics)*

	N	V	A	I	D	Ab	G	L
Sg	mat*is*	mat*e*	mat*im*	mat*yā*	mat*aye*	mat*es*	mat*es*	mat*au*
Du	mat*ī*	mat*ī*	mat*ī*	mat*ibhyām*	mat*ibhyām*	mat*ibhyām*	mat*yos*	mat*yos*
Pl	mat*ayas*	mat*ayas*	mat*īs*	mat*ibhis*	mat*ibhyas*	mat*ibhyas*	mat*īnām*	mat*işu*

5.4 The effects of enhancing principal parts with gender specifications and/or stem demarcations

We now compare analyses of the four alternative types of plats in (3):

(3) Four types of plats for Sanskrit declensions:
   (a) Unenhanced, hearer-oriented plat (as in Table 5.1)
   (b) Hearer-oriented plat enhanced with stem demarcations
   (c) Hearer-oriented plat enhanced with gender specifications
   (d) Fully enhanced, speaker-oriented plat (as in Table 5.23)

In order to determine the effects of enhancing principal parts with gender specifications and stem demarcations – both separately and together – we compare the different types of plats in (3) with respect to the measures of IC complexity identified in §5.2. One difference emerges at the very outset: if the Sanskrit declensional plat is enhanced with gender specifications, the instrumental/dative/ablative dual and the instrumental plural merge into a single distillation.

5.4.1 Optimal principal-part numbers

Consider first those measures of complexity involving static principal-part analyses; these are presented in Table 5.24. What is especially striking about

Table 5.21. *The declension of* ŚUKRAŚOCIS *'brilliant' (declensions* **DC31**, **DC32**; *stem* śukraśocis-; *theme* śukraśoc-; *distinguishers in bold italics)*

		N	V	A	I	D	Ab	G	L
Sg	Masc, Fem	śukraśocis	śukraśocis	śukraśoci***ṣam***	śukraśociṣā	śukraśociṣe	śukraśociṣas	śukraśociṣas	śukraśociṣi
	Neut			śukraśocis					
Du	Masc, Fem	śukraśociṣau	śukraśociṣau	śukraśociṣau	śukraśocirbhyām	śukraśocirbhyām	śukraśocirbhyām	śukraśociṣos	śukraśociṣos
	Neut	śukraśoci***ṣī***	śukraśoci***ṣī***	śukraśoci***ṣī***					
Pl	Masc, Fem	śukraśociṣas	śukraśociṣas	śukraśociṣas	śukraśocirbhis	śukraśocirbhyas	śukraśocirbhyas	śukraśociṣām	śukraśoci***ḥṣu***
	Neut	śukraśoc***īṃṣi***	śukraśoc***īṃṣi***	śukraśoc***īṃṣi***					

the results in Table 5.24 is how effectively gender simplifies the static principal-part sets for Sanskrit declensions. When principal-part specifications do not include gender, four static principal parts are necessary; when principal-part specifications do include gender, only three are necessary. Moreover, specifying both gender and stem delimitation in principal parts does not produce a simpler static analysis than specifying gender alone, nor does specifying stem delimitation without gender produce a static analysis that is any simpler than that of an unenhanced principal-part specification.

Various additional features of the static analyses in Table 5.24 are noteworthy:

- In an optimal static analysis, a paradigm's nominative singular cell is always a principal part, whether or not principal-part specifications include gender and/or stem delimitation. This fact suggests that on average, a paradigm's nominative singular cell is less predictable and/or more predictive than any other cell in the paradigm.
- In any given optimal analysis, the principal parts always include the pairing of (i) either the vocative singular cell or the genitive plural cell with (ii) one of the three cells in (2), repeated here; this suggests that all such pairings are informative in the same way.

(2) accusative singular cell
     nominative/vocative/accusative dual cell
     nominative/vocative plural cell

- In an optimal analysis, a paradigm's accusative plural cell is a principal part if and only if gender is not part of the principal-part specification. This fact suggests that a paradigm's accusative plural cell reveals its gender better than any other cell.

The results of optimal dynamic principal-part analysis for the four types of plats in (3) are listed in Table 5.25. Here, too, the effects of specifying the gender of principal parts are striking. If gender is specified, every declension but one allows a dynamic principal-part analysis requiring only a single principal part; the exception is **DC25**, the masculine declension of DHĪMAT 'intelligent'. If gender is unspecified, several other declension classes require at least two dynamic principal parts. Specifying stem delimitation without gender reduces the number of such classes to an extent, though not to the extent allowed by specifying gender; moreover, specifying both gender and stem delimitation is no better than specifying gender by itself for minimizing the number of dynamic principal parts in an optimal analysis.

Table 5.22. *Disambiguation of the principal part* $\langle Xis, \{nom\ sg\}\rangle$

Grammatical information	Declension class	Singular									Dual					Plural						
		N	V	A	I	D	Ab	G	L	NVA	IDAb	GL	NV	A	I	DAb	G	L
(i) none	DC4	is	e	im	inā	aye	es	es	au	ī	ibhyām	yos	ayas	īn	ibhis	ibhyas	īnām	iṣu
	DC5	is	e	im	yā	aye	es	es	au	ī	ibhyām	yos	ayas	īs	ibhis	ibhyas	īnām	iṣu
	DC31m	is	is	iṣam	iṣā	iṣe	iṣas	iṣas	iṣi	iṣau	irbhyām	iṣos	iṣas	iṣas	irbhis	irbhyas	iṣām	ihṣu
	DC31f	is	is	iṣam	iṣā	iṣe	iṣas	iṣas	iṣi	iṣau	irbhyām	iṣos	iṣas	iṣas	irbhis	irbhyas	iṣām	ihṣu
	DC32	is	is	is	iṣā	iṣe	iṣas	iṣas	iṣi	iṣī	irbhyām	iṣos	īmṣi	īmṣi	irbhis	irbhyas	iṣām	ihṣu
(ii) gender	DC4	isM	eM	imM	ināM	ayeM	esM	esM	auM	īM	ibhyāmM	yosM	ayasM	īnM	ibhisM	ibhyasM	īnāmM	iṣuM
	DC5	isF	eF	imF	yāF	ayeF	esF	esF	auF	īF	ibhyāmF	yosF	ayasF	īsF	ibhisF	ibhyasF	īnāmF	iṣuF
	DC31m	isM	isM	iṣamM	iṣāM	iṣeM	iṣasM	iṣasM	iṣiM	iṣauM	irbhyāmM	iṣosM	iṣasM	iṣasM	irbhisM	irbhyasM	iṣāmM	ihṣuM
	DC31f	isF	isF	iṣamF	iṣāF	iṣeF	iṣasF	iṣasF	iṣiF	iṣauF	irbhyāmF	iṣosF	iṣasF	iṣasF	irbhisF	irbhyasF	iṣāmF	ihṣuF
	DC32	isN	isN	isN	iṣāN	iṣeN	iṣasN	iṣasN	iṣiN	iṣīN	irbhyāmN	iṣosN	īmṣiN	īmṣiN	irbhisN	irbhyasN	iṣāmN	ihṣuN
(iii) stem	DC4	i+s	e+	i+m	in+ā	ay+e	e+s	e+s	au+	ī+	i+bhyām	y+os	ay+as	ī+n	i+bhis	i+bhyas	īn+ām	i+ṣu
	DC5	i+s	e+	i+m	y+ā	ay+e	e+s	e+s	au+	ī+	i+bhyām	y+os	ay+as	ī+s	i+bhis	i+bhyas	īn+ām	i+ṣu
	DC31m	is+	is+	iṣ+am	iṣ+ā	iṣ+e	iṣ+as	iṣ+as	iṣ+i	iṣ+au	ir+bhyām	iṣ+os	iṣ+as	iṣ+as	ir+bhis	ir+bhyas	iṣ+ām	ih+ṣu
	DC31f	is+	is+	iṣ+am	iṣ+ā	iṣ+e	iṣ+as	iṣ+as	iṣ+i	iṣ+au	ir+bhyām	iṣ+os	iṣ+as	iṣ+as	ir+bhis	ir+bhyas	iṣ+ām	ih+ṣu

Morphosyntactic property sets and their distinguishers

	is+	is+	is+	iṣ+ā	iṣ+e	iṣ+as	iṣ+as	iṣ+i	iṣ+ī	ir+bhyām	iṣ+os	īmṣ+i	ir+bhis	ir+bhyas	iṣ+ām	iḥ+ṣu
(iv) DC32	**i+sM**	e+M	i+mM	in+āM	ay+eM	e+sM	au+M	i+M		i+bhyāmM	y+osM	ay+asM	ī+nM	i+bhisM	i+bhyasM	īn+āmM	i+ṣuM
both DC4	i+sF	e+F	i+mF	y+āF	ay+eF	e+sF	au+F	ī+F		i+bhyāmF	y+osF	ay+asF	ī+sF	i+bhisF	i+bhyasF	īn+āmF	ī+ṣuF
DC5	is+M	is+M	iṣ+amM	iṣ+āM	iṣ+eM	iṣ+asM	iṣ+iM	iṣ+auM		ir+bhyāmM	iṣ+osM	iṣ+asM	ī+nM	ir+bhisM	ir+bhyasM	iṣ+āmM	iḥ+ṣuM
DC31m	is+F	iṣ+F	iṣ+amF	iṣ+āF	iṣ+eF	iṣ+asF	iṣ+iF	iṣ+auF		ir+bhyāmF	iṣ+osF	iṣ+asF	ī+sF	ir+bhisF	ir+bhyasF	iṣ+āmF	iḥ+ṣuF
DC31f	is+F	iṣ+F	iṣ+amF	iṣ+āF	iṣ+eF	iṣ+asF	iṣ+iF	iṣ+auF		ir+bhyāmF	iṣ+osF	iṣ+asF	ī+sF	ir+bhisF	ir+bhyasF	iṣ+āmF	iḥ+ṣuF
DC32	is+N	is+N	iṣ+N	iṣ+āN	iṣ+eN	iṣ+asN	iṣ+iN	iṣ+iN		ir+bhyāmN	iṣ+osN	īmṣ+iN	īmṣ+iN	ir+bhisN	ir+bhyasN	iṣ+āmN	iḥ+ṣuN

In (i), the boxed principal part ⟨Xis, {nom sg}⟩ belongs to either DC4, DC5, DC31m, DC31f or DC32 but is not an identifier of any of these declensions, nor is it a predictor of any of the shaded exponences.

In (ii), the boxed principal part ⟨XisM, {nom sg}⟩ belongs to either DC4 or DC31m but is not an identifier of either, nor is it a predictor of any of the shaded exponences.

In (iii), the boxed principal part ⟨Xi+s, {nom sg}⟩ belongs to either DC4 or DC5 but is not an identifier of either; it is a predictor of all but the shaded exponences.

In (iv), the boxed principal part ⟨Xi+sM, {nom sg}⟩ is an identifier for DC4.

Table 5.23. Plat of declensional distinguishers for Sanskrit enhanced with specifications of gender and stem delimitation

Declension class	Singular									Dual					Plural					
	N	V	A	I	D	Ab	G	L	NVA	IDAb	GL	NV	A	I	DAb	G	L
DC1	a+sM	a+M	a+mM	enaM	āyaM	ātM	a+syaM	eM	+auM	ā+bhyāmM	ay+osM	ā+sM	ā+nM	aisM	e+bhyasM	ān+āmM	e+ṣuM
DC2	a+mN	a+N	a+mN	enaN	āyaN	ātN	a+syaN	eN	eN	ā+bhyāmN	ay+osN	ān+iN	ān+iN	aisN	e+bhyasN	ān+āmN	e+ṣuN
DC3	ā+F	eF	ā+mF	ay+āF	āy+aiF	āy+āsF	āy+āsF	āy+āmF	eF	ā+bhyāmF	ay+osF	ā+sF	ā+sF	ā+bhisF	ā+bhyasF	ān+āmF	ā+suF
DC4	i+sM	e+M	i+mM	in+āM	ay+eM	e+sM	e+sM	au+M	ī+M	i+bhyāmM	y+osM	ay+asM	ī+nM	i+bhisM	i+bhyasM	īn+āmM	i+ṣuM
DC5	i+sF	e+F	i+mF	y+āF	ay+eF	e+sF	e+sF	au+F	ī+F	i+bhyāmF	y+osF	ay+asF	ī+sF	i+bhisF	i+bhyasF	īn+āmF	i+ṣuF
DC6	i+N	i+N	i+N	in+āN	in+eN	in+asN	in+asN	in+iN	ī+N	i+bhyāmN	in+osN	in+iN	in+iN	i+bhisN	i+bhyasN	īn+āmN	i+ṣuN
DC7	u+sM	o+M	u+mM	un+āM	av+eM	o+sM	o+sM	au+M	ū+M	u+bhyāmM	v+osM	av+asM	ū+nM	u+bhisM	u+bhyasM	ūn+āmM	u+ṣuM
DC8	u+sF	o+F	u+mF	v+āF	av+eF	o+sF	o+sF	au+F	ū+F	u+bhyāmF	v+osF	av+asF	ū+sF	u+bhisF	u+bhyasF	ūn+āmF	u+ṣuF
DC9	u+N	u+N	u+N	un+āN	un+eN	un+asN	un+asN	un+iN	un+iN	u+bhyāmN	un+osN	un+iN	un+iN	u+bhisN	u+bhyasN	ūn+āmN	u+ṣuN
DC10	ī+F	ī+F	ī+mF	y+āF	y+aiF	y+āsF	y+āsF	y+āmF	y+auF	ī+bhyāmF	y+osF	y+asF	ī+sF	ī+bhisF	ī+bhyasF	īn+āmF	ī+ṣuF
DC11	ū+sF	u+F	ū+mF	v+āF	v+aiF	v+āsF	v+āsF	v+āmF	v+auF	ū+bhyāmF	v+osF	v+asF	ū+sF	ū+bhisF	ū+bhyasF	ūn+āmF	ū+ṣuF
DC12	ī+sF	ī+sF	iy+amF	iy+āF	iy+eF	iy+asF	iy+asF	iy+iF	iy+auF	ī+bhyāmF	iy+osF	iy+asF	iy+asF	ī+bhisF	ī+bhyasF	iy+āmF	ī+ṣuF
DC13	ū+sF	ū+sF	uv+amF	uv+āF	uv+eF	uv+asF	uv+asF	uv+iF	uv+auF	ū+bhyāmF	uv+osF	uv+asF	uv+asF	ū+bhisF	ū+bhyasF	uv+āmF	ū+ṣuF
DC14	ā+M	ar+M	ar+amM	r+āM	r+eM	ur+M	ur+M	ar+iM	ar+auM	r+bhyāmM	r+osM	ar+asM	r̄+nM	r+bhisM	r+bhyasM	r̥̄+āmM	r+ṣuM
DC15	ā+F	ar+F	ar+amF	r+āF	r+eF	ur+F	ur+F	ar+iF	ar+auF	r+bhyāmF	r+osF	ar+asF	r̄+sF	r+bhisF	r+bhyasF	r̥̄+āmF	r+ṣuF
DC16	ā+M	ar+M	ār+amM	r+āM	r+eM	ur+M	ur+M	ar+iM	ār+auM	r+bhyāmM	r+osM	ār+asM	r̄+nM	r+bhisM	r+bhyasM	r̥̄+āmM	r+ṣuM
DC17	ā+F	ar+F	ār+amF	r+āF	r+eF	ur+F	ur+F	ar+iF	ār+auF	r+bhyāmF	r+osF	ār+asF	r̄+sF	r+bhisF	r+bhyasF	r̥̄+āmF	r+ṣuF
DC18	r̥+N	r̥+N	r̥+N	r̥n+āN	r̥n+eN	r̥n+asN	r̥n+asN	r̥n+iN	r̥n+iN	r̥+bhyāmN	r̥n+osN	r̥n+iN	r̥n+iN	r̥+bhisN	r̥+bhyasN	r̥n+āmN	r̥+ṣuN
DC19	ā+M	an+M	ān+amM	n+āM	n+eM	n+asM	n+asM	n+iM	ān+auM	a+bhyāmM	n+osM	ān+asM	n+asM	a+bhisM	a+bhyasM	n+āmM	a+suM
DC20	a+N	a+N	a+N	n+āN	n+eN	n+asN	n+asN	n+iN	n+iN	a+bhyāmN	n+osN	ān+iN	ān+iN	a+bhisN	a+bhyasN	n+āmN	a+suN
DC21	ī+M	in+M	in+amM	in+āM	in+eM	in+asM	in+asM	in+iM	in+auM	i+bhyāmM	in+osM	in+asM	in+asM	i+bhisM	i+bhyasM	in+āmM	i+ṣuM
DC22	i+N	i(n)+N	i+N	in+āN	in+eN	in+asN	in+asN	in+iN	in+ī̄N	i+bhyāmN	in+osN	in+iN	in+iN	i+bhisN	i+bhyasN	in+āmN	i+ṣuN
DC23	an+M	an+M	ant+amM	at+āM	at+eM	at+asM	at+asM	at+iM	ant+auM	ad+bhyāmM	at+osM	ant+asM	at+asM	ad+bhisM	ad+bhyasM	at+āmM	at+suM
DC24	at+N	at+N	at+N	n+āN	at+eN	at+asN	at+asN	at+iN	at+ī̄N	ad+bhyāmN	at+osN	ant+iN	ant+iN	ad+bhisN	ad+bhyasN	at+āmN	at+suN
DC25	ān+M	an+M	ant+amM	at+āM	at+eM	at+asM	at+asM	at+iM	ant+auM	ad+bhyāmM	at+osM	ant+asM	at+asM	ad+bhisM	ad+bhyasM	at+āmM	at+suM
DC26	ān+M	an+M	āṃs+amM	as+āM	as+eM	as+asM	as+asM	as+iM	āṃs+auM	ad+bhyāmM	as+osM	āṃs+asM	as+asM	ad+bhisM	ad+bhyasM	as+āmM	ah+suM
DC27	as+N	as+N	as+N	as+āN	as+eN	as+asN	as+asN	as+iN	āṃs+iN	o+bhyāmN	as+osN	āṃs+iN	āṃs+iN	o+bhisN	o+bhyasN	as+āmN	ah+suN
DC28	vān+M	van+M	vāṃs+amM	uṣ+āM	uṣ+eM	uṣ+asM	uṣ+asM	uṣ+iM	vāṃs+auM	vad+bhyāmM	uṣ+osM	vāṃs+asM	uṣ+asM	vad+bhisM	vad+bhyasM	uṣ+āmM	vat+suM

DC29	vat+N	vat+N	vat+N	uṣ+āN	uṣ+eN	uṣ+asN	uṣ+asN	uṣ+iN	uṣ+iN	vad+bhyāmM	uṣ+osN	vāṃs+iN	vāṃs+iN	vad+bhisN	vad+bhyasN	uṣ+āmN	vat+suM
DC30m	ās+M	as+M	as+amM	as+āM	as+eM	as+asM	as+asM	as+iM	as+auM	o+bhyāmM	as+osM	as+asM	as+asM	o+bhisF	o+bhyasF	as+āmM	ah+suM
DC30f	ās+F	as+F	as+amF	as+āF	as+eF	as+asF	as+asF	as+iF	as+auF	o+bhyāmF	as+osF	as+asF	as+asF	o+bhisF	o+bhyasF	as+āmF	ah+suF
DC31m	is+M	is+M	iṣ+amM	iṣ+āM	iṣ+eM	iṣ+asM	iṣ+asM	iṣ+iM	iṣ+auM	ir+bhyāmM	iṣ+osM	iṣ+asM	iṣ+asM	ir+bhisM	ir+bhyasM	iṣ+āmM	ih+ṣuM
DC31f	is+F	is+F	iṣ+amF	iṣ+āF	iṣ+eF	iṣ+asF	iṣ+asF	iṣ+iF	iṣ+auF	ir+bhyāmF	iṣ+osF	iṣ+asF	iṣ+asF	ir+bhisF	ir+bhyasF	iṣ+āmF	ih+ṣuF
DC32	is+N	is+N	is+N	iṣ+āN	iṣ+eN	iṣ+asN	iṣ+asN	iṣ+iN	iṣ+īN	ir+bhyāmN	iṣ+osN	īṃs+iN	īṃs+iN	ir+bhisN	ir+bhyasN	iṣ+āmN	ih+ṣuN
DC33m	us+M	us+M	uṣ+amM	uṣ+āM	uṣ+eM	uṣ+asM	uṣ+asM	uṣ+iM	uṣ+auM	ur+bhyāmM	uṣ+osM	uṣ+asM	uṣ+asM	ur+bhisM	ur+bhyasM	uṣ+āmM	uh+ṣuM
DC33f	us+F	us+F	uṣ+amF	uṣ+āF	uṣ+eF	uṣ+asF	uṣ+asF	uṣ+iF	uṣ+auF	ur+bhyāmF	uṣ+osF	uṣ+asF	uṣ+asF	ur+bhisF	ur+bhyasF	uṣ+āmF	uh+ṣuF
DC34	us+N	us+N	us+N	uṣ+āN	uṣ+eN	uṣ+asN	uṣ+asN	uṣ+iN	uṣ+īN	ur+bhyāmN	uṣ+osN	ūṃṣ+iN	ūṃṣ+iN	ur+bhisN	ur+bhyasN	uṣ+āmN	uh+ṣuN
DC35m	t+M	t+M	t+amM	t+āM	t+eM	t+asM	t+asM	t+iM	t+auM	d+bhyāmM	t+osM	t+asM	t+asF	d+bhisM	d+bhyasM	t+āmM	t+suM
DC35f	t+F	t+F	t+amF	t+āF	t+eF	t+asF	t+asF	t+iF	t+auF	d+bhyāmF	t+osF	t+asF	t+asF	d+bhisF	d+bhyasF	t+āmF	t+suF
DC36	t+N	t+N	t+N	t+āN	t+eN	t+asN	t+asN	t+iN	t+īN	d+bhyāmN	t+osN	nt+iN	nt+iN	d+bhisN	d+bhyasN	t+āmN	t+suN
DC37	yan+M	yan+M	yañc+amM	ic+āM	ic+eM	ic+asM	ic+asM	ic+iM	yañc+auM	yag+bhyāmM	ic+osM	yañc+asM	yañc+asM	yag+bhisM	yag+bhyasM	ic+āmM	yak+suM
DC38	yak+N	yak+N	yak+N	ic+āN	ic+eN	ic+asN	ic+asN	ic+iN	ic+īN	yag+bhyāmN	ic+osN	yañc+iN	yañc+iN	yag+bhisN	yag+bhyasN	ic+āmN	yak+ṣuN

150 *Grammatically enhanced plats*

Table 5.24. *Optimal static principal-part analyses for the four types of plats in (3) (In the presence of gender specifications, Ipl is not a distillation.)*

Plat	Alternative analyses	Distillations											
		Singular					Dual			Plural			
		N	V	A	I	D	L	NVA	IDAb	GL	NV	A	I	G
(3a): unenhanced plat	a.	✓	✓	✓							✓			
	b.	✓	✓					✓			✓			
	c.	✓	✓								✓	✓		
	d.	✓			✓						✓			✓
	e.	✓						✓			✓		✓	✓
	f.	✓									✓	✓	✓	✓
(3b): plat enhanced by stem delimitation	a.	✓	✓	✓							✓			
	b.	✓	✓					✓			✓			
	c.	✓	✓								✓	✓		
	d.	✓			✓						✓			✓
	e.	✓						✓			✓		✓	✓
	f.	✓									✓	✓	✓	✓
(3c): plat enhanced by gender specifications	a.	✓	✓	✓							✓			
	b.	✓	✓					✓						
	c.	✓	✓								✓			
	d.	✓			✓									✓
	e.	✓						✓						✓
	f.	✓									✓			✓
(3d): plat enhanced by stem delimitation and gender specifications	a.	✓	✓	✓							✓			
	b.	✓	✓					✓						
	c.	✓	✓								✓			
	d.	✓			✓									✓
	e.	✓						✓						✓
	f.	✓									✓			✓

5.4.2 Cell predictor numbers

As we saw in §5.2.2, most Sanskrit declensions have a cell predictor number of 1 on every one of their optimal dynamic principal-part analyses; but in four declensions (**DC5**, **DC6**, **DC8**, and **DC25**), the cell predictor number varies from one optimal analysis to another. As Table 5.25 shows,

The effects of enhancing principal parts 151

including gender in principal-part specifications drives the cell predictor number down to 1 for every alternative analysis of the four exceptional declensions, making 1 the uniform cell predictor number across all declensions. If stem demarcations alone are included in principal-part specifications, cells are no more easily deduced than from unenhanced principal-part specifications. (If both gender and stem delimitation are included in principal-part specifications, the cell predictor number across all analyses of all declensions remains a uniform 1.)

5.4.3   Alternative analyses
Specifying gender tends to increase the number of optimal dynamic principal-part analyses, as seen in the shaded cells in Table 5.25; specifying stem delimitation without gender may also increase the number of optimal analyses, but does so much less pervasively; and specifying both gender and stem delimitation is scarcely better than specifying gender by itself for boosting the number of optimal analyses.

5.4.4   IC predictability and cell predictability
The results in Table 5.26 show that specifying gender enhances both cell predictability and IC predictability. By contrast, specifying stem delimitation does neither. Figures 5.1–5.4 provide a more detailed demonstration of this same point.[4] As a comparison of Figures 5.1 and 5.2 shows, specifying stem delimitation without gender does not result in higher degrees of predictability than are observed in the absence of stem delimitation. By contrast, Figures 5.3 and 5.4 show that specifying gender without stem delimitation enhances both IC predictability and cell predictability, and does so to no less an extent than specifying both gender and stem delimitation.

5.4.5   Cell predictiveness
The facts considered so far suggest that while gender specifications substantially reduce IC complexity, specifications of stem delimitation do not. Consider now the measure of cell predictiveness. Table 5.27 shows that specifications of gender enhance predictiveness and that specifications of stem delimitation generally do not. In the nominative singular and vocative singular, however, specifications of stem delimitation do enhance

---

[4] The instrumental plural counts as a distillation in Figure 5.2 (as in Figure 5.1) but not in Figures 5.3 and 5.4: that is, whether the instrumental plural is a distillation depends on whether the plat's distinguishers include gender specifications.

Table 5.25. *Optimal dynamic principal-part analyses of Sanskrit declensions for the four types of plats in (3) (Shaded numbers in (b) and (c) are higher than their counterparts in (a); shaded numbers in (d) are higher than their counterparts in (c).)*

Declension class	(a) Neither gender nor stem delimitation			(b) Stem delimitation only			(c) Gender only			(d) Both gender and stem delimitation		
	Principal parts	Cell predictor number	Alternative analyses	Principal parts	Cell predictor number	Alternative analyses	Principal parts	Cell predictor number	Alternative analyses	Principal parts	Cell predictor number	Alternative analyses
DC1	1	1.00	2	1	1.00	3	1	1.00	12	1	1.00	12
DC2	1	1.00	1	1	1.00	1	1	1.00	9	1	1.00	9
DC3	1	1.00	6	1	1.00	7	1	1.00	10	1	1.00	11
DC4	1	1.00	1	1	1.00	1	1	1.00	8	1	1.00	9
DC5	2	1.00–1.62	18	2	1.00–1.62	18	1	1.00	5	1	1.00	7
DC6	2	1.00–1.69	19	2	1.00–1.69	19	1	1.00	2	1	1.00	2
DC7	1	1.00	1	1	1.00	1	1	1.00	10	1	1.00	11
DC8	2	1.00–1.62	18	2	1.00–1.62	18	1	1.00	6	1	1.00	7
DC9	1	1.00	8	1	1.00	8	1	1.00	12	1	1.00	12
DC10	1	1.00	5	1	1.00	5	1	1.00	7	1	1.00	7
DC11	1	1.00	5	1	1.00	5	1	1.00	6	1	1.00	6
DC12	1	1.00	11	1	1.00	11	1	1.00	11	1	1.00	11
DC13	1	1.00	10	1	1.00	10	1	1.00	10	1	1.00	10
DC14	2	1.00	3	2	1.00	3	1	1.00	3	1	1.00	3
DC15	2	1.00	3	1	1.00	3	1	1.00	3	1	1.00	3
DC16	2	1.00	3	1	1.00	3	1	1.00	3	1	1.00	3
DC17	2	1.00	3	1	1.00	3	1	1.00	3	1	1.00	3
DC18	1	1.00	10	1	1.00	10	1	1.00	12	1	1.00	12
DC19	1	1.00	4	1	1.00	4	1	1.00	10	1	1.00	10

DC20	1	1.00	3	1	1.00	3	1	1.00	9
DC21	1	1.00	5	1	1.00	5	1	1.00	10
DC22	1	1.00	1	1	1.00	1	1	1.00	2
DC23	1	1.00	1	1	1.00	1	1	1.00	1
DC24	1	1.00	6	1	1.00	6	1	1.00	12
DC25	2	1.00–1.31	11	2	1.00–1.31	10	2	1.00	10
DC26	1	1.00	3	1	1.00	3	1	1.00	3
DC27	1	1.00	4	1	1.00	5	1	1.00	12
DC28	1	1.00	5	1	1.00	6	1	1.00	6
DC29	1	1.00	5	1	1.00	6	1	1.00	6
DC30m	1	1.00	4	1	1.00	5	1	1.00	5
DC30f							1	1.00	12
DC31m	1	1.00	4	1	1.00	4	1	1.00	12
DC31f							1	1.00	11
DC32	1	1.00	4	1	1.00	4	1	1.00	12
DC33m	1	1.00	3	1	1.00	3	1	1.00	5
DC33f							1	1.00	11
DC34	1	1.00	3	1	1.00	3	1	1.00	6
DC35m	1	1.00	4	1	1.00	4	1	1.00	12
DC35f							1	1.00	12
DC36	1	1.00	4	1	1.00	4	1	1.00	12
DC37	1	1.00	6	1	1.00	6	1	1.00	12
DC38	1	1.00	6	1	1.00	6	1	1.00	12

Table 5.26. *Average cell and IC predictability for the four types of plats in (3)*

Without gender or stem delimitation		With stem delimitation but not gender	
Average cell predictability 0.903	Average IC predictability 0.702	Average cell predictability 0.903	Average IC predictability 0.702
With gender but not stem delimitation		With both gender and stem delimitation	
Average cell predictability 0.965	Average IC predictability 0.894	Average cell predictability 0.966	Average IC predictability 0.894

predictiveness, both in the absence and the presence of gender specifications; in fact, they enhance it even more than gender specifications do in the nominative singular.

Tables 5.28–5.31 provide a more detailed view of this pattern. These tables focus on selected MPSs, namely the seven MPSs appearing in optimal static analyses of the unenhanced declensional plat. In these tables, CI indicates cells that are class identifiers, whose realization uniquely determines that of every other cell in the paradigm. OCP ('optimal co-predictor') indicates cells that join with one other cell to determine the realization of every other cell in the paradigm. As these tables show, specifying stem delimitation sometimes enhances predictiveness by converting nonpredictive distinguishers into class identifiers in the nominative singular and vocative singular: in the absence of gender, stem delimitation converts three cells into class identifiers; in the presence of gender, stem delimitation converts ten cells into class identifiers. Gender, however, remains the big story: in Tables 5.28–5.31, adding gender specifications to a plat engenders a hundred or more class identifiers.

These facts recall the No-Blur Principle of Cameron-Faulkner & Carstairs-McCarthy (2000:816):

(4)   The No-Blur Principle
        Among the rival affixes for any inflectional cell, at most one affix may fail to be a class-identifier, in which case that one affix is the class-default for that cell.

In Chapter 4, we argued that this principle is far too strong for the facts; cf. also Finkel & Stump 2009. Even so, it is striking how grammatical information serves to bring paradigms closer to conformity with this principle.

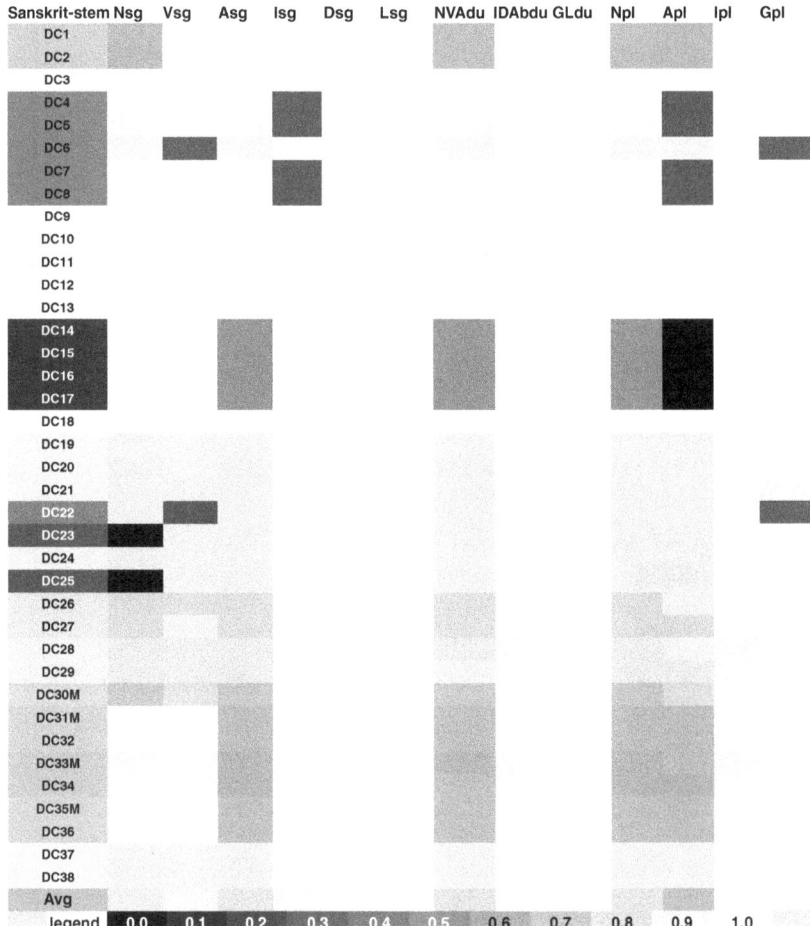

Figure 5.2. *IC and cell predictability for Sanskrit declensions in a plat with specifications for stem delimitation but lacking gender specifications (distillations are on the horizontal axis, ICs on the vertical axis; lighter shade represents higher predictability)*

5.5 Conclusions

The results discussed in this chapter afford two main conclusions. First, we have proposed that IC complexity is a typological variable that can be measured in at least six ways – that canonically, IC complexity is manifested as (a) a high optimal principal-part number, (b) a high cell predictor number, (c) a small number of alternative principal-part analyses, (d) low IC predictability, (e) low

156 *Grammatically enhanced plats*

Figure 5.3. *IC and cell predictability for Sanskrit declensions in a plat with gender specifications but lacking specifications for stem delimitation (distillations are on the horizontal axis, ICs on the vertical axis; lighter shade represents higher predictability)*

Conclusions 157

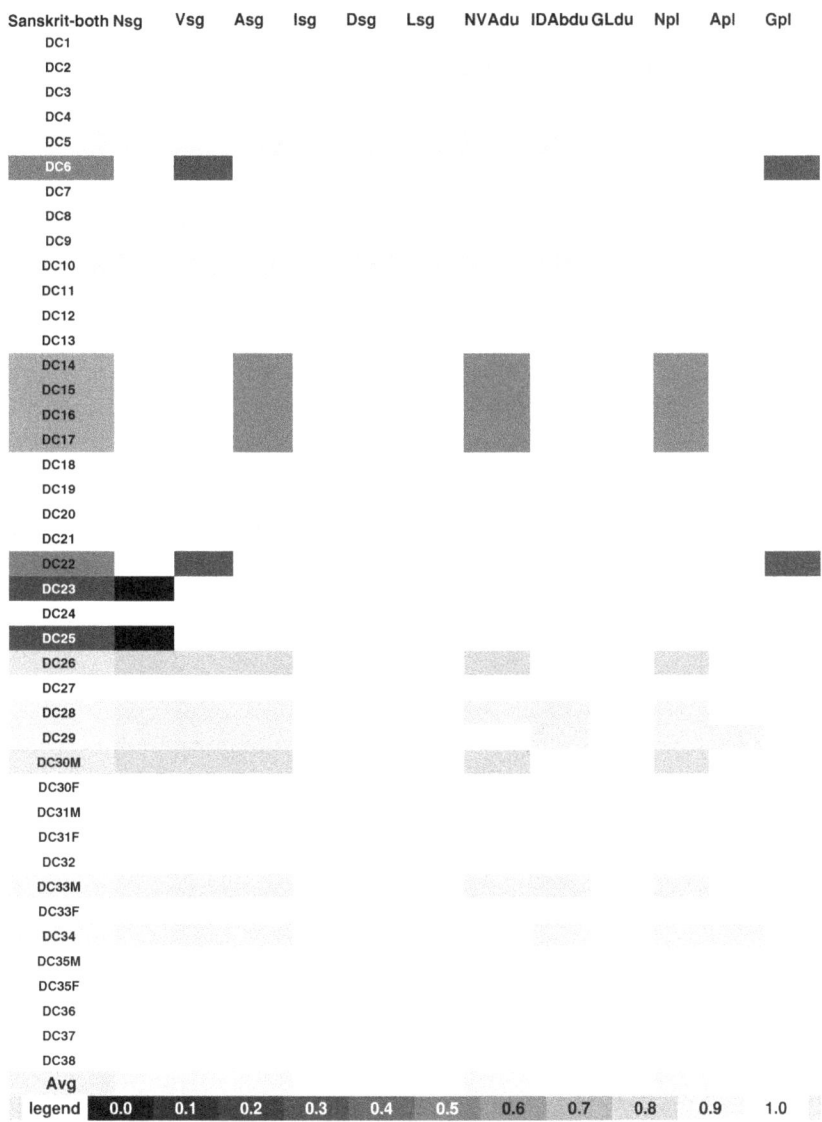

Figure 5.4. *IC and cell predictability for Sanskrit declensions in a plat fully enhanced with specifications for both gender and stem delimitation (distillations on the horizontal axis, ICs on the vertical axis; lighter shade represents higher predictability)*

Table 5.27. *Average predictiveness of cells realizing the distillations of Sanskrit nominal paradigms for the four types of plats in (3)*

Specifications		Distillations													
		Singular						Dual				Plural			
Gender?	Stem?	N	V	A	I	D	L	NVA	IDAb	GL	NV	A	I	G
no	no	0.408	0.522	0.943	0.504	0.647	0.559	0.890	0.336	0.471	0.877	0.785	0.384	0.351
no	yes	0.618	0.592	0.943	0.504	0.647	0.559	0.890	0.336	0.471	0.877	0.785	0.384	0.351
yes	no	0.561	0.787	0.987	0.769	0.885	0.787	0.960	0.800	0.814	0.947	0.800		0.823
yes	yes	0.756	0.836	0.987	0.769	0.885	0.787	0.960	0.800	0.814	0.947	0.800		0.823

Table 5.28. *Class identifiers (CI) and optimal co-predictors (OCP, shaded) under an analysis lacking specifications for gender or stem delimitation*

Declension class	Nsg	Vsg	Asg	NVAdu	NVpl	Apl	Gpl	Number of declension identifiers (out of 7)
DC1				CI		CI		2
DC2	CI							1
DC3			CI			CI		2
DC4						CI		1
DC5	OCP	OCP	OCP	OCP	OCP	OCP		0
DC6	OCP	OCP	OCP	OCP	OCP	OCP	OCP	0
DC7						CI		1
DC8	OCP	OCP	OCP	OCP	OCP	OCP		0
DC9	CI		CI	CI	CI	CI		5
DC10			CI	CI	CI			3
DC11			CI	CI	CI			3
DC12	CI	CI	CI	CI	CI	CI	CI	7
DC13		CI	CI	CI	CI	CI	CI	6
DC14			OCP	OCP	OCP	OCP		0
DC15			OCP	OCP	OCP	OCP		0
DC16			OCP	OCP	OCP	OCP		0
DC17			OCP	OCP	OCP	OCP		0
DC18	CI	CI	CI	CI	CI	CI		6
DC19			CI	CI	CI	CI		4
DC20	CI		CI	CI				3
DC21		CI	CI	CI	CI	CI		5
DC22		CI						1
DC23	CI							1
DC24	CI	CI	CI	CI	CI	CI		6
DC25	OCP		OCP	OCP	OCP	OCP	OCP	0
DC26			CI	CI	CI			3
DC27			CI	CI	CI	CI		4
DC28	CI	CI	CI	CI	CI			5
DC29	CI	CI	CI		CI	CI		5
DC30m	CI		CI	CI	CI			4
DC30f	–	–	–	–	–	–	–	
DC31m			CI	CI	CI	CI		4
DC31f	–	–	–	–	–	–	–	
DC32			CI	CI	CI	CI		4
DC33m			CI	CI	CI			3

160 *Grammatically enhanced plats*

Table 5.28. (*cont.*)

Declension class	Nsg	Vsg	Asg	NVAdu	NVpl	Apl	Gpl	Number of declension identifiers (out of 7)
DC33f	–	–	–	–	–	–	–	
DC34			CI		CI	CI		3
DC35m			CI	CI	CI	CI		4
DC35f	–	–	–	–	–	–	–	
DC36			CI	CI	CI	CI		4
DC37	CI	CI	CI	CI	CI	CI		6
DC38	CI	CI	CI	CI	CI	CI		6
Total CI	12	10	24	22	22	20	2	112
Total OCP	4	3	8	8	8	8	2	41

Table 5.29. *Class identifiers (CI) and optimal co-predictors (OCP, shaded) under an analysis with specifications for stem delimitation but lacking gender specifications*

Declension class	Nsg	Vsg	Asg	NVAdu	NVpl	Apl	Gpl	Number of declension identifiers (out of 7)
DC1	CI			CI		CI		3
DC2	CI							1
DC3		CI	CI			CI		3
DC4						CI		1
DC5	OCP	OCP	OCP	OCP	OCP	OCP		0
DC6	OCP	OCP	OCP	OCP	OCP	OCP	OCP	0
DC7						CI		1
DC8	OCP	OCP	OCP	OCP	OCP	OCP		0
DC9	CI		CI	CI	CI	CI		5
DC10			CI	CI	CI			3
DC11			CI	CI	CI			3
DC12	CI	CI	CI	CI	CI	CI	CI	7
DC13		CI	CI	CI	CI	CI	CI	6
DC14			OCP	OCP	OCP	OCP		0
DC15			OCP	OCP	OCP	OCP		0
DC16			OCP	OCP	OCP	OCP		0
DC17			OCP	OCP	OCP	OCP		0
DC18	CI	CI	CI	CI	CI	CI		6
DC19			CI	CI	CI	CI		4
DC20	CI		CI	CI				3
DC21		CI	CI	CI	CI	CI		5
DC22		CI						1

Table 5.29. (*cont.*)

Declension class	Nsg	Vsg	Asg	NVAdu	NVpl	Apl	Gpl	Number of declension identifiers (out of 7)
DC23	CI							1
DC24	CI	CI	CI	CI	CI	CI		6
DC25	OCP		OCP	OCP	OCP	OCP	OCP	0
DC26			CI	CI	CI			3
DC27	CI		CI	CI	CI	CI		5
DC28	CI	CI	CI	CI	CI			5
DC29	CI	CI	CI		CI	CI		5
DC30m	CI		CI	CI	CI			4
DC30f	–	–	–	–	–	–	–	
DC31m			CI	CI	CI	CI		4
DC31f	–	–	–	–	–	–	–	
DC32			CI	CI	CI	CI		4
DC33m			CI	CI	CI			3
DC33f	–	–	–	–	–	–	–	
DC34			CI		CI	CI		3
DC35m			CI	CI	CI	CI		4
DC35f	–	–	–	–	–	–	–	
DC36			CI	CI	CI	CI		4
DC37	CI	CI	CI	CI	CI	CI		6
DC38	CI	CI	CI	CI	CI	CI		6
Total CI	14	11	24	22	22	20	2	115
Total OCP	4	3	8	8	8	8	2	41

Table 5.30. *Class identifiers (*CI*) and optimal co-predictors (*OCP*, shaded) under an analysis with gender specifications but lacking specifications for stem delimitation*

Declension class	Nsg	Vsg	Asg	NVAdu	NVpl	Apl	Gpl	Number of declension identifiers (out of 7)
DC1	CI	CI	CI	CI	CI	CI	CI	7
DC2	CI		CI	CI			CI	4
DC3			CI	CI	CI	CI	CI	5
DC4		CI	CI	CI	CI	CI	CI	6
DC5			CI	CI	CI			3
DC6		CI					CI	2
DC7			CI	CI	CI	CI	CI	6

162 *Grammatically enhanced plats*

Table 5.30. (*cont.*)

Declension class	Nsg	Vsg	Asg	NVAdu	NVpl	Apl	Gpl	Number of declension identifiers (out of 7)
DC8		CI	CI	CI	CI			4
DC9	CI	CI	CI	CI	CI	CI	CI	7
DC10	CI	CI	CI	CI	CI			5
DC11		CI	CI	CI	CI			4
DC12	CI	CI	CI	CI	CI	CI	CI	7
DC13		CI	CI	CI	CI	CI	CI	6
DC14			CI	CI	CI			3
DC15			CI	CI	CI			3
DC16			CI	CI	CI			3
DC17			CI	CI	CI			3
DC18	CI	CI	CI	CI	CI	CI	CI	7
DC19		CI	CI	CI	CI	CI	CI	5
DC20	CI		CI	CI			CI	4
DC21	CI	CI	CI	CI	CI	CI	CI	7
DC22		CI					CI	2
DC23	CI							1
DC24	CI	CI	CI	CI	CI	CI	CI	7
DC25	OCP		OCP	OCP	OCP	OCP	OCP	0
DC26		CI	CI	CI				3
DC27	CI	CI	CI	CI	CI	CI	CI	7
DC28	CI	CI	CI	CI	CI			5
DC29	CI	CI	CI		CI	CI		5
DC30m	CI	CI	CI	CI	CI			5
DC30f	CI	CI	CI	CI	CI	CI	CI	7
DC31m		CI	CI	CI	CI	CI	CI	6
DC31f		CI	CI	CI	CI	CI	CI	6
DC32	CI	CI	CI	CI	CI	CI	CI	7
DC33m		CI	CI	CI	CI			4
DC33f		CI	CI	CI	CI	CI	CI	6
DC34	CI	CI	CI		CI	CI		5
DC35m	CI	CI	CI	CI	CI	CI	CI	7
DC35f	CI	CI	CI	CI	CI	CI	CI	7
DC36	CI	CI	CI	CI	CI	CI	CI	7
DC37	CI	CI	CI	CI	CI	CI	CI	7
DC38	CI	CI	CI	CI	CI	CI	CI	7
Total CI	22	30	38	36	36	24	26	212
Total OCP	1	0	1	1	1	1	1	6

Table 5.31. *Class identifiers (CI) and optimal co-predictors (OCP, shaded) under an analysis with specifications for both gender and stem delimitation*

Declension class	Nsg	Vsg	Asg	NVAdu	NVpl	Apl	Gpl	Number of declension identifiers (out of 7)
DC1	CI	CI	CI	CI	CI	CI	CI	7
DC2	CI		CI	CI			CI	4
DC3		CI	CI	CI	CI	CI	CI	6
DC4	CI	CI	CI	CI	CI	CI	CI	7
DC5	CI	CI	CI	CI	CI			5
DC6		CI					CI	2
DC7	CI	CI	CI	CI	CI	CI	CI	7
DC8	CI	CI	CI	CI	CI			5
DC9	CI	CI	CI	CI	CI	CI	CI	7
DC10	CI	CI	CI	CI	CI			5
DC11		CI	CI	CI	CI			4
DC12	CI	CI	CI	CI	CI	CI	CI	7
DC13		CI	CI	CI	CI	CI	CI	6
DC14			CI	CI	CI			3
DC15			CI	CI	CI			3
DC16			CI	CI	CI			3
DC17			CI	CI	CI			3
DC18	CI	CI	CI	CI	CI	CI	CI	7
DC19			CI	CI	CI	CI	CI	5
DC20	CI		CI	CI			CI	4
DC21	CI	CI	CI	CI	CI	CI	CI	7
DC22		CI					CI	2
DC23	CI							1
DC24	CI	CI	CI	CI	CI	CI	CI	7
DC25	OCP		OCP	OCP	OCP	OCP	OCP	0
DC26			CI	CI	CI			3
DC27	CI	CI	CI	CI	CI	CI	CI	7
DC28	CI	CI	CI	CI	CI			5
DC29	CI	CI	CI		CI	CI		5
DC30m	CI	CI	CI	CI	CI			5
DC30f	CI	CI	CI	CI	CI	CI	CI	7
DC31m	CI	CI	CI	CI	CI	CI	CI	7
DC31f	CI	CI	CI	CI	CI	CI	CI	7
DC32	CI	CI	CI	CI	CI	CI	CI	7
DC33m	CI	CI	CI	CI	CI			5
DC33f	CI	CI	CI	CI	CI	CI	CI	7
DC34	CI	CI	CI		CI	CI		5

Table 5.31. (cont.)

Declension class	Nsg	Vsg	Asg	NVAdu	NVpl	Apl	Gpl	Number of declension identifiers (out of 7)
DC35f	CI	CI	CI	CI	CI	CI	CI	7
DC35f	CI	CI	CI	CI	CI	CI	CI	7
DC36	CI	CI	CI	CI	CI	CI	CI	7
DC37	CI	CI	CI	CI	CI	CI	CI	7
DC38	CI	CI	CI	CI	CI	CI	CI	7
Total CI	30	32	38	36	36	24	26	222
Total OCP	1	0	1	1	1	1	1	6

average cell predictability, and (f) low cell predictiveness. Because other measures are also relevant, we return to this proposal in Chapter 11.

The second main conclusion to be drawn from this chapter is that grammatical information may serve to diminish IC complexity. In Sanskrit, gender specifications heighten both predictability and predictiveness, and stem delimitation heightens predictiveness but not predictability.

Together, these conclusions define a rich framework for further research in linguistic complexity as a domain of typological contrast among languages.

6 *Impostors and heteroclites*

In many languages, the construction of plats is complicated by the incidence of two phenomena: imposture and heteroclisis. Imposture (§6.1) is an ambiguity in the morphology of one or more of a lexeme's word forms that results in uncertainty about that lexeme's IC membership; heteroclisis (§6.2) is the property of lexemes that function as members of distinct ICs in different parts of their realized paradigms. As we show in this chapter, both impostor lexemes and heteroclite lexemes may have the effect of diminishing other lexemes' IC predictability and cell predictability. We discuss the significance of this fact for the representation issue raised in §2.2.[1]

6.1 Impostors and plat construction

In language pedagogy, principal parts serve two functions. First, they allow language learners to internalize entire realized paradigms with a minimum of rote memorization; they do this by furnishing the minimum number of cells in a realized paradigm that are necessary to infer all of the paradigm's remaining cells by means of a fixed set of deductive rules. This is the **deductive function** of principal parts – inferring the forms of a lexeme from its principal parts.

Second, principal parts allow language users to learn newly encountered lexemes by matching their inflection to that of known lexemes: if the new lexeme L_1 has cells that parallel the principal parts of a known lexeme L_2, the inference is that all of the cells in L_1's realized paradigm parallel their counterparts in L_2's realized paradigm. This is the **matching function** of principal parts – inferring the IC membership of a new lexeme from the fact that it matches the principal parts of a known lexeme.

---

[1] The data sets that we have employed in this chapter are:

impostors.czech   impostors.sanskrit

These are available at the *Morphological Typology* website www.cambridge.org/stump_finkel.

But matching can interact with principal parts in more than one way. On one hand, the principal parts of lexeme L_1 may match those of lexeme L_2: in that case, the remaining cells in the realized paradigm of L_1 follow the pattern of their counterparts in the realized paradigm of L_2. On the other hand, a cell in the realized paradigm of L_1 may match its counterpart in the realized paradigm of L_2, causing speakers to jump to the conclusion that the principal parts of L_1 follow the pattern of those of L_2; that is, language users sometimes infer an unfamiliar lexeme's principal parts on the basis of a perceived similarity to one or more familiar lexemes.[2] Inferences of this latter sort can lead to errors (or less judgmentally, to lexical reanalyses). For instance, because of the phonological similarity between *speed* and *need*, a language learner might infer that the principal parts of SPEED are like those of NEED, thus arriving at the principal-part set

{⟨*speed*, {inf}⟩, ⟨*speeded*, {past}⟩, ⟨*speeded*, {past ptcp}⟩}

rather than the traditional set

{⟨*speed*, {inf}⟩, ⟨*sped*, {past}⟩, ⟨*sped*, {past ptcp}⟩}.

Thus, inferences may begin with an unfamiliar lexeme's known principal parts to deduce the remainder of its realized paradigm, or they may begin with an unfamiliar lexeme's perceived similarity to some known lexeme to deduce the unfamiliar lexeme's principal parts (hence also the remainder of its paradigm). We refer to these two types of inferences as **motivated** and **unmotivated**, respectively.

In an adequate system of principal parts, frequency plays no role in motivated inferences of the deductive type. That is, if one knows a principal-part set for a lexeme L, then the remainder of the cells in L's realized paradigm are fully determined. For instance, if one encounters the following realizations of the archaic English verb HOISE /hɔɪz/ 'hoist', then there is no doubt what the remaining forms in its realized paradigm are. The fact that this verb exhibits a very infrequent pattern in the past tense and past participial forms (that of a suffixal *-t* with devoicing of a stem-final obstruent, as with *leave – left*) plays no role in the deductive inference.

---

[2] An important issue surrounds such inferences: are they instances of analogical reasoning, or do they involve the application of stochastic rules that are sensitive to islands of reliability (phonological contexts which recurrently coincide with a particular morphological pattern)? This issue should be amenable to empirical resolution, but the evidence marshaled so far is not clearly conclusive; see Albright & Hayes (2003), Ernestus & Baayen (2003, 2004), and Chandler (2010).

{⟨*hoise*, {inf}⟩, ⟨*hoist*, {past}⟩, ⟨*hoist*, {past ptcp}⟩}.

Frequency does, however, have an important role in unmotivated inferences. In particular, if an unfamiliar lexeme resembles a known lexeme that is high in frequency, the likelihood of influence is enhanced. Thus, in the *Corpus of Contemporary American English* (COCA: Davies 2008–present), tokens of the verb NEED (304,665) are nearly ten times as frequent as tokens of the verb FEED (31,124); this disparity enhances the likelihood that NEED will affect SPEED (a comparatively infrequent lexeme, with only 8,516 tokens). The influence is all the more likely given that the forms of NEED and SPEED that are alike for all speakers:

- infinitive: *(to) need*, *(to) speed*
- default present: *(they) need*, *(they) speed*
- 3sg present indicative: *needs, speeds*
- present participle: *needing, speeding*

are, as a group, much more frequent than the past-tense and past-participal forms. (In the COCA, the bulleted forms of the verb NEED are more than three times as frequent as *needed*, and the bulleted forms of the verb SPEED are nearly four times as frequent as *sped/speeded*.)

One might suppose that the frequency of NEED is of scant relevance, given that NEED follows the weak conjugation, a default instantiated by thousands of verbs. But frequency is not the only factor that enhances the likelihood of unmotivated inferences; a second important factor is the degree of similarity between the new, influenced form and the known, influencing form (Albright & Hayes 2003; Ernestus & Baayen 2003, 2004). One kind of evidence for this conclusion is the fact that strong verbs can, as an effect of frequency, pull similar verbs away from the default weak conjugation. Although the English verb DIVE was traditionally weak, the infinitive form *dive* resembles *drive*, one of the principal parts participating in the strong conjugational pattern *drive–drove*; in this way, the parallel form *dove* has come into use. Given the importance of frequency as a determinant of such lexical influences, the *dove* development might seem improbable, since the *drive–drove* pattern is instantiated by only a handful of verbs (e.g. DRIVE, STRIVE, STRIDE, RIDE, and WRITE). But verbs whose default present stem ends in /aɪv/ are fairly few in number and are fairly evenly divided between the *walk–walked* pattern and the *drive–drove* pattern. Moreover, the token frequency of DRIVE's forms (86,999 in COCA) far exceeds the combined token frequency of ARRIVE's forms (51,438) and THRIVE's forms (5,966). By virtue of its higher token frequency among phonologically similar forms, DRIVE attracts DIVE (a comparatively low-frequency verb, with 5,139 tokens) to its conjugation.

The lexeme DIVE is what we call an **impostor**: a lexeme whose IC membership is ambiguous because one or more of its realizations is morphologically ambiguous.³ In the case of DIVE, it is ultimately the stem *dive* that is ambiguous: is this a weak stem, which takes *-ed* in the formation of its past tense (with *dived* following the pattern of *thrived*) or is it a strong stem whose vowel /aɪ/ exhibits gradation in the past tense (with *dove* following the pattern of *drove*)? Some other impostors:

- SPEED: *speeded* (like *needed*) or *sped* (like *fed*)?
- KNEEL: *kneeled* (like *peeled*) or *knelt* (like *felt*)?
- DREAM: *dreamed* (like *seemed*) or *dreamt* (like *meant*)?
- OCTOPUS: *octopi* (like *alumni*) or *octopuses* (like *campuses*)?
- MONGOOSE: *mongooses* (like *cabooses*) or *mongeese* (like *geese*)?
- SHAMAN: *shamans* (like *Romans*) or *shamen* (like *postmen*)?

Impostors are important in the present context because they have the effect of driving down the predictability of some ICs and may, in addition, drive up the number of principal parts required by the plat to which they belong. Consider a Sanskrit example. In Sanskrit, *i*-stem nominals (including nouns and adjectives) have the neuter declension **DC6** exemplified in column A of Table 6.1;⁴ derivative adjectives with stems in *-in* have neuter forms in the contrasting declension **DC22** exemplified in column B. Three factors conspire to make these declensions extremely similar:

- they involve the same case suffixes,
- neuter *i*-stems epenthesize *n* before vowel-initial suffixes, and
- *in*-stems lose their *n* before consonant-initial suffixes.

---

³ We acknowledge that the impostor metaphor is not entirely apt. Ordinarily, 'impostor' names an asymmetrical relation: 'A is B's impostor' doesn't entail 'B is A's impostor'. But if THRIVE is an impostor with respect to the DRIVE conjugation (*thrived/*throve*), then DRIVE is likewise an impostor of the THRIVE conjugation (*drove/*drived*): impostor, in our sense, is a symmetrical relation. Also, we ordinarily think of impostors as being troublesome. We might accordingly expect morphological impostors to be similarly troublesome, like DIVE, SPEED, KNEEL, and so on. But though it is an impostor with respect to the FEED conjugation, NEED isn't the least bit troublesome; though it is parallel to *fed*, the form **ned* is universally rejected as the past tense of NEED. In this case, speakers are in confident agreement about an impostor because the impostor happens to embody a highly frequent pattern.

⁴ Adjectival *i*-stems may also follow a different neuter declension more closely resembling the corresponding masculine declension (Whitney 1889: §344); this alternative is not relevant to the example under discussion.

Table 6.1. *Neuter declension* **DC6** *of the i-stem* KRĪḌI *'playing' and neuter declension* **DC22** *of the in-stem* BALIN *'powerful' (shaded cells indicate points of contrast)*

		N	V	A	I	D	Ab	G	L
Singular	KRĪḌI	krīḍi	krīḍi	krīḍi	krīḍinā	krīḍine		krīḍinas	krīḍini
	BALIN	bali	bali(n)	bali	balinā	baline		balinas	balini
Dual	KRĪḌI		krīḍinī			krīḍibhyām		krīḍinos	
	BALIN		balinī			balibhyām		balinos	
Plural	KRĪḌI		krīḍīni		krīḍibhis	krīḍibhyas		krīḍīnām	krīḍiṣu
	BALIN		balīni		balibhis	balibhyas		balinām	baliṣu

As a consequence, the two declensions differ only in the genitive plural (where the *i*-stem but not the *in*-stem shows lengthening of the *i*, a pattern of lengthening typical of vowel-stem nominals) and, optionally, in the vocative singular (where the *in*-stem may preserve its stem-final *n*); thus, every lexeme that follows the neuter *i*-stem declension is an impostor of the neuter *in*-stem declension, and vice versa. The neuter forms of KRĪḌI 'playing' and BALIN 'powerful' in Table 6.1 exemplify this imposture.

Consider the predictabilities of declension **DC22** in the universe of unenhanced Sanskrit declensions presented in Chapter 5. If declension **DC6** is omitted from this universe, the average cell predictability and IC predictability of **DC22** are quite high: 0.939 and 0.910, respectively. But if these measures are recalculated in the same universe with declension **DC6** present, they are considerably lower: 0.836 and 0.448, respectively. The average cell predictability and IC predictability of **DC6** are comparable in this universe: 0.851 and 0.477, respectively. Declensions **DC6** and **DC22** detract from each other's predictability in the two cells in which they differ. The full sets of predictability measures are given in Table 6.2; as expected, these two declensions both have low cell predictability in the vocative singular and genitive plural, the only two cells in which they are distinguished.

Accordingly, these declensions together require either the vocative singular or the genitive plural to be a principal part. In the absence of declension **DC6** (that of neuter *i*-stems), the universe of Sanskrit declensions requires at least three static principal parts; the three possible analyses are given in (1). In the presence of **DC6**, at least four static principal parts are required, and there are six optimal analyses (as in (2)), each the result of adding either the vocative singular or the genitive plural to one of the analyses in (1).

Table 6.2. *Cell predictabilities and IC predictability of* **DC22** *(the in-stem declension [neuter forms]) in the Sanskrit declensional universe, excluding and including* **DC6** *(the i-stem declension [neuter forms])*

DC6 (neuter *i*-stem declension)	IC	Cell predictabilities															Avg	IC predictability
		Distillations																
		Singular							Dual					Plural				
		N	V	A	I	D	L	NVA	IDAb	GL	NV	A	I	G			
excluded	DC22	0.875	0.875	0.875	0.995	0.990	0.977	0.875	0.999	0.990	0.875	0.916	0.999	0.990	0.990	0.939	0.910
included	DC6	0.916	0.282	0.916	0.987	0.977	0.916	0.995	0.977	0.916	0.916	0.995	0.292	0.851	0.477
	DC22	0.875	0.239	0.875	0.995	0.990	0.990	0.875	0.999	0.990	0.875	0.875	0.999	0.292	0.836	0.448

(1)   Optimal static principal-part analyses for Sanskrit declensions excluding declension **DC6** (that of neuter *i*-stems)
Nsg – Asg – Apl
Nsg – NVAdu – Apl
Nsg – NVpl – Apl

(2)   Optimal static principal-part analyses for the Sanskrit declensions including declension **DC6** (that of neuter *i*-stems)
Nsg – Vsg – Asg – Apl   Nsg – Asg – Apl – Gpl
Nsg – Vsg – NVAdu – Apl   Nsg – NVAdu – Apl – Gpl
Nsg – Vsg – NVpl – Apl   Nsg – NVpl – Apl – Gpl

It is clear that a speaker of Sanskrit could have encountered novel forms that were genuinely ambiguous as to their membership in **DC6** or **DC22**; for this reason, lexemes switch back and forth between these declensions throughout the history of Sanskrit (Whitney 1889: §441).

In some instances, words are prevented from being impostors by supplementary grammatical information. Consider, for instance, declensions **DC1** and **DC2**. Members of these declensions are quite similar in their inflection: as the inflection of AŚVA 'horse' (masc) and DĀNA 'gift' (neut) in Table 6.3 shows, they inflect alike in all oblique cases (i.e. outside the nominative, vocative, and accusative).

Thus, members of **DC1** and **DC2** would appear to be impostors for each other's declensions. But all members of **DC1** are masculine nouns or masculine forms of adjectives, while all members of **DC2** are neuter nouns or neuter forms of adjectives. Accordingly, gender information suffices to keep members of **DC1** and **DC2** from acting as impostors with respect to each other's declensions. Nevertheless, when encountering unfamiliar lexemes, language users cannot

Table 6.3. *Declension* **DC1** *of the masculine* a-*stem* AŚVA *'horse' and declension* **DC2** *of the neuter* a-*stem* DĀNA *'gift' (shaded cells indicate points of contrast)*

		N	V	A	I	D	Ab	G	L
Singular	AŚVA	aśvas	aśva	aśvam	aśvena	aśvāya	aśvāt	aśvasya	aśve
	DĀNA	dānam	dāna	dānam	dānena	dānāya	dānāt	dānasya	dāne
Dual	AŚVA		aśvau			aśvābhyām		aśvayos	
	DĀNA		dāne			dānābhyām		dānayos	
Plural	AŚVA	aśvās		aśvān	aśvais	aśvebhyas		aśvānām	aśveṣu
	DĀNA		dānāni		dānais	dānebhyas		dānānām	dāneṣu

always determine their gender; nouns of indeterminate gender may then act as impostors. If the predictabilities of DC1 are calculated in the universe of Sanskrit declensions with declension DC2 absent, its average cell predictability and IC predictability are quite high: 0.983 and 0.984, respectively. If these same calculations are made with DC2 present (but without gender information), the average cell predictability and IC predictability of DC1 are considerably lower: 0.887 and 0.758, respectively. Thus, in the absence of gender information, members of DC2 act as impostors of DC1 (and vice versa).

Even so, DC2 does not drive up the number of principal parts required by the Sanskrit declensional plat. Without DC2, the universe of Sanskrit declensions requires four principal parts, the choice of possible principal-parts sets being as in (2). These same six sets suffice to distinguish DC1 from DC2 when the latter is restored to the declensional universe.

The two examples of imposture that we have considered so far share two important properties: (i) all of the members of IC A are impostors of IC B (and vice versa); and (ii) there are pervasive inflectional similarities between A and B. We refer to impostor relations exhibiting both of these characteristics as **essential** impostor relations. But some impostor relations lack one or both of these characteristics; we refer to these as **accidental** impostor relations. Consider an example of this latter type.

In Sanskrit, *a*-stem nominals are not, in general, impostors of the *in*-stem declensions; but some *a*-stem nominals have stems ending specifically in *ina*. The masculine noun ŚŪLINA 'Indian fig-tree', for example, is an impostor of the masculine *in*-stem declension DC21 because its accusative singular and nominative/vocative/accusative (= direct-case) dual forms are morphologically ambiguous: Are the accusative singular form *śūlinam* and the dual direct-case form *śūlinau* to be parsed as *śūlina-m*, *śūlina-au* (i.e. as a masculine *a*-stem like *aśva-m*, *aśva-au* ['horse']) or as *śūlin-am*, *śūlin-au* (i.e. as a masculine *in*-stem like *balin-am*, *balin-au* ['powerful'])? Notwithstanding these ambiguities, ŚŪLINA's *a*-stem morphology makes it different from BALIN in every other case/number combination, as Table 6.4 shows. Thus, ŚŪLINA's status as an impostor of the masculine *in*-stem declension DC21 is very different from KRĪḌI's status as an impostor of declension DC22 and from DĀNA's status as an impostor of declension DC1: whereas KRĪḌI and DĀNA have pervasive inflectional similarities to neuter *in*-stem nominals and masculine *a*-stem nominals, respectively, the inflection of ŚŪLINA has few similarities to that of a masculine *in*-stem nominal.

The numbers reveal this difference between ŚŪLINA on the one hand and KRĪḌI and DĀNA on the other. If the average cell predictability and IC predictability of

Table 6.4. *Declension* DC1 *of the masculine a-stem* ŚŪLINA *'Indian fig-tree' and masculine declension* DC21 *of the in-stem* BALIN *'powerful' (shaded cells indicate points of contrast)*

		N	V	A	I	D	Ab	G	L
Singular	ŚŪLINA	śūlinas	śūlina	śūlinam	śūlinena	śūlināya	śūlināt	śūlinasya	śūline
	BALIN	balī	balin	balinam	balinā	baline	balinas		balini
Dual	ŚŪLINA		śūlinau			śūlinābhyām		śūlinayos	
	BALIN		balinau			balibhyām		balinos	
Plural	ŚŪLINA	śūlinās		śūlinān	śūlinais	śūlinebhyas		śūlinānām	śūlineṣu
	BALIN		balinas		balibhis	balibhyas		balinām	baliṣu

the masculine *in*-stem declension DC21 are calculated in a universe of declensions from which the *ina* subtype of DC1 is excluded, the numbers are quite high: 0.933 and 0.909, respectively. If these figures are recalculated with the *ina* subtype of DC1 specifically included in the plat (as in Table 6.5), the numbers remain high: 0.930 and 0.907, respectively. As this example suggests, an accidental impostor of IC A does not detract as convincingly from the predictability of A as an essential impostor would.

It is important to take the phenomenon of imposture into consideration in constructing plats. Instances of essential imposture should be represented in any plat intended as a comprehensive representation of a inflection system's ICs; a plat of Sanskrit declensional morphology that omitted either or both of DC6 and DC22 simply would not be complete. Accidental imposture is another matter. It again raises the representation issue introduced in §2.2. In a hearer-oriented plat (one representing the phonological contrasts that a language user employs as a basis for determining a newly encountered lexeme's IC membership), the inclusion of accidental impostors is appropriate. Imagine, for example, a Sanskrit speaker encountering the lexeme ŚŪLINA 'Indian fig-tree' for the first time via the accusative singular token *śūlinam*. Because this is a possible form for either the *a*-stem declension DC1 or the masculine *in*-stem declension DC21, the speaker needs more information to decide whether to infer an *a*-stem paradigm or a masculine *in*-stem paradigm for ŚŪLINA; *śūlinam* by itself does not work as an adequate optimal principal part and actually detracts from the IC predictability of the masculine *in*-stem declension. On the other hand, it is not reasonable to include accidental impostors in a speaker-oriented plat (one representing the kinds of IC contrasts that a language user regards as morphologically significant and that could potentially be used in deducing a known lexeme's realized

Table 6.5. *Sanskrit declension plat modified by the inclusion of the **ina** subtype of **DC1** (shaded cells indicate points of contrast between **DC1INA** and **DC21**)*

IC	Singular								Dual				Plural					
	N	V	A	I	D	Ab	G	L	NVA	IDAb	GL	NV	A	I	DAb	G	L
DC1	as	a	am	ena	āya	āt	asya	e	au	ābhyām	ayos	ās	ān	ais	ebhyas	ānām	eṣu
DC1INA	inas	ina	inam	inena	ināya	ināt	inasya	ine	inau	inābhyām	inayos	inās	inān	inais	inebhyas	inānām	ineṣu
DC21	ī	in	inam	inā	ine	inas	inas	ini	inau	ibhyām	inos	inas	inas	ibhis	ibhyas	inām	iṣu

paradigm from principal parts). For instance, a Sanskrit speaker knows that there is a morphological distinction between the suffixation of -*m* to an *a*-stem nominal and the suffixation of -*am* to an *in*-stem nominal; if the speaker knows that *śūlinam* is an instance of the former morphological pattern, then no additional information is necessary in order to deduce an *a*-stem paradigm for ŚŪLINA; under these circumstances, *śūlina-m* by itself fully motivates that inference.

6.2 Heteroclites and plat construction

In English, verbs belonging to the (unproductive) IC of DRINK, SWIM, and SING have static principal parts instantiating the general schema /XɪY/ – /XæY/ – /XʌY/; compare *drink–drank–drunk*, *swim–swam–swum*, and *sing–sang–sung*. Intuitively, there is a one-to-one correspondence between a language's ICs and principal-part schemata of this sort. But if that is so, how should principal-part analyses accommodate lexemes whose inflection is heteroclite? A **heteroclite** lexeme is one whose paradigm inflects partly according to the pattern of one IC and partly according to the pattern of another (Maiden 2009; Stump 2006). Consider, for example, the Czech noun PRAMEN 'spring, source' in Table 6.6. In the singular, the inflection of PRAMEN follows the soft masculine inanimate declension, like that of POKOJ 'room' (and unlike that of MOST 'bridge'); yet, in the plural, PRAMEN instead follows the hard masculine inanimate declension, like MOST (and unlike POKOJ).

Heteroclites present a choice: we can pursue either the **autonomy hypothesis**, according to which a heteroclite defines its own IC, so that POKOJ, PRAMEN, and MOST embody three distinct ICs; or the **annexation hypothesis**, according to which a heteroclite is assimilated to the ICs that it apparently straddles, so that POKOJ, PRAMEN, and MOST only embody two ICs, as in Table 6.6. Only the autonomy hypothesis makes it possible to maintain the idea that ICs stand in a one-to-one correspondence to principal-part schemata: under the autonomy hypothesis, the principal-part sets of POKOJ, PRAMEN, and MOST embody three different schemata, each corresponding to a different IC. Under the annexation hypothesis, by contrast, the principal-part schema embodied by PRAMEN fails to correspond to its own IC; part of this schema goes with POKOJ's IC, whereas the complementary part goes with MOST's IC. Under the autonomy hypothesis, PRAMEN is an impostor with respect to the ICs of both POKOJ and MOST; under the annexation hypothesis, by contrast, it is not really an impostor, since none of its realizations is morphologically ambiguous – its singular realizations unambiguously conform to the IC of POKOJ, while its plural realizations unambiguously conform to the IC of MOST.

Table 6.6. *The heteroclite inflection of Czech* PRAMEN *'spring, source'*

		N	G	D	A	V	L	I	IC
POKOJ (m.) 'room'	Sg	pokoj	pokoje	pokoji	pokoj	pokoji	pokoji	pokojem	soft masculine inanimate declension
	Pl	pokoje	pokojů	pokojům	pokoje	pokoje	pokojich	pokoji	
PRAMEN (m.) 'spring'	Sg	pramen	pramene	prameni	pramen	prameni	prameni	pramenem	hard masculine inanimate declension
	Pl	prameny	pramenů	pramenům	prameny	prameny	pramenech	prameny	
MOST (m.) 'bridge'	Sg	most	mostu	mostu	most	moste	mostě	mostem	
	Pl	mosty	mostů	mostům	mosty	mosty	mostech	mosty	

Source: Heim 1982: 22, 41f, 176

Table 6.7. *Czech declensional plat*

	Singular						Plural					
	N	G	D	A	V	L	I	NV	G	D	A	L	I
BRATR₁	r	ra	rovi	ra	ře	rovi	rem	ři	rů	rům	ry	rech	ry
BRATR₂	r	ra	ru	ra	ře	ru	rem	ři	rů	rům	ry	rech	ry
HRAD	∅	u	u	∅	e	u	em	y	ů	ům	y	ech	y
KOST	∅	i	i	∅	i	i	í	i	í	em	i	ech	mi
KOTĚ	ě	ete	eti	ě	ě	eti	etem	ata	at	atům	ata	atech	aty
KOTEL₁	∅	u	u	∅	i	u	em	e	ů	ům	e	ech	i
KOTEL₂	∅	e	i	∅	i	i	em	y	ů	ům	y	ích	y
KUŘE	e	ete	eti	e	e	eti	etem	ata	at	atům	ata	atech	aty
MALÍŘ	∅	e	ovi	e	i	ovi	em	i	ů	ům	e	ích	i
MĚSTO	o	a	u	o	o	ě	em	a	∅	ům	a	ech	y
MOŘE	e	e	i	e	e	i	em	e	í	ím	e	ích	i
MOST	∅	u	u	∅	e	ě	em	y	ů	ům	y	ech	y
MUŽ	∅	e	i	e	i	i	em	i	ů	ům	e	ích	i
NÁBŘEŽÍ	í	í	í	í	í	í	ím	í	í	ím	í	ích	ími
PÁN₁	∅	a	ovi	a	e	ovi	em	i	ů	ům	y	ech	y
PÁN₂	∅	a	ovi	a	e	ovi	em	ové	ů	ům	y	ech	y
PÍSEŇ	∅	ě	i	∅	i	i	í	ě	í	ím	ě	ích	ěmi
POKOJ	∅	e	i	∅	i	i	em	e	ů	ům	e	ích	i
PRAMEN	∅	e	i	∅	i	i	em	y	ů	ům	y	ech	y
PŘEDSEDA	a	y	ovi	u	o	ovi	ou	ové	ů	ům	y	ech	y
RŮŽE	e	e	i	i	e	i	í	e	í	ím	e	ích	emi
SLŮNĚ	ě	ěte	ěti	ě	ě	ěti	ětem	ata	at	atům	ata	atech	aty
SOUDCE	e	e	i	e	e	i	em	i	ů	ům	e	ích	i
STAVENÍ	∅	∅	∅	∅	∅	∅	m	∅	∅	m	∅	ch	mi
ZACHRÁNCE	e	e	ovi	e	e	ovi	em	i	ů	ům	e	ích	i
ŽENA	a	y	ě	u	o	ě	ou	y	∅	ám	y	ách	ami

The choice between the autonomy hypothesis and the annexation hypothesis has consequences for constructing inflectional plats. Under the annexation hypothesis, the declension of PRAMEN is simply absent from the Czech declensional plat, where it is represented by the declension of POKOJ in the singular and that of MOST in the plural. But under the autonomy hypothesis, the declension of PRAMEN is included as an independent row in the plat, contrasting with both that of POKOJ and that of MOST. Because of its similarity to both of these declensions, it is an impostor of them both, and one would expect it to degrade the average IC predictability of Czech declensions and to drive up the number of necessary principal parts.

This prediction is confirmed. Using the plat in Table 6.7 and the themes in Table 6.8 (which together presume the sandhi modifications in (3)), we calculate

Table 6.8. *Czech declensions and the themes of their exemplars (in morphophonological representation)*

Declension	Gloss of exemplar	Theme of examplar	Declension	Gloss of exemplar	Theme of examplar
BRATR₁	'brother'	*brat*	NÁBŘEŽÍ	'waterfront'	*nábřež*
BRATR₂	'brother'	*brat*	PÁN₁	'gentleman'	*pán*
HRAD	'castle'	*hrad*	PÁN₂	'gentleman'	*pán*
KOST	'bone'	*kost*	PÍSEŇ	'song'	*písEn*
KOTĚ	'kitten'	*kot'*	POKOJ	'room'	*pokoj*
KOTEL₁	'cauldron'	*kotel*	PRAMEN	'spring'	*pramen*
KOTEL₂	'cauldron'	*kotel*	PŘEDSEDA	'chairman'	*předsed*
KUŘE	'chicken'	*kuř*	RŮŽE	'rose'	*růž*
MALÍŘ	'painter'	*malíř*	SLŮNĚ	'baby elephant'	*slůň*
MĚSTO	'city'	*měst*	SOUDCE	'judge'	*soudc*
MOŘE	'sea'	*moř*	STAVENÍ	'manor'	*stavení*
MOST	'bridge'	*most*	ZACHRÁNCE	'savior'	*zachránc*
MUŽ	'man'	*muž*	ŽENA	'woman'	*žen*

the IC predictabilities of Czech declensions, first excluding PRAMEN's declension, then including it. As the resulting figures in Table 6.9 show, the average IC predictability of the declensions in Table 6.7 is 0.515 without PRAMEN, but 0.486 with PRAMEN included. Interestingly, the declensions whose IC predictability suffers with the inclusion of PRAMEN are not those of POKOJ and MOST (from each which the declension of PRAMEN is after all quite different), but those of KOST 'bone' and KOTEL 'cauldron' (the latter of which exhibits two alternative declensions, here labeled KOTEL₁ and KOTEL₂). The details of this influence can be seen in Table 6.10, which shows the cell predictabilities of the KOST, KOTEL₁, and KOTEL₂ declensions with and without the PRAMEN declension; the inclusion of PRAMEN diminishes the predictability of several cells in the KOST and KOTEL₁ declensions, and because the PRAMEN and KOTEL₂ declensions differ only in the locative plural, they reduce each other's locative plural cell predictability to zero.

(3) Sandhi rules for the Czech declensional system as represented in Tables 6.7 and 6.8
E → e / __ l#   ň → n / __ {i, í, ě}
En → eň / __ #   t' → t / __ {ě, e}
E → ∅   áne → ane / __ #

Table 6.9. *IC predictability of Czech declensions without and with the* PRAMEN *declension (based on* m = 4*)*

Declension	Without PRAMEN	With PRAMEN
NÁBŘEŽÍ	0.994	0.994
STAVENÍ	0.993	0.993
ŽENA	0.939	0.939
MĚSTO	0.923	0.923
KOST	0.884	0.867
PÍSEŇ	0.853	0.853
PŘEDSEDA	0.795	0.795
SLŮNĚ	0.766	0.766
KUŘE	0.641	0.641
RŮŽE	0.624	0.624
KOTEL$_1$	0.557	0.546
KOTEL$_2$	0.527	0.155
BRATR$_1$	0.486	0.486
BRATR$_2$	0.486	0.486
KOTĚ	0.465	0.465
MOŘE	0.350	0.350
MOST	0.247	0.247
PÁN$_1$	0.219	0.219
PÁN$_2$	0.215	0.215
POKOJ	0.196	0.196
HRAD	0.189	0.189
MALÍŘ	0.181	0.181
ZACHRÁNCE	0.181	0.181
PRAMEN	—	0.158
SOUDCE	0.099	0.099
MUŽ	0.062	0.062
Avg	0.515	0.486

Table 6.11 shows the optimal static principal-part analyses for the Czech declensional system. Without PRAMEN, four static principal parts are necessary; the four alternative analyses all include the locative singular and the nominative/vocative plural as principal parts. With PRAMEN, five static principal parts are necessary; the six alternative analyses all include the locative plural as a principal part (in addition to the locative singular and the nominative/vocative plural). Here again, the number of principal parts required in an optimal analysis

Table 6.10. *Cell predictabilities of* KOST, KOTEL$_1$, *and* KOTEL$_2$ *without and with* PRAMEN *(based on m = 4)*

	IC	Distillation														Avg cell predictability	IC predictability
		Singular							Plural								
		N	G	D	A	V	L	I	NV	G	D	A	L	I		
without PRAMEN	KOST	0.974	0.839	0.966	0.941	0.957	0.966	0.919	0.860	0.924	0.839	0.839	0.851	0.844	0.901	0.884
	KOTEL$_1$	0.933	0.641	0.651	0.836	0.639	0.506	0.969	0.554	0.945	0.961	0.640	0.678	0.636	0.738	0.557
	KOTEL$_2$	0.855	0.700	0.676	0.623	0.680	0.676	0.897	0.462	0.888	0.895	0.509	0.733	0.510	0.700	0.527
with PRAMEN	KOST	0.974	0.816	0.966	0.941	0.957	0.966	0.897	0.838	0.902	0.816	0.816	0.851	0.821	0.889	0.867
	KOTEL$_1$	0.933	0.615	0.625	0.836	0.639	0.491	0.969	0.539	0.945	0.961	0.625	0.678	0.621	0.729	0.546
	KOTEL$_2$	0.855	0.700	0.676	0.623	0.680	0.676	0.897	0.462	0.888	0.895	0.509	0.000	0.510	0.644	0.155
	PRAMEN	0.884	0.573	0.592	0.688	0.616	0.592	0.884	0.516	0.893	0.909	0.592	0.000	0.598	0.641	0.158

Shaded cells exhibit diminished predictability in the plat including PRAMEN's heteroclite declension.

Table 6.11. *Static principal-part analyses for Czech declensions, without and with the heteroclite declension of* PRAMEN

Without PRAMEN	With PRAMEN	
Nsg – Asg – Lsg – NVpl	Nsg – Asg – Lsg – NVpl – Lpl	Asg – Vsg – Lsg – NVpl – Lpl
Nsg – Lsg – NVpl – Ipl	Nsg – Lsg – Isg – NVpl – Lpl	Vsg – Lsg – Isg – NVpl – Lpl
Asg – Vsg – Lsg – NVpl	Nsg – Lsg – NVpl – Lpl – Ipl	Vsg – Lsg – NVpl – Lpl – Ipl
Vsg – Lsg – NVpl – Ipl		

is not proportional to the number of exponences, ICs or distillations in a plat; it is proportional to the amount of similarity that exists between different ICs within a plat. The heteroclite declension of PRAMEN does not add any new exponences or increase the number of distillations; it is, however, very similar to other declensions in the plat (differing in only a single cell from the KOTEL$_2$ declension).

Heteroclites are like accidental impostors in the sense that whether one includes them in an inflectional plat depends on what the plat is intended to represent. Inclusion of heteroclites (the autonomy hypothesis) is appropriate for hearer-oriented plats: at a purely phonological level, the full set of inflectional exponences exhibited by a heteroclite lexeme is distinct from those of the ICs whose boundary it straddles. On the other hand, excluding heteroclites (the annexation hypothesis) is appropriate for plats intended to represent the kinds of IC contrasts that a language user regards as morphologically significant. A speaker of Czech knows that the distinction between the soft and hard masculine inanimate declensions is well motivated by a significant number of nominal lexemes and that the inflection of the lexeme PRAMEN 'source' is unique simply because it aligns this well-motivated declensional distinction with the morphosyntactic distinction between singular and plural; the inflection of PRAMEN does not, in itself, motivate the postulation of an additional IC distinction. If language users deduce PRAMEN's full realized paradigm from principal parts, they know that PRAMEN participates in the same implicative relations as POKOJ in the singular and the same relation as MOST in the plural.

We return to the representation issue in Chapter 12, where we examine the formal consequences of distinguishing hearer-oriented and speaker-oriented plats.

7 *Stems as principal parts*

7.1 Principal parts can be indexed stems as well as realized cells

Up to now, we have regarded a lexeme's principal parts as a set of cells in its realized paradigm that distinguishes its IC membership (that is, a set of cells that determines all of the remaining cells in its realized paradigm). In this chapter, we investigate a second possibility, that a lexeme's principal parts are a set of indexed stems that are used in the definition of its realized paradigm and that optimally distinguish its IC membership.[1]

In an inflectional system in which ICs are distinguished at the outer layer of a word's morphology, it is useful to regard principal parts as realized cells. Latin declensions are a case in point. As Table 7.1 shows, the Latin declensions are distinguished by the terminations exhibited by their members; accordingly, the principal parts of a Latin noun are traditionally regarded as whole-word forms.

In many systems, however, it is more useful to regard principal parts as **indexed stems** (stem forms that are indexed according to their distribution in a realized paradigm). In French, for example, nearly all verbs exhibit the same inflectional terminations, so a French verb's conjugation-class membership is distinguished not by the outer layer of its morphology, but by the modulation and alternation of its stems (Bonami & Boyé 2002; cf. also Montermini & Boyé 2012 for a similar perspective on Italian). In this chapter, we examine the consequences of this fact for the analysis of principal parts in French. We begin with a preliminary discussion of the morphology of French verbs (§7.2); we draw attention to the fact that the number and identity of indexed stems that one

---

[1] An earlier version of the material in this chapter was presented as "Stem alternations and principal parts in French verb inflection" at Décembrettes 6, December 4–6, 2008, Bordeaux.
  The data sets that we have employed in this chapter are:
  stems.french.abstract   stems.french.concrete   stems.french.referral-new
  These are available at the *Morphological Typology* website www.cambridge.org/stump_finkel.

Table 7.1. Latin declensional endings

Declension	Singular							Plural						
	N	G	D	A	V	Ab	L	N	G	D	A	V	Ab	L
First	-a	-ae	-ae	-am	-a	-ā	-ae	-ae	-ārum	-īs	-ās	-ae	-īs	-īs
Second	-us	-ī	-ō	-um	-e	-ō	-ī	-ī	-ōrum	-īs	-ōs	-ī	-īs	-īs
	—	-ī	-ō	-um	—	-ō	-ī	-ī	-ōrum	-īs	-ōs	-ī	-īs	-īs
	-um	-ī	-ō	-um	-um	-ō	-ī	-a	-ōrum	-īs	-a	-a	-īs	-īs
Third	-s	-is	-ī	-em	-s	-e	-e	-ēs	-um	-ibus	-ēs	-ēs	-ibus	-ibus
	—	-is	-ī	—	—	-e	-e	-a	-um	-ibus	-a	-a	-ibus	-ibus
Third (*i*-stems)	-is	-is	-ī	-em	-is	-e	-e	-ēs	-ium	-ibus	-ēs	-ēs	-ibus	-ibus
	-s	-is	-ī	-em	-s	-e	-e	-ēs	-ium	-ibus	-ēs	-ēs	-ibus	-ibus
	-e	-is	-ī	-e	-e	-ī	-ī	-ia	-ium	-ibus	-ia	-ia	-ibus	-ibus
Fourth	-us	-ūs	-uī	-um	-us	-ū	-ū	-ūs	-uum	-ibus	-ūs	-ūs	-ibus	-ibus
	-ū	-ūs	-ū	-ū	-ū	-ū	-ū	-ua	-uum	-ibus	-ua	-ua	-ibus	-ibus
Fifth	-ēs	-ēī	-ēī	-em	-ēs	-ē	-ē	-ēs	-ērum	-ēbus	-ēs	-ēs	-ēbus	-ēbus

postulates for a verb's paradigm depend on one's account of stem phonology. We accordingly distinguish two plats for the analysis of French verb morphology. One plat is speaker-oriented; its structure presupposes that a verb's indexed stems have underlying forms that are subject to manipulation by rules of sandhi. The other plat is hearer-oriented; its structure presupposes that the form of a verb's indexed stems is simply their superficial phonological form. We show that the analysis of a verb's theme and IC membership depends on whether one employs the speaker-oriented or the hearer-oriented plat (§7.3). Using the methods developed in earlier chapters for analyzing implicative relations in realized paradigms, we examine the consequences of assuming that a French verb's principal parts are indexed stems. Our discussion includes static principal-part analysis (§7.4), dynamic principal-part analysis (§7.5), and cell and IC predictability measures (§7.6). We then compare our French results with the results for other languages presented in earlier chapters (§7.7). In §7.8, we investigate a different approach to the use of stems in principal-part analysis; this "stem-referral approach" is based on a plat in which a French verb paradigm's patterns of stem syncretism are directly encoded. We summarize our conclusions in §7.9.

7.2 The morphology and phonology of French verbs

As the basis for our discussion of the French system of verb inflection, we focus on the seventy-two conjugations listed in Table 7.2, in which each conjugation is named after an exemplar. These conjugations are based on the nondefective conjugations distinguished in *Bescherelle* (2006), a standard (some would say *the* standard) reference for French verb inflection. Our list of conjugations is, however, somewhat different from that of *Bescherelle*, for three reasons.

- *Bescherelle* draws some conjugation-class distinctions whose only motivation is orthographic. For instance, the conjugations of MANGER 'eat', PLACER 'place', and AIMER 'like' are distinguished because (i) MANGER requires an orthographic *e* in contexts in which PLACER and AIMER do not, and (ii) PLACER sometimes requires an orthographic cedilla, which MANGER and AIMER never do: *mangeons* 'we eat', *plaçons* 'we place', *aimons* 'we like'. Yet, MANGER, PLACER, and AIMER belong to the same conjugation, as phonemic transcription reveals: /mɑ̃ʒɔ̃/, /plasɔ̃/, /ɛmɔ̃/.[2]

---

[2] Here and below, we enclose phonemic representations in slashes // and underlying morphophonological representations in vertical strokes ||.

Table 7.2. *Seventy-two conjugations (each named after an exemplar) and their models in* Bescherelle *(2006)*

Conjugation		Model in *Bescherelle*	Conjugation		Model in *Bescherelle*
ÊTRE	'be'	1	DEVOIR	'have to'	44
AVOIR	'have'	2	POUVOIR	'can'	45
AIMER	'like'	7	MOUVOIR	'move'	46
COLLER	'paste'	7	VALOIR	'be worth'	49
BEURRER	'butter'	7	VOULOIR	'want'	50
DÉJEUNER	'have lunch'	7	ASSEOIR$_1$	'seat'	51
ÉCROUER	'imprison'	7	ASSEOIR$_2$	'seat'	52
ÉCHOUER	'fail'	7	SURSEOIR	'stay'	54
REFLUER	'ebb'	7	RENDRE	'give back'	58
REMUER	'stir'	7	PRENDRE	'take'	59
LEVER	'raise'	10	BATTRE	'beat'	60
CÉDER	'give up'	11	METTRE	'put'	61
COPIER	'copy'	16	PEINDRE	'paint'	62
APPUYER	'press'	18	JOINDRE	'join'	63
BROYER	'grind'	18	CRAINDRE	'fear'	64
ENVOYER	'send'	19	VAINCRE	'conquer'	65
FINIR	'finish'	20	FAIRE	'do'	67
HAÏR	'hate'	21	PLAIRE	'please'	68
ALLER	'go'	23	CONNAÎTRE	'be acquainted with'	69
TENIR	'hold'	24	NAÎTRE	'be born'	70
ACQUÉRIR	'acquire'	25	REPAÎTRE	'feed'	72
SENTIR	'feel'	26	CROÎTRE	'grow'	73
VÊTIR	'clothe'	27	CROIRE	'believe'	74
COUVRIR	'cover'	28	BOIRE	'drink'	75
CUEILLIR	'pick'	29	CONCLURE	'end'	77
ASSAILLIR	'assail'	30	INCLURE	'include'	77
BOUILLIR	'boil'	32	COUDRE	'sew'	79
DORMIR	'sleep'	33	MOUDRE	'grind'	80
COURIR	'run'	34	SUIVRE	'follow'	81
MOURIR	'die'	35	VIVRE	'live'	82
SERVIR	'serve'	36	LIRE	'read'	83
FUIR	'flee'	37	DIRE	'say'	84
RECEVOIR	'receive'	40	RIRE	'laugh'	85
VOIR	'see'	41	ÉCRIRE	'write'	86
POURVOIR	'provide'	42	CONFIRE	'preserve'	87
SAVOIR	'know'	43	CUIRE	'cook'	88

- *Bescherelle* sometimes fails to draw distinctions that have morphophonological (and even orthographic) reality. For instance, it assigns CONCLURE 'end' and INCLURE 'include' to the same conjugation, even though they differ in their past-participle formations: *conclue* /kɔ̃kly/, but *incluse* /ɛ̃klyz/ (both in their feminine singular form).
- *Bescherelle* abstracts away differences resulting from the application or nonapplication of automatic phonological processes. For instance, it assigns ÉCHOUER 'fail' and AIMER 'like' to the same conjugation, even though the former verb exhibits a phonologically conditioned alternation that has no analogue in the inflection of the latter verb: before a consonant or word-finally, /eʃw/ becomes /eʃu/ (*échouez* /eʃwe/ 'you (pl) fail', *échouent* /eʃu/ 'they fail'), but /ɛm/ remains unchanged (*aimez* /eme/ 'you (pl) like', *aiment* /ɛm/ 'they like').

There is nevertheless some redundancy among the conjugations in Table 7.2; that is, some of the exemplars in Table 7.2 exemplify the same conjugation. There are three reasons for this redundancy.

- One of the functions of the PPA is to identify sameness of IC membership; we have therefore purposely included some verbs that we assume to belong to the same conjugation to check that the PPA's output accords with our assumption. For example, we include both PEINDRE 'paint' and CRAINDRE 'fear', which the PPA correctly identifies as members of a single conjugation.
- Two verbs may exemplify the same conjugation class in the speaker-oriented plat but distinct conjugations in the hearer-oriented plat. For instance, AIMER 'like' and COLLER 'paste' belong to distinct conjugations in the hearer-oriented plat: compare *aime* /ɛm/ : *aimons* /ɛmɔ̃/ 'I like : we like' (with no alternation in stem vocalism) with *colle* /kɔl/ : *collons* /kolɔ̃/ 'I paste : we paste' (with an /ɔ/ ~ /o/ alternation). In the speaker-oriented plat, by contrast, they belong to the same conjugation: at an abstract level, |ɛm| and |ɛmɔ̃| ('I like' and 'we like') are parallel to |kƆl| and |kƆlɔ̃| ('I paste' and 'we past'), where the morphophoneme |Ɔ| is realized phonologically as /ɔ/ or /o/ according to context.
- It is useful to include exceptional verbs as a guarantee that principal-part analyses are compatible with their exceptional properties. For instance, the verb DÉJEUNER 'have lunch' belongs to the same conjugation as AIMER, but is remarkable because of an exceptional

Table 7.3. *The forty-nine cells in a French verb's synthetic paradigm*

		Singular			Plural		
		1st	2nd	3rd	1st	2nd	3rd
Indicative	Present	1	2	3	4	5	6
	Imperfect	7	8	9	10	11	12
	Simple past	13	14	15	16	17	18
	Future	19	20	21	22	23	24
Conditional		25	26	27	28	29	30
Subjunctive	Present	31	32	33	34	35	36
	Past	37	38	39	40	41	42
Imperative			43		44	45	

		Past participle	
Infinitive	Present participle	masc	fem
46	47	48	49

regularity. Alone among verbs with a penultimate /ə/ in forms like /deʒənɔ̃/ 'we have lunch', DÉJEUNER does not exhibit the /ɛ/~ /ə/ alternation of verbs like LEVER 'raise': this alternation is exhibited by /lɛv/, /ləvɔ̃/ 'I raise, we raise', but not by /deʒən/, /deʒənɔ̃/ 'I have lunch, we have lunch'.[3] Any viable principal-part analysis for French verbs should reflect this difference between DÉJEUNER and verbs like LEVER.

In French, a verb's synthetic paradigm ordinarily has forty-nine cells; these are numbered 1–49 in Table 7.3.

Each of the French verb forms in a synthetic paradigm consists of either a bare stem or a stem followed by a termination. How one identifies these terminations depends on whether one assumes that words have underlying phonological representations distinct from their superficial representations. Consider, for example, the verb form *aimions* /ɛmjɔ̃/ 'we liked'. Like most first-person plural imperfect verb forms, *aimions* ends with /jɔ̃/, which might therefore be regarded as the termination used to realize the property set {1pl impf}. There are, however, verbs whose first-person plural imperfect form has /ɔ̃/ rather than /jɔ̃/, e.g. *craignions* /kʁɛɲ-ɔ̃/ 'we feared', *cueillions* /kœj-ɔ̃/ 'we picked'. Because such verbs have stems ending in a palatal sonorant, we could

---

[3] Thanks to Olivier Bonami for pointing out this peculiarity.

188 *Stems as principal parts*

assume that when these stems join with the termination /jɔ̃/, the rule of phonology in (1) causes the termination to be realized as /ɔ̃/.

(1)   j → Ø / [palatal sonorant] ___

Alternatively, we could assume that in the first-person plural imperfect, the termination is in fact /ɔ̃/, and that the stem used in combination with this termination invariably ends in a palatal sonorant (ordinarily /j/): /ɛmj-ɔ̃/, /kʁɛɲ-ɔ̃/, /køj-ɔ̃/. Because it postulates abstract underlying representations such as |kʁɛɲ-jɔ̃| and |køj-jɔ̃|, we sometimes call the former analysis the abstract analysis; the contrasting analysis, which eschews abstract underlying representations, is the concrete analysis.

If one assumes the concrete analysis, the plat of terminations involved in the inflection of French verbs is the hearer-oriented plat in Table 7.4; the table's

Table 7.4. *Hearer-oriented plat of French verb terminations (concrete phonological analysis)*

		Singular			Plural		
		1st	2nd	3rd	1st	2nd	3rd
Indicative	Present	–	–	–	/ɔ̃/*	/e/**	–
	Imperfect	/ɛ/	/ɛ/	/ɛ/	/ɔ̃/	/e/	/ɛ/
	Simple past	–	–	–	/m/	/t/	/ʁ/
	Future	/ʁɛ/	/ʁa/	/ʁa/	/ʁɔ̃/	/ʁe/	/ʁɔ̃/
Conditional		/ʁɛ/	/ʁɛ/	/ʁɛ/	/jɔ̃/	/je/	/ʁɛ/
Subjunctive	Present	–	–	–	/ɔ̃/	/e/	–
	Past	/s/	/s/	–	/sjɔ̃/	/sje/	/s/
Imperative			–		/ɔ̃/	/e/***	

Infinitive	Present participle	Past participle	
		masc	fem
–	/ɑ̃/	–	–

Shaded cells indicate points of contrast between the concrete and abstract analyses.
*But ÊTRE: /sɔm/ 'we are'.
**But ÊTRE: /ɛt/ 'you (pl) are';
  FAIRE: /fɛt/ 'you (pl) do';
  DIRE: /dit/ 'you (pl) say'.
***But FAIRE: /fɛt/ 'you (pl) do!';
  DIRE: /dit/ 'you (pl) say!'

Table 7.5. *Speaker-oriented plat of French verb terminations (abstract phonological analysis)*

		Singular			Plural		
		1st	2nd	3rd	1st	2nd	3rd
Indicative	Present	–	–	–	/ɔ̃/*	/e/**	–
	Imperfect	/ɛ/	/ɛ/	/ɛ/	/jɔ̃/	/je/	/ɛ/
	Simple past	–	–	–	/m/	/t/	/ʁ/
	Future	/ʁɛ/	/ʁa/	/ʁa/	/ʁɔ̃/	/ʁe/	/ʁɔ̃/
Conditional		/ʁɛ/	/ʁɛ/	/ʁɛ/	/ʁjɔ̃/	/ʁje/	/ʁɛ/
Subjunctive	Present	–	–	–	/jɔ̃/	/je/	–
	Past	/s/	/s/	–	/sjɔ̃/	/sje/	/s/
Imperative			–		/ɔ̃/	/e/***	

Infinitive	Present participle	Past participle	
		masc	fem
–	/ɑ̃/	–	–

Shaded cells indicate points of contrast between the concrete and abstract analyses.
*But ÊTRE: /sɔm/ 'we are'.
**But ÊTRE: /ɛt/ 'you (pl) are';
 FAIRE: /fɛt/ 'you (pl) do';
 DIRE: /dit/ 'you (pl) say'
***But FAIRE: /fɛt/ 'you (pl) do!';
 DIRE: /dit/ 'you (pl) say!'

notes indicate the few exceptions to the otherwise general use of these terminations in the inflection of French verbs. Under the abstract analysis, the plat of terminations is instead the speaker-oriented plat in Table 7.5. The shaded cells in the two tables highlight their six points of contrast.

It is clear from the generality of the terminations in Tables 7.4 and 7.5 that the conjugational distinctions among French verbs are expressed in their stems rather than in their terminations. For each verb in French, we postulate a set of indexed stems: stem forms whose distribution in a verb's realized paradigm is determined by their indices. The number and representation of indexed stems involved in a verb's conjugation vary according to whether one assumes an abstract or a concrete analysis of their phonology. Under the concrete analysis, a verb has twenty indexed stems; under the abstract analysis, it has nineteen. The distributional properties of these indexed stems are presented in Table 7.6. Stem 10a (used in the first- and second-person plural of the conditional) is only

190 *Stems as principal parts*

Table 7.6. *The indexed stems in a French verb's synthetic paradigm (in the concrete analysis, Stem 10a is used in the first- and second-person plural of the conditional; in the abstract analysis, Stem 10a is absent and Stem 10 is used in its place)*

		Singular			Plural		
		1st	2nd	3rd	1st	2nd	3rd
Indicative	Present	Stem 1	Stem 2	Stem 3	Stem 3	Stem 4	Stem 5
	Imperfect	Stem 6			Stem 7		Stem 6
	Simple past	Stem 8		Stem 9			Stem 8
	Future	Stem 10					
Conditional		(Stem 10a)					
Subjunctive	Present	Stem 11			Stem 12		Stem 11
	Past	Stem 9					
Imperative			Stem 13		Stem 14	Stem 15	

Infinitive	Present participle	Past participle	
		masc	fem
Stem 16	Stem 17	Stem 18	Stem 19

distinguished in the concrete analysis; in the abstract analysis, Stem 10 is instead employed throughout the conditional. As Table 7.6 shows, the indexed stems are fundamentally morphomic (Aronoff 1994): the range of morphosyntactic contexts in which a given indexed stem appears does not necessarily exhibit any morphosyntactic coherence. For instance, Stem 8 appears in the first-person singular and third-person plural of the simple past, not a natural class of contexts.

The verbs AIMER 'like', ALLER 'go', AVOIR 'have', COPIER 'copy', ÉCHOUER 'fail', ÊTRE 'be', FAIRE 'make, do', and RECEVOIR 'receive' have the indexed stems in Table 7.7. (In the interests of readability, we omit the enclosing slashes from the phonemic representations in the concrete part of this table and the vertical strokes from the underlying morphophonological representations in the abstract part of the table.) In both the concrete and the abstract analyses, there is frequent syncretism among indexed stems, both for the verbs in Table 7.7 and elsewhere; but every distinction between any two indexed stems in Table 7.6 is justified by a phonological distinction in the conjugation of at least one verb in our sample.

Table 7.7. Indexed stems of eight French verbs in the concrete and abstract analyses

	Lexeme	Theme	Present indicative					Imperfect indicative		Simple past			Future	Conditional		Present subjunctive		Imperative			Infinitive	Participles		
			Singular			Plural					Indicative		Subjunctive								Present	Past	
											1sg, 3pl	Default pl	Default	Subjunctive		Sg, 3pl	Default pl	Sg, 3pl	Default pl	2sg	1pl	2pl			Masculine	Feminine
			1st person	Default	1st person	2nd person	3rd person	Sg, 3pl	Default pl															
			Stem 1	Stem 2	Stem 3	Stem 4	Stem 5	Stem 6	Stem 7	Stem 8	Stem 9	Stem 10	Stem 10a	Stem 11	Stem 12	Stem 13	Stem 14	Stem 15	Stem 16	Stem 17	Stem 18	Stem 19
C O N C R E T E	AIMER	ɛm	ɛm	ɛm	ɛm	ɛm	ɛm	ɛm	ɛmj	ɛmɛ	ɛma	ɛmə	ɛmə	ɛmʁ	ɛm	ɛmj	ɛm	ɛm	ɛm	ɛme	ɛm	ɛm	ɛm
	ALLER	al	vɛ	va	al	al	vɔ̃	al	alj	ale	ala	i	iʁ	aj	alj	va	al	al	ale	al	ale	ale
	AVOIR	∅	ɛ	a	av	av	ɔ̃	av	avj	y	y	o	oʁ	ɛ	ɛj	ɛ	ɛj	ɛj	avwaʁ	ɛj	y	y
	COPIER	kop	kopi	kopi	kopj	kopj	kopi	kopj	kopj	kopje	kopja	kopi	kopiʁ	kopj	kopj	kopi	kopj	kopj	kopje	kopj	kopje	kopje
	ÉCHOUER	eʃ	eʃɥi	eʃu	eʃw	eʃw	eʃu	eʃw	eʃuj	eʃwe	eʃwa	eʃu	eʃuʁ	eʃw	eʃuj	eʃu	eʃw	eʃw	eʃwe	eʃw	eʃwe	eʃwe
	ÊTRE	∅	sɥi	ɛ	sɔm	ɛt	sɔ̃	ɛt	etj	fy	fy	sə	səʁ	swa	swaj	swa	swaj	swaj	ɛtʁ	ɛt	ete	ete
	FAIRE	f	fɛ	fʁ	fəz	fɛt	fɔ̃	fəz	fəzj	fi	fi	fə	fəʁ	fas	fasj	fɛ	fəz	fɛt	fɛʁ	fəz	fɛ	fɛt
	RECEVOIR	ʁəs	ʁəswa	ʁəswa	ʁəsəv	ʁəsəv	ʁəswav	ʁəsəv	ʁəsəvj	ʁəsy	ʁəsy	ʁəsəv	ʁəsəvʁi	ʁəswav	ʁəsəvj	ʁəswa	ʁəsəv	ʁəsəv	ʁəsəvwaʁ	ʁəsəv	ʁəsy	ʁəsy
A B S T R A C T	AIMER	ɛm	ɛm	ɛm	ɛm	ɛm	ɛm	ɛm	ɛm	ɛmɛ	ɛma	ɛmə	ɛmə	ɛm	ɛm	ɛm	ɛm	ɛm	ɛme	ɛm	ɛm	ɛm
	ALLER	al	vɛ	va	al	al	vɔ̃	al	al	ale	ala	i		aj	al	va	al	al	ale	al	ale	ale
	AVOIR	∅	ɛ	a	av	av	ɔ̃	av	av	y	y	o		ɛ	ɛ	ɛ	ɛj	ɛj	avwaʁ	ɛj	y	y
	COPIER	kopj	kopj	kopj	kopj	kopj	kopj	kopj	kopj	kopje	kopja	kopj		kopj	kopj	kopj	kopj	kopj	kopje	kopj	kopje	kopje
	ÉCHOUER	eʃw	eʃw	eʃw	eʃw	eʃw	eʃw	eʃw	eʃw	eʃwe	eʃwa	eʃw		eʃw	eʃw	eʃw	eʃw	eʃw	eʃwe	eʃw	eʃwe	eʃwe
	ÊTRE	∅	sɥi	ɛ	sɔm	ɛt	sɔ̃	ɛt	ɛt	fy	fy	sə		swa	swa	swa	swaj	swaj	ɛtʁ	ɛt	ete	ete
	FAIRE	f	fɛ	fʁ	fəz	fɛt	fɔ̃	fəz	fəz	fi	fi	fə		fas	fas	fɛ	fəz	fɛt	fɛʁ	fəz	fɛ	fɛt
	RECEVOIR	ʁəs	ʁəswa	ʁəswa	ʁəsəv	ʁəsəv	ʁəswav	ʁəsəv	ʁəsəv	ʁəsy	ʁəsy	ʁəsəv		ʁəswav	ʁəsəv	ʁəswa	ʁəsəv	ʁəsəv	ʁəsəvwaʁ	ʁəsəv	ʁəsy	ʁəsy

192 *Stems as principal parts*

A verb's principal parts are a proper subset of its inventory of indexed stems. Not all of a verb's indexed stems need to be listed lexically, because the form of each stem is deducible from the verb's theme (which must be listed lexically, either on its own or as part of a lexically listed stem or word form) and the conjugation class to which the verb belongs. A verb's conjugation-class membership may be represented lexically in either of two ways. On one hand, it may be represented as an inflection-class diacritic, i.e. as the name of the class to which the verb belongs. On the other hand, it may be represented as a set of principal parts. We propose that a French verb's principal parts are, in all cases, a proper subset of its full inventory of indexed stems. For example, the verb AIMER (theme /ɛm/) has two optimal dynamic principal parts; in the concrete analysis, these are Stems 8 and 10 (i.e. the first-person singular/third-person plural simple-past stem /ɛmɛ/ and the future stem /ɛmə/). Thus, the lexical entry of AIMER might simply specify theme: /ɛm/, Stem 8: /ɛmɛ/, and Stem 10: /ɛmə/; from this information, all of AIMER's other stems (as well as its fully inflected word forms) are deducible. In Chapter 9, we return to the question of how best to represent a lexeme's IC membership its lexical entry.

7.3 Themes, stems, and conjugation classes in French

In general, each stem form consists of a theme with or without a stem formative. The irregular verbs ÊTRE 'be' and AVOIR 'have' have null themes, since neither the stems of ÊTRE nor those of AVOIR share a nonempty initial substring. On the other hand, we assume that the suppletive verb ALLER 'go' has the theme /al/ and that this theme is overridden in forms such as /vɛ/ 'I go', /iʁɛ/ 'I will go' and /aj/ '(that) I go'. Table 7.8 lists the theme of every verb in our sample. In several cases, the form of a verb's theme depends on whether one assumes an abstract or a concrete approach to its phonology; these alternatives are shaded in Table 7.8.

In the concrete analysis, the seventy-two verbs in Table 7.8 fall into sixty-four distinct conjugation classes. In the abstract analysis, we reduce the number of distinct conjugations from 64 to 57 by postulating rules of sandhi. These rules allow what would otherwise be distinct conjugations to be assimilated by treating their difference as a difference in susceptibility to a rule of sandhi rather than as a true morphological difference; that is, they allow conjugations that are superficially different to be identified at a more abstract level of phonological representation.

The rules of sandhi assumed in this analysis are listed in (2), where C, C_n represent consonants, O an obstruent, V a vowel, $ a syllable boundary and # a

Table 7.8. *Themes of seventy-two French verbs*

Lexeme		Theme Concrete analysis	Theme Abstract analysis	Lexeme		Theme Concrete analysis	Theme Abstract analysis
ÊTRE	'be'	/∅/	|∅|	DEVOIR	'have to'	/d/	|d|
AVOIR	'have'	/∅/	|∅|	POUVOIR	'can'	/p/	|p|
AIMER	'like'	/ɛm/	|ɛm|	MOUVOIR	'move'	/m/	|m|
COLLER	'paste'	/k/	|kɔl|	VALOIR	'be worth'	/v/	|v|
BEURRER	'butter'	/b/	|bŒʁ|	VOULOIR	'want'	/v/	|v|
DÉJEUNER	'have lunch'	/deʒən/	|deʒən|	ASSEOIR₁	'seat₁'	/as/	|as|
ÉCROUER	'imprison'	/ekʁu/	|ekʁu|	ASSEOIR₂	'seat₂'	/as/	|as|
ÉCHOUER	'fail'	/eʃ/	|eʃw|	SURSEOIR	'stay'	/syʁs/	|syʁs|
REFLUER	'ebb'	/ʁəfly/	|ʁəfly|	RENDRE	'give back'	/ʁɑ̃/	|ʁɑ̃|
REMUER	'stir'	/ʁəm/	|ʁəmɥ|	PRENDRE	'take'	/pʁ/	|pʁ|
LEVER	'raise'	/l/	|ləv|	BATTRE	'beat'	/ba/	|ba|
CÉDER	'give up'	/s/	|sEd|	METTRE	'put'	/m/	|m|
COPIER	'copy'	/kop/	|kopj|	PEINDRE	'paint'	/p/	|p|
APPUYER	'press'	/apɥi/	|apɥi|	JOINDRE	'join'	/ʒw/	|ʒw|
BROYER	'grind₁'	/bʁwa/	|bʁwa|	CRAINDRE	'fear'	/kʁ/	|kʁ|
ENVOYER	'send'	/ɑ̃v/	|ɑ̃v|	VAINCRE	'conquer'	/vɛ̃/	|vɛ̃|
FINIR	'finish'	/fini/	|fini|	FAIRE	'do'	/f/	|f|
HAÏR	'hate'	/ai/	|ai|	PLAIRE	'please'	/pl/	|pl|
ALLER	'go'	/al/	|al|	CONNAÎTRE	'be acquainted with'	/kon/	|kon|
TENIR	'hold'	/t/	|t|	NAÎTRE	'be born'	/n/	|n|
ACQUÉRIR	'acquire'	/ak/	|ak|	REPAÎTRE	'feed'	/ʁəp/	|ʁəp|
SENTIR	'feel'	/sɑ̃/	|sɑ̃|	CROÎTRE	'grow'	/kʁ/	|kʁ|
VÊTIR	'clothe'	/vɛ/	|vɛ|	CROIRE	'believe'	/kʁ/	|kʁ|
COUVRIR	'cover'	/kuv/	|kuv|	BOIRE	'drink'	/b/	|b|
CUEILLIR	'pick'	/k/	|kŒj|	CONCLURE	'end'	/kɔ̃kly/	|kɔ̃kly|
ASSAILLIR	'assail'	/asaj/	|asaj|	INCLURE	'include'	/ɛ̃kly/	|ɛ̃kly|
BOUILLIR	'boil'	/bu/	|bu|	COUDRE	'sew'	/ku/	|ku|
DORMIR	'sleep'	/dɔʁ/	|dɔʁ|	MOUDRE	'grind₂'	/mu/	|mu|
COURIR	'run'	/kuʁ/	|kuʁ|	SUIVRE	'follow'	/sɥi/	|sɥi|
MOURIR	'die'	/m/	|m|	VIVRE	'live'	/v/	|v|
SERVIR	'serve'	/sɛʁ/	|sɛʁ|	LIRE	'read'	/l/	|l|
FUIR	'flee'	/fɥi/	|fɥi|	DIRE	'say'	/di/	|di|
RECEVOIR	'receive'	/ʁəs/	|ʁəs|	RIRE	'laugh'	/ʁ/	|ʁi|
VOIR	'see'	/v/	|v|	ÉCRIRE	'write'	/ekʁi/	|ekʁi|
POURVOIR	'provide'	/puʁv/	|puʁv|	CONFIRE	'preserve'	/kɔ̃fi/	|kɔ̃fi|
SAVOIR	'know'	/s/	|s|	CUIRE	'cook'	/kɥi/	|kɥi|

Shaded cells indicate points of contrast between the concrete and abstract analyses.

word boundary. Some of these rules specify the realization of the vowel morphophonemes |E|, |Ɔ|, |Œ|, |Ə|.

(2) (a) |jj| → /j/   Example: |køj-jɔ̃| → /køjɔ̃/   'we picked'
    (b) |ɲj| → /ɲ/ |кʁɛɲ-jɔ̃| → /кʁɛɲɔ̃/   'we feared'
    (c) |C₁wC₂| → /C₁uC₂/ |eʃw-jɔ̃| → /eʃujɔ̃/   'we failed'
    (d) |C₁ɥC₂| → /C₁yC₂/ |ʁəmɥ-jɔ̃| → /ʁəmyjɔ̃/   'we stirred'
    (e) |OCj| → /OCij/ |ʁəsəv-ʁjɔ̃| → /ʁəsəvʁijɔ̃/   'we received'
    (f) |Cj|# → /Ci/# |kopj| → /kopi/   's/he copies'
    (g) |C₁jC₂| → /C₁iC₂/ |kopj-ʁɔ̃| → /kopiʁɔ̃/   'we'll copy'
    (h) |Cw|# → /Cu/# |eʃw| → /eʃu/   's/he fails'
    (i) |Cɥ|# → /Cy/# |ʁəmɥ| → /ʁəmy/   's/he stirs'
    (j) $|CiV| → $/CjV/ |ʁi-ɑ̃| → /ʁjɑ̃/   'laughing'
    (k) |EC|# → /ɛC/# |sEd| → /sɛd/   'gives up'
    (l) |EC₁əC₂V| → /ɛC₁əC₂V/ |sEdəʁɔ̃| → /sɛdəʁɔ̃/   'we will give up'
    (m) |EC₁əC₂C₃V| → /ɛC₁əC₂C₃V/ |sEdəʁjɔ̃| → /sɛdəʁjɔ̃/   'we would give up'
    (n) |E| → /e/ |sEdɔ̃| → /sedɔ̃/   'we give up'
    (o) |ƆC|# → /ɔC/# |kƆl| → /kɔl/   's/he pastes'
    (p) |Ɔ| → /o/ |kƆlɔ̃| → /kolɔ̃/   'we paste'
    (q) |ŒC|# → /œC/# |kŒj| → /kœj/   's/he picks'
    (r) |ŒC₁əC₂V| → /œC₁əC₂V/ |kŒjəʁɔ̃| → /kœjəʁɔ̃/   'we'll pick'
    (s) |ŒC₁əC₂C₃V| → /œC₁əC₂C₃V/ |kŒjəʁjɔ̃| → /kœjəʁjɔ̃/   'we would pick'
    (t) |Œ| → /ø/ |kŒjɔ̃| → /køjɔ̃/   'we pick'
    (u) |ƏC|# → /ɛC/# |lƏv| → /lɛv/   's/he raises'
    (v) |ƏC₁əC₂V| → /ɛC₁əC₂V/ |lƏvəʁɔ̃| → /lɛvəʁɔ̃/   'we'll raise'
    (w) |ƏC₁əC₂C₃V| → /ɛC₁əC₂C₃V/ |lƏvəʁjɔ̃| → /lɛvəʁjɔ̃/   'we would raise'
    (x) |Ə| → /ə/ |lƏvɔ̃| → /ləvɔ̃/   'we raise'

If we assume no sandhi, there are few redundancies among the seventy-two conjugations in Table 7.2, as the first column of Table 7.9 shows; if we assume the sandhi rules in (2), there are additional redundancies, as in the second column of Table 7.9.

Up to now, our analyses have employed plats that have MPSs on the horizontal axis, ICs on the vertical axis, and inflectional exponences at the intersections of MPSs with ICs. Because we are taking a French verb's principal parts to be indexed stems rather than realized cells, the plats we use for doing principal-part analysis in French are somewhat different. The horizontal axis in

Table 7.9. *Identical French conjugations*

Conjugations that are identical in the absence of sandhi (concrete phonology)	Conjugations that are identical under the sandhi rules in (2) (abstract phonology)
AIMER = DÉJEUNER	AIMER = COLLER, BEURRER, DÉJEUNER, LEVER, CÉDER
APPUYER = BROYER	APPUYER = BROYER
ASSEOIR$_1$ = SURSEOIR	ASSEOIR$_1$ = SURSEOIR
CONNAÎTRE = REPAÎTRE	CONNAÎTRE = REPAÎTRE
PEINDRE = CRAINDRE	PEINDRE = CRAINDRE
POURVOIR = CROIRE	POURVOIR = CROIRE
RECEVOIR = DEVOIR	RECEVOIR = DEVOIR
ÉCROUER = REFLUER	ÉCROUER = ÉCHOUER, REFLUER, REMUER, COPIER

these plats is the list of indexed stems, and the exponence at the intersection of Stem *n* with IC J is the stem formative distinguishing Stem *n* in IC J. For instance, the IC of ENVOYER (theme /ɑ̃v/) lists /-waj/ as its stem formative in the Stem 3 column; thus, /ɑ̃vwaj-/ is the form of its Stem 3. These plats do not include the terminations in Tables 7.4 and 7.5, nor do they contain the full set of 49 MPSs for which French verbs inflect.

The inventory of stem formatives that join with the themes in Table 7.8 to produce each verb's inventory of indexed stems varies according to whether one employs a concrete or an abstract phonological representation. In the concrete analysis, each verb has twenty stems (the full set of stems distinguished in Table 7.6, including Stem 10a); the corresponding stem formatives are listed in Table 7.10, the "concrete plat." In the abstract analysis assuming the rules of sandhi in (2), each verb has nineteen stems (the stems distinguished in Table 7.6 excluding Stem 10a); the corresponding stem formatives are listed in Table 7.11, the "abstract plat." (In the interests of readability, we omit the enclosing slashes and vertical strokes from the representations in these plats.) In these plats, formatives marked '!' are word-level overrides of the combination of an indexed stem with an expected termination, e.g. **!sɔm** (orthographically *sommes* 'we are'), which lacks the expected termination ɔ̃ (orthographically -*ons*). Formatives marked '@' are stem-level overrides of an expected theme, e.g. **@i**, which overrides the expected theme **al** (the theme of ALLER 'go') but which nevertheless takes the expected terminations for the future and the conditional; unlike '!', '@' does not override the

Table 7.10. Concrete plat of stem formatives for seventy-two French conjugations

Conjugation	Stem 1	Stem 2	Stem 3	Stem 4	Stem 5	Stem 6	Stem 7	Stem 8	Stem 9	Stem 10	Stem 10a	Stem 11	Stem 12	Stem 13	Stem 14	Stem 15	Stem 16	Stem 17	Stem 18	Stem 19
ÊTRE	-sɥi	-ɛ	-sɔm	-ɛt	-sɔ̃	-et	-etj	-fy	-fy	-sə	-sɛʁ	-swa	-swaj	-swa	-swaj	-etʁ	-etʁ	-et	-ete	-ete
AVOIR	-ɛ	-a	-av	-av	-ɔ̃	-av	-avj	-y	-y	-o	-oʁ	-ɛ	-ɛj	-ɛ	-ɛj	-avwaʁ	-avwaʁ	-ɛj	-y	-y
AIMER	-ɔl	-a	—	—	—	—	-j	-ɛ	-a	-ə	-əʁ	—	-j	—	-j	-e	-e	—	-e	-e
COLLER	-ɔl	-ɔl	-ɔl	-ɔl	-ɔl	-ɔl	-olj	-ɔle	-ola	-ole	-olaʁ	-ɔl	-olj	-ɔl	-ɔl	-ole	-ole	-ol	-ole	-ole
BEURRER	-œʁ	-œʁ	-œʁ	-œʁ	-œʁ	-œʁ	-œʁj	-œʁɛ	-œʁa	-œʁə	-œʁaʁ	-œʁ	-œʁj	-œʁ	-œʁ	-œʁe	-œʁe	-œʁ	-œʁe	-œʁe
DÉJEUNER	—	—	—	—	—	—	-j	-ɛ	-a	-ə	-əʁ	—	-j	—	-j	-e	-e	—	-e	-e
ÉCROUER	—	—	—	—	—	—	-j	-ɛ	-a	-ə	-ʁ	—	-j	—	-j	-e	-e	—	-e	-e
ÉCHOUER	-u	-u	-w	-w	-u	-w	-uj	-wɛ	-wa	-ɛ	-uʁ	-u	-uj	-u	-w	-we	-we	-w	-we	-we
REFLUER	—	—	—	—	—	—	-j	-ɛ	-a	—	-ʁ	—	-j	—	—	-e	-e	—	-e	-e
REMUER	-y	-y	-ɥ	-ɥ	-y	-ɥ	-yj	-ɥɛ	-ɥa	-y	-yʁ	-y	-yj	-y	-ɥ	-ɥe	-ɥe	-ɥ	-ɥe	-ɥe
LEVER	-ɛv	-ɛv	-əv	-əv	-ɛv	-əv	-əvj	-əvɛ	-əva	-əvə	-əvaʁ	-ɛv	-əvj	-ɛv	-əv	-əve	-əve	-əv	-əve	-əve
CÉDER	-ɛd	-ɛd	-ed	-ed	-ɛd	-ed	-edj	-edɛ	-eda	-edə	-edaʁ	-ɛd	-edj	-ɛd	-ed	-ede	-ede	-ed	-ede	-ede
COPIER	-i	-i	-j	-j	-i	-j	-j	-jɛ	-ja	-i	-iʁ	-i	-j	-i	-j	-je	-je	-j	-je	-je
APPUYER	—	—	-j	-j	—	-j	-j	-jɛ	-ja	—	-ʁ	—	-j	—	-j	-je	-je	-j	-je	-je
BROYER	—	—	-j	-j	—	-j	-j	-jɛ	-ja	—	-ʁ	—	-j	—	-j	-je	-je	-j	-je	-je
ENVOYER	-wa	-wa	-waj	-waj	-wa	-waj	-waj	-wajɛ	-waja	-ɛ	-ɛʁ	-wa	-waj	-wa	-waj	-waje	-waje	-waj	-waje	-waje
FINIR	—	—	-s	-s	-s	-s	-sj	—	—	—	-ʁ	-s	-sj	-s	-s	-ʁ	-ʁ	-s	—	—
HAÏR	-ɛ	-ɛ	-s	-s	-s	-s	-sj	—	—	—	-ʁ	-s	-sj	-s	-s	-ʁ	-ʁ	-s	—	—
ALLER	!vɛ	!va	—	—	!vɔ̃	—	-j	-ɛ	-a	@i	@iʁ	!aj	-j	!va	—	-e	-e	—	-e	-e
TENIR	-jɛ̃	-jɛ̃	-ən	-ən	-jɛn	-ən	-ənj	-ɛ̃	-ɛ̃	-jɛ̃d	-jɛ̃dʁi	-jɛn	-ənj	-jɛ̃	-ən	-əniʁ	-əniʁ	-ən	-əny	-əny
ACQUÉRIR	-jɛʁ	-jɛʁ	-eʁ	-eʁ	-jɛʁ	-eʁ	-eʁj	-i	-i	-eʁ	-eʁʁ	-jɛʁ	-eʁj	-jɛʁ	-eʁ	-eʁiʁ	-eʁiʁ	-eʁ	-i	-iz
SENTIR	—	—	-t	-t	-t	-t	-tj	-ti	-ti	-ti	-tiʁ	-t	-tj	—	-t	-tiʁ	-tiʁ	-ti	-ti	-ti
VÊTIR	—	—	-t	-t	-t	-t	-tj	-ti	-ti	-ti	-tiʁ	-t	-tj	—	-t	-tiʁ	-tiʁ	-t	-ty	-ty
COUVRIR	-ʁ	-ʁ	-ʁ	-ʁ	-ʁ	-ʁ	-ʁij	-ʁi	-ʁi	-ʁi	-ʁiʁ	-ʁij	-ʁij	-ʁ	-ʁ	-ʁiʁ	-ʁiʁ	-ʁ	-ɛʁt	-ɛʁt
CUEILLIR	-œj	-œj	-oj	-oj	-œj	-oj	-oj	-ojɛ	-oja	-ɛjə	-ɛjaʁ	-oj	-oj	-œj	-oj	-ojiʁ	-ojiʁ	-oj	-oji	-oji
ASSAILLIR	—	—	—	—	—	—	—	-i	-i	-i	-iʁ	—	—	—	—	-iʁ	-iʁ	—	-i	-i
BOUILLIR	—	—	-j	-j	-j	-j	-j	-ji	-ji	-ji	-jiʁ	-j	-j	—	-j	-jiʁ	-jiʁ	-j	-ji	-ji

DORMIR	—	—	-m	-m	-mj	-mi	-mi	-miʁ	-m	-m	-miʁ	-m	-m	-mi	-mi	-mi
COURIR	—	—	—	—	-j	-y	-y	-ʁ	—	—	-ʁ	—	—	-y	-y	-y
MOURIR	-œʁ	-œʁ	-uʁ	-uʁ	-uʁj	-uʁy	-uʁ	-uʁiʁ	-œʁ	-uʁ	-uʁiʁ	-uʁ	-uʁ	-œʁ	-œʁ	-œʁ
SERVIR	—	—	-v	-v	-vj	-vi	-vi	-viʁ	-v	-v	-viʁ	-v	-v	-vi	-vi	-vi
FUIR	—	—	-j	-j	-j	—	—	-ʁ	-j	-j	—	-j	-j	—	—	—
RECEVOIR	-wa	-wa	-əv	-əv	-əvj	-y	-ɛv	-əvwaʁ	-əv	-əv	-əvwaʁ	-əv	-əv	-y	-y	-y
VOIR	-wa	-wa	-waj	-waj	-waj	-i	-ɛ	-waʁ	-waj	-waj	-waʁ	-waj	-waj	-y	-y	-y
POURVOIR	-wa	-wa	-waj	-waj	-waj	-y	-waj	-waʁ	-waj	-waj	-waʁ	-waj	-waj	-y	-y	-y
SAVOIR	-ɛ	-ɛ	-av	-av	-aʃj	-y	-a	-aʁ	-aʃ	-aʃ	-avwaʁ	-aʃ	-aʃ	-y	-y	-y
DEVOIR	-wa	-wa	-əv	-əv	-əvj	-y	-ə	-əvʁ	-əv	-əv	-əvwaʁ	-əv	-əv	-y	-y	-y
POUVOIR	-ø	-ø	-uv	-uv	-uvj	-y	-u	-uʁ	-uv	-uv	-uvwaʁ	-uv	-uv	-y	-y	-y
MOUVOIR	-ø	-ø	-uv	-uv	-uvj	-y	-uv	-uvʁ	-uv	-uv	-uvwaʁ	-uv	-uv	-y	-y	-y
VALOIR	-o	-o	-al	-al	-alj	-aly	-od	-odʁ	-al	-al	-alwaʁ	-al	-al	-aly	-aly	-aly
VOULOIR	-ø	-ø	-ul	-ul	-ulj	-uly	-ud	-udʁ	-ul	-ul	-ulwaʁ	-ul	-ul	-uly	-uly	-uly
ASSEOIR1	-wa	-wa	-waj	-waj	-waj	-i	-wa	-waʁ	-waj	-waj	-waʁ	-waj	-waj	-i	-i	-iz
ASSEOIR2	-je	-je	-cj	-cj	-cj	-i	-je	-jeʁ	-cj	-cj	-cjʁ	-cj	-cj	-i	-i	-iz
SURSEOIR	-wa	-wa	-waj	-waj	-waj	-i	-wa	-waʁ	-waj	-waj	-waʁ	-waj	-waj	-i	-i	-iz
RENDRE	—	-d	-d	-d	-dj	-di	-d	-dʁ	-d	-d	-dʁ	-d	-d	-dy	-dy	-dy
PRENDRE	-ɑ̃	—	-ən	-ən	-ənj	-i	-ən	-ɑ̃dʁ	-ən	-ən	-ɑ̃dʁ	-ən	-ən	-i	-i	-iz
BATTRE	—	—	-t	-t	-tj	-ti	-t	-tʁ	-t	-t	-tʁ	-t	-t	-ty	-ty	-ty
METTRE	-ɛ	-ɛ	-ɛt	-ɛt	-ɛtj	-i	-ɛt	-ɛtʁ	-ɛt	-ɛt	-ɛtʁ	-ɛt	-ɛt	-i	-i	-iz
PEINDRE	-ɛ̃	-ɛ̃	-ɛɲ	-ɛɲ	-ɛɲ	-ɛɲi	-ɛd	-ɛ̃dʁ	-ɛɲ	-ɛɲ	-ɛ̃dʁ	-ɛɲ	-ɛɲ	-ɛ̃	-ɛ̃	-ɛ̃t
JOINDRE	-ɛ̃	-ɛ̃	-aɲ	-aɲ	-aɲ	-aɲi	-ɛd	-ɛ̃dʁ	-aɲ	-aɲ	-ɛ̃dʁ	-aɲ	-aɲ	-ɛ̃	-ɛ̃	-ɛ̃t
CRAINDRE	-ɛ̃	-ɛ̃	-ɛɲ	-ɛɲ	-ɛɲ	-ɛɲi	-ɛd	-ɛ̃dʁ	-ɛɲ	-ɛɲ	-ɛ̃dʁ	-ɛɲ	-ɛɲ	-ɛ̃	-ɛ̃	-ɛ̃t
VAINCRE	—	—	-k	-k	-kj	-ki	-k	-kʁ	-k	-k	-kʁ	-k	-k	-ky	-ky	-ky
FAIRE	-ɛ	-ɛ	-əz	-əz	-asj	-i	-ə	-əʁ	-əz	-əz	-əʁ	-əz	-əz	-ɛ	-ɛ	-ɛt
PLAIRE	-ɛ	-ɛ	-ɛz	-ɛz	-ɛzj	-y	-ɛ	-ɛʁ	-ɛz	-ɛz	-ɛʁ	-ɛz	-ɛz	-y	-y	-y
CONNAÎTRE	-ɛ	-ɛ	-ɛs	-ɛs	-ɛsj	-y	-ɛt	-ɛtʁ	-ɛs	-ɛs	-ɛtʁ	-ɛs	-ɛs	-y	-y	-y
NAÎTRE	-ɛ	-ɛ	-ɛs	-ɛs	-ɛsj	-aki	-ɛt	-ɛtʁ	-ɛs	-ɛs	-ɛtʁ	-ɛs	-ɛs	-e	-e	-e
REPAÎTRE	-ɛ	-ɛ	-ɛs	-ɛs	-ɛsj	-y	-ɛt	-ɛtʁ	-ɛs	-ɛs	-ɛtʁ	-ɛs	-ɛs	-y	-y	-y
CROÎTRE	-wa	-wa	-was	-was	-wasj	-y	-wat	-watʁ	-was	-was	-watʁ	-was	-was	-y	-y	-y

Table 7.10. (*cont.*)

Conjugation	Stem 1	Stem 2	Stem 3	Stem 4	Stem 5	Stem 6	Stem 7	Stem 8	Stem 9	Stem 10	Stem 10a	Stem 11	Stem 12	Stem 13	Stem 14	Stem 15	Stem 16	Stem 17	Stem 18	Stem 19
CROIRE	-wa	-wa	-waj	-waj	-wa	-waj	-waj	-y	-y	-wa	-wa	-waj	-wa	-waj	-waj	-waʁ	-waj	-y	-y	-y
BOIRE	-wa	-wa	-yv	-yv	-wav	-yv	-yvj	-y	-y	-wa	-wav	-yvj	-wa	-yv	-yv	-waʁ	-yv	-y	-y	-y
CONCLURE	–	–	–	–	–	–	-j	–	–	-ʁ	–	-j	–	–	–	-ʁ	–	–	–	–
INCLURE	–	–	–	–	–	–	-j	–	–	-ʁ	–	-j	–	–	–	-ʁ	–	–	–	-z
COUDRE	–	-z	-z	-z	-z	-z	-zj	-zi	-zi	-dʁi	-z	-zj	–	-z	-z	-dʁ	-z	-zy	-zy	-zy
MOUDRE	–	-l	-l	-l	-l	-l	-lj	-ly	-ly	-dʁi	-l	-lj	–	-l	-l	-dʁ	-l	-ly	-ly	-ly
SUIVRE	–	-v	-v	-v	-v	-v	-vj	-vi	-vi	-vʁi	-v	-vj	–	-v	-v	-vʁ	-v	-vi	-vi	-vi
VIVRE	-i	-i	-iv	-iv	-iv	-iv	-ivj	-ɛky	-ɛky	-ivʁi	-iv	-ivj	-i	-iv	-iv	-ivʁ	-iv	-ɛky	-ɛky	-ɛky
LIRE	-i	-i	-iz	-iz	-iz	-iz	-izj	-y	-y	-iʁ	-iz	-izj	-i	-iz	-iz	-iʁ	-iz	-y	-y	-y
DIRE	–	–	-z	!dit	-z	-zj	-zj	–	–	-ʁ	-z	-zj	–	-z	!dit	-ʁ	-z	-t	–	-t
RIRE	-i	-i	-ij	-ij	-i	-ij	-ij	-i	-i	-iʁ	-i	-ij	-i	-ij	-ij	-iʁ	-ij	-i	-i	-i
ÉCRIRE	–	–	-v	-v	-v	-v	-vj	-vi	-vi	-ʁ	-v	-vj	–	-v	-v	-ʁ	-v	–	–	-t
CONFIRE	–	–	-z	-z	-z	-z	-zj	–	–	-ʁ	-z	-zj	–	-z	-z	-ʁ	-z	–	–	-t
CUIRE	–	-z	-z	-z	-z	-z	-zj	-zi	-zi	-ʁ	-z	-zj	–	-z	-z	-ʁ	-z	–	–	-t

Table 7.11. *Abstract plat of stem formatives for seventy-two French conjugations*

Conjugation	Stem 1	Stem 2	Stem 3	Stem 4	Stem 5	Stem 6	Stem 7	Stem 8	Stem 9	Stem 10	Stem 11	Stem 12	Stem 13	Stem 14	Stem 15	Stem 16	Stem 17	Stem 18	Stem 19
ÊTRE	-sɥi	-ɛ	-sɔm	-ɛt	-sɔ̃	-ɛt	-ɛt	-fy	-fy	-sə	-swa	-swa	-swa	-swaj	-swaj	-etʁ	-et	-ete	-ete
AVOIR	-ɛ	-a	-av	-av	-ɔ̃	-av	-av	-y	-y	-o	-ɛ	-ɛ	-ɛ	-ɛj	-ɛj	-avwaʁ	-ɛj	-y	-y
AIMER	—	—	—	—	—	—	—	-ɛ	-a	-ɔ	—	—	—	—	—	-e	—	-e	-e
COLLER	—	—	—	—	—	—	—	-ɛ	-a	-ɔ	—	—	—	—	—	-e	—	-e	-e
BEURRER	—	—	—	—	—	—	—	-ɛ	-a	-ɔ	—	—	—	—	—	-e	—	-e	-e
DÉJEUNER	—	—	—	—	—	—	—	-ɛ	-a	-ɔ	—	—	—	—	—	-e	—	-e	-e
ÉCROUER	—	—	—	—	—	—	—	-ɛ	-a	-ɔ	—	—	—	—	—	-e	—	-e	-e
ÉCHOUER	—	—	—	—	—	—	—	-ɛ	-a	—	—	—	—	—	—	-e	—	-e	-e
REFLUER	—	—	—	—	—	—	—	-ɛ	-a	—	—	—	—	—	—	-e	—	-e	-e
REMUER	—	—	—	—	—	—	—	-ɛ	-a	—	—	—	—	—	—	-e	—	-e	-e
LEVER	—	—	—	—	—	—	—	-ɛ	-a	-ɔ	—	—	—	—	—	-e	—	-e	-e
CÉDER	—	—	—	—	—	—	—	-ɛ	-a	-ɔ	—	—	—	—	—	-e	—	-e	-e
COPIER	—	—	—	—	—	—	—	-ɛ	-a	—	—	—	—	—	—	-e	—	-e	-e
APPUYER	—	—	-j	-j	-j	-j	-j	-jɛ	-ja	—	—	—	—	-j	-j	-je	-j	-je	-je
BROYER	—	—	-j	-j	-j	-j	-j	-jɛ	-ja	—	—	—	—	-j	-j	-je	-j	-je	-je
ENVOYER	-wa	-wa	-waj	-waj	-wa	-wa	-wa	-wajɛ	-waja	-ɛ	-wa	-wa	-wa	-waj	-waj	-waje	-waj	-waje	-waje
FINIR	!ɛ	!ɛ	-s	-s	-s	-s	-s	—	—	—	-s	-s	-s	-s	-s	-ʁ	-s	—	—
HAÏR	!vɛ	!va	-s	-s	!vɔ̃	-s	-s	—	—	—	-s	-s	-s	-s	-s	-ʁ	-s	—	—
ALLER	-jɛ̃	—	—	—	!vɔ̃	—	—	-ɛ	-a	@i	!aj	-ɛ	!va	—	—	-e	—	-e	-e
TENIR	-jɛ̃	-jɛ̃	-ən	-ən	-jɛn	-ən	-ən	-ɛ̃	-ɛ̃	-jɛ̃d	-jɛn	-ən	-jɛ̃	-ən	-ən	-əniʁ	-ən	-əny	-əny
ACQUÉRIR	-jɛʁ	-jɛʁ	-eʁ	-eʁ	-jɛʁ	-eʁ	-eʁ	-i	-i	-eʁ	-jɛʁ	-eʁ	-jɛʁ	-eʁ	-eʁ	-eʁiʁ	-eʁ	-i	-iz
SENTIR	—	—	-t	-t	-t	-t	-t	-ti	-ti	-ti	-t	-t	-t	-t	-t	-tiʁ	-t	-ti	-ti
VÊTIR	—	—	-t	-t	-t	-t	-t	-ti	-ti	-ti	-t	-t	-t	-t	-t	-tiʁ	-t	-ty	-ty
COUVRIR	-ʁ	-ʁ	-ʁ	-ʁ	-ʁ	-ʁ	-ʁ	-ʁi	-ʁi	-ʁi	-ʁ	-ʁ	-ʁ	-ʁ	-ʁ	-ʁiʁ	-ʁ	-ɛʁt	-ɛʁt
CUEILLIR	—	—	—	—	—	—	—	-i	-i	-ə	—	—	—	—	—	-iʁ	—	-i	-i
ASSAILLIR	—	—	—	—	—	—	—	-i	-i	-i	—	—	—	—	—	-iʁ	—	-i	-i
BOUILLIR	—	—	-j	-j	-j	-j	-j	-ji	-ji	-ji	-j	-j	-j	-j	-j	-jiʁ	-j	-ji	-ji

Table 7.11. (cont.)

Conjugation	Stem 1	Stem 2	Stem 3	Stem 4	Stem 5	Stem 6	Stem 7	Stem 8	Stem 9	Stem 10	Stem 11	Stem 12	Stem 13	Stem 14	Stem 15	Stem 16	Stem 17	Stem 18	Stem 19
DORMIR	—	—	-m	-m	-m	-m	-mi	-mi	-mi	-m	-m	-m	-m	-m	-miʁ	-m	-mi	-mi	-mi
COURIR	—	—	—	—	—	—	-y	-y	—	—	—	—	—	—	-iʁ	—	-y	-y	-y
MOURIR	-œʁ	-œʁ	-uʁ	-uʁ	-œʁ	-uʁ	-uʁy	-uʁy	-uʁ	-œʁ	-œʁ	-œʁ	-uʁ	-uʁ	-uʁiʁ	-uʁ	-œʁ	-œʁ	-œʁ
SERVIR	—	—	-v	-v	-v	-v	-vi	-vi	-vi	-v	-v	—	-v	-v	-viʁ	-v	-vi	-vi	-vi
FUIR	—	—	-j	-j	-j	—	—	—	—	—	—	—	-j	-j	-ʁ	-j	—	—	—
RECEVOIR	-wa	-wa	-əv	-wav	-əv	-əv	-y	-y	-əv	-wav	-wav	-wa	-əv	-əv	-əvwaʁ	-əv	-y	-y	-y
VOIR	-wa	-wa	-waj	-wa	-waj	-wa	-i	-i	-ɛ	-wa	-wa	-wa	-waj	-waj	-waʁ	-waj	-y	-y	-y
POURVOIR	-wa	-wa	-waj	-waj	-waj	-wa	-y	-y	-wa	-wa	-wa	-wa	-waj	-waj	-waʁ	-waj	-y	-y	-y
SAVOIR	-ɛ	-ɛ	-av	-av	-av	-av	-y	-y	-o	-av	-av	-av	-av	-av	-avwaʁ	-aʃ	-y	-y	-y
DEVOIR	-wa	-wa	-əv	-wav	-əv	-əv	-y	-y	-əv	-wav	-qis	-wa	-əv	-əv	-əvwaʁ	-əv	-y	-y	-y
POUVOIR	-ø	-ø	-uv	-uv	-uv	-uv	-y	-y	-u	-uv	-qis	-ø	-uv	-uv	-uvwaʁ	-uv	-y	-y	-y
MOUVOIR	-ø	-ø	-uv	-uv	-œv	-uv	-y	-y	-uv	-œv	-əv	-ø	-uv	-uv	-uvwaʁ	-uv	-y	-y	-y
VALOIR	-o	-o	-al	-al	-al	-al	-aly	-aly	-od	-aj	-aj	-o	-al	-al	-alwaʁ	-al	-aly	-aly	-aly
VOULOIR	-ø	-ø	-ul	-ul	-œl	-ul	-uly	-uly	-ud	-œj	-œj	-ø	-ul	-ul	-ulwaʁ	-ul	-uly	-uly	-uly
ASSEOIR₁	-wa	-wa	-waj	-waj	-waj	-wa	-i	-i	-wa	-wa	-wa	-wa	-waj	-waj	-waʁ	-waj	-i	-i	-iz
ASSEOIR₂	-je	-je	-ɛj	-ɛj	-ɛj	-ɛ	-i	-i	-je	-ɛ	-ɛ	-je	-ɛj	-ɛj	-waʁ	-ɛj	-i	-i	-iz
SURSEOIR	-wa	-wa	-waj	-waj	-waj	-wa	-i	-i	-wa	-wa	-wa	-wa	-waj	-waj	-waʁ	-waj	-i	-i	-iz
RENDRE	-ɑ̃	-ɑ̃	-d	-d	-d	-d	-di	-di	-d	-d	-d	-d	-d	-d	-dʁ	-d	-dy	-dy	-dy
PRENDRE	-ɑ̃	-ɑ̃	-ən	-ən	-ən	-ən	-i	-i	-ɑ̃d	-ɛn	-ɛn	-ɑ̃	-ən	-ən	-ɑ̃dʁ	-ən	-i	-i	-iz
BATTRE	—	-ɛ	-t	-t	-t	-t	-ti	-ti	-t	-t	-t	-ɛ	-t	-t	-tʁ	-t	-ty	-ty	-ty
METTRE	-ɛ	-ɛ	-ɛt	-ɛt	-ɛt	-ɛt	-i	-i	-ɛt	-ɛt	-ɛt	-ɛ	-ɛt	-ɛt	-ɛtʁ	-ɛt	-i	-i	-iz
PEINDRE	-ɛ̃	-ɛ̃	-ɛɲ	-ɛɲ	-ɛɲ	-ɛɲ	-ɛɲi	-ɛɲi	-ɛɲd	-ɛɲ	-ɛɲ	-ɛ̃	-ɛɲ	-ɛɲ	-ɛ̃dʁ	-ɛɲ	-ɛ̃	-ɛ̃	-ɛ̃t
JOINDRE	-ɛ̃	-ɛ̃	-aɲ	-aɲ	-aɲ	-aɲ	-aɲi	-aɲi	-aɲd	-aɲ	-aɲ	-ɛ̃	-aɲ	-aɲ	-ɛ̃dʁ	-aɲ	-ɛ̃	-ɛ̃	-ɛ̃t
CRAINDRE	-ɛ̃	-ɛ̃	-ɛɲ	-ɛɲ	-ɛɲ	-ɛɲ	-ɛɲi	-ɛɲi	-ɛɲd	-ɛɲ	-ɛɲ	-ɛ̃	-ɛɲ	-ɛɲ	-ɛ̃dʁ	-ɛɲ	-ɛ̃	-ɛ̃	-ɛ̃t
VAINCRE	—	—	-k	-k	-k	-k	-ki	-ki	-k	-k	-k	-k	-k	-k	-kʁ	-k	-ky	-ky	-ky
FAIRE	-ɛ	-ɛ	-əz	-əz	-ɔ̃	-əz	-i	-i	-ə	-as	-as	-ɛ	-əz	!fɛt	-əʁ	-əz	-ɛ	-ɛ	-ɛt
PLAIRE	-ɛ	-ɛ	-ɛz	-ɛz	-ɛz	-ɛz	-y	-y	-ɛ	-ɛz	-ɛz	-ɛ	-ɛz	-ɛz	-ɛʁ	-ɛz	-y	-y	-y

Verb	1	2	3	4	5	6	7	8	9	10	11	12	13	14	15	16
CONNAÎTRE	-ɛ	-ɛ	-ɛs	-ɛs	-ɛs	-ɛ	-ɛs	-y	-y	-ɛt	-ɛs	-ɛs	-ɛtʁ	-ɛs	-y	-y
NAÎTRE	-ɛ	-ɛ	-ɛs	-ɛs	-ɛs	-ɛ	-ɛs	-aki	-aki	-ɛt	-ɛs	-ɛs	-ɛtʁ	-ɛs	-e	-e
REPAÎTRE	-ɛ	-ɛ	-ɛs	-ɛs	-ɛs	-ɛ	-ɛs	-y	-y	-ɛt	-ɛs	-ɛs	-ɛtʁ	-ɛs	-y	-y
CROÎTRE	-wa	-wa	-was	-was	-was	-wa	-was	-y	-y	-wat	-was	-was	-watʁ	-was	-y	-y
CROIRE	-wa	-wa	-waj	-waj	-wa	-wa	-waj	-y	-y	-wa	-wa	-waj	-waʁ	-waj	-y	-y
BOIRE	-wa	-wa	-yv	-yv	-wav	-wa	-yv	-y	-y	-wa	-wav	-yv	-waʁ	-yv	-y	-y
CONCLURE	—	—	—	—	—	—	—	—	—	—	—	—	-ʁ	—	—	—
INCLURE	—	—	—	—	—	—	—	—	—	—	—	—	-ʁ	—	—	-z
COUDRE	—	—	-z	-z	-z	—	-z	-zi	-zi	-d	-z	-z	-dʁ	-z	-zy	-zy
MOUDRE	—	—	-l	-l	-l	—	-l	-ly	-ly	-d	-l	-l	-dʁ	-l	-ly	-ly
SUIVRE	—	—	-v	-v	-v	—	-v	-vi	-vi	-v	-v	-v	-vʁ	-v	-vi	-vi
VIVRE	-i	-i	-iv	-iv	-iv	—	-iv	-ɛky	-ɛky	-iv	-iv	-iv	-ivʁ	-iv	-ɛky	-ɛky
LIRE	-i	-i	-iz	-iz	-iz	-i	-iz	-y	-y	-i	-iz	-iz	-iʁ	-iz	-y	-y
DIRE	—	—	-z	!dit	-z	—	-z	—	—	—	-z	!dit	-ʁ	!dit	-t	-t
RIRE	—	—	-j	-j	—	—	-j	—	—	—	—	-j	-ʁ	-j	—	—
ÉCRIRE	—	—	-v	-v	-v	—	-v	-vi	-vi	—	-v	-v	-ʁ	-v	—	—
CONFIRE	—	—	-z	-z	-z	—	-z	—	—	—	-z	-z	-ʁ	-z	-t	-t
CUIRE	—	—	-z	-z	-z	—	-z	-zi	-zi	—	-z	-z	-ʁ	-z	-t	-t

202 *Stems as principal parts*

expected termination (thus: iʁɔ̃, orthographically *irons* 'we will go', with the expected termination).

7.4 Static principal-part analysis

Under the concrete analysis, the seventy-two verbs in our sample require only five static principal parts. As Table 7.12 shows, all five of the alternative optimal analyses include three essential stems as optimal static principal parts:

- Stem 8 (that of the first-person singular simple past),
- Stem 10 (that of the first-person singular future),
- Stem 19 (that of the feminine form of the past participle).

Under the abstract phonological analysis, the seventy-two verbs require six static principal parts. As Table 7.13 shows, all six of the alternative optimal analyses include four essential stems – the three just listed plus Stem 17 (that of the present participle). The present participial stem is not only not essential in the concrete analysis; it does not figure as a principal part in any of the five optimal analyses in Table 7.12.

This difference between the concrete and abstract plats is ultimately traceable to just two conjugations: those of FUIR 'flee' and RIRE 'laugh'. In the abstract plat that we employ here, these two conjugations are alike in their inflection except in their present participal form: disyllabic /fɥijɑ̃/ but monosyllabic /ʁjɑ̃/. In this plat, the theme of RIRE is assumed to be |ʁi|, so that the present participial form /ʁjɑ̃/ arises from the underlying form |ʁi-ɑ̃| through the application of the sandhi rule in (2j); in the inflection of FUIR, by contrast, the present participial inflection involves the suffixed stem formative /j/, whose appearance in the

Table 7.12. *Optimal static principal-part analyses for French (concrete analysis)*

Distillation:	1	2	3	4	5	6	7	8	9	10	11	12	13	14	15	16	17
Indexed stem:	1	2	3	4	5	7	8	10	11	12	13	14	15	16	17	18	19
Analyses a	✓							✓	✓				✓				✓
b		✓	✓					✓	✓								✓
c		✓						✓	✓				✓				✓
d				✓				✓	✓		✓						✓
e								✓	✓		✓	✓					✓

Table 7.13. *Optimal static principal-part analyses for French (abstract analysis)*

Distillation:	1	2	3	4	5	6	7	8	9	10	11	12	13	14	15	16	17
Indexed stem:	1	2	3	4	5	7	8	10	11	12	13	14	15	16	17	18	19
Analyses a	✓		✓		✓	✓									✓		✓
b	✓				✓	✓							✓		✓		✓
c		✓	✓		✓	✓									✓		✓
d		✓			✓	✓							✓		✓		✓
e				✓	✓	✓				✓					✓		✓
f					✓	✓				✓			✓		✓		✓

inflection of FUIR is (in this plat) otherwise paralleled in that of RIRE (e.g./ʁijɔ̃/ 'we laugh' alongside /fɥijɔ̃/ 'we flee'). Thus, in the abstract plat employed here, Stem 17 must be a principal part, since it is the only point at which the conjugations of FUIR and RIRE differ. In the concrete analysis, Stem 17 needn't be a principal part, because FUIR and RIRE have very different inflections: FUIR has the theme /fɥi/, but RIRE has the theme /ʁ/, and for this reason, their distinguishers contrast in a number of stems, not just in Stem 17 (see again Table 7.10).

Yet, the difference between FUIR and RIRE in the abstract plat may simply be an artifact of specific choices in the plat's construction. In particular, the contrast between *riant* /ʁjɑ̃/ 'laughing' and *rions* /ʁijɔ̃/ 'we laugh' may not be as categorical as the abstract plat implies. In fact, both words exhibit alternating pronunciations: /ʁjɑ̃/ ~ /ʁijɑ̃/ and /ʁjɔ̃/ ~ /ʁijɔ̃/; to the extent that /ʁjɑ̃/ and /ʁijɔ̃/ are favored, this may simply be a consequence of the fact that *rions* is more likely than *riant* to appear sentence finally and hence to receive nuclear stress. Thus, an alternative to the abstract plat is conceivable, in which both FUIR and RIRE have themes in |i| (|fɥi| and |ʁi|) and are subject to two successive rules of sandhi, the first converting |i| to /j/ before a vowel, the second epenthesizing /i/ before /j/ in complex onsets of the form /(C)Cj/ – obligatorily in onsets of the form /CCj/, optionally otherwise, with nuclear stress favoring epenthesis. In this alternative plat, the conjugations of FUIR and RIRE would be alike, and only five static principal parts would be necessary. As this example shows, minute choices in the formulation of an inflectional system's plat can have significant consequences for the analysis of that system's implicative relations; we return to this point in Chapter 12.[4]

---

[4] Many thanks to Olivier Bonami for discussion of this issue.

7.5 Dynamic principal-part analysis

When we compute the dynamic principal parts of the seventy-two French verbs, the results are surprisingly similar whether we employ a concrete or an abstract phonological analysis. For each conjugation J, Table 7.14 shows J's optimal dynamic principal-part number, J's cell predictor number, the number of optimal dynamic analyses for J, and the ratio of actual to possible optimal dynamic analyses, all under the concrete phonological analysis; Table 7.15 shows the same information under the abstract phonological analysis. The figures in the two tables are remarkably consistent. Typically, several optimal analyses are available for a given lexeme (approximately 10, on average); the average number of principal parts required to deduce a given member of a verb's paradigm is usually one, with 1.82 being the upper extreme; and predicting a verb's entire paradigm never requires more than two dynamic principal parts, and most often requires only one.

7.6 IC predictability and cell predictability

Tables 7.16 and 7.17 present the cell predictabilities and IC predictability of each French conjugation (under a concrete and an abstract phonology, respectively). These figures reveal considerable variation in the predictability of paradigms. In a concrete analysis, there are five maximally transparent conjugations – CÉDER 'give up', COLLER 'paste', COUVRIR 'cover', REMUER 'stir', and VALOIR 'be worth'; in each of these conjugations, any indexed stem suffices as the sole principal part. In an abstract analysis, French has three maximally transparent conjugations – those of COUVRIR, VALOIR, and MOURIR 'die' (whose paradigm is less than fully transparent in a concrete analysis). The cell predictability measures show that certain distillations tend to be highly predictable across most conjugations: Stems 1, 2, and 13 (those of the first- and second-person singular of the present indicative and the second-person singular imperative).

Both tables also present conjugations with extremely low predictability, the extreme case being that of CONFIRE 'preserve', with an IC predictability of 0.071 in both tables. But no conjugation in either table has more than one distillation whose realization is totally unpredictable (with a cell predictability of 0.000).

The tables differ, however, in the number of unpredictable stems they reveal. In the concrete plat analyzed in Table 7.16, there are six unpredictable stems: Stem 8 for (a) the conjugations of CUIRE 'cook' and CONFIRE, Stem 10 for (b)

Table 7.14. *Overview of optimal dynamic principal-part analyses of French conjugations (concrete analysis)*

Conjugations	Dynamic principal-part number n	Cell predictor number	Number p of optimal dynamic analyses	Ratio of p to the number of possible principal-part sets of cardinality n
CÉDER, COLLER, COUVRIR, REMUER, VALOIR	1	1.00	17	100.0% of 17
CUEILLIR, ÉCHOUER, ÊTRE	1	1.00	16	94.1% of 17
ACQUÉRIR, DORMIR, VAINCRE, VIVRE	1	1.00	14	82.4% of 17
VOULOIR	1	1.00	13	76.5% of 17
BEURRER, MOUDRE, MOURIR, RENDRE	1	1.00	12	70.6% of 17
CROÎTRE	1	1.00	11	64.7% of 17
FAIRE, JOINDRE, LEVER, PEINDRE, TENIR	1	1.00	10	58.8% of 17
ASSEOIR$_2$, LIRE, METTRE, PLAIRE	1	1.00	9	52.9% of 17
BOIRE, BOUILLIR, PRENDRE, SAVOIR	1	1.00	7	41.2% of 17
ALLER, RIRE	1	1.00	6	35.3% of 17
ENVOYER	1	1.00	4	23.5% of 17
HAÏR, MOUVOIR	1	1.00	3	17.6% of 17
ASSAILLIR, AVOIR, BATTRE, COUDRE, DIRE, POUVOIR, RECEVOIR, SENTIR, SERVIR, SUIVRE	1	1.00	2	11.8% of 17
INCLURE, NAÎTRE	1	1.00	1	5.9% of 17
COPIER	2	1.00	60	44.1% of 136
ÉCRIRE	2	1.00	40	29.4% of 136
CONNAÎTRE	2	1.00	33	24.3% of 136
FINIR	2	1.00	27	19.9% of 136
CUIRE, VÊTIR	2	1.00	4	2.9% of 136
APPUYER	2	1.06	24	17.6% of 136
CONFIRE	2	1.06	2	1.5% of 136
ASSEOIR$_1$	2	1.12	27	19.9% of 136
POURVOIR	2	1.12	9	6.6% of 136
FUIR	2	1.29	20	14.7% of 136
AIMER	2	1.29	16	11.8% of 136
ÉCROUER	2	1.29	4	2.9% of 136
CONCLURE	2	1.41	5	3.7% of 136
COURIR	2	1.53	42	30.9% of 136
VOIR	2	1.82	4	2.9% of 136
Average	1.25	1.05	11.56	42.20%

Table 7.15. *Overview of optimal dynamic principal-part analyses of French conjugations (abstract analysis)*

Conjugations	Dynamic principal-part number n	Cell predictor number	Number p of optimal dynamic analyses	Ratio of p to the number of possible principal-part sets of cardinality n
COUVRIR, MOURIR, VALOIR	1	1.00	17	100.0% of 17
ÊTRE	1	1.00	16	94.1% of 17
ACQUÉRIR, DORMIR, VAINCRE, VIVRE, VOULOIR	1	1.00	14	82.4% of 17
MOUDRE, RENDRE	1	1.00	12	70.6% of 17
CROÎTRE	1	1.00	11	64.7% of 17
FAIRE, JOINDRE, PEINDRE, TENIR	1	1.00	10	58.8% of 17
ASSEOIR$_2$, LIRE, METTRE, PLAIRE, RECEVOIR	1	1.00	9	52.9% of 17
BOIRE, BOUILLIR, PRENDRE, SAVOIR	1	1.00	7	41.2% of 17
ALLER	1	1.00	6	35.3% of 17
APPUYER, ENVOYER	1	1.00	4	23.5% of 17
HAÏR, MOUVOIR, POUVOIR	1	1.00	3	17.6% of 17
AVOIR, BATTRE, COUDRE, DIRE, SENTIR, SERVIR, SUIVRE	1	1.00	2	11.8% of 17
INCLURE, NAÎTRE	1	1.00	1	5.9% of 17
ÉCRIRE	2	1.00	40	29.4% of 136
CONNAÎTRE	2	1.00	33	24.3% of 136
FINIR	2	1.00	27	19.9% of 136
ASSAILLIR	2	1.00	15	11.0% of 136
CUIRE, VÊTIR	2	1.00	4	2.9% of 136
CUEILLIR	2	1.00	3	2.2% of 136
CONFIRE	2	1.06	2	1.5% of 136
ASSEOIR$_1$	2	1.12	27	19.9% of 136
POURVOIR	2	1.12	9	6.6% of 136
FUIR	2	1.12	4	2.9% of 136
AIMER, CONCLURE, ÉCROUER	2	1.29	4	2.9% of 136
COURIR	2	1.41	40	29.4% of 136
RIRE	2	1.41	4	2.9% of 136
VOIR	2	1.82	4	2.9% of 136
Average	1.30	1.05	9.68	36.38%

the conjugations of AIMER 'like' and ÉCROUER 'imprison', and Stem 19 for (c) the conjugations of INCLURE 'include' and CONCLURE 'end'. These stems are unpredictable because for each of the three pairs of conjugations in (a)–(c), both members of the pair exhibit exactly the same stem formatives in every distillation but one – that of Stem 8 in the case of (a) CUIRE and CONFIRE, that of Stem 10 in the case of (b) AIMER and ÉCROUER, and Stem 19 in the case of (c) INCLURE and CONCLURE. In the abstract plat, by contrast, there are ten unpredictable stems: those that are unpredictable under the concrete analysis, Stem 17 in the FUIR and RIRE conjugations (which, as we have already seen, is the only distillation for which these conjugations have distinct stem formatives under the abstract analysis), and Stem 10 in the conjugations of ASSAILLIR 'assail' and CUEILLIR 'pick'.

The case of ASSAILLIR and CUEILLIR reveals an important difference between phonologically concrete, hearer-oriented plats and phonologically abstract, speaker-oriented plats. In the abstract plat in Table 7.11, ASSAILLIR and CUEILLIR differ only in Stem 10 (the future/conditional stem): in the ASSAILLIR conjugation, Stem 10 has the stem formative /i/, while in the CUEILLIR conjugation, Stem 10 has the stem formative /ə/ – e.g. /asaj-i-ʁɛ/ '(I) will assail', but /kœj-ə-ʁɛ/ '(I) will pick'. In the concrete plat in Table 7.10, by contrast, the ASSAILLIR and CUEILLIR conjugations differ at several points because of the /œ/ ~ /ø/ alternation exhibited by CUEILLIR; for example, CUEILLIR exhibits a stem contrast between /kœj/ '(I) pick' and /køjɛ/ '(I) was picking', but ASSAILLIR exhibits no corresponding contrast (/asaj/ '(I) assail', /asajɛ/ '(I) was assailing'). The recurrence of the /œ/ ~ /ø/ alternation makes it possible to distinguish the CUEILLIR conjugation from the ASSAILLIR conjugation in several stems in the concrete plat; thus, the Stem-10 difference between the two conjugations is predictable from other differences. But in the abstract analysis, all forms of CUEILLIR are based on the theme |kŒj| (e.g. |kŒj| '(I) assail', |kŒjɛ| '(I) was assailing'), and the /œ/ ~ /ø/ alternation is absent from the plat, being automatically introduced by sandhi rules realizing the morphophoneme |Œ|, namely those in (2q–t). The conclusion is that the abstract plat is simpler than the concrete plat insofar as it makes fewer distinctions. The concrete plat is, accordingly, more informative than the abstract plat: it allows ICs to be distinguished more easily, and therefore has a higher average cell predictability (0.909 vs 0.891), has a higher average IC predictability (0.722 vs 0.647), and distinguishes certain conjugations that the abstract plat does not distinguish at all (Table 7.9).

The grayscale representations of Tables 7.16 and 7.17 in Figures 7.1 and 7.2 (in which the numbers on the horizontal axis are distillation numbers) show that low

Table 7.16. Cell predictabilities and IC predictability of sixty-four French conjugations (concrete analysis) [based on m = 4]

Distillations:	1	2	3	4	5	6	7	8	9	10	11	12	13	14	15	16	17	Avg cell predictability	IC predictability
Indexed stems:	1	2	3	4	5	7	8	10	11	12	13	14	15	16	17	18	19		
CÉDER	1.000	1.000	1.000	1.000	1.000	1.000	1.000	1.000	1.000	1.000	1.000	1.000	1.000	1.000	1.000	1.000	1.000	1.000	1.000 (3213 out of 3213)
COLLER	1.000	1.000	1.000	1.000	1.000	1.000	1.000	1.000	1.000	1.000	1.000	1.000	1.000	1.000	1.000	1.000	1.000	1.000	1.000 (3213 out of 3213)
COUVRIR	1.000	1.000	1.000	1.000	1.000	1.000	1.000	1.000	1.000	1.000	1.000	1.000	1.000	1.000	1.000	1.000	1.000	1.000	1.000 (3213 out of 3213)
REMUER	1.000	1.000	1.000	1.000	1.000	1.000	1.000	1.000	1.000	1.000	1.000	1.000	1.000	1.000	1.000	1.000	1.000	1.000	1.000 (3213 out of 3213)
VALOIR	1.000	1.000	1.000	1.000	1.000	1.000	1.000	1.000	1.000	1.000	1.000	1.000	1.000	1.000	1.000	1.000	1.000	1.000	1.000 (3213 out of 3213)
CUEILLIR	0.999	0.999	0.999	0.999	0.999	0.999	0.999	0.999	1.000	0.999	0.999	0.999	0.999	0.999	0.999	0.999	0.999	0.999	1.000 (3212 out of 3213)
ÉCHOUER	0.999	0.999	0.999	0.999	0.999	0.999	0.999	1.000	0.999	0.999	0.999	0.999	0.999	0.999	0.999	0.999	0.999	0.999	1.000 (3212 out of 3213)
ÊTRE	0.999	1.000	0.999	0.999	0.999	0.999	0.999	0.999	0.999	0.999	0.999	0.999	0.999	0.999	0.999	0.999	0.999	0.999	1.000 (3212 out of 3213)
ACQUÉRIR	0.997	0.997	0.997	0.997	0.997	0.997	1.000	0.997	0.997	0.997	0.997	0.997	0.997	0.997	0.997	0.997	0.998	0.997	0.998 (3206 out of 3213)
DORMIR	1.000	1.000	1.000	1.000	1.000	1.000	0.997	0.997	0.997	0.997	1.000	0.997	0.997	0.997	0.997	0.997	0.997	0.997	0.998 (3206 out of 3213)
VAINCRE	1.000	1.000	1.000	1.000	1.000	1.000	0.997	0.997	0.997	0.997	1.000	0.997	0.997	0.997	0.997	0.997	0.997	0.997	0.998 (3206 out of 3213)
VIVRE	1.000	1.000	1.000	1.000	1.000	1.000	0.997	0.997	0.997	0.997	1.000	0.997	0.997	0.997	0.997	0.997	0.997	0.997	0.998 (3206 out of 3213)
VOULOIR	0.999	0.999	0.996	0.996	0.996	0.996	0.996	0.996	0.997	0.996	0.999	0.996	0.996	0.996	0.996	0.996	0.996	0.997	0.998 (3205 out of 3213)
BEURRER	1.000	1.000	0.988	0.988	1.000	0.988	0.988	0.988	1.000	0.988	1.000	0.988	0.988	0.988	0.988	0.988	0.988	0.991	0.991 (3183 out of 3213)
FAIRE	0.998	0.996	0.988	0.988	0.990	0.988	0.992	0.989	0.988	0.988	0.998	0.988	0.988	0.992	0.988	0.988	0.988	0.991	0.991 (3185 out of 3213)
MOUDRE	1.000	1.000	0.988	0.988	0.988	0.988	0.988	0.997	0.988	0.988	1.000	0.988	0.988	0.997	0.988	0.988	0.988	0.991	0.991 (3183 out of 3213)
MOURIR	1.000	1.000	0.988	0.988	1.000	0.988	0.988	0.988	1.000	0.988	1.000	0.988	0.988	0.988	0.988	0.988	0.988	0.991	0.991 (3183 out of 3213)
RENDRE	1.000	1.000	0.988	0.988	0.988	0.988	0.988	0.997	0.988	0.988	1.000	0.988	0.988	0.997	0.988	0.988	0.988	0.991	0.991 (3183 out of 3213)
ASSEOIR$_2$	0.988	0.988	0.988	0.988	0.988	0.988	0.988	0.988	0.988	0.994	0.988	0.994	0.994	0.991	0.994	0.992	0.992	0.990	0.991 (3183 out of 3213)
LIRE	0.993	0.993	0.982	0.982	0.982	0.982	0.986	0.991	0.982	0.982	0.993	0.982	0.982	0.991	0.982	0.988	0.988	0.986	0.986 (3169 out of 3213)
METTRE	0.996	0.996	0.982	0.982	0.982	0.982	0.988	0.991	0.982	0.982	0.996	0.982	0.982	0.991	0.982	0.985	0.984	0.986	0.986 (3169 out of 3213)
CROÎTRE	0.997	0.997	0.977	0.977	0.977	0.977	0.988	0.977	0.977	0.977	0.997	0.977	0.977	0.977	0.977	0.997	0.997	0.984	0.983 (3157 out of 3213)
PLAIRE	0.995	0.986	0.973	0.973	0.973	0.973	0.991	0.974	0.973	0.973	0.986	0.973	0.973	0.976	0.973	0.993	0.993	0.979	0.979 (3145 out of 3213)
JOINDRE	1.000	1.000	0.961	0.961	0.961	0.961	0.961	1.000	0.961	0.961	1.000	0.961	0.961	1.000	0.961	1.000	1.000	0.977	0.969 (3115 out of 3213)
LEVER	0.961	0.961	1.000	1.000	0.961	1.000	0.961	0.961	0.961	1.000	0.961	1.000	1.000	0.961	1.000	0.961	0.961	0.977	0.969 (3115 out of 3213)
PEINDRE	1.000	1.000	0.961	0.961	0.961	0.961	0.961	1.000	0.961	0.961	1.000	0.961	0.961	1.000	0.961	1.000	1.000	0.977	0.969 (3115 out of 3213)
TENIR	0.961	0.961	1.000	1.000	0.961	1.000	0.961	0.961	0.961	1.000	0.961	1.000	1.000	0.961	1.000	0.961	0.961	0.977	0.969 (3115 out of 3213)
PRENDRE	0.958	0.958	0.997	0.997	0.958	0.997	0.961	0.958	0.958	0.997	0.958	0.997	0.997	0.958	0.997	0.960	0.959	0.974	0.967 (3108 out of 3213)
RIRE	0.987	0.987	0.944	0.944	0.977	0.944	0.955	0.995	0.977	0.944	0.987	0.944	0.944	0.959	0.977	0.954	0.954	0.963	0.956 (3073 out of 3213)
RECEVOIR	0.958	0.958	0.935	0.935	0.938	0.935	0.949	0.896	0.938	0.935	0.958	0.935	0.935	0.896	0.935	0.958	0.958	0.938	0.919 (2953 out of 3213)
BOIRE	0.996	0.996	0.893	0.893	0.935	0.893	0.971	0.925	0.935	0.893	0.996	0.893	0.893	0.935	0.893	0.988	0.988	0.936	0.917 (2945 out of 3213)

CONJUGATIONS

Verb																	Total
SAVOIR	0.996	0.898	0.988	0.988	0.892	0.988	0.997	0.988	0.892	0.892	0.892	0.988	0.892	0.988	0.998	0.946	0.916 (2943 out of 3213)
AVOIR	0.991	0.885	0.980	0.980	0.891	0.980	0.990	0.980	0.885	0.891	0.891	0.980	0.891	0.991	0.991	0.940	0.910 (2924 out of 3213)
BOUILLIR	0.961	0.961	0.987	0.987	0.847	0.996	0.847	0.996	0.847	0.987	0.987	0.988	0.847	0.988	0.847	0.926	0.880 (2828 out of 3213)
ALLER	0.777	0.777	0.997	0.997	0.777	0.986	0.959	0.777	0.777	0.997	0.997	0.997	0.959	0.997	0.961	0.909	0.825 (2652 out of 3213)
ASSAILLIR	0.976	0.976	0.976	0.976	0.973	0.765	0.776	0.765	0.973	0.976	0.976	0.976	0.845	0.961	0.775	0.896	0.816 (2623 out of 3213)
COPIER	0.776	0.776	0.959	0.959	0.771	0.776	0.922	0.776	0.771	0.959	0.959	0.992	0.922	0.922	0.922	0.887	0.795 (2555 out of 3213)
ENVOYER	0.999	0.999	0.996	0.996	0.996	0.961	0.566	0.996	0.961	0.999	0.996	0.996	0.566	0.566	0.566	0.877	0.660 (2121 out of 3213)
COUDRE	1.000	1.000	0.988	0.988	0.988	0.996	0.675	0.988	0.996	1.000	0.988	0.988	0.566	0.557	0.557	0.853	0.653 (2098 out of 3213)
ÉCRIRE	0.997	0.997	0.961	0.961	0.961	0.961	0.961	0.961	0.961	0.997	0.961	0.961	0.563	0.563	0.546	0.873	0.632 (2030 out of 3213)
COURIR	0.954	0.954	0.929	0.929	0.941	0.768	0.495	0.768	0.941	0.954	0.929	0.929	0.563	0.496	0.496	0.799	0.601 (1931 out of 3213)
MOUVOIR	0.997	0.997	0.994	0.994	0.994	0.416	0.996	0.416	0.994	0.997	0.994	0.994	0.994	0.997	0.997	0.893	0.542 (1743 out of 3213)
POUVOIR	0.996	0.996	0.994	0.994	0.994	0.415	0.995	0.415	0.994	0.996	0.994	0.994	0.994	0.996	0.996	0.892	0.542 (1742 out of 3213)
HAÏR	0.416	0.416	0.988	0.988	0.988	0.988	0.997	0.416	0.988	0.416	0.988	0.988	0.988	0.999	0.994	0.890	0.542 (1743 out of 3213)
NAÎTRE	0.998	0.997	0.986	0.986	0.986	0.414	0.996	1.000	0.986	0.997	0.986	0.986	0.999	0.999	0.994	0.889	0.542 (1740 out of 3213)
CONNAÎTRE	0.996	0.988	0.968	0.968	0.968	0.414	0.977	0.996	0.968	0.988	0.968	0.968	0.977	0.416	0.416	0.876	0.527 (1694 out of 3213)
APPUYER	0.776	0.776	0.935	0.935	0.984	0.977	0.566	0.984	0.776	0.776	0.935	0.935	0.566	0.566	0.566	0.776	0.516 (1658 out of 3213)
FINIR	0.416	0.416	0.935	0.935	0.660	0.935	0.977	0.935	0.416	0.416	0.935	0.935	0.994	0.994	0.961	0.858	0.501 (1611 out of 3213)
FUIR	0.949	0.949	0.684	0.684	0.785	0.926	0.549	0.785	0.949	0.949	0.684	0.684	0.566	0.566	0.407	0.741	0.464 (1490 out of 3213)
ASSEOIR$_1$	0.994	0.994	0.982	0.982	0.982	0.982	0.416	0.982	0.982	0.994	0.982	0.982	0.682	0.982	0.265	0.815	0.421 (1353 out of 3213)
BATTRE	1.000	1.000	0.997	0.997	0.997	0.997	0.411	0.997	0.997	1.000	0.997	0.997	0.229	0.265	0.265	0.856	0.396 (1273 out of 3213)
SENTIR	1.000	1.000	0.997	0.997	0.997	0.997	0.229	0.997	1.000	1.000	0.997	0.997	0.997	0.566	0.566	0.856	0.396 (1273 out of 3213)
SERVIR	1.000	1.000	0.997	0.997	0.997	0.997	0.997	0.997	1.000	1.000	0.997	0.997	0.229	0.229	0.229	0.856	0.396 (1273 out of 3213)
SUIVRE	1.000	1.000	0.997	0.997	0.997	0.997	0.997	0.997	1.000	1.000	0.997	0.997	0.997	0.566	0.566	0.856	0.396 (1273 out of 3213)
DIRE	0.994	0.994	0.944	0.944	0.944	0.944	0.847	0.944	0.944	0.994	0.944	0.944	0.843	0.843	0.810	0.812	0.396 (1273 out of 3213)
POURVOIR	0.996	0.996	0.935	0.935	0.935	0.935	0.219	0.935	0.996	0.996	0.935	0.935	0.665	0.416	0.416	0.776	0.250 (804 out of 3213)
AIMER	0.776	0.776	0.959	0.959	0.766	0.845	0.683	0.845	0.776	0.959	0.959	0.959	0.683	0.684	0.684	0.769	0.217 (696 out of 3213)
INCLURE	0.955	0.955	0.777	0.777	0.914	0.810	0.549	0.810	0.955	0.776	0.777	0.777	0.566	0.566	0.000	0.739	0.217 (697 out of 3213)
VOIR	0.996	0.996	0.975	0.975	0.975	0.975	0.109	0.975	0.996	0.955	0.975	0.975	0.555	0.297	0.297	0.770	0.185 (593 out of 3213)
CONCLURE	0.949	0.949	0.685	0.685	0.888	0.785	0.549	0.785	0.949	0.996	0.685	0.685	0.566	0.566	0.000	0.705	0.145 (465 out of 3213)
VÊTIR	1.000	1.000	0.997	0.997	0.997	0.997	0.997	0.997	0.997	1.000	0.997	0.997	0.229	0.229	0.229	0.817	0.132 (425 out of 3213)
CUIRE	0.997	0.997	0.961	0.961	0.961	0.961	0.000	0.961	0.961	0.997	0.961	0.961	0.563	0.563	0.546	0.752	0.124 (398 out of 3213)
ÉCROUER	0.776	0.776	0.934	0.934	0.763	0.842	0.565	0.842	0.776	0.776	0.934	0.934	0.565	0.566	0.566	0.734	0.124 (398 out of 3213)
CONFIRE	0.994	0.994	0.944	0.944	0.944	0.944	0.000	0.944	0.944	0.994	0.944	0.944	0.681	0.681	0.648	0.750	0.071 (227 out of 3213)
Avg	0.956	0.952	0.966	0.933	0.952	0.964	0.782	0.933	0.943	0.952	0.963	0.930	0.832	0.811	0.788	0.909	0.722

Boxed cells have maximally predictable realizations; shaded cells have unpredictable realizations.

Table 7.17. Cell predictabilities and IC predictability of fifty-seven French conjugations (abstract analysis) [based on m = 4]

Distillations:	1	2	3	4	5	6	7	8	9	10	11	12	13	14	15	16	17	Avg cell predictability	IC predictability
Indexed stems:	1	2	3	4	5	6	7	8	9	10	11	12	13	14	15	16	17		
COUVRIR	1.000	1.000	1.000	1.000	1.000	1.000	1.000	1.000	1.000	1.000	1.000	1.000	1.000	1.000	1.000	1.000	1.000	1.000	1.000 (3213 out of 3213)
MOURIR	1.000	1.000	1.000	1.000	1.000	1.000	1.000	1.000	1.000	1.000	1.000	1.000	1.000	1.000	1.000	1.000	1.000	1.000	1.000 (3213 out of 3213)
VALOIR	1.000	1.000	1.000	1.000	1.000	1.000	1.000	1.000	1.000	1.000	1.000	1.000	1.000	1.000	1.000	1.000	1.000	1.000	1.000 (3213 out of 3213)
ÊTRE	0.999	1.000	0.999	0.999	0.999	0.999	0.999	0.999	0.999	0.999	0.999	0.999	0.999	0.999	0.999	0.999	0.999	0.999	1.000 (3212 out of 3213)
ACQUÉRIR	0.997	0.997	0.997	0.997	0.997	0.997	1.000	0.997	0.997	0.997	0.997	0.997	0.997	0.997	0.997	0.997	0.998	0.997	0.998 (3206 out of 3213)
DORMIR	1.000	1.000	0.997	0.997	0.997	0.997	0.997	0.997	0.997	0.997	1.000	0.997	0.997	0.997	0.997	0.997	0.997	0.997	0.998 (3206 out of 3213)
VAINCRE	1.000	1.000	0.997	0.997	0.997	0.997	0.997	0.997	0.997	0.997	1.000	0.997	0.997	0.997	0.997	0.997	0.997	0.997	0.998 (3206 out of 3213)
VIVRE	1.000	1.000	0.997	0.997	0.997	0.997	0.997	0.997	0.997	0.997	1.000	0.997	0.997	0.997	0.997	0.997	0.997	0.997	0.998 (3206 out of 3213)
C VOULOIR	1.000	1.000	0.997	0.997	0.997	0.997	0.997	0.997	0.997	0.997	1.000	0.997	0.997	0.997	0.997	0.997	0.997	0.997	0.998 (3206 out of 3213)
O LIRE	0.993	0.993	0.990	0.990	0.990	0.990	0.994	0.991	0.990	0.990	0.993	0.990	0.990	0.994	0.990	0.996	0.996	0.992	0.993 (3189 out of 3213)
N FAIRE	0.998	0.996	0.988	0.988	0.990	0.988	0.992	0.989	0.988	0.988	0.997	0.988	0.988	0.991	0.988	0.988	0.988	0.990	0.991 (3184 out of 3213)
J MOUDRE	1.000	1.000	0.988	0.988	0.988	0.988	0.988	0.997	0.988	0.988	1.000	0.988	0.988	0.997	0.988	0.988	0.988	0.991	0.991 (3183 out of 3213)
U RENDRE	1.000	1.000	0.988	0.988	0.988	0.988	0.988	0.997	0.988	0.988	1.000	0.988	0.988	0.997	0.988	0.988	0.988	0.991	0.991 (3183 out of 3213)
G ASSEOIR$_2$	0.988	0.988	0.988	0.988	0.988	0.988	0.993	0.988	0.988	0.994	0.988	0.994	0.994	0.991	0.994	0.992	0.992	0.990	0.991 (3183 out of 3213)
A METTRE	0.996	0.996	0.982	0.982	0.982	0.982	0.988	0.991	0.982	0.982	0.996	0.982	0.982	0.991	0.982	0.985	0.984	0.986	0.986 (3169 out of 3213)
T CROÎTRE	0.997	0.997	0.977	0.977	0.977	0.977	0.988	0.977	0.977	0.977	0.977	0.977	0.977	0.977	0.977	0.977	0.977	0.984	0.983 (3157 out of 3213)
I PLAIRE	0.995	0.986	0.973	0.973	0.973	0.973	0.991	0.974	0.973	0.973	0.986	0.973	0.973	0.976	0.973	0.993	0.993	0.979	0.979 (3145 out of 3213)
O JOINDRE	1.000	1.000	0.961	0.961	0.961	0.961	0.961	1.000	0.961	0.961	1.000	0.961	0.961	1.000	0.961	1.000	1.000	0.977	0.969 (3115 out of 3213)
N PEINDRE	1.000	1.000	0.961	0.961	0.961	0.961	0.961	1.000	0.961	0.961	1.000	0.961	0.961	1.000	0.961	1.000	1.000	0.977	0.969 (3115 out of 3213)
S TENIR	0.961	0.961	1.000	1.000	0.961	1.000	0.961	0.961	0.961	1.000	0.961	1.000	1.000	0.961	1.000	0.961	0.961	0.977	0.969 (3115 out of 3213)
PRENDRE	0.958	0.958	0.997	0.997	0.958	0.997	0.961	0.958	0.958	0.997	0.958	0.997	0.997	0.958	0.997	0.960	0.959	0.974	0.967 (3108 out of 3213)
RECEVOIR	0.997	0.997	0.935	0.935	0.977	0.935	0.988	0.935	0.977	0.935	0.997	0.935	0.935	0.935	0.935	0.997	0.997	0.961	0.950 (3051 out of 3213)
BOIRE	0.996	0.996	0.893	0.893	0.935	0.893	0.971	0.925	0.935	0.893	0.996	0.893	0.893	0.935	0.893	0.988	0.988	0.936	0.917 (2945 out of 3213)
SAVOIR	0.996	0.898	0.988	0.988	0.892	0.988	0.997	0.988	0.892	0.892	0.892	0.892	0.892	0.988	0.892	0.998	0.998	0.946	0.916 (2943 out of 3213)
AVOIR	0.991	0.885	0.980	0.980	0.886	0.980	0.990	0.988	0.885	0.885	0.892	0.891	0.891	0.980	0.891	0.991	0.991	0.940	0.910 (2924 out of 3213)
BOUILLIR	0.998	0.998	0.988	0.988	0.847	0.997	0.847	0.991	0.847	0.847	0.777	0.847	0.847	0.847	0.898	0.847	0.847	0.927	0.880 (2828 out of 3213)
ALLER	0.777	0.777	0.996	0.996	0.777	0.998	0.959	0.777	0.777	0.777	0.998	0.777	0.996	0.959	0.997	0.961	0.961	0.910	0.825 (2652 out of 3213)
ENVOYER	0.999	0.999	0.996	0.996	0.996	0.996	0.566	0.685	0.996	0.996	0.999	0.996	0.996	0.566	0.996	0.566	0.566	0.877	0.660 (2121 out of 3213)
APPUYER	0.998	0.998	0.935	0.935	0.843	0.994	0.566	0.820	0.843	0.994	0.998	0.935	0.935	0.566	0.685	0.566	0.566	0.834	0.660 (2121 out of 3213)

COUDRE	**1.000**	**1.000**	0.988	0.838	0.988	0.675	0.566	0.988	0.988	**1.000**	0.988	0.838	0.566	0.988	0.557	0.557	0.853	0.653 (2098 out of 3213)
ÉCRIRE	0.997	0.997	0.961	0.961	0.961	0.961	0.566	0.961	0.961	0.997	0.961	0.961	0.563	0.961	0.563	0.546	0.873	0.632 (2030 out of 3213)
COURIR	0.954	0.954	0.892	0.892	0.941	0.446	0.560	0.988	0.941	0.954	0.892	0.892	0.563	0.929	0.447	0.447	0.805	0.563 (1808 out of 3213)
MOUVOIR	0.997	0.997	0.994	0.994	0.994	0.996	0.416	0.416	0.416	0.997	0.994	0.994	0.994	0.994	0.997	0.997	0.893	0.542 (1743 out of 3213)
POUVOIR	0.997	0.997	0.994	0.994	0.994	0.996	0.416	0.416	0.416	0.997	0.994	0.994	0.994	0.994	0.997	0.997	0.893	0.542 (1743 out of 3213)
HAÏR	0.416	0.416	0.988	0.988	0.988	0.997	**1.000**	0.416	0.988	0.416	0.988	0.988	0.999	0.988	0.999	0.994	0.890	0.542 (1743 out of 3213)
NAÎTRE	0.998	0.997	0.986	0.986	0.986	0.414	0.996	0.986	0.986	0.997	0.986	0.986	0.996	0.986	0.416	0.416	0.889	0.542 (1740 out of 3213)
CONNAÎTRE	0.996	0.988	0.968	0.968	0.968	0.414	0.977	0.968	0.968	0.988	0.968	0.968	0.977	0.968	0.416	0.416	0.876	0.527 (1694 out of 3213)
FINIR	0.416	0.416	0.935	0.935	0.935	0.977	0.997	0.935	0.935	0.416	0.935	0.935	0.994	0.935	0.994	0.961	0.858	0.501 (1611 out of 3213)
ASSEOIR$_1$	0.994	0.994	0.982	0.982	0.982	0.416	0.411	0.982	0.982	0.994	0.982	0.982	0.682	0.982	0.265	0.265	0.815	0.421 (1353 out of 3213)
BATTRE	**1.000**	**1.000**	0.997	0.997	0.997	0.997	0.229	0.997	0.997	**1.000**	0.997	0.997	0.229	0.997	0.566	0.566	0.856	0.396 (1273 out of 3213)
SENTIR	**1.000**	**1.000**	0.997	0.997	0.997	0.997	0.566	0.997	0.997	**1.000**	0.997	0.997	0.566	0.997	0.229	0.229	0.856	0.396 (1273 out of 3213)
SERVIR	**1.000**	**1.000**	0.997	0.997	0.997	0.997	0.229	0.997	0.997	**1.000**	0.997	0.997	0.229	0.997	0.566	0.566	0.856	0.396 (1273 out of 3213)
SUIVRE	**1.000**	**1.000**	0.997	0.997	0.997	0.997	0.229	0.997	0.997	**1.000**	0.997	0.997	0.229	0.997	0.566	0.566	0.856	0.396 (1273 out of 3213)
DIRE	0.994	0.994	0.944	0.944	0.944	0.416	0.847	0.944	0.944	0.994	0.944	0.229	0.843	0.944	0.843	0.810	0.812	0.396 (1273 out of 3213)
POURVOIR	0.996	0.996	0.935	0.935	0.935	0.079	0.219	0.935	0.935	0.996	0.935	0.935	0.665	0.935	0.416	0.416	0.776	0.250 (804 out of 3213)
INCLURE	0.955	0.955	0.685	0.685	0.914	0.549	0.685	0.961	0.914	0.955	0.685	0.685	0.566	0.777	0.566	0.000	0.735	0.217 (697 out of 3213)
ASSAILLIR	0.958	0.958	0.933	0.933	0.948	0.565	0.000	0.994	0.948	0.958	0.933	0.933	0.683	0.958	0.565	0.564	0.813	0.216 (695 out of 3213)
VOIR	0.996	0.996	0.975	0.975	0.975	0.109	0.079	0.975	0.975	0.996	0.975	0.975	0.555	0.975	0.297	0.297	0.770	0.185 (593 out of 3213)
VÊTIR	**1.000**	**1.000**	0.997	0.997	0.997	0.997	0.229	0.997	0.997	**1.000**	0.997	0.997	0.229	0.997	0.229	0.229	0.817	0.132 (425 out of 3213)
AIMER	0.776	0.776	0.934	0.934	0.766	0.565	0.000	0.995	0.766	0.776	0.934	0.934	0.565	0.959	0.566	0.566	0.753	0.124 (398 out of 3213)
CUIRE	0.997	0.997	0.961	0.961	0.961	0.000	0.566	0.961	0.961	0.997	0.961	0.416	0.563	0.961	0.563	0.546	0.752	0.124 (398 out of 3213)
ÉCROUER	0.776	0.776	0.897	0.897	0.763	0.565	0.000	0.992	0.763	0.776	0.897	0.897	0.565	0.934	0.566	0.566	0.743	0.124 (398 out of 3213)
FUIR	0.986	0.986	0.685	0.685	0.785	0.549	0.820	0.785	0.935	0.986	0.685	0.685	0.566	0.000	0.566	0.407	0.709	0.124 (398 out of 3213)
RIRE	0.985	0.985	0.566	0.566	0.835	0.631	0.846	0.835	0.935	0.985	0.566	0.566	0.648	0.000	0.648	0.434	0.704	0.124 (398 out of 3213)
CONCLURE	0.949	0.949	0.566	0.566	0.888	0.549	0.685	0.888	0.935	0.949	0.566	0.566	0.685	0.685	0.566	0.000	0.695	0.124 (398 out of 3213)
CUEILLIR	0.958	0.958	0.933	0.933	0.948	0.447	0.000	0.994	0.948	0.958	0.933	0.933	0.564	0.958	0.446	0.445	0.785	0.124 (397 out of 3213)
CONFIRE	0.994	0.994	0.944	0.944	0.944	0.000	0.685	0.944	0.944	0.994	0.944	0.229	0.681	0.944	0.681	0.648	0.750	0.071 (227 out of 3213)
Avg	0.960	0.956	0.949	0.912	0.951	0.979	0.788	0.730	0.930	0.956	0.946	0.909	0.797	0.925	0.769	0.740	0.891	0.647

212 *Stems as principal parts*

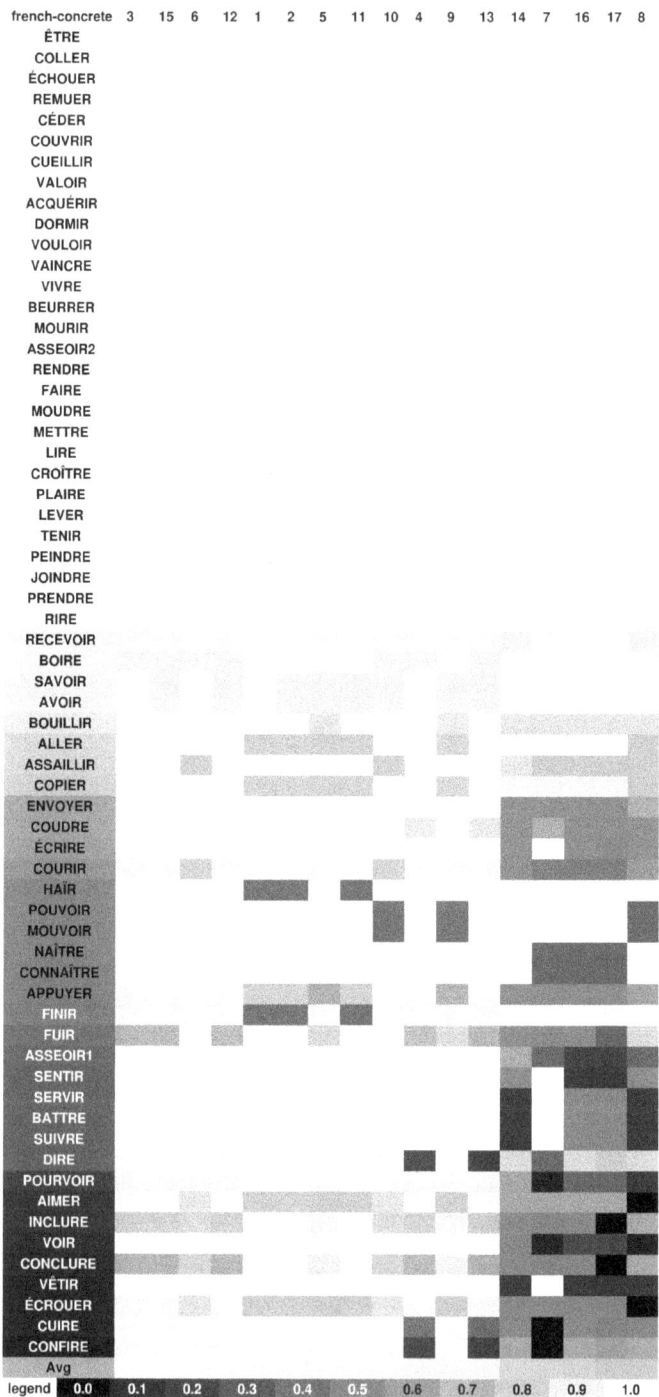

Figure 7.1. *Predictabilities of French conjugations (concrete analysis)*

IC predictability and cell predictability 213

Figure 7.2. *Predictabilities of French conjugations (abstract analysis)*

Table 7.18. *Paradigm transparency in four languages*

	Fur	Icelandic	Comaltepec Chinantec	French
Conjugations	19	162*	67	abstract 57 concrete 64
Distillations	9	21	12	17
Dynamic principal-part number, averaged across ICs	1.58	1.56	1.84	abstract 1.30 concrete 1.25
Number of alternative dynamic principal-part analyses for a conjugation, averaged across conjugations	3.26	28.18	5.96	abstract 9.68 concrete 11.56
Ratio of actual to possible optimal dynamic principal-part analyses, averaged across conjugations (%)	17.3	23.9	20.3	abstract 36.4 concrete 42.2
IC predictability, averaged across conjugations	0.485	0.570	0.391	abstract 0.647 concrete 0.722
Average cell predictability, averaged across conjugations	0.743	0.845	0.815	abstract 0.891 concrete 0.909
Cell predictor number, averaged across conjugations	1.04	1.09	1.08	1.05

*Jörg 1989 lists 162, but there are only 146 distinct ICs.

cell predictability is a diffuse property of French conjugations; recall the comparatively condensed pattern of low cell predictability in Fur (Figure 4.1 in §4.6).

7.7 Cross-linguistic comparison

If we set our French results alongside those for Fur, Icelandic, and Comaltepec Chinantec (as in Table 7.18), several patterns emerge. On one hand, the systems of verb inflection in these languages clearly differ widely along certain dimensions, including the number of conjugation classes, the number of distillations for which verbs inflect, and the average number of dynamic principal parts needed to identify a verb's conjugation; with respect to the last of these dimensions, Comaltepec Chinantec and French vary quite widely. These languages also vary widely in their number of alternative dynamic principal-part analyses (averaged across conjugations), in the ratio of actual to possible optimal principal-part analyses (averaged across conjugations), and in their average IC predictability. On the other hand, the languages show less variation in their average cell predictability, and they show a high degree of uniformity with respect to their cell predictor number (averaged across conjugations). Thus, French adds further evidence of the pattern in (3) (noted earlier in §3.3).

(3) The **depth-of-inference contrast**
Languages vary widely in the number of dynamic principal parts they require to distinguish a given IC; but languages show a high degree of uniformity in allowing a given form in a lexeme's paradigm to be deduced from a low number of dynamic principal parts (the average number being not much more than one).

That is, the identification of a lexeme's IC may require a complex inference based on several word forms; deducing particular word forms sometimes involves inferences of similar complexity, but on average, it involves much simpler inferences, most often from no more than one other word form. We view the depth-of-inference contrast as a more precise formulation of the Low Entropy Conjecture (Malouf & Ackerman 2010c), according to which paradigms tend universally to exhibit low expected conditional entropy. We return to a discussion of entropy measures in Chapter 8.

7.8   Stem referrals and principal parts

As we observed in §7.2, a French verb ordinarily has forty-nine cells in its synthetic paradigm; see again Table 7.3. We have shown that if one considers the stem distinctions in all French verb paradigms, then the cumulative result is a schematic paradigm distinguishing nineteen or twenty indexed stems (depending on whether the assumed phonological analysis is concrete or abstract); see again Table 7.6. No verb, however, has this many distinct stem forms. On the contrary, every verb's indexed stems show considerable syncretism, but verbs vary in the ways in which this syncretism is distributed among their indexed stems. In this section, we discuss an alternative approach to the analysis of French principal parts based on these patterns of stem syncretism; we call this the **stem-referral approach**. Unlike the **formative-based approach** of §7.3, in which stem formatives (or the significative absence thereof) are treated as the only marks of a French verb's conjugation class membership, the stem-referral approach distinguishes conjugations both by the stem formatives that they employ and by the particular patterns of stem syncretism that they exhibit.[5]

---

[5] We wish to thank Matthew Baerman for conversations that led to our investigation of the stem-referral approach. Matthew proposed the idea of a **signature**: the pattern of syncretism exhibited

The plat that we use for the stem-referral approach is given in Table 7.19. This "stem-referral plat" assumes an abstract phonological analysis. Each column corresponds to one of the nineteen indexed stems in the abstract, formative-based analysis. Each indexed stem S has, as its exponence in a given conjugation, either a stem formative or a referral to the form of indexed stem with which S is syncretized. The stem-referral plat is therefore speaker-oriented. The plat's patterns of referral are part of a French speaker's knowledge of verb morphology; they have no phonological reality (for instance, the exponence '3' refers to a stem in /-waj/ in the conjugation of ENVOYER but to a stem in /-s/ in that of FINIR).

Consider the conjugation of CONNAÎTRE 'be acquainted with' in Table 7.19. Although nineteen indexed stems are needed to determine the full paradigm of CONNAÎTRE, there are only five distinct stem forms, those of Stem 1 /konɛ/), Stem 3 (/konɛs/), Stem 8 (/kony/), Stem 10 (/konɛt/), and Stem 16 (/konɛtʁ/); Stems 2 and 13 share the form of Stem 1, Stems 4–7, 11, 12, 14, 15, and 17 share the form of Stem 3, and Stems 9, 18, and 19 share the form of Stem 8. As Table 7.19 shows, French verbs vary in the amount of syncretism they exhibit: ÊTRE 'be' exhibits very little, while CONCLURE 'end' is highly syncretic: all but one of its indexed stems are syncretized with Stem 1 (/kɔ̃kly/).

In this plat, the same conjugations fall together as in the abstract, formative-based plat; see again the redundancies in Table 7.9. Thus, the seventy-two conjugations in our initial sample are reduced to fifty-seven in Table 7.19. On the other hand, all nineteen indexed stems are distillations in this plat. Like the abstract, formative-based analysis, the stem-referral analysis yields six optimal static principal parts. Here, there are four alternative analyses (Table 7.20), with four indexed stems essential to every analysis:

---

by a lexeme's paradigm. More precisely, the signature of an IC J with respect to a set S of MPSs is a partition P of S such that (i) for every s ∈ P, every member of s has the same exponence, and (ii) for all s_1, s_2 ∈ P, if s_1's members share exponence E_1 and s_2's members share exponence E_2, then $E_1 = E_2$ iff $s_1 = s_2$. This notion makes it possible to construct a plat in which paradigms exhibiting the same signature are assigned to the same IC. In a plat of this sort, the English verbs WALK and DIG belong to the same IC, because they exhibit the same pattern of syncretism: past tense form (*I walked/dug*) = irrealis form (*if I walked/dug*) = past participial form (*I have walked/dug*). The stem-referral plat in Table 7.19 is similar but not identical to a signature-based plat: it does represent two ICs as alike to the extent that they exhibit similar stem-referrals, but nevertheless distinguishes ICs if they exhibit different morphology. In a plat of this sort, the conjugations of WALK and DIG would differ in the past tense column, in which WALK would have -*ed* but DIG would have /ɪ/ ⟶ /ʌ/ (or something similar); in all other columns, the two conjugations would be alike (including the two columns specifying a referral to the past tense form).

Table 7.19. *Stem-referral for seventy-two French conjugations*

Conjugation	Stem 1	Stem 2	Stem 3	Stem 4	Stem 5	Stem 6	Stem 7	Stem 8	Stem 9	Stem 10	Stem 11	Stem 12	Stem 13	Stem 14	Stem 15	Stem 16	Stem 17	Stem 18	Stem 19
ÊTRE	-sɥi	-ɛ	-sɔm	!ɛt	-sɔ̃	-et	6	8	-sə	-swa	11	11	-swaj	14	-etʁ	6	-ete	18
AVOIR	-ɛ	-a	-av	3	-ɔ̃	3	-y	8	-o	1	11	11	-ɛj	14	-avwaʁ	14	8	8
AIMER	—	1	1	1	1	1	-ɛ	-a	-ə	1	1	1	1	1	-e	1	16	16
COLLER	—	1	1	1	1	1	-ɛ	-a	-ə	1	1	1	1	1	-e	1	16	16
BEURRER	—	1	1	1	1	1	-ɛ	-a	-ə	1	1	1	1	1	-e	1	16	16
DÉJEUNER	—	1	1	1	1	1	-ɛ	-a	-ə	1	1	1	1	1	-e	1	16	16
ÉCROUER	—	1	1	1	1	1	-ɛ	-a	1	1	1	1	1	1	-e	1	16	16
ÉCHOUER	—	1	1	1	1	1	-ɛ	-a	1	1	1	1	1	1	-e	1	16	16
REFLUER	—	1	1	1	1	1	-ɛ	-a	1	1	1	1	1	1	-e	1	16	16
REMUER	—	1	1	1	1	1	-ɛ	-a	-ə	1	1	1	1	1	-e	1	16	16
LEVER	—	1	1	1	1	1	-ɛ	-a	-ə	1	1	1	1	1	-e	1	16	16
CÉDER	—	1	1	1	1	1	-ɛ	-a	-ə	1	1	1	1	1	-e	1	16	16
COPIER	—	1	1	1	1	1	-ɛ	-a	1	1	1	1	1	1	-e	1	16	16
APPUYER	—	-j	3	1	3	1	-jɛ	-ja	1	1	1	1	3	3	-je	3	16	16
BROYER	—	-j	3	1	3	1	-jɛ	-ja	1	1	1	1	3	3	-je	3	16	16
ENVOYER	-wa	-waj	3	1	3	1	-wajɛ	-waja	-ɛ	1	1	1	3	3	-waje	3	16	16
FINIR	—	-s	3	3	3	3	1	1	8	3	3	3	3	3	-ʁ	3	1	1
HAÏR	!ɛ	-s	3	3	3	3	—	-a	8	3	3	3	3	3	-ʁ	3	8	8
ALLER	!vɛ	!va	—	!vɔ̃	3	3	-ɛ	-a	@i	!aj	3	2	3	3	-e	3	16	16
TENIR	-jɛ̃	-jɛ̃	-ən	-jɛn	3	3	-ɛ̃	8	-jɛ̃d	5	3	1	3	3	-əniʁ	3	-əny	18
ACQUÉRIR	-jɛʁ	-jɛʁ	-eʁ	3	1	3	-i	8	3	1	3	1	3	3	-eʁiʁ	-eʁiʁ	8	19
SENTIR	—	-t	-t	3	3	3	-ti	8	8	3	3	3	3	3	-tiʁ	3	8	8
VÊTIR	—	-t	-t	3	3	3	-ti	8	8	3	3	3	3	3	-tiʁ	3	-ty	18
COUVRIR	-ʁ	1	1	1	1	-ʁi	7	7	7	1	7	1	1	1	-ʁiʁ	1	-ɛʁ	19

Table 7.19. (cont.)

Conjugation	Stem 1	Stem 2	Stem 3	Stem 4	Stem 5	Stem 6	Stem 7	Stem 8	Stem 9	Stem 10	Stem 11	Stem 12	Stem 13	Stem 14	Stem 15	Stem 16	Stem 17	Stem 18	Stem 19
CUEILLIR	–	1	1	1	1	1	-i	8	-ɔ	1	1	1	1	1	-iʁ	1	8	8	8
ASSAILLIR	–	1	1	1	1	1	-i	8	8	1	1	1	1	1	-iʁ	1	8	8	8
BOUILLIR	–	-j	3	3	3	3	-ji	8	8	3	3	3	3	3	-jiʁ	3	8	8	8
DORMIR	–	-m	3	3	3	3	-mi	8	8	3	3	3	3	3	-miʁ	3	8	8	8
COURIR	–	1	1	1	1	1	-y	8	1	1	1	1	1	1	-iʁ	1	8	8	8
MOURIR	-œʁ	-uʁ	3	3	1	3	-uʁy	8	3	3	3	3	3	3	-uʁiʁ	3	-ɔʁ	19	19
SERVIR	–	-v	3	3	1	3	-vi	8	8	3	3	3	3	3	-viʁ	3	8	8	8
FUIR	–	-j	3	3	1	3	1	1	1	1	1	1	3	3	-ʁ	3	1	1	1
RECEVOIR	-wa	-əv	3	3	3	3	-y	8	3	5	3	3	3	3	-əvwaʁ	3	8	8	8
VOIR	-wa	-waj	3	1	3	1	-i	8	-ɛ	1	1	1	3	3	-waʁ	3	-y	18	18
POURVOIR	-wa	-waj	3	1	3	1	-y	8	1	1	1	1	3	3	-waʁ	3	8	8	8
SAVOIR	-ɛ	-av	3	3	3	3	-y	8	-o	-aʃ	11	11	11	11	-avwaʁ	11	8	8	8
DEVOIR	-wa	-əv	3	-wav	3	3	-y	8	3	5	3	3	3	3	-əvwaʁ	3	8	8	8
POUVOIR	-ø	-uv	3	-œv	3	3	-y	8	-u	-ɥis	11	1	3	3	-uvwaʁ	3	8	8	8
MOUVOIR	-ø	-uv	3	-œv	3	3	-y	8	3	5	3	3	3	3	-uvwaʁ	3	8	8	8
VALOIR	-o	-al	3	3	3	3	-aly	8	-od	-aj	3	3	3	3	-alwaʁ	3	8	8	8
VOULOIR	-ø	-ul	3	-œl	3	3	-uly	8	-ud	-œj	3	3	3	3	-ulwaʁ	3	8	8	8
ASSEOIR₁	-wa	-waj	3	1	3	3	-i	8	1	1	1	1	3	3	-waʁ	3	8	8	-iz
ASSEOIR₂	-je	-ɛj	3	3	3	-ɛ	-i	8	1	3	7	3	3	3	-waʁ	3	8	8	-iz
SURSEOIR	-wa	-waj	3	1	3	1	-i	8	1	3	1	1	3	3	-waʁ	3	8	8	-iz
RENDRE	–	-d	3	3	3	3	-di	8	3	3	3	3	3	3	-dʁ	3	-dy	18	-iz
PRENDRE	-ɑ̃	-ən	3	-ɛn	3	3	-i	8	-ɑ̃d	5	3	3	3	3	-ɑ̃dʁ	3	8	-iz	-iz
BATTRE	–	-t	3	3	3	3	-ti	8	3	3	3	3	3	3	-tʁ	3	-ty	18	-iz
METTRE	-ɛ	-ɛt	3	3	3	3	-i	8	3	3	3	3	3	3	-ɛtʁ	3	8	8	-iz
PEINDRE	-ɛ̃	-ɛɲ	3	3	3	3	-ɛɲi	8	-ɛ̃d	3	3	3	3	3	-ɛ̃dʁ	3	1	1	-ɛ̃t
JOINDRE	-ɛ̃	-ɑɲ	3	3	3	3	-ɑɲi	8	-ɛ̃d	3	3	3	3	3	-ɛ̃dʁ	3	1	1	-ɛ̃t

CRAINDRE	-ɛ̃	1	-ɛɲ	3	3	3	-ɛɲi	8	-ɛ̃d	3	3	1	3	-ɛ̃dʁ	3	—	-ɛ̃t
VAINCRE	—	1	-k	3	3	3	-ki	8	3	3	3	1	3	-kʁ	3	-ky	18
FAIRE	-ɛ	1	-əz	!fɛt	-ɔ̃	3	-i	8	-ə	-as	11	1	3	-ɛʁ	4	—	-ɛt
PLAIRE	-ɛ	1	-ɛz	3	3	3	-y	8	1	3	3	1	3	-ɛʁ	3	8	8
CONNAÎTRE	-ɛ	1	-ɛs	3	3	3	-y	8	-ɛt	3	3	1	3	-ɛtʁ	3	8	8
NAÎTRE	-ɛ	1	-ɛs	3	3	3	-aki	8	-ɛt	3	3	1	3	-ɛtʁ	3	-e	18
REPAÎTRE	-ɛ	1	-ɛs	3	3	3	-y	8	-ɛt	3	3	1	3	-ɛtʁ	3	8	8
CROÎTRE	-wa	1	-was	3	3	3	-y	8	-wat	3	3	1	3	-watʁ	3	8	8
CROIRE	-wa	1	-waj	3	1	3	-y	8	1	1	3	1	3	-waʁ	3	8	8
BOIRE	-wa	1	-yv	3	-wav	3	-y	8	1	5	3	1	3	-waʁ	3	8	8
CONCLURE	—	1	1	1	1	1	1	1	1	1	1	1	1	-ʁ	1	—	1
INCLURE	—	1	1	1	1	1	1	1	1	1	1	1	1	-ʁ	1	—	-z
COUDRE	—	1	-z	3	3	3	-zi	8	-d	3	3	1	3	-dʁ	3	-zy	18
MOUDRE	—	1	-l	3	3	3	-ly	8	-d	3	3	1	3	-dʁ	3	8	8
SUIVRE	—	1	-v	3	3	3	-vi	8	3	3	3	1	3	-vʁ	3	8	8
VIVRE	-i	1	-iv	3	3	3	-ɛky	8	3	3	3	1	3	-ivʁ	3	8	8
LIRE	-i	1	-iz	3	3	3	-y	8	1	3	3	1	3	-iʁ	3	8	8
DIRE	—	1	-z	!dit	3	3	1	1	1	3	3	1	3	-ʁ	4	1	-t
RIRE	—	1	-j	3	1	3	1	1	1	1	1	1	3	-ʁ	3	1	1
ÉCRIRE	—	1	-v	3	3	3	-vi	8	1	3	3	1	3	-ʁ	3	1	-t
CONFIRE	—	1	-z	3	3	3	1	1	1	3	3	1	3	-ʁ	3	1	-t
CUIRE	—	1	-z	3	3	3	-zi	8	1	3	3	1	3	-ʁ	3	1	-t

Table 7.20. *Optimal static principal-part analyses for French (stem-referral analysis)*

Indexed stem	1	2	3	4	5	6	7	8	9	10	11	12	13	14	15	16	17	18	19
Analyses a	✓	✓			✓	✓											✓		✓
b	✓	✓							✓	✓							✓		✓
c	✓								✓	✓					✓		✓		✓
d	✓								✓	✓					✓		✓		✓

- Stem 3 (the first-person plural present indicative stem)
- Stem 10 (the future/conditional stem)
- Stem 17 (the present participial stem)
- Stem 19 (the feminine stem of the past participle).

Although the exponence of Stem 3 is most often a stem formative in the stem-referral plat, that of Stem 17 is nearly always a referral, mostly to Stem 3.

In the formative-based analyses, no conjugation requires more than two dynamic principal parts; in the stem-referral analysis, however, two conjugations (those of CONFIRE and FUIR) require three dynamic principal parts. Still, the stem-referral analysis entails only a modest increase in the average dynamic principal-part number and a minuscule increase in the average cell predictor number, as Table 7.21 shows.

Table 7.21 presents the predictability measures for the stem-referral analysis. These differ in several ways from the corresponding measures under the formative-based analyses in Tables 7.16 and 7.17. The high and low extremes for average cell predictability and IC predictability are lower in Table 7.21 than in either Table 7.16 or 7.17; thus, there are no maximally transparent conjugations in Table 7.21. There are very few instances (only four) of stems that are maximally predictable in their ICs. On the other hand, only eight conjugations have stems that are unpredictable (compared to six and ten in the concrete and abstract formative-based analyses), and none of these eight conjugations has more than one unpredictable stem. Under the stem-referral analysis, both the average IC predictability and the average cell predictability are lower than under either of the formative-based analyses.

Over all, considerations of parsimony favor the formative-based approach to principal-part analysis developed in §7.3: in particular, the concrete formative-based approach yields a lower number of principal parts (whether static or dynamic) and higher predictabilities. Nevertheless, the stem-referral approach provides useful confirmation of the depth-of-inference contrast: however high an IC system's dynamic principal-part number may be, its cell predictor number tends to remain low.

7.9 Conclusions

The evidence discussed in this chapter supports three main conclusions. The first is that the implicative relations among the cells in a lexeme's paradigm may pertain basically to the formation and alternation of the stems involved in their definition. Because the implicative relations among the cells in a French verb's realized paradigm depend not on its word forms' terminations (which are remarkably constant across conjugations) but on their stems, it is simpler to regard a French verb's principal parts as indexed stems rather than as realized cells. The methods of principal-part analysis developed in the preceding chapters directly accommodate this alternative conception of principal parts; we anticipate that this alternative conception will be desirable for the analysis of many languages' IC systems.

The second conclusion is that the implicative relations among a realized paradigm's cells vary according to the kind of plat from which they are gauged: the results yielded by a hearer-oriented plat (in which IC distinctions are represented in concrete phonological terms) differ from those yielded by a speaker-oriented plat (in which IC distinctions are represented in a more abstract way, one that takes account of language users' knowledge of the rules of sandhi and the morphophonological alternations in which an IC system's realized paradigms participate).

The results in this chapter compare in an interesting way with those of Chapter 5. In Chapter 5, we saw that including grammatical information in a plat diminishes the measurable complexity of the IC system that it represents. In this chapter, we have seen that omitting information from a plat may make the plat itself simpler, yet this simplification may increase the complexity of the IC system that it represents. In the abstract, speaker-oriented plat, distinctions between automatic phonological alternants and between morphophonological alternants are omitted; because of these omissions, the abstract plat represents the French system of conjugations as more complex, in the sense that it tends more strongly to inhibit motivated inferences about a lexeme's full paradigm of forms from subsets of those forms. The speaker-oriented stem-referral plat discussed in §7.8 also omits information; the plat in Table 7.19 represents referrals to Stem n identically across ICs (as 'n'), even though Stem n may itself vary in its form from one IC to another. Accordingly, this plat represents the French system

Table 7.21. *Cell predictabilities and IC predictability of fifty-seven French conjugations (stem-referral analysis) [based on m = 4]*

19 stems, all distillations

	1	2	3	4	5	6	7	8	9	10	11	12	13	14	15	16	17	18	19	Avg	IC predictability
ÊTRE	0.992	0.992	0.992	0.992	0.992	0.992	0.998	0.992	1.000	0.992	0.992	0.999	0.999	0.992	0.998	0.992	0.992	0.992	0.992	0.994	0.994 (5003 out of 5035)
ALLER	0.952	0.952	0.952	0.985	0.952	0.992	0.969	0.959	0.959	0.952	0.952	0.962	0.952	0.991	0.984	0.959	0.979	0.976	0.976	0.966	0.962 (4842 out of 5035)
COUVRIR	0.900	1.000	0.988	0.988	0.998	0.988	0.900	0.900	0.900	0.900	0.998	0.901	0.999	0.988	0.988	0.900	0.991	0.900	0.904	0.949	0.920 (4631 out of 5035)
FAIRE	0.909	0.989	0.856	0.856	0.860	0.991	0.959	0.882	0.959	0.860	0.856	0.878	0.979	0.975	0.872	0.879	0.954	0.888	0.856	0.908	0.885 (4454 out of 5035)
AVOIR	0.958	0.784	0.943	0.979	0.788	0.985	0.790	0.972	0.998	0.943	0.794	0.965	0.950	0.784	0.790	0.943	0.784	0.982	0.976	0.900	0.827 (4162 out of 5035)
TENIR	0.760	0.974	0.818	0.965	0.760	0.998	0.937	0.760	0.937	0.760	0.861	0.914	0.969	0.991	0.961	0.760	0.936	0.760	0.804	0.875	0.808 (4066 out of 5035)
VOULOIR	0.804	0.969	0.730	0.959	0.730	0.992	0.905	0.730	0.937	0.730	0.730	0.804	0.953	0.972	0.942	0.730	0.893	0.905	0.861	0.857	0.783 (3943 out of 5035)
VALOIR	0.730	0.969	0.730	0.944	0.804	0.992	0.861	0.730	0.905	0.730	0.730	0.812	0.937	0.956	0.912	0.730	0.877	0.861	0.804	0.843	0.783 (3943 out of 5035)
SAVOIR	0.913	0.803	0.878	0.976	0.761	0.991	0.783	0.937	0.992	0.878	0.719	0.905	0.879	0.719	0.719	0.878	0.719	0.968	0.952	0.861	0.774 (3897 out of 5035)
MOURIR	0.670	0.973	0.670	0.956	0.859	0.989	0.901	0.670	0.894	0.846	0.861	0.878	0.968	0.980	0.951	0.670	0.730	0.670	0.806	0.839	0.735 (3701 out of 5035)
PRENDRE	0.615	0.973	0.673	0.946	0.615	0.992	0.861	0.747	0.937	0.615	0.730	0.824	0.963	0.980	0.937	0.615	0.861	0.775	0.694	0.808	0.691 (3479 out of 5035)
ACQUÉRIR	0.592	0.979	0.592	0.945	0.800	0.972	0.857	0.670	0.930	0.782	0.804	0.831	0.970	0.957	0.933	0.592	0.592	0.694	0.728	0.801	0.672 (3386 out of 5035)
ASSEOIR$_2$	0.573	0.989	0.573	0.936	0.729	0.988	0.573	0.759	0.904	0.697	0.697	0.574	0.979	0.976	0.925	0.672	0.916	0.805	0.720	0.789	0.657 (3306 out of 5035)
VAINCRE	0.656	0.974	0.521	0.893	0.801	0.996	0.838	0.521	0.804	0.637	0.757	0.812	0.963	0.982	0.885	0.521	0.886	0.521	0.637	0.769	0.615 (3095 out of 5035)
ENVOYER	0.730	0.975	0.714	0.953	0.903	0.960	0.904	0.505	0.505	0.599	0.904	0.904	0.974	0.958	0.951	0.505	0.878	0.637	0.637	0.795	0.603 (3034 out of 5035)
APPUYER	0.673	0.975	0.607	0.884	0.820	0.905	0.881	0.477	0.477	0.635	0.821	0.881	0.974	0.902	0.882	0.477	0.675	0.637	0.625	0.748	0.579 (2917 out of 5035)
BOUILLIR	0.629	0.986	0.514	0.893	0.693	0.937	0.637	0.457	0.806	0.563	0.650	0.637	0.969	0.916	0.875	0.457	0.811	0.689	0.625	0.723	0.563 (2837 out of 5035)
CROÎTRE	0.521	0.962	0.427	0.914	0.637	0.986	0.703	0.604	0.845	0.427	0.556	0.633	0.914	0.930	0.864	0.427	0.851	0.781	0.698	0.720	0.540 (2717 out of 5035)
RENDRE	0.656	0.974	0.404	0.893	0.801	0.996	0.838	0.404	0.804	0.521	0.757	0.812	0.963	0.982	0.885	0.521	0.886	0.404	0.543	0.739	0.521 (2625 out of 5035)
VIVRE	0.521	0.969	0.404	0.921	0.730	0.992	0.804	0.404	0.861	0.521	0.656	0.755	0.937	0.956	0.889	0.404	0.833	0.730	0.637	0.733	0.521 (2625 out of 5035)
DORMIR	0.521	0.969	0.378	0.873	0.772	0.976	0.637	0.378	0.804	0.521	0.521	0.588	0.937	0.939	0.841	0.378	0.851	0.637	0.563	0.698	0.500 (2519 out of 5035)
HAÏR	0.373	0.969	0.447	0.882	0.782	0.985	0.714	0.373	0.730	0.489	0.698	0.665	0.937	0.949	0.851	0.521	0.860	0.582	0.508	0.701	0.496 (2497 out of 5035)
POUVOIR	0.769	0.962	0.711	0.948	0.711	0.985	0.851	0.788	0.960	0.343	0.343	0.378	0.925	0.930	0.899	0.711	0.883	0.921	0.889	0.785	0.472 (2377 out of 5035)
MOUDRE	0.637	0.969	0.311	0.883	0.783	0.986	0.730	0.311	0.804	0.427	0.709	0.681	0.937	0.950	0.852	0.521	0.861	0.521	0.447	0.701	0.446 (2247 out of 5035)
NAÎTRE	0.730	0.972	0.563	0.910	0.844	0.998	0.880	0.304	0.861	0.563	0.795	0.833	0.953	0.974	0.895	0.656	0.919	0.304	0.378	0.754	0.441 (2220 out of 5035)
RECEVOIR	0.521	0.962	0.262	0.953	0.427	0.986	0.804	0.641	0.921	0.378	0.563	0.747	0.937	0.953	0.923	0.262	0.831	0.795	0.714	0.715	0.407 (2049 out of 5035)
VOIR	0.705	0.989	0.673	0.939	0.792	0.959	0.778	0.404	0.637	0.355	0.794	0.778	0.987	0.955	0.935	0.505	0.833	0.262	0.285	0.714	0.407 (2048 out of 5035)
LIRE	0.362	0.962	0.246	0.857	0.621	0.960	0.662	0.426	0.804	0.398	0.540	0.592	0.914	0.904	0.806	0.262	0.815	0.730	0.642	0.658	0.394 (1985 out of 5035)
METTRE	0.436	0.969	0.219	0.884	0.633	0.992	0.726	0.427	0.861	0.327	0.566	0.653	0.937	0.954	0.854	0.335	0.778	0.527	0.354	0.654	0.373 (1876 out of 5035)

PLAIRE	0.378	0.952	0.213	0.834	0.588	0.976	0.667	0.433	0.804	0.355	0.488	0.541	0.882	0.888	0.755	0.236	0.799	0.633	0.526	0.629	0.367 (1850 out of 5035)
JOINDRE	0.730	0.975	0.206	0.889	0.879	0.997	0.889	0.206	0.804	0.730	0.836	0.854	0.963	0.984	0.881	0.730	0.920	0.804	0.730	0.790	0.362 (1822 out of 5035)
PEINDRE	0.730	0.975	0.206	0.889	0.879	0.997	0.889	0.206	0.804	0.730	0.836	0.854	0.963	0.984	0.881	0.730	0.920	0.804	0.730	0.790	0.362 (1822 out of 5035)
COUDRE	0.730	0.974	0.404	0.849	0.844	0.996	0.838	0.331	0.730	0.311	0.801	0.812	0.963	0.982	0.841	0.427	0.918	0.195	0.311	0.698	0.353 (1777 out of 5035)
DIRE	0.730	0.992	0.411	0.190	0.815	0.960	0.826	0.505	0.505	0.781	0.799	0.798	0.989	0.956	0.206	0.777	0.893	0.793	0.461	0.710	0.349 (1758 out of 5035)
BOIRE	0.825	0.962	0.175	0.928	0.340	0.976	0.637	0.593	0.889	0.346	0.433	0.579	0.937	0.943	0.898	0.285	0.854	0.763	0.650	0.668	0.337 (1696 out of 5035)
BATTRE	0.500	0.974	0.521	0.893	0.801	0.996	0.838	0.521	0.804	0.206	0.757	0.812	0.963	0.982	0.885	0.090	0.886	0.311	0.427	0.701	0.269 (1352 out of 5035)
MOUVOIR	0.656	0.962	0.447	0.953	0.447	0.986	0.861	0.599	0.937	0.194	0.214	0.378	0.963	0.953	0.923	0.447	0.831	0.818	0.747	0.692	0.259 (1305 out of 5035)
SUIVRE	0.521	0.969	0.385	0.883	0.709	0.986	0.730	0.385	0.804	0.206	0.635	0.681	0.937	0.950	0.852	0.070	0.817	0.427	0.334	0.646	0.253 (1273 out of 5035)
SERVIR	0.521	0.969	0.378	0.873	0.772	0.976	0.637	0.378	0.804	0.206	0.698	0.588	0.937	0.939	0.841	0.064	0.851	0.427	0.353	0.643	0.247 (1246 out of 5035)
FINIR	0.615	0.976	0.113	0.498	0.578	0.937	0.565	0.447	0.447	0.615	0.545	0.544	0.970	0.930	0.494	0.682	0.700	0.608	0.132	0.600	0.227 (1145 out of 5035)
COURIR	0.754	0.992	0.794	0.794	0.922	0.794	0.847	0.099	0.637	0.198	0.925	0.847	0.989	0.794	0.794	0.509	0.817	0.624	0.596	0.722	0.226 (1139 out of 5035)
CONNAÎTRE	0.521	0.952	0.262	0.898	0.705	0.986	0.750	0.169	0.861	0.262	0.605	0.646	0.882	0.898	0.819	0.378	0.819	0.378	0.262	0.634	0.199 (1003 out of 5035)
INCLURE	0.882	1.000	0.730	0.730	0.954	0.730	0.865	0.626	0.626	0.728	0.954	0.865	0.999	0.730	0.730	0.636	0.804	0.636	0.000	0.749	0.196 (988 out of 5035)
ÉCRIRE	0.582	0.975	0.206	0.618	0.751	0.982	0.734	0.206	0.378	0.373	0.708	0.699	0.963	0.969	0.610	0.365	0.846	0.365	0.187	0.606	0.193 (974 out of 5035)
ASSAILLIR	0.810	0.996	0.846	0.846	0.925	0.846	0.856	0.183	0.730	0.000	0.927	0.856	0.994	0.846	0.846	0.623	0.862	0.699	0.676	0.756	0.178 (895 out of 5035)
POURVOIR	0.435	0.969	0.311	0.844	0.525	0.861	0.559	0.136	0.673	0.302	0.536	0.559	0.958	0.838	0.821	0.306	0.687	0.456	0.206	0.578	0.162 (816 out of 5035)
ASSEOIR₁	0.453	0.986	0.396	0.888	0.593	0.914	0.581	0.206	0.673	0.244	0.597	0.581	0.982	0.905	0.880	0.404	0.721	0.314	0.049	0.598	0.162 (815 out of 5035)
SENTIR	0.521	0.969	0.378	0.873	0.772	0.976	0.637	0.378	0.804	0.311	0.698	0.588	0.937	0.939	0.841	0.169	0.851	0.206	0.132	0.630	0.154 (776 out of 5035)
AIMER	0.861	0.992	0.913	0.913	0.984	0.913	0.895	0.598	0.598	0.000	0.984	0.895	0.992	0.913	0.913	0.598	0.929	0.637	0.637	0.798	0.121 (610 out of 5035)
CONCLURE	0.882	1.000	0.637	0.637	0.931	0.637	0.842	0.626	0.626	0.728	0.931	0.842	0.999	0.637	0.637	0.636	0.730	0.636	0.000	0.715	0.121 (610 out of 5035)
RIRE	0.837	0.995	0.338	0.582	0.658	0.637	0.637	0.652	0.652	0.806	0.659	0.700	0.994	0.634	0.580	0.697	0.000	0.697	0.381	0.642	0.121 (610 out of 5035)
CUEILLIR	0.812	0.996	0.865	0.865	0.944	0.865	0.863	0.113	0.637	0.000	0.946	0.863	0.994	0.865	0.865	0.550	0.881	0.607	0.584	0.743	0.119 (599 out of 5035)
CUIRE	0.582	0.975	0.206	0.502	0.751	0.982	0.734	0.034	0.206	0.373	0.708	0.699	0.963	0.969	0.494	0.365	0.846	0.365	0.187	0.576	0.114 (576 out of 5035)
VÊTIR	0.656	0.974	0.543	0.889	0.841	0.992	0.781	0.543	0.804	0.206	0.797	0.755	0.963	0.979	0.881	0.113	0.915	0.113	0.206	0.682	0.109 (549 out of 5035)
ÉCROUER	0.851	0.992	0.875	0.875	0.983	0.875	0.894	0.582	0.582	0.000	0.983	0.894	0.992	0.875	0.875	0.582	0.898	0.637	0.637	0.783	0.108 (544 out of 5035)
FUIR	0.772	0.991	0.296	0.631	0.537	0.730	0.598	0.561	0.561	0.747	0.538	0.598	0.990	0.728	0.630	0.621	0.000	0.621	0.310	0.603	0.065 (325 out of 5035)
CONFIRE	0.689	0.976	0.064	0.206	0.671	0.960	0.659	0.206	0.206	0.615	0.639	0.637	0.970	0.953	0.202	0.608	0.774	0.608	0.132	0.567	0.025 (124 out of 5035)
Avg	0.674	0.970	0.525	0.845	0.763	0.946	0.787	0.503	0.760	0.508	0.732	0.747	0.959	0.919	0.822	0.535	0.815	0.632	0.541	0.736	0.423

of conjugations as more complex in comparison with the representation afforded by the concrete, formative-based, hearer-oriented plat.

The third conclusion supported by the evidence in this chapter is an empirical generalization, the depth-of-inference contrast, according to which the identification of a lexeme's IC membership may require complex inferences from multiple realized cells, but the deduction of an individual cell tends to involve a simpler inference, typically from a single cell.

8 *The Marginal Detraction Hypothesis*

8.1 Introduction

Our objective in this book is to elucidate a precise conception of an IC system's complexity. A natural part of this investigation is the question of whether certain ICs contribute more strongly than others to the complexity of the system to which they belong. In this chapter, we distinguish between central and marginal ICs. The more members an IC has, the more **central** it is in a language's inflectional morphology; the fewer members an IC has, the more **marginal** it is. This distinction relates purely to type frequency (the proportion of a language's lexemes in each of its ICs) and not at all to token frequency (the incidence of each lexeme or IC in a corpus). This definition should not be taken to suggest that we regard measures of token frequency as irrelevant to IC phenomena, but only that measures of type frequency reveal significant properties of IC systems. There is, of course, no logical necessity that central and marginal ICs should differ in their characteristics; indeed, the null hypothesis is that there is no systematic difference between the properties of central ICs and those of marginal ICs. Empirical evidence to the contrary is therefore significant.[1] We provide evidence for the following hypothesis:

(1) The Marginal Detraction Hypothesis
Marginal ICs tend to detract most strongly from the IC predictability of other ICs.

This hypothesis assumes the measure of IC predictability presented in §4.4. Intuitively, IC predictability is the fraction of subsets of a paradigm's cells that

---

[1] An earlier version of the material presented in this chapter was presented as "Blinkered vision. Sources of opacity in inflectional paradigms" at the Workshop on Information Theory and Simulations in Morphology, Center for Human Development, UC San Diego, January 15–16, 2011.
 The data sets that we have employed in this chapter are:

  marginal.english   marginal.hypothetical
  marginal.french   marginal.icelandic

These are available at the *Morphological Typology* website www.cambridge.org/stump_finkel.

suffice as predictors of all of its other cells (given a particular **universe** of contrasting ICs) – i.e. the fraction of subsets of a paradigm's cells that constitute adequate (though not necessarily optimal) dynamic principal-part sets for that paradigm. We begin our discussion by explaining the notion of detraction from an IC's predictability (§8.2), then investigate this notion in the context of Icelandic verb inflection. After a brief survey of Icelandic conjugation classes (§8.3), we present a plat for their analysis, including various contrasting sub-plats (§8.4), which we use to show that in Icelandic, marginal conjugations detract from the IC predictability of central conjugations more than central conjugations detract from the IC predictability of marginal conjugations (§8.5). In §8.6, we propose a partial explanation for this observation, namely the fact that in Icelandic, marginal conjugations require more distillations than central conjugations. We discuss the significance of this fact in §8.7, where we propose a deeper explanation for the observed asymmetry in detractiveness among marginal and central conjugations. In §8.8, we reëxamine our French data from Chapter 7, demonstrating that it provides further confirmation for the Marginal Detraction Hypothesis.

8.2   Detraction from an IC's predictability

Imagine an English-like language in which all verbal lexemes conform to the conjugation in row (a) of Table 8.1 (the conjugation of SING, SINK, and SWIM). In this hypothetical case, the paradigm of a verb like SING has an IC predictability of 1 (= absolute predictability), since SING's membership in conjugation (a) is deducible from those of its forms realizing any of the seven groups of

Table 8.1. *A simple example of detraction from IC predictability*

	Stem vocalism				IC predictability of a member of conjugation (a) with the successive addition of conjugations (b)–(d)
Conjugation	Present	Past	Past participle	Sample lexemes	
(a)	-I-	-æ-	-ʌ-	SING, SINK, SWIM	1.000
(b)	-I-	-ʌ-	-ʌ-	CLING, STICK, DIG	0.571
(c)	-I-	-æ-	-æ-	SIT, SPIT	0.286
(d)	-ʌ-	-æ-	-ʌ-	RUN	0.143

properties in (2) (= nonempty members of the power set of {pres, past, past ptcp}).

(2) $$\left\{\begin{array}{l} \{\text{pres}\}, \\ \{\text{past}\}, \\ \{\text{past ptcp}\}, \\ \{\text{pres, past}\}, \\ \{\text{pres, past ptcp}\}, \\ \{\text{past, past ptcp}\}, \\ \{\text{pres, past, past ptcp}\} \end{array}\right\}$$

Suppose now that we successively add new conjugations to the universe of conjugations in (a). In a language in which all verbal lexemes conform to the two conjugations in Table 8.1 (a) and (b), the IC predictability of SING's paradigm drops to 0.571, because its membership in conjugation (a) is only deducible from four of the seven groups of forms characterized in (2) (namely those groups that include the past form): without *sang*, the forms *sing* and *sung* do not reveal whether SING follows SINK (*sink–sank–sunk*) or CLING (*cling–clung–clung*).

In a language in which all verbal lexemes conform to the conjugations in Table 8.1 (a)–(c), the IC predictability of SING's paradigm drops still further, to 0.286, since its membership in conjugation (a) is only deducible from two of the seven groups of forms characterized in (2) (namely those groups that include both the past and past participle): without both *sang* and *sung*, it cannot be decided whether SING follows SINK, CLING, or SIT. And in a language in which all verbal lexemes conform to the conjugations in Table 8.1 (a)–(d), the IC predictability of SING's paradigm falls to 0.143, since its membership in conjugation (a) is only deducible from one of the groups of forms in (2) (namely {pres, past, past ptcp}); that is, *sing*, *sang*, and *sung* are all three necessary to distinguish SING from CLING, SIT, and RUN (and to liken it to SINK).

As this example shows, adding a new IC to a universe of ICs may detract from the predictability of an IC belonging to that universe (from 1.000 to 0.143, in the case of conjugation (a)). Though we will not offer a proof here, we believe that the reverse is never true – that adding a new IC can never heighten the predictability of an existing IC.[2]

---

2 If adding an IC to the universe of ICs increases the number of distillations, it is logically possible for this addition to heighten the predictability of an existing IC if its predictability is calculated in the context of the larger set of distillations. Consider, for example, the hypothetical plat in Table (ia): it has two distillations and an average IC predictability of 0.778. If one adds the ICs in (ib) to this plat, then the resulting plat has a higher number of distillations (three) and also a higher average IC predictability (0.886). This apparent increase in IC predictability is purely a consequence of the fact that there are now more candidate predictions available. Comparing the IC

228 *The Marginal Detraction Hypothesis*

Facts such as those summarized in Table 8.1 raise a natural question: Do all conjugations detract from IC predictability in the same way, or are some more likely to detract from the IC predictability of a universe of conjugations? Our hypothesis is that marginal conjugations tend to detract from IC predictability more than central ones. As we now show, evidence from Icelandic supports this hypothesis.

8.3 Conjugation classes in Icelandic

An Icelandic verb typically has thirty synthetic forms in its realized paradigm; we exemplify these forms with the realized paradigm of BÍTA 'bite' in Table 8.2.

Conjugations in Icelandic are of two broadly different types, as in other Germanic languages. **Weak** verbs form their past tense by means of a dental suffix; **Strong** verbs instead form their past tense by means of ablaut. (Some verbs – the **preterite-present** verbs – exhibit Strong deponent forms in the present tense and Weak forms in the past tense. We regard these as neither Weak nor Strong, but as heteroclite; see §6.2; also Maiden 2009; Stump 2006.) Weak conjugations are of four main types, each of which exhibits various subtypes. Some general differences among the Weak conjugations are listed in Table 8.3;

---

predictability figures 0.778 and 0.886 is misleading, since the higher number of distillations in the augmented plat biases that plat in favor of a higher IC predictability. To counteract this bias, the average IC predictability of the plat in (ia) should be calculated on the basis of the same three distillations that are required once (ib) is added to it. The (ia) plat's average IC predictability, calculated in this way, is instead 0.905; on this view, the plat's average IC predictability does indeed decrease with the addition of (ib). So granted that we calculate paradigm predictabilities in a "fair" way, it is apparently the case that adding distillations to a plat either leaves its average IC predictability unaffected or decreases it.

(i) A hypothetical plat

(a)

	V	W	X	Y	Z
I	a	f	i	n	s
II	b	f	j	o	t
III	c	g	k	p	u

(b)

IV	d	h	l	q	v
V	e	i	l	r	w

But our conjecture is that if the number of distillations is held constant before and after the addition of the novel IC, then this addition cannot increase the predictability of an existing class. In our calculations in §8.5 and §8.8 below, we follow the practice of holding the set of distillations constant, always equating it with the set of distillations required by the full plat.

Table 8.2. *Synthetic paradigm of Icelandic* BÍTA *'bite'*

	Indicative		Subjunctive			Infinitive: *bíta*
	Present	Past	Present	Past	Imperative	1st participle: *bítandi* 2nd participle: *bitið*
1sg	bít	beit	bíti	biti		
2sg	bítur	beist	bítir	bitir	bít	
3sg	bítur	beit	bíti	biti		
1pl	bítum	bitum	bítum	bitum	bítum	
2pl	bítið	bituð	bítið	bituð	bítið	
3pl	bíta	bitu	bíti	bitu		

Source: Jörg 1989: 83.

Table 8.3. *Distinctions among the Weak conjugations in Icelandic*

	Infinitive	Indicative		Second participle	Example
		Present 1sg	Past 1sg		
V1	suffix *-ja*	–	*-di/-ði/-ti*	*-ið*	'confuse': *glepja, glep, glapti, glapið*[1]
V2	stem vowel is front *(e i y ý ei ey æ);* suffix *-a*	*-i*	*-di/-ði/-ti*	*-t*	'dispute': *deila, deili, deildi, deilt*
V3	stem vowel is back *(a á o ó u ú),* also *ö i;* suffix *-a*	*-i*	*-di/-ði/-ti*	*-að*	'dare': *þora, þori, þorði, þorað*
V4	suffix *-a*	*-a*	*-aði*	*-að*	'call': *kalla, kalla, kallaði, kallað*

[1] The *e ~ a* alternation in the inflection is an effect of *i*-mutation, not an instance of the kind of ablaut characteristic of Strong verbs.
Source: Jörg 1989: 20.

differences in their present indicative endings are listed in Table 8.4. (In Tables 8.3 and 8.5 below, examples are cited by means of their traditional, static sets of principal parts: the infinitive, the first-person singular past indicative, the first-person plural past indicative and the second participle.)

Strong conjugations are of eight main types, each of which exhibits various subtypes. Some general differences among the Strong conjugations are listed in

Table 8.4. *Indicative present endings in the Weak conjugations in Icelandic*

	V1			V2		V3	V4
Conjugation:	post-consonantal	post-vocalic	after *r*	post-consonantal	after *g/k*		
1sg	–	–	–	-i	-i	-i	-a
2sg	-ur	-rð	-ð	-ir	-ir	-ir	-ar
3sg	-ur	-r	–	-ir	-ir	-ir	-ar
1pl	-jum	-jum	-jum	-um	-jum	-um	-um
2pl	-jið	-ið	-jið	-ið	-ið	-ið	-ið
3pl	-ja	-ja	-ja	-a	-ja	-a	-a

Source: Jörg 1989: 20.

Table 8.5 (along with the reduplicating conjugations RI (a) and (b)); differences in their present indicative endings are listed in Table 8.6.

Drawing upon the analysis of the Icelandic conjugation system in Jörg 1989, we have investigated the IC predictability of the 162 conjugations in Table 8.7. The preterite-present conjugations are labeled as PretPres_*n* (where *n* = 1 through 9) and the reduplicating conjugations, as RIa_1 and RIb_1; the labels of Strong conjugations begin with 'S', and those of Weak conjugations, with 'V'; and conjugations that are (according to Jörg's analysis) irregular have labels containing 'irr'.

8.4 Plats and subplats

As in the preceding chapters, we calculate IC predictability from a language's plat. The plat for Icelandic verbs is quite large, consisting of thirty MPSs (corresponding to the thirty cells in an Icelandic verb's synthetic paradigm) and 162 rows (corresponding to the 162 conjugations). In view of its size, we put the full plat in the supplementary material on the book's website (www.cambridge.org/stump_finkel). The fragment of this plat in Table 8.8 gives a rough idea of what the whole plat looks like. As this fragment shows, the exponences in our plat may involve both stem ablaut and suffixation. For instance, the infinitive exponence *í-a* listed for Conjugation S1a_1 reflects both the stem vocalism and the suffix of an infinitive form such as *bíta* 'bite'. Thus, an exponence of the form X–Y has stem vocalism X and suffix Y; either or both of X and Y may, of course, be empty, depending on the conjugation and the morphosyntactic property set being expressed. For instance, the second-person singular imperative exponence *í-* listed for Conjugation S1a_1 involves a stem vocalism but no suffix: *bít!* 'bite!'

Table 8.5. *Distinctions in stem vocalism among the Strong conjugations in Icelandic*

		Inf	Past sg	Past pl	2nd Ptcp	Examples
S1	(a)	-í-	-ei-	-i-	-i-	'grasp': grípa, greip, gripum, gripið
	(b)				-e-	'wait': bíða, beið, biðum, beðið
S2	(a)	-jó-				'offer': bjóða, bauð, buðum, boðið
	(b)	-jú-	-au-	-u-	-o-	'fly': fljúga, flaug, flugum, flogið
	(c)	-ú-				'drink': súpa, saup, supum, sopið
S3	(a)	-e- (-ja-/-já-)	-a-		-o-	'escape': sleppa, slapp, sluppum, sloppið
		-in- (-en-)		-u-		'spin': spinna, spann, spunnum, spunnið
	(b)	(-yn-)	(-ö-)		-u-	'sing': syngja, söng, sungum, sungið
S4	(a)	(-o-)	(-o-)	(-o-)	-o-	'come': koma, kom, komum, komið
		-e-	-a-	-á-		'carry': bera, bar, bárum, borið
	(b)				-u-	'take': nema, nam, námum, numið
S5	(a)	(-é-)			(-é-)	'eat': éta, át, átum, étið
		-e-	-a-/-á-	-á-	-e-	'give': gefa, gaf, gáfum, gefið
	(b)	-i-				'ask': biðja, bað, báðum, beðið
S6	(a)	-a-	-ó-	-ó-	-a-	'dig': grafa, gróf, grófum, grafið
	(b)	(e/á/o/ey/æ)			(after g/k) -e-	'drive': aka, ók, ókum, ekið
S7	(a)	-ei-	-é-	-é-	-ei-	'play': leika, lék, lékum, leikið
	(b)	-au-	-jó-	-ju-	-au-	'increase': auka, jók, jukum, aukið
	(c)	-a-	-é-	-é-	-a-	'fall': falla, féll, féllum, fallið
	(d)	-á-	-é-	-é-	-á-	'blow': blása, blés, blésum, blásið
R1	(a)	-ó-	-er-	-er-	-ó-	'grow': gróa, greri, grerum, gróið
	(b)	-ú-			-ú-	'turn': snúa, sneri, snerum, snúið

Source: Jörg 1989: 21.

Table 8.6. *Indicative present endings in the Strong conjugations in Icelandic*

	postvocalic	after *r*	after *s*	after *ín/x*	postconsonantal
1sg	–	–	–	–	–
2sg	-rð	-ð	-t	–	-ur
3sg	-r	–	–	–	-ur
1pl			-um		
2pl			-ið		
3pl			-a		

Source: Jörg 1989: 22.

The method in our Icelandic analysis is to calculate IC predictability in different subplats of the Icelandic verb plat and to compare the results. For the most part, the IC predictability of a given conjugation either remains constant or diminishes as it is calculated in progressively larger subplats of the full plat. Our choice of subplats is based on two cross-cutting distinctions among Icelandic conjugations: the Strong/Weak distinction (see §8.3 above) and the amassed/singleton distinction.

In our terminology, an **amassed** conjugation is one that includes more than one lexeme, and a **singleton** conjugation is one that only includes a single lexeme. Thus, a singleton conjugation is maximally marginal. Table 8.9 distinguishes the Icelandic conjugations that are amassed from those that are singleton; we base this classification on the appendix of Jörg (1989), which classifies 1034 Icelandic verbs according to their conjugation. We emphasize that a lexeme belonging to a singleton conjugation is not necessarily infrequent in its use; indeed, the opposite is often true.

Given the Strong/Weak and the amassed/singleton distinctions, we distinguish eight subplats of the full Icelandic plat; these are listed in (3). As heteroclites, the preterite-present verbs are excluded from all Weak and Strong subplats; we do, however, include heteroclite conjugations as autonomous conjugations in the full plat. We treat the two reduplicative conjugations as members of all Strong subplats.

(3) the subplat of Strong conjugations the subplat of Strong amassed conjugations
      the subplat of Weak conjugations the subplat of Strong singleton conjugations
      the subplat of amassed conjugations the subplat of Weak amassed conjugations
      the subplat of singleton conjugations the subplat of Weak singleton conjugations

8.5 IC predictability and amassed vs singleton conjugation classes

In our first set of calculations, we look at the IC predictability of Weak amassed conjugations – in isolation, in the universe of all Weak conjugations, in the universe of all amassed conjugations, and in the universe of all conjugations. The Venn diagram in Figure 8.1 indicates the nesting of universes in these calculations.

Comparing these calculations is complicated by the fact that the same morphosyntactic property sets may be grouped into distillations in different ways in different subplats. We avoid this complication by holding the distillations constant across all four IC-predictability calculations; in particular, we use the distillations required by the universe of all conjugations as the standard set of distillations for all subplats. Table 8.10 shows the results of these calculations. In this table and those that follow, the IC predictability of conjugation X is listed as '=' in universe U whenever X has the same IC predictability in U as in the table's narrowest universe (the Weak amassed universe, in the case of Table 8.10).

The figures in Table 8.10 show that when the Weak amassed conjugations are combined with the Strong amassed conjugations to create the universe of amassed conjugations, their IC predictability is not much diminished (hence the prevalence of equal signs in column C and the closeness of the average paradigm predictabilities 0.520 and 0.518 in the bottom row). By contrast, when the Weak amassed conjugations are combined with the Weak singleton conjugations, their IC predictability is substantially diminished – nearly as much as when they are combined with all other conjugations; compare the equal signs in columns B and D and the average paradigm predictabilities of 0.447 and 0.432 in the bottom row.

In our second set of calculations, we look at the IC predictability of Strong amassed conjugations – in isolation, in the universe of all Strong conjugations, in the universe of all amassed conjugations, and in the universe of all conjugations. The figures in Table 8.11 are similar to those in Table 8.10: they show that when the Strong amassed conjugations are combined with the Weak amassed ones to create the universe of amassed conjugations, their IC predictability is not diminished much: compare the average paradigm predictabilities of 0.641 and 0.638 in the bottom line of the table. The figures in Table 8.11 also parallel those in Table 8.10 insofar as when the Strong amassed conjugations are combined with the Strong singleton ones, their IC predictability is dramatically diminished, nearly as much as when they are combined with the totality of other conjugations.

Table 8.7. The 162 conjugations in this study (based on Jörg 1989)

Conjugation	exemplar	gloss	Jörg*	Conjugation	exemplar	gloss	Jörg*	Conjugation	exemplar	gloss	Jörg*	Conjugation	exemplar	gloss	Jörg*
PretPres_1	EIGA	'have to'	#150	S3irr_12	SNERTA	'concern'	#098	S7d_2	BLÁSA	'blow'	#137	V2irr_2	BREIÐA	'spread'	#031
PretPres_2	MUNA	'remember'	#152	S4a_1	BERA	'carry'	#099	S7d_3	GRÁTA	'weep'	#139	V2irr_3	BYGGJA	'build'	#032
PretPres_3	KUNNA	'know, be able'	#151	S4a_2	STELA	'steal'	#100	S7irr_1	HEITA	'be named'	#140	V2irr_4	KVEIKJA	'light'	#033
PretPres_4	MUNA	'remember'	#152	S4b_1	NEMA	'study'	#101	S7irr_2	HANGA	'hang'	#141	V2irr_5	BENDA	'bend'	#034
PretPres_5	VITA	'know'	#153	S4irr_1	SOFA	'sleep'	#102	S7irr_3	GANGA	'walk'	#142	V2irr_6	ELTA	'chase'	#035
PretPres_6	VILJA	'want'	#154	S4irr_2	KOMA	'come'	#103	S7irr_4	FÁ	'get, may'	#143	V2irr_7	SLÖKKVA	'extinguish'	#036
PretPres_7	ÞURFA	'need'	#155	S4irr_3	VEFA	'weave'	#104	S7irr_5	HLAUPA	'run'	#144	V2irr_8	SÖKKVA	'sink'	#037
PretPres_8	MUNU	'will'	#156	S4irr_4	TROÐA	'trample'	#105	S7irr_6	BÚA	'reside'	#145	V2irr_9	KAUPA	'buy'	#038
PretPres_9	SKULU	'shall'	#157	S5_0	VERA	'be'	#1.1	S7irr_7	SPÝJA	'vomit'	#146	V2irr_10	SÆKJA	'fetch'	#039
R1a_1	GRÓA	'grow'	#148	S5a_1	GEFA	'give'	#106	S7irr_8	LJÁ	'lend'	#147	V2irr_11	ÞYKJA	'seem'	#040
R1b_1	SNÚA	'turn'	#149	S5a_2	LEKA	'leak'	#107	V1a_1	GLEPJA	'confuse'	#001	V2irr_12	YRKJA	'cultivate'	#041
S1a_1	BÍTA	'bite'	#070	S5a_3	META	'rate'	#108	V1b_1	FLÝJA	'flee'	#002	V2irr_13	MEINA	'mean'	#042
S1a_2	GRÍPA	'grasp'	#069	S5b_1	BIÐJA	'ask'	#109	V1c_1	YRJA	'scrape'	#003	V2irr_14	SEGJA	'say'	#043
S1b_1	BÍÐA	'wait'	#071	S5b_2	SITJA	'sit'	#110	V1irr_1	SPYRJA	'ask'	#016	V2irr_15	ÞEGJA	'be silent'	#044
S1irr_1	KVÍÐA	'be anxious'	#072	S5irr_1	SVIMMA	'swim'	#115	V1irr_2	DVELJA	'stay'	#004	V3_0	HAFA	'have'	#1.2
S1irr_2	GÍNA	'be open'	#073	S5irr_2	ÉTA	'eat'	#111	V1irr_3	LEGGJA	'lay'	#005	V3a_0	AGA	'wet'	#1.4
S1irr_3	RÍSA	'rise'	#074	S5irr_3	LIGGJA	'lie'	#112	V1irr_4	KEFJA	'dip'	#006	V3a_1	ÞORA	'dare'	#045
S1irr_4	HNÍGA	'fall'	#075	S5irr_4	SJÁ	'see'	#113	V1irr_5	ETJA	'egg on'	#007	V3a_2	STARA	'stare'	#046
S1irr_5	VÍKJA	'diverge'	#076	S5irr_5	FREGNA	'be told'	#114	V1irr_6	VEKJA	'awaken (tr)'	#008	V3b_1	SÁ	'sow'	#047
S2a_1	BJÓÐA	'offer'	#077	S6a_1	FARA	'leave, go'	#117	V1irr_7	HRYNJA	'collapse'	#009	V3c_1	ÞOLA	'bear'	#048
S2a_2	BRJÓTA	'break'	#078	S6a_2	GRAFA	'dig'	#116	V1irr_8	TYGGJA	'chew'	#010	V3c_2	LOÐA	'stick'	#049
S2b_1	FLJÚGA	'fly'	#079	S6b_1	AKA	'drive'	#118	V1irr_9	HYGGJA	'think'	#011	V3d_1	VAKA	'be awake'	#050
S2c_1	SÚPA	'drink'	#080	S6irr_1	VALDA	'cause'	#119	V1irr_10	FLYTJA	'convey'	#012	V3d_2	GAPA	'gape'	#051
S2irr_1	KJÓSA	'choose'	#081	S6irr_2	VAÐA	'ford'	#120	V1irr_11	BERJA	'beat'	#013	V3d_3	BROSA	'smile'	#052
S3_0	VERÐA	'become'	#1.3	S6irr_3	VAXA	'grow'	#121	V1irr_12	BLEÐJA	'strip off leaves'	#014	V3irr_1	ÞVO	'wash'	#053

S3a_1	SLEPPA	'escape'	#082	S6irr_4	DRAGA	'pull'	#122	V1irr_13	BRYÐJA	'crunch'	#054
S3a_2	BRESTA	'burst'	#083	S6irr_5	VEGA	'weigh'	#123	V1irr_14	ÞIGGJA	'accept'	#055
S3a_3	DETTA	'fall'	#084	S6irr_6	HEFJA	'begin'	#124	V1irr_15	FRÝJA	'challenge'	#056
S3b_1	SPINNA	'spin'	#085	S6irr_7	SVERJA	'swear'	#125	V1irr_16	FELA	'hide'	#057
S3b_2	VINNA	'work'	#086	S6irr_8	DEYJA	'die'	#126	V1irr_17	SELJA	'sell'	#058
S3irr_1	BREGÐA	'move quickly'	#087	S6irr_9	FLÁ	'skin'	#127	V1irr_18	SETJA	'set'	#059
S3irr_2	GJALDA	'repay'	#088	S6irr_10	HLÆJA	'laugh'	#128	V1irr_19	SKE	'happen'	#060
S3irr_3	HVERFA	'vanish'	#089	S6irr_11	HÖGGVA	'hew'	#129	V1irr_20	SKILJA	'understand'	#061
S3irr_4	SVELTA	'starve'	#090	S6irr_12	STANDA	'stand'	#130	V1irr_21	ÞREYJA	'yearn'	#062
S3irr_5	SVELGJA	'gulp'	#091	S6irr_13	FELA	'entrust'	#131	V1irr_22	HEYJA	'perform'	#063
S3irr_6	FINNA	'find'	#092	S7a_1	LEIKA	'play'	#132	V1irr_23	TÆJA	'rip'	#064
S3irr_7	SPRINGA	'burst'	#093	S7b_1	AUKA	'augment'	#133	V2a_1	DEILA	'dispute'	#065
S3irr_8	HRINDA	'push'	#094	S7b_2	AUSA	'scoop'	#134	V2b_1	HEYRA	'hear'	#066
S3irr_9	VINDA	'wind'	#095	S7c_1	FALLA	'fall'	#135	V2c_1	LÝSA	'light'	#067
S3irr_10	HRÖKKVA	'break'	#096	S7c_2	HALDA	'hold'	#136	V2irr_1	HENGJA	'hang'	#068
S3irr_11	SYNGJA	'sing'	#097	S7d_1	RÁÐA	'advise'	#138				

#015	V3irr_2	LAFA	'dangle'		
#017	V3irr_3	HORFA	'look at'		
#018	V3irr_4	HVOLFA	'capsize'		
#019	V3irr_5	LIFA	'live'		
#020	V3irr_6	GÓNA	'gape'		
#021	V3irr_7	SAMA	'befit'		
#022	V3irr_8	DRÚPA	'droop'		
#023	V3irr_9	FLÁ	'skin'		
#024	V3irr_10	LJÁ	'lend'		
#025	V3irr_11	NÁ	'achieve'		
#026	V3irr_12	TJÁ	'express'		
#027	V4a_1	KALLA	'shout'		
#028	V4b_1	ÆTLA	'intend'		
#029	V4b_2	HLÝJA	'warm'		
#030	V4irr_1	BYRJA	'begin'		

* The numbers in this column identify the relevant exemplar paradigms in Jörg 1989.

Table 8.8. *A fragment of the plat for Icelandic verbs*

Conjugation	inf	impv2sg	impv1pl	impv2pl	1stPtcp	2ndPtcp
S1a_1	í-a	í-	í-um	í-ið	í-andi	i-ið
S1b_1	í-a	í-	í-um	í-ið	í-andi	e-ið
S2a_1	jó-a	jó-	jó-um	jó-ið	jó-andi	o-ið
S2b_1	jú-a	jú-	jú-um	jú-ið	jú-andi	o-ið
S2c_1	ú-a	ú-	ú-um	ú-ið	ú-andi	o-ið
S3a_1	e-a	e-	e-um	e-ið	e-andi	o-ið
S3b_1	i-a	i-	i-um	i-ið	i-andi	u-ið
S4a_1	e-a	e-	e-um	e-ið	e-andi	o-ið
S4b_1	e-a	e-	e-um	e-ið	e-andi	u-ið
S5a_1	e-a	e-	e-um	e-ið	e-andi	e-ið
S5b_1	i-ja	i-	i-jum	i-jið	i-jandi	e-ið
S6a_1	a-a	a-	ö-um	a-ið	a-andi	a-ið
S6b_1	a-a	a-	ö-um	a-ið	a-andi	e-ið
S7a_1	ei-a	ei-	ei-um	ei-ið	ei-andi	ei-ið
S7b_1	au-a	au-	au-um	au-ið	au-andi	au-ið
S7c_1	a-a	a-	ö-um	a-ið	a-andi	a-ið
S7d_1	á-a	á-	á-um	á-ið	á-andi	á-ið

The results so far support the fairly unsurprising generalization (A).

Generalization (A)

> Weak and Strong conjugations generally do not detract from each other's IC predictability, but Weak conjugations detract from the IC predictability of other Weak conjugations and Strong conjugations from that of other Strong conjugations.

This result is unsurprising because one expects that a conjugation will detract more from the IC predictability of similar conjugations and less from the IC predictability of dissimilar conjugations, hence Weak detracts from Weak, and Strong from Strong. Interestingly, though, this generalization is more valid for amassed conjugations than for singleton ones. That is, mutual detractiveness between Weak and Strong conjugations is more evident among singleton conjugations than among amassed conjugations, as in Figure 8.2.

Thus, consider now the IC predictability of Weak singleton conjugations – in isolation, in the universe of all Weak conjugations, in the universe of all singleton conjugations, and in the universe of all conjugations. As the figures in Table 8.12 show, combining Strong singleton conjugations with Weak singleton conjugations diminishes their IC predictability substantially more than the combination of Strong amassed with Weak amassed conjugations (cf. Table 8.10). Consider likewise the IC predictability of Strong singleton conjugations in Table 8.13: combining Weak singleton conjugations with Strong singleton conjugations clearly diminishes IC predictability, while on average, the combination of Weak amassed conjugations with Strong amassed conjugations barely does so (cf. Table 8.11).

A stronger generalization is therefore (B).

> *Generalization (B)*
>
> The tendency for Strong conjugations and Weak conjugations to detract from each other's IC predictability is greater in the universe of singleton conjugations than in the universe of amassed conjugations.

Overall, Tables 8.10–8.13 also support generalization (C).

> *Generalization (C)*
>
> Singleton conjugations tend to have greater IC predictability than their amassed counterparts, and Strong conjugations tend to have greater IC predictability than their Weak counterparts.

The relevant evidence for this conclusion is summarized in Table 8.14.

Finally, Tables 8.10–8.13 support generalization (D).

> *Generalization (D)*
>
> Notwithstanding their own higher IC predictability, singleton conjugations detract from the IC predictability of amassed conjugations more than amassed conjugations detract from that of singleton conjugations.

This generalization is confirmed by the facts summarized in Tables 8.15 and 8.16.

As these facts show, the Icelandic verb system confirms the Marginal Detraction Hypothesis in (1), especially in the domain of Strong verbs. Clearly there is a significant difference between singleton and amassed conjugations. There is also a significant difference between Strong and Weak conjugations, reflected in the differing degrees to which they confirm the Marginal Detraction Hypothesis. What are the reasons for these differences? In the following sections, we uncover the basis for an explanation.

8.6 The isomorphic ideal

Recall from §2.1.1 that a distillation is a set of morphosyntactic property sets whose exponences exhibit the same pattern of sames and differents across all ICs.

Table 8.9. *Amassed and singleton conjugations in Icelandic*

Amassed			Singleton		
Conjugation	members*	Conjugation	members*	Conjugation	members*
PretPres_1	3	V1c_1	2	PretPres_2	1	S7a_1	1
PretPres_3	3	V1irr_1	2	PretPres_4	1	S7b_1	1
PretPres_7	2	V1irr_10	3	PretPres_5	1	S7b_2	1
R1a_1	2	V1irr_11	4	PretPres_6	1	S7c_1	1
R1b_1	2	V1irr_12	5	PretPres_8	1	S7d_1	1
S1a_1	6	V1irr_13	4	PretPres_9	1	S7d_2	1
S1a_2	14	V1irr_18	3	S1b_1	1	S7irr_1	1
S1irr_2	4	V1irr_2	14	S1irr_1	1	S7irr_2	1
S1irr_4	3	V1irr_20	2	S1irr_3	1	S7irr_3	1
S1irr_5	2	V1irr_3	2	S3_0	1	S7irr_5	1
S2a_1	4	V1irr_4	4	S3a_2	1	S7irr_7	1
S2a_2	12	V1irr_5	4	S3a_3	1	S7irr_8	1
S2b_1	13	V1irr_6	3	S3b_2	1	V1irr_14	1
S2c_1	2	V1irr_7	15	S3irr_11	1	V1irr_15	1
S2irr_1	5	V2a_1	60	S3irr_12	1	V1irr_16	1
S3a_1	5	V2b_1	29	S3irr_5	1	V1irr_17	1
S3b_1	3	V2c_1	60	S3irr_6	1	V1irr_19	1
S3irr_1	2	V2irr_1	10	S3irr_7	1	V1irr_21	1
S3irr_10	3	V2irr_10	2	S3irr_8	1	V1irr_22	1
S3irr_2	4	V2irr_2	28	S4a_2	1	V1irr_23	1
S3irr_3	5	V2irr_3	19	S4b_1	1	V1irr_8	1
S3irr_4	3	V2irr_4	17	S4irr_1	1	V1irr_9	1
S3irr_9	3	V2irr_5	14	S4irr_2	1	V2irr_11	1

S4a_1	3	V2irr_6	32	S4irr_3	1	V2irr_12	1
S4irr_4	2	V2irr_8	2	S5_0	1	V2irr_13	1
S5a_1	5	V3a_1	4	S5b_1	1	V2irr_14	1
S5a_2	2	V3a_2	5	S5b_2	1	V2irr_15	1
S5a_3	4	V3b_1	16	S5irr_1	1	V2irr_7	1
S5irr_2	2	V3c_1	5	S5irr_4	1	V2irr_9	1
S5irr_3	2	V3d_1	4	S5irr_5	1	V3_0	1
S6a_1	2	V3d_2	2	S6irr_1	1	V3a_0	1
S6a_2	6	V3irr_3	3	S6irr_10	1	V3c_2	1
S6b_1	4	V3irr_5	14	S6irr_11	1	V3d_3	1
S6irr_9	3	V3irr_6	2	S6irr_12	1	V3irr_1	1
S7c_2	2	V3irr_8	8	S6irr_13	1	V3irr_10	1
S7d_3	2	V4a_1	97	S6irr_2	1	V3irr_11	1
S7irr_4	2	V4b_1	282	S6irr_3	1	V3irr_12	1
S7irr_6	2	V4irr_1	5	S6irr_4	1	V3irr_2	1
V1a_1	7			S6irr_5	1	V3irr_4	1
V1b_1	8			S6irr_6	1	V3irr_7	1
				S6irr_7	1	V3irr_9	1
				S6irr_8	1	V4b_2	1
		78 in all	950 in all			84 in all	84 in all

*Number of members listed in the appendix of Jörg 1989.

240 *The Marginal Detraction Hypothesis*

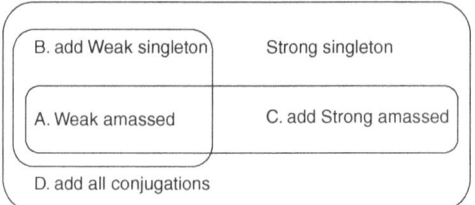

Figure 8.1. *The nesting of universes in our first set of calculations*

Thus, in the hypothetical plat in Table 8.17, the morphosyntactic property sets V and Z belong to a single distillation, since both conform to the patterns in (4).

(4) In columns V and Z in Table 8.17,
  (a) I and II have the same exponence
  (b) II, III, IV and V have distinct exponences

Saying that two morphosyntactic property sets belong to the same distillation is equivalent to saying that their patterns of exponence are isomorphic. In the hypothetical plat in Table 8.17, the property sets V and Z have isomorphic patterns of exponence because there is a one-to-one correspondence between exponences of V and exponences of Z: exponence **a** corresponds to exponence **d**, **g** to **i**, **j** to **l**, and **m** to **o**.

Consider now the hypothetical plat in Table 8.18. This plat embodies a kind of canonical ideal, since by virtue of the pattern in (5), there is a single distillation to which all of the morphosyntactic property sets in Table 8.18 belong. Accordingly, no member of any IC in Table 8.18 requires more than a single dynamic principal part, and any word form in a lexeme's paradigm suffices as its sole dynamic principal part. We will refer to any plat in which all morphosyntactic property sets belong to the same distillation as adhering to the **isomorphic ideal**; in such a plat, the pattern of exponence associated with any morphosyntactic property set is isomorphic to that of every other morphosyntactic property set. Naturally, plats in actual human languages do not, in general, conform to the isomorphic ideal, but we can distinguish subplats of a language's plat according to the extent to which they deviate from it. As we now show, the conjugations in the Icelandic verb plat exhibit systematic variation in the extent of their deviation. This variation is directly relevant to understanding the phenomenon of marginal detraction in Icelandic and the fact that Strong verbs exhibit this phenomenon more than Weak verbs.

(5) In columns V–Z in Table 8.18, I, II, III, IV, and V all have distinct exponences.

Table 8.10. *IC predictability of Weak amassed conjugations calculated in: A. isolation, and in three larger universes: B. all Weak conjugations, C. all amassed conjugations, and D. all conjugations*

	IC predictability of Weak amassed conjugations			
		in the universe resulting from adding		
Weak amassed conjugations	A. in the universe of Weak amassed conjugations	B. Weak singleton conjugations	C. Strong amassed conjugations	D. all other conjugations
V1c_1	0.048	=	=	=
V1irr_1	0.179	=	=	=
V1irr_10	0.179	=	=	=
V1irr_12	0.179	=	=	=
V1irr_13	0.179	=	=	=
V1irr_2	0.006	=	=	=
V1irr_5	0.179	=	=	=
V2a_1	0.543	=	=	=
V2c_1	0.543	=	=	=
V2irr_1	0.543	=	=	=
V2irr_2	0.179	=	=	=
V2irr_4	0.543	=	=	=
V2irr_5	0.966	=	=	=
V2irr_6	0.895	=	=	=
V3d_1	0.834	=	=	=
V3irr_5	0.167	=	=	=
V4a_1	0.966	=	=	=
V4b_1	0.179	=	=	=
V4irr_1	0.179	=	=	=
V3c_1	0.855	=	=	0.854
V1b_1	1.000	=	0.998	0.743
V1irr_11	0.333	=	0.330	0.330
V1a_1	0.834	0.817	=	0.817
V1irr_18	0.743	0.179	=	0.179
V1irr_3	0.996	0.993	=	0.993
V1irr_7	0.048	0.014	=	0.014
V2b_1	0.072	0.021	=	0.021
V2irr_10	1.000	0.958	=	0.958
V2irr_3	0.390	0.254	=	0.254
V3a_1	0.854	0.762	=	0.762
V3a_2	0.848	0.461	=	0.461
V3b_1	0.464	0.423	=	0.423
V1irr_20	0.805	0.743	0.801	0.508
V1irr_6	0.464	0.115	0.453	0.115
V2irr_8	0.996	0.464	0.962	0.464
Avg	0.520	0.447	0.518	0.432

242 *The Marginal Detraction Hypothesis*

Table 8.11. *IC predictability of Strong amassed conjugations calculated in: A. isolation, and in three larger universes: B. all Strong conjugations, C. all amassed conjugations, and D. all conjugations*

	IC predictability of Strong amassed conjugations			
		in the universe resulting from adding		
Strong amassed conjugations	A. in the universe of Strong amassed conjugations	B. Strong singleton conjugations	C. Weak amassed conjugations	D. all other conjugations
RIa_1	0.978	=	=	=
S1irr_4	0.103	=	=	=
S1irr_5	0.667	=	=	=
S2a_1	0.179	=	=	=
S2a_2	0.048	=	=	=
S2b_1	0.922	=	=	=
S2c_1	0.844	=	=	=
S2irr_1	0.333	=	=	=
S3irr_2	0.949	=	=	=
S1a_1	0.048	0.005	=	0.005
S1irr_2	0.333	0.048	=	0.048
S3a_1	0.631	0.022	=	0.022
S3b_1	0.873	0.294	=	0.294
S3irr_1	1.000	0.999	=	0.999
S3irr_3	0.993	0.739	=	0.739
S3irr_9	0.895	0.420	=	0.420
S4a_1	0.406	0.327	=	0.327
S5a_1	0.066	0.016	=	0.016
S5a_2	0.171	0.100	=	0.100
S5irr_3	0.993	0.953	=	0.861
S6a_1	0.327	0.297	=	0.296
S6a_2	0.064	0.024	=	0.024
S6b_1	0.320	0.123	=	0.123
S6irr_9	0.848	0.752	=	0.752
S7c_2	0.848	0.333	=	0.333
S7d_3	0.992	0.333	=	0.333
S7irr_4	0.855	0.847	=	0.847
RIb_1	0.928	0.926	0.926	0.926
S3irr_10	0.975	0.705	0.941	0.705
S4irr_4	0.923	0.600	0.889	0.600
S5irr_2	1.000	0.949	0.962	0.944
S7irr_6	0.999	0.979	0.999	0.979
Avg	0.641	0.499	0.638	0.496

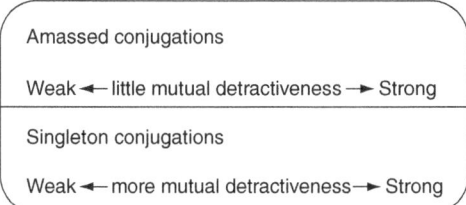

Figure 8.2. *Mutual detractiveness between Weak and Strong conjugations in singleton and amassed universes*

8.7 Distillations and amassed vs singleton conjugations

We begin by calculating the number of distillations required by four subplats – the Weak singleton, the Weak amassed, the Strong singleton, and the Strong amassed. Tables 8.19 and 8.20 show the grouping of a synthetic paradigm's thirty morphosyntactic property sets into distillations for each of these four subplats. As these tables show, singleton conjugations require more distillations than amassed conjugations, and among singleton conjugations, Strong conjugations require more distillations than Weak ones. The findings reveal that as a group, the Weak singleton and Strong singleton conjugations stray from the isomorphic ideal to a greater extent than the complementary group of Weak amassed and Strong amassed conjugations, and that among singleton conjugations, Strong conjugations stray more than Weak ones.

Table 8.21 shows that the Icelandic conjugations, taken in their entirety, require twenty-one distillations – more than any of the four subplats represented in Tables 8.19 and 8.20. The subplat consisting of all Weak conjugations requires sixteen distillations (Table 8.22), as does the subplat consisting of all strong conjugations (Table 8.23); sixteen is slightly more than the number of distillations required by any of the four subplats in Tables 8.19 and 8.20 but is still well below the twenty-one distillations required by the full plat. The subplat consisting of all amassed conjugations requires twelve distillations (Table 8.24), but strikingly, the subplat consisting of all singleton conjugations requires twenty-one distillations (Table 8.25) – the full set of distillations required by the plat as a whole. This fact provides additional evidence that as a group, the singleton conjugations (unlike the complementary group of amassed conjugations) stray from the isomorphic ideal to the same extent as the plat as a whole. No other systematic subplat engenders such a high degree of deviation from the isomorphic ideal.

What is the significance of this fact? One cannot say that a set of conjugations that strays from the isomorphic ideal inevitably becomes less predictable; after

Table 8.12. *IC predictability of Weak singleton conjugations calculated in: A. isolation, and in three larger universes: B. all Weak conjugations, C. all singleton conjugations, and D. all conjugations*

Weak singleton conjugations	IC predictability of Weak singleton conjugations			
		in the universe resulting from adding		
	A. in the universe of Weak singleton conjugations	B. Weak amassed conjugations	C. Strong singleton conjugations	D. all other conjugations
V2irr_12	0.895	=	=	=
V2irr_15	0.320	=	=	=
V3a_0	0.966	=	=	=
V3irr_10	0.464	=	=	=
V3irr_12	0.464	=	=	=
V3irr_7	0.463	=	=	=
V4b_2	0.996	=	=	=
V1irr_14	1.000	=	0.987	0.895
V1irr_22	0.975	=	0.901	0.901
V1irr_9	0.996	=	0.993	0.993
V2irr_9	1.000	=	0.966	0.966
V3_0	0.509	=	0.439	0.439
V3irr_11	0.969	=	0.956	0.956
V1irr_21	0.332	0.293	=	0.293
V1irr_23	0.961	0.927	=	0.927
V2irr_11	0.895	0.887	=	0.887
V2irr_13	0.574	0.521	=	0.521
V3c_2	0.179	0.167	=	0.167
V3irr_4	0.087	0.021	=	0.021
V1irr_15	0.331	0.268	0.281	0.267
V1irr_16	0.838	0.667	0.697	0.543
V1irr_17	0.955	0.179	0.859	0.179
V1irr_19	0.998	0.997	0.978	0.977
V1irr_8	0.962	0.437	0.834	0.370
V2irr_14	0.278	0.228	0.274	0.224
V2irr_7	0.999	0.446	0.895	0.376
V3irr_1	0.993	0.887	0.980	0.887
V3irr_2	0.226	0.074	0.181	0.074
Avg	0.701	0.630	0.672	0.608

Table 8.13. *IC predictability of Strong singleton conjugations calculated in: A. isolation, and in three larger universes: B. all Strong conjugations, C. all singleton conjugations, and D. all conjugations*

	IC predictability of Strong singleton conjugations			
		in the universe resulting from adding		
Strong singleton conjugations	A. in the universe of Strong singleton conjugations	B. Strong amassed conjugations	C. Weak singleton conjugations	D. all other conjugations
S3_0	0.686	=	=	=
S3a_2	0.179	=	=	=
S3irr_7	0.571	=	=	=
S4irr_1	0.833	=	=	=
S4irr_3	0.636	=	=	=
S5irr_1	0.978	=	=	=
S6irr_1	1.000	=	=	=
S6irr_12	0.966	=	=	=
S6irr_7	0.982	=	=	=
S7a_1	0.803	=	=	=
S7b_1	0.666	=	=	=
S7d_1	0.333	=	=	=
S7d_2	0.333	=	=	=
S7irr_5	0.663	=	=	=
S7irr_8	0.949	=	=	=
S3irr_12	0.464	=	0.453	0.453
S6irr_13	0.171	=	0.133	0.133
S7irr_1	0.797	=	0.796	0.796
S1b_1	0.482	0.179	=	0.179
S1irr_1	0.482	0.464	=	0.464
S1irr_3	0.482	0.179	=	0.179
S3a_3	0.032	0.022	=	0.022
S3b_2	0.872	0.412	=	0.412
S3irr_5	0.979	0.727	=	0.727
S3irr_8	0.572	0.312	=	0.312
S4a_2	0.098	0.019	=	0.019
S4b_1	0.179	0.178	=	0.178
S4irr_2	0.841	0.664	=	0.664
S5_0	0.909	0.892	=	0.892
S5b_1	0.959	0.954	=	0.954
S5irr_4	0.945	0.944	=	0.944
S5irr_5	0.994	0.966	=	0.966
S6irr_10	0.966	0.895	=	0.895

Table 8.13. (cont.)

Strong singleton conjugations	IC predictability of Strong singleton conjugations			
	A. in the universe of Strong singleton conjugations	in the universe resulting from adding		
		B. Strong amassed conjugations	C. Weak singleton conjugations	D. all other conjugations
S6irr_2	0.572	0.481	=	0.481
S6irr_3	0.798	0.767	=	0.767
S6irr_4	0.666	0.392	=	0.392
S6irr_5	0.691	0.569	=	0.569
S7c_1	0.692	0.319	=	0.319
S7irr_3	0.855	0.848	=	0.848
S7irr_7	0.999	0.997	=	0.742
S3irr_11	0.993	0.975	0.848	0.831
S3irr_6	1.000	0.987	0.983	0.983
S6irr_11	0.995	0.722	0.891	0.722
S6irr_6	0.934	0.881	0.831	0.741
S6irr_8	0.985	0.978	0.911	0.904
S7b_2	1.000	0.949	0.966	0.949
S7irr_2	0.803	0.802	0.732	0.731
Avg	0.719	0.662	0.706	0.646

Table 8.14. *Average IC predictability of different conjugations (from Tables 8.10–8.13) [calculated in the universe of all conjugations]*

Amassed conjugations		Singleton conjugations	
Weak amassed	Strong amassed	Weak singleton	Strong singleton
0.432	0.496	0.608	0.646

all, the singleton conjugations stray most dramatically from this ideal, yet by virtue of their high irregularity, they are more predictable than the amassed conjugations, as Table 8.14 shows. But because the exponences of morphosyntactic property sets belonging to the same distillation are interpredictable, the IC predictability of a plat is in general enhanced to the extent that its morphosyntactic property sets are grouped into a small number of distillations. Singleton

Table 8.15. *How singleton and amassed conjugations detract from each other's IC predictability (Weak and Strong universes contrasted)*

	When singleton conjugations are added to amassed, the average IC predictability of amassed conjugations decreases to	When amassed conjugations are added to singleton, the average IC predictability of singleton conjugations decreases to
Weak conjugations	0.447 from 0.520 (14% decrease)	0.630 from 0.701 (10% decrease)
Strong conjugations	0.499 from 0.641 (22% decrease)	0.662 from 0.719 (8% decrease)

Table 8.16. *How singleton and amassed conjugations detract from each other's IC predictability (Weak/Strong universes contrasted with amassed/singleton universes)*

A.	IC predictability of X in the universe consisting of			
	all amassed conjugations	all Weak conjugations	all Strong conjugations	Difference (%)
X = Weak amassed conjugations	0.518	0.447		14
X = Strong amassed conjugations	0.638		0.499	22
B.	IC predictability of Y in the universe consisting of			
	all singleton conjugations	all Weak conjugations	all Strong conjugations	Difference (%)
Y = Weak singleton conjugations	0.672	0.630		6
Y = Strong singleton conjugations	0.706		0.662	6

Table 8.17. *A hypothetical plat (property sets V and Z have isomorphic patterns of exponence)*

	V	W	X	Y	Z
I	a	a	b	c	d
II	a	e	e	f	d
III	g	e	h	h	i
IV	j	k	h	l	l
V	m	m	n	l	o

Table 8.18. *A hypothetical plat (patterns of exponence of all property sets are isomorphic)*

	V	W	X	Y	Z
I	a	e	d	c	b
II	b	a	e	d	c
III	c	b	a	e	d
IV	d	c	b	a	e
V	e	d	c	b	a

conjugations therefore detract from the IC predictability of the plat as a whole because they separate the plat's morphosyntactic property sets into a larger number of distillations: MPSs that belong to a single distillation (whose exponences are therefore interpredictable) in the universe of amassed conjugations do not always belong to the same distillation (and so do not always have interpredictable exponences) once singleton conjugations are included in the universe of conjugations. In particular, instances in which the exponences of a singleton conjugation X intersect those of an amassed conjugation Y will tend to diminish the interpredictability of Y's exponences.

8.8 Discussion

In §§8.5–7, we have encountered several generalizations about Icelandic conjugations. We have seen that the conjugations fall into two groups – the traditional Weak and Strong groups – such that members of one group tend not to detract from the IC predictability of members of the other group; they are sufficiently different in their morphology that they do not "get in each other's way"; on the

Table 8.19. *Grouping of morphosyntactic property sets into distillations in the Weak conjugations*

Singleton (12 distillations)	Amassed (11 distillations)
Inf IndPres3pl	Inf IndPres3pl
1stPtcp IndPres1pl SbjvPres1pl	1stPtcp IndPres1pl SbjvPres1pl
Impv1pl	Impv1pl
IndPres2pl SbjvPres1sg SbjvPres2sg SbjvPres3sg SbjvPres2pl SbjvPres3pl	IndPres2pl SbjvPres1sg SbjvPres2sg SbjvPres3sg SbjvPres2pl SbjvPres3pl
Impv2sg	Impv2sg
2ndPtcp	2ndPtcp
IndPres1sg	IndPres1sg
IndPres2sg IndPres3sg	IndPres2sg IndPres3sg
IndPast3sg	IndPast3sg
IndPast1sg IndPast2sg	IndPast1sg IndPast2sg
IndPast1pl IndPast2pl IndPast3pl	IndPast1pl IndPast2pl IndPast3pl
SbjvPast1pl SbjvPast2pl SbjvPast3pl	SbjvPast1pl SbjvPast2pl SbjvPast3pl
SbjvPast1sg SbjvPast2sg	SbjvPast1sg SbjvPast2sg
SbjvPast3sg	SbjvPast3sg

Table 8.20. *Grouping of morphosyntactic property sets into distillations in the Strong conjugations*

Singleton (15 distillations)	Amassed (11 distillations)
Inf 1stPtcp	Inf 1stPtcp
Impv1pl	Impv1pl
IndPres1pl IndPres3pl SbjvPres1pl	IndPres1pl IndPres3pl SbjvPres1pl
Impv2sg	Impv2sg
2ndPtcp	2ndPtcp
IndPres1sg	IndPres1sg
Impv2pl	Impv2pl
IndPres2pl SbjvPres1sg SbjvPres2sg SbjvPres3sg SbjvPres2pl SbjvPres3pl	IndPres2pl SbjvPres1sg SbjvPres2sg SbjvPres3sg SbjvPres2pl SbjvPres3pl
IndPres2sg IndPres3sg	IndPres2sg IndPres3sg
IndPast1pl IndPast3pl	IndPast1pl IndPast3pl
IndPast2pl	IndPast2pl
IndPast1sg IndPast3sg	IndPast1sg IndPast3sg
IndPast2sg	IndPast2sg
SbjvPast1pl SbjvPast2pl SbjvPast3pl	SbjvPast1pl SbjvPast2pl SbjvPast3pl
SbjvPast1sg SbjvPast2sg SbjvPast3sg	SbjvPast1sg SbjvPast2sg SbjvPast3sg

250 *The Marginal Detraction Hypothesis*

Table 8.21. *Grouping of morphosyntactic property sets into distillations in all conjugations (twenty-one distillations)*

Inf
IndPres3pl
IndPres1sg
IndPres2sg
IndPres3sg
Impv2sg
Impv1pl
1stPtcp
IndPres1pl SbjvPres1pl
impv2pl
IndPres2pl
SbjvPres1sg SbjvPres2sg SbjvPres3sg SbjvPres2pl SbjvPres3pl
2ndPtcp
IndPast2sg
IndPast1sg
IndPast3sg
IndPast1pl IndPast3pl
IndPast2pl
SbjvPast1sg SbjvPast2sg
SbjvPast3sg
SbjvPast1pl SbjvPast2pl SbjvPast3pl

Table 8.22. *Grouping of morphosyntactic property sets into distillations in all Weak conjugations (sixteen distillations)*

Inf
IndPres3pl
IndPres1sg
IndPres2sg IndPres3sg
Impv2sg
Impv1pl
1stPtcp IndPres1pl SbjvPres1pl
Impv2pl
IndPres2pl SbjvPres1sg SbjvPres2sg SbjvPres3sg SbjvPres2pl SbjvPres3pl
2ndPtcp
IndPast2sg IndPast1sg
IndPast3sg
IndPast1pl IndPast3pl IndPast2pl
SbjvPast1sg SbjvPast2sg
SbjvPast3sg
SbjvPast1pl SbjvPast2pl SbjvPast3pl

Table 8.23. *Grouping of morphosyntactic property sets into distillations in all Strong conjugations (sixteen distillations)*

Impv1pl
IndPres1pl SbjvPres1pl IndPres3pl
1stPtcp Inf
IndPres1sg
IndPres2sg
IndPres3sg
Impv2pl
IndPres2pl SbjvPres1sg SbjvPres2sg SbjvPres3sg SbjvPres2pl SbjvPres3pl
Impv2sg
2ndPtcp
IndPast1sg IndPast3sg
IndPast2sg
IndPast1pl IndPast3pl
IndPast2pl
SbjvPast1sg SbjvPast2sg SbjvPast3sg
SbjvPast1pl SbjvPast2pl SbjvPast3pl

Discussion 251

Table 8.24. *Grouping of morphosyntactic property sets into distillations in all amassed conjugations (twelve distillations)*

Inf IndPres3pl
IndPres1sg
IndPres2sg IndPres3sg
Impv2sg
Impv1pl 1stPtcp IndPres1pl SbjvPres1pl
Impv2pl IndPres2pl SbjvPres1sg SbjvPres2sg SbjvPres3sg SbjvPres2pl SbjvPres3pl
2ndPtcp
IndPast2sg
IndPast1sg IndPast3sg
IndPast1pl IndPast3pl IndPast2pl
SbjvPast1sg SbjvPast2sg SbjvPast3sg
SbjvPast1pl SbjvPast2pl SbjvPast3pl

Table 8.25. *Grouping of morphosyntactic property sets into distillations in all singleton conjugations (twenty-one distillations)*

Inf
1stPtcp
IndPres1pl SbjvPres1pl
IndPres3pl
IndPres1sg
IndPres2sg
IndPres3sg
IndPres2pl
SbjvPres1sg SbjvPres2sg SbjvPres3sg SbjvPres2pl SbjvPres3pl
Impv2sg
Impv1pl
Impv2pl
2ndPtcp
IndPast1sg
IndPast2sg
IndPast1pl IndPast3pl
IndPast2pl
IndPast3sg
SbjvPast1sg SbjvPast2sg
SbjvPast1pl SbjvPast2pl SbjvPast3pl
SbjvPast3sg

other hand, members of the same group are sufficiently similar in their morphology that they do detract from each other's IC predictability (generalization (A)). This distinction between Weak and Strong conjugations is clearest in the case of central conjugations. Marginal conjugations, by contrast, seem to blur the distinction between Weak and Strong conjugations, so that Weak (or Strong) marginal conjugations show a greater tendency to detract from the IC predictability of Strong (or Weak) conjugations (generalization (B)).

Singleton conjugations are, as a group, more predictable than amassed conjugations (generalization (C), part one). This result is at least partly because inflectional characteristics that contribute to a conjugation's singletonness also contribute to its distinctiveness. For instance, one reason why a conjugation might be singleton is because it involves suppletion, as in the case of English GO, whose forms *go–went* immediately suffice to distinguish its inflection from that of superficially similar verbs: OWE (*owe–owed*), GROW (*grow–grew*), BEND (*bend–bent*), and so on.

Strong conjugations are also more predictable than Weak conjugations in Icelandic (generalization (C), part two). This is unsurprising, given the high degree of IC differentiation afforded by stem ablaut in the Strong conjugations (Table 8.5) and not in the Weak conjugations (Table 8.3).

Finally, singleton conjugations detract from the IC predictability of amassed conjugations more than amassed conjugations detract from that of singleton conjugations (generalization (D)). This empirical observation supports the Marginal Detraction Hypothesis in (1). The evidence presented in §8.7 provides a partial explanation for generalization (D): marginal ICs tend to detract most strongly from the predictability of other ICs because they require more distillations. As a consequence of this fact, when their patterns of exponence intersect with those of amassed conjugations, they actually diminish the interpredictability of the latter patterns' exponences.

These facts suggest that languages should exhibit a historical tension: on the one hand, one would expect to see innovations that would eliminate a language's singleton conjugations, since they tend to elevate the number of distillations and hence to detract from the IC predictability of the language's plat (generalization (D)); on the other hand, the persistence of singleton conjugations should be favored by the fact that they are inherently more predictable than amassed conjugations (generalization (C), part one). A plausible hypothesis that we have yet to investigate is that token frequency is central to resolving this tension in a language's diachronic development.

But why is there a correlation between marginality and detractiveness? That is, why do ICs that require more distillations have the fewest members? The explanation for this correlation may be historical in origin. Complex systems of

ICs are made more difficult to learn by ICs that systematically require more distillations, because these classes make it more difficult to deduce as-yet-unencountered forms of regular lexemes. Such ICs are detractive precisely because they have partial similarities to other, more regular ICs. Because of these similarities, their member lexemes are subject to gradual diachronic incorporation into these other, more regular classes, a process that gradually marginalizes the detractive classes by robbing them of their members. Ultimately, detractive ICs are either eliminated by this process or are left with a small number of members whose high token frequency makes them resistant to reanalysis.

Historical evidence suggests that this scenario is plausible. In Old English, for example, the third-person singular past and the third-person plural past belong to the same distillation in the universe of Weak verbs; by contrast, these morphosyntactic property sets belong to two distinct distillations in the universe of Strong verbs. Thus, for the Weak conjugations in Table 8.26, the third singular and third plural past-tense forms are interpredictable – either is deducible from the other. But in the case of the Strong conjugations in Table 8.26, the third singular past-tense forms are not deducible from the corresponding third plural past-tense forms; the latter all have *u* as their stem-internal vowel, but the former vary in their stem vocalism. But English has changed: now all the Strong verbs in Table 8.26 fit the originally Weak pattern of having a single past-tense distillation. Indeed, by phonological change, the plural suffixes in Table 8.26 have eroded, so that most verbs have not only a single distillation in the past tense, but a single form as well. The lone exception is BE, whose past-tense forms *was* and *were* differ in their phonology. But not even these forms necessitate distinct distillations: because these forms are uniquely suppletive, each implies the other. Thus, English verbs are a case in which detractive ICs have been eliminated in favor of a smaller number of distillations.

Table 8.26. *The third-person singular and third-person plural past-tense forms of six Old English verbs*

Conjugation type	Gloss	Singular	Plural
Weak	FREMMAN 'bring about'	*frem-ede*	*frem-edon*
	HǢLAN 'heal'	*hǣl-de*	*hǣl-don*
	HOPIAN 'hope'	*hop-ode*	*hop-odon*
Strong	BEORCAN 'bark'	*bearc*	*burc-on*
	CRĒOPAN 'creep'	*crēap*	*crup-on*
	SINGAN 'sing'	*sang*	*sung-on*

8.9 French evidence for the Marginal Detraction Hypothesis

We now reëxamine the French system of conjugations to determine whether it confirms the Marginal Detraction Hypothesis. We employ the seventy-two conjugations of our analyses in Chapter 7, whose type frequencies (kindly supplied to us by Olivier Bonami) are listed in Table 8.27. We employ the concrete plat given earlier in Table 7.10.

The conjugation with the highest type frequency is that of AIMER, which has 4139 member lexemes in Bonami's sample; at the opposite extreme are the conjugations of ALLER 'go', DÉJEUNER 'have lunch', ÊTRE 'be', HAÏR 'hate', MOURIR 'die', POUVOIR 'can', REPAÎTRE 'feed', SAVOIR 'know', SURSEOIR 'stay' and VOULOIR 'want', each of which has only a single member lexeme.

Table 8.27. *Type frequencies of seventy-two French conjugations*

Conjugation	Type frequency	Conjugation	Type frequency	Conjugation	Type frequency
AIMER	4139	BATTRE	9	ASSEOIR$_1$	2
CÉDER	499	COURIR	8	ASSEOIR$_2$	2
COLLER	423	JOINDRE	8	AVOIR	2
FINIR	332	DIRE	7	BOIRE	2
COPIER	262	ACQUÉRIR	5	BOUILLIR	2
LEVER	196	CONFIRE	5	CONCLURE	2
APPUYER	83	RECEVOIR	5	CROIRE	2
REMUER	63	ASSAILLIR	4	DEVOIR	2
BROYER	53	CROÎTRE	4	ENVOYER	2
RENDRE	52	LIRE	4	FUIR	2
ÉCHOUER	33	PLAIRE	4	NAÎTRE	2
BEURRER	31	VALOIR	4	POURVOIR	2
TENIR	30	VÊTIR	4	RIRE	2
CUIRE	24	VOIR	4	VAINCRE	2
PEINDRE	17	COUDRE	3	ALLER	1
METTRE	15	CRAINDRE	3	DÉJEUNER	1
REFLUER	12	CUEILLIR	3	ÊTRE	1
SENTIR	12	DORMIR	3	HAÏR	1
CONNAÎTRE	11	INCLURE	3	MOURIR	1
ÉCRIRE	11	MOUDRE	3	POUVOIR	1
ÉCROUER	11	MOUVOIR	3	REPAÎTRE	1
FAIRE	11	SERVIR	3	SAVOIR	1
PRENDRE	11	SUIVRE	3	SURSEOIR	1
COUVRIR	10	VIVRE	3	VOULOIR	1

Our French data are therefore quite different from our Icelandic data. In Icelandic, just over half the conjugations are singleton (i.e. single-member) conjugations, while in French, only a handful of conjugations are singleton. Although we use singleton conjugations as the marginal conjugations in our analysis of Icelandic, it is not practical to do the same in French – there are simply too few singleton conjugations for a comparison of singleton conjugations with amassed conjugations to be balanced.

As we saw in §8.7, the number of distillations required by the singleton subplat of Icelandic is 21, the same as the number of distillations required by the full plat. By contrast, the subplat of singleton conjugations in our French data (given in Table 8.28) only requires four distillations, despite the fact that the full French plat requires seventeen distillations. The small number of ICs in the French singleton subplat makes it possible for most of the plat's MPSs to have a different exponence in each IC and hence to belong to a single distillation. In Icelandic, by contrast, there are eighty-four singleton conjugations; the larger the number of conjugations, the less likely it becomes for an MPS to have distinct exponences for every conjugation, heightening the likelihood that MPSs will belong to distinct distillations.

Because the French singleton subplat is so small, we employ a different bipartite subdivision of ICs in our French analysis: central conjugations are those having a type frequency of ten or more, and marginal conjugations are those having a type frequency of nine or fewer. By this sorting, the conjugations in the first column of Table 8.27 are central, and those in the second and third columns are marginal. Unlike Icelandic, French does not exhibit a distinction between Strong and Weak conjugations; our French calculations are therefore based purely on type frequency.

With central and marginal conjugations distinguished in this way, we now calculate the IC predictability of marginal conjugations in the universe of marginal conjugations and in the universe of all conjugations; the resulting figures are given in Table 8.29. As these figures show, adding central conjugations to marginal conjugations causes their average IC predictability to fall from 0.749 to 0.704, a drop of only six percent. By contrast, when we calculate the paradigm predictabilities of the central conjugations in the universe of central conjugations and in the universe of all conjugations, we get the very different results in Table 8.30. Here, we see that when marginal conjugations are added to central conjugations, their average IC predictability falls from 0.902 to 0.758, a drop of sixteen percent. Thus, these French figures support a generalization analogous to our generalization (D) for Icelandic: marginal conjugations tend to detract from the IC predictability of central conjugations more than central

Table 8.28. *The subplat of singleton conjugations in French (concrete plat: distillations shaded)*

Indexed stem	1	2	3	4	5	6	7	8	9	10	10a	11	12	13	14	15	16	17	18	19
CON ÊTRE	-sɥi	-ɛ	!sɔm	!ɛt	-sɔ̃	-ɛtɛ	-etjɔ̃	-fy	-fy	-sɛʁɛ	-səʁjɔ̃	-swa	-swajɔ̃	-swa	-swajɔ̃	-swaje	-etʁ	-etɑ̃	-ete	-ete
HAÏR	!ɛ	!ɛ	-sɔ̃	-se	-s	-sɛ	-sjɔ̃	—	—	-ʁɛ	-ʁjɔ̃	-s	-sjɔ̃	!ɛ	-sɔ̃	-se	-ʁ	-sɑ̃	—	—
ALLER	!vɛ	!va	-ɔ̃	-e	!vɔ̃	-ɛ	-jɔ̃	-ɛ	-a	@iʁɛ	@iʁjɔ̃	!aj	-jɔ̃	!va	-ɔ̃	-e	-e	-ɑ̃	-e	-e
JUG MOURIR	-œʁ	-œʁ	-uʁɔ̃	-uʁe	-œʁ	-uʁɛ	-uʁjɔ̃	-uʁy	-uʁy	-uʁʁɛ	-uʁʁjɔ̃	-œʁ	-uʁjɔ̃	-œʁ	-uʁɔ̃	-uʁe	-uʁiʁ	-uʁɑ̃	-ɔʁ	-ɔʁt
SAVOIR	-ɛ	-ɛ	-avɔ̃	-ave	-av	-avɛ	-avjɔ̃	-y	-y	-oʁɛ	-oʁjɔ̃	-aʃ	-aʃjɔ̃	-aʃ	-aʃɔ̃	-aʃe	-avwaʁ	-aʃɑ̃	-y	-y
POUVOIR	-ø	-ø	-uvɔ̃	-uve	-œv	-uvɛ	-uvjɔ̃	-y	-y	-uʁɛ	-uʁjɔ̃	-ɥis	-ɥisjɔ̃	-ø	-uvɔ̃	-uve	-uvwaʁ	-uvɑ̃	-y	-y
VOULOIR	-ø	-ø	-ulɔ̃	-ule	-œl	-ulɛ	-uljɔ̃	-uly	-uly	-udʁɛ	-udʁijɔ̃	-œj	-uljɔ̃	-ø	-ulɔ̃	-ule	-ulwaʁ	-ulɑ̃	-uly	-uly

Table 8.29. *IC predictability of marginal conjugations in: A. the universe of marginal conjugations, and B. the universe of all conjugations*

Marginal conjugations	A. in isolation	B. add all other conjugations	B / A
CUEILLIR	1.000	1.000	1.000
ÊTRE	1.000	1.000	1.000
VALOIR	1.000	1.000	1.000
ACQUÉRIR	0.998	0.998	1.000
DORMIR	0.998	0.998	1.000
VAINCRE	0.998	0.998	1.000
VIVRE	0.998	0.998	1.000
VOULOIR	0.998	0.998	1.000
ASSEOIR$_2$	0.991	0.991	1.000
MOUDRE	0.991	0.991	1.000
LIRE	0.986	0.986	1.000
CROÎTRE	0.983	0.983	1.000
BOIRE	0.917	0.917	1.000
SAVOIR	0.916	0.916	1.000
BOUILLIR	0.880	0.880	1.000
ASSAILLIR	0.816	0.816	1.000
ENVOYER	0.660	0.660	1.000
COURIR	0.601	0.601	1.000
MOUVOIR	0.542	0.542	1.000
POUVOIR	0.542	0.542	1.000
ASSEOIR$_1$	0.421	0.421	1.000
BATTRE	0.396	0.396	1.000
DIRE	0.396	0.396	1.000
SERVIR	0.396	0.396	1.000
SUIVRE	0.396	0.396	1.000
POURVOIR	0.250	0.250	1.000
INCLURE	0.217	0.217	1.000
VOIR	0.185	0.185	1.000
CONCLURE	0.145	0.145	1.000
AVOIR	0.911	0.910	0.999
PLAIRE	0.984	0.979	0.995
MOURIR	1.000	0.991	0.991
RIRE	0.982	0.956	0.974
JOINDRE	1.000	0.969	0.969
RECEVOIR	0.950	0.919	0.967
COUDRE	0.746	0.653	0.875
ALLER	0.969	0.825	0.851
FUIR	0.643	0.464	0.722
HAÏR	0.991	0.542	0.547
NAÎTRE	0.997	0.542	0.544
VÊTIR	0.396	0.132	0.333
CONFIRE	0.269	0.071	0.264
Avg	0.749	0.704	0.940

258 *The Marginal Detraction Hypothesis*

Table 8.30. *IC predictability of central conjugations in: A. the universe of central conjugations, and B. the universe of all conjugations*

Central conjugations	A. in isolation	B. add all other conjugations	B/A
CÉDER	1.000	1.000	1.000
COLLER	1.000	1.000	1.000
COUVRIR	1.000	1.000	1.000
ÉCHOUER	1.000	1.000	1.000
REMUER	1.000	1.000	1.000
METTRE	0.986	0.986	1.000
TENIR	0.969	0.969	1.000
PRENDRE	0.967	0.967	1.000
AIMER	0.217	0.217	1.000
FAIRE	0.995	0.991	0.996
RENDRE	0.998	0.991	0.993
BEURRER	1.000	0.991	0.991
LEVER	1.000	0.969	0.969
PEINDRE	1.000	0.969	0.969
COPIER	0.825	0.795	0.964
APPUYER	0.776	0.516	0.665
ÉCRIRE	0.969	0.632	0.652
ÉCROUER	0.197	0.124	0.629
CONNAÎTRE	0.991	0.527	0.532
FINIR	0.983	0.501	0.510
SENTIR	0.998	0.396	0.397
CUIRE	0.969	0.124	0.128
Avg	0.902	0.758	0.840

conjugations detract from that of marginal conjugations. These facts support the Marginal Detraction Hypothesis. At the same time, the figures in Tables 8.29 and 8.30 do not support an analogue of the first part of generalization (C) for Icelandic. Marginal conjugations are not more predictable than central conjugations in French; indeed, the reverse is true. The reason for this difference between French and Icelandic may stem from the different ways in which we have delineated the boundary between marginal and central in these languages.

Just as we saw (§8.7) that the detractiveness of singleton conjugations correlates with an elevated number of distillations in Icelandic, marginal conjugations in French likewise require more distillations. In French, the central conjugations together require only nine distillations; by contrast, the marginal conjugations together require seventeen distillations, which equals the number of distillations required by the entire plat. Table 8.31 shows the sorting of

French evidence for the Marginal Detraction Hypothesis 259

Table 8.31. *Distillations required by the full French concrete plat and by the marginal and central subplats*

All (17 distillations)	Marginal (17 distillations)	Central (9 distillations)
PresInd1sg	PresInd1sg	PresInd1sg
PresInd2sg	PresInd2sg	PresInd2sg
PresInd3sg	PresInd3sg	PresInd3sg
impv2sg	impv2sg	impv2sg
PresInd2pl	PresInd2pl	PresInd2pl
impv2pl	impv2pl	impv2pl
PresInd1pl	PresInd1pl	PresInd1pl
impf1sg	impf1sg	impf1sg
impf2sg	impf2sg	impf2sg
impf3sg	impf3sg	impf3sg
impf3pl	impf3pl	impf3pl
impv1pl	impv1pl	impv1pl
PresPtcp	PresPtcp	PresPtcp
PresInd3pl	PresInd3pl	PresInd3pl
PresSbjv1sg	PresSbjv1sg	PresSbjv1sg
PresSbjv2sg	PresSbjv2sg	PresSbjv2sg
PresSbjv3sg	PresSbjv3sg	PresSbjv3sg
PresSbjv3pl	PresSbjv3pl	PresSbjv3pl
impf1pl	impf1pl	impf1pl
impf2pl	impf2pl	impf2pl
PresSbjv1pl	PresSbjv1pl	PresSbjv1pl
PresSbjv2pl	PresSbjv2pl	PresSbjv2pl
PastInd1sg	PastInd1sg	PastInd1sg
PastInd2sg	PastInd2sg	PastInd2sg
PastInd3sg	PastInd3sg	PastInd3sg
PastInd1pl	PastInd1pl	PastInd1pl
PastInd2pl	PastInd2pl	PastInd2pl
PastInd3pl	PastInd3pl	PastInd3pl
PastSbjv1sg	PastSbjv1sg	PastSbjv1sg
PastSbjv2sg	PastSbjv2sg	PastSbjv2sg
PastSbjv3sg	PastSbjv3sg	PastSbjv3sg
PastSbjv1pl	PastSbjv1pl	PastSbjv1pl
PastSbjv2pl	PastSbjv2pl	PastSbjv2pl
PastSbjv3pl	PastSbjv3pl	PastSbjv3pl
Fut1sg	Fut1sg	Fut1sg
Fut2sg	Fut2sg	Fut2sg

Table 8.31. (cont.)

All (17 distillations)	Marginal (17 distillations)	Central (9 distillations)
Fut3sg	Fut3sg	Fut3sg
Fut1pl	Fut1pl	Fut1pl
Fut2pl	Fut2pl	Fut2pl
Fut3pl	Fut3pl	Fut3pl
Cond1sg	Cond1sg	Cond1sg
Cond2sg	Cond2sg	Cond2sg
Cond3sg	Cond3sg	Cond3sg
Cond1pl	Cond1pl	Cond1pl
Cond2pl	Cond2pl	Cond2pl
Cond3pl	Cond3pl	Cond3pl
Inf	Inf	Inf
PastPtcpMasc	PastPtcpMasc	PastPtcpMasc
PastPtcpFem	PastPtcpFem	PastPtcpFem

Table 8.32. *Average IC predictabilities for the French subplats when marginal conjugations are those with three or fewer members, and central conjugations those with four or more*

Average IC predictability of the marginal subplat in the universe of			Average IC predictability of the central subplat in the universe of		
A. marginal conjugations	B. all conjugations	B / A	C. central conjugations	D. all conjugations	D / C
0.815	0.737	0.904	0.767	0.712	0.928

morphosyntactic property sets into distillations in the full concrete plat and in the marginal and central subplats.

Despite the overall congruence of the French results given above with our Icelandic results, the French data do present a complication. We have chosen more or less arbitrarily to set the boundary between marginal and central conjugations in French between nine and ten: conjugations with ten or more members count as central, and those with fewer than ten as marginal. But if we instead set the boundary at between three and four, we get cloudier results. In this alternative analysis, the average paradigm predictabilities are as in Table 8.32. These figures show that with the boundary between three and four, marginal conjugations do not differ appreciably from central conjugations in their capacity to detract from the predictability of other conjugations – indeed, they detract slightly less than central conjugations do; thus, these results differ from those in Tables 8.29 and 8.30. With the boundary between three and four, marginal conjugations still require more distillations than central conjugations (the former require fifteen, while the latter require only ten), but the number required by the marginal conjugations is not as high as that required by the full plat (seventeen distillations).

These facts show that it matters where one draws the line between marginal and central conjugations for purposes of calculating detraction. For French, it appears that some conjugations having between four and ten members have an important role in detracting from the average IC predictability of the full concrete plat: if they are treated as marginal rather than central, they cause the average IC predictability of central conjugations to drop by sixteen rather than seven percent; if they are treated as central rather than marginal, they cause the average IC predictability of marginal conjugations to drop by just under ten rather than six percent. These facts suggest that languages differ with respect to exactly which of their marginal members are most detractive of paradigm predictability; for example, they may be exclusive inflection classes (as in Icelandic) or small but amassed inflection classes (as in French). But this cross-linguistic variability does not alter the apparent validity of the general observation that inflection classes with few members tend to require more distillations and for this reason detract most significantly from the IC predictability of inflection classes that have numerous members and that, in isolation, require fewer distillations.

In Chapter 4, we saw that an inflectional system's ICs are unbalanced in the sense that they may vary widely in their IC predictability. The correlation between marginality and detractiveness that we have investigated in this chapter is another locus of imbalance among a language's ICs. It is reasonable to expect that there are other significant asymmetries as well.

9 Inflection classes, implicative relations, and morphological theory

In the preceding chapters, we have been concerned with analyzing the implicative relations among the cells in a language's realized paradigms. Because these relations afford a precise conception of an IC system's complexity, they open a new avenue for the typological comparison of inflectional morphologies. In this chapter,[1] we discuss a related issue in the theoretical domain, namely: How should implicative relations and inflection classes be modeled in a formal theory of morphology? We distinguish between two possible ways of representing a lexeme's IC membership, and orthogonally, between two approaches to the formulation of a language's rules of inflectional realization (§9.1). Drawing upon these distinctions, we characterize two possible architectures for a formal theory of inflection, each a kind of canonical extreme (§9.2). We show that neither of these extremes is adequate – that a hybrid architecture incorporating characteristics of both approaches is preferable. In §9.3, we propose a hybrid theory of this sort, illustrating with a small but rich fragment of Sanskrit declensional morphology. This chapter is not an analysis of implicative relations per se, but of the position that such relations occupy within the broader formal definition of a language's inflectional morphology.

9.1 Two kinds of lexical representation and two kinds of inflectional rule

Traditionally, principal parts have always had a very specific instructional function: specifying what is unpredictable about a lexeme's realized paradigm, and doing so as concisely as possible, so that language learners can internalize this paradigm with a minimum of rote memorization. If lexemes have principal parts that are alike, then these lexemes are alike throughout their realized paradigms.

---

[1] Portions of this chapter were presented in a rather different form at the Workshop on Morphology and Formal Grammar, Université Paris Diderot, July 8, 2010.

This practical function also has an analogue in grammatical theory: because a lexeme's principal parts may effectively play the same role as its IC specification, they are relevant to the theoretical task of representing lexemes parsimoniously in the lexicon. Thus, a formal grammar of Latin might specify the declension-class membership of the noun FRŪCTUS 'fruit' diacritically (as [4th declension]) or by means of the principal parts *frūctus–frūctūs* (with the uniform convention that a noun's principal parts are its nominative singular and genitive singular forms). Orthogonal to the distinction between these two possible modes of lexical representation is a distinction between two possible types of rules for the realization of inflected forms: rules of exponence deduce the realization of a given cell ⟨L, σ⟩ in the paradigm of a lexeme L from the morphosyntactic property set σ together with information about L's stem(s); implicative rules, by contrast, deduce a given cell in a lexeme's realized paradigm from the realization of one or more other cells in the paradigm. We find it helpful to visualize exponence-based rules as specifying inflectional relations that are "vertical" (as in (1)) and implicative rules as specifying inflectional relations that are "horizontal" (as in (2)). Up to now, we have mainly been concerned with the kinds of implicative relations expressed by rules of this latter sort.

(1)   ⟨WALK, {3sg pres ind}⟩
         ↓
       /wɔks/

(2)   ⟨/wɔkɪŋ/, {pres ptcp}⟩ → ⟨/wɔks/, {3sg pres ind}⟩

9.2 Two canonical extremes for a theory of inflection

Consider the English verb forms phonemically transcribed in Table 9.1. One can imagine at least two ways of defining this fragment of the English conjugation system in formal terms.

Table 9.1. *A fragment of the English conjugational system*

Lexeme	Morphosyntactic property set				
	{inf}	{past}	{past ptcp}	{3sg pres ind}	{pres ptcp}
THRIVE	/θɹaɪv/	/θɹaɪvd/	/θɹaɪvd/	/θɹaɪvz/	/θɹaɪvɪŋ/
TEND	/tɛnd/	/tɛndəd/	/tɛndəd/	/tɛndz/	/tɛndɪŋ/
SEND	/sɛnd/	/sɛnt/	/sɛnt/	/sɛndz/	/sɛndɪŋ/
DRIVE	/dɹaɪv/	/dɹoʊv/	/dɹɪvən/	/dɹaɪvz/	/dɹaɪvɪŋ/

Table 9.2. *Conjugation-class diacritics and stems for the fragment of English in Table 9.1*

Lexeme	Conjugation-class diacritic	Default stem	Preterite stem	Past participial stem
THRIVE	[Weak]	/θɹaɪv/	–	–
TEND	[Weak]	/tɛnd/	–	–
SEND	[T]	/sɛnd/	–	–
DRIVE	[Strong]	/dɹaɪv/	/dɹoʊv/	/dɹɪv/

In the first approach, the lexical entries of THRIVE, TEND, SEND, and DRIVE each list three principal parts: the realized cells for the MPSs {inf}, {past}, and {past ptcp}. The cells realizing {3sg pres ind} and {pres ptcp} are then defined by implicative rules that deduce one cell in a realized paradigm from one or more other cells in that paradigm. The relevant implicative rules are formulated in (3).

(3) Implicative rules for the fragment of English in Table 9.1

(a) ⟨/X/, {inf}⟩ → ⟨/Xz/, {3sg pres ind}⟩
(b) ⟨/X/, {inf}⟩ → ⟨/Xɪŋ/, {pres ptcp}⟩

In the second approach, the lexical entries of THRIVE, TEND, SEND, and DRIVE each list a conjugation-class diacritic and a set of one or more stems; these are given in Table 9.2. For each verb, the five realizations in Table 9.1 are then defined by rules of exponence, which deduce the realization of a paradigmatic cell from the stem and morphosyntactic property set associated with that cell. These rules are formulated (in phonemic terms) in Table 9.3.

The first approach to the formal definition of the inflectional patterns in Table 9.1 embodies what we have called the pure word-and-paradigm morphology (PWPM) hypothesis (§1.2.1); the second embodies the **pure exponence-based morphology (PEM) hypothesis**. The two approaches are extreme examples of what Blevins (2006) distinguishes as abstractive and constructive approaches to morphology. The hypotheses that they embody are polar opposites with respect to two criteria. First, the PWPM hypothesis entails that a lexeme's IC membership is represented purely by means of lexically listed principal parts. By contrast, the PEM hypothesis represents a lexeme's IC membership by means of an IC diacritic and one or more lexically listed stems. Second, the PWPM hypothesis employs implicative rules formulated entirely in terms of realized cells, while PEM

Table 9.3. *Rules of exponence for the fragment of English in Table 9.1*
Given a lexeme L having /X/ as its Default stem, L has the following forms:

Class of L	A. {past}	B. {past ptcp}	C. {inf}	D. {3sg pres ind}	E. {pres ptcp}
(i) [Weak]	/Xd/[1]	/Xd/[1]	/X/	/Xz/	/Xɪŋ/
(ii) [T]	/Xt/[2]	/Xt/[2]	/X/	/Xz/	/Xɪŋ/
(iii) [Strong]	L's preterite stem	/Yən/, where /Y/ is L's past participial stem	/X/	/Xz/	/Xɪŋ/

[1] Sandhi:/Yd+d/→/Ydəd/
[2] Sandhi:/Yd+t/→/Yt/

Table 9.4. *Differences between the PWPM and PEM hypotheses*

Criterion	PWPM	PEM
IC membership	represented by means of a set of lexically listed principal parts	represented by means of a diacritic+one or more stems
Rules	implicative rules formulated in terms of realized cells	rules of exponence formulated in terms of stems

employs rules of exponence formulated in terms of stems, not all of which appear as independent word forms in realized cells. These differences are summarized in Table 9.4.

The PWPM and PEM hypotheses are (in the sense of Corbett 2005, 2007, 2009) canonical extremes: each pushes particular criteria to their logical endpoints – opposite endpoints, in these cases. But the PWPM and PEM hypotheses do not represent the only possible theoretical approaches to inflectional morphology. Logically, the criteria in Table 9.4 are independently variable. For example, lexically listed principal parts are not inherently incompatible with rules of exponence. For that matter, the options for each criterion in Table 9.4, though presented as opposites, are not necessarily mutually exclusive. One could, for example, imagine a theory incorporating implicative rules making reference to stems, or one incorporating both implicative rules and rules of exponence. Thus, morphologists are faced with a representational choice, not only between the PWPM and PEM hypotheses, but among a variety of hybrid theories as well.

For the lexical representation of IC membership, the choice between the diacritic+stem approach and the principal-part approach is not straightforward, since each approach has apparent advantages. The diacritic+stem approach has the obvious advantage of compactness: IC membership can often be marked more concisely by means of a stem bearing an IC diacritic than by a sequence of principal parts. Moreover, the diacritic+stem approach represents each IC with its own diacritic, so that the number of distinct ICs is transparently reflected in the number of distinct diacritics. For many linguists, these advantages are decisive.

But the principal-part approach has competing advantages.[2] Principal parts are concise embodiments of the implicative patterns in a realized paradigm. Speakers clearly use their knowledge of such patterns in deducing unheard forms of a newly encountered lexeme (e.g. to deduce the participle *texting* on encountering the past-tense form *texted*). Unlike IC diacritics, principal parts identify the particular cells in a realized paradigm that afford the most reliable inferences of this sort. And unlike IC diacritics, principal-part specifications reveal important typological differences among inflectional systems; as we saw in Chapter 2, principal parts are the basis for three cross-cutting dimensions of variation among languages.

The choice between the principal-part and the diacritic+stem approaches to the lexical representation of IC membership is complicated by the fact that the distinction between them is sometimes blurred. In Chapter 3, we discussed the traditional analysis of the Sanskrit conjugational system, according to which a verb's realized paradigm has four separate sectors, each regulated by its own, independent set of IC distinctions. To account for a system of this sort under the diacritic+stem approach, one must assume that each lexeme has multiple diacritic+stem pairings; but a set of such pairings is not very different from a set of principal parts, particularly if principal parts can be stems, as argued in Chapter 7. Even in languages whose IC systems do not exhibit the sort of partitioning observed in Sanskrit, irregular lexemes sometimes require a set of

---

[2] A possible objection to the principal-part approach is that it entails redundancy in lexical representations; for instance, the principal-part set *break – broke – broken* multiply repeats the consonantism of the lexeme BREAK. This objection, however, implies a conception of the lexicon as a redundancy-free archive of unpredictable lexical information – a conception implying that the production and interpretation of language are heavily computational. An alternative conception (compatible with both of the approaches to lexical representation discussed here) is that the lexicon contains redundant information and that the production and interpretation of language are less heavily computational, often simply involving the retrieval of stored information; cf. Prasada & Pinker (1993); Baayen *et al.* (1997); Hare *et al.* (2001); Alegre & Gordon (1999).

principal-part-like specifications, whether or not one assumes the principal-part approach to representing IC membership; in English, for example, the irregularity of the verb GO must be specified lexically by a set of forms (*go–went–gone*) that is identical to its traditional principal parts.

Partitioning and irregularity coincide in Latin. The present system, perfect system, and perfect passive participial stems of FERRE 'bear' (*fer-*, *tul-*, *lāt-*) stand in a suppletive relationship and so must be listed, whether or not one assumes the principal-part approach; correspondingly, the traditional principal parts of FERRE 'bear' are *ferō–tulī–lātum–ferre*. Moreover, the conjugation-class membership of present system, perfect system, and perfect passive participial stems varies independently even in the inflection of regular verbs; for example, the verbs LAUDĀRE 'praise', CREPĀRE 'crack', and IUVĀRE 'help' all inflect as first-conjugation verbs in the present system, but they inflect differently both in the perfect system (*laudāvī/*lauduī/*laudī, crepuī/*crepāvī/*crepī, iūvī/*iūvāvī/*iūvuī*) and in their perfect passive participles (*laudātum/*lauditum/*lautum, crepitum/*crepātum/*cretum, iūtum/*iūvātum/*iūvitum*). Thus, a verb's lexical entry must contain either its present system, perfect system, and perfect passive participial stems (each carrying an appropriate conjugation-class diacritic) or its present system, perfect system, and perfect passive participial principal parts.

These considerations suggest that for the lexical representation of lexemes' IC membership, the dichotomy of the diacritic+stem and principal-part approaches is a false one.

The choice between implicative rules and rules of exponence is similarly complicated. Minimally, a theory of inflectional morphology should furnish a means of defining a phonological realization for each cell in a lexeme's paradigm. The phonological realization of some such cells must be lexically specified, but a language's inflectional morphology allows the phonological realization of most cells to be deduced. Implicative rules and rules of exponence are two approaches to formulating such deductions.

Prima facie, there are good reasons to assume that rules of exponence and implicative rules both have a role in defining a language's inflected forms. First, many languages exhibit directional syncretisms, instances in which the form realizing one cell is systematically identical to the form realizing some contrasting cell; in Sanskrit, for instance, a neuter noun's nominative forms (singular, dual, and plural) are always identical to its corresponding accusative forms, whatever their morphology might be. To account for such cases, it is usual in realizational theories of morphology to supplement rules of exponence with **rules of referral** – rules that specify that two contrasting cells in a paradigm have identical realizations. Rules of referral are, in fact, one type of implicative rule: they deduce the form realizing one cell from that realizing another cell. Thus, implicative rules such as those in (3) might be seen as "generalized" rules of referral that specify a particular formal relation (not necessarily identity) between the realizations of two different cells. Analogical changes such as *dive/dived* > *dive/dove* (on the analogy of *drive/drove*) might be seen as involving such "generalized" (**nonsyncretistic**) referrals between phonologically distinct members of a paradigm.

But even if implicative rules such as those in (3) are postulated, there is still a need for rules of exponence. To see this need, consider the realized declensional paradigms of the Sanskrit nominals in Table 9.5 (to whose full analysis we turn in the section that follows).[3] These paradigms reveal two important reasons for postulating rules of exponence.[4]

First, some inflectional patterns resist easy definition as whole-word implicative patterns, without reference to stems. One class of problematic patterns involves inward phonological conditioning – instances in which the phonological context created by an affix determines a choice among stems. Consider, for example, the Sanskrit nominals MARUT 'wind' (masc), VIDVĀMS 'knowing' (masc forms), and RĀJĀN 'king' (masc) in Table 9.5. In the so-called Weak cases (shaded in Table 9.5), VIDVĀMS and RĀJĀN exhibit an alternation in the form of their stem: *vidvat-* ~ *viduṣ-*, *rāja-* ~ *rājñ-*. By contrast, MARUT exhibits no such alternation in the Weak cases: a single stem *marut-* (or its sandhi variant *marud-*) is used throughout the realized paradigm of MARUT. As inspection of the realized paradigms of the three nominals reveals, the conditions governing the alternation exhibited by VIDVĀMS and RĀJĀN are easily stated in terms of stems, as in (4).

(4)   In the Weak cases, VIDVĀMS and RĀJĀN assume their Default Weak ("Middle") stem (*vidvat-*, *rāja-*) before a suffix-initial consonant and their Weak Prevocalic ("Weakest") stem (*viduṣ-*, *rājñ-*) before a suffix-initial vowel.

Because reference to word-internal stems and affixes is excluded under the PWPM hypothesis, this generalization is not directly expressible under that

---

[3] Throughout this chapter, the names we use for Sanskrit lexemes are based on their default stems; for example, the lexeme PITAR 'father' has the default stem *pitar-*. In the analysis that we propose, the default stems of the lexemes 'knowing', 'king', and 'descendant' are their lengthened-grade stems *vidvāṃs-*, *rājān-*, and *naptār-*; we therefore give these lexemes the names VIDVĀMS, RĀJĀN, and NAPTĀR. This is contrary to convention; for example, Monier-Williams' dictionary of Sanskrit represents them as *vidvat* (the weak preconsonantal stem), *rājan* (the normal-grade stem) and *naptṛ* (the weak preconsonantal stem).

[4] Language change provides other kinds of motivation for the postulation of rules of exponence. For instance, the change of the English possessive suffix from a head inflection (*the Wyves Tale of Bathe*) to an edge inflection (*the wife of Bath's tale*) is plausibly a change in a rule of exponence, less plausibly a change in the inference of one member of a paradigm from another.

Table 9.5. Realized declensional paradigms of nine Sanskrit nominals: MARUT 'wind' (masc), VIDVĀMS 'knowing' (masc forms), RĀJĀN 'king' (masc), AŚVA 'horse' (masc), ĀSYA 'mouth' (neut), AGNI 'fire' (masc), ŚATRU 'enemy' (masc), PITAR 'father' (masc), NAPTĀR 'descendant' (masc) (Shading indicates the "Weak" cells in the realization of gradational nominals.)

		NOM	VOC	ACC	INS	DAT	ABL	GEN	LOC
Singular	MARUT	marut	marut	marut-am	marut-ā	marut-e	marut-as	marut-as	marut-i
	VIDVĀMS	vidvān	vidvan	vidvāms-am	viduṣ-ā	viduṣ-e	viduṣ-as	viduṣ-as	viduṣ-i
	RĀJĀN	rājā	rājan	rājān-am	rājñ-ā	rājñ-e	rājñ-as	rājñ-as	rājñ-i
	AŚVA	aśva-s	aśva	aśva-m	aśvena	aśvāya	aśvāt	aśva-sya	aśve
	ĀSYA	āsya-m	āsya	āsya-m	āsyena	āsyāya	āsyāt	āsya-sya	āsye
	AGNI	agni-s	agne	agni-m	agnin-ā	agnay-e	agne-s	agne-s	agnau
	ŚATRU	śatru-s	śatro	śatru-m	śatruṇ-ā	śatrav-e	śatro-s	śatro-s	śatrau
	PITAR	pitā	pitar	pitar-am	pitr-ā	pitr-e	pitur	pitur	pitar-i
	NAPTĀR	naptā	naptar	naptār-am	naptr-ā	naptr-e	naptur	naptur	naptar-i
Dual	MARUT		marut-au			marud-bhyām		marut-os	
	VIDVĀMS		vidvāms-au			vidvad-bhyām		viduṣ-os	
	RĀJĀN		rājān-au			rāja-bhyām		rājñ-os	
	AŚVA		aśvau			aśvābhyām		aśvayos	
	ĀSYA		āsye			āsyābhyām		āsyayos	
	AGNI		agnī			agni-bhyām		agny-os	
	ŚATRU		śatrū			śatru-bhyām		śatrv-os	
	PITAR		pitar-au			pitr-bhyām		pitr-os	
	NAPTĀR		naptār-au			naptr-bhyām		naptr-os	
Plural	MARUT	marut-as	marut-as	marut-as	marud-bhis	marud-bhyas	marud-bhyas	marut-ām	marut-su
	VIDVĀMS	vidvāms-as	vidvāms-as	viduṣ-as	vidvad-bhis	vidvad-bhyas	vidvad-bhyas	viduṣ-ām	vidvat-su
	RĀJĀN	rājān-as	rājān-as	rājñ-as	rāja-bhis	rāja-bhyas	rāja-bhyas	rājñ-ām	rāja-su
	AŚVA	aśvās	aśvās	aśvān	aśvais	aśve-bhyas	aśve-bhyas	aśvānām	aśve-ṣu
	ĀSYA	āsyāni	āsyāni	āsyāni	āsyais	āsye-bhyas	āsye-bhyas	āsyānām	āsye-ṣu
	AGNI	agnay-as	agnay-as	agnīn	agni-bhis	agni-bhyas	agni-bhyas	agnīnām	agni-ṣu
	ŚATRU	śatrav-as	śatrav-as	śatrūn	śatru-bhis	śatru-bhyas	śatru-bhyas	śatrūṇām	śatru-ṣu
	PITAR	pitar-as	pitar-as	pitṝn	pitr-bhis	pitr-bhyas	pitr-bhyas	pitṝṇām	pitṛ-ṣu
	NAPTĀR	naptār-as	naptār-as	naptṝn	naptr-bhis	naptr-bhyas	naptr-bhyas	naptṝṇām	naptṛ-ṣu

approach. Thus, if the inflection of VIDVĀMS and RĀJAN is defined by means of purely implicative rules, the generalization in (4) is missed, and there is no more reason to expect the implicative pattern in (5a) (which conforms to (4)) than that in (5b) (which does not conform to (4)). In PEM, by contrast, the generalization in (4) can be stated as a morphological metageneralization – a rule about rules of exponence (Stump 2001:47ff; Zwicky 1994). A metageneralization of this sort requires rules of exponence realizing the Weak cases to apply to a gradational lexeme's Weak Prevocalic stem if they introduce a vowel-initial suffix and otherwise to the lexeme's Default Weak stem.

(5) (a) $\langle Xas, \{\text{GEND}:\alpha \text{ gen sg}\}\rangle \to \langle Xe, \{\text{GEND}:\alpha \text{ dat sg}\}\rangle$
(e.g. $\langle viduṣas, \{\text{masc gen sg}\}\rangle \to \langle viduṣe, \{\text{masc dat sg}\}\rangle$)
(b) $\langle Xsu, \{\text{GEND}:\alpha \text{ loc pl}\}\rangle \to \langle Xe, \{\text{GEND}:\alpha \text{ dat sg}\}\rangle$
(e.g. $\langle vidvatsu, \{\text{masc loc pl}\}\rangle \to *\langle vidvate, \{\text{masc dat sg}\}\rangle$)

The second reason why we need rules of exponence is to account for certain kinds of implicative patterns in a language's paradigms: in many cases, such patterns are better seen as relations among realization rules (including rules of exponence) than as relations among realizations. To appreciate this point, consider now the nouns AŚVA 'horse' (masc), ĀSYA 'mouth' (neut), AGNI 'fire' (masc), ŚATRU 'enemy' (masc), PITAR 'father' (masc), and NAPTĀR 'descendant' (masc) in Table 9.5.

In Sanskrit, all nouns having a genitive singular of the form X-sya (e.g. aśva-sya 'horse's', āsya-sya 'mouth's') have an accusative singular of the form X-m (aśva-m, āsya-m); their nominative singular, however, is X-s for masculine nouns (e.g. AŚVA: aśva-s) but X-m for neuter nouns (ĀSYA: āsya-m). What these two nominative singular forms have in common is that they are based on the same stem as is used in the genitive singular (aśva-, āsya-) rather than, say, the stem used in the dative plural (aśve-, āsye-). Thus, some implicative relations determine a word form's stem without determining the word form in its entirety: all nouns having a genitive singular of the form X-sya have a nominative singular based on the same stem X. This relation may be seen as a relation between realization rules: the application of the -sya rule (a rule of exponence) to stem X in the genitive singular inflection of a given lexeme L implies the application a rule selecting stem X in L's nominative singular inflection.

Implicative relations may also determine a word form's affixal inflection without determining its stem. In Sanskrit, all nouns having a locative singular of the form Xau (agnau 'in a fire', śatrau 'at an enemy') have -s as their affixal exponent of the genitive singular; but the stem of the genitive singular is Xe for some such nouns (e.g. AGNI: agne-s) and Xo for others (ŚATRU: śatro-s). Such implicative relations may likewise be seen as relations between realization rules; for instance, the application of the rule selecting the AU-Stem in the locative singular inflection of a given lexeme L implies the application of the rule suffixing -*s* (a rule of exponence) in L's genitive singular inflection.

Such evidence reveals that the implicative relations exhibited by a language's inflectional morphology are not simply relations among fully realized word forms. They may also be relations among the realization rules defining a lexeme's inflection, at least some of which are rules of exponence. Indeed, we wish to raise the possibility that all implicative relations between full word forms are in fact reducible to implicative relations among realization rules; moreover, we propose that many such relations should simply be seen as theorems of a precise realizational definition of a language's inflectional system.

We conclude that neither implicative rules nor rules of exponence are dispensable in morphological theory. One might object that a theory that incorporates both rules of exponence and implicative rules will inevitably lead to redundancies; but our stored linguistic knowledge certainly is not nonredundant. People store whole phrases and sentences whose parts they know how to parse syntactically (Schmitt & Underwood 2004; Tremblay *et al.* 2011); it is equally plausible that they store paradigmatic relations between words whose exponence they know how to parse morphologically.

If one accepts the coexistence of rules of exponence with implicative rules (as we do), one is left with the need to decide when one or the other or both are called for. In the following section, we propose a theoretical approach to inflectional morphology that employs the diacritic+stem approach to lexical representation and accommodates both implicative rules and exponence-based rules in a principled manner. The hypothesis embodied by this approach is that implicative rules are of two sorts: rules of referral defining patterns of syncretism are basic, whereas rules defining systematic patterns among phonologically distinct realizations of a lexeme are theorems of the formal, primarily exponence-based, definition of a language's inflectional system.

9.3 A hybrid conception of inflectional morphology

The conception of inflectional morphology that we propose is a hybrid relative to the canonical extremes considered in §9.2. In our conception, a lexeme L's lexical entry minimally includes its Default stem and a specification of its IC membership, represented diacritically as the name of a set of lexemes; the lexical listing of one or more realized cells in L's paradigm is not excluded, and these may or may not be optimal principal parts. Certain realization rules are basic to the definition of an inflectional system; these are in general restricted to specific ICs. Such rules are of two broadly different types, which themselves subsume different subtypes: rules of stem realization include stem-formation rules and stem-selection rules, while rules of word-realization include rules of exponence and traditional rules of referral. Implicative rules of the nonsyncretistic sort are non-basic, existing as theorems of the basic realization rules and their interaction; the relations that they specify include both W-relations and R-relations (§4.1).

In order to elucidate the properties of this conception of inflectional morphology, we use a small illustrative fragment of the Sanskrit declensional system. Our fragment comprises the nine nominal (noun and adjective) lexemes given earlier in Table 9.5: MARUT 'wind', VIDVĀMS 'knowing', RĀJĀN 'king', AŚVA 'horse', ĀSYA 'mouth', AGNI 'fire', ŚATRU 'enemy', PITAR 'father', and NAPTĀR 'descendant'. In the following subsections, we present the components of our analysis of this fragment, including the representation of IC membership (§9.3.1), the definition of the Sanskrit paradigm function (§9.3.2), and the rules of stem realization and word-realization on which the paradigm function depends (§§9.3.3–4). We then discuss the status of principal parts in our analysis (§9.3.5) and their role in deriving implicative rules as theorems of the analysis (§9.3.6).

9.3.1 IC membership

The IC membership of the lexemes in our fragment may be characterized as follows:

- MARUT 'wind' belongs to the class of ***nongradational C(onsonant)-stem*** nominals,
- the gradational C-stem lexeme VIDVĀMS 'knowing' belongs to the class of **vāms-*stem*** nominals,
- the gradational C-stem lexeme RĀJĀN 'king' belongs to the class of **ān-*stem*** nominals,
- the nongradational V(owel)-stem lexemes AŚVA 'horse' (masc) and ĀSYA 'mouth' (neut) belong to the class of **a-*stem*** nominals,
- the nongradational V-stem lexemes AGNI 'fire' and ŚATRU 'enemy' belong to the class of **i/u-*stem*** nominals, and
- the gradational V-stem[5] lexemes PITAR 'father' and NAPTĀR 'descendant' belong to the **r-*stem*-I** class and the **r-*stem*-II** class (respectively).

---

[5] Because lexemes belonging to the **r-*stem*** classes have important declensional similarities to *a*-stem and *i/u*-stem nominals and because each **r-*stem*** noun has one stem ending in a vowel-like syllable nucleus *r̥* (its Weak stem in Table 9.7), we include them among the V-stem nominals for morphological purposes.

A hybrid conception of inflectional morphology   273

This classification implies an IC system whose classes are sometimes nested and sometimes partially overlap, as in Table 9.6. Thus, we assume the set-theoretic relationships in (6). Where a lexeme L belongs to an IC J and there is no proper subject J′ of J such that (a) L belongs to J′ and (b) at least one realization rule is defined as applying to members of J′, we say that L **narrowly belongs** to J; where L narrowly belongs to J and J is a proper subset of J′, we say that L **broadly belongs** to J′. For example, VIDVĀMS narrowly belongs to the **vāṃs-*stem*** class and broadly belongs to the ***C-stem gradational*** and ***nominal*** classes. The lexical entry of each lexeme L contains a diacritic denoting the IC to which L narrowly belongs and L's Default stem.

(6)   (a) MARUT ∈ ***C-stem, nongradational*** ⊂ ***nominal***
       (b) VIDVĀMS ∈ **vāṃs-*stem*** ⊂ ***C-stem, gradational*** ⊂ ***nominal***
       (c) RĀJĀN ∈ **ān-*stem*** ⊂ ***C-stem, gradational*** ⊂ ***nominal***
       (d) AŚVA, ĀSYA ∈ **a-*stem*** ⊂ ***V-stem, nongradational*** ⊂ ***nominal***
       (e) AGNI, ŚATRU ∈ **i/u-*stem*** ⊂ ***V-stem, nongradational*** ⊂ ***nominal***
       (f) PITAR ∈ **r-*stem*-I** ⊂ **r-*stem*** = ***V-stem, gradational*** ⊂ ***nominal***
       (g) NAPTĀR ∈ **r-*stem*-II** ⊂ **r-*stem*** = ***V-stem, gradational*** ⊂ ***nominal***

9.3.2   The Sanskrit paradigm function

We draw our techniques about the formulation and interaction of morphological rules from Paradigm Function Morphology (Stump 2001) and Network Morphology (Brown & Hippisley 2012; Corbett & Fraser 1993), both inferential-realizational theories of inflection that make essential use of default/override relations. In Paradigm Function Morphology, all realization rules contribute to the definition of a language's paradigm function. A **paradigm function** is a function from the cells in lexemes' paradigms to the corresponding cells in their realized paradigms. For example, the value of the Sanskrit paradigm function PF for the cell ⟨AŚVA, {masc nom pl}⟩ is the realized cell ⟨*aśvās*, {masc nom pl}⟩:

$$\text{PF}(\langle \text{AŚVA}, \{\text{masc nom pl}\}\rangle) = \langle \textit{aśvās}, \{\text{masc nom pl}\}\rangle.$$

The domain of a language's paradigm function is the set containing every cell in the paradigm of every lexeme (regardless of its syntactic category). Here, we are only concerned with the nominals (nouns and adjectives) in our fragment. Accordingly, we do not propose an all-encompassing definition of the Sanskrit paradigm function; instead, we simply formulate the clause in that definition responsible for the inflection of nominals:

(7)   The Sanskrit paradigm function (partial definition)
       Where L is a nominal that narrowly belongs to IC J,
       PF(⟨L, σ⟩) = [⟨L, σ⟩ : |J, σ|].

Table 9.6. Six declension classes and their superclasses in Sanskrit (✓ = membership)

			MARUT 'wind'	VIDVĀṂS 'knowing'	RĀJĀN 'king'	AŚVA 'horse'	ĀSYA 'mouth'	AGNI 'fire'	ŚATRU 'enemy'	PITAR 'father'	NAPTĀR 'descendant'
Nominal											
	Nongradational		✓	✓							
	Gradational			✓	✓					✓	✓
	C-stem		✓	✓	✓						
		vāṃs-stem		✓							
		ān-stem			✓						
	V-stem					✓	✓	✓	✓	✓	✓
		a-stem				✓	✓				
		i/u-stem						✓	✓		
	r-stem	I								✓	
		II									✓

Here, we use the notation '|J, σ|' ("J's rule for σ") to represent the narrowest (most specific) word-realization rule realizing the property set σ in the inflection of members of IC J; this rule may be (a) a rule defined as applying specifically to members of J, or, in the absence of such a rule, (b) a rule defined as applying to members of a superclass of J. We also use the notation '[⟨L, σ⟩ : R]' to represent the result of applying rule R to ⟨L, σ⟩. Thus, [⟨L, σ⟩ : |J, σ|] is the result of applying J's rule for σ to the cell ⟨L, σ⟩.

Definition (7) depends on the definition of the individual realization rules for the inflection of Sanskrit nominals. These realization rules include stem-realization rules and word-realization rules. Consider now the rules of each of these two types.

9.3.3 Stem-realization rules

For any lexeme L, morphosyntactic property set σ and phonological context K, we employ the notation *Stem*(⟨L, σ, K⟩) to represent the stem used for L in expressing σ in K; for example, *Stem*(⟨RĀJAN, {masc gen sg}, [___V]⟩) = *rājñ-*, the stem used for the masculine noun RĀJAN 'king' in expressing the genitive singular, whose suffix -*as* is vowel-initial.[6] The value of *Stem*(⟨L, σ, K⟩) in any given instance is determined by **stem-realization rules** of two sorts: (i) a **stem-selection rule** indicates where a stem with a particular index *i* appears within its lexeme's realized paradigm, and thus has the form

$$Stem(\langle L, \sigma, K \rangle) = L\text{'s } i\text{-Stem}$$

(where σ defines a morphosyntactic context and K, a phonological context); and (ii) a **stem-formation rule** derives the phonological shape of a stem with one index *j* from that of a stem with a distinct index *i*, and thus has the form

> Where the *i*-stem of L is X, the *j*-stem of L is *f*(X) (for some morphological operation *f*).

In the fragment of the Sanskrit declensional system at issue here, a nominal lexeme has one to four indexed stems, as in Table 9.7. The indices of a lexeme L's indexed stems depend on the IC to which L belongs; for instance, lexemes in the **gradational C-stem** class have a Default stem (DefStem), a Strong stem (StrStem), a Weak stem (WkStem), and a Weak Prevocalic stem (WkPVStem); by contrast, lexemes in the **i/u-*stem*** class have a DefStem, a StrStem, an N-Stem, and an AU-Stem. Only a lexeme's DefStem need be listed lexically. The

---

[6] Here and below, we represent prevocalic and preconsonantal contexts as '[___V]' and '[___C]'; '[___]' represents word-final position.

Table 9.7. *Indexed stems for nine Sanskrit nominal lexemes (shaded stems are lexically listed)*

IC	Lexeme	Default stem (DefStem)	Strong stem (StrStem)	Weak stem (WkStem)	Weak Prevocalic stem (WkPVStem)	Nominative singular stem (NsgStem)	Ā-Stem	N-Stem	E-Stem	AU-Stem
C-stem	MARUT 'wind'	*marut-*	–	–	–	–	–	–	–	–
	VIDVĀṂS 'knowing'	*vidvāṃs-*	*vidvāṃs-*	*vidvat-*	*viduṣ-*	–	–	–	–	–
	RĀJAN 'king'	*rājān-*	*rājan-*	*rāja-*	*rājñ-*	–	–	–	–	–
a-stem	AŚVA 'horse' (masc)	*aśva-*	–	–	–	–	*aśvā-*	–	*aśve-*	–
	ĀSYA 'mouth' (neut)	*āsya-*	–	–	–	–	*āsyā-*	*āsyān-*	*āsye-*	–
i/u-stem	AGNI 'fire'	*agni-*	*agne-*	–	–	–	–	*agnin-*	–	*agnau-*
	ŚATRU 'enemy'	*śatru-*	*śatro-*	–	–	–	–	*śatrun-*	–	*śatrau-*
r-stem-I	PITAR 'father'	*pitár-* (= StrStem)	*pitar-*	*pitṛ-*	*pitr-*	*pitār-*	–	–	–	–
r-stem-II	NAPTĀR 'descendant'	*naptār-* (= NsgStem)	*naptar-*	*naptṛ-*	*naptr-*	*naptār-*	–	–	–	–

phonological shape of other indexed stems is deduced by means of stem-formation rules, and the distribution of stems within a lexeme's realized paradigm (including that of its DefStem) is specified by means of stem-selection rules.

Stem-realization rules are formulated so as to apply to a particular IC. Consider first the stem-realization rules defined as applying to members of the ***gradational*** class. These do not include stem-formation rules, which apply to more specific classes. There are, however, some stem-selection rules that apply to the ***gradational*** class: these are the rules governing stem selection in the inflection of gradational nominals, including both gradational C-stem nominals (such as VIDVĀMS and RĀJĀN) and gradational V-stem nominals (such as PITAR and NAPTĀR). These rules presuppose that a gradational nominal has four stems: DefStem, StrStem, WkStem, and WkPVStem. The choice of stem in the inflection of a gradational C-stem nominal L depends on the morphosyntactic property set being realized and on the phonological context created by the rule of word-realization expressing that property set in L's inflection. The stem-selection rule (8a.ii) says that in the oblique (= instrumental, dative, ablative, genitive, and locative) cases and in the accusative plural, the realization of L is based on its WkStem; but in a prevocalic context, (8a.ii) is overridden by (8a.i), which instead prescribes the use of L's WeakPVStem. The stem-selection rule in (8b) specifies the use of L's StrStem in the vocative singular, and the stem-selection rule in (8c) specifies the use of L's DefStem as a default.

(8) Stem-selection rules applying to the ***gradational*** class
Where L is a nominal in the ***gradational*** (***C-stem*** or ***V-stem***) class, σ is a morphosyntactic property set and K is a phonological context:

(a) If σ is oblique or {acc pl} ⊆ σ, then
  (i) where K = [___V], ***Stem***(⟨L, σ, K⟩) = L's WkPVStem;
  (ii) for other values of K, ***Stem***(⟨L, σ, K⟩) = L's WkStem.
(b) If {voc sg} ⊆ σ, then ***Stem***(⟨L, σ, K⟩) = L's StrStem.
(c) By default, ***Stem***(⟨L, σ, K⟩) = L's DefStem.

Competition among realization rules is in all cases resolved by the general principle that the narrowest rule (the rule applicable in the most restrictive circumstances) prevails over more general competitors. Specifically, we refer to the following principle as **Pāṇini's principle**.

If realization rules R_1 and R_2 are in competition, R_1 is narrower than (and therefore overrides) R_2 iff
either (a) R_1 is defined as applying to a proper subclass of the class to which R_2 is defined as applying,
or (b) R_1 and R_2 are defined as applying to the same class, but R_1 is defined for a smaller number of morphosyntactic property sets than R_2.

Thus, in the case at hand, rules (8b) and (8c) compete for the definition of ***Stem***(⟨RĀJĀN, {masc voc sg}, K⟩). Although both rules apply to the class of gradational nominals, rule (8b) is only defined for {voc sg} property sets ({masc voc sg}, {fem voc sg}, {neut voc sg}), whereas (8c) is defined for any property set. Thus, by Pāṇini's principle, (8b) overrides (8c):

Stem(⟨RĀJĀN, {masc voc sg}, K⟩) = L's StrStem ≠ L's DefStem.

Consider also the stem-selection rules in (9), which apply to the ***gradational V-stem*** class.

(9)   Stem-selection rules applying to the ***gradational V-stem*** class
       Where L is a nominal in the ***gradational V-stem*** class, σ is a morphosyntactic property set and K is a phonological context:
       (a) If {loc sg} ⊆ σ, then ***Stem***(⟨L, σ, K⟩) = L's StrStem.
       (b) If {nom sg} ⊆ σ, then ***Stem***(⟨L, σ, K⟩) = L's NsgStem.

Because the ***gradational V-stem*** class is a subclass of the ***gradational*** class, rules (8a.i) and (9a) compete to determine the value of ***Stem***(⟨PITAR, {masc loc sg}, [___V]⟩). Pāṇini's principle entails that (9a) prevails:

Stem(⟨PITAR, {masc loc sg}, [___V]⟩) = L's StrStem ≠ L's WkPVStem

Similarly, rules (8c) and (9b) compete to determine the value of ***Stem***(⟨PITAR, {masc nom sg}, K⟩). Pāṇini's principle entails that (9b) prevails:

Stem(⟨PITAR, {masc nom sg}, K⟩) = L's NsgStem ≠ L's DefStem

Consider now the stem-selection rule in (10), which applies to the ***nongradational C-stem*** class. This rule is maximally simple; it associates a nongradational C-stem nominal L with a single stem (L's DefStem) appearing in every cell of L's realized paradigm; this Default stem is simply listed in L's lexical entry. No stem-formation rule is needed for the ***nongradational C-stem*** class, since the only stem involved in the inflection of a nongradational C-stem nominal is its lexically listed DefStem.

(10)   Stem-selection rule applying to the ***nongradational C-stem*** class
       Where L is a nominal in the ***nongradational C-stem*** class, σ is a morphosyntactic property set and K is a phonological context,
       Stem(⟨L, σ, K⟩) = L's DefStem.
       Example: ***Stem***(⟨MARUT, σ, K⟩) = *marut*;
                MARUT's DefStem *marut* is listed in its lexical entry.

Stem-formation rules are, however, necessary for nominals whose selection is determined by (8) and (9). For nominals belonging to the **vāṃs-*stem*** and

A hybrid conception of inflectional morphology 279

ān-*stem* classes (= the ***gradational C-stem*** classes), StrStem, WkStem, and WkPVStem are deduced by means of the stem-formation rules in (11) and (12). The stem-formation rule in (11) applies to members of the **vāṃs-*stem*** class, using a lexeme's lexically listed DefStem X*vāṃs-* to define its WkPVStem X*uṣ-*, its WkStem X*vat-* and its StrStem X*vaṃs-*; together with the stem-selection rules in (8), the stem-formation rule in (11) entails the equations in (13). The stem-formation rule in (12) applies to members of the **ān-*stem*** class, using a lexeme's lexically listed DefStem X*ān-* to define its WkPVStem X*n-*, its WkStem X*a-*, and its StrStem X*an-*; together with the stem-selection rules in (8), the stem-formation rule in (12) entails the equations in (14).

(11) Stem-formation rule applying to the **vāṃs-*stem*** class
      If a nominal belonging to the **vāṃs-*stem*** class has X*vāṃs-* as its DefStem, then it has

      - X*uṣ-* as its WkPVStem,
      - X*vat-* as its WkStem, and
      - X*vaṃs-* as its StrStem.

(12) Stem-formation rule applying to the **ān-*stem*** class
      If a nominal belonging to the **ān-*stem*** class has X*ān-* as its DefStem, then it has

      - X*n-* as its WkPVStem,
      - X*a-* as its WkStem, and
      - X*an-* as its StrStem.

(13) ***Stem***(⟨VIDVĀṂS, {masc ins sg}, [___V]⟩) = *viduṣ-*
      Stem(⟨VIDVĀṂS, {masc ins pl}, [___C]⟩) = *vidvat-*
      Stem(⟨VIDVĀṂS, {masc voc sg}, K⟩) = *vidvaṁs-*
      Stem(⟨VIDVĀṂS, {masc nom du}, K⟩) = *vidvāṁs-*

(14) ***Stem***(⟨RĀJAN, {masc ins sg}, [___V]⟩) = *rājn-* (→ *rājñ-* by automatic sandhi)
      Stem(⟨RĀJAN, {masc ins pl}, [___C]⟩) = *rāja-*
      Stem(⟨RĀJAN, {masc voc sg}, K⟩) = *rājan-*
      Stem(⟨RĀJAN, {masc nom du}, K⟩) = *rājān-*

For nominals belonging to the **r-*stem*** classes (= the ***gradational V-stem*** class), StrStem, WkStem, and WkPVStem are deduced by means of the stem-formation rules in (15). According to (15a), if a nominal belonging to the **r-*stem*-I** class has DefStem X*ar-*, then it has StrStem X*ar-*, NsgStem X*ār-*, WkStem X*r̥-*, and WkPVStem X*r-*; by (15b), if a nominal belonging to the **r-*stem*-II** class has DefStem X*ār-*, then it has StrStem X*ar-*, NsgStem X*ār-*, WkStem X*r̥-*, and WkPVStem X*r-*. Note that the stems of nominals belonging to the **r-*stem*-I** class are exactly like those of nominals in the **r-*stem*-II** class except that for nominals in the **r-*stem*-I** class, DefStem = StrStem ≠ NsgStem,

280 *Inflection classes, implicative relations, and morphological theory*

while for nominals in the **r-*stem*-II** class, DefStem = NsgStem ≠ StrStem; see again Table 9.7. It might appear that these equivalences make DefStem redundant for nominals in the **r-*stem*** class, but the formulation of the stem-selection rules in (8) and (9) is simplified if DefStem, StrStem and NsgStem are maintained as distinct indices for the stems of nominals belonging to the **r-*stem*** class. Together with these stem-selection rules, the stem-formation rules in (15) entail the equations in (16).

(15) Stem-formation rules applying to the **r-*stem*** (= ***gradational V-stem***) classes

(a) If a nominal belonging to the **r-*stem*-I** class has Xar- as its DefStem, then it has
- Xar- as its StrStem,
- X$ār$- as its NsgStem,
- X$r̥$- as its WkStem, and
- Xr- as its WkPVStem.

(b) If a nominal belonging to the **r-*stem*-II** class has X$ār$- as its DefStem, then it has
- Xar- as its StrStem,
- X$ār$- as its NsgStem,
- X$r̥$- as its WkStem, and
- Xr- as its WkPVStem.

(16) $Stem(\langle\text{PITAR}, \{\text{masc ins sg}\}, [\_\_\_V]\rangle) = pitr$-
$Stem(\langle\text{PITAR}, \{\text{masc ins pl}\}, [\_\_\_C]\rangle) = pitr̥$-
$Stem(\langle\text{PITAR}, \{\text{masc voc sg}\}, K\rangle) = pitar$-
$Stem(\langle\text{PITAR}, \{\text{masc nom du}\}, K\rangle) = pitar$-
$Stem(\langle\text{PITAR}, \{\text{masc nom sg}\}, K\rangle) = pitār$-
$Stem(\langle\text{NAPTĀR}, \{\text{masc ins sg}\}, [\_\_\_V]\rangle) = naptr$-
$Stem(\langle\text{NAPTĀR}, \{\text{masc ins pl}\}, [\_\_\_C]\rangle) = naptr̥$-
$Stem(\langle\text{NAPTĀR}, \{\text{masc voc sg}\}, K\rangle) = naptar$-
$Stem(\langle\text{NAPTĀR}, \{\text{masc nom du}\}, K\rangle) = naptār$-
$Stem(\langle\text{NAPTĀR}, \{\text{masc nom sg}\}, K\rangle) = naptār$-

The stem-formation rule in (17) and the stem-selection rules in (18) are defined as applying to the **a-*stem*** class. According to (17), if a nominal in the **a-*stem*** class has Xa- as its lexically listed DefStem, then it has Ā-Stem X$ā$-, E-Stem Xe-, and N-Stem X$ān$. The distribution of these stems is defined by (18). Together with the stem-formation rule in (17), the stem-selection rules in (18) determine the equations in (19).

(17) Stem-formation rule applying to the **a-*stem*** class
If a nominal belonging to the **a-*stem*** class has Xa- as its DefStem, then it has
- X$ā$- as its Ā-Stem,
- Xe- as its E-Stem, and
- X$ān$- as its N-Stem.

A hybrid conception of inflectional morphology   281

(18)   Stem-selection rule applying to the **a-stem** class
         Where L is a nominal belonging to the **a-stem** class, σ is a morphosyntactic property set and K is a phonological context:

   (a) If σ is plural and K = [___C], then ***Stem***(⟨L, σ, K⟩) = L's E-Stem.
   (b) If {gen du} ⊆ σ, then ***Stem***(⟨L, σ, K⟩) = L's E-Stem.
   (c) If {ins du} ⊆ σ, then ***Stem***(⟨L, σ, K⟩) = L's Ā-Stem.
   (d) If σ = {neut acc pl}, ***Stem***(⟨L, σ, K⟩) = L's N-Stem.
   (e) By default, ***Stem***(⟨L, σ, K⟩) = L's DefStem.

(19)   ***Stem***(⟨AŚVA, {masc dat pl}, [___C]⟩) = *aśve-*
         Stem(⟨AŚVA, {masc gen du}, K⟩) = *aśve-*
         Stem(⟨AŚVA, {masc ins du}, K⟩) = *aśvā-*
         Stem(⟨ĀSYA, {neut acc pl}, K⟩) = *āsyān-*
         Stem(⟨AŚVA, {masc acc sg}, K⟩) = *aśva-*

The stem-formation rule in (20) and the stem-selection rules in (21) are defined as appyling to the **i/u-stem** class. According to (20), if a nominal belonging to the **i/u-stem** class has DefStem X*i*-, then it has StrStem X*e*-, N-Stem X*n*-, and AU-Stem X*au*-; similarly, if a nominal in the **i/u-stem** class has DefStem X*u*-, then it has StrStem X*o*-, N-Stem X*n*-, and AU-Stem X*au*-. The distribution of these stems is defined by (21). Together with the stem-formation rule in (20), the stem-selection rules in (21) determine the equations in (22).

(20)   Stem-formation rule applying to the **i/u-stem** class
         If a nominal belonging to the **i/u-stem** class has X*i*- as its DefStem, then it has
         • X*e*- as its StrStem,
         • X*in*- as its N-Stem, and
         • X*au*- as its AU-Stem;

         if it has X*u*- as its DefStem, then it has
         • X*o*- as its StrStem,
         • X*un*- as its N-Stem, and
         • X*au*- as its AU-Stem.

(21)   Stem-selection rules applying to the **i/u-stem** class
         Where L is a nominal belonging to the **i/u-stem** class, σ is a morphosyntactic property set, and K is a phonological context:

   (a) If {voc sg}, {dat sg}, {gen sg} or {nom pl} ⊆ σ, then ***Stem***(⟨L, σ, K⟩) = L's StrStem.
   (b) If {loc sg} ⊆ σ, then ***Stem***(⟨L, σ, K⟩) = L's AU-Stem.
   (c) If {ins sg} ⊆ σ, then ***Stem***(⟨L, σ, K⟩) = L's N-Stem.
   (d) By default, ***Stem***(⟨L, σ, K⟩) = L's DefStem.

282 *Inflection classes, implicative relations, and morphological theory*

Table 9.8. *Rules of stem formation and stem selection for nine Sanskrit nominals*

	MARUT 'wind'	VIDVĀMS 'knowing'	RĀJĀN 'king'	AŚVA 'horse'	ĀSYA 'mouth'	AGNI 'fire'	ŚATRU 'enemy'	PITAR 'father'	NAPTĀR 'descendant'
Stem-formation rule	–	(11)	(12)	(17)	(17)	(20)	(20)	(15)	(15)
Stem-selection rules	(10)	(8)	(8)	(18)	(18)	(21)	(21)	(8), (9)	(8), (9)

(22)   ***Stem***(⟨AGNI, {masc dat sg}, K⟩) = *agne-*
       Stem(⟨AGNI, {masc loc sg}, K⟩) = *agnau-*
       Stem(⟨AGNI, {masc ins sg}, K⟩) = *agnin-*
       Stem(⟨AGNI, {masc nom sg}, K⟩) = *agni-*

We have now seen how stem formation and stem selection are effected for each of the nine nominals under consideration; the rules for all of these nominals are summarized in Table 9.8.

9.3.4   *Word-realization rules*

For each cell ⟨L, σ⟩ in the paradigm of a lexeme L, the realization of ⟨L, σ⟩ is determined by the stem-realization rules discussed in §9.3.2 and by one or more rules of word-realization specifying how the selected stem is inflected for the expression of σ. Word-realization rules may take the form of rules of exponence or traditional rules of referral; the format for their formulation is given in (23). (Here and throughout, the notation 'σ:τ' refers to a morphosyntactic property set σ such that τ ⊆ σ; within a rule or equation, σ:τ and σ are to be understood as referring to the same property set.)

(23)   Format for the statement of word-realization rules: L, σ:τ → Y.
       Interpretation: Given some lexeme L and some property sets σ, τ such that τ ⊆ σ, the cell ⟨L, σ⟩ in L's paradigm is realized as ⟨Y, σ⟩.

Given this format, the full inventory of word-realization rules for the fragment of Sanskrit under consideration may be formulated as in (24). In each rule of exponence, the variable X is evaluated in accordance with the morphological metageneralizations in (25); by virtue of these metageneralizations, the model proposed here accounts for the phenomenon of inward phonological conditioned discussed in §9.2.

(24)   Word-realization rules for a fragment of Sanskrit

Rules of exponence applying to lexemes in the ***nominal*** class

Nom.a	L, σ:{nom sg}	→ X*s*
Nom.b	L, σ:{voc sg}	→ X
Nom.c	L, σ:{acc sg}	→ X*am*
Nom.d	L, σ:{ins sg}	→ X*ā*
Nom.e	L, σ:{dat sg}	→ X*e*
Nom.f	L, σ:{loc sg}	→ X*i*
Nom.g	L, σ:{masc nom du}	→ X*au*
Nom.h	L, σ:{neut acc du}	→ X*ī*
Nom.i	L, σ:{ins du}	→ X*bhyām*
Nom.j	L, σ:{gen du}	→ X*os*
Nom.k	L, σ:{nom pl}	→ X*as*
Nom.l	L, σ:{neut acc pl}	→ X*i*
Nom.m	L, σ:{ins pl}	→ X*bhis*
Nom.n	L, σ:{dat pl}	→ X*bhyas*
Nom.o	L, σ:{loc pl}	→ X*su*

Rules of referral applying to lexemes in the ***nominal*** class

Nom.p	Where Y = PF(⟨L, σ/{acc}⟩),	L, σ:{neut nom}	→ Y
Nom.q	Where Y = PF(⟨L, σ/{gen}⟩),	L, σ:{abl sg}	→ Y
Nom.r	Where Y = PF(⟨L, σ/{nom}⟩),	L, σ:{voc}	→ Y
Nom.s	Where Y = PF(⟨L, σ/{nom}⟩),	L, σ:{acc du}	→ Y
Nom.t	Where Y = PF(⟨L, σ/{ins}⟩),	L, σ:{dat du}	→ Y
Nom.u	Where Y = PF(⟨L, σ/{dat}⟩),	L, σ:{abl}	→ Y
Nom.v	Where Y = PF(⟨L, σ/{gen}⟩),	L, σ:{loc du}	→ Y

Rules of exponence applying to lexemes in the ***C-stem*** class

C-st.a	Where Y*n* = ***Stem***(⟨L, σ, [___]⟩), L, σ:{masc nom sg}	→ Y
C-st.b	L, σ:{gen sg}	→ X*as*
C-st.c	L, σ:{acc pl}	→ X*as*
C-st.d	L, σ:{gen pl}	→ X*ām*

Rules of exponence applying to lexemes in the ***V-stem*** class[7]

Where ***Stem***(⟨L, σ, [___ C]⟩) = Y,

V-st.a	L, σ:{acc sg}	→ Y*m* if Y is vowel-final
V-st.b	L, σ:{masc acc pl}	→ Y:*n*
V-st.c	L, σ:{gen pl}	→ Y:*nām*

---

[7] In V-st.b, V-st.c, and i/u-st.c, ':' represents an underspecified vowel mora inducing lengthening of a preceding vowel.

284 *Inflection classes, implicative relations, and morphological theory*

Rules of exponence applying to lexemes in the **a-*stem*** class	
a-*st*.a	L, σ:{ins sg} → X*ina*.
a-*st*.b	L, σ:{dat sg} → X*āya*.
a-*st*.c	L, σ:{abl sg} → X*āt*.
a-*st*.d	L, σ:{gen sg} → X*sya*.
a-*st*.e	L, σ:{ins pl} → X*ais*.

Rules of exponence applying to lexemes in the **i/u-*stem*** class	
i/u-*st*.a	L, σ:{gen sg} → X*s*.
i/u-*st*.b	L, σ:{loc sg} → X.
i/u-*st* t.c	L, σ:{nom du} → X:.

Rules of exponence applying to lexemes in the **r-*stem*** class	
r-*st*.a	Where Y*r* = ***Stem***(⟨L, σ, [___]⟩), L, σ:{masc nom sg} → Y.
r-*st*.b	Where Y*r* = ***Stem***(⟨L, σ, [___]⟩), L, σ:{gen sg} → Y*ur*.

(25) Morphological metageneralizations for the rules of exponence in (24)
For any rule of exponence L, σ → X*y*,

(a) X = ***Stem***(⟨L, σ, [___V]⟩) if *y* is vowel-initial
(b) X = ***Stem***(⟨L, σ, [___C]⟩) if *y* is consonant-initial
(c) X = ***Stem***(⟨L, σ, [___]⟩) if *y* is null

The word-realization rules in (24) – subject to the morphological metageneralizations in (25) – apply to cells in a lexeme's paradigm to yield cells in that lexeme's realized paradigm, as in the illustrative examples in (26). The phonological forms generated by the rules in (24) are subsequently subject to rules of automatic sandhi (for which see Whitney 1889: §§34–87); the effects of these processes are exemplified in the rightmost column of (26).

(26) Examples of the application of the word-realization rules in (24)

Class	Rule	applies to the cell		to yield the realized cell	Sandhi	
nominal	*Nom*.a	⟨AŚVA, σ:{masc nom sg}⟩	→	⟨*aśva-s*, σ⟩		
	Nom.b	⟨AŚVA, σ:{masc voc sg}⟩	→	⟨*aśva*, σ⟩		
	Nom.c	⟨RĀJAN, σ:{masc acc sg}⟩	→	⟨*rājān-am*, σ⟩		
	Nom.d	⟨AGNI, σ:{masc ins sg}⟩	→	⟨*agnin-ā*, σ⟩		
	Nom.e	⟨AGNI, σ:{masc dat sg}⟩	→	⟨*agne-e*, σ⟩	→	⟨*agnaye*, σ⟩
	Nom.f	⟨AŚVA, σ:{masc loc sg}⟩	→	⟨*aśva-i*, σ⟩	→	⟨*aśve*, σ⟩
	Nom.g	⟨AŚVA, σ:{masc nom du}⟩	→	⟨*aśva-au*, σ⟩	→	⟨*aśvau*, σ⟩
	Nom.h	⟨ĀSYA, σ:{neut acc du}⟩	→	⟨*āsya-ī*, σ⟩	→	⟨*āsye*, σ⟩
	Nom.i	⟨AŚVA, σ:{masc ins du}⟩	→	⟨*aśve-bhyām*, σ⟩		
	Nom.j	⟨AŚVA, σ:{masc gen du}⟩	→	⟨*aśve-os*, σ⟩	→	⟨*aśvayos*, σ⟩

	Nom.k	⟨AŚVA, σ:{masc nom pl}⟩	→	⟨aśva-as, σ⟩	→	⟨aśvās, σ⟩
	Nom.l	⟨ĀSYA, σ:{neut acc pl}⟩	→	⟨āsyān-i, σ⟩		
	Nom.m	⟨AGNI, σ:{masc ins pl}⟩	→	⟨agni-bhis, σ⟩		
	Nom.n	⟨AŚVA, σ:{masc dat pl}⟩	→	⟨aśve-bhyas, σ⟩		
	Nom.o	⟨AŚVA, σ:{masc loc pl}⟩	→	⟨aśve-su, σ⟩	→	⟨aśveṣu, σ⟩
	Nom.p	⟨ĀSYA, σ:{neut nom du}⟩	→	⟨āsya-ī, σ⟩	→	⟨āsye, σ⟩
	Nom.q	⟨AGNI, σ:{masc abl sg}⟩	→	⟨agne-s, σ⟩		
	Nom.r	⟨AŚVA, σ:{masc voc du}⟩	→	⟨aśva-au, σ⟩	→	⟨aśvau, σ⟩
	Nom.s	⟨AŚVA, σ:{masc acc du}⟩	→	⟨aśva-au, σ⟩	→	⟨aśvau, σ⟩
	Nom.t	⟨AŚVA, σ:{masc dat du}⟩	→	⟨aśve-bhyām, σ⟩		
	Nom.u	⟨AŚVA, σ:{masc abl pl}⟩	→	⟨aśve-bhyas, σ⟩		
	Nom.v	⟨AŚVA, σ:{masc loc du}⟩	→	⟨aśve-os, σ⟩	→	⟨aśvayos, σ⟩
C-stem	*C-st*.a	⟨RĀJĀN, σ:{masc nom sg}⟩	→	⟨rājā, σ⟩		
	C-st.c	⟨RĀJĀN, σ:{masc gen sg}⟩	→	⟨rājn-as, σ⟩	→	⟨rājñas, σ⟩
	C-st.d	⟨RĀJĀN, σ:{masc acc pl}⟩	→	⟨rājn-as, σ⟩	→	⟨rājñas, σ⟩
	C-st.e	⟨RĀJĀN, σ:{masc gen pl}⟩	→	⟨rājn-ām, σ⟩	→	⟨rājñām, σ⟩
V-stem	*V-st*.a	⟨AŚVA, σ:{masc acc sg}⟩	→	⟨aśva-m, σ⟩		
	V-st.b	⟨AŚVA, σ:{masc acc pl}⟩	→	⟨aśva-:n, σ⟩	→	⟨aśvān, σ⟩
	V-st.c	⟨AŚVA, σ:{masc gen pl}⟩	→	⟨aśva-:nām, σ⟩	→	⟨aśvānām, σ⟩
a-stem	*a-st*.a	⟨AŚVA, σ:{masc ins sg}⟩	→	⟨aśva-ina, σ⟩	→	⟨aśvena, σ⟩
	a-st.b	⟨AŚVA, σ:{masc dat sg}⟩	→	⟨aśva-āya, σ⟩	→	⟨aśvāya, σ⟩
	a-st.c	⟨AŚVA, σ:{masc abl sg}⟩	→	⟨aśva-āt, σ⟩	→	⟨aśvāt, σ⟩
	a-st.d	⟨AŚVA, σ:{masc gen sg}⟩	→	⟨aśva-sya, σ⟩		
	a-st.e	⟨AŚVA, σ:{masc ins pl}⟩	→	⟨aśva-ais, σ⟩	→	⟨aśvais, σ⟩
i/u-stem	*i/u-st*.a	⟨AGNI, σ:{masc gen sg}⟩	→	⟨agne-s, σ⟩		
	i/u-st.b	⟨AGNI, σ:{masc loc sg}⟩	→	⟨agnau, σ⟩		
	i/u-st.c	⟨AGNI, σ:{masc nom du}⟩	→	⟨agnī, σ⟩		
r-stem	*r-st*.a	⟨PITAR, σ:{masc nom sg}⟩	→	⟨pitā, σ⟩		
	r-st.b	⟨PITAR, σ:{masc gen sg}⟩	→	⟨pitur, σ⟩		

In realizing a cell ⟨L, σ⟩, each rule of exponence R in (24) makes reference to that stem for L appropriate for realizing σ in the phonological context created by the R's application; in that sense, the forms defined by the rules of exponence in (24) depend upon the rules of stem realization presented in §9.3.2. For example, rule *C-st*.c depends upon the stem-selection rule (8a.i) and the stem-formation rule (12) to select RĀJĀN's WkPVStem *rājñ-* for combination with the vowel-initial genitive singular suffix *-as*: *rājñ-as* 'king's'.

The rules of referral in (24) (*Nom*.p through *Nom*.v) involve the Sanskrit paradigm function PF defined in (7). The notation 'σ/{x}' in these rules represents the morphosyntactic property set that is like σ except that it has x in place of any incompatible property in σ, e.g. {abl pl}/{dative} = {dat pl}. Thus, the rule of referral *Nom*.u in (24) causes the ablative plural cell ⟨AŚVA, {masc abl pl}⟩ to be realized as PF(⟨AŚVA, {masc abl pl}/{dat}⟩), i.e. as PF(⟨AŚVA, {masc dat pl}⟩), AŚVA's dative plural realization.

The word-realization rules in (24) make the Sanskrit paradigm function in (7) fully interpretable. That is, we can now easily show that equations such as those in (27) are theorems of the proposed analysis. A proof of equation (27a.i) is given in (28).

(27)   (a) Because MARUT narrowly belongs to the ***nongradational C-stem*** class,
           (i) PF(⟨MARUT, σ:{masc gen sg}⟩) = ⟨*marutas*, σ⟩
           (ii) PF(⟨MARUT, σ:{masc acc pl}⟩) = ⟨*marutas*, σ⟩
       (b) Because VIDVĀMS narrowly belongs to the **vāṃs-*stem*** class,
           (i) PF(⟨VIDVĀMS, σ:{masc ins sg}⟩) = ⟨*viduṣā*, σ⟩
           (ii) PF(⟨VIDVĀMS, σ:{masc loc pl}⟩) = ⟨*vidvatsu*, σ⟩
       (c) Because AŚVA narrowly belongs to the **a-*stem*** class,
           (i) PF(⟨AŚVA, σ:{masc gen sg}⟩) = ⟨*aśvasya*, σ⟩
           (ii) PF(⟨AŚVA, σ:{masc acc pl}⟩) = ⟨*aśvān*, σ⟩
       (d) Because AGNI narrowly belongs to the **i/u-*stem*** class,
           (i) PF(⟨AGNI, σ:{masc ins sg}⟩) = ⟨*aginā*, σ⟩
           (ii) PF(⟨AGNI, σ:{masc loc pl}⟩) = ⟨*agniṣu*, σ⟩

(28)   Proof of (27a.i)

        PF(⟨MARUT, σ:{masc gen sg}⟩)
          = [⟨MARUT, σ⟩ : |***C-stem*** class, σ|]   [by (7)]
          = ⟨X-*as*, σ⟩, where X = **Stem**(⟨MARUT, σ, [___ V]⟩)   [by ***C-st*.b**, (25a)]
                  = MARUT's DefStem   [by (10)]
                  = *marut*-   [by Table 9.7]
          = ⟨*marutas*, σ⟩

9.3.5   *The status of principal parts*

Principal parts play no direct role in the analysis of the Sanskrit declensional system proposed in §§9.3.1–4. Indeed, nothing in this analysis necessitates the lexical storage of a lexeme's principal parts. Given the realization rules that we have proposed, the principal parts of each lexeme in our fragment are deducible from its DefStem and its IC membership (both lexically listed). But if the principal parts are themselves deducible in this way, what possible role could they have? Their role, we argue, is to provide a basis for (a) determining the IC membership of newly encountered lexemes, and (b) deriving nonsyncretistic implicative rules that allow language users to infer one realized cell from one or more others; (a) is what we have called the matching function of principal parts, and (b), their deductive function (§6.1).

There are various alternative principal-part analyses for the nine Sanskrit nominals under consideration; we give two of these alternatives in Table 9.9. One is a static analysis in which each lexeme has four principal parts (the

Table 9.9. *Two principal-part analyses for nine Sanskrit lexemes (Analysis (a): all four realized cells are static principal parts; Analysis (b): shaded forms are dynamic principal parts. In ĀSYA's cells, α = neut; otherwise, α = masc)*

	DefStem	σ₁= {α nom sg}	σ₂ = {α acc sg}	σ₃= {α acc pl}	σ₄= {α gen pl}
MARUT 'wind'	marut-	⟨marut, σ₁⟩	⟨marutam, σ₂⟩	⟨marutas, σ₃⟩	⟨marutām, σ₄⟩
VIDVĀMS 'knowing'	vidvāṃs-	⟨vidvān, σ₁⟩	⟨vidvāṃsam, σ₂⟩	⟨viduṣas, σ₃⟩	⟨viduṣām, σ₄⟩
RĀJĀN 'king'	rājān-	⟨rājā, σ₁⟩	⟨rājānam, σ₂⟩	⟨rājñas, σ₃⟩	⟨rājñām, σ₄⟩
AŚVA 'horse'	aśva-	⟨aśvas, σ₁⟩	⟨aśvam, σ₂⟩	⟨aśvān, σ₃⟩	⟨aśvānām, σ₄⟩
ĀSYA 'mouth'	āsya-	⟨āsyam, σ₁⟩	⟨āsyam, σ₂⟩	⟨āsyāni, σ₃⟩	⟨āsyānām, σ₄⟩
AGNI 'fire'	agni-	⟨agnis, σ₁⟩	⟨agnim, σ₂⟩	⟨agnīn, σ₃⟩	⟨agnīnām, σ₄⟩
ŚATRU 'enemy'	śatru-	⟨śatrus, σ₁⟩	⟨śatrum, σ₂⟩	⟨śatrūn, σ₃⟩	⟨śatrūṇām, σ₄⟩
PITAR 'father'	pitār-	⟨pitā, σ₁⟩	⟨pitaram, σ₂⟩	⟨pitṝn, σ₃⟩	⟨pitṝṇām, σ₄⟩
NAPTĀR 'descendant'	naptār-	⟨naptā, σ₁⟩	⟨naptāram, σ₂⟩	⟨naptṝn, σ₃⟩	⟨naptṝṇām, σ₄⟩

nominative singular, accusative singular, accusative plural, and genitive plural cells in its realized paradigm); the other is a dynamic analysis in which each lexeme has only one or two principal parts (the shaded cells in Table 9.9). We stress that there is no need to assume that a lexeme has at most one principal-part set nor that every principal-part set is optimal (§1.1). As a basis for discussion, however, we will restrict our attention to the two optimal analyses in Table 9.9.

If we abstract away the idiosyncratic phonological characteristics of individual lexemes (that is, if we replace their themes with a variable X), the formal analysis of Sanskrit in §§9.3.1–4 generates the schematic realized paradigms in Table 9.10; this is essentially the plat for our fragment of Sanskrit declensional morphology. The principal-part analyses in Table 9.9 generalize to the schematic realized paradigms in Table 9.10. Whether one employs the static or the dynamic principal-part analysis in Tables 9.9 and 9.10, a Sanskrit noun's principal-part set conforms to the generalizations in (29).

(29) (a) Where S is a set of cells in the realized paradigm of lexeme L, S is a principal-part set for L if there is a single IC J in Table 9.10 such that for every member $\langle X{:}y, \sigma\rangle$ of J's (static or dynamic) principal-part set, there is a matching member $\langle Z{:}y, \sigma\rangle$ of S (where X:y, Z:y represent themes marked with exponence y).
(b) If S = $\{\langle Y_1, \sigma_1\rangle, \ldots, \langle Y_n, \sigma_n\rangle\}$ is a principal-part set for L, then there is exactly one IC J such that for each i ($1 \leq i \leq n$), $\text{PF}(\langle L, \sigma_i\rangle) = [\langle L, \sigma_i\rangle : |J, \sigma_i|] = \langle Y_i, \sigma_i\rangle$; in that case, L narrowly belongs to J.

The generalizations in (29) make it possible to deduce a newly encountered Sanskrit noun's IC membership from a subset of the cells in its realized paradigm. For example, on encountering the accusative plural form *gajān* of the masculine noun GAJA 'elephant', one can immediately infer that GAJA belongs to the AŚVA declension, since $\{\langle gaj\bar{a}n, \{\text{masc acc pl}\}\rangle\}$ matches the dynamic principal-part set $\{\langle X\bar{a}n, \{\text{masc acc pl}\}\rangle\}$ in Table 9.10. In this way, the principal parts schematized in Table 9.10 allow language users to infer a newly encountered lexeme's IC membership (fulfilling the matching function of principal parts).

Once one knows a noun's IC membership, its full realized paradigm may be directly generated by the rules in §9.3.1–4. But these rules also engender a number of nonsyncretistic implicative rules, by means of the axiom in (30).

(30) Axiom for deducing nonsyncretistic implicative rules from a lexeme's principal-part set
If L is a lexeme that narrowly belongs to IC J and has the principal-part set $\{\langle w_1, \sigma_1\rangle, \ldots, \langle w_n, \sigma_n\rangle\}$, then for any cell $\langle L, \sigma_0\rangle$ in L's paradigm,
$$\{\langle w_1, \sigma_1\rangle, \ldots, \langle w_n, \sigma_n\rangle\} \rightarrow [\langle L, \sigma_0\rangle : |J, \sigma_0|]$$
is a valid implicative rule.

A hybrid conception of inflectional morphology 289

The nonsyncretistic implicative rules engendered by means of (30) express W-relations – relations among cells in the realized paradigm of a particular lexeme (§4.1). For example, given GAJA's principal-part set {⟨gajān, {masc acc pl}⟩}, (30) entails the implicative rule (31a), equivalently (31b). (By convention, we regard (31b) as equivalent to (31c).) In similar fashion, ⟨gajān, {masc acc pl}⟩ implies every cell in GAJA's realized paradigm, as in (32). In this way, the principal parts of a known or newly encountered lexeme L allow language users to deduce L's entire realized paradigm (fulfilling the deductive function of principal parts).

(31)   (a) {⟨gajān, {masc acc pl}⟩} → [⟨GAJA, σ:{masc nom sg}⟩ : |**a-*stem*** class, σ|]
       (b) {⟨gajān, {masc acc pl}⟩} → ⟨gajas, {masc nom sg}⟩
       (c) ⟨gajān, {masc acc pl}⟩ → ⟨gajas, {masc nom sg}⟩

(32) ⟨gajān, {masc acc pl}⟩ →
    ⟨gajas, {masc nom sg}⟩   ⟨gajau, {masc nom du}⟩   ⟨gajās, {masc nom pl}⟩
    ⟨gaja, {masc voc sg}⟩   ⟨gajau, {masc voc du}⟩   ⟨gajās, {masc voc pl}⟩
    ⟨gajam, {masc acc sg}⟩   ⟨gajau, {masc acc du}⟩
    ⟨gajena, {masc ins sg}⟩   ⟨gajābhyām, {masc ins du}⟩ ⟨gajais, {masc ins pl}⟩
    ⟨gajāya, {masc dat sg}⟩   ⟨gajābhyām, {masc dat du}⟩ ⟨gajebhyas, {masc dat pl}⟩
    ⟨gajāt, {masc abl sg}⟩   ⟨gajābhyām, {masc abl du}⟩ ⟨gajebhyas, {masc abl pl}⟩
    ⟨gajasya, {masc gen sg}⟩ ⟨gajayos, {masc gen du}⟩   ⟨gajānām, {masc gen pl}⟩
    ⟨gaje, {masc loc sg}⟩   ⟨gajayos, {masc loc du}⟩   ⟨gajeṣu, {masc loc pl}⟩

One might object that this analysis is redundant – that nonsyncretistic implicative rules such as those in (32) are rendered unnecessary by the primarily exponence-based rules proposed in §§9.3.1–4. Whether this is a reasonable objection is an empirical question. At present, we know of no evidence that language users always employ the same sort of rule in inferring a cell's realization. Our conjecture is that language users have more than one means at their disposal for deducing a given cell's realization, including both rules of exponence and nonsyncretistic implicative rules; given that the latter are derivable as theorems of the former, we regard the distinction between constructive and abstractive approaches to morphology (Blevins 2006) as a false dichotomy.

9.3.6 W-relations and R-relations

Implicative rules such as those in (32) represent W-relations. We distinguish W-relations from R-relations, which are not restricted to a particular realized paradigm, but generalize over whole classes of realized paradigms (§4.1). The implicative rules in (33) represent valid R-relations for our fragment of Sanskrit declensional morphology, as can be verified by comparing them with Table 9.10.

Table 9.10. *Schematic realized paradigms for the nine declension classes exemplified in Table 9.5*

				N	V	A	I	D	Ab	G	L
Singular	C-stem	Nonalternating			X	X	Xam	Xā	Xe	Xas	Xas	Xi
		Alternating	vāṃs-stem	Xvān	Xvan	Xvāṃsam	Xuṣā	Xuṣe	Xuṣas	Xuṣas	Xuṣi
			ān-stem	Xā	Xan	Xānam	Xnā	Xne	Xnas	Xñas	Xñi
	V-stem	a-stem	(masc)	Xas	Xa	Xam	Xena	Xāya	Xāt	Xasya	Xe
			(neut)	Xam	Xa	Xam	Xena	Xāya	Xāt	Xasya	Xe
		i/u-stem	(i-stem)	Xis	Xe	Xim	Xinā	Xaye	Xes	Xes	Xau
			(u-stem)	Xus	Xo	Xum	Xunā	Xave	Xos	Xos	Xau
		r-stem	I	Xā	Xar	Xaram	Xrā	Xre	Xur	Xur	Xari
			II	Xā	Xar	Xāram	Xrā	Xre	Xur	Xur	Xari
Dual	C-stem	Nonalternating			Xau			Xbhyām		Xos	
		Alternating	vāṃs-stem		Xvāṃsau			Xvadbhyām		Xuṣos	
			ān-stem		Xānau			Xabhyām		Xnos	
	V-stem	a-stem	(masc)		Xau			Xābhyām		Xayos	
			(neut)		Xe			Xābhyām		Xayos	
		i/u-stem	(i-stem)		Xī			Xibhyam		Xyos	
			(u-stem)		Xū			Xubhyām		Xvos	
		r-stem	I		Xarau			Xṛbhyām		Xros	
			II		Xārau			Xṛbhyām		Xros	

			Xas	Xas	Xbhis	Xbhyas	Xām	Xsu
C-stem	Nonalternating		Xas	Xas	Xbhis	Xbhyas	Xām	Xsu
	Alternating	vāṁs-stem	Xvāṁsas	Xuṣas	Xvadbhis	Xvadbhyas	Xuṣām	Xvatsu
		ān-stem	Xānas	Xnas	Xabhis	Xabhyas	Xnām	Xaṣu
V-stem	a-stem	(masc)	Xās	**Xān**	Xais	Xebhyas	Xānām	Xeṣu
Plural		(neut)	Xāni	Xāni	Xais	Xebhyas	Xānām	Xeṣu
	i/u-stem	(i-stem)	Xayas	**Xīn**	Xibhis	Xibhyas	Xīnām	Xiṣu
		(u-stem)	Xavas	**Xūn**	Xubhis	Xubhyas	Xūnām	Xuṣu
	r-stem	I	Xaras	**Xṝn**	Xṛbhis	Xṛbhyas	Xṝṇām	Xṛṣu
		II	Xāras	**Xṝn**	Xṛbhis	Xṛbhyas	Xṝṇām	Xṛṣu

(Shaded cells represent a static principal-part analysis; cells with a dark outline represent a dynamic principal-part analysis.)

292　*Inflection classes, implicative relations, and morphological theory*

(33)   (a) $\langle Xasya, \{\text{masc gen sg}\}\rangle \leftrightarrow \langle X\bar{a}t, \{\text{masc abl sg}\}\rangle$ (e.g. *aśvasya* ↔ *aśvāt*)
         (b) $\langle Xrbhy\bar{a}m, \{\text{masc ins du}\}\rangle \leftrightarrow \langle Xros, \{\text{masc gen du}\}\rangle$ (*pitṛbhyām* ↔ *pitros*)
         (c) $\langle Xus\bar{a}, \{\text{masc ins sg}\}\rangle \leftrightarrow \langle Xuṣe, \{\text{masc dat sg}\}\rangle$ (*viduṣā* ↔ *viduṣe*)
         (d) $\langle Xas, \{\text{masc gen sg}\}\rangle \rightarrow \langle Xe, \{\text{masc dat sg}\}\rangle$ (*marutas* → *marute*; not biconditional: *pitur, pitre*)
         (e) $\langle Xa, \{\text{masc voc sg}\}\rangle \rightarrow \langle Xam, \{\text{masc acc sg}\}\rangle$ (*aśva* → *aśvam*; not biconditional: *pitar, pitaram*)
         (f) $\langle Xur, \{\text{masc gen sg}\}\rangle \rightarrow \langle X\bar{a}, \{\text{masc nom sg}\}\rangle$ (*pitur* → *pitā*; not biconditional: *rājñas, rājā*)

The R-relations represented in (33) may be alternatively represented as relations among realization rules; for example, the R-relations expressed by (33a) and (33b) may be alternatively represented as in (34a) and (34b). According to (34a), the genitive singular cell of a nominal lexeme L is defined by means of rule **a-st**.d (the *-sya* rule) if and only if L's ablative singular cell is defined by means of rule **a-st**.c (the *-āt* rule); by (34b), the instrumental dual cell of a masculine lexeme L is defined by the **r-stem** class's rule for {masc ins du} if and only if L's genitive dual cell is defined by the **r-stem** class's rule for {masc gen du}.

(34)   (a) PF($\langle L, \sigma_1: \{\text{gen sg}\}\rangle$) = [$\langle L, \sigma_1\rangle$: **a-st**.d] iff PF($\langle L, \sigma_2: \{\text{abl sg}\}\rangle$) = [$\langle L, \sigma_2\rangle$: **a-st**.c].
         (b) PF($\langle L, \sigma_1: \{\text{masc ins du}\}\rangle$) = [$\langle L, \sigma_1\rangle$: |**r-stem** class, σ_1|] iff PF($\langle L, \sigma_2: \{\text{masc gen du}\}\rangle$) = [$\langle L, \sigma_2\rangle$: |**r-stem** class, σ_2|].

Besides being more general than W-relations, R-relations also sometimes differ from W-relations in a second way. As we observed in §9.2, not all of the implicative relations in a language's inflectional morphology are whole-word relations: R-relations may also be word-internal regularities involving stems and affixes – regularities that are not directly expressible as relations between realized cells. Recall the generalizations in (35):

(35)   (a) All nouns having a genitive singular of the form X*sya* have a nominative singular based on the same stem X (though its suffix is undetermined).
         (b) All nouns having a locative singular of the form X*au* have *-s* as their affixal exponent of the genitive singular (though its stem is undetermined).

Like the R-relations represented in (33), those in (35) can be represented as relations among realization rules, as in (36).

(36)   (a) If PF($\langle L, \sigma_1: \{\text{gen sg}\}\rangle$) = [$\langle L, \sigma_1\rangle$: **a-st**.d], then **Stem**($\langle L, \sigma_1: \{\text{gen sg}\}, K\rangle$) = **Stem**($\langle L, \sigma_2: \{\text{nom sg}\}, K\rangle$).
         (b) If PF($\langle L, \sigma_1: \{\text{loc sg}\}\rangle$) = [$\langle L, \sigma_1\rangle$: **i/u-st**.b], then PF($\langle L, \sigma_2: \{\text{gen sg}\}\rangle$) = [$\langle L, \sigma_2\rangle$: **i/u-st**.a].

Table 9.11. *Proof of (34a)*

Lexeme L	PF($\langle$L, σ_1:{gen sg}$\rangle$)	= [$\langle$L, $\sigma_1\rangle$: **a-st**.d]	PF($\langle$L, σ_2:{abl sg}$\rangle$)	= [$\langle$L, $\sigma_2\rangle$: **a-st**.c]
MARUT	$\langle marutas, \sigma_1\rangle$	no	$\langle marutas, \sigma_2\rangle$	no
VIDVĀMS	$\langle viduṣas, \sigma_1\rangle$	no	$\langle viduṣas, \sigma_2\rangle$	no
RĀJAN	$\langle rājñas, \sigma_1\rangle$	no	$\langle rājñas, \sigma_2\rangle$	no
AŚVA	$\langle aśvasya, \sigma_1\rangle$	yes	$\langle aśvāt, \sigma_2\rangle$	yes
ĀSYA	$\langle āsyasya, \sigma_1\rangle$	yes	$\langle āsyāt, \sigma_2\rangle$	yes
AGNI	$\langle agne\text{-}s, \sigma_1\rangle$	no	$\langle agne\text{-}s, \sigma_2\rangle$	no
ŚATRU	$\langle śatros, \sigma_1\rangle$	no	$\langle śatros, \sigma_2\rangle$	no
PITAR	$\langle pitur, \sigma_1\rangle$	no	$\langle pitur, \sigma_2\rangle$	no
NAPTĀR	$\langle naptur, \sigma_1\rangle$	no	$\langle naptur, \sigma_2\rangle$	no

Table 9.12. *Proof of (36b)*

Lexeme L	PF($\langle$L, σ_1:{loc sg}$\rangle$)	= [$\langle$L, $\sigma_1\rangle$: **i/u-st**.b]	PF($\langle$L, σ_2:{gen sg}$\rangle$)	= [$\langle$L, $\sigma_2\rangle$: **i/u-st**.a]
MARUT	$\langle maruti, \sigma_1\rangle$	no	$\langle marut\text{-}as, \sigma_2\rangle$	no
VIDVĀMS	$\langle viduṣi, \sigma_1\rangle$	no	$\langle viduṣ\text{-}as, \sigma_2\rangle$	no
RĀJAN	$\langle rājñi, \sigma_1\rangle$	no	$\langle rājñ\text{-}as, \sigma_2\rangle$	no
AŚVA	$\langle aśve, \sigma_1\rangle$	no	$\langle aśva\text{-}sya, \sigma_2\rangle$	no
ĀSYA	$\langle āsye, \sigma_1\rangle$	no	$\langle āsya\text{-}sya, \sigma_2\rangle$	no
AGNI	$\langle agnau, \sigma_1\rangle$	yes	$\langle agne\text{-}s, \sigma_2\rangle$	yes
ŚATRU	$\langle śatrau, \sigma_1\rangle$	yes	$\langle śatro\text{-}s, \sigma_2\rangle$	yes
PITAR	$\langle pitari, \sigma_1\rangle$	no	$\langle pitur, \sigma_2\rangle$	no
NAPTĀR	$\langle naptari, \sigma_1\rangle$	no	$\langle naptur, \sigma_2\rangle$	no

Each of the R-relations represented in (34) and (36) is a theorem of the analysis of Sanskrit that we have proposed; for example, there is no value of L in our fragment for which (34a) and (36b) are not true, as the proofs by extension in Tables 9.11 and 9.12 show. Nonsyncretistic implicative rules can therefore be seen as theorems of a language's basic realization rules and their interaction.

Like R-relations, W-relations are also expressible as implicative relations among realization rules; for instance, the W-relation in (31c) may be expressed as in (37). We therefore hypothesize that all of the implicative relations among cells in a language's realized paradigms can be seen as relations among the realization rules defining those paradigms.

(37)   If PF(⟨GAJA, σ_1:{masc acc pl}⟩) = [⟨GAJA, σ_1⟩ : *V-st*.b],
then PF(⟨GAJA, σ_2:{masc nom sg}⟩) = [⟨GAJA, σ_2⟩ : ***Nom***.a].

The conception of inflectional morphology that we have proposed here is intermediate between the PWPM and PEM hypotheses. Like the PWPM hypothesis, our approach gives implicative rules a role in the definition of a language's inflectional morphology and is compatible with the possibility that some cells in a lexeme's realized paradigm are stored in its lexical entry. Like the PEM hypothesis, our approach defines a language's inflectional morphology primarily by rules of exponence, but we assume that these are supplemented by one sort of implicative rule (rules of referral) to account for instances of syncretism. We derive nonsyncretistic implicative rules as theorems of an inflectional system's exponence-based definition; these nonsyncretistic implicative rules express both W-relations and R-relations.

We regard our approach to the Sanskrit fragment as superior to a PWPM approach in at least two ways. First, it provides a straightforward account of the phenomenon of inward phonological conditioning in defining the realized paradigms of gradational nominals; this account depends crucially on employing stems in the definition of word forms. Second, it provides a straightforward account of the fact that some implicative relations do not involve whole words, but instead involve rules that treat stems and affixes as morphotactic units. Thus, the approach to implicative relations proposed here is finer-grained than the PWPM approach, since it accounts for relations that are not directly expressible as relations among realized cells. In addition, it affords the hypothesis all implicative relations among the cells of realized paradigms are reducible to implicative relations among realization rules.

We regard our approach as superior to a PEM approach because it distinguishes words in a lexeme's realized paradigm that may be used to identify a newly encountered lexeme's IC membership and thereby to deduce the full realized paradigm of a known or newly encountered lexeme. Given the generalizations in (29) and the axiom in (30), such words derive implicative rules (expressing both W-relations and R-relations) that, plausibly, play a role in learning newly encountered lexemes and in recognizing and producing the realizations of known lexemes.

10 *Entropy, predictability, and predictiveness*

Recent research on morphological complexity (Ackerman *et al.* 2009; Milin *et al.* 2009; Moscoso del Prado Martín *et al.* 2004) has employed the information-theoretical measures of **entropy** and **conditional entropy** (Shannon 1951) as a way to quantify the degree to which cells in a lexeme's paradigm are predictable. In this chapter, we draw upon evidence from earlier chapters as a basis for comparing entropy measures with our measures of predictiveness and paradigm and cell predictability. We demonstrate that measures of entropy, predictability, and predictiveness reveal different patterns and are therefore complementary as elucidations of morphological complexity.[1]

10.1   Definitions

As Shannon (1951) demonstrated, one can measure the information content of an item x in some collection C based on its probability of occurrence. Intuitively, more common items carry little information, and uncommon items carry a great amount. The formula that computes the information content, measured in bits, is $-\log_2 P(x)$. If x is very likely, with probability approaching 1, then its information content is close to 0. If $P(x) = 0.5$, its information content is 1 bit. If x is very unlikely, its information content can be very large.

A collection C of items has a collective measure of variation $H(C)$ called its **entropy**. Low entropy means that the items do not vary much. The formula that

---

[1] The data sets that we have employed in this chapter are:

        entropy.finnish   entropy.icelandic
        entropy.french   entropy.finnish

These are available at the *Morphological Typology* website www.cambridge.org/stump_finkel.

Entropy, predictability, and predictiveness

Table 10.1. *Entropy values*

Collection					Entropy (bits × 100)
A	A				0
A	B				50
A	A	A			0
A	A	B			91
A	B	C			158
A	A	A	A		0
A	A	A	B		81
A	A	B	B		100
A	B	C	D		200
A	A	A	A	A	0
A	A	A	A	B	65
A	A	A	B	B	91
A	A	B	B	B	100
A	B	C	D	E	258

computes the entropy, again measured in bits, is the average of the information content of all the items weighted by their probability:

$$H(C) = -\sum_{x \in C} P(x)\log_2 P(x)$$

To give some intuition, Table 10.1 presents several collections and their entropy. In our tables, we multiply the entropy by 100, because we find these values easier to read. When the collection contains identical items, the entropy is 0; there is no variation at all. When all the items are different, the entropy is at its highest. Larger collections have larger maximum entropies. For example, the collection {A B C D} has entropy 2.00 (we show it as 200), but the larger collection {A B C D E} has entropy 2.58. One way to understand the entropy is that it represents the number of questions necessary to narrow down a particular value in the collection. In the collection {A B C D}, the first question could be "is the value either A or B?" The second question could be "is the value either A or C?" These two questions suffice, so the entropy is 2. On the other hand, for the collection {A B C D E}, we need more questions, but sometimes two questions suffice, so the entropy is between 2 and 3.

The concept of **conditional entropy** applies to items that have multiple components. The first component M_1 might make it easier to establish the value of the second component M_2. In that case, the conditional entropy of M_2 given the value of M_1 is less than the entropy of M_2 alone. The formula for conditional entropy of M_2 given M_1 is:

$$H(M_2|M_1) = - \sum_{x \in M_1} P(x) \sum_{y \in M_2} P(y|x) \log_2 P(y|x)$$

The reason entropy and conditional entropy enter into a discussion of principal parts is that we can measure the entropy of the exponences of an MPS in a plat, and we can measure the conditional entropy of the exponences of one MPS given the exponences of another MPS. The following section explores this idea.

10.2 Entropy applied to plats

Consider Table 10.2, a small plat of Finnish *i*-stem and *e*-stem nouns, based on Ackerman *et al.* (2009), in turn based on Buchholz (2004).[2]

We can compute the conditional entropy of each MPS given one other MPS, yielding the results shown in Table 10.3. This table has several points of interest.

- The conditional entropy values tend to be quite small, generally less than 1.0, confirming the Low Entropy Conjecture of Ackerman and Malouf (2010c).
- The conditional entropy of the partitive singular given the partitive plural is 0, as is the conditional entropy of the partitive plural given

Table 10.2. Finnish *i*-stem and *e*-stem nouns

Declension	Stem	nomSg	genSg	partSg	partPl	inessPl
OVI 'door'	ov	-i	-en	-ea	-ia	-issa
KIELI 'language'	kiel	-i	-en	-tä	-iä	-issä
VESI 'water'	ves	-i	-den	-tä	-iä	-issä
LASI 'glass'	las	-i	-in	-ia	-eja	-eissa
NALLE 'teddy bear'	nalle	—	-n	-a	-ja	-issa
KIRJE 'letter'	kirje	—	-en	-ttä	-itä	-issä
MPS entropy		92	179	225	225	146

[2] This table assumes two rules of sandhi: $sd \to d$, and $st \to tt$. The entropy measures disagree with the values given by Ackerman *et al.* (2009), partially because of our introduction of sandhi, which reduces entropy, and our choice of stem *las* for 'glass'. Entropy measures are quite sensitive to such choices. We return to this point when we show a derivation of this plat in Chapter 12.

298 *Entropy, predictability, and predictiveness*

Table 10.3. *Conditional entropy (× 100) of MPS (column) given MPS (row), from Table 10.2*

	nomSg	genSg	partSg	partPl	inessPl	Avg
nomSg	–	133	133	133	133	133
genSg	46	–	79	79	46	63
partSg	0	33	–	0	0	8
partPl	0	33	0	–	0	8
inessPl	79	79	79	79	–	79
Avg	31	69	72	72	44	58

Table 10.4. *Conditional entropy (× 100) of MPS (column) given MPS (row), from Table 10.2, omitting the redundant MPS {partPl}.*

	nomSg	genSg	partSg	inessPl	Avg
nomSg	–	133	133	133	133
genSg	46	–	79	46	57
partSg	0	33	–	0	11
inessPl	79	79	79	–	79
Avg	41	81	97	59	70

the partitive singular. The fact that either of these MPSs completely determines the other means that they belong to the same distillation. They act precisely the same way, both in rows and in columns of Table 10.3. We might as well ignore the row and column associated with the partitive plural. We therefore turn our attention to Table 10.4, which omits this redundancy. The only important difference is that the calculation of averages avoids redundant values. From this point forward, all of the MPSs to which we refer have the status of distillations.

- The conditional entropy of the nominative singular given the partitive singular is also 0, but the conditional entropy of partitive singular given nominative singular is 1.33. We explain this asymmetry by noting that the nominative singular has low (unconditional) entropy, whereas partitive singular has a high entropy. The large variation in the partitive singular is enough to completely predict the small amount of variation in the nominative singular.

- A low row average in Table 10.4 means that the associated MPS predicts other MPSs very well. Rows with low row average are therefore highly predictive. In our case, the partitive singular appears to be the most predictive, followed by the genitive singular. In fact, a static principal-part analysis of this plat shows that {gen sg, partitive sg} form the best set of static principal parts.
- A high column average in Table 10.4 means that the associated MPS is highly unpredictable. The most unpredictable MPSs are again the partitive singular and then the genitive singular.[3] As we observed in Chapter 5, canonical principal parts are those MPSs that are highly predictive and highly unpredictable.

These results are only suggestive. If we consider Sanskrit nominals,[4] we find that there are six optimal static principal-part analyses, all of which contain nominative singular. However, Table 10.5 shows that nominative singular does not appear either highly predictive (its row average is not particularly low) or

Table 10.5. *Entropy values (× 100) for Sanskrit nominals*

Measure	nomS	Vsg	Asg	Isg	Dsg	Lsg	Ndu	Idu	Gdu	Npl	Apl	Ipl	Gpl	Avg
nomS	–	62	88	72	62	62	88	57	62	88	99	57	67	72
Vsg	51	–	72	51	41	41	78	41	41	72	83	41	30	54
Asg	11	5	–	11	0	0	5	0	0	5	26	0	5	6
Isg	88	78	104	–	24	24	104	21	14	109	88	21	11	57
Dsg	64	53	80	11	–	0	80	11	0	85	85	11	7	40
Lsg	74	64	90	21	11	–	90	21	11	95	95	21	18	51
Ndu	16	16	11	16	5	5	–	5	0	11	32	11	5	11
Idu	95	90	116	44	47	47	116	–	40	116	127	7	23	73
Gdu	86	75	101	22	22	22	96	25	–	101	96	32	7	57
Npl	16	11	11	21	11	11	11	5	5	–	26	11	11	12
Apl	32	26	37	5	16	16	37	21	5	32	–	21	11	21
Ipl	88	83	109	37	40	40	114	0	40	114	120	–	23	67
Gpl	110	84	126	38	48	48	121	28	27	126	121	35	–	76
Avg	60	53	78	29	27	26	78	19	20	79	83	22	18	46

---

[3] Ackerman *et al.* (2009) call the column average the "predictedness" of the associated MPS; we call it the "predictability." They agree with our nomenclature that a row with low average entropy is associated with an MPS of high predictiveness.

[4] See Table 5.1.

300 *Entropy, predictability, and predictiveness*

highly unpredictable (its column average is not particularly high), so it is not an obvious choice as a principal part.

We can generalize conditional entropy so that the condition is a combination of MPSs. For instance, since we know that {gen singular, partitive sg} form the best set of static principal parts for the Finnish plat of Table 10.2, we can be sure that the entropy of the other MPSs conditional on the combination of the genitive singular and the partitive singular must be 0 everywhere. We can choose multiple combinations and average the MPS entropy conditional on those combinations, in the same spirit as our definition in Chapter 5 of paradigm predictability. Given a particular MPS M, we consider the collection C_M containing all combinations of 0 ... n MPSs such that $M \notin C_M$. We typically set $n = 4$. We then average conditional entropies to get the n-**MPS entropy of** M.

The formula for the n-MPS entropy of M is:

$$H_n(M) = \frac{\sum_{c \in C_M} H(M|c)}{|C_M|}$$

Table 10.6 shows the n-MPS entropies of the Finnish nouns of Table 10.2 for various values of n. The 0-MPS entropy agrees with the unconditional MPS entropy. The 3-MPS and 4-MPS entropy are identical, because there are no collections of 4 MPSs that do not include any given MPS, so the collections over which the computation averages are the same. The trend is clear: as more information is brought to bear, the residual entropy of an MPS decreases. At least in this plat, MPSs with relatively high entropy have relatively high n-MPS entropy. For example, the partitive singular has the highest entropy no matter how we condition it.

Table 10.6. MPS entropy measures for Finnish *i*-stem and *e*-stem nouns

Measure	nomSg	genSg	partSg	inessPl
MPS entropy	92	179	225	146
0-MPS entropy	92	179	225	146
1-MPS entropy	54	106	129	81
2-MPS entropy	36	75	83	51
3-MPS entropy	31	70	73	45
4-MPS entropy	31	70	73	45

10.3 The effect of type frequency

Because entropy is based on probabilities, it makes sense to include a measure of probability for every inflection class in the plat. Again, using the Finnish plat of Table 10.2, imagine that all declensions have the same type frequency,[5] except that the last one, KIRJE 'letter', has a frequency 1/10 as great as the others. Then the unusual pattern of this declension should have a reduced effect on the entropy chart. We show the resulting entropies in Table 10.7.

The entropy values have changed in various ways. The column for nominative singular shows that it is more predictable now, which makes sense, because one of its unusual values has become even more unusual. The row for nominative singular has slightly higher values now; nominative singular is not quite as predictive as before, which makes sense for the same reason.

We generally expect that inflection classes in which MPSs have the most unusual exponences are of low type frequency. We turn now to languages for which we have type frequency information: Icelandic and French.

10.3.1 Icelandic

We introduced our plat of Icelandic verbs in Chapter 8. This plat has 146 distinct conjugations and 30 MPSs, 21 of which can serve as distillations. (See Table 4.26 for the numbered list of distillations in the Icelandic plat.) When we do not take type frequency into account, we get the entropy chart shown in Table 10.8.

Table 10.7. *Entropy values (× 100) for Finnish nouns with artificial type frequency*

	nomSg	genSg	partSg	inessPl	Avg
MPS entropy	75	190	202	151	155
Conditional entropy of MPS (col) given MPS (row)					
nomSg	–	127	127	127	127
genSg	11	–	51	41	34
partSg	0	39	–	0	13
inessPl	51	80	51	–	61
Avg	20	82	76	56	59

---

[5] The **type frequency** of an inflection class is the number of lexemes in this class divided by the total number of lexemes. We distinguish this measure from the **token frequency** of an inflection class, which is the frequency with which lexemes in this class appear in a particular corpus. This latter measure is potentially quite variable from one corpus to another, given differences of discourse register and individual differences among language users.

Table 10.8. *Entropy values (× 100) for Icelandic verbs*

	1	2	3	4	5	6	7	8	9	10	11	12	13	14	15	16	17	18	19	20	21	Avg
MPS entropy	486	462	477	467	478	492	449	499	491	479	474	491	511	511	509	468	470	470	444	441	482	479
Conditional entropy of MPS (col) given MPS (row)																						
1	–	32	9	27	1	128	72	102	98	5	23	5	131	136	130	138	139	23	125	124	141	79
2	56	–	39	30	48	151	73	100	99	51	44	59	147	152	149	154	155	41	142	142	160	100
3	19	25	–	18	9	144	80	110	108	12	32	22	139	143	141	145	146	30	135	135	150	87
4	47	25	28	–	37	146	81	109	108	39	14	50	145	150	147	151	153	12	143	143	160	94
5	10	33	8	26	–	137	75	108	104	5	23	13	134	139	136	140	142	23	131	131	147	83
6	121	121	129	120	123	–	99	124	120	125	117	125	136	137	134	112	113	117	105	103	127	120
7	109	86	107	99	104	142	–	51	43	101	96	109	161	162	161	158	159	93	136	136	157	118
8	90	64	87	77	87	117	1	–	0	85	76	90	134	134	134	131	132	74	111	111	131	93
9	93	70	94	83	90	121	1	8	–	88	80	93	142	142	142	139	140	77	117	117	137	99
10	12	34	9	27	4	138	71	105	100	–	22	12	138	142	138	141	142	18	131	131	147	83
11	36	33	36	8	28	136	71	102	98	28	–	36	140	145	140	143	144	0	136	136	154	87
12	0	30	8	26	0	126	67	98	93	0	18	–	130	134	130	133	134	18	123	123	139	76
13	107	99	105	101	101	117	99	123	123	106	103	110	–	6	2	34	35	103	51	51	71	82
14	111	103	109	106	106	118	100	123	123	111	107	114	6	–	8	34	35	107	51	51	71	85
15	107	102	108	104	104	117	101	124	124	108	104	112	3	10	–	37	39	104	53	49	72	84
16	156	149	154	150	151	137	140	163	163	152	149	156	77	77	79	–	2	149	31	31	64	116
17	155	148	153	150	150	136	139	162	162	152	148	155	76	77	78	0	–	148	31	31	64	116
18	39	34	37	9	31	140	73	104	99	28	4	39	144	148	144	147	148	–	138	138	157	90
19	167	161	168	165	165	153	141	166	164	167	165	170	118	118	118	55	57	164	–	0	40	131
20	169	164	171	169	168	155	144	169	168	170	169	174	121	122	118	58	60	167	3	–	43	134
21	146	141	145	145	143	138	125	148	147	144	146	148	100	100	100	50	52	145	2	2	–	113
Avg	87	82	85	82	82	134	87	114	112	83	82	89	116	118	116	105	106	80	94	94	116	99

The same data, taking type frequency into account, is in Table 10.9. We take typefrequency information from the index of Jörg (1989).

The most obvious difference between these two entropy tables is that including type frequency reduces the average MPS entropy (3.27 as opposed to 4.79) as well as the average conditional entropy (0.68 as opposed to 0.99). This result agrees with the observation made by Bonami *et al.* (2011) in their analysis of Mauritian: the inflection classes exhibiting the lowest predictability have low type frequency. It also agrees with our Marginal Detraction Hypothesis (Chapter 8), according to which the least frequent inflection classes are responsible for most of the variation in a plat. Similarly, if we consider the inclusive fragment of Icelandic (only including conjugations with type frequency greater than 1), we reduce the average MPS entropy to 4.28, whereas the exclusive fragment (only including conjugations with type frequency 1) has an average MPS entropy of 4.57.

Interestingly, using the inverse of type frequency as a weight also reduces the entropy and conditional entropy from their unweighted values, but only slightly: the average MPS entropy becomes 4.75, and the average conditional entropy becomes 0.95. In a few cases, entropy actually increases (for MPS 7, it rises from 4.49 to 4.51). So we should take weighted values with a grain of salt: any weighting might reduce entropy values somewhat.

The two entropy tables disagree on which MPS (numbered 1–21) is the most predictive. Without frequency information, MPS 12 (3rd plural present indicative) is the most predictive; with frequency information, MPS 21 (1st plural past subjunctive) is the most predictive. The fact that most conditional entropy values are still fairly high (reaching as high as 1.59, even in the table based on frequency) indicates that Icelandic verbs need more than one principal part. In fact, our analysis shows that they need eight static principal parts, as discussed in Chapter 8. Of the sixty optimal analyses, 100 percent use MPS 21; only 20 percent use MPS 12. The entropy tables give no hint that MPS 6 (2nd past ptcp) is important, but every optimal static principal-part analysis includes it. So we see that conditional entropy gives us some insight into static principal parts, but not a complete picture.

10.3.2 French

In Chapter 7, we introduced our stem-based, hearer-oriented, concrete plat of French verbs. Our plat has sixty-four distinct conjugations and 20 MPSs, of which seventeen are distillations. (See Table 7.12 for the numbered list of

Table 10.9. Entropy values (× 100) for Icelandic verbs, using type frequency

MPS	1	2	3	4	5	6	7	8	9	10	11	12	13	14	15	16	17	18	19	20	21	Avg
entropy	301	331	290	267	290	352	316	334	333	290	268	302	369	368	368	358	358	268	360	359	377	327

Conditional entropy of MPS (col) given MPS (row)

	1	2	3	4	5	6	7	8	9	10	11	12	13	14	15	16	17	18	19	20	21	Avg
1	–	71	2	8	1	114	78	90	89	1	7	1	143	144	143	145	145	7	142	142	147	81
2	41	–	30	12	32	88	19	30	29	32	14	41	93	94	93	95	96	14	93	93	98	57
3	13	71	–	6	2	127	81	92	92	2	8	14	148	149	148	150	150	8	147	147	152	85
4	41	75	28	–	30	134	85	96	96	30	3	42	155	156	155	157	157	2	154	154	160	95
5	11	73	2	7	–	126	80	92	91	1	7	12	147	148	147	149	149	7	147	147	151	85
6	63	66	65	49	63	–	49	60	59	64	48	64	90	90	90	78	79	48	76	76	87	68
7	63	33	54	36	54	85	–	18	17	53	35	63	101	101	101	100	101	35	94	94	104	67
8	56	26	48	29	48	77	0	–	0	47	29	56	93	93	93	92	93	28	86	86	96	59
9	57	27	49	30	48	78	0	2	–	48	30	57	95	94	95	94	94	29	88	88	97	60
10	12	73	2	7	1	126	79	92	91	–	6	12	148	149	148	149	149	6	147	147	152	85
11	39	77	30	2	28	132	83	95	94	28	–	39	154	155	154	155	156	0	153	153	159	94
12	0	70	2	7	0	114	77	89	88	0	6	–	143	143	143	144	144	6	142	142	146	80
13	75	55	69	53	68	73	49	59	59	69	53	75	–	1	0	26	26	53	28	28	41	48
14	77	57	71	55	70	74	49	59	59	71	55	78	2	–	3	27	27	55	28	28	41	49
15	75	56	69	54	69	73	49	59	59	69	54	76	1	2	–	27	27	54	28	27	41	49
16	88	68	82	66	81	73	59	69	69	81	66	88	37	37	38	–	0	66	21	21	34	57
17	88	68	82	66	81	73	59	69	69	81	66	88	37	36	37	0	–	66	21	21	34	57
18	40	77	30	2	29	132	83	95	94	28	1	40	155	156	155	156	156	–	154	154	160	95
19	82	63	77	61	76	68	50	60	60	77	61	83	36	36	36	19	19	61	–	0	18	52
20	83	64	77	62	77	68	51	61	61	77	62	84	37	36	36	20	20	62	1	–	19	53
21	70	51	64	50	64	61	43	53	52	64	50	71	32	32	32	14	14	50	1	1	–	43
Avg	53	61	46	33	46	94	56	67	66	46	33	54	92	92	92	89	90	32	87	87	96	68

distillations in the French plat.) We show the entropy charts in Table 10.10 and Table 10.11; the latter takes type frequency information into account.[6]

There are five static principal parts. Each of the five optimal analyses uses distillations 7, 8, and 17. None of these MPSs has visibly high predictiveness in the tables, although MPSs 8 and 17 show low predictability in both tables. So we see that entropy gives us some insight into the interplay among MPSs, but it does not provide the same information as our set-theoretic approach.

10.3.3 Alternatives to type frequency

Applying type frequency gives heavier weight to inflection classes with many members. We can consider such classes "standard" or "central." On the other hand, token frequency, which relates to how common lexemes in individual classes appear in actual usage, can give a very different result. Conjugations with only one element are often irregular verbs such as BE or GO, which are extremely token-frequent. We have not investigated such token-frequency weights here, but we expect that they would not reduce the entropy measures as much as weighting by type frequency, because the inflection classes with the most variation (highest entropy) would be the most heavily weighted.

An alternative to weights, based either on type or token frequency, is to ignore those inflection classes with low frequency. We follow exactly this practice in Chapter 8, where we build subplats that exclude inflection classes, sometimes on the basis of low type frequency. Such a technique allows us to see the effect of certain inflection classes on the complexity of the entire plat without resorting to entropy calculations.

10.4 Static near-principal parts

We have seen that conditional entropy values can be much smaller than the corresponding unconditional values. If we condition an entropy calculation on not one, but several MPSs, we have seen in Table 10.6 that the remaining MPSs show an even smaller residual entropy. At the extreme, if we condition the calculation on a set of static principal parts, all residual entropies are zero. In fact, we can treat this fact as an alternative definition of static principal parts.

---

[6] The token frequencies that we employ here are derived from two sources. For verbs in the first and second conjugations (the former have an infinitive in -*er*, the latter an infinitive in -*ir* and a present participle in -*issant*), frequencies are based on the BDLEX database (with approximately 6,400 verbal lexemes overall); for the remaining conjugational patterns (which include many irregular patterns), frequencies are based on the index of *Bescherelle* 2006 (with approximately 12,000 verbal lexemes overall).

Table 10.10. Entropy values (× 100) for French verbs

	1	2	3	4	5	6	7	8	9	10	11	12	13	14	15	16	17	Avg
MPS entropy	340	340	498	503	501	489	429	475	504	493	347	498	503	484	493	425	454	457
Conditional entropy of MPS (col) given MPS (row)																		
1	–	6	179	184	163	173	180	158	170	179	6	182	187	170	179	176	193	155
2	6	–	182	187	167	176	185	161	170	179	13	182	187	173	179	181	198	158
3	21	24	–	5	25	6	55	60	28	13	24	3	8	55	3	62	65	29
4	21	24	0	–	25	6	53	59	28	13	24	3	3	54	3	61	64	28
5	3	6	23	28	–	19	55	49	6	22	3	23	28	58	20	63	67	30
6	24	27	15	20	31	–	59	60	34	6	27	18	23	62	18	66	71	35
7	91	96	124	127	127	119	–	128	130	126	96	127	130	104	127	26	50	108
8	23	27	83	88	75	75	82	–	75	78	27	86	91	41	83	65	84	68
9	6	6	23	28	3	19	55	46	–	19	6	23	28	58	20	63	67	29
10	27	27	18	23	31	3	62	60	31	–	27	15	20	65	15	69	74	35
11	0	6	175	180	157	169	178	155	163	173	–	175	180	166	172	174	192	151
12	24	24	3	8	25	10	58	63	28	10	24	–	5	58	0	65	68	30
13	24	24	3	3	25	10	56	62	28	10	24	0	–	57	0	64	67	29
14	26	30	69	73	75	68	49	33	78	74	30	72	76	–	72	35	55	57
15	27	27	9	14	28	15	63	66	31	15	27	6	11	63	–	71	74	34
16	92	97	136	140	139	131	30	115	142	138	97	139	143	94	139	–	29	112
17	80	85	110	114	114	107	26	106	117	113	85	113	117	85	113	0	–	93
Avg	30	33	72	76	75	69	77	86	78	73	33	72	77	85	71	77	88	69

Table 10.11. *Entropy values (× 100) for French verbs, using type frequency*

	1	2	3	4	5	6	7	8	9	10	11	12	13	14	15	16	17	Avg
MPS entropy	157	157	213	213	206	183	211	209	206	183	157	213	213	211	212	209	213	198
Conditional entropy of MPS (col) given MPS (row)																		
1	–	0	63	63	49	50	64	54	49	50	0	63	64	61	63	62	65	51
2	0	–	63	63	49	50	64	54	49	50	0	63	63	61	63	62	65	51
3	7	7	–	0	7	1	6	14	8	1	7	0	0	6	0	6	6	5
4	7	7	0	–	7	1	5	14	8	1	7	0	0	6	0	6	6	5
5	0	0	14	15	–	1	18	18	0	1	0	14	15	18	14	18	18	10
6	24	24	30	31	24	–	35	42	24	0	24	30	31	35	30	35	35	28
7	10	10	7	7	13	7	–	15	13	7	10	7	7	5	7	2	4	8
8	3	3	18	18	16	16	18	–	16	16	3	18	18	13	18	14	18	14
9	0	0	14	15	0	1	18	18	–	1	0	14	15	18	14	18	18	10
10	24	24	30	31	24	0	35	42	24	–	24	30	31	35	30	35	36	28
11	0	0	63	63	49	50	64	54	49	50	–	63	63	61	63	62	65	51
12	7	7	0	0	7	1	6	14	8	1	7	–	0	6	0	6	6	5
13	7	7	0	0	7	1	5	14	8	1	7	0	–	6	0	6	6	5
14	6	6	7	7	13	7	5	10	13	7	6	7	7	–	7	2	6	7
15	7	7	0	1	8	1	6	14	8	1	7	0	1	6	–	6	6	5
16	10	10	10	10	15	10	4	14	15	10	10	10	10	4	10	–	4	10
17	9	9	6	6	12	6	2	13	12	6	9	6	6	4	6	0	–	7
Avg	7	7	20	20	18	12	22	25	19	12	7	20	20	21	20	21	22	18

Entropy gives us a way to compute **near-principal parts**, by which we mean a set of MPSs that reduces the residual entropy of the remaining MPSs below some threshold. For example, we might wish to constrain the maximum conditional entropy to 0.10 or lower. More formally, we would like a minimal set S of MPSs such that $\max_{m \in \text{MPS}, m \notin S} H(m|S) \leq \epsilon$, where ϵ is the tolerance, perhaps 0.10.

The **simple heuristic**[7] to find static near-principal parts is to start with an empty S and add likely MPSs to it until the residual entropy of the remaining MPSs is small enough. A "likely MPS" is one that appears highly unpredictable; that is, its residual entropy is high. We have seen in Table 10.9 that the MPS for Icelandic verbs with the highest unconditional entropy (that is, the least predictable MPS) is 21 (1st plural past subjunctive). We pick it as the first member of S. The row for conditional entropies given MPS 21 has a maximum of 71 at MPS 12 (3rd plural present indicative). That is, MPS 12 has the highest residual entropy, so we select it next. Table 10.12 completes this process until the residual entropy is zero. It shows that if $\epsilon = 0.10$, three principal parts suffice, instead of the full set of eight.

Tables 10.13 and 10.14 show the simple heuristic applied to French, first without frequency information, then with frequency information weighting the entropy calculations. These tables show that type frequency information allows

Table 10.12. *Simple heuristic for static near-principal parts for Icelandic verbs, using type frequency*

MPSs successively added to S	Highest residual ($\times$ 100)
With S empty	377.3
21 SbjvPast1pl	70.6
12 IndPres3pl	30.0
6 2ndPtcp	9.0
8 IndPres2sg	5.0
2 Impv2sg	2.7
14 IndPast2sg	1.7
4 Impv2pl	0.2
13 IndPast1sg	0.0

---

[7] Properly, a heuristic algorithm, but we follow computer science convention and simply call it a "heuristic."

Table 10.13. *Simple heuristic for static near-principal parts for French verbs*

MPSs successively added to S	Highest residual ($\times$ 100)
With S empty	503.9
9 PresSbjv1sg	66.8
17 PastPtcpFem	15.6
8 Fut1sg	7.4
4 Pres2pl	3.1
1 Pres1sg	3.1
7 Past1sg	0.0

Table 10.14. *Simple heuristic for static near-principal parts for French verbs, using type frequency*

MPSs successively added to S	Highest residual ($\times$ 100)
With S empty	213.1
4 Pres2pl	13.9
8 Fut1sg	1.6
7 Past1sg	0.3
17 PastPtcpFem	0.2
2 Pres2sg	0.0

us to reduce the residual entropy to 0.10 with only two near-principal parts; without that information, it takes three near-principal parts. The 2nd plural present and the 1st singular future forms of a French verb are together very likely to imply all the other forms; the highest residual entropy, weighted by type frequency, is only 0.016.

Interestingly, the simple heuristic chooses quite a different set of near-principal parts when type frequency enters the calculation. The fact that the number of near-principal parts is different shows that the heuristic does not in general minimize the full set of near-principal parts.

Turning again to Sanskrit nominals, for which nominative singular is a static principal part in every optimal analysis, Table 10.15 shows that the simple heuristic only chooses it once the residual entropy has been reduced to 0.03 by three other principal parts, and it still does not reduce the residual all the way to 0.00.

Table 10.15. *Simple heuristic for static near-principal parts for Sanskrit nominals*

MPSs successively added to S	Highest residual (× 100)
With S empty	571.9
Npl	15.6
Isg	6.3
Apl	3.1
Nsg	3.1
Vsg	0.0

Table 10.16. *Lookahead heuristic for static near-principal parts for French verbs*

MPS	Highest residual (× 100)
4 Pres2pl	64.3
14 Inf	21.1
8 Fut1sg	12.5
7 Past1sg	6.3
1 Pres1sg	6.3
16 PastPtcpMasc	3.1
2 Pres2sg	3.1
17 PastPtcpFem	0.0

Of course, we can apply other heuristics. Instead of repeatedly choosing the currently most unpredictable MPS (the one with currently highest residual entropy), the **lookahead heuristic** chooses the most predictive MPS; that is, the MPS that most reduces the maximum of the remaining residual entropies. The lookahead heuristic is more expensive to compute than the simple heuristic, and it gives different results. Table 10.16 shows the results for French verbs, not taking into account type frequency; compare it with Table 10.13. Interestingly, the lookahead heuristic, although it is more promising than the simple heuristic after one step (reducing the maximum residual entropy to 0.643 instead of 0.668), then falls behind the simple heuristic, finally requiring eight near-principal parts instead of six. Both heuristics reach a stage where the next selection fails to improve the residual entropy when it stands at 0.031, although further selections again reduce the residual entropy.

10.5 Inflection-class entropy measures

So far, we have considered the entropy of individual MPSs. We can also measure the variability of inflection classes by related computations. Here we show two different approaches to characterizing inflection classes. They correspond roughly to measures of predictability and predictiveness, introduced in Chapters 4 and 5.

Our first measure is related to the n-MPS entropy, as shown in Table 10.6 for Finnish declensions. Given an exponence e of an MPS[8] m in a given inflection class i, let $P_{i,m}(e|S)$ be the probability of e given the exponences of i in the members of S. Then e contributes $-P_{i,m}(e|S)\log_2 P_{i,m}(e|S)$ to the S-MPS entropy of m. We average this contribution over all sets S of size $0 \ldots n$ of other MPSs, giving us the n-**conditional exponence entropy for m and i**:

$$H_{i,m,n} = -\sum_{|S|\leq n, m \notin S} P(e|S)\log_2 P(e|S)$$

The average of the n-conditional exponence entropy across all MPSs gives us the n-conditional exponence entropy for i. Because this value measures the residual entropy of cells of i conditional on other cells in the plat, we call it the **inflection-class predictable entropy (ICBE)**. Formally,

$$n - \text{ICBE}_i = \frac{\sum_{m \in \text{MPS}} H_{i,m,n}}{|\text{MPS}|}.$$

Table 10.17 shows the 4-ICBE for the Finnish nouns of Table 10.2. It also shows the inflection-class predictability (ICB), as defined in Chapter 5. LASI 'glass' has the lowest 4-ICBE, and KIELI 'language' has the highest, so we

Table 10.17. *Inflection-class predictable entropy (4-ICBE) (× 100), Finnish nouns*

Declension	Nsg	Gsg	Part_sg	Iness_pl	ICBE	ICB
OVI 'door'	14	27	17	18	19	0.733
KIELI 'language'	14	27	21	17	20	0.333
VESI 'water'	14	23	21	17	19	0.533
LASI 'glass'	14	10	10	10	11	0.933
NALLE 'teddy bear'	17	10	10	18	14	0.867
KIRJE 'letter'	17	27	16	17	19	0.733

---

[8] Recall that we are here restricting consideration to MPSs that belong to distinct distillations.

312 *Entropy, predictability, and predictiveness*

would expect LASI to be the most predictable and KIELI the least. This intuition is borne out by the ICB measure.

The second measure depends on the following definition. Given an exponence *e* of an MPS *m* in a given inflection class *i*, we define the **plat reduced by *i*, *m*** as the fragment of the plat containing only those inflection classes that have exponence *e* for MPS *m*. This reduced plat can be as small as the single inflection class *i*, if *i* is unique in its exponence of *m*.

In the reduced plat, we calculate the **inflection-class-MPS entropy** $H^*_{i,m}$ as an average of the entropies of all the other MPSs *m'* conditional on *m*:

$$H_{i,m} = \frac{\sum_{m' \neq m} H_{reduced}(m'|m)}{|\text{MPS}| - 1}.$$

Then the **inflection-class predictive entropy (ICVE)** is the average of the inflection-class-MPS entropies $H_{i,m}$ over all MPSs *m* in the reduced plat:

$$\text{ICVE}_i = \frac{\sum_m H_{i,m}}{|\text{MPS}|}.$$

A low value of ICVE_i means that the exponents in inflection class *i* are highly predictive of each other, because on average, each limits the entropy of the possible values in other cells of *i*. Another way to understand ICVE_i is that it measures the amount of information needed to distinguish inflection class *i* from other inflection classes, given that one knows the exponence of one MPS for *i*. Inflection classes that have many unique exponences have low inflection-class predictive entropy; these inflection classes are highly predictive. Those that share exponences with many other inflection classes have a high inflection-class predictive entropy; they are less predictive.

Table 10.18 shows the ICVE values, along with the component $H_{i,m}$ measures, for the Finnish declensions of Table 10.2. Declension LASI 'glass' has

Table 10.18. *Inflection-class predictive entropy (ICVE) (× 100), Finnish nouns*

declension	nomSg	genSg	partSg	inessPl	ICVE
OVI 'door'	150	114	0	100	91
KIELI 'language'	150	114	33	92	97
VESI 'water'	150	0	33	92	69
LASI 'glass'	150	0	0	0	38
NALLE 'teddy bear'	100	0	0	100	50
KIRJE 'letter'	100	114	0	92	76

relatively low ICVE, because it has several unique forms (*-in* for the genitive singular, *-ia* for the partitive singular, and *-eissa* for the inessive plural). These forms are highly predictive, so the entire declension is predictive. In contrast, KIELI 'language' is less predictive.

10.6   Summary

This chapter has followed an information-theoretic approach, unlike earlier chapters, which follow a set-theoretic approach. These two approaches represent two points on a spectrum of generality.

The information-theoretic approach is a more general tool. Researchers have applied it to phonology (for instance: Hall 2009) and to syntax (for instance: Liu *et al.* 2008) in addition to morphology.

The set-theoretic approach, by contrast, is targeted more specifically: principal parts are, after all, something unique to morphology, and our definitions of static, adaptive, and dynamic principal parts, along with measures of predictability and predictiveness, are tailored to exactly that uniqueness.

We see the connection between the two approaches when residual entropy (conditional on a set of MPSs) becomes zero, which means that the MPSs constitute a static principal-part set. For the set-theoretic approach, all non-zero entropy values are effectively the same. Our derived measures, such as paradigm predictability, measure under what circumstances we can reduce the entropy to zero.

The fact that the set-theoretic approach does not obviously generalize to other disciplines is not a defect, but an expected feature of a specific tool. It gives fine detail for questions surrounding principal parts; it does not try to address other linguistic questions.

11 *The complexity of inflection-class systems*

We regard the complexity of an IC system as the extent to which it inhibits motivated inferences about a given lexeme's realized paradigm from subsets of that paradigm's cells. Our central goal has been to identify objective, measurable correlates of this conception of an IC system's complexity. In this chapter, we situate this notion within the broader context of research into language complexity (§11.1). Logically, our conception of an IC system's complexity has a number of measurable correlates; here, we summarize these measures (§11.2) and compare their use in the analysis of twelve different IC systems (§11.3). In doing so, we demonstrate that they are logically independent: none of the measures is strictly reducible to any of the others, because they quantify different things, each reflecting a different aspect of an IC system's complexity.[1]

11.1 Implicative relations and the complexity of IC systems

In recent years, linguistic complexity has been an object of growing interest among typologists. At least four international conferences devoted to this subject have been held within the past ten years (at the University of Helsinki in 2005, at the University of California, San Diego in 2011, and at the British Academy and the University of Washington in 2012), and several ground-breaking publications on the topic have recently appeared, including Dahl (2004), Hawkins (2004),

---

[1] The data sets that we have employed in this chapter are:

complexity.A	complexity.F	complexity.kwerba
complexity.B	complexity.french	complexity.lithuanian
complexity.C	complexity.fur	complexity.ngiti
complexity.comaltepec-chinantec	complexity.G	complexity.palantla-chinantec
complexity.czech	complexity.icelandic	complexity.sanskrit
complexity.D	complexity.koasati	complexity.tulu
complexity.E		

These are available at the *Morphological Typology* website www.cambridge.org/stump_finkel.

Miestamo *et al*. (2008), Sampson *et al*. (2009), and Sinnemäki (2011). At the root of this interest in linguistic complexity is the universal intuition that one language may be more complex than another in some way; for example, any English speaker who has studied French will agree that at an intuitive level, the inflectional morphology of verbs is more complex in French than in English. But it is important to be clear about what is meant by "complexity."

Miestamo (2006, 2008) distinguishes two main approaches to defining complexity in linguistic typology. According to the **absolute approach**, a language system is more complex the more parts it has, where 'parts' can be construed in any of a variety of ways.[2] Thus, a system of agreement that is sensitive to case, number, and gender (like that of Latin demonstrative determiners) is more complex than one that is only sensitive to number (like that of English demonstrative determiners); here the 'parts' are inflectional categories. But one could also compare the length of two precise and maximally concise descriptions of some linguistic system; thus, one could compare a formal description of the inflectional morphology of Latin ILLE 'that' with an analogous (and inevitably much briefer) description of English THAT. Various researchers have employed compression algorithms in calculating complexity in this way; see, for example, Bane (2008), Dahl (2004: 21ff), Juola (1998), and Moscoso del Prado Martín (2011). (For the theoretical basis for this information-theoretic approach to complexity, see Kolmogorov 1965, Li & Vitányi 1997.)

The absolute approach contrasts with the **relative approach**, which equates a language system's complexity with its "cost" for language users – that is, with the degree of difficulty it poses for processing or acquisition.[3] Investigating linguistic complexity naturally requires different methods depending on which of these approaches to complexity one adopts: under the absolute approach, the complexity of a language system is observable in a theoretical model of that system, while under the relative approach, it is observable in the documented behavior of that system's users. A reasonable hypothesis is that a language system that is complex in one approach will be comparably complex in the other approach, but whether this is so is, of course, an empirical question.

---

[2] The notion of grammatical complexity developed by Nichols (2009) rests on an absolute approach of this sort; in her words, "A definition of grammatical complexity can be based on the usual understanding of a complex system as one consisting of many different elements each with a number of degrees of freedom" (p. 111).

[3] As Miestamo observes (2008: 25f), the relative approach is problematic, since what is difficult for one group of language users may not be for another; for instance, reductive phonological processes in rapid speech make the articulation of a sentence easier for the speaker but may make the processing of that sentence more difficult for the hearer.

Miestamo also distinguishes between global and local conceptions of linguistic complexity. **Global complexity** is a property of entire languages, whereas **local complexity** is a property of particular linguistic subsystems. Linguists have long assumed that all languages are equally complex – that if one language is simpler than another in one area of its grammar, that simplicity is counterbalanced by complexity in another area of its grammar.[4] Recent work on language typology has, however, raised doubts about this assumption – see, for example, Dahl (2009); Kusters (2008); McWhorter (2001, 2008); Sampson (2009); Shosted (2006); and Sinnemäki (2008). Comparisons of languages' global complexity are nevertheless difficult to assess, for at least two reasons (Miestamo 2008: 30; see also Deutscher 2009). First, languages are big. Because there is no practicable way of establishing the contribution of every part of a language's structure to that language's global complexity, certain subsystems must, in the end, be taken as representative; but a priori, how do we know which ones are genuinely representative and which are exceptional? Second, a language's subsystems are really like apples and oranges: how does one decide whether to accord them equal status as contributors to the language's complexity or, instead, to weight them differently (and to what degree)? Cross-linguistic comparisons of local complexity are on surer ground, since they can be based on closely corresponding categories or processes whose boundaries within a language's grammar are comparatively well delineated.

The notion of complexity with which we are concerned – that of a language's IC system – is local, and we define it according to the absolute approach. On first consideration, one might question the claim that our definition of an IC system's complexity is an absolute one. After all, if the complexity of an IC system is the extent to which it inhibits motivated inferences about a given lexeme's realized paradigm from subsets of that paradigm's cells, surely we mean that a complex IC system has a greater "cost" for the language user? It is reasonable to assume that an IC system that is more complex (in our sense) exacts a greater "cost," but our definition does not hinge on issues of processing or acquisition – at least not directly. Our conception of complexity concerns relations of logical implication that hold or do not hold among the cells in realized paradigms: an IC system "inhibits" motivated inferences to the extent that the realized cells that it defines do not have any implicative relation to one another. The presence or absence of such relations is an objectively observable

---

[4] In his *Course in Modern Linguistics*, Hockett famously asserted that "the total grammatical complexity of any language, counting both morphology and syntax, is about the same as that of any other. This is not surprising, since all languages have about equally complex jobs to do, and what is not done morphologically has to be done syntactically" (1958: 180).

property of paradigms in a formal theoretical model of a language's IC system and is directly detectable by computational means. According to Miestamo's criterion, a more complex language system has more parts. What, then, are the "parts" whose numerousness constitutes an IC system's complexity? They might be thought of as a typical lexeme's optimal principal parts (on some analysis): the more principal parts a typical lexeme requires, the more complex the IC system. But we favor a somewhat different conception of an IC system's complexity; after all, two systems may be alike in the number of principal parts they require yet differ in their complexity (in our sense). In our view, an IC system's complexity is inversely proportional to the number of motivated inferences afforded by the cells in its realized paradigms.

As we have seen, numerous factors may contribute to an IC system's complexity; accordingly, there are numerous measurable correlates of an IC system's complexity. We have introduced these correlates progressively over the course of several chapters. We summarize them here and demonstrate that they are logically independent.

11.2 Measurable correlates of an IC system's complexity

In order to understand our conception of an IC system's complexity, it is helpful to envisage again two canonical extremes between which a language's IC system may be situated (§4.1). On one hand, one can imagine an IC system in which no cell in any realized paradigm predicts any other cell in that paradigm. Plat A in Table 11.1 is a hypothetical example of such an IC system; there are no nontrivial implicative rules that are valid for Plat A. On the other hand, one can imagine an IC system in which every cell in every realized paradigm predicts every other cell in that paradigm. Plat B in Table 11.1 is a hypothetical example of this sort; within each IC in Plat B, every realized cell predicts every other realized cell. According to our conception of an IC system's complexity, the IC system in Plat A is maximally complex, while the one in Plat B is minimally complex. In actual languages, an IC system's degree of complexity is situated somewhere between the two extremes exemplified in Plats A and B; moreover, IC systems differ in both the degree of their complexity and the causes of it.

We have identified ten different correlates of an IC system's complexity. The first is the number of distillations. One source of complexity in an IC system is the presence of more than one distillation. In Plat A, every one of the MPSs ρ, σ, and τ is a distillation; that is, no property set has exponents that are isomorphic to those of any other property set. In Plat B, by contrast, ρ, σ, and τ belong to a single distillation; the exponents of each property set are isomorphic to those

Table 11.1. *Two hypothetical plats and their associated implicative rules*

Plat A				(no nontrivial implicative rules for Plat A)
	ρ	σ	τ	
I	a	a	a	
II	b	a	a	
III	a	b	a	
IV	a	a	b	
V	b	b	a	
VI	b	a	b	
VII	a	b	b	
VIII	b	b	b	

Plat B				Irreducible implicative rules for Plat B		
	ρ	σ	τ			
I	a	b	c	⟨X:a, ρ⟩ → ⟨X:b, σ⟩	⟨X:g, ρ⟩ → ⟨X:h, σ⟩	⟨X:m, ρ⟩ → ⟨X:n, σ⟩	⟨X:s, ρ⟩ → ⟨X:t, σ⟩
II	d	e	f	⟨X:a, ρ⟩ → ⟨X:c, τ⟩	⟨X:g, ρ⟩ → ⟨X:i, τ⟩	⟨X:m, ρ⟩ → ⟨X:o, τ⟩	⟨X:s, ρ⟩ → ⟨X:u, τ⟩
III	g	h	i	⟨X:b, σ⟩ → ⟨X:a, ρ⟩	⟨X:h, σ⟩ → ⟨X:g, ρ⟩	⟨X:n, σ⟩ → ⟨X:m, ρ⟩	⟨X:t, σ⟩ → ⟨X:s, ρ⟩
IV	j	k	l	⟨X:b, σ⟩ → ⟨X:c, τ⟩	⟨X:h, σ⟩ → ⟨X:i, τ⟩	⟨X:n, σ⟩ → ⟨X:o, τ⟩	⟨X:t, σ⟩ → ⟨X:u, τ⟩
V	m	n	o	⟨X:c, τ⟩ → ⟨X:a, ρ⟩	⟨X:i, τ⟩ → ⟨X:g, ρ⟩	⟨X:o, τ⟩ → ⟨X:m, ρ⟩	⟨X:u, τ⟩ → ⟨X:s, ρ⟩
VI	p	q	r	⟨X:c, τ⟩ → ⟨X:b, σ⟩	⟨X:i, τ⟩ → ⟨X:h, σ⟩	⟨X:o, τ⟩ → ⟨X:n, σ⟩	⟨X:u, τ⟩ → ⟨X:t, σ⟩
VII	s	t	u	⟨X:d, ρ⟩ → ⟨X:e, σ⟩	⟨X:j, ρ⟩ → ⟨X:k, σ⟩	⟨X:p, ρ⟩ → ⟨X:q, σ⟩	⟨X:v, ρ⟩ → ⟨X:w, σ⟩
VIII	v	w	x	⟨X:d, ρ⟩ → ⟨X:f, τ⟩	⟨X:j, ρ⟩ → ⟨X:l, τ⟩	⟨X:p, ρ⟩ → ⟨X:r, τ⟩	⟨X:v, ρ⟩ → ⟨X:x, τ⟩
				⟨X:e, σ⟩ → ⟨X:d, ρ⟩	⟨X:k, σ⟩ → ⟨X:j, ρ⟩	⟨X:q, σ⟩ → ⟨X:p, ρ⟩	⟨X:w, σ⟩ → ⟨X:v, ρ⟩
				⟨X:e, σ⟩ → ⟨X:f, τ⟩	⟨X:k, σ⟩ → ⟨X:l, τ⟩	⟨X:q, σ⟩ → ⟨X:r, τ⟩	⟨X:w, σ⟩ → ⟨X:x, τ⟩
				⟨X:f, τ⟩ → ⟨X:d, ρ⟩	⟨X:l, τ⟩ → ⟨X:j, ρ⟩	⟨X:r, τ⟩ → ⟨X:p, ρ⟩	⟨X:x, τ⟩ → ⟨X:v, ρ⟩
				⟨X:f, τ⟩ → ⟨X:e, σ⟩	⟨X:l, τ⟩ → ⟨X:k, σ⟩	⟨X:r, τ⟩ → ⟨X:q, σ⟩	⟨X:x, τ⟩ → ⟨X:w, σ⟩

Separate distillations are shaded. X:y represents the word form consisting of stem X with exponence y; §4.1. Greek letters represents MPSs and Roman numerals represent ICs.

Table 11.2. *Hypothetical Plat C and implicative rules for* IC 1

	ρ	σ	τ	υ
I	a	e	g	i
II	b	e	h	j
III	c	f	h	i
IV	d	f	g	j
⟨X:a, ρ⟩ ↔ {⟨X:e, σ⟩, ⟨X:g, τ⟩, ⟨X:i, υ⟩}				
{⟨X:e, σ⟩, ⟨X:g, τ⟩} ↔ {⟨X:a, ρ⟩, ⟨X:i, υ⟩}				
{⟨X:e, σ⟩, ⟨X:i, υ⟩} ↔ {⟨X:a, ρ⟩, ⟨X:g, τ⟩}				
{⟨X:g, τ⟩, ⟨X:i, υ⟩} ↔ {⟨X:a, ρ⟩, ⟨X:e, σ⟩ }				

Separate distillations shaded. Greek letters represents MPSs and Roman numerals represent ICs.

of the other property sets. Isomorphism promotes inferences, and lack of isomorphism inhibits inferences. For instance, if one knows that a verb's τ-cell has exponence **c** in Plat B, then one can motivatedly infer that its ρ-cell has exponence **a** and that its σ-cell has exponence **b**; but if one knows that a verb's τ-cell has exponence **a** in Plat A, no motivated inferences are possible.

The second correlate of an IC system's complexity is the size of a lexeme's optimal static principal-part set. A lexeme requires many principal parts because the implicative relations in which its realized cells participate are insufficient to allow its full paradigm to be motivatedly inferred from a single one of its cells; the need for many principal parts is therefore another correlate of an IC system's complexity. In each IC in Plat A, all three cells in a lexeme's realized paradigm must be principal parts. Lexemes belonging to the ICs in Plat B, on the other hand, require only a single static principal part (indeed, the number cannot be larger, since Plat B only has a single distillation). The number of an IC system's distillations and the size of its lexemes' optimal static principal-part sets are independent variables. For example, Plat C in Table 11.2 is like Plat A in that each of its MPSs is a separate distillation, but it is like Plat B in that a single static principal part (a realized paradigm's ρ-cell) suffices for its member lexemes.

The third correlate is the density of a lexeme's optimal static principal-part sets. If a lexeme has many alternative principal-part sets, its full realized paradigm can be motivatedly inferred in a variety of ways; a lower density of alternative principal-part sets affords fewer motivated inferences, and is therefore another correlate of an IC system's complexity. For example, Plat C has

Table 11.3. *Hypothetical Plat D and implicative rules for* IC I

	ρ	σ	τ	υ
I	a	b	b	a
II	a	b	a	b
III	a	a	b	b
IV	a	a	a	a
⟨X:**b**, σ⟩ → ⟨X:**a**, ρ⟩				
⟨X:**b**, τ⟩ → ⟨X:**a**, ρ⟩				
⟨X:**a**, υ⟩ → ⟨X:**a**, ρ⟩				
{⟨X:**b**, σ⟩, ⟨X:**b**, τ⟩} → ⟨X:**a**, υ⟩				
{⟨X:**b**, σ⟩, ⟨X:**a**, υ⟩} → ⟨X:**b**, τ⟩				
{⟨X:**b**, τ⟩, ⟨X:**a**, υ⟩} → ⟨X:**b**, σ⟩				

Separate distillations shaded. Greek letters represents MPSs and Roman numerals represent ICs.

four distillations and one principal part suffices for its member lexemes; Plat D in Table 11.3 has four distillations and requires two principal parts for each member lexeme. Of a lexeme's four candidate single-member principal-part sets ({ρ-cell}, {σ-cell}, {τ-cell}, {υ-cell}) in Plat C, only one (25 percent) is adequate (namely {ρ-cell}); but of a lexeme's six candidate two-member principal-part sets in Plat D –

{ρ-cell, σ-cell}	{σ-cell, τ-cell}
{ρ-cell, τ-cell}	{σ-cell, υ-cell}
{ρ-cell, υ-cell}	{τ-cell, υ-cell}

– three (50 percent) are adequate (those in the right-hand column).

The fourth correlate is the size of a lexeme's optimal dynamic principal-part set (averaged across ICs); here, also, the need for many principal parts is a correlate of an IC system's complexity. Although Plat C is more complex than Plat D by the third criterion, Plat D (with two optimal dynamic principal parts per lexeme) is, by this fourth criterion, more complex than Plat C (with a single optimal dynamic principal part per lexeme). Plat E in Table 11.4 is intermediate between Plats C and D by this criterion, since lexemes in Plat E have either one optimal dynamic principal part (ICs I and IV) or two (ICs II and III).

The fifth correlate is the ratio of optimal dynamic principal-part sets to candidate sets of the same size (averaged across ICs). The smaller this ratio,

Table 11.4. *Hypothetical Plat E and implicative rule for* IC I

	ρ	σ	τ	υ
I	a	f	g	h
II	a	b	g	h
III	a	b	c	h
IV	a	b	c	d

⟨X:a, ρ⟩ ↔ {⟨X:f, σ⟩, ⟨X:g, τ⟩, ⟨X:h, υ⟩}

All MPSs are distillations; an IC's optimal dynamic principal parts are shaded. Greek letters represents MPSs and Roman numerals represent ICs.

the fewer the motivated inferences that are afforded. In Plat E, this average (the average of 1/4, 1/6, 1/6, and 1/4) is 0.21; in Plat D, the average (of 3/6 in each IC) is 0.50, and in Plat C, the average (of 1/4 in each IC) is 0.25. For lexemes in Plat B, there is only one candidate principal-part set because there is only one distillation, and this principal-part set is adequate. For lexemes in Plat A, there is again only one candidate principal-part set, because the only optimal dynamic principal-part set contains every realized cell in a lexeme's paradigm; this principal-part set, too, is adequate.

The sixth correlate of an IC system's complexity is the cell predictor number, averaged across a system's ICs. The need to refer to more than one principal part in order to infer a realized cell entails that the inferences afforded by individual cells are insufficient and is therefore another correlate of an IC system's complexity. In Plat D, the average cell predictor number is 1.00: in any optimal dynamic principal-part analysis of any IC, there is one cell (the ρ-cell) that is deducible without reference to any other cell (its exponence must be **a**), two self-deducing cells (the two principal parts) and one cell requiring reference to both principal parts. By this criterion, Plat E is less complex than Plat D: its cell predictor number, averaged across its four ICs, is 0.75 – one cell (the ρ-cell) is deducible without reference to any other cell, and every other cell is either self-deducing (as a principal part) or deducible from a single principal part.

The seventh correlate is cell predictiveness, averaged both across cells within an IC and across ICs. The less predictive the cells in a realized paradigm, the fewer motivated inferences they afford. By this criterion, Plat D (whose overall average cell predictiveness is 0.250) is again more complex than Plat E (with an overall cell predictiveness of 0.417).

The eighth correlate of an IC system's complexity is that of IC predictability. The lower an IC's predictability, the fewer motivated inferences it affords. Compare Plats C, D, and E. Each plat has four distillations, hence fifteen candidate dynamic (possibly nonoptimal) principal-part sets for each IC. Twelve of these are adequate for each IC in Plat C and eight for each IC in Plat D; in E, ICs I and IV each have eight adequate candidates and ICs II and III each have four. Thus, Plats A–E are ranked according to IC predictability as in Table 11.5.

The ninth correlate of an IC system's complexity is that of cell predictability, averaged both across cells within an IC and across ICs. The less predictable a cell is, the smaller the number of motivated inferences in which it participates. By this criterion, Plat A is most complex: none of its cells is predictable, so its overall average cell predictability is 0. (Because Plat B has only a single distillation, its cell predictability number is likewise 0.) Of the remaining three plats, Plat C has the highest overall average cell predictability (0.594) and Plat D, the lowest (0.438).

The final correlate of an IC system's complexity is m-system entropy. For a given choice of m, the fewer the motivated inferences afforded by an IC system's realized paradigms, the higher the system's m-system entropy. When we calculate the 4-system entropy for Plats A through E, we get the results in Table 11.6. The complexity rankings suggested by the measures of IC predictability (in Table 11.5) and 4-system entropy (in Table 11.6) are not in full agreement: Plat E has a lower IC predictability than Plat D, suggesting that Plat E is more complex than Plat D; yet, Plat E also has a lower 4-system entropy than Plat D, suggesting that Plat D is more complex than Plat E. This result is ultimately not surprising, since IC predictability and 4-system entropy measure different things. IC predictability measures the proportion of candidate principal-part sets that are adequate for identifying a lexeme's IC membership in a given IC system; 4-system entropy measures the average degree of uncertainty about a lexeme L's IC membership given a subset of one to four cells in L's realized paradigm.

The difference between IC predictability and m-system entropy can be appreciated by considering the hypothetical inflectional plats in Table 11.7: each plat has twelve MPSs (labeled A–L), twelve ICs (labeled 1–12) and two inflectional exponents (**a** and **b**).

Consider first the measure of 4-system entropy. Plat F has a 4-system entropy of 0.37; Plat G has a 4-system entropy of 0.31, so deducing the realizations of the cells in Plat G involves slightly less uncertainty than deducing the realizations of the cells in Plat F. This result seems reasonable. In Plat G, every cell is informative: if a cell has exponent **b**, then any cells to its right also have exponent **b**, and if

Table 11.5. *IC predictability of Plats A–E in Tables 11.1–11.4*

	Plat	\multicolumn{4}{c}{Candidate dynamic (possibly nonoptimal) principal-part sets}	(i) Total	(ii) Adequate principal-part sets	Ratio of (ii) to (i)
		1 member	2 members	3 members	4 members			
More complex	A	3 (0 adequate)	3 (0 adequate)	1 (1 adequate)		7	1	0.14
↑	E	4 (0.5* adequate)	6 (2* adequate)	4 (2.5* adequate)	1 (1 adequate)	15	6*	0.40
↓	D	4 (0 adequate)	6 (3 adequate)	4 (4 adequate)	1 (1 adequate)	15	8	0.53
	C	4 (1 adequate)	6 (6 adequate)	4 (4 adequate)	1 (1 adequate)	15	12	0.80
Less complex	B	1 (1 adequate)				1	1	1.00

* Averaged across ICs.

Table 11.6. *The 4-system entropy (× 100) of Plats A–E*

	Plat	4-system entropy
More complex	B	300
↑	A	100
	D	56
↓	E	49
Less complex	C	44

Table 11.7. *Two hypothetical plats*

Plat F													Plat G											
	A	B	C	D	E	F	G	H	I	J	K	L		A	B	C	D	E	F	G	H	I	J	K	L
1	a	b	b	b	b	b	b	b	b	b	b	b	1	a	b	b	b	b	b	b	b	b	b	b	b
2	b	a	b	b	b	b	b	b	b	b	b	b	2	a	a	b	b	b	b	b	b	b	b	b	b
3	b	b	a	b	b	b	b	b	b	b	b	b	3	a	a	a	b	b	b	b	b	b	b	b	b
4	b	b	b	a	b	b	b	b	b	b	b	b	4	a	a	a	a	b	b	b	b	b	b	b	b
5	b	b	b	b	a	b	b	b	b	b	b	b	5	a	a	a	a	a	b	b	b	b	b	b	b
6	b	b	b	b	b	a	b	b	b	b	b	b	6	a	a	a	a	a	a	b	b	b	b	b	b
7	b	b	b	b	b	b	a	b	b	b	b	b	7	a	a	a	a	a	a	a	b	b	b	b	b
8	b	b	b	b	b	b	b	a	b	b	b	b	8	a	a	a	a	a	a	a	a	b	b	b	b
9	b	b	b	b	b	b	b	b	a	b	b	b	9	a	a	a	a	a	a	a	a	a	b	b	b
10	b	b	b	b	b	b	b	b	b	a	b	b	10	a	a	a	a	a	a	a	a	a	a	b	b
11	b	b	b	b	b	b	b	b	b	b	a	b	11	a	a	a	a	a	a	a	a	a	a	a	b
12	b	b	b	b	b	b	b	b	b	b	b	a	12	a	a	a	a	a	a	a	a	a	a	a	a
IC predictability: 0.293													IC predictability: 0.108												
4-system entropy (× 100): 37													4-system entropy (× 100): 31												

All **a** cells are shaded.

it has exponent **a**, then any cells to its left also have exponent **a**. These same inferences do not hold in Plat F, where only the cells with exponent **a** are informative: if a cell has exponent **a**, then all of the other cells in its row have exponent **b**; by contrast, very little can be inferred from the knowledge that a given cell in a given column has exponent **b** – only that the cell does not belong to the one IC that has exponent **a** in that column. Nevertheless, there is a strong likelihood that a given cell in Plat F has exponent **b**.

Now consider the measure of IC predictability. Plat F has a IC predictability of 0.293; Plat G has a IC predictability of 0.108. This means that there are more adequate principal-part sets in Plat F than in Plat G. In Plat F, any principal-part set that includes a cell with exponent **a** suffices to identify a given IC. In Plat G, by contrast, a principal-part set must include both a cell with exponent **a** and an adjoining cell with exponent **b** in order for an IC to be uniquely identified by that set. (For two ICs, however, a single principal part suffices: the B-cell for IC 1 and the L-cell for IC 12.)

From these considerations, it is clear that IC predictability cannot be reduced to 4-system entropy, nor can 4-system entropy be reduced to IC predictability. More broadly, all ten of the measures summarized here are logically independent, so each must be seen as a distinct correlate of an IC system's complexity; together, they are simply more informative than any conception that purports to reduce IC complexity to a single parameter. We now examine our conception of an IC system's complexity in the context of some real languages.

11.3 Complexity as a typological variable of IC systems

As we saw in Chapter 1, the traditional conception of principal parts is bound by three requirements: the uniqueness requirement (only one of a lexeme's principal-part sets is privileged with the label 'principal parts'); the uniformity requirement (lexemes belonging to the same syntactic category have the same cells in their realized paradigms as principal parts); and the optimality requirement (each set of principal parts is as small as it can be, given the requirement of uniformity). None of these three requirements is included in our conception of principal parts ("a set of cells in a lexeme L's realized paradigm from which one can deduce the remaining cells in L's realized paradigm"; §1.1). In order to elucidate the various measures of an IC system's complexity, we begin with the three requirements in place and progressively suspend them.

11.3.1 Distillations

In the interests of concreteness, we focus on the complexity of the twelve inflectional systems in (1). As we shall show, these systems are quite varied. We note at the outset that the plats that we have used to model these systems vary widely in size. Table 11.8 lists the number of MPSs in each of the twelve plats. Our Tuḷu plat is the largest, with eighty MPSs; the Comaltepec Chinantec plat, by contrast, has only twelve MPSs.[5]

---

[5] Our Koasati plat has ten MPSs, but Koasati verb paradigms have many more cells than this. Koasati has a great deal of verb morphology (Kimball 1991: 111ff), but much of this is invariant across its various conjugation classes. Because the forms of the present indicative exhibit all of the systematic conjugation-class distinctions, we have chosen to restrict our plat to present indicative MPSs and their exponences; other MPSs belong to the distillations defined by the present indicative MPSs.

326 *The complexity of inflection-class systems*

Table 11.8. *The number of MPSs and distillations in the paradigms defined by twelve inflectional systems ('Unique' MPSs are those with distinct exponence.)*

	ICs	MPSs	Distillations
Comaltepec Chinantec verbs	67	12	12
Czech nouns	28	13	13
French verbs	64	20*	17
Fur verbs	19	12	9
Icelandic verbs	162**	30	21
Koasati verbs	12	10	5
Kwerba verbs	4	12 (6 unique)	4
Lithuanian nouns	18	13	9
Ngiti verbs	10	16 (10 unique)	8
Palantla Chinantec verbs	46	12	11
Sanskrit nouns	38	18 (17 unique)	13
Tuḷu verbs	6	80 (48 unique)	7

* These are the twenty stems in a French verb's synthetic paradigm in the concrete plat.
** Jörg 1989 lists 162, but there are only 146 distinct ICs.

(1)   (a) Verbs in Comaltepec Chinantec (Oto-Manguean; Mexico)
          (Pace 1990)
      (b) Nouns in Czech (Slavic; Czech Republic)
          (Janda & Townsend 2000)
      (c) Verbs in French (Romance; France)
          [concrete plat of §7.3]
      (d) Verbs in Fur (Nilo-Saharan; Sudan)
          (Jakobi 1990)
      (e) Verbs in Icelandic (Germanic; Iceland)
          (Jörg 1989)
      (f) Verbs in Koasati (Muskogean; US)
          (Kimball 1991)
      (g) Verbs in Kwerba (Tor-Kwerba; Indonesia)
          (De Vries & De Vries 1997)
      (h) Nouns in Lithuanian (Baltic; Lithuania)
          (Marvan 1979)
      (i) Verbs in Ngiti (Nilo-Saharan; DR Congo)
          (Kutsch Lojenga 1994)
      (j) Verbs in Palantla Chinantec (Oto-Manguean; Mexico)
          (Merrifield 1968)
      (k) Nouns in Sanskrit (Indic; India)
          (Whitney 1889)
      (l) Verbs in Tuḷu (Dravidian; India)
          (Brigel 1872)

One might suppose that the large number of MPSs in a Tuḷu verb's realized paradigm heightens the complexity of Tuḷu's conjugation-class system, but it does not. The eighty cells in a Tuḷu verb's paradigm correspond to a mere seven distillations, whereas each of the twelve cells in a Comaltepec Chinantec verb's paradigm corresponds to a distinct distillation. That is, despite the size of Tuḷu verbs' realized paradigms, many of their MPSs are isomorphic in their exponence; for this reason, many more motivated inferences are possible about a verb's realized cells in Tuḷu than in Comaltepec Chinantec. We therefore propose a first simple measure of an IC system's complexity:

Measure 1. The more distillations an IC system has, the more complex it is.

Henceforth, we only consider those cells that are exemplars of distillations as the basis for reckoning a paradigm's principal parts.

11.3.2 Measuring an IC system's complexity without adhering to the requirement of uniqueness

Consider now the possibility of doing principal-part analysis with the requirement of uniqueness suspended. On this basis, we can compare the size and number of an inflectional system's optimal static principal-part sets. As the first column of figures in Table 11.9 shows, the twelve systems in (1) vary widely in the size of their optimal static principal-part sets.

These figures reflect a second way of measuring an IC system's complexity:

Measure 2. The larger the size of an IC system's optimal static principal-part sets, the more complex it is.

By this measure, the Icelandic conjugational system is highly complex, requiring no fewer than eight static principal parts. By this same measure, the Kwerba conjugational system is low in complexity: a single principal part suffices to determine a Kwerba verb's entire realized paradigm. We also see that the size of an inflectional system's optimal static principal-part sets correlates loosely but not perfectly with number of distillations as a measure of complexity.

Consider now the number of alternative optimal static principal-part sets for an inflectional system. As the first column of figures in Table 11.10 shows, this too is a domain of significant variation among the twelve inflectional systems in (1). Comparisons along this dimension of variation are complicated, however, by the fact that a paradigm is open to more alternative principal-part analyses the more principal parts it has (§4.3). Where lexeme L has k principal parts and n is the number of distillations for which L inflects, the largest possible number of optimal principal-part analyses for L is the binomial coefficient of n and k, that is,

Table 11.9. *The size of optimal static principal-part sets for twelve inflectional systems*

	Size of optimal static principal-part sets	Distillations in a lexeme's paradigm
Comaltepec Chinantec verbs	5	12
Czech nouns	5	13
French verbs	5	17
Fur verbs	5	9
Icelandic verbs	8	21
Koasati verbs	2	5
Kwerba verbs	1	4
Lithuanian nouns	3	9
Ngiti verbs	3	8
Palantla Chinantec verbs	6	11
Sanskrit nouns	4	13
Tuḷu verbs	2	7

Table 11.10. *Density of optimal static principal-part sets for twelve inflectional systems*

	Number of optimal static principal-part sets		
	actual	possible	Density
Comaltepec Chinantec verbs	6	792	0.008
Czech nouns	6	1287	0.005
French verbs	5	6188	0.001
Fur verbs	4	126	0.032
Icelandic verbs	60	203,490	< 0.001
Koasati verbs	1	10	0.100
Kwerba verbs	1	4	0.250
Lithuanian nouns	1	84	0.012
Ngiti verbs	6	56	0.107
Palantla Chinantec verbs	16	462	0.035
Sanskrit nouns	6	715	0.008
Tuḷu verbs	10	21	0.476

$$\binom{n}{k} = \frac{n!}{k!(n-k)!}$$

Thus, rather than compare inflectional systems according to their number of alternative optimal static principal-part sets, we compare systems according to the **density** of their principal-part sets (i.e. their ratio of actual to possible optimal static principal-part sets, given the system's number of distillations and the size of its optimal static principal-part sets); these ratios are given in the final column of Table 11.10.

The density of an IC system's optimal static principal-part sets is the basis for a third way of measuring its complexity:

> **Measure 3.** The lower the density of an IC system's optimal static principal-part sets, the more complex it is.

The Comaltepec Chinantec and Czech inflectional systems both require five optimal static principal parts, and there are six alternative optimal static analyses in both languages. But in Comaltepec Chinantec, the density of optimal static principal-part sets is higher because it has one less distillation than Czech; thus, by this measure, the IC system of Comaltepec Chinantec verbs is marginally less complex than that of Czech nouns.

These means of measuring an IC system's complexity, though informative, are not entirely satisfactory. Because they are based on static principal-part sets, Measures 2 and 3 implicitly adhere to the requirement that principal-part sets be uniform across ICs. But adherence to this requirement may artificially inflate the number of principal parts required to deduce an inflectional system's paradigm realizations. In Icelandic, for example, no conjugation requires reference to more than four principal parts in order to deduce the realization of its paradigms, but because different conjugations require reference to different principal parts, the requirement of uniformity inflates the size of each conjugation's principal-part set. In short, the requirement of uniformity may make IC systems look more complex than they really are.

11.3.3 Measuring an IC system's complexity without adhering to the requirements of uniqueness and uniformity

We now suspend both the requirement of uniqueness and that of uniformity: we assume not only that a lexeme may have alternative principal-part sets, but that lexemes may differ in exactly which cells of their paradigms constitute principal-part sets. In particular, we compare the size and number of the distinct optimal dynamic principal-part sets for each of a language's individual ICs. As an example, consider the system of French conjugations in Table 11.11.

330 *The complexity of inflection-class systems*

Table 11.11. *Sixty-four French conjugations (each named after an exemplar)*

ÊTRE	'be'	ASSAILLIR	'assail'	PEINDRE	'paint'
AVOIR	'have'	BOUILLIR	'boil'	JOINDRE	'join'
AIMER	'like'	DORMIR	'sleep'	VAINCRE	'conquer'
COLLER	'paste'	COURIR	'run'	FAIRE	'do'
BEURRER	'butter'	MOURIR	'die'	PLAIRE	'please'
ÉCROUER	'imprison'	SERVIR	'serve'	CONNAÎTRE	'be acquainted with'
ÉCHOUER	'fail'	FUIR	'flee'	NAÎTRE	'be born'
REMUER	'stir'	RECEVOIR	'receive'	CROÎTRE	'grow'
LEVER	'raise'	VOIR	'see'	BOIRE	'drink'
CÉDER	'give up'	POURVOIR	'provide'	CONCLURE	'end'
COPIER	'copy'	SAVOIR	'know'	INCLURE	'include'
APPUYER	'press'	POUVOIR	'can'	COUDRE	'sew'
ENVOYER	'send'	MOUVOIR	'move'	MOUDRE	'grind'
FINIR	'finish'	VALOIR	'be worth'	SUIVRE	'follow'
HAÏR	'hate'	VOULOIR	'want'	VIVRE	'live'
ALLER	'go'	ASSEOIR$_1$	'seat'	LIRE	'read'
TENIR	'hold'	ASSEOIR$_2$	'seat'	DIRE	'say'
ACQUÉRIR	'acquire'	RENDRE	'give back'	RIRE	'laugh'
SENTIR	'feel'	PRENDRE	'take'	ÉCRIRE	'write'
VÊTIR	'clothe'	BATTRE	'beat'	CONFIRE	'preserve'
COUVRIR	'cover'	METTRE	'put'	CUIRE	'cook'
CUEILLIR	'pick'				

Each of these conjugations has an optimal dynamic principal-part set with either one or two members, but the number of alternative optimal dynamic principal-part sets varies widely from one conjugation to another; Table 11.12 presents the relevant statistics.

We can compare the averages in the bottom row of Table 11.12 with the corresponding averages for other inflectional systems, as in Table 11.13.

The two columns in Table 11.13 reflect two more ways of measuring an IC system's complexity. The first of these relates to the first column of figures:

> **Measure 4**. The larger the size of an IC system's optimal dynamic principal-part sets, the more complex it is.

A second measure relates to the second column.

> **Measure 5**. The smaller the average ratio of actual to possible optimal dynamic principal-part analyses for an IC system, the more complex it is.

Both of these measures entail that the Palantla Chinantec system of verb conjugation is highly complex; its dynamic principal-part number (2.52) is

Table 11.12. *Size and number of optimal dynamic principal-part sets for sixty-four French conjugations*

Conjugations	Number of principal parts in an optimal dynamic set	Number of optimal dynamic sets	Ratio of actual to possible optimal dynamic analyses
INCLURE, NAÎTRE	1	1	5.9% of 17
ASSAILLIR, AVOIR, BATTRE, COUDRE, DIRE, POUVOIR, RECEVOIR, SENTIR, SERVIR, SUIVRE	1	2	11.8% of 17
HAÏR, MOUVOIR	1	3	17.6% of 17
ENVOYER	1	4	23.5% of 17
ALLER, RIRE	1	6	35.3% of 17
BOIRE, BOUILLIR, PRENDRE, SAVOIR	1	7	41.2% of 17
ASSEOIR$_2$, LIRE, METTRE, PLAIRE	1	9	52.9% of 17
FAIRE, JOINDRE, LEVER, PEINDRE, TENIR	1	10	58.8% of 17
CROÎTRE	1	11	64.7% of 17
BEURRER, MOUDRE, MOURIR, RENDRE	1	12	70.6% of 17
VOULOIR	1	13	76.5% of 17
ACQUÉRIR, DORMIR, VAINCRE, VIVRE	1	14	82.4% of 17
CUEILLIR, ÉCHOUER, ÊTRE	1	16	94.1% of 17
CÉDER, COLLER, COUVRIR, REMUER, VALOIR	1	17	100.0% of 17
CONFIRE	2	2	1.5% of 136
CUIRE, ÉCROUER, VÊTIR, VOIR	2	4	2.9% of 136
CONCLURE	2	5	3.7% of 136
POURVOIR	2	9	6.6% of 136
AIMER	2	16	11.8% of 136
FUIR	2	20	14.7% of 136
APPUYER	2	24	17.6% of 136
ASSEOIR$_1$, FINIR	2	27	19.9% of 136
CONNAÎTRE	2	33	24.3% of 136
ÉCRIRE	2	40	29.4% of 136
COURIR	2	42	30.9% of 136
COPIER	2	60	44.1% of 136
Average over all sixty-four conjugations	1.25	11.56	42.2%

Table 11.13. *Average size of optimal dynamic principal-part sets for twelve inflectional systems and average ratio of actual to possible optimal dynamic analyses*

	Average size of optimal dynamic principal-part sets	Average ratio of actual to possible optimal dynamic analyses (%)
Comaltepec Chinantec verbs	1.84	20.3
Czech nouns	1.68	21.8
French verbs	1.25	42.2
Fur verbs	1.58	17.3
Icelandic verbs	1.56	23.9
Koasati verbs	1.00	58.3
Kwerba verbs	1.00	43.8
Lithuanian nouns	1.17	50.0
Ngiti verbs	1.60	23.8
Palantla Chinantec verbs	2.52	10.5
Sanskrit nouns	1.21	30.0
Tuḷu verbs	1.00	38.1

the highest that we have seen in the languages that we have investigated. By the measure of average size of optimal dynamic principal-part sets, the conjugational systems of Koasati, Kwerba, and Tuḷu are low in complexity; the Koasati system is also ranked low in complexity by the measure of average ratio of actual to possible optimal dynamic analyses.

Two additional measures focus specifically on the role of individual cells in the networks of implicative relations that determine an IC system's complexity. An IC's cell predictor number is the number of optimal dynamic principal parts required to deduce a given realized cell, averaged across cells; this number can in turn be averaged across ICs. We thus arrive at Measure 6:

> **Measure 6**. The higher an IC system's cell predictor number (averaged across ICs), the more complex it is.

We can also compare IC systems according to the predictiveness of its cells, averaged across cells in a realized paradigm and across ICs:

> **Measure 7**. The lower an IC system's average cell predictiveness, the more complex it is.

Table 11.14. *Cell predictor number and cell predictiveness, both averaged across ICs, for twelve inflectional systems*

	Cell predictor number	Cell predictiveness
Comaltepec Chinantec verbs	1.08	0.440
Czech nouns	1.20	0.319
French verbs	1.05	0.597
Fur verbs	1.04	0.509
Icelandic verbs	1.09	0.385
Koasati verbs	1.00	0.738
Kwerba verbs	0.75	0.542
Lithuanian nouns	1.00	0.728
Ngiti verbs	1.02	0.464
Palantla Chinantec verbs	1.21	0.182
Sanskrit nouns	1.00	0.591
Tuḷu verbs	1.00	0.524

The results of these two measures for our twelve IC systems are given in Table 11.14. Both of these measures entail that the Palantla Chinantec conjugation system is highly complex; the Czech declensional is virtually as complex by the first measure, substantially less so by the second. Palantla Chinantec and Czech exhibit the highest cell predictor numbers that we have seen in any of the languages that we have investigated. Even so, they do not alter the fact that an IC system's average cell predictor number tends to be substantially lower than its dynamic principal-part number (unless these are both simply 1.00, as in Koasati and Tuḷu); this is the depth-of-inference contrast (§7.7).

The measure of cell predictor numbers ranks Kwerba especially low in complexity; the fact that the Kwerba cell predictor number is less than 1.00 reflects the fact that one of the four distillations for Kwerba verbs has the same exponence in all four ICs and can therefore be deduced without reference to any principal parts; see Table 3.1. The IC systems of Koasati verbs and Lithuanian nouns are ranked low in complexity by the cell predictiveness measure.

These means of assessing an IC system's complexity are still not entirely satisfactory. Because they focus purely on optimal dynamic principal-part sets, they take no account of the varying extents to which nonoptimal dynamic principal-part sets may contribute to the deducibility of a realized paradigm's cells. Adhering to the requirement of optimality may therefore make an IC system look more complex than it is.

11.3.4 Measuring an IC system's complexity without adhering to the requirements of uniqueness, uniformity, and optimality

We therefore suspend the requirement of optimality as well as those of uniqueness and uniformity. In this way, we can contrast individual ICs according to the ratio of actual dynamic principal-part sets (both optimal and nonoptimal) to candidate principal-part sets of a certain cardinality. Consider again the case of French. If, for each conjugation, we calculate the ratio of actual dynamic principal-part sets among candidate principal-part sets containing a maximum of four members, we get the results in Table 11.15; we have called this ratio a conjugation's IC predictability (§4.4). That is, a conjugation's IC predictability is the percentage of actual dynamic principal-part sets among possible sets of a specified maximum size m.

IC predictability is a dimension of significant contrast across languages. The twelve inflectional systems in (1) have the average IC predictabilities in Figure 11.1 (where the candidate principal-part sets are those whose maximum cardinality m is 4).

Average IC predictability is therefore another measure of an IC system's complexity:

> **Measure 8**. The lower an IC system's average IC predictability, the more complex it is.

This measure, like Measures 4 and 5, shows that the conjugational system of Palantla Chinantec is highly complex; like Measure 3, it entails that the conjugational system of Tuḷu is low in complexity.

Cell predictability (§4.6) is also a significant dimension of cross-linguistic variability. Given a particular cell K in a lexeme's realized paradigm P, K's cell predictability is the proportion of sets in {S | S is a K-less subset of distillation-realizing cells in P and S has no more than m members} that determine K's form. The average cell predictability of an IC J is the average cell predictability of the cells in a realized paradigm belonging to J; an IC system's average cell predictability is the average of its ICs' average cell predictabilities. The twelve inflectional systems in (1) have the average cell predictabilities in Figure 11.2 (where m is again set at 4).

Thus, average cell predictability is another measure of an IC system's complexity:

> **Measure 9**. The lower an IC system's average cell predictability, the more complex it is.

Table 11.15. *IC predictability of sixty-four French conjugations [based on* m = *4]*

Conj	IC predictability
CÉDER, COLLER, COUVRIR, REMUER, VALOIR	1.000 (3213 out of 3214)
CUEILLIR, ÉCHOUER, ÊTRE	0.999 (3212 out of 3214)
ACQUÉRIR, DORMIR, VAINCRE, VIVRE	0.998 (3206 out of 3214)
VOULOIR	0.997 (3205 out of 3214)
FAIRE	0.991 (3185 out of 3214)
ASSEOIR$_2$, BEURRER, MOUDRE, MOURIR, RENDRE	0.990 (3183 out of 3214)
LIRE, METTRE	0.986 (3169 out of 3214)
CROÎTRE	0.982 (3157 out of 3214)
PLAIRE	0.979 (3145 out of 3214)
JOINDRE, LEVER, PEINDRE, TENIR	0.969 (3115 out of 3214)
PRENDRE	0.967 (3108 out of 3214)
RIRE	0.956 (3073 out of 3214)
RECEVOIR	0.919 (2953 out of 3214)
BOIRE, SAVOIR	0.916 (2945 out of 3214)
AVOIR	0.910 (2924 out of 3214)
BOUILLIR	0.880 (2828 out of 3214)
ALLER	0.825 (2652 out of 3214)
ASSAILLIR	0.816 (2623 out of 3214)
COPIER	0.795 (2555 out of 3214)
ENVOYER	0.660 (2121 out of 3214)
COUDRE	0.653 (2098 out of 3214)
ÉCRIRE	0.632 (2030 out of 3214)
COURIR	0.601 (1931 out of 3214)
HAÏR, MOUVOIR, POUVOIR	0.542 (1743 out of 3214)
NAÎTRE	0.541 (1740 out of 3214)
CONNAÎTRE	0.527 (1694 out of 3214)
APPUYER	0.516 (1658 out of 3214)
FINIR	0.501 (1611 out of 3214)
FUIR	0.464 (1490 out of 3214)
ASSEOIR$_1$	0.421 (1353 out of 3214)
BATTRE, DIRE, SENTIR, SERVIR, SUIVRE	0.396 (1273 out of 3214)
POURVOIR	0.250 (804 out of 3214)
AIMER, INCLURE	0.217 (697 out of 3214)
VOIR	0.185 (593 out of 3214)
CONCLURE	0.145 (465 out of 3214)
VÊTIR	0.132 (425 out of 3214)
CUIRE, ÉCROUER	0.124 (398 out of 3214)
CONFIRE	0.071 (227 out of 3214)
Avg	0.722 (2321 out of 3214)

336 *The complexity of inflection-class systems*

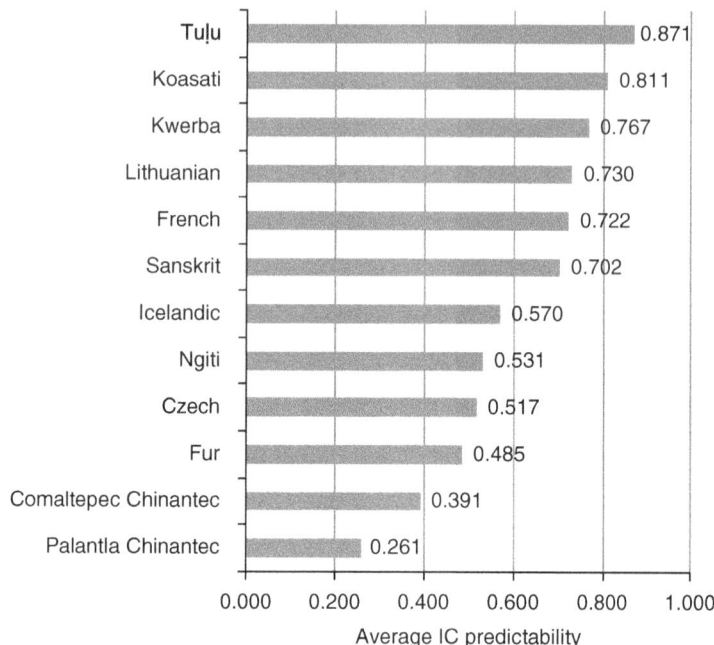

Figure 11.1. *Average IC predictability of twelve IC systems*

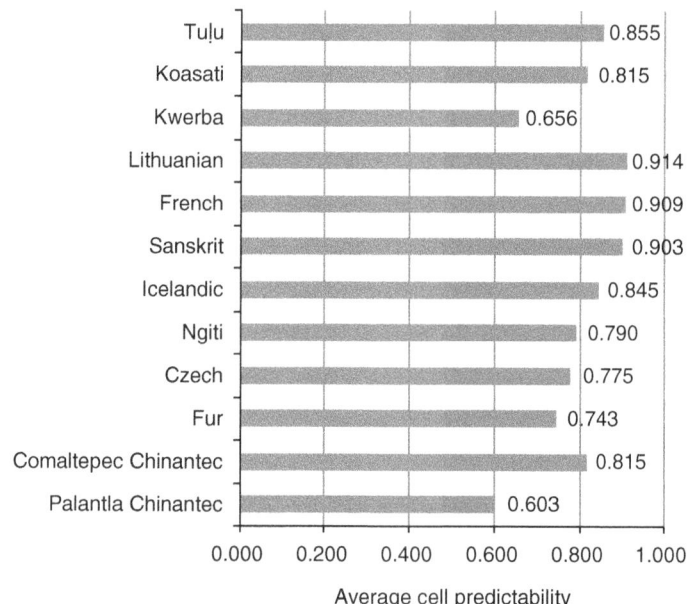

Figure 11.2. *Average cell predictability of twelve inflectional systems*

The contrast between the measures of average IC predictability and average cell predictability is striking. Although the average IC predictability of the Tuḷu system of conjugation is more than twice that of the Comaltepec Chinantec system, their average cell predictabilities are quite close. Thus, motivated inferences about a lexeme's IC membership are more abundant in Tuḷu than in Comaltepec Chinantec; but motivated inferences about the form of an individual realized cell are nearly equal in abundance in the two languages.

The Kwerba conjugation system is quite complex according to its average cell predictability. This result is initially surprising, given that most of the measures considered so far point to its relative simplicity. But the inflection of Kwerba verbs involves four distillations, one of whose realizations is highly informative (and is therefore the lone optimal static principal part) but not very predictable (its cell predictability, averaged over the four conjugations, is 0.438). Together, the small number of distillations and the low predictability of the cells realizing one of those distillations tend to skew the average cell predictability of the Kwerba verb system downward.

Candidate principal-part sets are also the basis for a different measure of an IC system's complexity: this is the measure of ***n*-MPS entropy** (§10.2).[6] The n-MPS entropy of an inflection-class system is the average n-MPS entropy of its property sets. Figure 11.3 shows the n-MPS entropy (with $n = 4$) of the inflectional systems in each language in (1). As with all entropy-based measures, low values reflect high predictability.

Thus, we have a final measure of an IC system's complexity:

> **Measure 10**. The higher an IC system's average n-MPS entropy, the more complex it is.

As the numbers in Figures 11.1 and 11.3 show, an IC system's average IC predictability and its n-MPS entropy reflect different aspects of complexity. An inflectional system's average IC predictability is a set-theoretic measure of the proportion of candidate principal part sets from which its realized paradigms can be motivatedly inferred. The measure of n-MPS entropy, by contrast, is an information-theoretic measure of the degree of uncertainty involved in deducing a realized paradigm. There is no necessary correspondence between an inflectional system's IC predictability and its n-MPS entropy. For example, the average IC predictability of Kwerba verbs is nearly three times that of Palantla Chinantec verbs; yet, these two conjugational systems are identical in

---

[6] The 'paradigm entropy' of Malouf & Ackerman (2010b) is like our n-MPS entropy with $n = 1$.

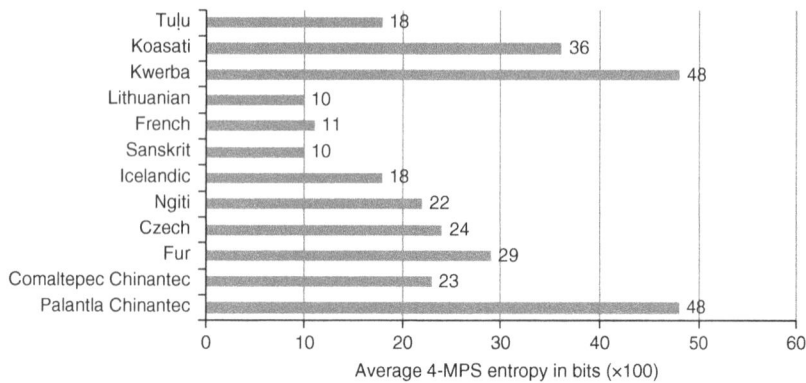

Figure 11.3. *Average 4-MPS entropy (× 100) of twelve IC systems*

their average 4-MPS entropy; Lithuanian and Koasati exhibit nearly the same IC predictability but very different 4-MPS entropies.

Summarizing, we have identified ten ways of measuring different aspects of an IC system's morphological complexity:

(a) the number of distillations the system has;
(b) the size of the system's optimal static principal-part sets;
(c) the density of the system's optimal static principal-part sets (given (a) and (b));
(d) the average size of optimal dynamic principal-part sets for the system's ICs;
(e) the average ratio of actual to possible optimal dynamic principal-part sets for the system's ICs;
(f) the system's average cell predictor number;
(g) the system's average cell predictiveness;
(h) the average IC predictability of the system's ICs;
(i) the average cell predictability of the system's ICs; and
(j) the n-MPS entropy.

We regard all of these measures as informative and are skeptical of any attempt to reduce an inflectional system's morphological complexity to any single measure. Rather than propose a definitive ranking of our twelve inflectional systems according to any single criterion of complexity, we feel that it is most revealing to place multiple rankings side by side. In Figure 11.4, we present a graph of the relative morphological complexity of the twelve inflectional systems according to

Table 11.16. *Linear transformations from the ten complexity measures to the composite scale of morphological complexity in Figure 11.3*

Where x is …	the transform of x is …
an IC system's number of distillations	$100x/21$
the size of an IC system's optimal static principal-part sets	$100x/8$
the density of an IC system's actual principal-part sets among its possible optimal static principal-part sets	$(0.5 - x) \times 200$
an IC system's average number of dynamic principal parts	$(x - 1) \times 100$
an IC system's average ratio of actual to possible optimal dynamic principal-part analyses	$100 - x$
an IC system's average cell predictor number	$(x - 0.75) \times 200$
an IC system's average cell predictiveness	$(1 - x) \times 100$
an IC system's average IC predictability	$(1 - x) \times 100$
an IC system's average cell predictability	$(1 - x) \times 200$
an IC system's average 4-MPS entropy	$100x/0.48$

the ten measures that we have discussed. In order to arrive at the composite scale of the IC systems' complexity on the graph's vertical axis, we have applied a different linear transformation to each of the ten measures; each of these transformations converts the measure to a scale from 0 (low complexity) to 100 (high complexity). The specific linear transformations that we have used are listed in Table 11.16. Taken together, the results in Figure 11.4 suggest that the Tuḷu and Koasati systems of conjugation are particularly low in complexity and that Palantla and Comaltepec Chinantec, Czech, and Fur are particularly high in complexity.

11.4 Conclusions

In this research, we have defined the complexity of an IC system as the extent to which it inhibits motivated inferences about a lexeme's full realized paradigm from subsets of its cells. The findings described here support two general conclusions about this conception of an IC system's complexity. The first conclusion is that complexity is itself complex – that IC systems may be complex in more than one dimension, and that there is no logical necessity that complexity in one dimension will translate into complexity in another dimension. Because complexity is a multifaceted property, there is no single measure that "captures" an IC system's complexity; on the contrary, two IC systems may be comparable in the extent to which they inhibit motivated

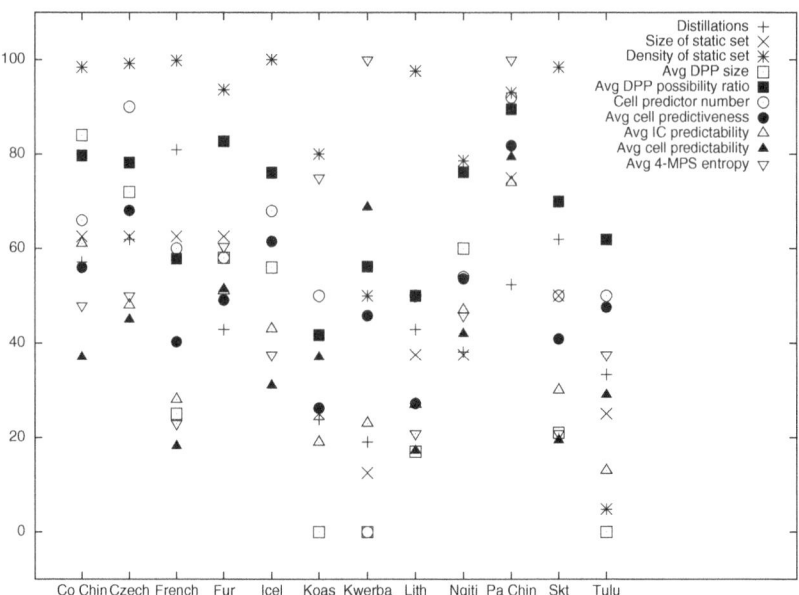

Figure 11.4. *The relative complexity of twelve IC systems according to ten measures*

inferences about lexemes' full realized paradigms, but the inhibiting causes may be very different in the two systems. We have therefore proposed ten measures, each gauging a different factor capable of contributing to an IC system's complexity.

Our second conclusion is that IC systems are not all identical in complexity: in some systems, motivated inferences about a lexeme's full realized paradigm are plentiful; in others, they are more restricted. A central concept in our investigation of this variation is the notion of principal parts. Principal parts have a long history of use in language pedagogy, but as we have shown, they have both typological and theoretical significance: they provide the basis for a range of measurements of an IC system's complexity.

Our findings raise important questions for other domains of linguistic research. Where two IC systems contrast in their complexity, is the more complex system more difficult to learn? For mature speakers, does the more complex system entail added difficulty in language production or perception? Experimental studies will be necessary to answer these questions in a definitive way; a reasonable hypothesis is that greater complexity produces greater difficulty, but only empirical psycholinguistic evidence can establish the nature and extent of such difficulty (if it exists).

Our findings also raise questions for the study of language change. How do complex IC systems arise? Are complex IC systems inherently unstable, invariably destined to evolve toward greater simplicity? A reasonable hypothesis is that complex IC systems arise as an effect of conditioned sound changes whose conditioning environments are obscured by later changes; such sound changes can cause a single IC to split into two or more distinct but similar ICs, and as we have seen, it is the similarity of a system's ICs that make it complex. Close inspection of the diachronic development of IC systems will make it possible to answer these questions.

In the domain of morphological theory, the question arises whether the length of an IC system's formal description is proportional to its complexity. Given the way we have defined an IC system's complexity, it is clear that no such correlation is logically necessary. Consider, for example, the hypothetical IC systems in Table 11.17: system A is, in our sense, more complex than system B (which is maximally transparent); nevertheless, the formal description of system B requires more stipulations than that of system A. Thus, if the complexity of real IC systems should prove to correlate with the size of their formal descriptions, that would be an unexpected and interesting finding.

In the research presented here, we have demonstrated that the traditional notion of principal parts is relevant to the typological comparison of inflectional systems. Principal-part analysis requires explicitness about a range of assumptions. In defining a lexeme L's principal parts as a set of cells in L's realized paradigm P from which one can reliably deduce the remaining cells in P (§1.1), we abandon the traditional assumption that a lexeme only has a single principal-part set (i.e. that the label 'principal parts' is reserved for a single, conventionally agreed-upon set among potentially many logical possibilities). This definition is compatible with different principal-part schemes, e.g. the static scheme (in which lexemes belonging to the same syntactic category have the same cells in their realized paradigms as principal parts) and the dynamic scheme (in which lexemes in the same category may have different cells as principal parts); it also affords the desirable possibility of comparing optimal principal-part schemes with nonoptimal schemes.

Principal parts reveal the implicative relations that bind the cells in a lexeme's realized paradigm. These implicative relations make it possible for language users to infer the IC membership of newly encountered lexemes and to deduce the full realized paradigms of both known and newly encountered lexemes. While the utility of these implicative relations for language users is apparent, there is disagreement about their theoretical status. According to one imaginable approach to the definition of a language's inflectional system, the only

Table 11.17. *Two hypothetical IC systems and their irreducible inferences and formal descriptions*

	System A					System B			
	ρ	σ	τ	υ		ρ	σ	τ	υ
I	-a	-b	-b	-b	I	-a	-b	-c	-d
II	-b	-a	-b	-b	II	-e	-f	-g	-h
III	-b	-b	-a	-b	III	-i	-j	-k	-l
IV	-b	-b	-b	-a	IV	-m	-n	-o	-p

Irreducible inferences of system A
In the realized paradigm of a lexeme L belonging to IC J, only the following sets of cells determine L's membership in J:
(a) each set containing the -a cell;
(b) the set containing all non-a cells.

Irreducible inferences of system B
In the realized paradigm of a lexeme L belonging to IC J, each nonempty set of cells determines L's membership in J.

Formal description of system A
Where X is L's stem,
Class I: L, ρ → **X-a**
Class II: L, σ → **X-a**
Class III: L, τ → **X-a**
Class IV: L, υ → **X-a**
Default for all classes: L, {} → **X-b**

Formal description of system B
Class I:
L, ρ → **X-a**
L, σ → **X-b**
L, τ → **X-c**
L, υ → **X-d**
Class III:
L, ρ → **X-i**
L, σ → **X-j**
L, τ → **X-k**
L, υ → **X-l**

Class II:
L, ρ → **X-e**
L, σ → **X-f**
L, τ → **X-g**
L, υ → **X-h**
Class IV:
L, ρ → **X-m**
L, σ → **X-n**
L, τ → **X-o**
L, υ → **X-p**

inflectional rules are rules expressing implicative relations among realized cells. This is an extreme view, whose compatibility with generalizations about stems, affixes, and morphophonological patterns is not clear. We have argued for a theory of inflection in which the cells in a lexeme's realized paradigm are defined by means of two sorts of realization rules: rules of stem realization (including rules of stem formation and stem selection) and rules of word-realization (including rules of inflectional exponence and rules of referral). In a theory of this sort, the implicative relations binding a realized paradigm's cells are derivable as theorems. This theory affords a more fine-grained approach to the implicative relations embodied by a language's inflectional paradigms:

besides accounting for implicative relations among cells in realized paradigms, it also accounts for implicative relations among realization rules – relations that are not always directly expressible as relations among realized cells; indeed, our theory raises the possibility that all of a realized paradigm's implicative relations are reducible to relations among realization rules.

The conviction underlying this research is that the structure of a language's inflectional paradigms and the differentiation of its ICs are important loci of systematic cross-linguistic variation. Our hope is that the methods applied here – in particular, the precise analysis of IC systems represented as plats – will facilitate further study in this domain of morphological typology. With that hope in mind, we conclude with discussions of the techniques of plat construction (Chapter 12) and of the PPA, the computational tool that we have developed for this research (Chapter 13) and which we gladly make available for anyone to use.

12 Sensitivity to plat presentation

Every principal-part analysis is based on a set of data encoding the inflectional properties of each member of a set of inflection classes. This information, which we represent in a plat, is subject to various manipulations that aim to simplify the presentation without losing data. However, these manipulations often influence the resulting analysis.[1]

In this chapter, we present examples that elucidate this problem. We show examples of manipulations based on introducing rules of sandhi, separating stem segments, introducing morphophonemes, representing phonetic instead of spelled surface forms, distinguishing multiple stem contexts, including syntactic information, and omitting problematic inflection classes. These manipulations tend to reduce the number of distinct inflection classes and the number of distillations. In doing so, they also affect all our measures of complexity: principal-part analyses, predictability/predictiveness measures, and entropy-based measures. Several of the manipulations raise questions of linguistic and psycholinguistic motivation, which must be resolved on a case-by-case basis.

12.1   Common features of each inflection class

We start by analyzing a plat of Finnish i-stem and e-stem nouns, which we discussed in Chapter 10. The plat of data, given by Ackerman *et al.* (2009), is in Table 12.1. This is a plat in its most concrete possible form. It is different from

---

[1] The data sets that we have employed in this chapter are:

sensitivity.10	sensitivity.english-morph	sensitivity.finnish.3
sensitivity.12	sensitivity.english-surface	sensitivity.finnish.4
sensitivity.13	sensitivity.finnish	sensitivity.finnish.5
sensitivity.13-stems	sensitivity.finnish.1	sensitivity.finnish.6
sensitivity.czech	sensitivity.finnish.2	sensitivity.sanskrit

These are available at the *Morphological Typology* website www.cambridge.org/stump_finkel.

Table 12.1. *Finnish* i-*stem and* e-*stem nouns*

Declension	nomSg	genSg	partSg	partPl	inessPl
OVI 'door'	*ovi*	*oven*	*ovea*	*ovia*	*ovissa*
KIELI 'language'	*kieli*	*kielen*	*kieltä*	*kieliä*	*kielissä*
VESI 'water'	*vesi*	*veden*	*vettä*	*vesiä*	*vesissä*
LASI 'glass'	*lasi*	*lasin*	*lasia*	*laseja*	*laseissa*
NALLE 'teddy bear'	*nalle*	*nallen*	*nallea*	*nalleja*	*nalleissa*
KIRJE 'letter'	*kirje*	*kirjeen*	*kirjettä*	*kirjeitä*	*kirjeissä*

Table 12.2. *Finnish* i-*stem and* e-*stem nouns, themes removed*

Declension	Theme	nomSg	genSg	partSg	partPl	inessPl
OVI 'door'	*ov*	*i*	*en*	*ea*	*ia*	*issa*
KIELI 'language'	*kiel*	*i*	*en*	*tä*	*iä*	*issä*
VESI 'water'	*ve*	*si*	*den*	*ttä*	*siä*	*sissä*
LASI 'glass'	*las*	*i*	*in*	*ia*	*eja*	*eissa*
NALLE 'teddy bear'	*nalle*	Ø	*n*	*a*	*ja*	*issa*
KIRJE 'letter'	*kirje*	Ø	*en*	*ttä*	*itä*	*issä*
Static principal parts				partPl		
Average inflection-class predictability				0.900 (see Table 12.3)		
Paradigm entropy				52 (see Table 12.4)		

the plats that we have used in earlier chapters: in the column headed by a given MPS σ, it lists entire word forms expressing σ rather than just the exponence of σ in each of the relevant inflection classes.

When we analyze this plat, we find that all the MPSs belong to the same distillation, because every entry in the plat is different. Our convention is to use one of the MPSs in a distillation as its exemplar. Whichever exemplar we choose, it corresponds to a lexeme's sole principal part. In other words, since every surface form appears exactly once in the table, we can uniquely determine the declension of a Finnish noun (if it is one of these six!) by any of its forms.

To make the plat less trivial, we abstract out all of the features shared by forms in the same row. In particular, we notice that every surface form within a declension contains the same initial string, its theme (§2.1.2). When we abstract out the themes, we get the plat shown in Table 12.2, which also lists the themes.

346 *Sensitivity to plat presentation*

Table 12.3. *Cell and inflection-class predictability, Finnish nouns, themes removed*

Declension	nomSg	genSg	partSg	partPl	inessPl	IC predictability
OVI 'door'	0.812	0.812	0.688	0.688	0.750	0.867
KIELI 'language'	0.750	0.875	0.625	0.625	0.750	0.833
VESI 'water'	0.875	0.875	0.938	0.875	0.875	0.967
LASI 'glass'	0.938	0.875	0.875	0.875	0.875	0.967
NALLE 'teddy bear'	0.875	0.812	0.812	0.812	0.875	0.933
KIRJE 'letter'	0.688	0.812	0.688	0.625	0.750	0.833
Avg	0.823	0.844	0.771	0.750	0.812	0.900

Table 12.4. *Entropy values (× 100) for Finnish nouns, themes removed*

	nomSg	genSg	partSg	partPl	inessPl	Avg
MPS entropy	146	179	225	258	192	200
Conditional entropy of MPS (col) given MPS (row)						
nomSg	–	79	113	113	113	104
genSg	46	–	79	79	46	63
partSg	33	33	–	33	33	33
partPl	0	0	0	–	0	0
inessPl	67	33	67	67	–	58
Avg	36	36	64	73	48	52

Now we start to see differences among the MPSs, whose patterns of exponence are no longer isomorphic; every MPS is therefore in a separate distillation. The partitive plural MPS, though, has unique values for each declension, so in an optimal analysis, it is the sole static principal part.

We can analyze this plat for cell and inflection-class predictability, as we show in Table 12.3. Some declensions, such as 'water' and 'glass', are more predictable than others, like 'letter'. The partitive singular MPS is the least predictable MPS. A single value summarizes the inflection-class predictability, 0.900, which is the average of the per-inflection class predictabilities. On average, ninety percent of the candidate principal-part analyses for the plat in Table 12.2 are viable.

Similarly, we can construct a conditional-entropy chart, much as we did in Chapter 10, and as we show in Table 12.4. As we expect, the partitive plural is

Table 12.5. *Finnish i-stem and e-stem nouns, themes removed, with templates*

Declension	Theme	nomSg	genSg	partSg	partPl	inessPl
Template		TC	TCn	TC	TC	TC
OVI 'door'	ov	i	e	ea	ia	issa
KIELI 'language'	kiel	i	e	tä	iä	issä
VESI 'water'	ve	si	de	ttä	siä	sissä
LASI 'glass'	las	i	i	ia	eja	eissa
NALLE 'teddy bear'	nalle	Ø	Ø	a	ja	issa
KIRJE 'letter'	kirje	Ø	e	ttä	itä	issä

highly predictive (as shown in its row) and most unpredictable (as shown in its column). The easiest single-number summary of the entropy (which Ackerman *et al.* (2009) call the "paradigm entropy") is the overall average number, in this case, 52 (representing an entropy of 0.52).

In Table 12.2, we have abstracted common features on a per-declension basis. We can also abstract common features on a per-MPS basis. In particular, the genitive singular forms always end with -*n*. Table 12.5 shows the plat with this common feature abstracted out. This simplification never changes the number of distillations, because the resulting MPS values are isomorphic to the original ones. However, it can reduce the number of distinct exponences; we now see that the exponence *i* appears both in the nominative singular and the genitive singular. In some cases, it can even make two or more MPSs identical in exponence. For example, the Latin singular imperfect active endings (-*m*, -*s*, -*t*) are invariant across conjugations and can therefore be abstracted away in a plat of Latin conjugations; what is left is a plat in which the exponence of the 1sg imperfect active is, within each conjugation, identical to that of the 2nd and 3rd persons of the imperfect active.

Table 12.5 includes a "template" row, which is an abbreviatory device. In the template, "T" stands for "theme" and "C" stands for "contents of the cell." Thus, the notation "TCn" in the genitive singular column says that the surface form is constructed by concatenating the theme (for instance, *kiel*), the contents of the cell (for instance, *e*), and the suffix *n* (producing *kielen*). Introducing a template does not change the results of any analysis, because it replaces one set of exponences with an isomorphic set. However, we often find that it abstracts out commonalities and lets us focus on differences.

12.2 Rules of sandhi

When we inspect the plat of Table 12.5, we see that the 'water' declension is unique in that it includes a consonant *s* in forms like the nominative singular, where the other declensions have only a vowel. We would like to move this *s* into the theme to make the plat more regular. We cannot simply abstract the *s* as part of the theme, though, because in the genitive singular and partitive singular, the consonant becomes *d* and *t*, respectively.

Instead, we introduce some rules of sandhi to make the plat more regular. Introducing sandhi is not always appropriate; it must be phonetically reasonable, and evaluating reasonability is often quite difficult.

Why do we want to make the plat more regular? After all, it is the irregularities across inflection classes that make them distinguishable. If our manipulations reduce the number of distinct inflection classes, that is a good thing; we then have fewer inflection classes to distinguish, so paradigms become easier to predict. But if the manipulations make inflection classes more alike without conflating them, that is a bad thing, since it makes inflection classes harder to distinguish.

The choice of plat depends on the representation issue, introduced in Chapter 2. If we want a hearer-oriented plat, then it does not make sense to introduce sandhi processes, since it may sometimes be that the very presence of a particular distinction most obviously distinguishes one inflection class from another. On the other hand, if we want a speaker-oriented plat, then it does make sense to apply sandhi processes, since, for example, the three phonemically distinct suffixes in the English verb forms /bʌdʒ-əz/, /kʌt-s/, and /lid-z/ presumably share a common underlying representation.

Whether or not we are justified in this case, for the sake of example we will say that the theme of 'water' is *ves* instead of *ve*,[2] but we will correct the exponences of the genitive singular and partitive singular by rules of sandhi:

$$s\ d \rightarrow d$$
$$s\ t \rightarrow t\ t$$

In practice, such rules need to be verified. For example, there may be other Finnish nouns whose stem ends in -*s* that behave similarly in this declension.

These rules of sandhi give us the plat of Table 12.6. This plat is simpler; it has more common elements (it now contains eighteen distinct exponences instead

---

[2] In so doing, we are stretching our definition of "theme."

Table 12.6. *Finnish* i-*stem and* e-*stem nouns, themes removed, sandhi rules*

Declension	Theme	nomSg	genSg	partSg	partPl	inessPl		
Template		TC	TCn	TC	TC	TC		
OVI 'door'	ov	i	e	ea	ia	issa	Sandhi rules	
KIELI 'language'	kiel	i	e	tä	iä	issä	old →	new
VESI 'water'	ves	i	de	tä	iä	issä	s d	d
LASI 'glass'	las	i	i	ia	eja	eissa	s t	tt
NALLE 'teddy bear'	nalle	∅	∅	a	ja	issa		
KIRJE 'letter'	kirje	∅	e	ttä	itä	issä		
	Static principal parts					genSg, partSg		
	Average inflection-class predictability					0.689		
	Paradigm entropy					70		

of twenty one). When we analyze this plat, we find that there are only four distillations; the partitive singular and plural now have identical patterns. Analysis reveals two static principal parts: genitive singular and partitive singular. So introducing rules of sandhi simplifies the plat in one direction (fewer exponences), but it increases complexity in another (more principal parts). In addition, the paradigm entropy has increased from 52 to 70, largely because we now ignore the partitive singular, so the cross-effect between the two partitive MPSs, which contributed before to a low entropy, has disappeared. The 'water' and 'language' declensions have become more similar, and as expected, greater similarity among inflection classes correlates with a lower average inflection-class predictability. The average inflection-class predictability falls from 0.900 (Table 12.2) to 0.689 (Table 12.6) if we introduce these sandhi rules in the Finnish plat.

We have also lost some implicative power, because rules of sandhi are not always reversible. For example, when we see the surface form *vettä*, even if we know the word is in the partitive singular and in the 'water' declension, we cannot predict its nominative singular: is it *vesi* or *⁺veti*?

Again, there's a large issue at stake here: If plats represent the phonological information that is directly perceptible to language users as a distinction between inflection classes, then the effects of sandhi should remain embedded as part of the exponences in the plat and not added as a corrective step. Each principal-part analysis must wrestle with this question.

350 *Sensitivity to plat presentation*

Table 12.7. *Finnish* i-*stem and* e-*stem nouns, two stems, sandhi rules*

Declension Template	Stem 1	Stem 2	nomSg S_1 C	genSg S_1 Cn	partSg S_1 CS_2	partPl S_1 CS_2	inessPl S_1 $CissS_2$
OVI 'door'	ov	a	i	e	e	i	∅
KIELI 'language'	kiel	ä	i	e	t	i	∅
VESI 'water'	ves	ä	i	de	t	i	∅
LASI 'glass'	las	a	i	i	i	ej	e
NALLE 'teddy bear'	nalle	a	∅	∅	∅	j	∅
KIRJE 'letter'	kirje	ä	∅	e	tt	it	∅

	Sandhi rules old → new
	s d d
	s t tt

Static principal parts	genSg, partSg
Average inflection-class predictability	0.656
Paradigm entropy	59

12.3 Multiple stem segments

We now notice that in some declensions, the final vowel in the partitive and inessive plural is *a*, but in others, it is *ä*. We can remove this distinction in the plat by stipulating that each lexeme has two stem segments, the one formed from the theme and the other being the final vowel, giving us the plat shown in Table 12.7. The templates now distinguish stems S_1 and S_2. Analysis reveals that there are still two static principal parts (genitive singular, partitive singular); the paradigm entropy has gone down to 59. The inessive plural has also benefited from a more descriptive template.

To be honest, most linguists familiar with Finnish would be very skeptical of this approach. We are using multiple stem segments to capture a simple phonological rule that we could better capture with a rule of sandhi: "If the stem contains one or more of the vowels *u, o, a*, the ending also has to have a back vowel (*u, o, a*). If the stem has no back vowels, the ending has to have a front vowel" (Karlsson 1999: 16). Although multiple stem segments are an unreasonable analysis of Finnish, they are essential in analyzing Semitic languages like Hebrew (verbs generally have three consonantal stems), and we have also found them useful in analyzing Icelandic (Chapter 8).

12.4 Morphophonemes

Now the extra 'e' in the partitive and inessive plural for 'glass' stands out. We might theorize that the underlying construction for inessive plural is always $S_1 iss S_2$, and that the apparent $S_1 eiss S_2$ is the result of some other process. In order to represent that theory, we take a potentially controversial step and introduce a morphophoneme.

Morphophonemes have many uses. For instance, in Czech, we use the morphophoneme *E* (we usually use capital letters) to represent a fleeting *e* that is preserved before word-final *l* and word-final *n* (changing the latter to *ň*), but elided elsewhere, for instance in PÍSEŇ 'song', whose forms include *písně* (genitive singular) and *píseň* (accusative singular). In Irish, we use a morphophoneme to represent eclipsis on the following consonant, changing, for instance, *d* to *nd* (pronounced [n]). Other morphophonemes represent lenition and other consonant mutations. In Dakota, we use a morphophoneme that becomes *e* at the end of a word, but is realized as *a* elsewhere. In Icelandic (Chapter 8), we use a morphophoneme to indicate consonant doubling, which occurs in some (but not all) forms of the S5irr and S6irr conjugations. For instance, the verb SVIMMA 'swim' has *svámum* in the 1st plural past indicative, but *svimmum* in the 1st plural imperative.

In our case, we introduce the morphophoneme *I* that by default becomes *i*, but which absorbs a preceding *e* to become simply *i*. We make the first stem of 'glass' *lase* and introduce additional rules of sandhi.

This particular morphophoneme may be a source of skepticism. The underlying distinction between |I| and |i| is absolutely neutralized in this approach: both surface as /i/. One might question the validity of absolute neutralizations in modeling a language's phonology on the grounds that they are not learnable: language learners faced with nothing but /i/ cannot be expected to learn that some instances are |i| and others |I|. As before in our discussion of sandhi, we leave that question open; we are not proposing an analysis of Finnish, but rather displaying the possible manipulations that one may apply to plats in general.

The new plat is shown in Table 12.8. In some ways it is less satisfying than Table 12.7, because the morphophoneme *I* occurs in so many places, but it does unify the inessive plural, whose MPS entropy has become 0; it is completely predictable and completely unpredictive. In fact, its template describes it entirely; the exponences are all Ø. Whether this is a change for the better or worse depends, as always, on our purpose in presenting a plat. Analysis reveals that the static principal parts for the plat remain the genitive singular and the

352 *Sensitivity to plat presentation*

Table 12.8. *Finnish* i-*stem and* e-*stem nouns, two stems, sandhi rules, morphophoneme*

Declension Template	Stem 1	Stem 2	nomSg S_1 C	genSg S_1 Cn	partSg S_1 CS_2	partPl S_1 CS_2	inessPl S_1 $issS_2$
OVI 'door'	ov	a	I	e	e	I	Ø
KIELI 'language'	kiel	ä	I	e	t	I	Ø
VESI 'water'	ves	ä	I	de	t	I	Ø
LASI 'glass'	lase	a	I	I	I	j	Ø
NALLE 'teddy bear'	nalle	a	Ø	Ø	Ø	j	Ø
KIRJE 'letter'	kirje	ä	Ø	e	tt	it	Ø

	Sandhi rules old → new	
	e l	i
	I	i
	s d	d
	s t	t t

Static principal parts	genSg, partSg
Average inflection-class predictability	0.622
Paradigm entropy	70

partitive singular, but the paradigm entropy has climbed back to 70, mostly because the inessive plural is no longer predictive.

12.5 More rules of sandhi

Now we notice that the declensions 'language' and 'water' are almost the same. We would like to unify them. The only point of difference is in the genitive singular, where 'water' has an extra *d*. We will put the *d* on the first stem for the lexeme, giving us VESD 'water', and correct the exponences with new rules of sandhi. The new plat is in Table 12.9, which now has three sandhi rules to account for stems ending in -*sd*.

Now there are only four declensions, and there is only one principal part: the partitive singular. The paradigm entropy has dropped to 65, mostly because there are fewer declensions.

We have reduced this plat as far as seems reasonable, and very likely too far. Choosing what simplifications we make to the plat is a sensitive business. It affects

Table 12.9. *Finnish* i-*stem and* e-*stem nouns, two stems, more sandhi rules, morphophoneme*

Declension Template	Stem 1	Stem 2	nomSg S_1 C	genSg S_1 Cn	partSg S_1 CS$_2$	partPl S_1 CS$_2$	inessPl S_1 issS$_2$
OVI 'door'	ov	a	I	e	e	I	Ø
KIELI 'language'	kiel	ä	I	e	t	I	Ø
VESI 'water'	vesd	ä	I	e	t	I	Ø
LASI 'glass'	lase	a	I	I	I	j	Ø
NALLE 'teddy bear'	nalle	a	Ø	Ø	Ø	j	Ø
KIRJE 'letter'	kirje	ä	Ø	e	tt	it	Ø

	Sandhi rules	
	old →	new
	e I	i
	I	i
	sd t	t t
	sd e	d e
	sd i	s i

Static principal parts	partSg
Average inflection-class predictability	0.710
Paradigm entropy	65

both our aesthetic sense (is the plat simple and elegant?) and the analysis that we then perform on the plat (principal parts, predictability, entropy). It also touches on the psycholinguistic dimension, insofar as plats represent the raw phonological data on which language users may base inferences about inflection-class membership.

In short, there is no single correct plat for any language, and what plat we choose depends on what we want the plat to represent, as discussed in Chapter 2. Honesty and reproducibility demand that we accompany any analysis with the plat on which it is based, and we need to justify our choice of rules of sandhi and the morphophonemes we introduce.

12.6 Morphophonological rules

Related to morphophonemes are morphophonological rules, which can be invoked by features in the plat that condition the realization of nearby elements through sandhi-like rules. For instance, in Pāli, we use a rule feature to indicate

354 *Sensitivity to plat presentation*

Table 12.10. *Fragment of a plat of English verbs in phonemic transcription*

IC	Lexeme	Stem	Theme	inf	3sg pres ind	past	pres ptcp	past ptcp
1	BUDGE	bʌdʒ	bʌdʒ	∅	əz	d	ɪŋ	d
2	LAST	læst	læst	∅	s	əd	ɪŋ	əd
3	PASS	pæs	pæs	∅	əz	t	ɪŋ	t
4	LOAD	loʊd	loʊd	∅	z	əd	ɪŋ	əd
5	PAY	peɪ	peɪ	∅	z	d	jɪŋ	d
6	SHOP	ʃɑp	ʃɑp	∅	s	t	ɪŋ	t
7	BUY	baɪ	b	aɪ	aɪz	ɔt	aɪjɪŋ	ɔt
8	FIGHT	faɪt	f	aɪt	aɪts	ɔt	aɪtɪŋ	ɔt
9	SEEK	sik	s	ik	iks	ɔt	ikɪŋ	ɔt
10	TEACH	tiʧ	t	iʧ	iʧəz	ɔt	iʧɪŋ	ɔt
11	MAKE	meɪk	meɪ	k	ks	d	kɪŋ	d
12	SEND	sɛnd	sɛn	d	dz	t	dɪŋ	t
13	SAY	seɪ	s	eɪ	ɛz	ɛd	eɪjɪŋ	ɛd
14	DO	du	d	u	ʌz	ɪd	uɪŋ	ʌn
15	CAST	kæst	kæst	∅	s	∅	ɪŋ	∅

gunation (strengthening) of the previous vowel, changing *i* and *ī* to *e* and *u* and *ū* to *o*, but leaving other vowels intact.

We turn to a detailed example of the English verbs BUDGE, LAST, PASS, LOAD, PAY, SHOP, BUY, FIGHT, SEEK, TEACH, MAKE, SEND, SAY, DO, and CAST. As we construct a plat, we might adopt a "surface-like" approach that adheres strictly to a theme-plus-distinguisher analysis of word forms in phonemic representation. In this approach, the fifteen verbs represent fifteen different inflection classes, as in Table 12.10, whose five MPSs fall into four distillations (past participle and past are in the same distillation).

We can reduce both the number of distinct inflection classes and the number of distillations in this plat by (i) equating a verb's theme with its stem, (ii) representing stems, themes, and affixal exponents as morphophonological expressions subject to several sandhi rules, and (iii) allowing the exponences in the plat to include morphophonological operations. Then we arrive at the more abstract plat in Table 12.11, in which there are only seven distinct inflection classes and only three distillations.

As a consequence of these differences in their construction, the plats in Tables 12.10 and 12.11 differ in their implicative relations. For example, the plat in Table 12.10 exhibits this implicative relation:

$$\langle /Xs/, \text{3sg pres ind}\rangle \mathbin{\&} \langle /Xd/, \text{past}\rangle \longrightarrow \langle /Yt/, \text{inf}\rangle$$

Table 12.11. *Fragment of a plat of English verbs in morphophonological representation*

IC	Lexeme	Stem and theme	inf	3sg pres ind	past	pres ptcp	past ptcp
1	BUDGE	bʌdʒ	Ø	z	d	ɪŋ	d
1	LAST	læst	Ø	z	d	ɪŋ	d
1	PASS	pæs	Ø	z	d	ɪŋ	d
1	LOAD	loʊd	Ø	z	d	ɪŋ	d
1	PAY	peɪ	Ø	z	d	ɪŋ	d
1	SHOP	ʃɑp	Ø	z	d	ɪŋ	d
2	BUY	baɪ	Ø	z	O	ɪŋ	O
2	FIGHT	faɪt	Ø	z	O	ɪŋ	O
2	SEEK	sik	Ø	z	O	ɪŋ	O
2	TEACH	tiʧ	Ø	z	O	ɪŋ	O
3	MAKE	meɪk	Ø	z	D	ɪŋ	D
4	SEND	sɛnd	Ø	z	T	ɪŋ	T
5	SAY	seɪ	Ø	Ez	Ed	ɪŋ	Ed
6	DO	du	Ø	Uz	Id	ɪŋ	Un
7	CAST	kæst	Ø	z	Ø	ɪŋ	Ø

Morphophonological rules

rule feature	meaning
O	Rime → ɔt
D	Final Consonant → d
T	Final Consonant → t
E	eɪ → ɛ
U	u → ʌ
I	u → ɪ

Sandhi rules (# is a word boundary)

old	→	new
[sibilant]z#		[sibilant]əz#
[voiceless]z#		[voiceless]s#
[oral alveolar stop]d#		[oral alveolar stop]əd#
[voiceless]d#		[voiceless]t#
[σ … ɪ] [σ ɪ …]		[σ … ɪ] [σ j ɪ …] where [σ X] is a syllable

Because this relation is restricted to particular phonological realizations of the affixes morphophonologically represented as |-z| and |-d|, this relation is obscured in Table 12.11. On the other hand, the plat in Table 12.11 exhibits this implicative relation:

$\langle |X|, \text{inf} \rangle \,\&\, \langle\, |Xd|, \text{past} \rangle \longrightarrow \langle |Xz|, \text{3sg pres ind} \rangle$

Because this latter relation pertains to morphophonological representations whose phonemic realizations are varied, it is obscured in Table 12.10.

As we have seen before in this chapter and in Chapter 2, our choice of plats reflects our understanding of what they represent. The exponences in the phonemic plat are a closer approximation to what language users hear. Thus, one might hypothesize that the implicative relations that the phonemic plat embodies are closer to the ones that language users employ in matching forms of newly encountered lexemes with the inflectional patterns of known lexemes. For example, the past-tense forms /kæst/ and /pæst/ are alike according to the phonemic plat, so they might be expected to complicate the learning of the distinct conjugations of CAST and PASS.

On the other hand, one might plausibly assume that the representations in the morphophonological plat more closely approximate mental representations. This plat has fewer inflection classes and fewer distillations precisely because its interpretation depends upon independent morphophonological principles and upon the lexicon: whereas the exponence /-z/ in Table 12.10 is in effect an audible string, the exponence |-z| in Table 12.11 is a generalization over three distinct strings, whose identity and distribution are determined by language-specific rules of sandhi. Moreover, the interpretation of exponences such as "Rime" in Table 12.11 depends on lexical knowledge: it is BUY's stem |baɪ| that allows its past-tense form |bɔt| to be deduced in accordance with the second plat. In this plat, the (pre-sandhi) past-tense forms |kæst| and |pæs-d| are not alike, representing a speaker's awareness that they differ in morphology despite their superficial similarity. Thus, the choice between the plats depends on whether one wishes to model inflection-class distinctions that are perceptually salient to the hearer or those that are grammatically significant to the speaker.

12.7 Surface-form representation

Our analysis of French verbs in Chapter 7 elucidates other problems that arise when we deal with a plat. The first problem involves our choice of surface form. For Finnish, we have chosen the written form. Finnish is spelled phonetically to a very large extent. However, French spelling has developed over centuries and maintains distinctions that are no longer pronounced.

To judge from the discussion in our *Larousse* dictionary (*Petit Larousse illustré*, 1974), French has approximately 149 conjugations (more or less,

Table 12.12. *Fragment of a plat of French verbs*

Lexeme	Inf	Pres 2sg	1pl pres	3pl pres	1sg impf	1sg simple past
ABSOUDRE 'exonerate'	*absoudre*	*absous*	*absolvons*	*absolvent*	*absolvais*	*absolus*
ACCROÎTRE 'increase'	*accroître*	*accrois*	*accroissons*	*accroissent*	*accroissais*	*accrus*
ACHETER 'buy'	*acheter*	*achètes*	*achetons*	*achètent*	*achetais*	*achetai*
ACQUÉRIR 'get'	*acquérir*	*acquiers*	*acquérons*	*acquièrent*	*acquérais*	*acquis*
ACQUIESCER 'agree'	*acquiescer*	*acquiesces*	*acquiesçons*	*acquiescent*	*acquiesçais*	*acquiesçai*
ALLÉGER 'lighten'	*alléger*	*alléges*	*allégeons*	*allégent*	*allégeais*	*allégeai*
ALLER 'go'	*aller*	*vas*	*allons*	*vont*	*allais*	*allai*
APERCEVOIR 'glimpse'	*apercevoir*	*aperçois*	*apercevons*	*aperçoivent*	*apercevais*	*aperçus*
APPELER 'call'	*appeler*	*appèlles*	*appelons*	*appèllent*	*appelais*	*appelai*
APPRENDRE 'learn'	*apprendre*	*apprends*	*apprenons*	*apprennent*	*apprenais*	*appris*
ARGUER 'deduce'	*arguer*	*argues*	*arguons*	*arguent*	*arguais*	*arguai*
ARRÊTER 'stop'	*arrêter*	*arrêtes*	*arrêtons*	*arrêtent*	*arrêtais*	*arrêtai*
ASSEOIR 'sit'	*asseoir*	*assois*	*assoyons*	*assoyent*	*assoyais*	*assis*
ASTREINDRE 'compel'	*astreindre*	*astreins*	*astreignons*	*astreignent*	*astreignais*	*astreignis*
AVOIR 'have'	*avoir*	*as*	*avons*	*ont*	*avais*	*eus*

depending on how defective verbs are reckoned). Table 12.12 shows some of the many forms for a few of these conjugations.

The rules of French spelling present numerous difficulties. For example, the consonant *c* followed by *e* or *i* is pronounced /s/, as is its variant *ç* before *o*, *a*, or *u*. The theme of the verb APERCEVOIR 'glimpse' is therefore *aperc*, although the spelling might change in some instances to *aperç*. We could represent this spelling peculiarity by a rule of sandhi. When we follow this path, we need

358 *Sensitivity to plat presentation*

approximately thirty rules of sandhi and four "morphographemes" just for spelling. For example, the morphographeme Q usually becomes *qu*, but it becomes *que* at the end of a word or before a consonant. The morphographeme Y becomes *i* at the end of a word, before a consonant, or before *en, nt* or *s*, but otherwise becomes *y*. Regularizing spelling in this way, we can simplify the plat of French verbs by reducing both the number of distinct conjugations (from 149 to 85) and the number of MPSs (27 distillations from 48 MPSs). But if we analyze this simplified plat, we arrive at twelve static principal parts – an implausibly large number.

We therefore prefer to represent French verbs entirely in phonemic representation, giving us the fragment shown in Table 12.13. Now it is clear that the theme of 'glimpse' is /apɛʁs/; the spelling peculiarity distinguishing *c* and *ç* has disappeared. In addition, the historical suffix *-s* on the 2nd singular present forms, which is no longer pronounced, has disappeared, as has the *-r* on some,

Table 12.13. *Fragment of a plat of French verbs in phonemic transcription*

Gloss	inf	2sg pres	1pl pres	3pl pres	1sg impf	1sg simple past
ABSOUDRE 'exonerate'	absudʁ	absu	absɔlvɔ̃	absɔlv	absɔlvɛ	absɔly
ACCROÎTRE 'increase'	akʁwatʁ	akʁwa	akʁwasɔ̃	akʁwas	akʁwasɛ	akʁy
ACHETER 'buy'	aʃəte	aʃɛt	aʃətɔ̃	aʃɛt	aʃəte	aʃəte
ACQUÉRIR 'get'	akeʁiʁ	akje	akeʁɔ̃	akjeʁ	akeʁɛ	aki
ACQUIESCER 'agree'	akjɛse	akjɛs	akjɛsɔ̃	akjɛs	akjɛse	akjɛse
ALLÉGER 'lighten'	aleʒe	aleʒ	aleʒɔ̃	aleʒ	aleʒɛ	aleʒɛ
ALLER 'go'	ale	va	alɔ̃	vɔ̃	alɛ	alɛ
APERCEVOIR 'glimpse'	apɛʁsəvwaʁ	apɛʁswa	apɛʁsəvɔ̃	apɛʁswav	apɛʁsəvɛ	apɛʁsy
APPELER 'call'	apəle	apɛl	apɛlɔ̃	apɛl	apɛlɛ	apɛlɛ
APPRENDRE 'learn'	apʁɑ̃dʁ	apʁɑ̃	apʁɛnɔ̃	apʁɛn	apʁɛnɛ	apʁi
ARGUER 'deduce'	aʁgɥe	aʁgy	aʁgɥɔ̃	aʁgy	aʁgɥɛ	aʁgɥɛ
ARRÊTER 'stop'	aʁɛte	aʁɛt	aʁɛtɔ̃	aʁɛt	aʁɛtɛ	aʁɛtɛ
ASSEOIR 'sit'	aswaʁ	aswa	aswajɔ̃	aswa	aswajɛ	asi
ASTREINDRE 'compel'	astʁɛ̃dʁ	astʁɛ̃	astʁɛɲɔ̃	astʁɛɲ	astʁɛɲɛ	astʁɛɲi
AVOIR 'have'	avwɑʁ	a	avɔ̃	ɔ̃	ave	ø

but not all, infinitive forms. The result is that the phonemic plat is a more accurate synchronic account of French. The complete plat has only 64 conjugations and 19 distillations; there are five static principal parts, which seems much more reasonable than twelve. When we reduce the fragment in Table 12.13 by abstracting out themes, we only have twelve inflection classes, because 'agree', 'lighten', 'call', and 'stop' have identical paradigms. In contrast, the spelled forms of 'lighten' and 'call' are hard to unite because of occasional doubling of the *l* in *appeler*.

12.8 Multiple stems

The plat of French verbs in Table 12.13 shows that verb stems vary across MPSs. The theme for 'exonerate' is /abs/, the only prefix common to all the MPSs shown. However, two of the MPSs agree on /absu/, and three agree on /absɔlv/. It does not seem reasonable to claim that the exponence in this conjugation for the 3rd plural present, for example, is /-ɔlv/. Every conjugation would disagree in this MPS, which would then become a sole static principal part; the principal-part analysis would be as uninformative as the one for our first Finnish plat in Table 12.1.

Instead of dealing with themes, which are invariant across an entire paradigm, we recast our plat to use stems. At best, a single stem applies across all MPSs (in which case we would call it a theme). But French does not seem to follow that pattern. At worst, every MPS requires a different stem. Luckily, French is not that extreme. For example, Table 12.13 lets us always use the same stem for 1st plural and 1st singular present imperfect. We therefore suggest using a set of indexed stems. An **indexed stem** is a stem whose distribution is determined by its association with a morphological index that has no necessary correspondence to the stem's form or to the MPS(s) that it is used to express. For simplicity, we use the numbers 1–15 as indices. A single indexed stem may be used in expressing a range of MPSs; the MPSs in this range needn't constitute a morphosyntactically coherent class. In all conjugations, the same indexed stem is used to express the same MPS(s). In a given inflection class, one indexed stem may be syncretic with another, but these patterns of syncretism vary across inflection classes.

It turns out that for French verbs, fifteen stems cover the forty-eight MPSs, except for very irregular verbs (ÊTRE 'be', FAIRE 'make'). We list the fifteen stems with a few examples in Table 12.14. Some stems (like 10: infinitive) apply to only a single MPS; others (like 7: future, conditional) apply to many (in this case, twelve MPSs).

Table 12.14. *Stems for three French verbs*

#	Stem	ALLER 'go'	ACHETER 'buy'	APPELER 'call'
1	1sg pres ind	vɛ	aʃɛt	apɛl
2	2/3sg pres ind	va	aʃɛt	apɛl
3	1/2pl pres ind, impf ind	al	aʃət	apɛl
4	3pl pres ind	vɔ̃	aʃɛt	apɛl
5	1/2pl pres sbjv	al	aʃɛt	apɛl
6	past	ala	aʃəta	apɛla
7	fut, cond	i	aʃɛt	apɛl
8	pres sbjv	aj	aʃət	apɛl
9	impf sbjv	al	aʃəta	apɛla
10	inf	al	aʃət	apɛl
11	sg impv	va	aʃɛt	apɛl
12	1pl impv	al	aʃɛt	apɛl
13	2pl impv	al	aʃɛt	apɛl
14	pres ptcp	al	aʃɛt	apɛl
15	past ptcp	ale	aʃəte	apɛle

Introducing MPS-specific stems allows us to reduce the forty-eight MPSs to only four distillations: infinitive, 1st singular present indicative, 2nd singular present indicative, and 2nd plural present indicative. There are only two static principal parts: infinitive and 2 plural present indicative. The eighty-eight apparently distinct conjugations implied by the *Larousse* dictionary (1974) have reduced to six conjugations: ABSOUDRE 'exonerate', ACHETER 'buy', ACQUÉRIR 'get', APERCEVOIR 'glimpse', DIRE 'say', and ÊTRE 'be'. Almost all the exponences in the plat are null; the MPS-specific content (covering the fact, for example, that all first-person plural present indicative forms end with /-ɔ̃/) combined with conjugation-specific stems covers almost all the variation within French.

We show the stems (2, 3, 4, 8, and 10) that we need for our fragment in Table 12.15. The resulting plat is in Table 12.16. It has only four conjugations, differing solely on their infinitive suffix: /-ʁ/ 'exonerate', /-e/ 'buy', /-iʁ/ 'get', and /-waʁ/ 'glimpse'. In other words, we started with a complex plat and a simple lexicon. After manipulating the plat, it has become very simple, but the lexicon (including all the stems) has become correspondingly complex. We use just a few rules of sandhi to simplify the plat: one to remove vowels before /ɛ/, and one to convert /y/ to /ɥ/ after a consonant and before a vowel.

Table 12.15. *Stems for the French verb fragment*

Gloss	Stem 2	Stem 3	Stem 4	Stem 8	Stem 10
ABSOUDRE 'exonerate'	absu	absɔlv	absɔlv	absɔly	absud
ACCROÎTRE 'increase'	akʁwa	akʁwas	akʁwas	akʁy	akʁwat
ACHETER 'buy'	aʃɛt	aʃət	aʃɛt	aʃət	aʃət
ACQUÉRIR 'get'	akje	akeʁ	akjeʁ	aki	akeʁ
ACQUIESCER 'agree'	akjɛs	akjɛs	akjɛs	akjɛs	akjɛs
ALLÉGER 'lighten'	aleʒ	aleʒ	aleʒ	aleʒ	aleʒ
ALLER 'go'	va	al	vɔ̃	aj	al
APERCEVOIR 'glimpse'	apɛʁswa	apɛʁsəv	apɛʁswav	apɛʁsy	apɛʁsəv
APPELER 'call'	apɛl	apɛl	apɛl	apɛl	apɛl
APPRENDRE 'learn'	apʁɑ̃	apʁɛn	apʁɛn	apʁi	apʁɑ̃d
ARGUER 'deduce'	aʁgy	aʁgy	aʁgy	aʁgyɛ	aʁgy
ARRÊTER 'stop'	aʁɛt	aʁɛt	aʁɛt	aʁɛt	aʁɛt
ASSEOIR 'sit'	aswa	aswaj	aswa	asi	aswa
ASTREINDRE 'compel'	astʁɛ̃	astʁɛɲ	astʁɛɲ	astʁɛɲi	astʁɛ̃d
AVOIR 'have'	a	av	ɔ̃	ø	av

12.9 Stem forms

We seem to have removed all variation from the plat of French verbs at this point. How can we justify that AVOIR 'have' is in the same conjugation as APERCEVOIR 'glimpse'? The answer is that the variation has moved from the plat to the pattern of stems. Although we can distinguish fifteen indexed stems in a verb's conjugation, Tables 12.14 and 12.15 show that for a given conjugation, two or more indexed stems may share the same stem form. For instance, ALLER 'go' has only eight distinct stems that cover its fifteen indexed stems. The stem form /al/, for example, is shared by the stems with the indices 3, 8, and 10. Other verbs have even more commonality. The verb APPELER 'call' has only three distinct stem forms.

The plat itself no longer distinguishes very many inflection classes, because almost all variation is in the stems. This observation leads us to examine **stem-referral patterns**; that is, which stems are identical with each other, as we did in Chapter 7 (§8).

The full plat of French verbs has forty-five stem-referral patterns, even though it has only six distinguishable conjugations if we ignore stem referrals. The conjugation exemplified by ABSOUDRE 'exonerate' has members with twenty-five different stem-referral patterns. In contrast, ÊTRE 'be' has only one member, with its own stem-referral pattern.

Table 12.16. Plat of French verb fragment with multiple stems, in phonemic transcription

	Lexeme	Gloss	Inf	2sg pres	1pl pres	3pl pres	1sg impf	1sg sbjv
Template			S10C	S2C	S3C̃	S4C	S3Ce	S8Cɛ
	ABSOUDRE	'exonerate'	ʁ	∅	∅	∅	∅	∅
	ACCROÎTRE	'increase'	ʁ	∅	∅	∅	∅	∅
	ACHETER	'buy'	e	∅	∅	∅	∅	∅
	ACQUÉRIR	'get'	iʁ	∅	∅	∅	∅	∅
	ACQUIESCER	'agree'	e	∅	∅	∅	∅	∅
	ALLÉGER	'lighten'	e	∅	∅	∅	∅	∅
	ALLER	'go'	e	∅	∅	∅	∅	∅
	APERCEVOIR	'glimpse'	waʁ	∅	∅	∅	∅	∅
	APPELER	'call'	e	∅	∅	∅	∅	∅
	APPRENDRE	'learn'	ʁ	∅	∅	∅	∅	∅
	ARGUER	'deduce'	e	∅	∅	∅	∅	∅
	ARRÊTER	'stop'	e	∅	∅	∅	∅	∅
	ASSEOIR	'sit'	ʁ	∅	∅	∅	∅	∅
	ASTREINDRE	'compel'	ʁ	∅	∅	∅	∅	∅
	AVOIR	'have'	waʁ	∅	∅	∅	∅	∅

Our small fragment of Table 12.12 has seven stem-referral patterns, as shown in Table 12.17. One popular pattern is the syncretism of stem 4 with stem 3, with stems 2, 8, and 10 remaining distinct in form. This pattern appears in the conjugations of ABSOUDRE, ACCROÎTRE, APPRENDRE, and ASTREINDRE. Another popular pattern is that all the stems are identical; this pattern appears in the conjugations of ACQUIESCER, ALLÉGER, APPELER, and ARRÊTER. Interestingly, AVOIR 'have' has the same stem-referral pattern as APERCEVOIR 'glimpse'. This evidence gives credence to placing them in the same conjugation.

12.10 Additional syntactic data

We can supplement the exponence of each cell in the plat with additional syntactic data that is not part of the cell's phonological specification. In particular, in §5.4 and §5.5 we consider adding gender and stem-delimitation specifications to the plat, both separately and together. Such additions have the opposite effect to sandhi: Instead of uniting inflection classes and increasing the

Table 12.17. *Referral patterns for the French verb fragment*

ABSOUDRE	4 → 3	
ACCROÎTRE	4 → 3	
APPRENDRE	4 → 3	
ASTREINDRE	4 → 3	
ACHETER	4 → 2	8, 10 → 3
ACQUÉRIR	10 → 3	
APERCEVOIR	10 → 3	
AVOIR	10 → 3	
ACQUIESCER	3–4, 8, 10 → 2	
ALLÉGER	3–4, 8, 10 → 2	
APPELER	3–4, 8, 10 → 2	
ARRÊTER	3–4, 8, 10 → 2	
ARGUER	3–4, 10 → 2	
ALLER	8, 10 → 3	
ASSEOIR	4, 10 → 2	

number of static principal parts, they tend to split inflection classes and reduce the number of static principal parts. An extreme case would be to introduce a column (we cannot call it an MPS, because it is not morphosyntactic) whose exponence is simply the inflection-class label, such as "conjugation 3, i-stem." Any optimum static principal-part analysis would have only one member, the distillation containing this column.

12.11 Dealing with impostors

Our discussion of impostors in Chapter 6 points out that language learners make mistakes in deducing the realization of a lexeme in some MPS based on a false analogy with a lexeme in somewhat similar inflection class. Some examples:

- (English)

Lexeme	Present participle	Past
NEED	*needing*	*needed*
SPEED	*speeding*	*speeded [should be *sped*]

Here, the strong verb SPEED is subject to a false analogy with the Weak verb NEED.

- (Sanskrit)

Lexeme	Declension	Nom sg	Gen pl
BALIN 'strong' (neut)	DC22	*bali*	*balinām*
KRĪḌI 'playing'	DC6	*krīḍi*	**krīḍinām* [should be *krīḍīnām*]

Here, the neuter *i*-stem declension- DC6 adjective KRĪḌI 'playing' is subject to a false analogy with the neuter *in*-stem declension-DC22 adjective BALIN 'strong'. These two words have pervasively identical endings except the genitive plural (and vocative singular, if one chooses an optional ending for DC22), because these declensions involve the same suffixes, and because neuter *i*-stems epenthesize *n* before vowel-initial suffixes and *in*-stems lose their *n* before consonant-initial suffixes.

- (Sanskrit)

Lexeme	Declension	Acc sg	Nom sg
BALIN 'strong' (masc)	DC21	*balinam*	*balī*
ŚŪLINA 'Indian fig-tree'	DC1	*śūlinam*	**śūlī* [should be *śūlinas*]

These two words have occasional identical endings, namely, in the accusative singular and dual non-oblique, due to the fact that the masculine *a*-stem declension-DC1 noun ŚŪLINA 'Indian fig-tree' happens to have *in* at the end of its theme.

- (Czech)

Lexeme	Gen sg	Loc pl
POKOJ 'room'	*pokoje*	*pokojích*
PRAMEN 'spring, source'	*pramene*	**prameních* [should be *pramenech*]

These two words agree in the singular but not the plural forms, because PRAMEN 'spring' is a **heteroclite lexeme**, taking the forms of soft masculine inanimate nouns (like POKOJ 'room') in the singular, but the forms of hard masculine inanimate nouns (like MOST 'bridge') in the plural.

The four examples above show different kinds of impostors. SPEED has an ambiguity because its stem rhymes with the stem of NEED. In the case of KRĪḌI 'playing', two Sanskrit declension classes are pervasively similar. In fact, lexemes switch back and forth between these declensions throughout the history of Sanskrit (Whitney 1889: §441). In the case of the DC1 ŚŪLINA 'Indian fig-tree', it shares a few points of similarity with DC21 because of an unfortunate theme ending. In the case of PRAMEN 'spring', ambiguity arises from heteroclisis.

Dealing with impostors 365

As we design a language plat, we must deal somehow with impostors. In the case that two inflection classes are pervasively similar, we can choose to omit one of those classes. Such omission tends to reduce the number of principal parts, because it is no longer necessary to include one of the few MPSs at which the inflection classes differ. Another effect of omission is to increase measures of predictability, because the conflicting inflection classes detract from each other's predictability in the few cells in which they differ. In the case of the pervasively similar Sanskrit declensions DC6 and DC22, for instance, omitting declension DC6 lowers the number of static principal parts in an optimal analysis from 4 to 3 and raises average paradigm predictability from 0.702 to 0.721. It has almost no effect on entropy measures.

In the case of unfortunate theme endings that lead to occasional ambiguous realizations, we can emphasize the imposture by including an inflection subclass for the offending theme. In our case of ŚŪLINA 'Indian fig-tree', we could posit a subdeclension of DC1 where the *ina* fragment is not considered part of the theme but rather part of the exponent of each cell's realization. The effect of including this additional inflection class is to raise the average paradigm predictability slightly, from 0.702 to 0.710; the number of principal parts does not change, and entropy measures are unaffected. However, it seems unnecessary for a plat to include such subclasses.

In the case of a heteroclite lexeme L that participates partly in inflection class I_1 and partly in inflection class I_2, we have several options.

1. Introduce a new hybrid inflection class I' for L. Because I' has a high degree of imposture with both I_1 and I_2, introducing it tends to increase the number of principal parts (one needs at least one principal part to distinguish I' from each of I_1 and I_2), and it decreases predictability. This option seems best for Pāli verbs, which follow one of seven patterns for present and future and one of three patterns for aorist; fifteen of the twenty-one possible combinations are attested. Under this option, we consider each of those combinations a separate conjugation. For Czech, we originally have four static principal parts. The average MPS entropy is 2.54, and the average inflection-class predictability is 0.517. Adding a hybrid inflection class increases the number of principal parts to five, slightly lowers the average MPS entropy to 2.50, and decreases the average inflection-class predictability to 0.488.
2. Introduce two new inflection classes I'_1 and I'_2 for L, where I'_1 agrees with I_1 where appropriate and is defective for the other cells, and I'_2

agrees with I_2 where appropriate and is defective for the other cells. We also need to split L into two "lexemes," L_1 in inflection class I_1 and L_2 in inflection class L_2. It seems unmotivated, though, to introduce an arbitrary split in L. For Czech, adding two split inflection classes does not affect the number of principal parts, but it slightly increases the average MPS entropy to 2.58, and it increases the average inflection-classes predictability to 0.532.

3. Consider L to be an outlier that belongs to no single inflection class, and do not hybridize I_1 and I_2. This option, although slightly dishonest (it does not capture all the lexemes of the language), might be acceptable if heteroclisis is quite rare in the language. On the other hand, if heteroclisis is quite common, this option is most likely indefensible.

12.12 Conclusions

We have strong incentives to modify language plats. When we see similar inflection classes or similar MPSs, we try to abstract away the differences in order to reduce either the number of distinct inflection classes or the number of distillations. But as we do so, we must be aware that abstraction also changes what the plat represents, ranging from what language learners hear to hypothetical mental representations.

The tools at our disposal include introducing rules of sandhi, separating stem segments, introducing morphophonemes, representing phonemic instead of spelled surface forms, distinguishing multiple stem contexts, including grammatical information, and introducing or omitting inflection classes to deal with impostors. Abstraction tends to reduce the number of distinct inflection classes and the number of distillations. In doing so, it also affects all our measures of complexity: principal-part analyses, predictability/predictiveness measures, and entropy-based measures.

As we modify plats, we must do so tastefully. Rules of sandhi and morphophonemes should be phonologically supported by the language. Perhaps the most sensitive modification is to introduce multiple indexed stems that reduce the plat to very few inflection classes and very few distillations, leading us to investigate stem-referral patterns as a derived plat.

Intellectual honesty demands that whenever we analyze a language plat, we clarify exactly what that plat contains. It must explicitly show the rules of sandhi, the stem segments, the stems, and the stem-referral patterns. If we calculate entropy measures that depend on frequency, the plat must contain frequency (either token frequency or type frequency) data.

All the plats used in the analyses in this book are available on the book's web site. Chapter 13 discusses our computational tools, which are also publicly available.

13 *The Principal-Parts Analyzer*

The research on which this book rests is informed by a range of computational algorithms, all of which are embodied in a computer program that we call the **Principal-Parts Analyzer** (PPA). In this chapter, we present some details of PPA: its input format, outputs, and algorithms. PPA is available directly from the authors, and its functions are accessible at www.cs.uky.edu/~raphael/linguistics/analyze.html.

As with any program, the PPA is a work in progress, and we update it frequently, fixing bugs and adding features. If you find a bug or want a feature, please let us know!

13.1 Input format

PPA takes an annotated plat as its input file. All characters in a line following the comment character % are ignored. The file should be in Unicode, encoded as UTF-8. The file has several sections, which usually appear in the order described here.

13.1.1 Template abbreviations

Template abbreviations are used in templates, discussed shortly. These abbreviations follow a format like this:

```
ABBR 1 1S1C % 1A will expand to 1S1C in templates
ABBR 2 2C1S % 2A will expand to 2C1S in templates
```

13.1.2 The plat itself

Table 13.1 is a partial plat for Finnish in the format required by PPA, showing the same data as Table 10.2.

The first column, which must be labeled IC, lists the inflection classes by name. In cases in which an IC does not have a special name or number, we name it with an exemplar lexeme.

Table 13.1. *PPA input format of Finnish* i-*stem and* e-*stem nouns*

IC	nomSg	genSg	partSg	partPl	inessPl
TEMPLATE	1A	1An	1A	1A	1A
OVI	i	e	ea	ia	issa
KIELI	i	e	tä	iä	issä
VESI	i	de	tä	iä	issä
LASI	i	i	ia	eja	eissa
NALLE	∅	∅	a	ja	issa
KIRJE	∅	e	ttä	itä	issä

The remaining columns, which must be labeled by the associated MPS, are the exponences. If there are more columns than comfortably fit on a line, the plat may be presented in multiple sections, which must be separated by a blank line. Each section looks just like the one shown in the table, but it should have different MPS names for the columns. The column labeled IC must be repeated at the beginning of every section. Many of the plats provided as supplemental material on the web have multiple sections; one example is marginal.french.data.

The individual entries in the plat show the exponence associated with the given IC and MPS. The exponence of an MPS M in an IC J is listed in row J in the column labeled M. Exponences follow these conventions.

- In the plat in Table 13.1, every exponence is a single continuous string. In instances in which an exponence comprises discontinuous components, they are separated by hyphens. In such instances, the components are represented in the plat's template as 1C, 2C, and so forth (C means "component"). This feature is useful for languages with root-and-pattern morphology. For example, Hebrew verbal lexemes have triconsonantal roots whose segments are separable by the components of a vocalic exponence. Thus, in the first-person singular future inflection of the lexeme DIBER 'speak' (root *dbr*), the three components of the vocalic exponence a-a-e- are interposed among the root's consonants: *adaber* 'I will speak'. In such cases, it is necessary to regard stems as well as exponences as consisting of multiple components. We refer to a stem's components as substems; thus, the Hebrew root *dbr* consists of three substems. For technical reasons, it is useful to regard a stem consisting of a single component as its own, sole, substem.
- An empty exponence may be represented by the null character ∅ (Unicode \u2205). In exponences with more than one component,

- an empty component can be omitted. For example, -de-- is equivalent to ∅-de-∅-∅.
- The template shows how to expand exponences into word forms. For instance, the genitive singular realization of VESI 'water' is determined by the exponence *de* in accordance with the template 1An. In this template, 1A refers to the abbreviation ABBR 1 in §13.1.1, which expands to 1S1C, so the template 1An is equivalent to 1S1Cn. Within this string, 1C refers to the first component of the exponence (*de*) and 1S to a lexeme's first substem. Elsewhere in the plat, that substem is declared to be *ves* for the noun VESI 'water'. So the genitive singular realization of VESI is *ves+de+n*, yielding *vesden*. This form is subject to subsequent sandhi modifications.
- If an exponence is expressed starting with !, it is not subject to template expansion. We use such exponences for exceptional forms. For instance, if the genitive singular of KIRJE were *kirjek*, not ending in *-n* and therefore violating the template for this MPS, we could write that exponence as !kirjek. This exponence would apply to every noun in the IC KIRJE. For that reason, the ! notation is only helpful for ICs with a single member.
- If an exponence is expressed starting with @, the first substem is replaced by the string following @, and ordinary template expansion occurs. If the genitive singular of KIRJE were *korjeen*, using a variant stem, we could write its exponence as @korje. Again, this exponence would apply to every noun in the IC KIRJE. For that reason, the @ notation is only helpful for ICs with a single member.

13.1.3 Sandhi specifications

PPA accepts optional sandhi specifications, which often make it possible to simplify plats, as discussed in Chapter 12. These specifications include character-class definitions, such as

```
CLASS vow a e i o u y
```

and replacement rules, such as

```
SANDHI s d ⇒ d % vesden ⇒ veden
SANDHI s t ⇒ t t % vestä ⇒ vettä
```

A complex rule of sandhi that appears in one of our French theories looks like this:

```
SANDHI ə_ɛ [:cons:] ə [:cons:] [:vow:] ⇒ ɛ $1 ə $2 $3
```

This rule converts the morphophoneme ə_ɛ to ɛ in a context where it is followed by any sequence of a consonant, ə, another consonant, and a vowel. The expressions $1 and so forth on the right-hand side refer to character classes used on the left-hand side.

13.1.4 Stem referrals

In languages in which lexemes have multiple stems and ICs differ with respect to which stems are used for each MPS, the PPA input can indicate that some stems refer to others. For instance, one of our analyses of French verbs (not used in this book) uses fifteen stems, but some conjugations need fewer, because the same stem has multiple uses. We have lines like these:

```
REFER ABSOUDRE 2, 11, 15 -> 1; 10 -> 7; 4, 5, 8, 12-14 -> 3; 9 -> 6
REFER ACCROÎTRE 2, 5, 8, 11-14 -> 1; 10 -> 2; 9, 15 -> 6; 4 -> 3
```

These lines tell us, among other stem referrals, that stem 2 for the IC typified by ABSOUDRE 'exonerate' is the same as stem 1; there is no need to specify stem 2 for any lexeme in this IC.

13.1.5 Lexeme declarations

PPA does not require a list of lexemes, but it can generate a word form for each listed lexeme in each MPS, and this output serves as a useful accuracy check.

Each lexeme is listed with a lexeme name, its IC (here named for the member lexeme), and its stem(s) (including any substems), as in this Finnish example:

```
LEXEME    OVI_door           OVI     1:ov
LEXEME    KIELI_language     KIELI   1:kiel
LEXEME    VESI_water         VESI    1:ves
LEXEME    LASI_glass         LASI    1:las
LEXEME    TUOL_chair         TUOL    1:tuol
LEXEME    NALLE_teddy_bear   NALLE   1:nalle
LEXEME    KIRJE_letter       KIRJE   1:kirje
```

Here are lexeme definitions for French verbs corresponding to the stem referrals above:

```
LEXEME exonerate ABSOUDRE 1:absu 3:absɔlv 6:absɔly 7:absud
LEXEME increase ACCROÎTRE 1:akʁwa 6:akʁy 3:akʁwas 7:akʁwat
```

The numbered entries in these examples are stems whose form is stipulated rather than syncretic; a lexeme's syncretized stems are implied by the stem referrals.

13.1.6 Keys

Any set of keys may be associated with any IC. These keys can be used to indicate membership in a fragment of the plat or to associate a numeric value with the IC. For instance, in our French theory, we have these lines:

```
KEYS    ÊTRE       FREQ=1       LOW
KEYS    AVOIR      FREQ=2       LOW
KEYS    AIMER      FREQ=4139    HIGH
KEYS    COLLER     FREQ=423     HIGH
KEYS    BEURRER    FREQ=31      HIGH
```

These keys represent the fact that, for instance, IC AIMER has type frequency 4139, which we consider high. We use keys to extract fragments and to weight entropy analyses.

13.1.7 Impostor analysis

We discuss impostors in Chapter 6. To identify word forms that can be attributed to multiple ICs, the input file may request that PPA analyze a given word form, possibly associated with an MPS, for IC membership. The following requests apply to the Finnish plat:

```
ANALYZE ANY=patteja inessPl=patteissa
ANALYZE partPl=pitiä
```

The first line requests that PPA analyze the hypothetical pre-sandhi word form *patteja*. PPA responds that such a form might be in either the LASI declension with stem *patt* or in the NALLE or KIRJE declensions with stem *patteja*. The input continues by specifying that the inessive plural of this lexeme is *patteissa*. PPA decides that only the lasi declension works for both word forms. In a sense, the input is playing the "twenty questions" game, but not interactively.

The second line is a new request, asking PPA to analyze the hypothetical word form *pitiä* in the partitive plural.[1] PPA responds that this word form could be either in the KIELI declension or the VESI declension, in either case with stem *pit*, and that the genitive singular would distinguish these two ICs.

At present, PPA only handles situations in which the stem is meant to be the first substem, that is, the form that the template references as 1S.

---

[1] This hypothetical form obeys the Finnish rules of vowel harmony.

13.2 Output sections

PPA always outputs a synopsis of the input plat. For our Finnish plat, we get:

```
6 inflection classes
16 distinct exponences
5 MPSs
5 unique MPSs
    nomSg genSg partSg partPl inessPl
4 distillations (pattern 23)
    nomSg genSg partSg inessPl
```

This output is self-explanatory except for the pattern 23 that represents the distillations. The pattern is a binary encoding of which MPSs are picked as distillations. The binary representation is 10111, which, reading from right to left, indicates that MPSs 1, 2, 3, and 5 represent distillations, but that MPS 4 is in a previous distillation. We use patterns like this to specify sets of MPSs; for instance, if we wish to force some MPSs to represent distillations, even if PPA would otherwise subsume those MPSs under other distillations.

In verbose mode, PPA prints more information, including the plat with all exponences reduced to numbers, a list of MPSs with their serial number, MPS equivalences[2] (in our case, that 4 is essentially identical to 3), and the essence.

PPA then outputs the result of any ANALYZE requests. For the requests shown above, we get:

```
Analyzing: ANY=patteja inessPl=patteissa
    given MPS ANY=patteja
        maybe IC LASI: stem patt, exponence patteja
        maybe IC NALLE: stem patteja, exponence patteja
        maybe IC KIRJE: stem patteja, exponence patteja
        to determine with probability 100
            genSg partSg partPl inessPl
        to determine with probability 67
            nomSg
    given MPS inessPl=patteissa
        maybe IC LASI: stem patt, exponence patteissa
        not IC NALLE; it would need a new stem patte
        not IC KIRJE; it does not match this word form
```

---

[2] As explained in the Introduction, if two MPSs have identical or isomorphic (that is, essentially identical) exponences, ignoring their templates, the higher-numbered one is subsumed into the distillation named by the lower-numbered one. Equivalences explain why some MPSs are not picked as distillations.

374   *The Principal-Parts Analyzer*

```
        Certainly in inflection class LASI.
Analyzing: partPl=pitiä
    given MPS partPl=pitiä
        maybe IC KIELI: stem pat, exponence pitiä
        maybe IC VESI: stem pat, exponence pitiä
        to determine with probability 100
            genSg
```

PPA can perform many optional calculations on the plat. These options are specified in the PPA invocation.

- **Principal parts**: static, adaptive, and dynamic. For Finnish, we get:

```
Quick static principal parts
    2,3 (genSg, partSg)
Best sets of static principal parts
    2,3 (genSg, partSg)
```

We need 2 adaptive principal parts:

```
*if distillation 3 (partSg) has variant (1Sia)
        the inflection class is LASI
*if distillation 3 (partSg) has variant (1Sttä)
        the inflection class is KIRJE
*if distillation 3 (partSg) has variant (1Sa)
        the inflection class is NALLE
*if distillation 3 (partSg) has variant (1Stä)
** if distillation 2 (genSg) has variant (1Sden)
        the inflection class is VESI
** if distillation 2 (genSg) has variant (1Sen)
        the inflection class is KIELI
*if distillation 3 (partSg) has variant (1Sea)
        the inflection class is OVI
```

and an extract of the dynamic principal parts:

	1 nomSg	2 genSg	3 partSg	4 inessPl	
NALLE					
	2 | 2	2	2	2	avg 1.00
	3 | 3	3	3	3	avg 1.00

```
NALLE: 1 principal parts; lowest average 1.00;
2 analyses; 50.0% of four possible analyses
```

The quick heuristic is fast even if the number of principal parts is very large. It is guaranteed to give a set of static principal parts. That set is not guaranteed to be optimal, but in our experience it usually is optimal. If there are more than four static principal parts, one must tell PPA to consider larger values of *m*, the number of distillations considered in analyses.

- **Grouping inflection classes**. A measure of similarity of two ICs is the number of distillations on which they agree. Based on this measure, PPA can build a "family tree" of ICs. For Finnish, it produces this tree:

```
Join5: e3_3 e5_3
    Join3: e1_1
        LASI: e2_3
    Join2: e2_1
        OVI: e3_1 e5_1
        Join1: e3_2 e5_2
            KIELI: e2_1
            VESI: e2_2
Join4: e1_2
    NALLE: e2_4 e3_4 e5_1
    KIRJE: e2_1 e3_5 e5_2
```

This output shows a tree with KIELI and VESI closest together, differing only in distillation 2 (genitive singular). The notation e2_1 means the first distinct exponence in distillation 2; KIELI uses that first exponence (*e*), but vesi uses the second one (*de*). Otherwise, these ICs are identical. Close to both these ICs is OVI, which disagrees in distillation 3 (partitive singular) and 5 (inessive plural). The *i*-stem ICs LASI, OVI, KIELI, and VESI all group under Join3; they all agree in distillation 1 (nominative singular: *i*). In contrast, the e-stem ICs NALLE and KIRJE group under Join4.

- Cell and IC predictabilities. For Finnish, we get

```
Predictability (based on m = 4)
            1     2     3     4    | Avg         IC predictability
OVI    0.625 0.625 0.375 0.500 | 0.531 0.733 (11 out of 15)
KIELI  0.500 0.000 0.250 0.500 | 0.312 0.333 (5 out of 15)
VESI   0.750 0.000 0.625 0.750 | 0.531 0.533 (8 out of 15)
LASI   0.875 0.750 0.750 0.750 | 0.781 0.933 (14 out of 15)
NALLE  0.750 0.625 0.625 0.750 | 0.688 0.867 (13 out of 15)
KIRJE  0.500 0.625 0.375 0.625 | 0.531 0.733 (11 out of 15)
Avg    0.667 0.438 0.500 0.646 | 0.562 0.689
```

Each numbered column shows the predictability of the associated distillation based on *m* = 4.

- **Signature equivalence classes**. The **signature** of an IC is a string of numbers representing the first MPS in which each exponence appears.[3] For the partial Finnish plat given above, it is this:

  ```
  OVI    1  2  3  4  5
  KIELI  1  2  3  4  5
  VESI   1  2  3  4  5
  LASI   1  1  3  4  5
  NALLE  1  1  3  4  5
  KIRJE  1  2  3  4  5
  ```

All exponences differ for OVI, but the exponence of the first two MPSs is identical for LASI. PPA calculates the signatures and detects when ICs share a signature:

  ```
  Signature equivalence classes
      class LASI: LASI, NALLE
      class OVI: OVI, KIELI, VESI, KIRJE
  ```

  The six distinct ICs have 2 distinct signatures.

- **Entropies**. PPA computes the unconditional and conditional entropies, as well as near-static principal parts and inflection-class entropies:

  Entropies (times 100) by distillation

dist	1	2	3	4	avg	max
uncond	92	179	225	146	161	
4-cond	31	70	73	45	55	73

  4-cond entropy by IC (predictability)

	1	2	3	4	avg
OVI	14	27	17	18	19
KIELI	14	27	21	17	20
VESI	14	23	21	17	19
LASI	14	10	10	10	11
NALLE	17	10	10	18	14
KIRJE	17	27	16	17	19
avg	15	21	16	16	17

  conditional entropy of MPS (col) given MPS (row)

	1	2	3	4	Avg	max
1	—	133	133	133	133	133
2	46	—	79	46	57	79
3	0	33	—	0	11	33
4	79	79	79	—	79	79
Avg	41	81	97	59	70	

---

[3] We are indebted to Matthew Baerman for suggesting this concept and encouraging us to add this facility to PPA.

Near-static principal parts (simple heuristic)

> Highest residual entropy is 2.251629, so choose MPS 3 (partSg)
> Highest residual entropy is 0.333333, so choose MPS 2 (genSg)
> result: (genSg, partSg)

Near-static principal parts (lookahead)

> Choose MPS 3 (partSg), reducing highest residual to 0.333333
> Choose MPS 2 (genSg), reducing highest residual to 0.000000
> result: (genSg, partSg)

Inflection-class entropies (times 100)

```
   IC    1    2    3    4  | Avg
  OVI   50   48    0   50  |  37
KIELI   50   44   17   39  |  37
 VESI   50    0   17   44  |  28
 LASI   50    0    0    0  |  13
NALLE   50    0    0   50  |  25
KIRJE   50   48    0   48  |  37
  Avg   50   23    6   38  |  29
```

- KATR. PPA can convert its input into a KATR theory (Finkel *et al.* 2002) that can be executed to generate the set of realized paradigms defined by the plat for the specified lexemes.[4] This facility is useful for debugging the PPA input; if the output disagrees with the truth, the input is wrong. The KATR theory includes the sandhi information, which is only present in the PPA input for this purpose. For Finnish, the result of running KATR on the resulting theory is:

```
Lexeme             nomSg  genSg   partSg   partPl   inessPl
OVI_door           ovi    oven    ovea     ovia     ovissa
KIELI_language     kieli  kielen  kieltä   kieliä   kielissä
VESI_water         vesi   veden   vettä    vesiä    vesissä
LASI_glass         lasi   lasin   lasia    laseja   laseissa
TUOLI_chair        tuoli  tuolin  tuolia   tuoleja  tuoleissa
NALLE_teddy bear   nalle  nallen  nallea   nalleja  nalleissa
KIRJE_letter       kirje  kirjeen kirjettä kirjeitä kirjeissä
```

---

[4] KATR is a generalization of DATR (Evans and Gazdar 1989; 1996).

- Adjustments. The invocation of PPA can specify various adjustments, including
  - The number of distillations m to consider in searching for principal parts and in calculating paradigm predictabilities. By default, $m = 4$.
  - Specific MPSs that must be considered to represent distinct distillations, even if they are contained in other distillations.
  - A numeric key (like FREQ above) that should weight entropy calculations.
  - A key value that defines a fragment of the plat to which analysis should be restricted.
  - A key value that defines a subset of the ICs to which output should be restricted.
  - A string that defines a subset of the MPSs to which analysis should be restricted.

13.3 Algorithms

PPA is a Perl script of about 4,000 lines. We continue to introduce enhancements and fix bugs. Most of the algorithms are straightforward, if tedious. Here we only touch on a few of the unusual ones.

After reading the input, PPA removes ICs that are to be filtered out based on a key value. It then removes ICs whose exponences are identical to an earlier one in the plat (adding their weight, if necessary, to the weight of the earlier one). It then removes MPSs that are identical to or have the same pattern as earlier MPSs, except for those optionally forced to remain. The result is the **essence** of the plat, containing only nonredundant ICs and distillations. At this point, PPA prints the synopsis.

Many of the analyses require a list of distillation sets in order of increasing complexity. PPA builds this pattern list recursively, yielding first the empty set, then sets with one distillation, then sets with two distillations, and so on, up to m distillations in the set. Because this step can be both time- and space-consuming, especially if there are many distillations, we restrict $m = 4$ unless the PPA invocation overrides this value.

Searching for best sets of static principal parts is straightforward: for each set in the pattern list, PPA checks whether its distillations completely determine all the remaining distillations, that is, if it constitutes a set of static principal parts. Typically, small sets at the start of the pattern list fail, but at some point, a set succeeds. PPA continues to try all other sets of the same size and then stops. The result therefore contains all the minimum sets of static principal parts.

PPA uses the same pattern list in searching for dynamic principal parts, on a per-inflection-class basis.

Adaptive principal parts are far harder to compute. PPA uses a recursive branch-and-bound search for a minimum-depth tree of adaptive principal parts. It uses a heuristic based on entropy to sort its choices, preferring distillations that reduce the residual entropy of the ICs not yet determined.

The algorithms for entropy calculations are the most convoluted. At the center of these algorithms is a method for computing the weighted conditional entropy of a distillation given a set of distillations.

The algorithm for computing the tree that groups ICs is modeled on the algorithm for Huffman coding (Huffman 1952); PPA builds the tree of ICs by repeatedly combining those two that are most similar into a meta-inflection class.

Glossary

absolute approach to complexity. According to the absolute approach to linguistic complexity, a language system is more complex the more parts it has, where 'parts' can be construed in any of a variety of ways; in this approach, complexity is regarded as an inherent and objectively measurable property of language systems. Opposite of **relative approach to complexity**. (See Miestamo 2008.)

accidental. Where lexeme L belongs to IC A and is an impostor relative to IC B, L is an accidental impostor if (i) only a small number of L's realized cells make it appear to be a member of B and (ii) the members of A are not in general impostors relative to B. Opposite of **essential**.

adaptive. In an adaptive principal-part scheme for an IC system, each lexeme has an ordered sequence of principal parts in which the exponence of the lexeme's nth principal part determines the MPS of the $(n + 1)$th principal part.

adequate. An adequate principal-part set for lexeme L is any set of cells in L's realized paradigm that uniquely determines all of the other realized cells in that paradigm (that is, one that uniquely determines L's IC membership).

amassed. An amassed IC includes more than one lexeme. Opposite of **singleton**.

annexation hypothesis. Different parts of a heteroclite lexeme's realized paradigm belong to different ICs. See also **autonomy hypothesis**.

autonomy hypothesis. A heteroclite lexeme belongs to an independent IC whose exponences happen to resemble those of other ICs. See also **annexation hypothesis**.

broadly belong. A lexeme belonging to any IC J broadly belongs to every proper superclass of J. See also **narrowly belong**.

cell. A cell in the paradigm of lexeme L is the pairing $\langle L, \sigma \rangle$ of L with a complete and coherent MPS σ for which L is inflectable. See also **realized cell**.

cell predictability. Intuitively, the cell predictability of a cell $\langle w, \sigma \rangle$ in a lexeme L's realized paradigm P_L is the ratio of (a) to (b), where (a) is the number of nonempty subsets of P_L's cells whose realization uniquely determines $\langle w, \sigma \rangle$ and (b) is the number of all nonempty subsets of P_L's cells. Cell predictability is measured by the following formula; see §4.6 for details.

$$\text{CELLP}_{\langle w, \sigma \rangle} = \frac{|[_m[D_{\langle w,\sigma \rangle}]]_{-\langle w,\sigma \rangle}|}{|[_m[P(D_L)\backslash \emptyset]]_{-\langle w,\sigma \rangle}|}$$

cell predictor number. Where P is the realized paradigm of a lexeme belonging to IC J, J's cell predictor number is the number of dynamic principal parts required to determine a cell in P, averaged across the distillations in P.

central. A central IC has relatively many members. Opposite of **marginal**.

complexity. The complexity of an IC system is the extent to which it inhibits motivated inferences about a given lexeme's realized paradigm from subsets of that paradigm's cells.

condensed. In a condensed IC system, a realized paradigm's least predictable cells tend to realize the same group of MPSs from one IC to another. Opposite of **diffuse**.

conditional entropy. The measure of conditional entropy applies to items that have multiple components. The first component M_1 might make it easier to establish the value of the second component M_2. In that case, the conditional entropy of M_2 given the value of M_1 is less than the entropy of M_2 alone. The formula for conditional entropy is

$$H(M_2|M_1) = - \sum_{x \in M_1} P(x) \sum_{y \in M_2} P(y|x) \log_2 P(y|x).$$

See also **entropy**.

deductive function. The deductive function of a lexeme L's principal parts is their use in inferring L's other realizations. See also **matching function**.

density. The density of an IC system's static principal-part sets is the ratio of actual to possible optimal static principal-part sets, given the system's number of distillations and the size of its optimal static principal-part sets.

depth-of-inference contrast. Languages vary widely in the number of dynamic principal parts they require to distinguish a given IC, but they show a high degree of uniformity in allowing a given form in a lexeme's paradigm to be deduced from a low number of dynamic principal parts (the average number being not much more than one).

diffuse. In a diffuse IC system, a realized paradigm's least predictable cells do not invariably realize the same MPSs across different ICs, but are dispersed in different ways in different ICs. Opposite of **condensed**.

382 *Glossary*

distillation. Where S is a set of MPSs whose exponences in some IC system are isomorphic, the distillation of S is a member of S chosen to represent all members of S; typically, the distillation of S is the first member of S on some specified ordering of its members.

distinguisher. The substring by which a word form is distinguished from all distinct word forms in its realized paradigm is its distinguisher; for instance, *ought* is the distinguisher of BRING's past-tense form *brought*. See also **theme**.

dynamic principal-part number. A lexeme's dynamic principal-part number is its number of dynamic principal parts on any optimal analysis. An IC's dynamic principal-part number is that of its member lexemes. An IC system's dynamic principal-part number is the average of its member ICs' dynamic principal-part numbers.

dynamic. In a dynamic principal-part scheme for an IC system, the optimal principal-part sets of lexemes belonging to distinct ICs may differ in number and needn't realize any of the same MPSs.

entropy. The entropy of a set C of items is a measure of variation in C, calculated by

$$H(C) = -\sum_{x \in C} P(x) \log_2 P(x).$$

See also **conditional entropy**.

essential. Where lexeme L belongs to IC A and is an impostor relative to IC B, L is an essential impostor if (i) all members A are impostors relative to B and (ii) there are pervasive inflectional similarities between A and B. Opposite of **accidental**.

exponence. The exponence of an MPS in some word form is the full set of exponents of that property set in that word form. Contrast **exponent**; see also **rule of exponence**.

exponent. An exponent is a minimal morphological realization of some morphosyntactic property or MPS; it is minimal in the sense that no proper subpart of it is itself an exponent. Contrast **exponence**.

formative-based approach. In the formative-based approach to principal-part analysis, the exponence of a given MPS or indexed stem is invariably a morphological formative (or the significative absence thereof). Opposite of **stem-referral approach**.

global complexity. In language typology, global complexity refers to the complexity of an entire language. Opposite of **local complexity**. (See Miestamo 2008.)

hearer-oriented. In a hearer-oriented plat, an IC system's exponences are represented as audible phonological distinctions, either in full phonetic detail or with the effects of automatic phonology factored out. Contrast **speaker-oriented**.

heteroclite. A heteroclite lexeme's paradigm inflects partly according to the pattern of one IC and partly according to the pattern of another.

IC. See **inflection class**.

IC diacritic. In the lexicon, an IC diacritic specifies a lexeme's IC membership by naming the IC to which L narrowly belongs.

IC identifier. An IC identifier is a cell that is a predictor of every other cell in a lexeme L's realized paradigm (that is, one that uniquely determines L's IC membership).

IC-MPS entropy. Given an IC J and a distillation M in a reduced plat, the IC-MPS entropy $H_{J,M}$ is an average of the entropies of all other MPSs M' conditional on M, calculated as

$$H_{J,M} = \frac{\sum_{M' \neq M} H_{reduced}(M'|M)}{|MPS| - 1}$$

IC predictability. Intuitively, the IC predictability of a lexeme L's IC is the fraction of adequate (though not necessarily optimal) dynamic principal-part sets among all nonempty subsets of cells in L's realized paradigm. The IC predictability of a lexeme L's IC is measured by the following formula; see §4.4 for details.

$$\text{ICP}_L = \frac{|_m[D_L']|}{|_m[P(D_L)\setminus\emptyset]|}$$

IC predictable entropy (ICBE). Where J is an IC, $n\text{-ICBE}_J$ is the component of the n-MPS entropy due to the exponence of J, averaged across all MPSs. This is calculated as

$$n\text{-ICBE}_J = \frac{\sum_{M \in MPS} H_{J,M,n}}{|MPS|}$$

IC predictive entropy (ICVE). In a reduced plat, the ICVE_J is the average of the IC-MPS entropies $H_{J,M}$ over all MPSs M in the reduced plat:

$$\text{ICVE}_J = \frac{\sum_M H_{J,M}}{|MPS|}$$

IC system. An IC system for a syntactic category C is a set S of ICs such that every lexeme belonging to C belongs to some IC in S.

IC transparency. The IC transparency of an IC J is a function of the implicative relations exhibited by the realized paradigms of L's members: the more implicative relations they embody, the greater J's paradigmatic transparency. In the realized paradigms of lexemes belonging to a **maximally transparent IC**, each cell's exponence determines that of every other cell; given any two cells K_1, K_2 in a realized paradigm belonging to an IC of this sort, there is an R-relation deducing K_1 from K_2. By contrast, in the realized paradigms of lexemes belonging to a **maximally opaque IC**, no cell or combination of cells determines the exponence of any other cell; in a realized paradigm belonging to an IC of this sort, there are no R-relations deducing any cell from any other cell or combination of cells.

implicative relation. An implicative relation among the cells of a lexeme's realized paradigm is a relation of the type "the realized cells $\langle w_1, \sigma_1 \rangle, \ldots, \langle w_n, \sigma_n \rangle$ determine the realized cell $\langle x, \tau \rangle$". See **W-relation**, **R-relation**.

implicative rule. An implicative rule is a realization rule that expresses an implicative relation among cells of a realized paradigm.

impostor. An impostor is a lexeme whose inflection-class membership is ambiguous because one or more of its realizations is morphologically ambiguous. Example: the verb SPEED's realization *speed* is ambiguous, since it could reflect membership in the conjugation class of feed (past tense *fed*) or in that of NEED (past tense *needed*).

indexed stem. An indexed stem is a stem whose distribution is determined by its association with a morphological index that has no necessary correspondence to the stem's form or to the MPS(s) that it is used to express.

inflection class (abbreviation: IC). An inflection class is a class J of lexemes such that (i) J's members are distinguished by a common pattern of inflection and (ii) membership in J has no syntactic significance. Conjugation classes and declension classes are ICs.

irreducible. See **reducible**.

isomorphic ideal. The isomorphic ideal is the property attained by an IC system in which each MPS's pattern of exponences across ICs is isomorphic to that of every other MPS (so that all MPSs belong to the same distillation).

local complexity. In language typology, local complexity refers to the complexity of a particular linguistic subsystem. Opposite of **global complexity**. (See Miestamo 2008.)

lookahead heuristic. The lookahead heuristic is a way to find static near-principal parts: start with an empty S and repeatedly add the most predictive remaining MPSs to it until the residual entropy of the remaining MPSs is small enough. Compare **simple heuristic**.

Marginal Detraction Hypothesis. Marginal ICs tend to detract most strongly from the IC predictability of other ICs.

marginal. A marginal IC has relatively few members. Opposite of **central**.

matching function. The matching function of a known lexeme's principal-part set S is the use of S in inferring the IC membership of an unfamiliar lexeme whose inflection matches S. See also **deductive function**.

maximally opaque IC. See **IC transparency**.

maximally transparent IC. See **IC transparency**.

minimal. An adequate set of principal parts is minimal if none of its proper subsets is adequate.

morphosyntactic focus number. An IC system's morphosyntactic focus number is a measure of its degree of morphosyntactic focus. It is measured as $1 - (i/(j \cdot k))$, where i is the number of distinct distillations realized by optimal static principal parts, j is the number of optimal static principal-part sets, and k is the number of members in each set. See also **morphosyntactically focused**, **morphosyntactically unfocused**.

morphosyntactic property. A morphosyntactic property is the specification of an inflectional category by one of its permissible values. Example: the morphosyntactic property 'NUMBER:singular' is a specification of the inflectional category of number. Where there is no risk of ambiguity, we abbreviate the morphosyntactic property C:v (where C is an inflectional category and v is one of C's permissible values) as v.

morphosyntactic property set (abbreviation: MPS). Given a syntactic category C, a morphosyntactic property set for C is a set of morphosyntactic properties appropriate to C. Example: {CASE:nominative, NUMBER:singular, GENDER:feminine} is a morphosyntactic property set for adjectives in Latin.

morphosyntactically focused. An IC system is morphosyntactically focused to the extent that the distillations realized by its optimal static principal parts are constrained; an IC system that has only one optimal static principal-part set is maximally focused. Opposite of **morphosyntactically unfocused**.

morphosyntactically unfocused. An IC system is morphosyntactically unfocused to the extent that the distillations realized by a lexeme's optimal static principal parts are morphosyntactically unconstrained; an IC system in which every distillation is realized by a principal part in one or another optimal static principal-part analysis is maximally unfocused. Opposite of **morphosyntactically focused**.

motivated inference. If one infers the forms of a lexeme from an adequate set of principal parts, the inferences are motivated. Example: the inference of *sings* and *singing* from the principal-part set *sing–sang–sung*. Opposite of **unmotivated inference**.

MPS. See **morphosyntactic property set**.

narrowly belong. A lexeme L belonging to IC J_1 narrowly belongs to J_1 iff there is no proper subclass J_2 of J_1 such that (i) L belongs to J_2 and (ii) at least one realization rule is defined as applying to members of J_2. Contrast **broadly belong**.

near-principal parts. A set of near-principal parts for some realized paradigm P is a set of cells in P that reduces the residual entropy of P's remaining cells below some threshold.

***n*-conditional exponence entropy.** Where J is an IC and *M* is a distillation, the *n*-conditional exponence entropy for *M* and J is calculated as

$$H_{J,M,n} = -\sum_{|S|\leq n, M\notin S} P(e|S)\log_2 P(e|S).$$

***n*-MPS entropy.** The *n*-MPS entropy of an MPS *M* is the average of the entropy of *M* conditional on members of C_M, the collection of MPSs not including *M* with up to *n* members. The formula for *n*-MPS entropy is

$$H_n(M) = \frac{\sum_{c\in C_M} H(M|C)}{|C_M|}.$$

nonsyncretistic. A relation that allows one cell in a realized paradigm to be determined by another cell in that paradigm is nonsyncretistic if the two cells exhibit different word forms.

optimal set of principal parts. A set S of principal parts (static, adaptive or dynamic) is optimal for IC J if and only if there is no adequate set of principal parts for J whose cardinality is less than that of S.

Pāṇini's principle. If realization rules R_1 and R_2 are in competition, R_1 is narrower than (and therefore overrides) R_2 iff either (a) R_1 is defined as applying to a proper subclass of the IC to which R_2 is defined as applying, or (b) R_1 and R_2 are defined as applying to the same IC, but R_1 is defined for a smaller number of MPSs than R_2.

paradigm. The paradigm of a lexeme L is a complete set of cells for L. For maximally transparent paradigm, maximally opaque paradigm, see **IC transparency**.

paradigm function. A paradigm function is a function from the cells in lexemes' paradigms to the corresponding cells in their realized paradigms.

paradigm schema. A syntactic category's paradigm schema is the set of MPSs realized by the paradigms of that category's members. For instance, the paradigm schema of a Latin noun is the set {{nom sg}, {voc sg}, {gen sg}, {dat sg}, {acc sg}, {abl sg}, {loc sg}, {nom pl}, {voc pl}, {gen pl}, {dat pl}, {acc pl}, {abl pl}, {loc pl}}.

plat. A plat is the representation of an IC system as a matrix in which distinct MPSs are represented as columns, distinct ICs are represented as rows, and the exponence of MPS σ in IC J is specified at the intersection of J and σ.

plat reduced by J, M. A plat reduced by J, M is a fragment of a plat containing only those ICs that have the same exponence as IC J for MPS M.

predictability. See **cell predictability**, **IC predictability**.

predictiveness. The predictiveness of a cell K in a realized paradigm is the fraction of the other cells in the paradigm that are fully determined by K.

predictor. Where K_1, K_2 are cells in a realized paradigm, K_1 is a predictor of K_2 if K_1 fully determines K_2.

preterite-present. In Germanic languages, preterite-present verbs have (i) present-tense forms exhibiting the morphology usual for Strong verbs in the past tense and (ii) past-tense forms exhibiting the morphology usual for Weak verbs in the past tense. See **Weak** and **Strong**.

principal parts. A set of principal parts for a lexeme L is a set of cells in L's realized paradigm P from which one can reliably deduce the remaining cells in P. If the cell ⟨w, σ⟩ is a principal part, we sometimes refer to the word form w (or to the MPS σ) as a principal part, but with the understanding that we are using w (or σ) as a shorthand for ⟨w, σ⟩.

pure exponence-based morphology (PEM). According to the PEM hypothesis, the realization rules that define a language's inflectional morphology include rules of exponence and not implicative rules. Opposite of **pure word-and-paradigm morphology**.

pure word-and-paradigm morphology (PWPM). The PWPM hypothesis subsumes three axioms: (i) the realization rules that define a language's inflectional morphology are purely implicative rules; (ii) the **stored principal part hypothesis** (q. v.); (iii) because a lexeme's IC membership is determined by its principal-part set, neither IC diacritics nor inflectional stems are stored in the mental lexicon, nor do they figure in the formulation of realization rules. Opposite of **pure exponence-based morphology**.

realization. Where ⟨L, σ⟩ is a cell in the paradigm of lexeme L, ⟨L, σ⟩ is expressed morphologically as a word form w; w is in this context the realization of L, of σ, and of ⟨L, σ⟩. If w realizes ⟨L, σ⟩, we also sometimes refer to the realized cell ⟨w, σ⟩ as a realization ⟨L, σ⟩.

realized cell. Where the cell ⟨L, σ⟩ in the paradigm of lexeme L has realization w, L has ⟨w, σ⟩ as a realized cell.

realized paradigm. A lexeme's realized paradigm is its complete set of realized cells.

reducible. Where $S_1 \to S_2$ is a valid W- or R-relation, $S_1 \to S_2$ is reducible iff either (i) there is a proper subset S' of S_1 such that $S' \to S_2$ is a valid relation or (ii) S_2 is not a singleton set; otherwise, $S_1 \to S_2$ is **irreducible**.

relative approach to complexity. According to the relative approach to linguistic complexity, a language system is more complex if it has a higher "cost" for language users. Opposite of the **absolute approach to complexity**. (See Miestamo 2008.)

root property set. In an adaptive system of principal parts, the root property set is the MPS realized by the first principal part for all ICs.

R-relation. An R-relation is an implicative relation among realization rules. See also **W-relation**.

rule of exponence. Where $\langle L, \sigma \rangle$ is a cell in the paradigm of lexeme L and X is a stem of L, a rule of exponence is a realization rule that applies to the pairing $\langle X, \sigma \rangle$ to realize σ through the inflection of X.

rule of referral. A rule of referral is a realization rule that specifies that two contrasting cells in a paradigm are realized by identical forms.

signature. An IC's signature is the pattern of syncretism exhibited by its paradigms. In particular, the signature of an IC J with respect to a set S of MPSs is a partition P of S such that (i) for every $s \in P$, every member of s has the same exponence, and (ii) for all $s_1, s_2 \in P$, if s_1's members share exponence E_1 and s_2's members share exponence E_2, then $E_1 = E_2$ iff $s_1 = s_2$.

simple heuristic. A simple heuristic for finding static near-principal parts is to start with an empty set S and repeatedly add the MPS with the highest residual entropy to it until the residual entropy of the remaining MPSs is sufficiently small. Compare **lookahead heuristic**.

singleton. A singleton IC includes only a single lexeme. Opposite of **amassed**.

speaker-oriented. In a speaker-oriented plat, an IC system's exponences are represented as contrasts that a language user recognizes as morphologically significant, incorporating morpholexical as well as phonological information. Contrast **hearer-oriented**.

static principal-part number. A lexeme's static principal-part number is its number of static principal parts on any optimal analysis. An IC's static principal-part number is that of its member lexemes. An IC system's static principal-part number is that of its member ICs.

static. In a static principal-part scheme for an IC system, the same cells function as principal parts in the realized paradigm of every lexeme belonging to a given syntactic category. See also **uniform**.

stem-formation rule. A stem-formation rule is a stem-realization rule that determines the phonological shape of the stem S bearing a particular index if S is not lexically listed.

stem-realization rule. A stem-realization rule is one kind of realization rule, either a **stem-selection rule** or a **stem-formation rule**.

stem-referral approach. In the stem-referral approach to principal-part analysis, the exponence of an indexed stem S is represented either as a stem formative or, to the extent possible, as the index of a distinct indexed stem with which S is syncretized. Opposite of **formative-based approach**.

stem-referral pattern A stem-referral pattern is a pattern of syncretism between distinct indexed stems.

stem-selection rule. A stem-selection rule indicates the conditions in which a stem with a particular index is used in the definition of a lexeme's realized paradigm.

stored principal part (SPP) hypothesis. A lexeme L's entry in the mental lexicon includes a set of principal parts for L. Stored principal-part sets may or may not be unique, uniform or optimal.

Strong. In Germanic languages, Strong verbs form their past tense by means of ablaut. Opposite of **Weak**. See also **preterite-present**.

theme. The theme of a realized paradigm is the invariant substring shared by all word forms in that paradigm; for instance, *br* is the theme of the paradigm of BRING. See also **distinguisher**. In some instances, the boundary between a word form's theme and its distinguisher happens to coincide with a boundary between stem and affix (as in the forms of the verb WALK).

thick. A thick paradigm is one in which all principal parts are necessary to determine each cell (under a particular optimal dynamic principal-part analysis). A thick paradigm's IC is also thick, as is an IC system consisting entirely of thick ICs. Opposite of **thin**.

thin. A thin paradigm is one in which each cell is determined by a single principal part (under a particular optimal dynamic principal-part analysis). A thin paradigm's IC is also thin, as is an IC system consisting entirely of thin ICs. Opposite of **thick**.

token frequency. Where J is an IC, the token frequency of J is the frequency with which members of J appear in a particular corpus.

type frequency. Where J is an IC of lexemes belonging to syntactic category C, the type frequency of J is the ratio of J's members to the total number of lexemes in C.

uniform set of principal parts. The principal-part sets of a class C of lexemes are uniform if each member of C has the same members of its realized paradigm as its principal-part set. Traditionally, **unique principal-part sets** (q. v.) are uniform.

unique set of principal parts. In traditional grammar, a lexeme L is assumed to have a unique set of principal parts, in the sense that the label "principal parts" is reserved for one of L's (potentially multiple) principal-part sets; the identity of L's unique principal-part set is agreed upon as a matter of convention. Example: By convention, a Latin noun's unique set of principal parts consists of its nominative singular and genitive singular realizations.

universe. A universe of ICs is a set of ICs with respect to which some calculation is performed; the universe may be the full set of ICs in a system or one of its proper subsets.

unmotivated inference. If one infers that the principal parts of lexeme L_1 match those of lexeme L_2 because of a perceived similarity between L_1 and L_2, the inference is unmotivated. Example: the inference of *brang* and *brung* from the similarity of *bring* and *ring*. Opposite of **motivated inference**.

unpredictable. A cell K is unpredictable in the paradigm of some lexeme L if and only if no other cell in L's paradigm has a realization that is informative about K's realization.

Weak. In Germanic languages, Weak verbs form their past tense by means of a coronal suffix. Opposite of **Strong**. See also **preterite-present**.

word-realization rule. A word-realization rule is one kind of realization rule, either a **rule of exponence** or a **rule of referral**.

W-relation. A W-relation is an implicative relation among cells in the realized paradigm of a specific lexeme. See also **R-relation**.

References

Ackerman, F., J. P. Blevins, & R. Malouf 2009, Parts and wholes: implicative patterns in inflectional paradigms. In J. P. Blevins & J. Blevins (eds.), *Analogy in grammar: form and acquisition*. Oxford University Press, pp. 54–82.
Ackerman, F., G. Stump, & G. Webelhuth 2011, Lexicalism, periphrasis and implicative morphology. In B. Borsley & K. Börjars (eds.), *Non-transformational theories of grammar*. Oxford: Blackwell, pp. 325–358.
Albright, A. 2002, The identification of bases in morphological paradigms. UCLA doctoral dissertation.
  2008, Inflectional paradigms have bases too: evidence from Yiddish. In A. Bachrach & A. Nevins (eds.), *Inflectional identity*. Oxford University Press, pp. 271–312.
Albright, A. & B. Hayes 2003, Rules vs analogy in English past tenses: a computational/experimental study. *Cognition* 90: 119–161.
Alegre, M. & P. Gordon 1999, Frequency effects and the representational status of regular inflections. *Journal of memory and language* 40: 41–61.
Anderson, S. R. 1992, *A-morphous morphology*. Cambridge University Press.
Aronoff, M. 1994, *Morphology by itself: stems and inflectional classes*. Cambridge, MA and London: MIT Press.
Baayen, R. H., T. Dijkstra, & R. Schreuder 1997, Singulars and plurals in Dutch: evidence for a parallel dual-route model. *Journal of memory and language* 37: 94–117.
Baayen, R. H., J. McQueen, T. Dijkstra, & R. Schreuder 2003, Frequency effects in regular inflectional morphology: revisiting Dutch plurals. In R. H. Baayen & R. Schreuder (eds.), *Morphological structure in language processing*. Berlin: Mouton de Gruyter, pp. 355–390.
Baayen, R. H., R. Schreuder, N. de Jong, & A. Krott 2002, Dutch inflection: the rules that prove the exception. *Studies in theoretical psycholinguistics* 30(2): 61–92.
Baayen, R. H., H. Wurm, & J. Aycock, 2007 Lexical dynamics for low-frequency complex words. *The mental lexicon* 2: 419–463.
Baerman, M. 2012. Paradigmatic chaos in Nuer. *Language* 88, 467–494.
Baerman, M., D. Brown, & G. G. Corbett 2010, *Morphological complexity: a typological perspective. Manuscript*, University of Surrey.
Bane, M. 2008, Quantifying and measuring morphological complexity. In Charles B. Chang & Hannah J. Haynie (eds.), *Proceedings of the 26th West Coast*

Conference on Formal Linguistics. Somerville, MA: Cascadilla Proceedings Project, pp. 69–76.

Bescherelle: La conjugaison pour tous. 2006, Paris: Hatier.

Blevins, J. P. 2006, Word-based morphology. *Journal of linguistics* 42: 531–573.

Bonami, O. & G. Boyé 2002, Suppletion and dependency in inflectional morphology. In F. Van Eynde, L. Hellan & D. Beermann, (eds.), *The proceedings of the 8th International Conference on Head-Driven Phrase Structure Grammar*. Stanford: CSLI Publications, pp. 51–70.

Bonami, O., G. Boyé, & F. Henri 2011, Measuring inflectional complexity: French and Mauritian. Paper presented at the Workshop on Quantitative Measures in Morphology and Morphological Development, Center for Human Development, UC San Diego, January 15–16, 2011.

Brigel, Rev. J 1872, *A grammar of the Tuḷu language*. Mangalore: Basel Mission Book & Tract Depository.

Brown, D. & R. Evans 2010, Inflectional defaults and principal parts: an empirical investigation. In S. Müller (ed.), *Proceedings of the HPSG10 Conference, Université Paris Diderot*. Stanford: CSLI Publications, pp. 234–254.

Brown, D. & A. Hippisley 2012, *Network morphology: a defaults-based theory of word structure*. Cambridge University Press.

Buchholz, E. 2004, *Grammatik der finnischen Sprache*. Bremen: Hempen Verlag.

Bybee, J. 1995, Regular morphology and the lexicon. *Language and cognitive processes* 10: 425–455.

Cameron-Faulkner, T. & A. Carstairs-McCarthy 2000, Stem alternants as morphological signata: evidence from blur avoidance in Polish nouns. *Natural language and linguistic theory* 18: 813–835.

Carstairs, A. 1987, *Allomorphy in inflexion*. London: Croom Helm.

Carstairs-McCarthy, A. 1991, Inflection classes: two questions with one answer. In F. Plank (ed.), *Paradigms: the economy of inflection*. Berlin: Mouton de Gruyter, pp. 213–253.

  1994, Inflection classes, gender and the Principle of Contrast. *Language* 70: 737–788.

Chandler, S. 2010, The English past tense: analogy redux. *Cognitive linguistics* 21: 371–417.

Corbett, G. G. 1991, *Gender*. Cambridge University Press.

  2005, The canonical approach in typology. In Z. Frajzyngier, A. Hodges & D. S. Rood (eds.), *Linguistic diversity and language theories* (Studies in Language Companion Series 72). Amsterdam: John Benjamins, pp. 25–49.

  2007, Canonical typology, suppletion and possible words. *Language* 83: 8–42.

  2009. Canonical inflectional classes. In F. Montermini, G. Boyé, & J. Tseng (eds.), *Selected Proceedings of the 6th Décembrettes*. Somerville, MA: Cascadilla Proceedings Project, pp. 1–11.

Corbett, G. G. & N. M. Fraser 1993, Network morphology: a DATR account of Russian nominal inflection. *Journal of linguistics* 29: 113–142.

Dahl, Ö. 2004, *The growth and maintenance of linguistic complexity*. Amsterdam and Philadelphia: John Benjamins.

  2009, Testing the assumption of complexity invariance: the case of Elfdalian and Swedish. In G. Sampson, D. Gil, & P. Trudgill (eds.) 2009, *Language complexity as an evolving variable*. Oxford University Press, pp. 50–63.

Davies, M. 2008–present, The Corpus of Contemporary American English (COCA): 425 million words, 1990–present. Available online at www.americancorpus.org/.
de Groot, C. 2008, Morphological complexity as a parameter of linguistic typology: Hungarian as a contact language. In M. Miestamo, K. Sinnemäki, & F. Karlsson (eds.), *Language complexity: typology, contact, change*. Amsterdam: Benjamins, pp. 191–215.
De Vries, J. A. & S. A. De Vries 1997, An overview of Kwerba verb morphology. *Papers in Papuan linguistics* 3 (*Pacific Linguistics*, A-87): 1–35.
Deutscher, G. 2009, "Overall complexity": a wild goose chase? In G. Sampson, D. Gil, & P. Trudgill (eds.) 2009, *Language complexity as an evolving variable*. Oxford University Press, 243–251.
Dictionnaire du français contemporain. Paris: Larousse, 1971.
Dressler, W. U., M. Kilani-Schoch, N. Gagarina, L. Pestal, & M. Pochtrager. 2006, On the typology of inflection class systems. *Folia linguistica* 40(1–2): 51–74.
Ernestus, M. & R. H. Baayen 2003, Predicting the unpredictable: Interpreting neutralized segments in Dutch. *Language* 79: 5–38.
  2004, Analogical effects in regular past tense production in Dutch. *Linguistics* 42: 873–903.
Evans, R. & G. Gazdar 1989, Inference in DATR. In H. L. Somers & M. McGee Wood (eds.), *Proceedings of the Fourth Conference of the European Chapter of the Association for Computational Linguistics*. Manchester: Association for Computational Linguistics, pp. 66–71.
  1996, DATR: A language for lexical knowledge representation. *Computational linguistics* 22: 167–216.
Finkel, R. & G. Stump 2006a, Principal parts and degrees of paradigmatic transparency. Paper presented at the Conference on Analogy in Grammar: Form and Acquisition, Max Planck Institute for Evolutionary Anthropology, Leipzig, September 22–23.
  2006b, Principal parts and the intersection of conjugational paradigms. Paper presented at the 12th International Morphology Meeting, Budapest, May 25–28.
  2007, Principal parts and morphological typology. *Morphology* 17: 39–75.
  2008a, Principal parts and degrees of paradigmatic transparency. Paper presented at the Southeast Morphology Meeting, University of Surrey, Guildford, United Kingdom, September 26.
  2008b, Principal parts and French conjugation classes. Paper presented at Décembrettes 6: Colloque International de Morphologie, "Morphologie et classes flexionnelles," Université de Bordeaux, France, December 4–5.
  2009, Principal parts and degrees of paradigmatic transparency. In James P. Blevins & Juliette Blevins (eds.), *Analogy in grammar: form and acquisition*. Oxford University Press, pp. 13–53.
  2010, Predictability, predictiveness and paradigm complexity. Paper presented at the workshop "Morphological complexity: implications for the theory of language," Harvard University, January 22.
  2011a, Blinkered vision: Sources of opacity in inflectional paradigms. Paper presented at the Workshop on Quantitative Measures in Morphology and Morphological Development, Center for Human Development, UC San Diego, January 15–16.

2011b, Entropy, predictability and predictiveness. Paper presented at the Workshop on the Challenges of Complex Morphology to Morphological Theory, Linguistic Society of America Summer Institute, Boulder, CO, July 27.

2012, What are principal parts, and what can they tell us about an inflectional system's morphological complexity? Paper presented at the Conference on Morphological Complexity, British Academy, London, January 15.

Finkel, R., L. Shen, G. Stump, & S. Thesayi 2002, KATR: a set-based extension of DATR (Technical Report 346–02). Lexington, KY: University of Kentucky Department of Computer Science. (ftp.cs.uky.edu/cs/techreports/346–02.pdf).

Göksel, A. & C. Kerslake 2005, *Turkish: a comprehensive grammar*. London and New York: Routledge.

Grant, J. 1823, *Institutes of Latin grammar* (2nd edn., enlarged). London: G. & W. B. Whittaker.

Greenberg, J. H. 1960, A quantitative approach to the morphological typology of language. *International journal of American linguistics* 26: 178–194.

Hall, K. C. 2009, A probabilistic model of phonological relationships from contrast to allophony. PhD thesis, The Ohio State University.

Hare, M., M. Ford, & W. Marslen-Wilson 2001, Ambiguity and frequency effects in regular verb inflection. In J. Bybee & P. Hopper (eds.), *Frequency and the emergence of linguistic structure*. Amsterdam: John Benjamins, pp. 181–200.

Hawkins, J. A. 2004, *Efficiency and complexity in grammars*. Oxford University Press.

Heim, M. 1982, *Contemporary Czech*. Columbus, OH: Slavica.

Hockett, C. F. 1958, *A course in modern linguistics*. New York: Macmillan.

Huffman, D. A. 1952, A method for the construction of minimum-redundancy codes. *Proceedings of the Institute of Radio Engineers (I.R.E.), September 1952*, pp. 1098–1102.

Humboldt, W. von 1836, *Über die Verschiedenheit des menschlichen Sprachbaues und ihren Einfluss auf die geistige Entwickelung des Menschengeschlechts*. Berlin: F. Dümmler.

Jakobi, A. 1990, *A Fur grammar*. Hamburg: Helmut Buske Verlag.

Janda, L. A. & C. E. Townsend 2000, *Czech*. Munich: LINCOM EUROPA.

Jörg, C. 1989, *Isländische Konjugationstabellen / Icelandic Conjugation Tables / Tableaux de Conjugaison Islandaise / Beygingatöflur Íslenskra Sagna*. Hamburg: Helmut Buske Verlag.

Juola, P. 1998, Measuring linguistic complexity: the morphological tier. *Journal of quantitative linguistics* 5(3): 206–213.

Karlsson, F. 1999, *Finnish: an essential grammar*. London and New York: Routledge.

Kimball, G. D. 1991, *Koasati grammar*. Lincoln & London: University of Nebraska Press.

Kolmogorov, A. N. 1965, Three approaches to the quantitative definition of information. *Problems in information transmission* 1: 1–7.

Kusters, W. 2008, Complexity in linguistic theory, language learning and language change. In M. Miestamo, K. Sinnemäki, & F. Karlsson (eds.), *Language complexity: typology, contact, change*. Amsterdam and Philadelphia: John Benjamins, pp. 3–22.

Kutsch Lojenga, C. 1994, *Ngiti: A Central-Sudanic language of Zaire* (Nilo-Saharan Linguistic Analyses and Documentation, vol. IX). Köln: Rüdiger Köppe Verlag.

LaFontaine, H. & N. McKay 2005, *550 Dakota verbs*. St. Paul, MN: Minnesota Historical Society Press.

Li, M. & P. Vitányi 1997, *An introduction to Kolmogorov complexity and its applications* (2nd edn.). New York: Springer.

Liu, Q., Z. He, Y. Liu, & S. Lin 2008, Maximum entropy-based rule selection model for syntax-based statistical machine translation. In *Proceedings of the Conference on Empirical Methods in Natural Language Processing*, EMNLP '08, Honolulu, Hawaii. Association for Computational Linguistics, pp. 89–97.

Maiden, M. 2009, Where does heteroclisis come from? Evidence from Romanian dialects. *Morphology* 19: 59–86.

Malouf, R. & F. Ackerman 2010a, An evolutionary explanation for the Paradigm Economy Principle. Paper presented at 2010 Meeting of the Linguistic Society of America, Baltimore.

2010b, Paradigm entropy as a measure of morphological simplicity. Paper presented at the workshop "Morphological complexity: implications for the theory of language," Harvard University, January 22.

2010c, Paradigms: the low entropy conjecture. Paper presented at the Workshop on Morphology and Formal Grammar, Université Paris Diderot, July 8.

2011a, Paradigmatics, syntagmatics, and the agglutinative analogue. Paper presented at the Workshop on Quantitative Measures in Morphology and Morphological Development, Center for Human Development, UC San Diego, January 15–16.

2011b, The low entropy conjecture: the challenges of Modern Irish nominal declension. Paper presented at the Workshop on the Challenges of Complex Morphology to Morphological Theory, Linguistic Society of America Summer Institute, Boulder, CO, July 27.

Marvan, J. 1979, *Modern Lithuanian declension: a study of its infrastructure*. Ann Arbor: University of Michigan.

Matthews, P. H. 1972, *Inflectional morphology: a theoretical study based on aspects of Latin verb conjugation*. Cambridge University Press.

McWhorter, J. 2001, The world's simplest grammars are creole grammars. *Linguistic typology* 5: 125–166.

2008, Why does a language undress? Strange cases in Indonesia. In M. Miestamo, K. Sinnemäki, & F. Karlsson (eds), *Language complexity: typology, contact, change*. Amsterdam and Philadelphia: John Benjamins, pp. 167–190.

Merrifield, W. R. 1968, *Palantla Chinantec grammar*. Serie Científica (Museo Nacional de Antropología) 9. Mexico: Museo Nacional de Antropología.

Miestamo, M. 2006, On the feasibility of complexity metrics. In K. Kerge & M.-M. Sepper (eds), *Finest linguistics: proceedings of the annual Finnish and Estonian Conference of Linguistics, Tallinn, May 6–7, 2004*. Tallinn: Tallinn University Department of Estonian, pp. 11–26.

2008, Grammatical complexity in a cross-linguistic perspective. In M. Miestamo, K. Sinnemäki, & F. Karlsson (eds), *Language complexity: typology, contact, change*. Amsterdam and Philadelphia: John Benjamins, pp. 23–41.

Miestamo, M., K. Sinnemäki, & F. Karlsson (eds.) 2008, *Language complexity: typology, contact, change*. Amsterdam: John Benjamins.

Milin, P., V. Kuperman, Al. Kostić, and R. H. Baayen 2009, Words and paradigms bit by bit: an information-theoretic approach to the processing of paradigmatic structure in inflection and derivation. In J. P. Blevins & J. Blevins (eds.), *Analogy in grammar: form and acquisition*. Oxford University Press, pp. 214–252.

Montermini, F. & G. Boyé 2012, Stem relations and inflection class assignment in Italian. *Word structure* 5: 69–87.

Moscoso del Prado Martín, F. 2011, The mirage of morphological complexity. Paper presented at the Workshop on Quantitative Measures in Morphology and Morphological Development, Center for Human Development, UC San Diego, January 15–16.

Moscoso del Prado Martín, F., A. Kostic, & R. H. Baayen 2004, Putting the bits together: an information-theoretical perspective on morphological processing. *Cognition* 94 (1): 1–18.

Nichols, J. 1992, *Linguistic diversity in space and time*. University of Chicago Press.

   2007, The distribution of complexity in the world's languages: Prospectus. Paper presented at the Linguistic Society of America Annual Meeting, Anaheim, California, January.

   2009, Linguistic complexity: a comprehensive definition and survey. In G. Sampson, D. Gil, & P. Trudgill (eds.) 2009, *Language complexity as an evolving variable*. Oxford University Press, pp. 1101–1105.

Nichols, J., with J. Barnes & D. A. Peterson 2006, The robust bell curve of morphological complexity. *Linguistic typology* 10: 96–108.

Pace, W. J. 1990, Comaltepec Chinantec verb inflection. In W. R. Merrifield & C. R. Rensch (eds.), *Syllables, tone, and verb paradigms (Studies in Chinantec languages 4)*. Summer Institute of Linguistics & The University of Texas at Arlington, pp. 21–62.

Petit Larousse illustré, 1974. Paris: Librairie Larousse.

Prasada, S. & S. Pinker 1993, Generalization of regular and irregular morphological patterns. *Language and cognitive processes* 8: 1–56.

Robins, R. H. 1959, In defence of WP. *Transactions of the Philological Society* 58: 116–144.

Sampson, G. 2009, A linguistic axiom challenged. In G. Sampson, D. Gil, & P. Trudgill (eds.) 2009, *Language complexity as an evolving variable*. Oxford University Press, pp. 1–18.

Sampson, G., D. Gil, & P. Trudgill (eds.) 2009, *Language complexity as an evolving variable*. Oxford University Press.

Sapir, E. 1921, *Language: an introduction to the study of speech*. New York: Harcourt, Brace & Co.

Schlegel, F. von 1808, *Über die Sprache und Weisheit der Indier: Ein Beitrag zur Begründung der Alterthumskunde*. Heidelberg: Mohr & Zimmer.

Schmitt, N. & G. Underwood 2004, Exploring the processing of formulaic sequences through a self-paced reading task. In N. Schmitt (ed.), *Formulaic sequences*. Amsterdam and Philadelphia: John Benjamins, pp. 171–189.

Shannon, C. E. 1951, Prediction and entropy of printed English. *The Bell system technical journal* 30: 50–64.

Shosted, R. K. 2006, Correlating complexity: a typological approach. *Linguistic Typology* 10: 1–40.
Sinnemäki, K. 2008, Complexity trade-offs in core argument marking. In M. Miestamo, K. Sinnemäki, & F. Karlsson (eds), *Language complexity: typology, contact, change*. Amsterdam and Philadelphia: John Benjamins, pp. 67–88.
2011, Language universals and linguistic complexity: three case studies in core argument marking. University of Helsinki doctoral dissertation.
Stump, G. T. 2001, *Inflectional morphology: a theory of paradigm structure*. Cambridge University Press.
2006, Heteroclisis and paradigm linkage. *Language* 82: 279–322.
2010, Paradigm templates, stem patterns and lexical representations. Paper presented at the Workshop on Morphology and Formal Grammar, Université Paris Diderot, July 8.
Tremblay, A., B. Derwing, G. Libben, & C. Westbury 2011, Processing advantages of lexical bundles: evidence from self-paced reading and sentence recall tasks. *Language learning* 61: 569–613.
Wheelock, F. M. 1963, *Latin: an introductory course based on ancient authors*. New York: Barnes & Noble.
Whitney, W. D. 1889, *Sanskrit grammar* (2nd edn.; 1950 reprint). Cambridge, MA: Harvard University Press.
Wimmer, L. F. A. 1871, *Altnordische Grammatik* (tr. by E. Sievers). Halle: Verlag der Buchhandlung des Waisenhauses.
Wurzel, W. U. 1984, *Flexionsmorphologie und Natürlichkeit*. Berlin: Akademie-Verlag. Translated, by M. Schentke, as *Inflectional morphology and naturalness* (Dordrecht: Kluwer, 1989).}
Zoëga, G. T. 1910, *A concise dictionary of Old Icelandic*. London: Oxford University Press.
Zwicky, A. M. 1985, How to describe inflection. In M. Niepokuj, M. Van Clay, V. Nikiforidou, & D. Feder (eds.), *Proceedings of the Eleventh Annual Meeting of the Berkeley Linguistics Society*. Berkeley Linguistics Society, pp. 372–386.
1994, Morphological metageneralizations: morphology, phonology, and morphonology. Paper presented at the Kentucky Foreign Language Conference, University of Kentucky, April.

Index

accidental impostor. *See* impostor
Ackerman, Farrell, 17, 61, 109, 114, 215, 295, 297, 299, 344, 347
adaptive principal-part scheme. *See* principal parts
adequate set of principal parts. *See* principal parts
Albright, Adam, 16, 107, 166, 167
Alegre, Maria, 18, 51
amassed conjugation, 232–37, 255–61
analogy, 16, 268, 363
Anderson, Stephen R., 6, 17
annexation hypothesis, 175–81
Aronoff, Mark, 15, 190
autonomy hypothesis, 175–81
Aycock, Joanna, 18

Baayen, R. Harald, 16, 18, 166, 167
Baerman, Matthew, 3, 215, 376
Bane, Max, 315
Blevins, James P., 6, 17, 264, 289
Bonami, Olivier, 6, 182, 187, 254, 303
Boyé, Gilles, 6, 182
Brigel, Rev. J., 54, 326
broadly belongs to an inflection class, 273
Brown, Dunstan, 15, 273
Buchholz, Eva, 297
Bybee, Joan, 18

Cameron-Faulkner, Thea, 5, 84, 103, 104, 154
canonical typology, 3, 58, 74, 81, 114, 119, 126, 130, 155, 240, 262, 265, 271, 299, 317
Carstairs-McCarthy, Andrew, 5, 15, 84, 103, 104, 106, 130, 154
cell
  defined, 9
  realized, 10
  uninformative, 90–91
  unpredictable, 99
cell predictability, 79, 84, 99–103, 108–14, 119, 126–30, 151, 164, 169–72, 178, 204–15, 220, 322, 334–37, 338
cell predictiveness, 25, 130, 151–54, 155, 305, 311, 313, 321, 332–33, 338, 344, 366
cell predictor number, 60, 61, 77, 78, 79, 97, 119, 123, 126, 150, 155, 204, 215, 220, 221, 321, 332, 333, 338, 339
Chandler, Steve, 16, 166
Chinantec
  Comaltepec, 4, 5, 54, 57, 61, 76, 78, 84, 88, 107–11, 114, 214–15, 325–27, 326–28, 329, 332–33, 337, 339
  Palantla, 326–28, 330, 332–33, 334, 337, 339
class-identifier. *See* inflection-class identifier
complexity, 3, 20–21
  absolute approach, 315–17
  global, 316
  local, 316–17
  measures of an inflection-class system's complexity, 317–39
  of an inflection-class system, 3, 7, 9, 21–25, 53, 55, 61, 62, 83, 113–14, 119–30, 225, 262, 314–43
  relative approach, 315
conditional entropy. *See* entropy
Corbett, Greville G., 81, 136, 265, 273
Czech, 175–81, 326–28, 329, 332–33, 339, 351, 364, 365–66

Dahl, Östen, 3, 20, 314–16
Dakota, 54, 57, 61, 76, 78, 351
DATR, 377
Davies, Mark, 109, 167
de Groot, Casper, 20
de Jong, Nivja, 18

De Vries, James A., 54, 326
De Vries, Sandra A., 54, 326
density of optimal principal-part sets. *See* principal parts
depth-of-inference contrast, 215, 221, 333
Deutscher, Guy, 316
Dijkstra, Ton, 18
distillation, 42, 58–61, 69–77, 85–88, 92, 95, 99–103, 108–9, 123, 143, 181, 204–15, 216, 226, 227, 233, 237–61, 298, 301, 303, 338, 345–47, 354, 366, 373–79
distinguisher, 43–45, 46, 51, 52, 118, 122, 130–41, 154, 203, 354
Dressler, Wolfgang U., 15
dynamic principal-part scheme. *See* principal parts

English, 2, 10, 16, 42–44, 49, 50, 51, 109, 111, 166–68, 175, 216, 226, 252, 253, 263, 264, 267, 268, 315, 348, 354–56, 363
  entropy, 7, 109–14, 295–313, 349, 350, 351, 352–53, 365–66, 372, 376–79, *See* plat
  conditional, 7, 61, 109–14, 296–300, 346–47
  inflection-class predictable entropy (ICBE), 311
  inflection-class predictive entropy (ICVE), 312
  inflection-class-MPS entropy, 312
  Low Entropy Conjecture, 61, 215, 297
  m-system entropy, 322–25
  n-conditional exponence entropy, 311
  n-MPS entropy, 300, 337–39
Ernestus, Mirjam, 16, 166, 167
essential impostor. *See* impostor
Evans, Roger, 15, 377
exponence, 21, 42–46
exponent, 21

Finnish, 297–301, 311–13, 344–53, 369–70, 371, 372–77
Ford, Michael, 18
formative-based approach to principal-part analysis. *See* principal parts
Fraser, Norman M., 273
French, 5, 44, 52, 182–224, 226, 254–61, 301, 303, 306, 307, 308, 309, 310, 315, 326–28, 329, 330, 332–33, 334, 356–62, 363, 370–71, 372
frequency
  token, 167, 225, 252, 253, 301, 305, 367
  type, 7, 225, 254–55, 301–5, 307, 308, 309, 310, 367, 372
Fur, 4, 5, 54, 55, 57–60, 61, 76, 78, 84–109, 114, 115–16, 207–15, 326–28, 332–33, 339

Gazdar, Gerald, 377
Gil, David, 315
Göksel, Ash, 54
Gordon, Peter, 18, 51
Grant, John, 12–13, 18, 49
Greenberg, Joseph H., 4, 19

Hall, Kathleen Currie, 313
Hare, Mary, 18
Hawkins, John A., 3, 20, 314
Hayes, Bruce, 16, 166, 167
hearer-oriented plat. *See* plat
Hebrew, 350, 369
Heim, Michael, 176
heteroclite, 118, 175–81, 228, 232, 364–66
heuristic, 374, 379
  lookahead, 310, 377
  simple, 308–10, 377
Hippisley, Andrew, 273
Hockett, Charles F., 316
Huffman, David A., 379
Humboldt, Wilhelm von, 19

IC. *See* inflection class
Icelandic, 4, 5, 6, 23, 54, 57, 60, 61, 74, 76, 78, 84, 107, 108, 109, 113, 114, 214, 226, 228–52, 254–61, 301, 302, 303, 304, 308, 326–28, 329, 332–33, 350, 351
implicative relation, 12, 15–17, 23–25, 46, 48–51, 79–81, 289–94, 314–17, 341–43, 354–56
  deducing, 288–89
  irreducible, 373
  nonsyncretistic, 268, 272, 286–89, 294
  reducible, 373
  R-relation, 80–81, 272, 289–94
  W-relation, 80, 272, 289, 292, 293–94
implicative rule, 17, 18–19, 262, 272–86, 317
impostor, 165–77, 363–66, 372
  accidental, 172–75, 181
  essential, 172–75
indexed stem, 182–84, 189, 192–94, 204, 202–15, 277, 359–60, 361, 366
inflection class (IC), 11, 84–87, 228–30
  central, 225
  deducing membership, 286–88

inflection class (IC) (cont.)
  deviations from maximal transparency, 88–94
  diacritic, 17, 18–19, 264–67, 271, 273
  marginal, 225
  maximally opaque, 81
  maximally transparent, 81
  predictability, 79, 84, 94–103, 108–14, 119, 126–30, 151, 155, 169–78, 204–15, 220, 225–61, 322–25, 334–38
  transparency, 53, 79–115
  transparency criteria, 91, 99
  transparency defined, 83–84
inflection-class identifier, 103–6, 130, 134, 136
inflection-class system, 11
  condensed, 108–9
  degree of morphosyntactic focus, 74–77
  diffuse, 109
  thick, 58–61
  thin, 58–61
irreducible implicative relation. *See* implicative relation
isomorphic ideal, 237–46

Jakobi, Angelika, 54, 85, 86, 100, 105, 108, 326
Janda, Laura A., 326
Jörg, Christine, 54, 57, 108, 214, 229, 230, 231, 232, 234, 235, 303, 326
Juola, Patrick, 20, 315

Karlsson, Fred, 3, 20, 315, 350
KATR, 377
Kerslake, Celia, 54
Kimball, Geoffrey D., 54, 56, 325, 326
Koasati, 4, 55, 56–57, 60, 61, 76, 78, 325, 326–28, 330–33, 332–33, 338–39
Kolmogorov, Andrey Nikolaevich, 315
Krott, Andrea, 18
Kusters, Wouter, 20, 316
Kutsch Lojenga, Constance, 36, 46, 47, 54, 326
Kwerba, 4, 54, 55, 57, 60, 61, 76, 78, 326–28, 332–33, 337

LaFontaine, Harlan, 54
Latin, 4, 10–15, 16, 18, 21, 25, 35, 49, 50, 54, 57, 61, 76, 78, 79–80, 182, 183, 263, 267, 315, 347
lexical representation, 3, 15–19, 37, 262, 263–66, 271

lexical storage. *See* stored principal part (SPP) hypothesis
Li, Ming, 315
Lithuanian, 326–28, 332–33, 338
Liu, Qun, 313
Low Entropy Conjecture. *See* entropy

Maiden, Martin, 175, 228
Malouf, Robert, 6, 61, 109, 114, 215, 297, 325
Mandarin Chinese, 11
marginal conjugation, 255–61
Marginal Detraction Hypothesis, 225–61
Marslen-Wilson, William, 18
Marvan, Jiří, 326
Matthews, Peter Hugoe, 6, 17
McKay, Neil, 54
McQueen, James M., 18
McWhorter, John, 316
Merrifield, William R., 326
Miestamo, Matti, 3, 20, 315, 316, 317
Milin, Petar, 7, 109, 295
minimal set of principal parts. *See* principal parts
Montermini, Fabio, 182
morphological metageneralization, 270, 282, 284
morphological typology, 19–25, 53–54
morphophoneme, 351–52
morphophonology, 353–56
morphosyntactic focus number, 75
morphosyntactic property, 10
Moscoso del Prado Martín, Fermín, 7, 109, 295, 315
motivated inference, 3, 5, 21–23, 55, 77, 114, 166–67, 221, 316–22, 327, 337, 339–40

narrowly belongs to an inflection class, 273, 286–88
Network Morphology, 273
Ngiti, 35–39, 46, 47, 54, 57, 61, 76, 77, 78, 326–28, 332–33
Nichols, Johanna, 3, 20
No-Blur Principle, 103–7, 154

Old English, 253
Old Norse, 26–29
optimal set of principal parts. *See* principal parts

Pace, Wanda Jane, 54, 326
Pali, 353
Pāṇini's principle, 277

paradigm
  defined, 9
  realized, 10
  schema, 10
Paradigm Economy Principle, 106
paradigm function, 273, 286
Paradigm Function Morphology, 273
pedagogical use of principal parts. *See* principal parts
Pinker, Steven, 18, 51
plat, 4, 7–8, 21, 35, 40–52, 67–70, 81–83, 85, 117–64, 186, 188–89, 194–202, 204–14, 216–20, 221–24, 230–33, 237–48, 252, 254–61, 288, 297–305, 311–12, 317, 326, 343, 344–67, 368–70, 372–74, 376, 377
  entropy, 300
  essence, 378
  grammatically enhanced, 117–64, 362
  hearer-oriented, 51–52, 117, 118, 119, 132–43, 173, 181, 184, 186, 188, 207, 221–24, 303, 348
  hypothetical, 41, 81–83, 227, 237–40
  reduced, 312
  representation issue, 51–52
  speaker-oriented, 52, 117, 130–43, 173, 181, 184, 186, 189, 207, 216, 221, 348
  subplat, 230–32
  with heteroclites, 175–81
  with impostors, 165–75
Prasada, Sandeep, 18, 51
predictability. *See* cell predictability, inflection class
predictiveness. *See* cell predictiveness
predictor, 130, 134–36, 141, 226
preterite-present verb (Icelandic), 228
principal parts, 9–39, 53–54, 81–83
  adaptive scheme, 31–33, 55, 372, 374, 379
  adequate set, 29–30, 32–34, 37, 41, 94–95, 166, 173, 226, 262, 320–24
  alternative analyses, 35–37, 151
  deductive function, 165, 286, 289
  defined, 11
  density of optimal sets, 319, 329
  dynamic scheme, 33–34, 54–62, 85–87, 204, 372, 374
  formative-based approach, 220, 373
  grammatical information, 46–48
  matching function, 165, 286, 288
  minimal set, 373
  near-principal parts, 305–10, 376–77
  omitted lexemes, 49–51
  optimal set, 14, 18, 35–37, 143–45, 325, 327–29
  pedagogical use, 1, 9, 12, 14, 15, 16, 18, 37, 41, 165, 262, 340
  realized cells as, 11
  static scheme, 29–30, 55–58, 62–77, 202–3, 327–29, 372, 374, 378
  stem referral approach, 215–21, 361–62
  stems as, 182–84
  typology of systems, 53–78
  uniform set, 14, 18, 25, 35, 37, 325
  unique set, 14, 18, 37, 325
Principal-Parts Analyzer (PPA), 3, 35, 368–79
  algorithms, 378–79
  impostor analysis, 372
  input plat, 368–70
  keys, 372
  lexeme declarations, 371
  output, 373–78
  sandhi specifications, 370
  stem referrals, 371
  template abbreviations, 368
principal-part number, 58, 61, 77, 78, 97, 119–22, 143–45, 155, 204, 220–21, 330, 333
pure exponence-based morphology (PEM), 264–65, 294
pure word-and-paradigm morphology (PWPM), 17, 264–65, 294

realization, 275
realization rule. *See* stem-realization rule, word-realization rule
reducible implicative relation. *See* implicative relation
representation issue. *See* plat
Robins, R. H., 17
root property set (of adaptive principal parts), 31
R-relation. *See* implicative relation
rule of exponence, 6, 17, 19, 263–72, 282, 285, 289, 294
rule of referral, 267, 271–72, 282, 285, 294, 342
Russian, 15

Sampson, Geoffrey, 315, 316
sandhi, 348–49, 352–53

Index

Sanskrit, 4, 5, 6, 42–44, 45, 46–48, 54, 57, 61, 62–74, 76, 77, 78, 117–54, 158, 164, 168–75, 262, 266, 268–94, 299, 309, 310, 326–28, 332–33, 364, 365
Sapir, Edward, 19
Schlegel, Friedrich von, 19
Schmitt, Norbert, 271
Schreuder, Robert, 18
Shannon, Claude E., 7, 295
Shosted, Ryan K., 20, 316
signature, 215, 376
single surface base hypothesis, 107
singleton conjugation, 232–37
Sinnemäki, Kaius, 3, 20, 315, 316
speaker-oriented plat. *See* plat
static principal-part scheme. *See* principal parts
stem referral approach to principal-part analysis. *See* principal parts
stem segments, 350
stem-formation rule, 272, 277, 278–81, 285
stem-realization rule, 272, 275–82, 285, *See* stem-formation rule, stem-selection rule
stem-referral pattern, 361–62, 366–67
stem-selection rule, 19, 272, 275–79, 280, 281, 285
stored principal-part (SPP) hypothesis, 17–18, 19, 51, 103, 113, 114, 286, 294
Strong verb (Icelandic), 228
Sudoku, 1

theme, 43, 118, 134–39, 177, 184, 192–203, 207, 288, 344–50, 354, 357–59, 364–65
thick inflection-class system. *See* inflection-class system
thin inflection-class system. *See* inflection-class system
Townsend, Charles E., 326
transparency of an inflection class. *See* inflection class
Tremblay, Antoine, 271
Trudgill, Peter, 315
Tuḷu, 4, 23, 54, 57, 60, 61, 72, 74, 76, 78, 325, 326–28, 332–33, 334, 337, 339
Turkish, 11, 54

Underwood, Geoffery, 271
uniform set of principal parts. *See* principal parts
unique set of principal parts. *See* principal parts
universe of inflection classes, 169–75, 225–28, 233, 248, 253, 255
unmotivated inference. *See* motivated inference

Vitányi, Paul M. B., 315

Weak verb (Icelandic), 228
Webelhuth, Gert, 17
Wheelock, Frederic M., 54
Whitney, William Dwight, 45, 54, 62, 63, 64, 65, 67, 68, 69, 70, 168, 171, 284, 326, 364
Wimmer, Ludvig F. A., 26
word-realization rule, 272, 275, 277, 282–86, 342, *See* rule of exponence, rule of referral
W-relation. *See* implicative relation
Wurm, Lee H., 18
Wurzel, Wolfgang U., 17

Zoëga, Geir T., 27, 28
Zwicky, Arnold M., 6, 17, 270